WHAT MANNER OF MAN IS THIS?

A digest of the divine and human life of Christ before and after birth

---

Earl E. Cummings, B.S., Th.M., D.D.

Matthew 8:27
Mark 4:41 • Luke 8:25

Published by the Author
1991

Publishers of Original C. H. Spurgeon Works:
*New Park Street Pulpit, Metropolitan Tabernacle Pulpit,
The Treasury of David* and *The Sword and the Trowel*

Pilgrim PUBLICATIONS
BOX 66, PASADENA, TEXAS 77501

COPYRIGHT © 1991 BY EARL E. CUMMINGS

ISBN-1-56186-515-X

Order from
Pilgrim Publications
or
Dr. Earl E. Cummings
Route 3, Box 168
Rusk, Texas 75785

Contents

The Author's Prayer v
About the Author vii
Preface ix
Foreward xi
Explanation of Symbols xiii
Note From the Author xiv
Introducing the Manner of This Man 1
MINI Outline 9

Chapter	1	Christ, the Mystery Man, Identified 9
Chapter	2	Tracing Our Family Tree to the Heart of God's Love 21
Chapter	3	Watching the Creator Create All Things Seen and Unseen, Past, Present and Future 34
Chapter	4	Walking With Our Lord on Ancient Paths of Truth: 1 50
Chapter	5	Walking With Our Lord on Ancient Paths of Truth: 2 73
Chapter	6	Viewing the Long-Looked-For-Messiah in New Testament Fulfillment 93
Chapter	7	Journeying With Jesus on Soul-Winning Tours and Evangelical Crusades 114

Chapter	8	Journeying With Jesus in Healing Campaigns Both on the Masses and Individuals	129
Chapter	9	Journeying With Jesus on His Preaching/Teaching Crusades	152
Chapter	10	Ascending to Meet Our Lord in the Air: The Heavenly Homecoming	175
Chapter	11	Descending With Our Lord on Earth to Reign With Our Ruling King in the Last World Community	196
Chapter	12	Assisting Our Lord in the Final Judgment of the World's Wicked Dead — Eternal Woe ..	219

And
Assigning the World's Righteous to the Permanent Home at last — Eternal Bliss 226

Subject Index 237
Index of Scriptures 242

The Author's Prayer

Dear living, loving Lord,

"In Thy light shall we see light." Grant, Gracious God, that Thy dearly-beloved and only-begotten darling Son, who was in the bosom of the Father, and sent as the eternal Word into the deep darkness of this sin-cursed, present evil world, be soon crowned with the diadem of many crowns, when those from every tribe and tongue bow their feeble knees at His pierced feet, as an expression of their eternal gratitude for bestowing on us so great a salvation, which He purchased at the priceless cost of His precious blood at the holy place called Calvary.

May it please the Lord, the Maker of the heavens and the earth, before whom now I bow, that Your unprofitable servant, this unknown vessel of mercy, be so filled and overflowing with the Holy Spirit, that by Thy grace he will reflect the penetrating rays of heaven's light that one day will replace even the sun in the celestial city of the saved.

Lord, help us to walk by faith in that progressive light that shines more and more unto the perfect day. That divine Light which has brought to us that unspeakable gift of eternal life through Thy love and by Thy grace comes to Your chosen ones that seek Him, love Him, and serve Him with all of their hearts.

Bless, O God, with loving favor and tender mercy all who read this book, which is dedicated to the honor and glory of Jesus Christ the Lord of heaven, who will become the Savior on earth to every person that hears with the inner ear and sees with the spiritual eye, and He who said, "I am the Way, the Truth, and the Life; no man cometh unto the Father but by Me." May believing readers remember this divine declaration:

"If any man serve Me, him will My Father honor."

I ask that your directing Spirit may see fit to use each written word that is in harmony with heaven's unity and that corresponds with Christ's purity, to gently lead the sheep of Your pastures into a deeper knowledge of Your truth, and that they may be steadfast in abiding in Your good and acceptable and perfect will to the eternal glory of our great God. I humbly submit these human requests in the Divine Name, the sweet Name, the lovely Name, the prayer-answering Name, the devil-defeating Name, the God-honoring Name of Jesus.

Thank you, Lord, for enabling me to prepare a manuscript of this magnitude about You. Amen.

Appreciation

I would be guilty of a great lapse in memory if I failed as I so often do to extend to my one and only wife my highest appreciation for her untiring labor of love and loyal devotion for assisting me in every way in preparing this book for the press.

Also for our darling daughter, Earlene Lamnek, for her attractive calligraphy, and Kalman Kincses for his fitting description of the cover. May the Lord reward them fully.

—*E. E. C.*

About the Author

Unlike many writers, I have no famous celebrity to endorse my book. Nor am I in great demand as a conference speaker, because crowd-pleasing preachers have replaced, for the most part, preachers of truth, and human goals have been emphasized rather than God's glory. Nor have I built fabulous empires around myself as a nationally- or internationally-known leader or a widely-traveled evangelist. Be sure their sins will find them out.

I am just an unknown, a no-name person doing a little here and there for my most worthy Lord, who is my life's Sponsor and Sustainer.

In this book I try to avoid calling attention to myself, but rather to Him who is truly deserving of any credit that might come from this book. If I should refer to myself, I hope it will be as the beloved Apostle Paul did, to make a point, that men may praise my Lord and not me.

However, this much I will share. I was the youngest of ten children, and at the age of twelve God saved me by hearing His Word from my elder brother. When eighteen, I entered the Medical Corp in the Armed Forces. For nearly three years I accompanied our doughboys at the front of our country's battles in the European Theater of Operation of World War II. Being spared through three invasions, nine campaigns in the 39th Infantry, 9th Division, under General Patton, I finally returned home with a number of famous-battle decorations which stated, "Heroism beyond the call of duty."

When twenty-five I married a lovely girl whom God gave me. In due time four fine children were born, all being saved through the family altar, that ought to alter any family.

My work in the army was administering first aid to the wounded and dying on the battlefield. God had also called me to preach and administer first aid, using the "medication" of His Word, to the souls of men.

From many years of diligent study, the author holds three degrees: Bachelor of Science, Master of Theology, and Doctor of Divinity.

My seven-fold ministry has been directed to many kinds of people: teaching young people in a public school, preaching to prisoners, speaking in nursing homes, serving with a large produce company as a chaplain for migrant workers, centering in a ministry of church planting as the founding father of nine churches, and maintaining a daily fifteen-minute faith radio broadcast in New York, California, and Texas over fifteen years.

Now at length the Lord has led me to a literary ministry. If it pleases Him, I pray that more will be saved and helped spiritually through this book than in all my other endeavors for Jesus' sake.

God love you in Jesus,

Earl E. Cummings

Preface

Many have undertaken to write on the greatest doctrine in the Bible, the Doctrine of Christology. By God's grace, so shall I.

Some have honored Him with fine books, even great books, and thank God for every ready writer that has brought praise and glory to Jesus in a literary way. Others have not been so used. As a matter of fact, "deceivers" in this literary world are legion. Many have "crucified Christ afresh, and put Him to an open shame," not with the old nails of pain, but with the new prick of the pen.

First, in discrediting His deity they present Him as a created angel or being.

Second, they attempt to destroy His dignity disregarding His miraculous incarnation.

Third, they fail to recognize his impeccable purity as more than a man.

Fourth, they defy His divine doctrines as uninspired as He went teaching and preaching God's truth.

Fifth, going to the heart of the Gospel, they deny His vicarious substitutionary death and the power of the Lamb's blood that still cries out for God's vengeance and Christ's atonement.

Sixth, they denounce the "many infallible proofs" of His resurrection and attempt to "overthrow the faith of some."

Seventh, they have unknowingly set forth the manner, time, and effect of His return in a way foreign to the truth of Scriptures, thus bringing mass confusion to the great Doctrine of Eschatology.

"They are of the world; therefore, speak they of the world, and the world heareth them" (1 John 4:5).

"For many deceivers are entered into the world, who confess not that Jesus Christ is come in the flesh. This is a deceiver and an antichrist" (2 John 1:7).

Therefore, the "damnable doctrines" (destructive heresies) spoken of in 2 Peter 2:1 which flood the literary market today are nothing less than soul-destroying counterfeits against the stable truths of the Bible.

The Devil has long been the prime opponent and imitator of Christ. His agents, under the guise and masked veil of these respectable representatives within ecclesiastical Christendom, are making their assaults and have greatly disarmed the church, attempting to disfigure the Christ of whom we preach.

If we could write with a golden pen all the most wonderful things that have ever been read, and all the gracious words that have ever been said about the Lord Jesus Christ, it would still be inadequate and insufficient to say the least. In the Bible, Jesus speaks for Himself from Matthew 11:27: "*All* things are delivered unto Me of My Father: and *no man* knoweth the Son, but the Father; neither knoweth any man the Father, save the Son, and he to whomsoever the *Son will reveal him.*"

Foreword

Who is this Christ of the Bible to you? Some think of Him only as a good man like Confucius, Mohammed, or Buddha, who left us a good example to follow, so they say.

Others believe Him as God's Son, who was born in this world, lived among men, died on the cross, rose from the grave, and will come back some future date; but they have never trusted Him as their personal Savior. Most people in Christendom and members of different denominations know Him only as a historical figure.

The faith of an agnostic, the faith of a heretic, the faith of a hypocrite, and the faith of a modernist will not do. Only "the faith of God's elect" that comes by hearing the truth of God's Word, that causes a person to believe everything that the Father has said about His Son, is saving faith.

This unfeigned faith is linked with an unbreakable, invisible chain to Christ, so that we trust Him under all circumstances, believing He knows best in every situation; knowing that Jesus will bring us through every trial by exercising faith to trust in Him to open every God-honoring door of deliverance; relying on Him to remove obstacles and every mountain of difficulty; looking to Him with unquenchable faith to flatten every insurmountable wall of impossibility; clinging to Christ when all others forsake Him in the midst of a multitude of miseries and pressures. We are to stand on His promises even when death stares us in the face.

This is the saving faith that pleases God. This kind of faith is not only good to die with, but to live with.

Do you, dear friend, have this saving faith in some measure or proportion? If not, I trust in the foregoing pages that God in His mercy, love, and grace will enable you to trust Christ, rely upon Him, believe in Him, cling to Him for the salvation of your soul, and in the forgiveness of your sins to the rejoicing of your heart, now and forevermore. Amen.

Explanation of Symbols

Capitals are used in referring to Christ, in names or titles.

Parentheses ( ) are intended to signify a word or phrase to clarify the original text, unless it is obvious that it does not apply, such as *(Please read)*.

Brackets [ ] are given as qualified explanations yet not appearing in the original text.

Note: The King James Version is used throughout, except when a verse is unclear or uncertain, in which case a free translation is suggested by the author to aid in better understanding the verse.

Italic Words: Example: Psalm 3 verse 8, "Salvation *belongeth* unto the Lord. Selah." **(Selah means, pause and think on that.)**

The Italic letters that slant to the right, form the word "belongeth" meaning it is added to make the sentence clearer in Scripture.

For my purpose in this book, it is used to emphasize each word, that you may give special attention to such.

Note From the Author

The wisest man in the world, known as Solomon, said in Ecclesiastes 12:12, "... of making many books there is no end."

It appears to me that the above Scripture becomes more increasingly true in all kinds of books that flood the market.

Some seem to feel that a book to be scholarly must have a number of references from men of renown and distinction. It must also be well-documented to support and confirm whatever argument, proposal or doctrine the author may be addressing.

In my book, I purposely avoid the use of references of men outside the Bible, regardless of how noteable and famous they have become, because at best they are still fallible and subject to error.

Herein we set forth the infallible and unerring Word of the living God as our references to substantiate the truth.

Should there be any error within the pages of this book (God forbid), it would be found not in the inspiration of Holy Writ but in our interpretation.

May it please God to use the seedlings of truth and blow the chaff away by the wind of time.

Introducing the Manner of This Man

What Christ has done for millions, He can do for you. Where do you fit in from this parade of people who will march before your eyes in response to His eternal love?

- To the accused, He is the "Counselor" who never lost a case, Isaiah 9:6.
- To the archaeologist, He is the "Rock of salvation," Psalm 62:2.
- To the artist, He is "altogether lovely," Song of Solomon 5:16, and "fairer than the children of men," Psalm 45:2.
- To the astronomer, He is the "Bright and Morning Star," Revelation 22:16, and the "Sun of Righteousness," Malachi 4:2.
- To the baker, He is the "Bread of Life," John 6:48.
- To the banker, He is the "hidden Treasure," Colossians 2:3.
- To the believer, He is "above all," John 3:31; "before all," Colossians 1:17; "greater than all," John 10:29; "in all," Colossians 1:18; "Lord of all," Acts 10:36; and "over all," Romans 9:5.
- To the biologist, He is the "Lion of the tribe of Judah," Revelation 5:5.
- To the blind, He is the "Light of the world," John 8:12.
- To the bride, He is the "Bridegroom," Revelation 21:2,9.
- To the butcher, He is the "Lamb of God," John 1:29.
- To the carpenter, He is the "Builder" of the house, Psalm 127:1.

- To the Christ-rejector, He is the "Judge of the quick (living) and the dead," 2 Timothy 4:1.
- To the Christian, He is the firm "Foundation," 1 Corinthians 3:11; 1 Timothy 6:19.
- To the church body, He is the "Head," Colossians 1:18.
- To the composer of music, He is the Giver of "songs in the night," Job 35:10.
- To the dead, He is the "Resurrection and the Life," John 11:25.
- To the deaf and dumb, He is the divine "Healer," Matthew 4:23.
- To the educator, He is the great "Teacher," John 1:38.
- To the engineer, He is the "new and living Way," Hebrews 10:20.
- To the farmer, He is the "Sower of the good seed," Matthew 13:37.
- To the florist, He is the "Rose of Sharon, the Lily of the Valley," Song of Solomon 2:1.
- To the homeless, He is the Architect of "many mansions," John 14:2.
- To the horticulturist, He is the fruitful "Branch," Zechariah 6:12.
- To the hungry, He is the "Food" for their soul, John 6:55. They shall "hunger no more," Revelation 7:16.
- To the inventor, He is the Maker of "all things new," Revelation 21:5.
- To the jeweler, He is "the Pearl of great price," Matthew 13:46.
- To the Jew, He is the "Messiah," John 1:41.
- To the Gentile, He is the "Desire of all nations," Haggai 2:7.
- To the laborer, He is their "Rest," Matthew 11:29.
- To the legislator, He is the "Lawgiver," Isaiah 33:22.
- To the librarian, He is the "Book of Life," Revelation 17:8.
- To the linguistic, He is the "Alpha and the Omega," Revelation 1:8; 22:13.
- To the lonely, He is the "Friend that sticketh closer than a brother," Proverbs 18:24.

INTRODUCING THE MANNER OF THIS MAN

- To the meek, He is their Benefactor to "inherit the earth," Matthew 5:5.
- To the minister, He is the "Chief Shepherd," of the fold, 1 Peter 5:4.
- To the naked, He is the "Robe of Righteousness," Isaiah 61:10.
- To the newspaper man, He is the "good news of great joy," Luke 2:10.
- To the orphan, He is the "Everlasting Father," Isaiah 9:6.
- To the poor in spirit, He is the "King of the Kingdom," John 18:36.
- To the preacher, He is the "Word of God," Titus 2:5, Hebrews 4:12.
- To the scholar, He is the "Wisdom of God," 1 Corinthians 1:24.
- To the sculptor, He is the "Image of God," 2 Corinthians 4:4.
- To the servant, He is the "Good Master," Mark 10:17.
- To the sheep, He is the "Good Shepherd," John 10:11.
- To the sick, He is the great "Physician," Luke 4:23.
- To the sinner, He is the "Seeker and Savior," Luke 19:10.
- To the soldier, He is the "Captain of their salvation," Hebrews 2:10.
- To the temple, He is the "Chief Corner Stone," Psalm 118:22, Matthew 21:42.
- To the thirsty, He is the "living Fountains of water," Revelation 7:17.
- To the time-keeper, He is the Author of the "ages," Hebrews 1:2—Free Translation (refer to page 94).
- To the troubled heart, He is their "Comforter," John 14:16.
- To the weak, He is their "Strength," Psalm 27:1.
- To the writer He is the "Editor, the Source of Eternal Salvation," Hebrews 5:9—Free Translation.

Millions have come to Him and have experienced a change of heart, and now know Him as the Savior of their soul, the Master of their mind, and the Lord of their life.

Who is this awesome Person to you?

It must also be true but sad, that millions more have missed Him by simply turning Him away as He passed by.

I pray that He who is the "Desire of the Ages," the "Messenger of the Covenant," the "Redeemer of Israel," the "Light to the Gentiles," the "Blessed Hope" of the Church, the "Blessed and only Potentate" in the world, and the "Great High Priest" of "our profession," shall hear your call, and come to your aid and rescue you from sin, and save you by His grace so that you will never fall. Then as you read this book, your heart will burn with rejoicing from that "joy unspeakable" which Jesus gives. He henceforth will become more real to you every day, in every way, from here to and throughout eternity. Bless God!

Major Outline

I. CHAPTER 1—CHRIST, THE MYSTERY MAN, IDENTIFIED

Christ, the Mystery Man, Identified
OR
Christ, the Son of God and Man (The World's Only Savior)

II. CHAPTER 2—CHRIST AND THE COVENANT

Tracing Our Family Tree to the Heart of God's Love
OR
Christ, the Heart of the Father's Plan in Eternity (The Everlasting Covenant)

III. CHAPTER 3—CHRIST, THE CREATOR

Watching the Creator Create All Things Seen and Unseen, Past, Present and Future
OR
Christ, the Creator of All Creation, Old and New

IV. CHAPTER 4—CHRIST'S COMING PREVIEWED

Walking With Our Lord on Ancient Paths of Truth: 1
OR
Christ Recognized in the Old Testament Symbols, Types and Appearances

V. CHAPTER 5—CHRIST'S COMING PROPHESIED

Walking With Our Lord on Ancient Paths of Truth: 2
OR
Christ of the Old Testament in Messianic Prophecies

VI. CHAPTER 6—CHRIST'S FIRST ADVENT

Viewing the Long-Looked-For Messiah in New Testament Fulfillment
OR
Christ in the Forefront of the Gospels—From the Birthplace to the Site of Temptation)

VII. CHAPTER 7—CHRIST, THE REDEEMING PROPHET

Journeying With Jesus on Soul-Winning Tours and Evangelical Crusades
OR
Christ, the Prophet of Redemption: His Work in the Soul (Salvation)

VIII. CHAPTER 8—CHRIST, THE HEALING PROPHET

Journeying With Jesus in Healing Campaigns Both on the Masses and Individuals
OR
Christ, the Prophet, Restoring Health to the Body: His Work (Miracles)

IX. CHAPTER 9—CHRIST, THE PREACHING PROPHET

Journeying With Jesus on His Preaching/Teaching Crusades
OR
Christ, the Preaching Prophet: His Word in the Heart (Doctrine)

X. CHAPTER 10—CHRIST'S SECOND ADVENT

Ascending to Meet Our Lord in the Air: The Heavenly Homecoming

OR

Christ's Judgment Seat to Reward the Works of the Righteous (His Church)

XI. CHAPTER 11—CHRIST RULES THE NATIONS

Descending With Our Lord on Earth to Reign With Our Ruling King in the Last World Community

OR

Christ's Judgment of the Living Nations With a Loving Eye on Israel in the Millennial Age

XII. CHAPTER 12—CHRIST REIGNS IN THE NEW WORLD FOREVER

Assisting Our Lord in the Final Judgment of the World's Wicked Dead—Eternal Woe

AND

Christ Appoints the Righteous Their Place in the Father's Everlasting Kingdom—Eternal Bliss

Chapter 1

Christ, the Mystery Man, Identified
-or-
Christ, the Son of God and Man (The World's Only Savior)

I. The name of Jesus
   A. Gabriel's announcement to Mary (Luke 1:31)
   B. Gabriel's announcement to Joseph (Matthew 1:21)
   C. Christ's first descent in the form of man to earth—The fulfillment of many Old Testament prophesies (Isaiah 7:14, 9:6,7; Micah 5:2)

II. The threefold text, essentially the same—a reminder of the Trinity (Matthew 8:27; Mark 4:41; Luke 8:25)
   A. Jesus stills the storm in each of the Synoptic Gospels (verses above)
   B. Jesus stills the storms in the heart (Psalm 107:29,30; Romans 11:33)
   C. A passage to ponder regarding following Christ "daily" (Luke 9:23)

III. Those left unchanged after their contact with Christ
   A. Inadequate, incomplete, and insecure faith
      1. Nicodemus had feigned faith (John 3:12; 19:38,39)
      2. Many that first believed in Jesus had feigned faith (John 2:23,24, 6:44,45); bread-and-butter disciples (John 6:66)
      3. Many that believed in His miracles and His words had feigned faith (Zechariah 4:6; Matthew 9:8,33; John 2:23)
      4. Many that heard Jesus preach His famous "Sermon on the

Mount" were astonished but remained lost (Matthew 7:28)

B. An appeal to the lost to come to Christ for salvation (Matthew 11:28; John 6:37)

IV. Questionnaire and Answers

• • •

Ponder the passages herein as nails driven in wood—so shall your life stand up in the storm till the Sun breaks through.

• • •

How This Book Came to Be Written

The subject of this book fits the title like a glove. It is Psalm 45:1: "My heart overflows with a noble theme, I address the King (Christ) as touching the things I write. My tongue is the pen of a ready writer" (Free Translation).

This remarkable Psalm is a love song describing the mystical relationship between Christ and His Church.

The writer's heart is filled with the presence of the Bridegroom overflowing into the bride's mind that finds expression through the tongue and hand. Its words harmoniously identify Christ the King who is worthy indeed of a goodly matter. "My tongue is the pen of a ready writer."

Perhaps it would interest my reader the way I found this text. Could it be that you have tried the same method as I, which is very unscientific, but spiritual. I believe God speaks through His Word.

When I start each day off in my morning devotion, between three and five, I ask the Lord to speak to my heart and reveal His will to me for that day. I let the pages fall open where they will. The first words my eyes fell on was this prayer-answering passage. That morning started me on the wonderful experience of writing this book.

The Sweetest Name in the Bible

The theme before us is the most sublime and loftiest that engages the mind of man. Before the death angel overtakes me, even though as far as I know there is no shadow of death before me nor a dark valley below me, yet my heart throbs with a yearning, burning desire to write this book, be it ever so humble, on the greatest Person who ever lived, or ever shall live, who is given the name, the sweet name, the most wonderful name, the holy name, the condescending name, the transforming name, the never-dying name of *Jesus,* meaning Savior.

Although His name is thoughtlessly, recklessly, abusively used in profanity, yet it is:

The sweetest name on mortal tongue,
The sweetest carol ever sung.

Yes, it is the most serene and significant name known among the sons of men, the most meaningful name born of woman. It is the God-given name of Jesus, His only-begotten, dearly-beloved and darling Son, whom the angel Gabriel announced before the birth of Christ to the Virgin Mary, Luke 1:31.

Joseph, a descendant of King David, who was promised in marriage to Mary, was told in a dream:

Matthew 1:21, "Thou shalt call His name JESUS, for He shall save His people from their sins."

His coming in the fullness of time was the fulfillment of prophecy, Micah 5:2; Isaiah 7:14; 9:6,7.

Christ the *anointed One,* the *Messiah,* denotes the "God-Man." This unusual Man known to us is the most prominent Person in the Bible. Many sides of the Savior's life are seen in Holy Scripture. The aim and object of God's one Book is that we may *know Him* and *make Him known.* John 20:31; 21:25.

The Old Testament promises Christ, and the New Testament produces Christ. The Old Testament conceals Christ, and the New Testament reveals Christ.

The whole Bible is a beautiful portrait of God's Son, Jesus Christ our Lord. The most popular name that applies to Him is "Lord," for it is written more than five thousand times. The Lordship of Christ is one of the most effective doctrines in the Bible. This question that I am about to ask is true with me, and I hope it is true with all who read these lines: "Is Jesus your Lord *as well as* your Savior?"

"If you do not crown Christ Lord *of* all, you do not crown Him Lord *at* all." If your answer to the Lordship of Christ is still negative, I hope and pray that the Lord Himself will become known to you in all of His beauty and majesty, by His Eternal Spirit.

I am reminded of a great old hymn with this chorus:

Let the beauty of Jesus be seen in me,
All His wonderful passion and purity.
Oh Thou Spirit divine, all my nature refine,
Till the beauty of Jesus be seen in me.

It is my desire to dedicate this book to my Lord Jesus Christ. Be it famous or forgotten, I will have spent my time and money advancing the One referred to in the title, *What Manner Of Man Is This!*

Many people know about Christ historically; but if the truth were known in the whole body of Christendom, not many know Him personally. This was the state of most people when they spoke about Him in the New Testament.

The Three-Fold Text

First, let us see where this great text is found. This triune text of our book is found in Matthew 8:27, Mark 4:41, and Luke 8:25. The scene is essentially the same. This thought could be meaningful about God's Word, that when the Father says something once, it is most certainly true; but if God says in essence the same thing three times, it seems to me God is emphasizing the importance of the point. Know this also that we should read each Gospel that relates to the same incident to get the full picture.

When Jesus "stilled the storm," only the disciples spoke these remarkable words, "What manner of Man is this! For He *commandeth* even the winds and water, and they obey Him." I think I like Luke's choice of the three.

After we Christians have been with Jesus as His disciples, followed Him for many wonderful and difficult years, we still marvel and stand amazed at the magnitude of His wisdom in ordering our steps according to His divine plan.

In this next verse we catch a glimpse of Jesus as the wisdom of God. In Colossians 2, the inspired writer says at the end of verse 2 and verse 3, "... to the acknowledgement of (or in order to know) the mystery of God, and of the Father, and (especially) of Christ, in whom are hid all the treasures of wisdom and knowledge" (Free Translation).

In the future, more than in the past, we will continue to marvel about the *manner* of this magnificent Person. However, I want you to see similar phenomenal performances when people were startled and stunned by His mighty power in word and deed but were not changed, because they continued to know Him only after the flesh.

A man that presumes he was called of God performed miracles but never knew Him personally, never really committed himself to Christ as Lord. These kind of people might be considered as part-time Christians, Sabbath Day Christians, seasonal Christians, holiday Christians, or flat-tire Christians, who call upon God when they are in trouble.

In Luke 9:23 Jesus said, "If any man will come after Me, let him deny himself, and take up his cross *daily,* and follow Me."

We must follow Him every day, in every way.

The Interview of Jesus With Nicodemus

I believe the Lord at this point would have me to elaborate on the inadequate, incomplete, insufficient faith that is not saving faith. Many may marvel at the Master's words, ways and wonderful works, but still remain lost.

John 3:1–21 tells us about a very important man in the Jewish religion. He was named Nicodemus, a Pharisee (similar to today's Fundamentalist), who was of the best of the two active Jewish religious groups in the New Testament. The other group was the Sadducees (more like a Modernist).

Nicodemus was a ruler of the Jews, ruling the council of the Sanhedrins. He was a master of the nation of Israel, and yet he was a lost man, blind spiritually. He needed to be born again, like many who are in high places today. He could only say, "We (members of the council) know that Thou art a teacher come from God [no man is ever saved by believing in Jesus as a teacher]: for no man can do these miracles that Thou doest, except God be with him." (No man was ever saved believing only that Jesus was a *MAN* sent from God, and that He could perform miracles.) Many men have been sent from God, as John the Baptist. John was not able to save any person, nor perform a single miracle, nor did he make any such claim.

Believing Jesus as a teacher, or a *great* teacher, cannot save, nor can believing in His miracles save. You must believe in the entire record of Christ's life, death and resurrection.

1 John 5:10,11, "He that *believeth on the Son of God* hath the witness

(Holy Spirit) in himself: he that believeth not God hath made Him a liar, because he believeth not *the record* that God gave of His Son. And this is the record, that God hath given to us *eternal* life, and this life is *in His Son.*"

I am unlike other preachers, who believe that Nicodemus was saved. I beg to differ. Listen!

In John 3:12 Jesus said, "If I have told you earthly things, and ye *believe not,* how shall ye believe if I tell you of heavenly things?" In essence, Jesus was saying to this earthly, powerful, but lost, man, "You haven't even believed in the first step, the elementary things about the new birth, so why go any further and explain things that are more advanced spiritually and heavenly?" (Free Translation).

"Ah, but Brother Cummings, aren't you forgetting something? Are you not aware that Nicodemus joined Joseph of Arimathea in removing our Lord's body from the cross, and placed Him in Joseph's new tomb? Isn't that good enough?" Nicodemus saw nothing wrong in risking his reputation by removing the body of Jesus from the tree. He believed, as a good Pharisee, that it was against his religion to allow a malefactor to remain on the cross during the Sabbath Day. True, he showed generosity in bringing a hundred-pound weight of spices to assist Joseph in the task of burying the dead. What was a hundred pounds of spices to the ruler of the Jews, a very wealthy man? It was a good deed to say the least, but good deeds never saved anyone.

Ephesians 2:8,9, "For by grace are ye saved through faith; and that not of yourselves: it is the gift of God: not of works, lest any man should boast."

If we could only read that Nicodemus, in spite of his high position, stepped down from his pride and later believed on Jesus as His Savior! But nothing is said anymore than what Jesus previously said, "He believeth not."

This was not true of Joseph, for he was a believer. The Holy Spirit was careful to make this distinction. John 19:38, "Joseph . . . being a *disciple of Jesus.*" This was not said of Nicodemus, even though they worked together for a noble cause. You will find some day that your most familiar friends, who worked by your side in church, never made it. Remember that the Gospel of John was the last Gospel written, fifty-five to sixty years after the death of Christ. If a popular man like Nicodemus had become saved, and became a disciple of Jesus later,

John would have mentioned it as he did about Joseph, but still nothing was said of his reception of Christ.

The Faltering, Unsteady, Unsaved, Temporary Followers of Christ

As to the people who had insecure and inadequate faith to save them, John 2:23,24 tells us, "Now when He (Jesus) was in Jerusalem at the passover, in the feast day, (notice) many *believed* in His name, when they saw the *miracles* which He did. But Jesus did not commit Himself unto them, because He knew all (what was in) men (depravity)."

He knew man was a depraved creature, and that is exactly right. These people were swayed by the miracles Jesus performed. For a time they believed until difficult doctrines or teachings came from His lips when He said in John 6:65, "No man can come to Me, *except* it were *given* unto him of my Father."

The word *given,* if compared with other Scripture, will lead you to see the *Doctrine of Election,* which is the exercise of God's free will back in eternity.

John 6:44, Jesus said, "No man can come unto Me except the Father which hath sent Me *draw* Him."

John 6:66, "From that time *many of His disciples* went back and walked *no more* with Him."

As I have walked with Christ regarding these sovereign matters of God's grace, many such people did to me, in a mild sort of way, as they did to Christ. They left Him for good because they would rather believe they were free, when in truth they were still in *bondage* to sin, and refused to believe the revealed Word from Scripture.

So many people fall in this category. They will go anywhere to see a miracle and follow Christ because of His miraculous power—until He steps on their toes, goes contrary to their wills, casts aside their pet dogmas and traditions. They are often offended, then they decide to walk no more with him.

1 John 2:19 says, "They went out from us, but they were not of us, for if they had been of us, they would no doubt have continued with us; but they went out, that they might be made manifest that they were not all of us." How true!

The Word Heard Without the Power to Quicken Is Powerless

In addition to insufficient faith placed on miracles, rather than in the Master, we have a company of people excited, not only about His miracles, but His *Word* of authority.

Believing in the miracle of healing and His mighty Word is not enough to change your heart and transform your life. If this be the case, you will be left in your sins and suffer the consequence of *eternal punishment*. You must come to the end of yourself and see your nothingness, failures, guilt and sins. At the same time you will see His completeness and adequacy, that He alone saves. Not His works in others. Not His words that have fallen on your ears, or His words that you have memorized in your heart, but *in Him* alone. Not what He said or did during His ministry, but believe *in Him* for what He is, the only begotten Son of God. Hear what our Lord said in John 5:39: "Search the Scriptures; for *in them* ye think ye have eternal life: and they are they which *testify of Me*."

For what saith the Old Testament Scriptures? "Not by might nor by power, but by *My Spirit*, saith the Lord." It is not what He does for others, but what *He personally can do for you*. If you put your trust in other professing Christians, it may be that one day you will be disappointed. You will never be disappointed if you trust Christ only.

> *Nothing in my hand I bring*
> *Simply to Thy cross I cling.*

Following are a few New Testament Scriptures for your consideration, evaluation and examination, in the operation of feign, or false faith.

Matthew 9:8,33, "But when the multitudes saw it, they *marvelled*, and glorified God, which had given such power unto *men*" (classifying Jesus with other men).

Would you say that the "multitudes" were all believers because they saw Jesus display His miraculous power in healing the paralytic, forgiving and saving his lost soul? NO! They are not all saved that verbally say, "Praise the Lord!" The twelve disciples were saved, except Judas. The four carrying the bed on which the sick man lay were all saved. "For the Lord saw *their faith*." This is the faith that saves by putting one's trust in Jesus. The paralytic man was saved by his faith,

CHRIST, THE MYSTERY MAN IDENTIFIED

as he *desired* to be brought to Jesus. He was made every whit whole. (God's Spirit must put that desire in our hearts.)

Even though many marvelled when they saw what was done, yet most were left in their sins. Some were coming close to committing the unpardonable sin by charging Jesus with *blasphemy*. This was one step away from charging the Holy Spirit with blasphemy, by whom Jesus performed miracles and cast out evil spirits. (See verse 34 in Matthew, Chapter 8.)

Once again, Matthew 7:28,29. These verses are at the end of the greatest series of sermons ever delivered, known as The Sermon on the Mount: "When Jesus had ended these sayings, the people were *astonished* at His doctrine. For He taught them as one having authority, and not as the scribes."

Great congregations can be swept off their feet and come to the preacher at his beckoning call; but if they know not Jesus Christ in the full forgiveness of sins, believing He died on Calvary's Cross, calling upon Him in faith to save their sin-stained, hell-bound soul, then they do not have saving faith. Such will be left in a reformed state, but not a *regenerated* state of being saved by the grace of God. Beware of preachers that are very persuasive in getting big numbers to come forward.

Matthew 7:15,21,22,23: "Beware of false prophets, which come to you in sheep's clothing, but inwardly they are ravening wolves. Not every one that saith unto Me, Lord, Lord, shall enter into the kingdom of heaven; but he that doeth the will of My Father which is in heaven. Many will say to Me in that day, Lord, Lord, have we not prophesied in Thy name? and in Thy name have cast out devils (demons)? and in Thy name done many wonderful works? And then will I profess unto them, I never knew you: depart from Me, ye that work iniquity."

If we preachers could truly bear in mind that the only Person that can really satisfy the soul of the lost, as well as the soul of the saved, is Christ!

Listen to these weighty words. Not our particular denomination, but Christ. Not the church, but Christ. Not doctrine, but Christ. Not forms, but Christ. Not ceremonies, but Christ. Christ, the God-Man, giving His life for ours through the blood of the cross. Christ, the divine Storehouse of all light and truth. Christ, the infinite Vessel, filled with the Holy Spirit. Christ, the Enlightener, the Teacher, the Quickener, the Com-

from the tribe of Judah and both were descendants of the family of David (Luke 1:28,33; 2:4,5).
5. "He will save," or "Savior" (Matthew 1:21).
6. "Messiah" or "The Anointed One" (Luke 2:26).
7. God's purpose in the revelation of the printed page is salvation (John 20:30,31; 21:25).
8. "Lord," used about 5,000 times.
9. Most people then and now only know Jesus after the flesh and not spiritually.
10. All three (Matthew 8:27; Mark 4:41; Luke 8:25).
11. A miracle over nature.
12. False.
13. False.
14. Nicodemus.
15. Pharisees and Sadducees.
16. To be born again (John 3:3).
17. No (1 John 5:11).
18. No (John 3:12).
19. Yes (John 6:66).
20. (a) Repent toward God of all sin (Luke 24:47—Repentance).
(b) Turn to Jesus and believe in Him for salvation. Acts 16:31, Believe on (*in* is a better word from most translations) the *Lord Jesus Christ* (Jesus must be believed as Lord). Romans 10:9,10.

Chapter 2

Tracing Our Family Tree to the Heart of God's Love
-or-
Christ, the Heart of the Father's Plan in Eternity
(The Everlasting Covenant)

I. Who is Jesus in relation to God?
   A. Can *Christ* be proven as God?
      1. He is more than man (Matthew 8:27)
      2. He was the "Word" and the "Word was God" (John 1:1)
      3. He is One of the eternal Three (2 Corinthians 13:14; John 20:28; Matthew 28:19)
      4. He was "virgin born" (John 1:14)
      5. He is "God manifested in the flesh" (1 Timothy 3:16)
      6. He is to be "Judge" of all men (John 5:22)
         a. Judgment of the saved (Romans 14:10)
         b. Judgment of the lost (Revelation 20:11)

II. The *two types* of Covenants explained
   A. The Conditional Covenant based on works (Jeremiah 33:31–33)
      1. Example—Mosaic Covenant
      2. Key phrase: "If *ye* will" (Exodus 19:5)
   B. The Unconditional Covenant based on grace
      1. Example—Abrahamic Covenant and others
      2. Key phrase: "*I will*" (Genesis 12:1–3)

III. Treating neglected Scriptures
   A. God exercises His freedom of choice in the selection of men
      1. His Covenant for them (Hebrews 13:20)

      2. His promise to them (Titus 1:2)

      3. His love in them (Revelation 1:5)

      4. His salvation for them (Revelation 7:9,10)

      5. His Son, the Lamb, dies for them (Revelation 13:8)

      6. His record in a book of them (Revelation 17:8)

      7. His gift to His Son of them (John 6:37)

      8. His choice of them (Ephesians 1:4)

      9. His grace given to them (2 Timothy 1:9)

     10. His ordination of them (Acts 13:48)

  B. Man's condition after the fall, examined

      1. Some thoughts concerning the condition of the nature of man in bondage, with a depraved nature, a heart desperately wicked, blind, and spiritually dead

      2. God must put forth His power if man is to be redeemed by grace, or otherwise all would be lost.

V. Questionnaire and Answers

• • •

Love is the rarest ruby of God's jewels; if you have it, you are thrice blessed, Jeremiah 31:3.

Having said something regarding the mighty works and words of this ageless Mystery Man in Chapter 1, let us now proceed to see Him in the distant eternal past, as revealed in Holy Scripture.

Who is Jesus in relation to God? Is He only a man, or *more* than a man? He is both the Son of Man and the Son of God. The Bible says, *"prove all things,"* 1 Thessalonians 5:21. Can Christ be proven as God? If so, why is He thought of in many churches today as a good man, the ideal man, the perfect man, but not the God-Man? I believe the reason Jesus is so misrepresented is because the majority in Christendom do not know the truth about Him. Jesus said regarding the last days of this Dispensation of Grace, "And many false prophets shall rise and *deceive* many," Matthew 24:11.

In Romans 8:9, St. Paul writes, "... if any man have not the *Spirit* of Christ, he is none of His." The only one that can know the truth about Christ is he to whom the Holy Spirit is to reveal Him. This is clear from

1 Corinthians 2:14: "But the *natural man* receiveth not the things of the Spirit of God: for they are foolishness unto him: neither can he know them, because they are spiritually discerned."

Again, another chosen New Testament writer speaks in like manner from his first Epistle, 1 John 4:5,6: "They are of the world: therefore speak they of the world, and the world heareth them. We are of God: *he that knoweth God heareth us:* he that is not of God heareth *not* us. Hereby know we the *spirit of truth,* and the *spirit of error."*

To sum up what was said by Jesus, Paul, and John above: Jesus told us regarding the last days (and I believe we are living in them now), about false prophets appearing that would cause *"many"* to be "deceived." Paul wrote about those who had not the "Spirit of Christ," and he speaks of such as "the natural man." John sets forth *two groups.* The first is the largest group, because he says "the *world* heareth them" and they have the "spirit of error." Then John speaks of the smaller group—those that have the "spirit of truth," who are not deceived: "He that knoweth God"—that is, those who are in Christ spiritually and personally because they "hear" the truth from them that "are of God."

I asked awhile ago this timely question: Can Christ be proven as God? My answer is, unequivocally, Yes. Paul, the first *great mystery* writer, says in 1 Timothy 3:16, "God *was manifest in the flesh."* Was that not Jesus? So then, Jesus is God.

We shall now take a look at the "Word" in the word. One of the best Scriptures in the Bible at this point is in the Gospel of John, Chapter 1, verse 1: "In the beginning was the *Word,* and the *Word* was with God, and the *Word* was God." Perhaps you have read this verse, but do you really believe it? Observe that the "Word" is used three times, and each time it is capitalized, and rightly so. Why? Because it most certainly refers to Christ as the second Person in the Godhead. *Every time reference is made of Him in this book it will be capitalized,* so that Christ may be lifted up from every page.

Now what does John 1:1 really say? It says, *"In the beginning was the 'Word'"* (that is Christ), for verse 14 says, "And the Word was made flesh and dwelt among us . . . " Then we see that the "Word" is used the second time as "with God." That is, He existed "with God" in the eternal past and was then called "the Word." In the next place the "Word" is used in this convincing way: *"was God."* From verse 14 that we quoted

Tree to the Heart of God's Love, or Christ the Heart of the Father's Plan in Eternity," I shall now endeavor to show, as the Eternal Spirit enables me, how we were *included* in this everlasting covenant. What I say will not be man's opinion, but rather authentic, because it is taken from the Word of God. Even though it may seem to you fantastic, it should not be doubted, for it is drawn from the source of all truth.

Have you ever heard this expression, "If God said it, I believe it, and that settles it?" No, it does not settle it simply because I believe it. It does not matter whether I believe it or you believe it to make it so. It will stand because *God decreed it*. God does not need our approval to make a thing so. It was settled the moment God spoke it. Psalm 119:89, "Forever, O Lord, thy Word is settled in heaven."

Please come with me into an almost *unexplored territory* in our generation, as I want to take you back before time was, and before anything was. I want you to see the only One in existence, and that is God. Psalm 90:2, "Before the mountains were brought forth, or even Thou hadst formed the earth and the world, even from everlasting to everlasting Thou art God." Look with awe at the eternal One, in the eternal past.

I want to take you up in the Spirit to where God was then. I want us to look into God's dear heart of love, and then glance into His magnificent mind and see the impeccable qualities of His immortal Soul. This God is the only true self-existing God. He is, to say the least, a very mysterious, wise and loving Being. Listen! I want you to see the Holy Three in council and conference with the thought of man in mind.

A covenant is created from their deliberations. The first Person as the Father sees with His omnipotent eye the end from the beginning. His infinite mind designed a perfect plan never before conceived or equalled. His Son gladly agreed to accept the content of this covenant with an eternal outreach. To Him it was a covenant that would result in His own remarkable temporary, but meaningful, death. For us who believe, it is a covenant of life, yea, eternal life in a policy penned in blood, containing guarantees and promises that cannot be broken, written by the hand of the Almighty (Adonai). The contract included millions upon millions of human beings that would be brought out from under the penalty of death, and by God's amazing grace it would be in the most wonderful way a covenant to liberate and set men free. *Thank you, Lord Jesus!*

This was a covenant not of *chance,* but of *choice,* based not on *wrath,* but *love;* built not on *works,* but *grace.* You now need to see and understand the content of this covenant and those involved, as we by God's help put it together from different choice Scriptures.

If anyone would check the concordance, he would notice the word "covenant" frequently found throughout the Bible. According to my count from *Young's Analytical Concordance,* "covenant" is recorded about three hundred times. Putting it simply, a covenant is a solemn, or formal, or legal agreement, usually between two parties. *Covenants in the Word of God are divided in two.*

The Conditional Covenant

This first one is based on the promises of God *if obedient* to His commands. Such would be the *Mosaic Covenant* that is considered a *covenant of works.* This type would carry the phrase *"if ye will,"* Exodus 19:5. However, even this conditional and temporary covenant was later providentially changed to an eternal and unconditional covenant, in the light of man's former failures. This seems to be brought out in Jeremiah 31:31-33, "Behold, the days come, saith the Lord, that I will make a *new covenant* with the house of *Israel,* and with the house of Judah: not according to the covenant that I made with their fathers in the day that I took them by the hand to bring them out of the land of Egypt; which my covenant they brake although I was an husband unto them, saith the Lord: but this shall be the covenant that I will make with the house of Israel; after those days, saith the Lord, I will put my law in their inward parts, and write it in their hearts: and will be their God, and they shall be my people."

Part of the covenant was clarified, repeated, and replaced. Hebrews 8:6 points out a *better covenant of grace.*

The Unconditional Covenant

This covenant, as you may suppose, does not have the words "if ye will," but rather, *"I will."* God does it all. This type is relative to that given to Abraham. Genesis 12:1-3, "Now the Lord had said unto Abram, Get thee out of thy country, and from thy kindred, and from thy father's house, unto a land that *I will* shew thee: and *I will* make of thee a great nation, and *I will* bless thee, and make thy name great; and thou shalt be a blessing: and *I will* bless them that bless thee, and curse them that curseth thee: and in thee, *thy seed* [Christ], shall all families of the earth be blessed."

The first verse seems to be conditional, but the rest is unconditional. In this Abrahamic Covenant you will notice the change from "if ye will" to "I will" mentioned four times in those three verses. This is characteristic of all God's eternal covenants, such as the Noahic, Davidic, and down to the New Covenant which centers in the *sacrifice of the Son*.

Now we will take you into a number of Scriptures unfamiliar to most people who would do well to take heed and pay close attention, for coming up is a great central truth you might miss if you are not "in the Spirit." Pray that the dear Lord will enlighten you to lay claim to this treasure, if you are truly saved. If you are not a true born-again believer, you can become one by God's matchless grace, love, and favor. With a penitent heart, call on the Lord Jesus and He will forgive you and save you now. Then as you continue to read, you will be given an understanding heart to believe what now is to be uncovered from the infallible pages of God's Word by His Spirit. Please pray that you will see the light of truth, for to reject this valuable portion of God's Word could be fatal.

The following Scriptures I will number and briefly explain by the help of the Holy Spirit. I will emphasize the word or words for you to ponder.

1. We believers have this assurance in Titus 1:2, "In hope of eternal life, which God, that cannot lie, *promised before the world began*."

   When was this promise of eternal life made? It was designed in eternity. It was a promise extended to His elect. It was made in Christ when He accepted the terms of the contract or covenant of grace. He would do the work of dying for us as our substitute, and as God's suffering Servant, even the death of the cross.

2. Hebrews 13:20, "Now the God of peace that brought again from the dead *our* Lord Jesus, that *great Shepherd of the sheep*, through the *blood of the everlasting covenant*."

   When a person is to be saved God's way, the penitent sinner will be led to believe and receive Christ and will find peace through the blood of His cross, and henceforth is called in the Word as one of God's sheep, belonging to the Great Shepherd. It is He that will make you perfect (mature) in every good work, through Jesus Christ. We are to reach maturity in time and perfection in eternity when we are glorified.

3. We now can sing as in Revelation 1:5, "Unto Him that *loved us, and washed us* (believers) *from our sins in His own blood.*" One thought about this verse: the word *loved*. The objects loved are the subjects of His selection. We were chosen in love before the foundation of the world. Ephesians 1:4, "According as *He hath chosen* us in Him before the foundation of the world, that we should be holy and without blame before Him *in love.*"

4. John, the inspired writer, writes in Revelation 7: 9,10, "After this I beheld, and, lo, *a great multitude, which no man could number*, of all nations, and kindreds, and people, and tongues, stood before the throne, and before the Lamb, clothed with white robes, and palms in their hands; and cried with a loud voice, saying, *Salvation* is of (belongs to) our God which sitteth upon the throne, and unto the Lamb."

As one of the minor prophets said in his book, "*Salvation is of the Lord,*" Jonah 2:9. Salvation is of the Lord in origin, operation, and consummation. He planned to save us, He saves us in due time, and He keeps us saved until we are glorified and perfected.

5. Let me give it directly from Revelation 13:8, "And all that dwell upon the earth shall worship him (the beast) whose *names are not written* in the book of life of the *Lamb slain from the foundation of the world.*"

The Lamb represents Jesus. The Book of Life is where all of God's precious ones, saved by the Redeemer's blood, were written down before the foundation of the world. This corresponds with the *everlasting covenant between God and His Son*.

I cannot pass by this too lightly. I repeat! God's plan was finished in the everlasting covenant, and the Lamb's Book of Life was composed, compiled, and completed with all the names of the redeemed before the first man was ever created. God knows all of His elect ones by name, and all were written before time was. John 10:3, "He calleth His own sheep by name, and leadeth them out."

6. Revelation 17:8, "And they that dwell upon the earth shall wonder *whose names were not written in the Book of Life from the foundation of the world.*"

My, how this verse defies the popular preacher of today! This means all of the elect were recorded in the Lamb's Book of Life before the foundation of the world. God in the beginning knew those that were to be saved because He exercised His free will in choosing them. Everyone that was *"chosen," "elected," "predestined,"* and *"ordained"* to be saved will be brought home to heaven in the end, because they were picked out by God in the beginning. The four above words are taken from the Bible. It is not my opinion but God's eternal Word. *"Hear Him."*

I find no problem in believing this. Do you? All those in God's family are of His choice and adopted in His Son. Christ is the glorious Head of the Church, and all His members are chosen ones. Christ is the High Priest and represents the chosen race of the redeemed. We are chosen to salvation through His sanctifying Spirit to *believe the truth,* 2 Thessalonians 2:13. We are chosen to service and to live useful lives witnessing the truth for Him, as I endeavor to do, because it is true. We are chosen to eternal life and that is through Christ.

We are saved purely by grace and not of works. Our good works are to be a part of our new life in Christ Jesus. If it were left up to lost men to seek the Savior for salvation, none would be saved, for "no man seeketh after God," Romans 3:11. Our depraved nature would see to that. We once were children of the devil and gave our allegiance to him, but now we have undergone a divine change due only to God's mercy upon us. God broke through Satan's prison house of captives and liberated me and set me free, not because of anything that I did—I am delivered by His choice, His grace, and His blood. Praise God! We would still be in bondage if Christ had not set us free. "If the *Son* shall make *you free,* you will be free indeed." We were completely without strength, dead in sin, blind in sin, lost in sin, helpless in sin. Moreover, "it is not *by the will of the flesh* that we are *born again,* but by *His Spirit*" (John 1:13). None of us deserve to be saved, but on this side of Calvary any unworthy, awakened penitent sinner can come to Christ for His so great salvation, and receive it as a gift. The word "deserved" could be written over the gates of hell for all who go there. Likewise, "undeserved" could be written over heaven's gates, for none who enter deserve it.

7. For Jesus Himself says in John 6:37, "All that the *Father giveth Me* shall come to Me; and him that cometh to Me I will in no wise

cast out." That's sovereign grace and unmerited favor.

8. Ephesians 1:4 brings this all out into the open: "According as He (God) hath chosen us in Him (Christ) *before* the foundation of the world [he chose the nobodies of this world to make them somebody]" . . . "that *no flesh* should *glory in His presence*" [the foolish, the weak, the outcast, and the despised, 1 Corinthians 1:27–29].

The time when we were chosen is established in these verses. Does believing you were *chosen in Christ* offend you? I'm glad He chose me. Aren't you?

Let us go on to the end of verse 4: ". . . that we should be *holy* [the reason chosen] and without blame before Him in love." *Chosen in Christ*, chosen before the foundation of the world, chosen to be holy, chosen from the heart of God's love, we are His elect children of light. *"Predestined* to be adopted according to the good pleasure of His will." *Saved* to praise Him for His glorious grace. *Forgiven and redeemed* because of His mercy. All these precious thoughts are brought out in the above verses. It is God's divine revelation. If you remove one part of the truth, you cannot understand the whole.

9. 2 Timothy 1:9 is powerful on this neglected subject: "Who hath saved us, and called us with an holy calling, not according to *our works,* but according to His own *purpose and grace,* which was *given us in Christ Jesus before the world began.*" How wonderful to be taken away from Satan and given to Christ. Thank God for His omnipotence. He knows the end from the beginning because He *decreed* and willed it so.

10. Acts 13:48: "And when the Gentiles heard this, they were glad, and glorified the word of the Lord: and *as many as were ordained to eternal life believed.*"

A child can be made to see, but for many theologians and popular preachers, they are left in the dark; but "if the blind lead the blind," what happens? Matthew 11:25, "At that time Jesus answered and said, I thank Thee, O Father, Lord of heaven and earth, because Thou hast *hid these things from the wise and prudent,* and hast *revealed* them unto *babes*" [babes in Christ that have the faith of a child.]

The verse in Acts is a part of Paul's interesting and exciting missionary journey. I'm sure Paul believed as I, and hopefully as you, the truth of this verse: "And when the Gentiles heard this, they were glad, and glorified the word of the Lord: and *as many as were ordained to eternal life believed.*" God did not foresee that they would have faith, but rather He gave them what Paul calls *"the faith of God's elect,"* and caused them to hear Paul preach. They believed because faith was given to them as a divine gift. It was God who gave them to Christ in the eternal covenant and ordained them to be the recipients of His marvelous grace.

Psalm 110:3, *"Thy people shall be willing in the day of Thy power."* Faith is not the *cause,* but the *consequence* of the new birth.

Now, beloved of the Lord, if you are still with me, you have weathered a great storm of controversy. Those of our friends who object to this view and defend the *free will* of man, standing for man's dignity in this day of noticeable depravity, have a long way to go to catch up to the uncontaminated truth of God's Word. I pray that the Holy Spirit will give you what is lacking and yet use you for God's glory in Christ Jesus.

One lingering word to the awakened soul: The *Doctrine of Election* is designed not to hinder, but to help you see your undone condition in sin, while putting you in a position, when all hope is gone, to sue Him for favor. He will lead you to *repentance, trusting* only in Him as the Lord Jesus Christ. It would not hurt to call on Him now for salvation. The Scripture says in Romans 10:13, "Whosoever (or anyone that) shall call upon the name of the Lord *shall be saved.*"

We must now close this chapter, trusting in the help of the Spirit of God, who I hope has brought you to see these Scriptures that confirm what we have said, as we have traced our steps to the throne and viewed the heart of God's love in Jesus Christ on our behalf. Bless God for His love given freely to us unworthy sinners!

• • •

Questionnaire

1. Can Christ be proven to be more than a man?
2. Why is Jesus' birth considered a miracle?

3. Is each Person in the Godhead equal?
4. Does the Scripture teach more than one judgment?
5. What are the two types of covenants?
6. Would the Abrahamic Covenant be considered a covenant of works?
7. What does the unconditional covenant teach, works or grace?
8. What is the condition of all men, partially or totally depraved?
9. Does God have a right to choose whom He will?
10. If all are under condemnation, do any of us deserve to be saved?

• • •

Answers

1. Yes
2. Virgin born
3. Yes
4. Yes
5. Conditional and unconditional
6. No
7. Grace
8. Totally depraved
9. Yes
10. No

Chapter 3

Watching the Creator Create All Things Seen and Unseen, Past, Present and Future
-or-
Christ, the Creator of All Creation, Old and New

Thought

To create, Christ had only to speak; to save, He had to suffer, Psalm 33:9.

Introduction
- The theory of evolution—Darwinism (no proof)
- Christ, the Supreme Creator—Scriptural proof (Genesis 1:1,26; Colossians 1:16,17; John 1:3,4; Ephesians 3:9; Hebrews 1:1,2)
- Which would you prefer to believe, evolution or the Bible?

• • •

I. The invisible Angelic World—*Angelology*

  A. Twenty-five questions about angels—test

  B. Proof from Scripture about angels (Matthew 25:41; Colossians 1:16; Ephesians 3:9; Psalm 33:6; Hebrews 1:6,7,10; 1 Corinthians 6:3—references to angels)

  C. Answering the questions about angels (end of chapter)

II. The visible material world—*Anthropology*

  A. Considering the gap view between Genesis 1:1 and 1:2

  B. Creation of man

  1. First, spiritual image of the Godhead (Genesis 1:26)

  2. Second, physical formation from materials in the ground (Genesis 2:7; Ecclesiates 7:29)

       3. Made from each member of the Godhead
          (1 Thessalonians 5:23)
III. The creation anew in Christ Jesus as His bride—*Ecclesiology*
    A. Supernatural birth (John 1:13; 3:3,5,7; 2 Corinthians 5:17; Ephesians 4:24; Colossians 3:10)
    B. His workmanship (Ephesians 2:10)
IV. The creation of the new heaven and new earth—*Eschatology*
    A. All things new (Isaiah 42:9)
    B. What is heaven like? (Isaiah 65:17; 2 Peter 3:13; Revelation 21:1)
    C. Our future home (Revelation 21:11–27; 22:1–5)
V. Questionnaire and Answers

• • •

To create, Christ had only to speak; to save, He had to suffer, Psalm 33:9.

In the former chapter we introduced Christ as a member of the eternal Three, including the everlasting Covenant of Grace, while touching on the *Doctrine of Decrees*. In this chapter we wish to present *Christ as the Creator* of all things.

We shall now turn our thoughts, as an introduction, to the beginning of time, when God determined to create—and then all that He *was* to create in Christ. We shall *first* pursue, in this third chapter, these two stages of the early ages:

- *The creation of the spiritual world,* centering in the teaching of angelology.
- *The creation of the material world,* centering in the teaching of anthropology.

The *second* part of the chapter will consist of watching Christ as He works in two new areas of operation:

- *The formation of His church,* which makes up the Body and Bride of Christ.
- *The creation of the new heaven and the new earth* wherein the new Jerusalem will be the future capital of Christ's new creation.

We must in the beginning of this discussion concede that God is the origin of all things, and that all things belong to Him and are subject to Him, and were made for His ultimate glory. We will sidetrack the main issue for a few moments to consider the various views that approach the creation position *without God* as the source.

Darwinism recognizes Darwin as the father of the theory of evolution and natural selection. He explains the survival of the fittest, but cannot explain the arrival of the fittest. *It has no reasonable beginning, only a fatal ending.*

The evolution position has creatures without a Creator, a universe without an Author. *Evolution* and creation cannot mix and do not agree. For what agreement has light with darkness? I hear someone say, "But there is some good in the process of evolution." Perhaps so! There is some good in the garbage can, but I do not care to go in after it. Do you? I hope you don't. It is a dead-end street.

If you want to believe in evolution as the god of your destiny, that is your business. As for me, I believe that *Dualism* opposes pure creation. The *Platonic View* holds to Plato. The *Aristotelean* concept combines with Christianity. *Pantheism* holds to a plurality of gods and does not know the true triune God. The Hellenic culture, along with the *Alexandrian* philosophy all rolled up into one, is based on a false premise and a foundation of sinking sand. *They* start with a void of emptiness and darkness, and out of nothingness forms a particle of matter from which a spark of divinity appears. From that spark comes forth good and evil coinciding with the divine. From that point in time, developed over millions and billions of years, is the universe as we have it today, *so they say*. Take your pick, but know this: The God of the Bible did not evolve. He is eternal. He never had a beginning. He always was. Eternity is superior to time.

Time has a beginning and an ending. Eternity is beginningless and endless. God rules the ages because He was before time was, as He created time. He inhabits eternity. *"From everlasting to everlasting, Thou art God."* There was no *time* before eternity but God, and that is good enough for my poor finite mind to fathom. It seems more practical to think on this wise. We should not try to follow the development starting with men that reaches up to God, but start with God and condescend to man. Where you start is important. God first, then man. Not man first, then God.

Before we treat the four main points of this chapter, allow me to nail down the main theme, *Christ as the Creator*. Most people think of Christ as only the Savior. Scriptures confirm that, and more. When we think of creation we think of God as the Creator, and so He is. For that matter, each Person in the mystical trinity has the capacity and capability of creating, which is making something out of nothing.

Bear with me as I shall share with you some familiar passages to prove my point:

Genesis 1:1, "In the beginning *God* created the heaven(s) and the earth." He is the first Person. What depth and beauty there is in this first verse of the Bible!

Genesis 1:2, "And the *Spirit* of God moved upon the face of the waters." He is the third Person.

Compare Psalm 104:30, "Thou sendest forth Thy Spirit, they are created: and Thou renewest the face of the earth," and Genesis 1:26, "And God said, Let *us* make man in *our* image, after *our* likeness . . ."

The central Person mentioned in the Godhead is Christ, and He is the heart of the work of creation.

Verses That Point to Christ as Creator

In Colossians 1:16,17, this truth comes to the surface. "For by Him [Christ] were all things created, that are in heaven, and that are in earth, visible and invisible, whether they be thrones, or dominions, or principalities, or powers: all things were created by Him, and for Him: and He is before all things, and by Him all things consist."

He is the all-sufficient One. What a wonderful and meaningful verse that illuminates our understanding about creation! The object of my book, as well as God's Book, is to set forth Christ in all of His glory, including the work of creation. Pause for a moment and let these divine verses sink down into your heart:

John 1:3,4, "All things were made by Him [Christ] and without Him was not anything made that was made. In Him was *life*; and the life was the light of men."

Ephesians 3:9, "And to make all men see what is the fellowship of the mystery, which from the beginning of the world hath been hid in God, *who created all things* by Jesus Christ."

Henceforth, when we speak of creation we must agree and keep in mind that Christ is the active Agent in creation. This not only applies to the universe and everything in it, but the above passages point out that Christ as the life-giver is the *Giver* of spiritual and eternal life as well. Jesus as God has self-existing life, and can but speak the Word and life comes forth, as in the case of Lazarus. Let this verse vibrate in your soul: "By the word of the Lord were the heavens made; and all the host of them by the breath of His mouth," Psalm 33:6. And verse 9: "For He [Christ] *spake,* and it was done; He commanded and it stood fast."

Here we hear the Word speak, and things began to appear as they came into existence.

Let this last Scripture suffice to show that Christ is the Sovereign Creator: "God, who at sundry (various) times and divers (different) manners (ways) spake in time past unto the fathers by the prophets, hath in these last days [of this dispensation] spoken unto us by *His Son,* whom He hath appointed heir of all things, by whom also *He made the worlds,*" Hebrews 1:1,2.

This is God's own testimony crediting Christ, His only begotten and dearly-beloved Son, with the mystery, majesty, and the might of all creation.

Questions on Angelology

Now we come to consider what we set out to do, and that was to present Christ as the Creator of: (1) the invisible, or angelic, world; (2) the material, or visible, world; (3) the Christian and saved world in development; and (4) the new world to come.

With the help of the Spirit to inspire and the Scriptures to inform, we now move into the realm of reality that we cannot see, but know with a spiritual knowledge that it is there. To test your insight into the unknown and unseen, we base this questionnaire only on the Bible. This will serve as a measuring rod, not to discipline, but to inform my dear readers as to what you now know about angelology.

The beloved Brother Paul said, "For the things which are seen are temporary, but the things which are *not* seen are eternal." How true!

Here are twenty-five questions to test yourself or anyone else:

1. Were all angels created at once, or were they, as our first parents, created beings told to replenish the earth?
2. Were all angels the work of God's first creation, or did the evil

WATCHING THE CREATOR CREATE ALL THINGS

angels appear suddenly from unknown outer space and fight with God's angels?
3. Were all angels bad and some became good, or were all angels made good and some became bad?
4. Were all angels created by God as bodiless beings, or were some created with bodies?
5. Were the angels and man created simultaneously, or was there a great interval between the creation of man and angels?
6. Did the fall of man occur before or after the fall of the disobedient angels?
7. Are the angels of God greater in power and intelligence than man?
8. Can angels multiply, or does their number ever increase or decrease?
9. Are angels able to reproduce, or are they sexless as well as bodiless beings?
10. Are angels born and do they die like mortal man?
11. Were angels put on probation as was man in the garden of Eden?
12. Were some angels elected by the foreknowledge of God?
13. Do the evil angels have a leader, or do they move about as locusts, without a king?
14. Do the evil fallen angels, or demons, desire to occupy the bodies of fallen man?
15. Can an angel appear as a man?
16. Can angels eat food?
17. Can evil angels be restored and regain a right standing with God as men can?
18. Does the devil appear holding a pitchfork, dressed in red garments, having horns, hoofs, and a pointed tail?
19. Did Jesus ever engage in warfare with Satan?
20. Do the angels know all things?
21. Do children of God have guardian, holy angels?
22. Are some angels higher in rank, with different endowments and duties than other angels?

23. Can a bodiless being such as an evil angel or spirit feel pain or be confined to a prison?
24. Can Satan and his forces perform miracles?
25. Do the holy and elect angels rejoice when the soul of a sinner is saved?

Invisible Creation of the Angelic Spirit World

I wonder how you made out on this Bible competency test. Hopefully you gained some insight into the Doctrine of Angelology from what we said and will yet say as we develop the subject a little further. Even though we, like Jesus in human form, were made a little lower than the angels, someday we will be in our Lord's visible presence, and, like Him, we will not be inferior, but superior to angels. No angel of God has ever experienced salvation, for they have never sinned. Because we are the redeemed of the Lord at a great cost, we also are brought closer to our Lord than angels will ever be.

As for the fallen angels, Jesus tells us of the original purpose of hell, that it was prepared for them: "Depart from Me, ye cursed, into the everlasting fire prepared *for the devil and his angels,*" Matthew 25:41. However, these people that are told to "depart" are not spirit beings, but human beings. In Revelation 21:8, we are told the reason why.

Now, dear reader, as we watch our Lord create the invisible world, may we pick up a new thought or two in this first creation of Christ, and may the Holy Spirit give us understanding hearts as we proceed.

From Colossians 1:16 we recall that Christ is said to be the "Creator of all things." That means the things in heaven as well as on earth. The invisible as well as the visible. This obviously includes angels, so that He is the creator of the host of angels. Is it right for creatures created by Christ to worship Him? "Thou Lord, in the beginning, hast laid the foundation of the earth; and the *heavens* are the works of thine hand," Hebrews 1:10. Verses 6 and 7 say, "And let all the angels of *God worship Him* [Christ]." And of the angels He said, "Who *maketh His* angels spirits."

In 1 Timothy 5:21, we are told about *elect angels*. This election must antedate the creation of angels. God, who knows the end from the beginning, knows those that are His. For He made a choice among the angels as well as among men before time was, according to His sovereign purpose. We cannot describe what we cannot see with our eyes and what we do not understand with our hearts, but we do believe what we read from God's Word.

We know now that angels are ministers of divine providence, finite, bodiless beings, greater in intelligence and power than man in his present state, and will be inferior to man in his future state. We know from Scripture that they know nothing of growth, age, or death. They are servants of God, having different duties and assignments. They control the weather, wind, and water. They are put in charge of things, such as the one that has the keys to the "bottomless pit." There are angels of death as well as birth.

There is no hint in the Bible that there are female angels, for they are sexless beings. Angels appear largely at times of importance, similar to the appearance of miracles when the Bible was being written. They were seen in the Garden of Eden, protecting the tree of life with a flaming sword. The law was ordained or made effective by angels. Angels appeared many times in the Old Testament, but when the *"Angel of the Lord"* is spoken of, it refers to Christ, who made different theophantic appearances in the Old Testament. When Jesus was born, angels accompanied His birth. When He was tempted, angels ministered unto Him. When Jesus was facing crucifixion, He said (in Matthew 26:53), "Thinkest thou that I cannot now pray to My Father, and He shall presently give Me more than twelve legions of angels?" They were present at the resurrection and ascension. They will be used as reapers when Christ returns to the earth in His second advent. In the future, we believers will judge angels, 1 Corinthians 6:3. So much for the first creation of angelic beings, created by the hand of Christ our Sovereign Lord.

Visible Creation of the Material World

We have learned from part one that Christ, being the Creator, created all things "visible and invisible," Colossians 1:16. I have discovered over the past forty years of diligent study of the Bible that the Word is inexhaustible. Do you recall looking at a verse the second time and seeing more in it than you did the first time?

I want you now to prayerfully view the first two verses of the Bible, and perhaps a new look will come from this part of the Scripture that can revolutionize your thinking.

The Gap Theory: Fiction or Fact?

"In the beginning God created the heaven(s) and the earth," Genesis 1:1. Whatever God in Christ does is *good,* "very good." When He created the physical universe, I'm sure He created it beautifully.

Ecclesiastes 3:11 says, "He hath made everything beautiful in His time." It certainly is not like God to create something like the description in verse 2. Listen to the second verse in the Bible that I believe could span a million years between verse 1 and verse 2: "And the earth was without form, and void [that cannot be the way Christ created it]; and darkness was upon the face of the deep," Genesis 1:2.

Here our Sovereign Lord is shown as existing before creation and before His universe. To *create* means to call into existence something that never was. To *make* means to form something out of some substance already in existence. It was some kind of material that was void in the darkness, buried in the depth of the waters. It is believed that the word *"was"* in verse 2 needs to be rendered *"became."* Let us see the spiritual truth of Genesis 2:1, "Thus the heavens and the earth were finished." This can be rendered "brought to perfection." What caused God's creation to become a wasteland, void of beauty? In Isaiah 45:18 we see that "He created it not in vain, He formed it to be inhabited."

What caused the world to become a ruined mass? Could it be that Satan and his fallen, evil angels rebelled against the purpose of God and were cast down to the earth from heaven? Made a mess of it as they always try to do? I think so! The devil, you know, visited Eve in the Garden of Eden sometime after the creation of man and his mate.

I think this is sufficient evidence that the spirit world of angels was divided due to sin, when this earth became the habitation of evil spirits. It seems even now they are still doing their worst to destroy both the souls and bodies of men in God's re-creation. But take heart—God will soon put an end to evil and cast the evildoers into their eternal abode.

Skipping over the physical creation, we will witness the making of man on the sixth twenty-four hour day. He was to be the crown of God's creation as the last thing that He made before He rested on the seventh day (Sabbath).

The Creation of Man

Now notice some interesting things about the *creation* and *making* of man. First, man was created by Christ in the spiritual image—not physical, because God had no physical image, but made in the spiritual image of the Trinity. Genesis 1:26, "And God said, Let *us* make man in our *image,* after our *likeness.*"

In the similitude of angels, in an invisible, spiritual substance, we came to be an eternal soul from the eternal existing proprieties and in the spiritual image and likeness of God. At this point we were much like the angels as bodiless beings, until we received a material body.

I know God walked with man in the garden in the cool of the day. That body had to be a theophanic appearance. God often appeared to fellowship and communicate with man. That we will study more about in the next chapter. "God is Spirit," says John. Jesus says, "A spirit hath not flesh and blood." What did the Trinity communicate and deposit in man's being?

The key passage on the creation of man we shall discuss by the help of the Holy Spirit from Genesis 2:7: "And the Lord God *formed man* of the dust of the *ground,* and breathed into his nostrils the breath of life; and man became a living soul."

From Chapter 1, we saw God create man in a spiritual likeness to Himself as an invisible and immortal person. In Chapter 2, He put that spiritual being into the form of a human body and separated us as male and female. Therefore, one part of our being that came from God is eternal, the other, from the dust of the ground, is material and temporary.

Created and made is God's order. Creating something out of nothing in the first invisible creation. Second, God formed, fashioned, and framed the mass of matter regarding the second visible creation, fresh from His divine hands.

Remember Genesis 1:26, "And God said, Let *us* make man in *our* image, after *our* likeness."

Man was made from His Maker as a tripartitus being in likeness to the trinity. Paul says in 1 Thessalonians 5:23, "I pray God your whole *spirit, soul,* and *body* be preserved blameless unto the coming of our Lord Jesus Christ." Here is the first key to understanding the makeup of man as I see it.

God in Christ, through the Spirit, made man upright, Ecclesiastes 7:29. When Christ, through the Spirit of God, breathed in his nostrils the breath of life, he became a living soul (or being). Man was made a beautiful creature, resembling His triune Creator. *When man fell* in disobedience to God's Word, the beauty of God, Jesus and the Holy Spirit vanished, and he *became a depraved creature,* losing his likeness of God. Sin brought instant *separation* that same day. *Spiritual death* took the place of the spiritual life which he first knew in sweet fellowship with God, his Maker and Master. Now only by God's sovereign mercy and divine grace can man be restored to God's fellowship and favor again.

Allow me to run a thought or two on this theme by again and enlarge on it for clarification. Man was not made as a plant, nor as a four-footed beast, even though made on the same day that God made the animal kingdom. Notice carefully again that *God made man as the climax, conclusion, and crown of His visible creation.* Then we are told that God created male and female. That is, we were both made and created from the same eternal, invisible substance and essence of the Godhead. Think on that! We have a part of God's being. Man came from God first on His *spiritual side,* after he was formed from the earth with his physical, mortal, and material properties, which made up his *human side.* We were *created* and *made* from some of the same attributes of God's spiritual nature. God made us His *offspring* when He communicated to us something from and out of Himself that shall never die. This something was an invisible individual that shall live forever, called the *soul.* We will live as long as God lives somewhere throughout all eternity. Hopefully, your lot will be to join Him in heaven, or else descend down to a devil's hell. Thank you, Lord, for saving many by grace, and yet there is still room for more. The Bible says on man's human level, *"Whosoever will,* let him come." *Dear friend, do you have the will* and desire to come to Christ? If so, it is the *Spirit working in your heart.* Then come just as you are, but come right now, and heaven will be your eternal home.

The Creation of the Members of the Body of Christ

Our third step in this episode of creation should thrill us through and through, if we are among the saved and not deceived by the devil.

Our thought has to do with being delivered from sin and Satan's power, by being made anew in Christ Jesus. If we are now saved, we bear the image of our heavenly Lord. *They that were born but once will* die twice. *They that were, and are, and will be born twice, will peradventure die only once,* if our heavenly Lord tarries. If the Lord comes while we are still here in the body, we will be then *translated* and never taste of physical death. Praise God!

How can this be? It can be, because God said it in His wonderful Word. If you can listen with your inner ear what God is about to say, and see with your spiritual eye of faith what He is about to reveal, then you have been *born anew.* He alone has this supernatural power. We can no more produce the second birth than we could the first birth. "Yes," but somebody says, "how about the *freedom of the will?*" Your Scripture is found in *John 1:13.* That teaches that man cannot be born the second time from the will of man, or the flesh, but of the will of God only. God can produce the new birth by the regenerating power of the Holy Spirit.

Now take heed to this very important part of re-creation by our Redeeming Creator, our Kinsman Redeemer. If you are in need of a new heart—for the first one became exceedingly sinful and deceptive after the fall, of whose descendants we are in the flesh, that is Adam. Should you still have the old evil heart, make your appeal as David did when he cried out in Psalm 51:10, "*Create* in me a clean heart, O God, and renew a right (steadfast) spirit within me." That's what man needs, a *clean heart,* for "the *pure in heart . . .* shall see God."

I pray that you may see the beauty and significance of this special verse: "Therefore, if any man (person) be in Christ, he is a new creature (creation): old things are passed away; behold, all things are become new," 2 Corinthians 5:17.

Paul's favorite expression is the mysterious oft-repeated term, "*in Christ.*" Follow this phrase and see where it will take you in Scripture. I hope "in Christ," if there is still any question about your salvation. "For we are His workmanship, *created in Christ Jesus* unto good works," Ephesians 2:10.

Where do our good works come from? Christ Jesus, "which God hath before ordained that we should walk in them."

Ephesians 3:8,9,10, "Unto me, who am less than the least of all saints, is this grace given, that I should preach among the Gentiles the *unsearchable riches of Christ:* and to make all men see what is the fellowship of the mystery, which from the beginning of the world hath been hid in God, who created *all* things by Jesus Christ; to the intent that now unto the principalities and powers in heavenly places might be known by the *church* the manifold wisdom of God." Christ's unsearchable riches becomes ours in Him as His body, the church.

Ephesians 4:24, "And that ye put on the new man, which after God is *created in righteousness and true holiness.*" Since we have *His (Christ's) righteousness,* we cannot be cast out anymore than God would cast out His own Son.

Colossians 3:10, "And have put on the new man, which is renewed in knowledge after the image of *Him* that created him." Our knowledge is renewed in Christ who created us anew the second time, spiritually. The sum and substance of these thoughts are that Christ created the things invisible in the first creation of angels, spirited beings. Christ created the material universe, including man as a human being with body, soul, and spirit, which came from the triune God. He also created in Christ *the redeemed* of the Lord, who were called out to form the church of the living God. Don't you love to be in the fellowship of joyous Christians who have the sweet spirit of Jesus, and love and hug one another?

Are we not brothers and sisters in Christ? Did not our beloved Paul write more than once, "Greet one another with an holy kiss?" Do you not remember on one occasion when he was to depart from them that they "fell on his neck and kissed him" because they believed that they would "see his face no more?"

Galatians 3:28, "There is neither Jew nor Greek, there is neither bond nor free, there is neither male nor female: for ye are all *one* [equal] *in Christ Jesus.*"

Before the fall, Adam and Eve were made equal, although Adam was made first. Think of this! Eve was taken out of Adam's side to be equal with him, under his arm to be protected by him, and near his heart to be loved by him. So shall it be in the second Paradise. Christ our Bridegroom will never let us go, never divorce us, never cast us out.

Ephesians 1:9,10, "Having made known unto us the mystery of His will, according to His good pleasure which He hath *purposed in Himself:* that in the dispensation of the fulness of times He might gather together in one all things [can include all saints] in Christ, both which are in *heaven,* and which are on *earth;* even in Him."

The Creation of a New World That Will Not Pass Away

Now we shall move to a few closing thoughts concerning that *grand finale* of Christ, creating all things new in the world to come. Isaiah 42:9, "Behold, the former things are come to pass, and *new things* do I declare: *before they spring forth I tell you of them.*" Isaiah 65:17, "For, behold, I create *new heavens* and a *new earth:* and the former shall not be remembered, nor come into mind."

The companion verse of this prophecy is in *Revelation 21:1*. John, the apostle of love, who closes the Bible as John the Revelator, through the Spirit says, "I saw a new heaven and a new earth, for the first heaven and the first earth were *passed away.*" This means what it says. The first heaven and earth will not be renovated, but pass away, and no place is to be found for them. The new replaces the old, which is burned up.

The Lord God says, "Behold, I make *all things new.*" A "new city," a "holy and great city," coming down from God out of this new heaven. She is prepared like a bride is on her wedding day. What a descriptive beauty this city is in all of her majestic glory! Read about all the wonderful new things God, through His Son, has prepared for them that love Him (Revelation 21:11–27; 22:1–5). It is our eternal home where God keeps the register of the heavenly citizens in the Lamb's Book of Life.

Think long on this next and last remarkable verse in 2 Peter 3:13, "Nevertheless *we,* according to His promise, look for *new* heavens and a *new* earth, wherein dwelleth righteousness."

Those who have the righteousness of Christ will live in a land where no sin abounds or is found. No lawlessness reigns and ruins. No police force is needed to come to our rescue. A city without jails, hospitals, funeral homes, orphans, or poor people. There will be no pain, no sickness, no death, "for the former things have passed away."

There will never be crape on the doorknob
No funeral train in the sky,
No grave on the hillside of glory,
For there we shall never more die.

Thank you, my living, loving Lord, for making it possible for a someone like me to live forever with a beautiful Person like You in the city of God.

• • •

Answers to Questions on Angels (Pages 38–40)
1. All angels were created at once and do not reproduce.
2. All angels were created as the work of God in Christ.
3. All angels were made good, and some became bad.
4. All angels were created as bodiless beings.
5. Man was created after the angelic creation.
6. Man fell after the fall of angels.
7. Yes.
8. Never multiply.
9. Angels are sexless beings.
10. Angels are not born and never can die.
11. Apparently so. They must have had a free will.
12. Yes. (This reveals the wisdom of God.)
13. Yes.
14. Yes.
15. Yes.
16. Yes.
17. No.
18. No.
19. Yes.
20. No.
21. Yes.
22. Yes.
23. Yes.
24. Yes.
25. Yes.

• • •

Questionnaire
1. Name two false theories on creation.
2. Which of the members of the Trinity is credited with the creation of all things?

3. Is it best to start with man and build up to God, or start with God and descend to man?
4. What is the "Gap" view in Genesis 1, verse 2?
5. Was man created in the spiritual or physical image of God?
6. Is man made by his Creator with two or three parts to his being?
7. Which is true: When man fell into sin, did he become *partially depraved* or *totally depraved*?
8. *True or false:* If you are in Christ, you have been created anew.
9. Will Christ renovate the old heaven and earth, or will He create a new heaven and a new earth?
10. Name the four phases of creation.

• • •

Answers

1. Evolution, or Darwinism; Dualism; Platonicism; Pantheism, etc.
2. Christ.
3. Start with God and descend to man.
4. Lucifer became the devil cast out of heaven along with the fallen angels, and caused the earth to be filled with darkness without form and void. The gap between Genesis 1:1 and 1:2.
5. Spiritual image.
6. Three parts.
7. Totally depraved.
8. True.
9. Create a new heaven and earth.
10. (a) Creation of spiritual world, (b) creation of material world, (c) creation or formation of Church, and (d) creation of New Heaven and a New Earth.

Chapter 4

Walking With Our Lord on Ancient Paths of Truth: 1
-or-
Christ Recognized in the Old Testament Symbols, Types and Appearances
(Daniel 7:9–10 • Jeremiah 6:16)

Introduction

Christ's words in the New Testament points to holy men of old that wrote about Him. "And beginning at Moses and all the prophets, he expounded unto them in *all* the Scriptures the things concerning Himself" (Luke 24:27).

• • •

I. Symbolism
    A. What are symbols, and what do they teach?
    B. *Seven symbols of the Savior*
        1. The Scepter of God (Genesis 49:10)
        2. The Manna from Heaven (Exodus 16:4)
        3. The Smitten Rock (Exodus 17:6)
        4. The Brazen Serpent (Numbers 21:8)
        5. The Messianic Star (Numbers 24:17)
        6. Noah's Ark (Genesis 7:1)
        7. The Beautiful Branch (Isaiah 4:2)

II. Typology
    A. What are types, and what do they teach?
    B. *Three types of the Prototype Christ*
        1. The First Adam and Second Adam (Genesis 2:7; 1 Corinthians 15:45)

2. Melchizedek—A Perfect Type of Christ (Genesis 14:18–20)

   3. Isaac—A Beautiful Type of Christ (Genesis 22)

III. Appearances

   A. "The *Angel* of His presence saved them"—Christ (Isaiah 63:9)

   B. *Our Lord's seven appearances in the Form of "the Angel of the Lord"*—Christ

      1. Hagar, the Egyptian (Genesis 16:7–11)

      2. Abraham, the first Jew (Genesis 22:11–18)

      3. Jacob, the prince with God and men (Genesis 28:12–15)

      4. Moses, the law-giver (Exodus 3:2–6—a comparison of Moses and Christ is inserted for further study)

      5. Joshua, the successful successor of Moses (Joshua 5:13–15)

      6. Gideon, the mighty man of valor (Judges 6:11–14)

      7. Samson's parents, from whom was born the strongest man in the world (Judges 13:13–18)

IV. Questionnaire and Answers

• • •

In Jeremiah 6:16, God the Almighty says, "*Stand* at the crossroads, and behold, inquire and ask [of God] for the old *ancient paths* [of truth], where is found the good, godly, and eternal way [Christ the Way] and walk [by faith] in it, and you shall find the rest for your soul" (Free Translation).

On the "ancient paths" of the Old Testament you will see the footprints of Jesus in the historical and prophetical inspired Books, that can impart spiritual rest and reassurance to your soul.

The following remarkable Scriptures on prophecies that we will refer to *point to Christ* in whom all prophecy will reach its fulfillment, conclusion, and consummation. For the Word says in Revelation 19:10, "The testimony of Jesus is the spirit of prophecy." I believe this means that all the essential truths of prophecy must *center in Christ*.

In Romans 15:4 we read, "For whatsoever things were written aforetime were written for our *learning,* that we, through patience and comfort of the Scriptures, might have hope" [hope in Christ].

Therefore, emerging from the little-known or read, yet infallible, inexhaustible, and indestructible books of the Old Testament appears one familiar and famous Person, better known to us out of the widely read twenty-seven Books of the amazing, thrilling, and stimulating New Testament—none other than the *Lord Jesus Christ* Himself. He is the outstanding figure and theme of the Holy Bible.

From the Jewish Bible, called by Christians the Old Testament, we intend to set forth again by the help of the Holy Spirit our loving Savior, in addition to Christ in Eternity, Christ in Creation, and now Christ in the beloved Old Testament. Let us walk with our Lord down three ancient, ageless, and awesome paths of truth that I pray will cause us to think much more of Christ and His Word than ever before.

We shall now consider these three steady steps in the ancient paths of truth:

- Stepping in the light of symbols
- Stepping in the light of types
- Stepping in the light of mystical appearances

During a certain critical time in the New Testament, two Greeks said to the Apostle Philip, "Sir, we would see Jesus," John 12:20–22. These are exactly my sentiments as we search out ancient Scriptures, that in *them* "we would see Jesus." As the wise men of old that set out, led of the Spirit, may we find Him, and then let us journey with Him on holy ground within the sacred pages that was predetermined and predestined by God His Father along every path, trail, and road He trod on the old land of promise known to us as Palestine, or modern Israel. However, *my prayer is that not only every awakened Gentile reading these pages may see Jesus as the Greeks did that day, but sons of Abraham also.*

As the Hebrew writer wrote in Hebrews 2:9, first addressing the Jews, "But we would see Jesus ... crowned with glory and honor; that He [Jesus] by the grace of God should taste death for every *son* (son of Abraham)," (Free Translation).

Bear with me once more on an important passage in the New Testament before we explore the Old.

Jesus preached to a captive audience on the first meaningful day of His resurrection what I might call "His Seven-Mile Sermon" to the two men going to Emmaus from Jerusalem. Read with me these very fitting post-resurrection Scriptures that give the underlining contents of the Old Testament.

In Luke 24:25-27, Jesus speaks to His two bewildered disciples, "O foolish ones and slow of heart to believe all that the prophets have spoken! Ought not Christ to have suffered these things and to enter into His glory? And beginning at Moses [the first five books of the Bible] and *all* the prophets [Major and Minor] He expounded unto them in *all* the Scriptures the things concerning *Himself*."

May the risen Lord do likewise for us who believe, that our hearts might burn within us. That He might open our dim eyes like He did the privileged Cleopas and his companion. That we too may understand the precious truth that Christ can be seen from the concealed passages of the Old Testament as well as in the revealed writings of the New. *God bless this chapter to all who read its prayer-immersed pages. May the Holy Spirit, our promised and given Comforter, who from the Father and the Son, may take the things of Christ and reveal them to all who have a burning desire to know and love Him as Savior, and thereafter as Sovereign Lord, gently guide us into all truth.*

We shall start with what I believe to be the most important and, to many, undiscovered symbols and types of Christ found in the blessed Old Testament.

Symbolism

A symbol is something that stands for, or suggests something else by reason of relationship, association, comparison, emblem, or resemblance. In short, a symbol is a token of identity. To give you a New Testament comparison: Believer's Baptism is a *symbol* of salvation outwardly as to what has happened inwardly. In the Lord's Supper, unleavened bread and the red wine of the vine when processed *symbolizes* the bruised body and the bleeding royal blood from Emmanuel's veins. "The Lord our Passover."

It appears to me that symbols and types sometimes can be used interchangeably, but for my purpose, let me say that generally symbols bear a likeness to things, whereas types apply more so to people.

A type sets forth a living model, a perfect example, a pure pattern, a familiar form, a real figure of the prototype, and that will unquestionably be *Christ*. Types foreshadow the original. In our case, symbols and types that we will use from the Old Testament will show a remarkable resemblance, and more often than not, a perfect example of its Figure, Jesus Christ, the embodiment of all Scripture, Romans 5:14.

I plan to use *seven symbols* and *three types* very briefly from the Holy Scriptures pointing out Old Testament passages, and then show its fulfillment. This should be helpful to *Sunday School teachers, teachers in Christian day schools,* as well as *students in Bible colleges or seminaries* who would like to study the complete *Doctrine of Christology.* But most of all, *preachers* I hope, who will secure a copy for their own enrichment. As a matter of fact, *anyone who loves Jesus* and wants to know Him better, even those that *love not our Lord that such may be brought under conviction,* and *be converted by God's transforming power* and my feeble scribbling.

Seven Symbols of Salvation

The Scepter of God—which represents a Rod to Rule, or the Staff to Reign.

"The scepter (staff) shall not depart from Judah, nor a lawgiver (rod) from between His feet, until Shiloh (Messiah) come; and unto Him (Christ) shall the gathering of the people be," Genesis 49:10 (Free Translation).

"But unto the *Son* he saith, Thy throne, O *God,* is forever and ever. A scepter of righteousness is the scepter of Thy kingdom," Hebrews 1:8 (Free Translation).

The above verses obviously are addressed to Christ as the Son, with a capital "S." Also the *coming King* of the ages, King of the Jews, King of Saints, and the King of the Kingdom of God.

The Manna from Heaven—Christ the Bread of Life from Heaven.

"Then said the Lord unto Moses, Behold, I will rain *bread from heaven* for you; and the people shall go out and gather a certain rate (portion) every day, that I may prove them . . ." Exodus 16:4.

"Your fathers did eat manna in the wilderness, and are dead. This is the bread which cometh down from heaven, that a man may eat thereof, and not die," John 6:49,50.

Jesus says, *"I am that Bread of Life,"* John 6:48.

The thought here is that we are to feast on Christ and His truths daily for our sustenance and spiritual strength.

The Smitten Rock—Christ the Living Water.

"Behold, I will stand before thee there upon *the Rock* in Horeb; and thou shalt smite the rock, and there shall come *water* out of it, that the people may drink . . . ," Exodus 17:6.

Matthew 16:18, ". . . upon this *Rock* I will build My church . . ."

1 Corinthians 10:4, ". . . for they drank of that spiritual *Rock* that followed them: and that Rock was *Christ*."

In both the Old as well as the New Testament, Christ in each of the above Scriptures is seen: in Matthew as the Founder of His Church; in 1 Corinthians as the Giver of Living Water to His people through the *smitten* Rock that speaks of the cross.

The Brazen Serpent—Christ, the Gift of Eternal Life.

"And the Lord said unto Moses, Make thee a fiery (bronze) serpent, and set it upon a pole: and it shall come to pass, that every one (whosoever) that is bitten, when he *looketh* upon it, shall live," Numbers 21:8.

"As Moses lifted up the serpent in the wilderness, even so *must* the Son of man be lifted up: that whosoever *believeth* in Him should not perish, but have *eternal life*," John 3:14,15.

What a beautiful illustration of the story of salvation in our Savior Jesus Christ. There is life in the look of faith to Christ who died in the sinner's stead. Through Him, every poisonous stain of sin from Satan's bite is immediately removed, and we are washed as white as snow.

"For the wages of sin is death; but the gift of God is *eternal life* through Jesus Christ our Lord," Romans 6:23.

The Messianic Star—Christ the Expected King of the Jews.

Numbers 24:17, "I shall see *Him*, but not now: I shall behold Him, but not nigh: there shall come a *Star* (Christ) out of Jacob . . ."

Matthew 2:2, "Saying, Where is *He* that is born *King of the Jews*? For we have seen *His Star* in the east, and are come to worship Him."

Only God is worthy of our worship, and Jesus is God. He says of Himself in Revelation 22:16, ". . . I am the *Root* [beginning] and the *Offspring* [Divine Descendant] of David, and the *Bright and Morning Star*."

God forbid that we should be so taken up with the cares of this world and not expect Christ to come at any moment. This was a mistake of the Nation of Israel when He came the first time.

Noah's Ark—Christ the only protection that shelters us from the storm of God's wrath and judgment.

Genesis 7:1, "And the Lord said unto Noah, Come thou and all thy house into the ark . . ."

Verse 7, "And Noah went in, and his sons, and his wife, and his sons' wives with him, into the ark . . ."

Verse 16, ". . . the Lord shut them in."

Noah found grace along with the rest of his family that were spared from God's judgment.

Romans 8:1, "There is therefore *now* no condemnation (judgment) to them which are *in Christ Jesus,* who walk not after the flesh, but after the Spirit."

We are shut in to God's Grace in Christ and shut out to God's wrath that must yet fall upon those found in their own sins, unforgiven, unsaved, and unprepared to meet Him.

The Beautiful Branch—Christ the source of a fruitful life.

Isaiah 4:2, "In that day shall the *Branch* of the Lord be beautiful and glorious, and the fruit of the earth shall be excellent and comely (very fair) for them that are escaped of Israel."

John 15:4,5, "Abide in Me, and I in you. As the branch cannot bear fruit of itself, except it abide in the vine; no more can ye, except ye abide in Me. I am the *Vine,* ye are the branches: He that abideth in Me, and I in him, the same bringeth forth *much* fruit: for without Me ye can do nothing."

How fruitful is your life? Are you a fruit bearer for Christ? Those that do not abide in Him are only dead branches and will be cut off from the land of the living, gathered up, and burned. Will you not take stock of your Christian life and answer these questions?

Are you a healthy tree or a sickly one? Productive in bearing fruit or barren? God expects us to be in Christ, fruitbearers, not religious nuts.

These verses seem to teach that every Christian that has spiritual life in Christ is to be a fruit bearer in some way, otherwise you are none of His. I want to bear fruit. Don't you?

Typology

After mentioning in the briefest terms *seven symbols of salvation* regarding the Son of God and the Savior of men, we now move deeper into this chapter to present the first three and perhaps the most interesting and informative types of Christ out of the seven.

Here is the list of these men to study as types of Christ: Adam, Melchizedek, Isaac, Joseph, Moses, Joshua, David, and even Elijah. Before we give you the first three of the above personal types of Christ from the Old Testament, may I say a word about true types.

You would do well to remember in the following pages that the antitype of the New Testament is the true Christ that was prefigured as a type of Christ in the Old Testament.

A true type must contain three definite characteristics:

- The type must correspond in likeness to the person it foreshadows (Conformity to Christ).

- The type and antitype must be foreordained in God's predestined plan.

- The type, moreover, must also point to the future which is not necessarily true with symbols.

Dear friend, if you profess Christ, are you a good image and likeness of the Savior? We are to reflect in word and deed what Jesus would do outwardly, if He lives within (1 Corinthians 15:49).

Adam: A Comparative Type of Christ in Four Ways

1. The first Adam was made a "living soul," Genesis 2:7. The second Adam (Christ) was made a "life-giving Spirit," 1 Corinthians 15:45 (Free Translation).

2. The first Adam was the progenitor and federal head of the human race, Genesis 1:28. The Second Adam was the Spiritual Head and Progenitor of the saved race, 1 Corinthians 15:47,49; 2 Corinthians 5:17.

3. In Adam all died, Romans 5:12. In Christ shall all be made alive 1 Corinthians 15:22; John 10:10.

4. Adam brought sin into the world, Romans 5:12. Christ takes away the sin of the world, John 1:29.

Melchizedek: A Perfect Type of Christ in Five Ways

When this mysterious person is referred to in manifesting the Person of Christ, I shall use capitalization because I believe *His appearance* in the Old Testament is an *early edition* of the life of our Lord. This Old Testament character is, I think my favorite, because Melchizedek is the most perfect type of Christ of all, Genesis 14:18–20.

1. In His significant *name:*

Hebrews 7:2, "First being by interpretation [when translated means] King of Righteousness, and after that also King of Salem, which is King of Peace."

Jesus, thrice King of Righteousness, will be King of Jerusalem, and now as in time to come, King of Peace. Melchizedek's name connects him to Christ. Praise His *wonderful name,* Isaiah 9:6.

2. In His *divinely* appointed ordinance:

The elements of *"bread and wine"* which depict Christ's body and blood, foreshadows the Lord's Supper. Melchizedek was the first to use these sacred elements which point to Jesus' teaching about His memorial death at Calvary, Genesis 14:18; Luke 22:15–20.

3. In His *priestly* office:

Genesis 14:18, "He was the priest of the most high God."

Melchizedek is the first priest mentioned in the Bible, long before the Aaronic priesthood of the Levitical line. ". . . after the similitude of Melchizedek [and not Aaron], there arises another priest [Christ]," Hebrews 7:15. This is superior to the old order that has terminated in Christ. For it follows not the death of Aaron but "the power of an endless life." *There is no need for any priesthood on earth today.* Jesus supersedes all others, and His office today is not on earth but in heaven.

4. In His perpetual, eternal character:

Pertaining again to Melchizedek as a perfect resemblance of Christ, Hebrews 7:3 says, "Without father, without mother, without descent [meaning lineage and following no earthly or ancestral lineage as applied to Christ's divine side], having neither beginning of days, nor end of life; but made like unto the *Son of God . . .*"

Lest someone think wrongly regarding the phrase "without father, without mother," we must bear in mind that Christ existed as *"the Word"* before He was *"born in the flesh,"* John 1:1; 1 John 4:2.

5. In His receiving tithes from man:

Genesis 14:20, "And he (Abraham) gave Him (Melchizedek) tithes of all."

Hebrews 7:4, "Now consider how great this man was, unto whom even the patriarch Abraham gave the tenth of the spoils."

The only one deserving of the tithe is God. For the tithe is the Lord's, and Jesus is God. Therefore, Melchizedek in justly impersonating Christ received the tithe from the father of the faithful, Abraham. Do you believe in tithing? Remember the words of the Lord Jesus when He said, "It is more blessed to give than to receive," Acts 20:35. Moreover, Jesus taught in Matthew 23:23, *"These ought you to have done,* and not to leave the other undone." Referring to the tithe, Christians ought to reflect Christ in different ways: in love, loyalty, and truth.

Isaac: A Beautiful Type of Christ in Three Major Ways

1. *In His birth,* Romans 4:17–25; 9:7–9.

He was a promised Son.

Genesis 21:1, "And the Lord visited Sarah as He had said, and the Lord did unto Sarah as He had spoken."

God's promises in Christ are all "yea, yea, and Amen" (numbering, according to a friend in Canada, 8,810 promises), and most of them are in Christ. This was made good to Sarah. They shall all be made good to us, if you only believe.

He was a supernatural Son.

Genesis 21:2, "For Sarah conceived and bare Abraham a son in his old age . . ."

Sarah was ninety and Abraham was one hundred years old, according to Genesis 17:17. Have you received a miraculous supernatural birth? I have, and you must, John 3:3,7.

He was the only son.

Genesis 22:2, "Take now thy son, thine *only son* Isaac, whom thou lovest . . ." Do you love Him with all your heart?

John 3:16, "For God so loved the world that He gave *His only begotten Son . . .*"

2. *In His Sacrifice,* Genesis 22:1–14; Hebrews 11:17,18.

The supreme test of love is sacrifice. In this second step we focus on a forecast of Calvary.

Isaac was obedient to his father.

Philippians 2:8, "And being found in fashion as a man He humbled Himself, and became obedient unto death, even the death of the cross."

Abraham spared not his own son Isaac.

Romans 8:32, "He that *spared not* His own Son, but delivered Him up for us all . . ." Not all without exception, but all without distinction.

The Son of God who died was a perfect offering for man's sins. If all the world's best died to save one of the world's worst, it could not be. Each man is a sinner and guilty before God. Their offering would be a sinful offering that God, as a Holy God, could not accept. One or many men could never equal the sacrifice of Christ. *Only His sinless Son* could do that.

Abraham was given a ram from God, as a substitute for Isaac.

Genesis 22:13, "And Abraham lifted up his eyes, and looked, and behold behind him a ram caught in a thicket by his horns: and Abraham went and took the ram, and offered him up for a burnt offering in the stead of his son."

John 1:29, "Behold, the Lamb of God which taketh (beareth) away the sin of the world." What a beautiful picture of our Lord's substitutionary work for us!

I deserve to die. That would be my expected wages because of sin. God in His mercy provided a substitute to die in my stead. Thank you, Jesus!

Abraham officiated as his own priest in adoration to God by offering up his son. In pagan religious ceremonies, this was the custom of the time. God does not want human sacrifices, but He does want an *obedient heart*. Sacrificing His Son on the altar was the only way sinners, unclean, could be cleansed.

Abraham expected that God would raise his son up again: "Abraham said to the two men with him [which could represent the *two malefactors* crucified with Christ], Abide ye here with the donkey; and I and the lad (or young man) will go yonder and worship, and come again to you'" (Genesis 22:5).

Hebrews 11:19 proves that Abraham believed God would raise him up from among the dead. John 8:56 expresses Abraham's faith in the coming Messiah, which is the same saving faith of all those saints, like Abraham in the whole of the Old Testament, Galatians 3:8,16.

3. *On His Marriage.*

At this juncture it would be well to retire to the entire twenty-fourth chapter of Genesis to be further blessed with the whole picture from the thoughts that will ensue.

In this third and final step in the analogy of Isaac as a type of Christ, we see beyond Christ's supernatural birth and His blessed redemptive qualities to our Lord as the *Beloved Bridegroom* with His *betrothed bride.* A brief study of *Christ and His Church.*

Three things are called to our attention in relation to this Marriage. But first in all fairness to God, we need to say that Abraham is an excellent type of God the Father. *He chooses a bride for His Son,* and directs His chief servant Eliezer, who represents the Holy Spirit, where to find her. This is a glorious truth. We should be reminded that all the members that make up the holy church, as the body of Christ, are the elect and chosen ones by the Father.

Ephesians 1:4-13, "According as He hath *chosen us* in Him before the foundation of the world, that we should be holy and without blame before Him in *love:* having *predestinated us* unto the adoption of children by Jesus Christ to Himself, according to the good pleasure of *His will.* To the praise of the glory of His grace, wherein He hath made us accepted in the Beloved. In whom we have *redemption* through His blood, the *forgiveness* of sins, according to the riches of *His grace.* Wherein He hath abounded toward us in all wisdom and prudence; having made known unto us the mystery of His will, according to His good pleasure which He hath *purposed in Himself:* that in the dispensation of the fulness of times He might *gather together* in one all things *in Christ,* both which are in heaven, and which are on earth; even in Him: in whom also we have obtained an *inheritance,* being predestinated according to the purpose of Him who worketh all things after the counsel of His own will: that we should be to the praise of *His glory,* who first trusted in Christ. In whom ye also trusted, after that ye heard the Word of truth, the *Gospel* of your salvation: in whom also after that ye believed, ye were sealed with that *Holy Spirit of promise*".

The bridegroom Isaac is the beautiful type of Christ.

Hebrews 11:18, "That in Isaac shall *thy seed* [Christ's seed] be called."

The bride Rebekah is the *called out* one, a true type of the church.

Acts 15:14, "Simeon (Simon Peter) hath declared how God at the first did visit the Gentiles, to *take out* of them a people for His name."

John 14:26, "But the Comforter, which is the Holy Ghost (Spirit) whom the Father will send in My name, He will teach you all things, and bring all things to your remembrance, whatsoever I have said unto you."

The servant *Eliezer* is a fitting type of the work of the *Holy Spirit* sent forth by the father *Abraham*, typical of God, to win by *love*, and make willing a desirable *bride*, typical of the *church*, in behalf of his dear son *Isaac*; typical of *Jesus*, in bringing her to the father's house, typical of heaven, where he waits for her. The unfolding of this lovely story is the longest chapter in Genesis and is worth your personal attention. God bless you as you read it, and believe on the Christ of Holy Scripture.

Christ: The "Angel of the Lord" of the Old Testament

In the third chapter on creation, angels were mentioned as created beings by Christ, who is credited with the creation of all things. Now on Ancient Paths, we want to say a little more in depth about the large role angels play in Scripture, and climax this summary in *Christ* as *"the Angel of the Lord."*

Isaiah 63:9, "When they (His people) were afflicted so was God, and the *Angel of God's presence saved* them in His love and pity He (Christ) redeemed them: and He lifted them up and carried them, all the days of old (times)" (Free Translation).

Christ is the Redeeming Angel of the Lord in the Old Testament. Notice in Genesis 48:16, "The Angel (capitalized) which redeemed me from all evil . . ."

Christ is the *only* Redeemer of God as a member of the admirable and adorable Godhead. He is not a created being, but a divine Being. He is distinct from the other angels, for this expression, *"The Angel of the Lord,"* is referred to about seventy times in the Old Testament. Each time the word angel as above is used ought to be capitalized as it is in a number of places in the Old Testament when referring to Christ Jesus our Sovereign Lord. As a matter of fact, the usages of the word angel, cherub, cherubim, seraphim, and archangel, when summed up, amount to 453 times, according to my calculation. The tally looks like this:

WALKING WITH OUR LORD—PART 1

Cherub means *held fast* .... 25 times

Cherubim means *held fast*.
First angel spoken of in the Bible,
used to protect the tree of life .... 65 times

Seraphim means *burning* .... 2 times

Angel(s) means *messenger(s)*—Old Testament .... 111 times

Angel(s) means *messenger(s)*—New Testament .... 178 times

Archangel means *chief messenger* .... 2 times

"The Angel of the Lord, or of God,
or of His presence," is identified as Christ .... 70 times

This phrase is taken from the 111 times out of the Old Testament. In the New Testament, the phrase "the Angel of the Lord" does not appear *after* the birth of Christ. A crowning verse that teaches that angels are in subjection to Christ is 1 Peter 3:22.

Jesus in the Old Testament is the revealer of God the Father as He is in the New, but more fully. A book could be written with the title, "The Angel of the Lord," but limited space will allow only for the following.

The people that "the Angel of the Lord" made appearances to, found in the Old Testament, are: Hagar, Genesis 16:7,8; Abraham, Genesis 22:11; Jacob, Genesis 28:12; Moses, Exodus 3:2; Joshua (in the midst of Israel), Judges 2:4,6; Balaam, Numbers 22:22–35; Gideon, Judges 6:11–22; Manoah, Samson's father, Judges 13:13–21; David, 1 Chronicles 21:16; Ornan, 1 Chronicles 21:20; Elijah, 2 Kings 1:3; Isaiah, Isaiah 37:36; and Zechariah, Zechariah 12:8–10).

Thus we have thirteen visible appearances of the Angel of the Lord to different people in different periods.

The Angel of the Lord Appears First to Hagar

Hagar, an Egyptian slave girl for Sarah, Abraham's wife, is found in the first appearance of Christ as "the Angel of the Lord."

Genesis 16:7–11, "And *the Angel of the Lord* found her by a fountain (spring) of water in the wilderness, by the fountain in the way to Shur. And He said, Hagar, Sarai's maid, whence camest thou? and whither wilt thou go? And she said, I flee from the face of my mistress Sarai.

And *the Angel of the Lord* said unto her, Return to thy mistress, and submit thyself under her hands. And *the Angel of the Lord* said unto her, *I will* multiply thy seed exceedingly, that it shall not be numbered for multitude. And *the Angel of the Lord* said unto her, Behold, thou art with child, and shalt bear a son, and shalt call his name Ishmael; because the Lord hath heard thy affliction." Ishmael means "God shall hear."

If you wish to read verse 12 in the same chapter, you will find that Ishmael's descendents in this prophecy became the Arab tribes which characterize their action as hard to reach and reason with. Example: Israel and the Arab terrorist nations today.

The Angel of the Lord Appears to Abraham

Genesis 22:11,12,15–18, "And *the Angel of the Lord* called unto him out of heaven, and said, 'Abraham, Abraham:' and he said, Here am I. And he said, Lay not thine hand upon the lad, neither do thou anything unto him: for now I know that thou fearest God, seeing thou hast not withheld thy son, thine only son from Me.

"And *the Angel of the Lord* called unto Abraham out of heaven the second time, and said, By Myself have I sworn, saith the Lord, for because thou hast done this thing, and hast not withheld thy son, thine only son: that in blessing *I will* bless thee, and in multiplying I will multiply thy seed as the stars in the heaven, and as the sand which is upon the sea shore; and thy seed shall possess the gate of his enemies; and in thy seed shall all the nations of the earth be blessed; because thou hast obeyed *My voice*."

Here Abraham was obedient in his supreme test of love to God in offering up his only son from whom God would bless and multiply his seed abundantly beyond measure. Oh, how we need to obey the Words of God and reap the blessings He has in store for us! In Abraham's seed, by the way, Christ came, and that prediction is in Genesis 12:3: "In Thee [Christ, the seed on the human side as the Son of Abraham, not in Abraham, but in Christ] shall all the families of the earth be blessed."

The Angel of the Lord Appears to Jacob

Jacob, our next privileged patriarch, is found with the equivalent of a conversion experience in Genesis 28:12. Before we read about Jacob's first real encounter with God, permit me to acquaint you with Jacob's state of mind.

WALKING WITH OUR LORD—PART 1

He flees from Esau, his brother, whom Jacob thinks is out to kill him. A family feud is over the birthright that he deceptively acquired. Isaac pronounces a blessing on him. Jacob departs alone on his way to his Uncle Laban's house in Padanaram, which was his mother Rebekah's brother. He reaches a point of exhaustion, and selects a stone for his pillow and falls asleep.

Genesis 28:12, "And he dreamed, and behold a ladder set up on the earth, and the top of it reached to heaven: and behold the angels of God ascending and descending on it."

John 1:51, "And He saith unto him, Verily, verily, I say unto you, hereafter ye shall see heaven open, and *the angels of God* ascending and descending upon the Son of man (Christ)."

Jesus says to Nathanael, who had just confessed Christ not only as teacher, but as the Son of God, and the King of Israel. "Hereafter you shall see heaven open and the angels of God ascending and descending upon the Son of man." *Jesus is man's ladder to heaven*. Beloved, if we are saved, we too shall say and see greater things about Christ's coming in glory, when God opens heaven for us. Now let us examine the Scriptures before us, concerning Jacob's conversion.

Genesis 28:13, "And behold the Lord stood above it, and said *I am* the Lord God of Abraham thy father, and the God of Isaac; the land where thou liest, to thee will I give it, and to thy seed."

The promise to Abraham and Isaac is restated and reaffirmed to him. We are told that it was *the Angel of the Lord* that spoke with him, in somewhat of the same way that *the Angel of the Lord* spoke with his grandfather. In Hosea 12:4, the prophet makes it clear that it was at the first where this incident took place. That it was *the Angel of the Lord* that stood above him, and met him there at Bethel, where Jacob committed his life to the Lord.

Further, in Genesis 31:11–13, "And *the Angel of God* spake unto me in a dream, saying, Jacob: And I said, Here am I. And He said, Lift up now thine eyes, and see, all the rams which leap upon the cattle are ringstraked, speckled, and grisled: for I have seen all that Laban doeth unto thee. I am the *God* of Beth-el, where thou anointedst the pillar, and where thou vowedst a vow unto Me: now arise, get thee out from this land, and return unto the land of thy kindred."

Here again *"the Angel of God"* spoke with Jacob, some twenty years later, confirming the covenant, and commanding that he return home. In obedience to the divine command he gathers up his possessions, and leaves secretly for his native land. On the way back a great fear came upon him regarding Esau, whom he thought aimed to destroy him and all that he had. He was afraid not only for his own life, but his entire family. After some manipulating, he puts a plan in operation. In distress, Jacob sent his family ahead in two separate bands or companies, and he remained behind to pray.

Then in Genesis 32:24–30, it says, "And Jacob was left alone; and there wrestled a *Man* with him until the breaking of the day. And when He saw that he prevailed not against him (Jacob), He touched the hollow of his thigh; and the hollow of Jacob's thigh was out of joint, as he wrestled with Him. And he said, Let me go, for the day breaketh. And he said, I will not let thee go, except thou bless me. And He said unto him, What is thy name? And he said, Jacob. And He said, 'Thy name shall be called no more Jacob, but Israel: for as a prince hast thou power *with God* and *with men,* and hast prevailed. And Jacob asked Him, and said, Tell me, I pray Thee, thy name. And He said, Wherefore is it that thou dost ask after My name? And He blessed him there. And Jacob called the name of the place Peniel: for I have seen *God* face to face, and my life is preserved."

The *Man* that he wrestled with that night till the break of day should be capitalized, as it refers to the Man Christ Jesus in angelic form. This third personal, unforgettable encounter with *the Angel of the Lord* is commendable and mysterious. It is a scene not of a vision nor of a dream, but a real transaction. A person with great mental anxiety holds on to the Lord before meeting his depressing trial that swayed his unshakeable faith, believing that he must have the victory before releasing the grip on God's promises, and faith prevailed. He asked for the blessing of protection and preservation for himself and his own, basing his argument on the covenant relation, and won.

The name of this valiant man was changed that night from Jacob, meaning supplanter, deceiver, schemer, to Israel, meaning contending as a prince with God and with men. With this remarkable accomplishment, *the Angel of the Lord* touched his thigh. The socket sinews of the hip joint was disconnected so that he might ever remember this victorious and yet humbling experience. From henceforth he must walk with a limp, caused by the touch of God. In addition to these three mountaintop, crowning adventures, he is yet to have one more. This one God directs, not to him alone, but his family.

Genesis 35:9, "And God appeared unto Jacob again, when he came out of Pandanaram, and blessed him."

The reason why God blessed him is because he was obedient to His command. Genesis 35:1 says, "And God said unto Jacob, Arise, go up to Beth-el and dwell there and make there an altar unto God."

He was to build his family around this altar where he came to know the Lord, as a monument of God's grace. Jacob said to his household in Genesis 35:2, "*Put away the strange gods that are among you and be clean...*"

Bethel, house of God, was the place where he and his family were to worship. Christians need to return to the God of their fathers, to the house of God, and worship Him, putting all their gods away to serve the one and only God of the Bible, who alone can bless your life beyond measure, and give you the victory in Jesus.

The Angel of the Lord Appears to Moses

Moses, one of the mightiest and humblest men of the Old Testament, "the Angel of the Lord" appears to next, as a burning Seraphim.

Exodus 3:2–6, "And *the Angel of the Lord* appeared unto him in a flame of fire out of the midst of a bush: and he looked, and, behold, the bush burned with fire, and the bush was not consumed. And Moses said, I will now turn aside, and see this great sight, why the bush is not burnt. And when the Lord saw that he turned aside to see, God called unto him out of the midst of the bush, and said, Moses, Moses. And he said, Here am I. And He said, Draw not nigh hither: put off thy shoes from off thy feet, for the place whereon thou standest is holy ground. Moreover He said, I am the God of thy father, the God of Abraham, the God of Isaac, and the God of Jacob. And Moses hid his face; for he was afraid to look upon God." We see God in the face of Jesus here, as in other places, Christ, "the Angel of the Lord."

This burning bush was a wild acacia tree, dry and brittle. Its flames astonished Moses that it did not burn in a moment. This fire represented the nation of Israel, punished for her disobedience but preserved by God's power and mercy. It has always been so. Both the nation of Israel, as well as the Church, has suffered great persecution, and shall continue off and on until the return of Christ.

If Abraham was rightly called the "friend of God," so can we. The Bible says God is "no respecter of persons." God in Christ has freely favored us with His mercy, by our blessings we learn through obedience, which is a true mark of our relationship as heirs of God and joint heirs with Christ.

Moses displays the long-suffering of God, for it is said of him in Hebrews 3:2 that he was "faithful in all his house." Can that, at the end of our life's journey, be said of us? God grant it!

The Angel of the Lord that appeared to Moses and addressed him with a climactic commission is doubtless the divine Being, Jesus, elsewhere called *the Angel of the covenant*, and Jehovah–Jesus. Moses had already made a decision forty years ago when the Spirit of God had moved upon him in Egypt when he believed he was divinely chosen to be the deliverer of the nation of Israel.

Hebrews 11:24–27, "By faith Moses, when he was come to years, refused to be called the son of Pharaoh's daughter; choosing rather to suffer affliction with the people of God, than to enjoy the pleasures of sin for a season; esteeming the reproach of *Christ* greater riches than the treasures in Egypt: for he had respect unto the recompence of the reward. By faith he forsook Egypt, not fearing the wrath of the king: for he endured, as seeing *Him* who is invisible."

Now at the age of eighty Moses is now ready to be God's leader for His people in bondage. When God calls in Christ, you are never too old to serve Him.

Just now I feel led to insert a positive parallel, a stimulating similitude and marked likeness between Moses and Jesus.

- Both men were providentially protected after birth, Exodus 2:2–10; Matthew 2:14,15.
- Both men dealt with evil forces (Pharaoh could represent Satan), Exodus 7:11, Matthew 4:1.
- Both men fasted forty days and nights (Moses twice), Exodus 34:28; Matthew 4:2.
- Both men had power to restrain the sea (Red Sea and Sea of Galilee), Exodus 14:21; Matthew 8:26.
- Both men miraculously fed multitudes, Exodus 16:15; Matthew 14:20,21.

WALKING WITH OUR LORD—PART 1

- Both men introduced and established rituals (Passover and Memorial Supper), Exodus 12:14; Luke 22:19.
- Both men appeared alive after death, Matthew 17:3; Acts 1:3.

The Angel of the Lord Appears to Joshua

Joshua 5:13-15, "And it came to pass, when Joshua was by Jericho, that he lifted up his eyes and looked, and, behold, there stood a *Man* over against him with his sword drawn in His hand: and Joshua went unto Him, and said unto Him, Art Thou for us, or for our adversaries? And He said, Nay; but as *Captain* of the host of the Lord am I now come. And Joshua fell on his face to the earth, and *did worship,* and said unto Him, What saith my Lord unto his servant? And the captain of the Lord's host said unto Joshua, Loose thy shoe from off thy foot; for the place whereon thou standest is holy. And Joshua did so."

Joshua, the likeable and dependable personal attendant to Moses, became his successor and developed into a great general in conquering Canaan. He is one of the most noteworthy and blameless men in the Old Testament.

Preceding the fall of Jericho, *"The Angel of the Lord"* appeared to him much like his advent to Moses (Exodus 3:5), only this time as the Son of God in shining armor. His sword is drawn as the commanding Prince of the armies of the Lord's host. This appearance, like on other occasions, "the Angel of the Lord" was the object of worship, as only God is worthy of worship.

We need more worshippers like Joshua, not kneeling, but prostrate on our faces, if we are to be conquerors for Christ in the pulling down of the devil's stronghold and fortified cities. Anyplace where we meet the Lord is holy ground. If our command is anything like Joshua, who was to drive out the enemies of the Lord and possess the Promised Land, we need to defeat our adversaries in the name of, not captain only as our conquering Commander, but our present Princely Priest, and our sudden soon-coming, all-powerful King.

The Angel of the Lord Appears to Gideon

Gideon is the next worthy one that receives a visitation from the Holy One of Israel.

Judges 6:11-14, "And there came the Angel of the Lord, and sat under an oak which was in Ophrah, that pertained unto Joash the Abiezrite: and his son Gideon threshed wheat by the winepress, to hide it from the Midianites. And *the Angel of the Lord appeared unto him,* and said unto him, The Lord is with thee, thou mighty man of valour. And Gideon said unto Him, Oh my Lord, if the Lord be with us, why then is all this befallen us? and where be all His miracles which our fathers told us of, saying, Did not the Lord bring us up from Egypt? but now the Lord hath forsaken us, and delivered us into the hands of the Midianites. And the Lord looked upon him, and said, Go in this thy might, and thou shalt save Israel from the hand of the Midianites: have not *I sent thee?"*

Gideon met the "Angel of the Lord" when beating the wheat in the winepress, while hiding from the Midianites. This is a brave work in preserving food for his people. If the enemy knew it, he would die. Because of this, the Lord addresses him as a mighty man of fearless valor and continued courage.

Notice, the full title of the Angel is not mentioned in verse 14, but the famous name of the Lord is left. The Lord commissions him with the words, "Go in this thy might, and you shall save Israel . . . have not I sent you?" These words could not come from a messenger of the Lord as some angel, but the divine Son Himself. After the Lord proved Himself to Gideon, nothing could turn him away from his assigned course, regardless of how much his army was reduced. With fearless faith, Gideon set the Midianites aflight with only three hundred men, after some military testing, as he followed to the letter the instructions of the Lord.

The Angel of the Lord Appears to Samson's Parents

Samson's parents are the next to prepare the way of the Lord in producing a son.

Judges 13:13–18, "And *the Angel of the Lord* said unto Manoah, Of all that I said unto the woman let her beware. She may not eat of anything that cometh of the vine, neither let her drink wine or strong drink, nor eat any unclean thing; all that I commanded her let her observe. And Manoah said unto *the Angel of the Lord,* I pray Thee, let us detain Thee, until we shall have made ready a kid for Thee. And *the Angel of the Lord* said unto Manoah, Though thou detain Me, I will not eat of thy bread: and if thou wilt offer a burnt offering, thou must offer it to the Lord. For Manoah knew not that He was an *Angel of the Lord.*

And Manoah said unto *the Angel of the Lord,* What is Thy name, that when Thy sayings come to pass we may do Thee honour? And *the Angel of the Lord* said unto him, Why askest thou thus after My name, seeing it is secret?"

Within these verses *"the Angel of the Lord"* is referred seven times to Manoah, the father of Samson. His wife is given a strict diet to be followed during her pregnancy. If our American mothers would take better heed to what was told Manoah's wife in the Word as to what goes into their mouths, their children would no doubt be much healthier and wiser, instead of the retardation and deformity that we have today. What we need are more parents that will listen to the Word of God then we may realize our children are gifts from the Lord, brought up in a Christian environment with reverential fear and godly admonition of the Lord, as illustrated from the Scriptures.

What would happen if God gave us a tribe of holy Samsonites that would be moved with the Spirit within upon the masses of evil from without, with hidden power to turn the world upside down, as was said about the Christians of the first century? This power in the Spirit is ours to use today.

One final word about the *"Angel of the Lord"* being Christ is seen in His name called "Secret, better Wonderful" from verse 18. I would ask that you only read with me Isaiah 9:6, especially this portion, "and His name shall be called Wonderful." Could anyone doubt that the *"Angel of the Lord"* in the Old Testament is none other than our Lord Jesus Christ?

In conclusion to this first part of the Old Testament in Chapter 4, I leave you this precious passage in Psalm 34:7, *"The Angel of the Lord"* [Jesus Christ] encampeth round about them that fear Him and *delivereth* them."

Have you ever been "delivered (liberated) from the wrath to come" by this death-destroying and life-giving One? If you have never been delivered from your sins by His pardoning power and his redeeming Grace, then come this moment to Jesus.

1 Thessalonians 1:10 is addressed to the saints, "And to wait for His Son from heaven, whom He raised from the dead, even Jesus, which *delivered us from the wrath to come."*

• • •

Questionnaire
1. Define a symbol.
2. Name four symbols of the Savior.
3. Define a type.
4. Name two types of Christ given in this chapter.
5. Name five people He appeared to.
6. Give two ways Moses was like Christ.

• • •

Answers
1. Token of identity of something.
2. Scepter, Manna, Rock, Star, Brazen Serpent, Ark, and Branch.
3. A person resembling another.
4. Adam, Melchizedek, and Isaac.
5. Hagar, Abraham, Jacob, Moses, Joshua, Gideon, and Samson's parents.
6. Both were protected in birth and dealt with Satanic powers. Both fasted for forty days and both appeared alive after death.

Chapter 5

Walking With Our Lord on Ancient Paths of Truth: 2
-or-
Christ of the Old Testament in Messianic Prophecies

Introduction
The theme of the Old Testament is Christ, and the heart of the Doctrine of Christology, points to the Cross, and the Crown (Isaiah 53:1–12).

• • •

I. Reflecting on *Christ the center of Old Testament prophecy*
    A. Opening comments on Prophecy (1 Peter 1:10,11)
    B. Ten *messianic prophecies fulfilled,* which proves the authority and accuracy of God's Word.
        1. The first prophecy about Christ (Genesis 3:15)
        2. The place of Christ's birth (Micah 5:2)
        3. The person who gave Him birth (Isaiah 7:14)
        4. The perilous event following His birth (Jeremiah 31:15)
        5. The preparation before and after His birth (Isaiah 40:3–5)
        6. The people most blessed by His ministry (Isaiah 9:2)
        7. The preeminence of His prophectic ministry (Deuteronomy 18:15)
        8. The Physician of no equal in His healing ministry (Isaiah 61:1,2)
        9. The priestly portion of His sacrificial ministry (Psalm 110:4)

10. The photo forecast of His Kingly ministry (Zechariah 9:9)
   C. The seven painful prophetic portraits from *His substitutionary ministry* (Isaiah 53:1–12—when bearing the sins of God's people on the Cross)
      1. Pain from a false friend (Zechariah 11:12)
      2. Pain from false witnesses (Psalm 35:11)
      3. Pain from a paralyzing whip (Isaiah 50:6)
      4. Pain from mocking, lying lips (Psalm 22:7,8)
      5. Pain from agonizing thirst (Psalm 69:21)
      6. Pain from prints of the nails (Psalm 22:16)
      7. Pain in petitioning God for others and himself (Psalm 109:3,4; 22:1)
   D. Placed in a rich man's grave (Isaiah 53:9)
   E. Pleasant portions on Paradise regained through the death and resurrection of Christ (Psalm 16:10)
II. Realizing *Christ as the Sovereign Judge* of all men from the visions of Daniel
   A. Scriptural visions in general (Numbers 12:6; Proverbs 29:18)
   B. Visions in Daniel of the power and glory of Christ.
      1. The vision of Christ, the Stone (Daniel 2:28,32–45)
      2. The vision of Christ, the World's Judge (Daniel 7:9–14)
   C. Concluding comments in closing the Old Testament
III. Questionnaire and Answers

• • •

My beloved reader, know this, that there are hundreds of prophecies in the Old Testament that can be divided into two groups: the fulfilled and unfulfilled Scripture.

As we search them out, may the Holy Spirit lead us to know the truth that the Spirit of Christ inspired the prophets to write about the grace that was to come to us in this Church Age. They testified in the now fulfilled portion about the suffering of Christ, and in the unfulfilled part of prophecy about the glory of Christ that would follow.

1 Peter 1:10,11, "Of which salvation the prophets have inquired and searched diligently, who prophesied of the grace that should come unto you: Searching what, or what manner of time the *Spirit of Christ, which was in* them did signify, when it testified beforehand the sufferings of Christ, and the glory that should follow."

The world through the preaching of the gospel has seen Christ as the *Lamb*, in sacrifice and suffering. Next, the world will see Christ as a *Lion* when He comes in power and great glory, as our Sovereign King to rule and to reign over the whole earth.

The twofold advents are amazingly manifested in the Psalms. Psalm 22 has been referred to as the *"Psalm of the Savior's Cross."* Psalm 24 is called the *"Psalm of the Sovereign's Crown."*

I shall now endeavor to prove the authenticity of the Bible by stating a few verses of prophecy in the Old Testament, and show where that same prophecy was completely fulfilled hundreds and some thousands of years later exactly as God said it would in regard to our Lord's first advent. These fulfilled prophecies ought to persuade all, that God knows the end from the beginning.

My purpose for this is to convince the gainsayers of their danger in doubting the infallibility of Holy Writ, and assure and confirm the faith of believers that they can trust every Scripture in the Bible as inspired by the Spirit of God. Therefore, let me conclude this introduction to prophecy that every promise and prediction made by God through the Old Testament Prophets and New Testament Apostles will all be fulfilled in God's time. I shall deal only with the main Messianic prophecies that have been *fulfilled* to the letter, and leave the *unfulfilled* prophecies relating to our Lord's second advent for the last chapters.

Messianic Prophecies Fulfilled

The most ancient *prophecy* in the Bible about the Messiah is the *seed* of a woman to bear forth Christ:

Genesis 3:15, "And I will put enmity between thee and the woman, and between thy seed and *her seed, it* [Christ] shall bruise thy head, and thou [Satan] shalt bruise *His* heel."

This prophecy was written by Moses about 1,450 years before Christ was born. However, scholars estimate the fall of man occurred somewhere between 6,000 B.C. to 4,000 B.C. Therefore, the prophecy could have been about 6,000 years old when it was *fulfilled* in the death of Christ.

Galatians 4:4, "But when the fulness of time was come, *God sent forth His Son made of a woman* . . ."

The *place* of birth of the infant Messiah:

Micah 5:2, "But thou, *Bethlehem* Ephratah, though thou be little [town] among the thousands of Judah, yet out of thee shall He (Messiah) come forth unto Me (God) that is to be Ruler in Israel, whose going forth have been from of old, *from everlasting.*"

The place of His birth is clearly defined as Bethlehem. This Person, the Messiah (Christ) would be born there who would become Ruler of Israel during the Millennial Reign. This Person to be born was of old, even from eternity as God's Son, and speaks of Christ's Deity.

Luke 2:4–6, "And Joseph also went up from Galilee, out of the city of Nazareth, into Judaea, unto the city of David, which is *called Bethlehem;* (because he was of the house and lineage of David:) to be taxed with Mary his espoused wife, being great with child. And so it was, that, while they were there, the days were accomplished that she should be delivered."

We see in verse 4 that Jesus was born in the Judean Province, in the little town of Bethlehem, as God had foretold through His prophet Micah, about 710 years before the birth of His Son.

The *person* to bear the promised Messiah:

Isaiah 7:14, "Therefore the Lord Himself shall give you a sign: Behold, a *virgin* shall conceive, and bear a Son [Jesus] and shall call His name *Immanuel.*"

Notice, the person in His birth is not a *young maiden,* although she was that and more. She, by necessity, *must be a virgin,* otherwise Christ would have been born in sin and the prophecy would be amiss. Do you believe the *incarnation* to be a divine imperative? I would hope so, because this is not a minor matter, as some doubt and discredit the virgin birth.

In Luke 1:27, God says through the angel Gabriel that this woman was named Mary and she was a virgin, "and the virgin's name was

Mary." Then in verse 31, He says, "And, behold, thou shalt conceive in thy womb and bring forth a Son, and shalt *call His name Jesus.*"

Over in Matthew's Gospel, Chapter 1, verse 23, we are given the meaning of the name *"Emmanuel,"* which being interpreted is *God with us.*" In the Old Testament it was God *for* us. In the New Testament it was God *with* us. Today, to the believer it is God *in* us. "Christ in you" is "the hope of glory," Colossians 1:27. He is nearer to us than breathing, closer than hands or feet.

The *perilous* event following the birth of the young Messiah:

Jeremiah 31:15, "Thus saith the Lord, A voice was heard in Ramah, lamentation and bitter weeping; Rachel weeping for her children refused to be comforted for her children, because they were not."

Did you observe the opening phrase, *"Thus saith the Lord?"* When a prophet or a preacher speaks for God, it ought to be, God speaking through him.

Matthew 2:16–18, "Then Herod, when he saw that he was mocked of the wise men, was exceedingly wroth, and sent forth, and *slew all the children that were in Bethlehem, and in all the coasts thereof, from two years old and under,* according to the time which he had diligently inquired of the wise men. *Then was fulfilled* that which was spoken by *Jeremiah* the prophet, saying, Thus saith the Lord, A voice was heard in Ramah, lamentation, and bitter weeping; Rachel weeping for her children refused to be comforted for her children, because they were not."

I indirectly blame the wise men for this tragedy of the massacre of all those innocent children. If the wise men had kept their eyes on "His Star," and not leaned on their own reasoning by going to Jerusalem, the capital where they supposed the King would be found and announced the birth of King Jesus to Herod saying, "Where is He that is born King of the Jews?" Herod would not have known where to find Him. Nevertheless, the Scriptures for better or for worse must be fulfilled, and cannot be broken. Refer to Hosea 11:1, and the *fulfillment* in Matthew 2:14,15.

The *preparation* in the personage of John the Baptist, as the forerunner in the Messiah's ministry:

Malachi 3:1, "Behold, I (God) send My messenger, and he [John the

Baptist] shall prepare the way before Me. And the Lord (Messiah), whom you seek, shall suddenly come in His temple [in Jerusalem], even the Messenger *(Angel) of the covenant,* whom ye delight in: behold, He shall come, says the Lord of Hosts." Refer to Luke 1:76 and Mark 11:15–17 for the *fulfillment* (Free Translation). Compare Genesis 48:16, Redeeming Angel.

Matthew 11:10,11, "For this is He, of whom it is written, Behold, I send My messenger before Thy face, which shall prepare Thy way before Thee. Verily I say unto you, Among them that are born of women there hath not risen a greater than John the Baptist: notwithstanding he that is least in the kingdom of heaven is greater than he." Compare also Isaiah 40:3,4 with its *fulfillment* in John 1:23.

The *people* of the Gentiles are affected by His ministry:

Isaiah 9:1,2 shows the location of verse 1 that the area where Jesus was to visit in the beginning of His ministry was Zebulun and Naphtali: "The people (Gentiles) that walked in darkness have seen a *great Light:* they that dwell in the land of the shadow of death, upon them hath the light shined."

The "great Light" seen by the Gentiles in that region was more than natural light. They actually saw Jesus, "the Light of the world."

Mattew 4:13–16: "And leaving Nazareth, He (Jesus) came and dwelt in Capernaum, which is upon the sea coast, in the borders of Zebulun and Naphtali. *that it might be fulfilled* which was spoken by *Isaiah the prophet,* saying, The land of Zebulun, and the land of Naphtali, by way of the sea, beyond Jordan, Galilee of the Gentiles; the people which sat in darkness saw a *great Light;* and to them which sat in the region and shadow of death light is sprung up."

This prophecy, as well as all others concerning the first advent, was fulfilled to the letter, and so shall it be when Jesus comes again.

The *Physician* of no equal in His ministry:

Isaiah 61:1,2, "The Spirit of the Lord God is upon Me; because the LORD hath anointed Me to preach the good tidings unto the meek; He hath sent Me to bind up the brokenhearted, to proclaim liberty to the captives, and the opening of the prison to them that are bound; to proclaim the acceptable year of the LORD . . . to comfort all that mourn."

Because of Jesus, there is no heartache on earth that heaven's Physician cannot heal. A touch from His holy hand by one's faith can do wonders, yea, perform miracles through Him even today. For His healing power is inexhaustible and His love is condescending.

Luke 4:18,19, "The Spirit of the Lord is upon Me, because He hath anointed Me to preach the *gospel* [when the true gospel is preached through the Holy Spirit, *God* puts such a *spell* on the service that people can never forget; that is why it is referred to as God's spell] to the poor; He hath sent Me to heal the brokenhearted, to preach deliverance to the captives, and recovering of sight to the blind, to set at liberty them that are bruised, to preach the acceptable year of the Lord." *This was fulfilled.*

Praise God in the highest for sending Jesus to minister to the lowest!

The *preeminence* of His prophetic ministry:

Deuteronomy 18:15, "The Lord thy God will raise up unto thee a *Prophet* from the midst of thee (Jewish people), of thy brethren, like unto me; *unto Him (Christ) ye shall hearken.*"

The threefold ministry of Christ was *Prophet, Priest and King*. As a Prophet, He was the spokesman of God to men, Jesus the Word of God. As a Priest, He was the spokesman for the people to God, intercession and sacrifice. As King, He will rule during the Millennium in a Monotheistic government. God in Christ as the Prince of Peace will rule the world for a thousand years.

Acts 3:20-23, "And He shall send Jesus Christ, which before was preached unto you: whom the heaven must receive (retain) until the times of restitution (restoration) of all things, which God hath spoken by the mouth of *all* His holy prophets since the world began. For Moses truly said unto the fathers, A *Prophet* shall the Lord our God raise up unto you of your brethren, like unto me; *him shall ye hear* in all things whatsoever He shall say unto you. And it shall come to pass, that every soul, which will not hear (believe) *that Prophet,* shall be destroyed from among the people."

On the Mount of Transfiguration a voice came from heaven that said to Peter, James, and John, "This is My beloved Son; *hear ye Him.*" You remember the scene given on "the holy mount, from God's excellent glory," when two men, Moses and Elijah, appeared with Christ. Each of these men were prophets, but the One we are told now to hear is Jesus. For when the disciples looked up again after the vision, they saw "*Jesus only.*" I think if we see the beauty of Jesus in all of His splendor, we might hear God announce anew that it is "Jesus only" for salvation; "Jesus only" regarding prophecy; "Jesus only" can assure us of the home in heaven; and "Jesus only" is the answer for the sin-sick, troubled soul. Can we write or preach about a better Person?

The *High Priest* of Heaven serves us in His Ministry, first on earth, as in the case of Peter. Jesus said to Him, "I have prayed for thee that thy faith fail not." Now He as our High Priest prays faithfully for us in heaven.

Psalm 110:4, "The Lord hath sworn, and will not repent (or revoke it), Thou art a Priest for ever after the order of Melchizedek."

Hebrews 5:5,6, "So also Christ glorified not Himself to be made an High Priest; but He that said unto Him (Christ), Thou art My Son, today have I begotten Thee. As He saith also in another place, Thou art a Priest for ever after the order of Melchizedek." Remember, Melchizedek is a perfect type of Christ.

The *photo forecast* of His Kingly ministry:

We have heard Him as the preaching Prophet whom we believe to be the very Word of God. We have felt His cleansing power in the forgiveness of sins. Now let us see Him with the eye of faith as He comes to reign on the earth.

Zechariah 9:9, "Rejoice greatly, O daughter of Zion; shout, O daughter of Jerusalem: behold, thy King cometh unto thee: He is just, and *having salvation;* lowly, and riding upon an ass (donkey); and upon a colt the foal of an ass (donkey)."

John 12:14,16, "And Jesus, when He had found a young ass, sat thereon; as it is written, Fear not, daughter of Zion: behold, thy King cometh, sitting on an ass's colt. These things understood not His disciples at the first: but when Jesus was glorified, then remembered they that these things were written of Him, and that they had done these things unto Him."

May we too remember these *wonderful fulfillments* by keeping these prophecies regarding His living ministry in our hearts.

The Painful Persecution of Prophetic Portraits About the Cross: Isaiah 53:1–12

While bearing the sins of the ungodly under God's wrath, mixed with love, we now enter the Holy of Holies to consider a few of the main prophecies that point to His cross.

Mental suffering from a false friend:

Zechariah 11:12, "And I said unto them, If ye think good, give me my price; and if not, forbear. So they weighed for My price thirty pieces of silver." What a price to pay for the young 33-year-old Prince from Paradise!

He is a Friend that sticketh closer than a brother. That is what He is to us. What kind of friend are we to Him?

Matthew 26:15, "And said unto them, What will ye give me, and I will deliver Him unto you? And they covenanted with him (Judas) for thirty pieces of silver."

Judas must now wish that it would have been better if he had never been born. This will also be true of all who think more of money than they do of the Master.

Mental and physical suffering from false witnesses:

Psalm 35:11, "False witnesses did rise up; they laid to my charge things that I knew not" (false accusations about Christ).

Mark 14:57, "And there arose certain, and bare *false witness* against Him, saying . . ." Be sure to read verse 65 also in connection with this.

God help us to be always true, never false in living for Jesus. Our teeth may be false, but let our tongue be true.

Unbearable suffering from the paralyzing whip:

Isaiah 50:6, "I gave My back to the smiters, and My cheeks to them that plucked off the hair: I hid not My face from shame and spitting."

Matthew 26:67, "Then did they *spit in His face,* and *buffeted Him*; and others *smote Him* with the palms of their hands."

Matthew 27:26, "Then released he Barabbas unto them: and when he had *scourged Jesus,* he delivered Him to be crucified."

Shameful suffering from the lips of mockers:

Psalm 22:7,8, "All they that see me laugh Me to scorn: they shoot out the lip, they shake the head, saying, He trusted on the Lord that He would deliver Him: let Him deliver Him, seeing He delighted in Him."

Luke 23:35, "And the people stood beholding. And the rulers also with them derided Him, saying, He saved others; let Him save Himself, if He be Christ, the chosen of God."

Bodily suffering from the nails that held His frame:

Psalm 22:16, "For dogs have compassed Me: the assembly of the wicked have inclosed Me: they pierced My hands and My feet."

John 20:25,27, "The other disciples therefore said unto him, We have seen the Lord. But he said unto them, Except I shall see in His hands the print of the nails, and put my finger into the print of the nails, and thrust my hand into His side, I will not believe. (A full week passes.) Then saith He to Thomas, Reach hither thy finger, and behold My hands; and reach hither thy hand, and thrust it into My side: and be not faithless but believing."

Sum total of physical suffering from unquenchable thirst:

Psalm 69:21; John 19:28–30, "They gave Me also gall for My meat: and in My thirst they gave Me vinegar to drink."

Matthew 27:34, "They gave Him vinegar to drink mingled with gall: and when He had tasted thereof, He would not drink."

Soul suffering in petitioning God for others and Himself:

Psalm 109:3,4: "They compassed Me about also with words of hatred; and fought against Me without a cause. For My love they are My adversaries: but *I give Myself unto prayer.*"

Psalm 22:1, "*My God, My God, why hast Thou forsaken Me?* Why art Thou so far from helping Me, and from the words of My roaring?"

Luke 23:34, "Then said Jesus, *Father, forgive them; for they know not what they do.*" Notice also Isaiah 53:12, "...and made intercession for the transgressors."

Matthew 27:46, "And about the ninth hour Jesus cried with a loud voice, saying, Eli, Eli, lama sabachthani? that is to say, My God, My God, why hast Thou forsaken Me?"

Thank you, Lord Jesus, for being made sin on my behalf, that I might live on Your behalf!

I regret leaving out numerous other Scriptures that were prophesied and later fulfilled as to everything that Jesus suffered during those six hours while hanging on the cruel cross. Space does not allow it here; nevertheless, I want you to know that Jesus suffered more than any man ever suffered physically, mentally, and spiritually.

Isaiah 52:14, "... His visage (body) was so *marred more* than any man, and *His form more* than the sons of men."

Bless God for His Son's demonstration of unmatched love on the cross for us!

From a beloved hymn come these thoughts:

See, from His head, His hands, His feet,
Sorrow and love flow mingled down.
Did e'er such love and sorrow meet,
Or thorns compose so rich a crown?

Placed in a rich man's grave: 2 Corinthians 8:9

Isaiah 53:9, "And He made His grave with the wicked, and *with the rich in His death*; because He had done no violence, neither was any deceit in His mouth."

Matthew 27:57–60, "When the even was come, there came a *rich man* of Arimathæa, named Joseph, who also himself was *Jesus' disciple*: He went to Pilate, and begged the body of Jesus. Then Pilate commanded the body to be delivered. And when Joseph had taken the body, he wrapped it in a clean linen cloth, and laid it in his *own new tomb,* which he had hewn out of rock: and he rolled a great stone to the door of the sepulchre, and departed."

Paradise regained through the death and resurrection of Christ:

Psalm 16:10; Acts 2:27, "For Thou wilt not leave My soul in hell, neither wilt Thou suffer Thine Holy One (Christ) to see corruption."

Acts 2:31, "He seeing this before spake of the resurrection of Christ, that His soul was not left in hell, neither His flesh did see corruption."

Psalm 68:18, "Thou (Christ) has ascended on high, Thou hast led captivity captive: Thou hast received gifts for (from among) men . . ."

Ephesians 4:8, "Wherefore He saith, when He (Christ) ascended up on high, He led captivity captive and gave gifts unto men."

Here are some Scriptures to help understand the above. In Luke 16:26 notice the word *gulf* that separates the righteous from the wicked. Paradise was not yet opened until after Christ's death.

In 1 Peter 3:19 consider the word *preached* where "He went and preached to the *spirits* in prison," the waiting place, when Christ would release them.

When Jesus died He did descend into hell [the unseen state of the dead] as the Scriptures say, but it was the compartment of hell where the righteous were at rest while waiting for Christ to die. The souls of the wicked across the gulf shall remain in the same place until the *Final Judgment*. Jesus led this long train of captives, who died in faith during Old Testament times to Paradise, where they will receive gifts at the Judgment Seat of Christ, along with the whole body of resurrected saints and the translated Church.

Visions of Christ

The study of visions is no small topic in the Word, but important to understanding the whole. It is an undeniable fact that God communicated with man through the method of dreams and visions.

Numbers 12:6, "If there be a prophet among you, I the Lord will make Myself known unto him in a *vision,* and will speak unto him in a *dream.*"

This method is not restricted to early man, but more mature and enlightened saints. Godly men have received such in the New Testament as well. A few examples would be: Joseph, Zacharius, women that witnessed the resurrection, apostles that witnessed the transfiguration, and Peter and Paul in a special way.

In Joel's prophecy regarding the descent of the Holy Spirit on the Day of Pentecost, when Peter preached to a throng in Jerusalem, he quoted from Joel 2:28, interpreting what was happening in the economy of the new Dispensation of Grace.

Acts 2:17,18, "And it shall come to pass in the last days, saith [not Joel, but] God, *I will* pour out My Spirit upon all flesh: and your *sons* and your *daughters* shall prophesy, and your young men shall see *visions,* and your old men shall *dream* dreams: and on My servants and on my handmaidens I will pour out in those days of *My Spirit;* and they shall prophesy."

When God withholds His revelation in visions given to prophets, the *people perish* in the darkness (Proverbs 29:18).

Hosea 12:10, "I have also spoken by the prophets, and I have multiplied *visions* and used similitudes, by the ministry of the prophets."

Ezekiel 1:1 says, "... the heavens were opened, and I saw *visions of God.*"

Daniel was called of God, "greatly beloved."

Daniel 2:19, "Then was the secret revealed to Daniel in the night *vision.* Then Daniel blessed the God of heaven."

Visions and dreams from God usually meant God's blessings were to follow in the near or distant future. God's prophets had the idea, and rightly so, that a vision from the Most High was inspired insight. Isaiah opens his prophetic writings with these words, "The *vision* of Isaiah . . ."

The prophets of God, unlike priests, were not taken from a particular family like Aaron, but called from various walks of life as preachers are today. They were chosen and called of God in a special way.

Psalm 89:19, "Then Thou spakest in *vision* to thy holy one, and saidst, I have laid help upon one that is mighty; *I have* exalted one *chosen* out of the people."

Visions from our merciful God seemed to come to people in the past, in times of great spiritual decline. There are *open* visions and there are *closed* visions (Isaiah 29:11; 1 Samuel 3:1). There are times when God gives a vision while sleeping in the bed, as was the case in Daniel 4:5, and at other times when the eye was opened (Numbers 24:4,16). But Peter and Cornelius were praying miles apart when they had a vision from God. He brought them together, working on both ends, causing His servant Peter to be prepared to deal with perhaps his first Gentile converts in Cornelius' home (Acts 10:3,17).

Saul of Tarsus was saved through a vision (Acts 26:19), who later was to be called Paul. As Peter was chosen by God to witness to Cornelius, both were given a vision. So it was true with Ananias and Paul. Ananias was chosen to witness to Paul (Acts 9:10).

As you see, visions are used in various ways through the Bible. Visions and dreams have much in common. They are given to the young and the old, the prophet and the layman to further the cause of salvation and divine service. *In the Bible, visions run through it from Genesis to Revelation, in twenty-six different Books, numbering one hundred times in all.* Out of this number, *forty-two times* the word "vision" is found in one book, and that book is *Daniel.* We now will begin a brief and interesting study of the visions that Daniel had of Christ and get back to continue our teachings of Christ in the Old Testament.

Before we consider the visions in this visionary book, we need to know the aim of the Book. First, let me say what the aim of the Book is not.

It is not to give the life of Daniel, for it gives neither his descendants nor his death. It is not to give the history of the Israelites in their seventy years of captivity while in Babylon.

But it is to reveal how God works in the kingdoms of the world by His divine guidance, miracles of power in foreknowing the end from the beginning, while showing the kingdoms that die and the kingdom that lives on with its King in the Millennium and into eternity. In short, its purpose is to show the supremacy of God and His power over the nations of the world and His providence extended to His people.

After reading the twelve chapters of Daniel, which offer seed thoughts for many devotions, lessons, and sermons, I find that *Christ Jesus our Lord is referred to fourteen times,* and possibly more, in this great prophetic book. I will only locate them for you with brief comments, and select but two. Later I will enlarge upon the ones that are marked with an asterisk (*).

Daniel's Vision of Christ

The vision of *Christ as the "Stone"* :*

Chapter 2:28,32–45: I believe Jesus is implied in verses 34,45, and 47 in this first vision spoken of by Daniel.

The vision of *four in the fire:*

Chapter 3:15-30: Jesus is referred to in verse 25 as the "Son of God," although in the Hebrew it is written, "like a son of the gods." That was the viewers' opinion. Nevertheless, a fourth person was with the three Hebrew children in the fire, and I believe the fourth to be Jesus (Isaiah 43:2). He is with us in the fire of persecution.

The vision of *Christ's Kingdom:*

This kingdom is referred to as "His Kingdom" (Chapter 4:3). Nebuchadnezzar's kingdom was temporary, Christ's kingdom is eternal (Luke 1:31-33).

The vision of *Christ in the "lion's den"* :

This was the appearance of Jesus, "The Angel of the Lord," as in other places. Chapter 6:22, the "Angel" that is spoken of from God is rendered in the Hebrew, although, this verse with a capital "A" makes a distinction from other angels.

Paul the Apostle tells us that "the *Lord* stood with me . . ., and I was delivered out of the mouth of the lion" (2 Timothy 4:17).

The next reference of Christ is connected with the same deliverance in verse 27. Here I believe Jesus is actually implied in the Hebrew when rendering such words that fit Jesus as, "*He* delivers, *He* works wonders in heaven and earth, and His kingdom" (verse 26). The same Person is in chapter 4:3.

The vision of *Christ as Judge of the world:**

This section is very impressive in the light of Christ's assigned and appointed authority in the Judicial power of the Godhead (John 5:22).

Chapter 7, verse 9: In this passage, *"The Ancient of days,"* must doubtless refer to Christ and the final judgment of the wicked, while believers are present with the Lord.

Also verses 13 and 14 refer to Christ as the *Son of Man,* and continues to teach about *"His dominion* as an everlasting dominion."

In verse 22 of the same chapter, we see Him who is spoken of as the "Ancient of days" again. This is at least the eleventh time Jesus is referred to, and where the saints assist in the judgment. Then in verse 27, Jesus is referred to again as in previous places, speaking of "His kingdom" (Christ) and all who serve Him.

The vision of *Christ as "Prince of princes, the Messiah Prince:"*

I believe that Chapter 8, verse 25, is concerning Christ in a more familiar term: Jesus as the "Prince of princes" and the "Prince of peace," *who will destroy the false prophet and beast who both oppose Christ* (Revelation 19:19,20).

The last vision of *Christ in Daniel, compared to Revelation—His appearance:*

In Chapter 10, verses 5–9, is a description of Jesus Christ our Lord in the vision which corresponds to Daniel 7:9 and Revelation 1:13–15. Here we have but touched the hem of the garment of God's glory in Christ. It is your privilege to follow through with these visions of our Lord given to Daniel.

Now we shall say something more as the Lord leads my hand and your heart to know and understand, that *the second greatest event in the annals of human history is when Jesus returns to earth some years after the world's first greatest event, the birth of Christ.*

Once again my purpose in this book is to present the power and glory of Christ *before* He was born, and *during* His life on earth, and long *after* His death—also reaching into the Millennium and eternity with Christ, the *King of the ages*. Therefore, we will look with only a passing glance at the four world powers. Then notice the *"STONE"* which is the climax of this vision, as well as the others regarding the *centrality of Christology*, elsewhere.

The *"Great Image"* destroyed by the divine "Stone" (Daniel 2:31-34):

The meaning of the metals is as follows:

The *"head of gold"* represents Nebuchadnezzar or the first world power, Babylon, verses 32,38,39.

The *"breast and arms of silver"* represent Darius and Cyrus combined, making the Medo-Persian Empire the second world power, inferior to Babylon, verses 32,39.

The *"belly and thighs of brass* (bronze)" represent Alexander the Great, "which shall bear rule over all the earth," the Grecian Empire, the third world power, verses 32,39.

The *"legs of iron,* and the *feet* part of *iron and clay"* represent the powerful Roman Empire as "strong as iron," verses 33,40-43.

Octavian, the heir of Julius Cæsar, took the name of "Cæsar Augustus" and extended the empire to over a hundred million people of different races, who enjoyed the *Pax Romana,* or the Roman Peace, that lasted for two hundred years.

These four kingdoms seemed to increase in strength, but they experienced inward deterioration and division. When Alexander died young, his empire was divided between his generals. When Rome reached her zenith of power, it was divided in two, between the East and West as "legs." Later it was divided into different kingdoms as "toes."

All these represented the Gentile world system that would be suddenly destroyed by Christ, the "Stone."

The "Stone" that smote the image (Daniel 2:34,35,44,45):

"Thou sawest until a Stone was cut out without hands, which smote the image upon its feet that were of iron and clay, and broke them to pieces, and the *Stone* that smote the image became a great mountain and filled the whole earth."

This has reference to the Millennium, following Christ's judgment of the nations in the final battle of Armageddon.

Verses 44,45, "And in the days of these kings shall the God of heaven set up a kingdom, which shall never be destroyed: and the kingdom shall not be left to other people, but it shall break in pieces and consume all these kingdoms, and it shall stand for ever. Forasmuch as thou sawest that the *Stone* was cut out of the mountain without hands, and that it broke in pieces the iron, the brass, the clay, the silver, and the gold; the great God hath made known to the king what shall come to pass hereafter: and the dream is certain, and the *interpretation there of sure.*"

The "Stone" [Christ] has two special features seen in 1 Peter 2:7,8. First, the Stone of Salvation, and second, the Stone of Separation.

"*Unto you, therefore, who believe He is precious, but unto them who are disobedient,* the *Stone* which the builders disallowed, the *same* is made the *head* of the corner, and a Stone of stumbling and a Rock of offense (Isaiah 8:14) even to them who stumble at the word, being disobedient whereunto also *they were appointed.*"

Those who think Jesus to be precious are "*living stones,*" with Him being the *chief corner-Stone* (cap-Stone) making up His "spiritual house." Those who do not believe Him and will not trust Him, but reject Him, will themselves be rejected in the last day in the *Great White Throne Judgment.*

Matthew 21:44, "And whosoever shall fall on this *Stone* shall be broken: but on whomsoever It shall fall, It (Christ) will grind him to powder."

I believe the first part of this marvelous verse, difficult to interpret, is addressed to the candidates of salvation. Those that come to Christ in their sins and wicked ways, realizing their need of salvation and knowing that their lives are filled with selfish ambitions and sinful practices, may come to Him to have these evil habits *broken.* They gently trust in Christ as Savior while yielding themselves to be *not run* over, but lovingly *ruled* over by Christ as their Lord. The fact is, we shall through love be ruled by Christ our King, or dominated by the enemy of our soul, Satan. To us He is marvelous in our eyes of faith. Compare also Romans 9:21–24.

Now to the rest of the quotation from Matthew: ". . . but on whomsoever It (Christ) shall fall, It (Christ) will grind him to powder."

Are you stumbling over the Scriptures and turning a cold shoulder to Christ and His teachings? Or has His Word been an offense to you? Beware! One day you will fall on your knees begging for forgiveness and acceptance into His Kingdom, where every knee shall bow in heaven, on earth and under the earth, in hell (Philippians 2:10,11), acknowledging that He is Lord of all.

If you fail at this point, the verdict will be irreversible. You will be cast into outer darkness, where there shall be weeping and gnashing of teeth.

Why take such a hopeless chance of certain doom? Come to Christ without delay and be made a subject of the King right now. In the light of the above Scriptures that the Holy Spirit, through me, has made known to you, come quickly to Him. *Build not on the sinking sands of your sins, but on Christ the solid Rock, your sure Foundation and Fortress.* Then you will be a part of His church, and a member of the everlasting Kingdom. Cry out to Jesus this moment: "Lord, save me by breaking me from all my sinful ways, lest I perish and be ground to powder!"

We must close this section of our studies in the Old Testament, with a final look at the last vision given to Daniel of Christ, that corresponds to the New Testament, especially the book of Revelation where Jesus is pictured as the Judge of the Great White Throne Judgment: "As I beheld *thrones* (for believers) put in place, and the *Ancient of Days* took His seat, [Christ our King, now as Judge of the world's dead] whose garment or robe was white as snow, and the hair of His head like pure wool: His throne was like flaming fire. A thousand thousands ministered to Him, and ten thousand times ten thousand [a massive number] stood up before Him. The court [then] was seated and the books were opened" (Daniel 7:9,10 and Revelation 1:13–15,18; 3:21; 5:10; 20:11–15, Free Translation).

What an amazing vision given to us from the Old Testament of the final judgment! This is a preview of things to come, written several thousand years before this climactic event ever occurs.

A clearer glimpse of Him on the throne that relates to the same scene is found in Daniel 10:5,6: "Then I lifted up mine eyes, and looked, and behold, a *certain man* [Son of man, this man must be Christ] clothed in linen, whose loins (mid-section) were girded with fine gold of Uphaz: His body was like the beryl, and his face as the appearance of lightning, and his eyes as lamps of fire, and his arms and his feet like in colour to polished brass, and the voice of his words like the voice of a multitude." Compare Revelation 1:13.

Revelation 1:16: "... His countenance was as the sun shineth in His strength, ... and His eyes as lamps (torches) of fire," Revelation 1:14; 2:18; 19:12. "And His voice as the sound of many waters," Revelation 1:15.

In verse 8 of Daniel, Chapter 10, this vision for the first time is called a *"great vision,"* which is in essence the last of the series of visions. Doubtless *the Person that Daniel saw was Christ,* dressed in royal splendor, ready to take His final roll as Judge. The "Judge of the quick (living first) and the dead (last)."

All of us must stand one day before Him. His judgment must be based on justice. Either you will stand before Him on that day justified or condemned. Your condemnation will be just, if you have not trusted in *the Jesus of the Bible* as your only Lord and Savior; then He will be your Judge and His sentence will stand for all eternity.

Romans 5:1, "Therefore being *justified by faith,* we have peace with God through our Lord Jesus Christ."

Romans 8:1, "There is therefore now *no condemnation* to them which are in Christ Jesus, who walk not after the flesh, but after the Spirit."

Hebrews 10:28,29,31,37, "He that despised Moses' law died without mercy under two or three witnesses: of how much *sorer punishment,* suppose ye, shall he be thought worthy, *who hath trodden under foot the Son of God,* and hath counted the *blood of the covenant,* wherewith he was sanctified, an *unholy thing,* and hath *done despite unto the Spirit of grace*? It is a fearful thing to fall into the hands of the living God. For yet a little while, and He that shall come will come, and will not tarry."

Matthew 25:46, "And these shall go away into *everlasting punishment*: but the *righteous into life eternal.*"

We have walked with our Lord, led of His Spirit to notice the interesting symbols, types, mystical appearances, and fulfilled prophecies relating to our Lord's first advent. We feel sure that we have seen the Christ of the Old Testament many times and in many ways, while walking across these "Ancient Paths of Truth."

We shall next cross the border of the four silent centuries to reach the four Gospels of the New Testament, where again, in a more intimate nearness, we shall journey with Jesus from the cradle to the cross, and from the cross to the crown.

Dear friend, I do hope that it can be said of you, as Philip said to Nathanæl, "We have found Him, of whom Moses in the law, and the *prophets*, did write, Jesus of Nazareth the [lawful, legal] Son of Joseph" (John 1:45).

• • •

Questionnaire

1. What Person is the center of Old Testament prophecy?
2. Based on 1 Peter 1:10,11, what two central themes did most prophecies about Christ contain?
3. Where is the first prophecy about Christ found?
4. Name five books in the Old Testament that contain prophecies of Christ.
5. Name five portraits of the suffering of Christ.
6. In which book is the vision of Christ as a Great Stone found, Isaiah or Daniel?

• • •

Answers

1. Christ
2. His suffering, His glory
3. Genesis 3:15
4. Genesis; Micah; Isaiah; Jeremiah; Zechariah
5. A false friend; false witness; mocking; whipping; nail prints
6. Daniel

Chapter 6

Viewing the Long-Looked-For Messiah in New Testament Fulfillment
-or-
Christ in the Forefront of the Gospels—From the Birthplace to the Site of Temptation

Purpose
To view the Gospels from the greatest story ever told, to the greatest literature ever written, about the greatest Person that ever lived.

Opening verses
Hebrews 1:1–3

• • •

I. God's time line of the ages
   A. The close of this Dispensation of Grace (Matthew 24:14)
      1. Prospects of His near Second Coming (John 14:3)
      2. What if Jesus had never come the first time?
   B. God is still calling out His people; His Church must be complete before He returns (Matthew 16:18; 26:28; 2 Peter 3:9, "usward")

II. God's greatest event in secular or religious history (John 1:14)
   A. The greatest influence on the world (John 21:25)
   B. The greatest art gallery of any Person
      Penpals of Holy Writ as they painted picture passages from the New Testament

III. God's miraculous birth and the boyhood of Jesus
   A. A supernatural birth (Matthew 1:21–23)
   B. The mystified doctors of the Law (Luke 2:46,47)
   C. The lost lad found in the temple (Luke 2:48,49)

IV. God's blessings on the baptism of His Son and all that follow His example
   A. When, where, why, and how was He baptized?
   B. Scripture references (Matthew 3:13–17; Mark 1:9–11; Luke 3:21–23; John 1:30–34)
V. God's test for His Son in dueling with the Devil (Matthew 4:1–11; Luke 4:1–13)
   A. Were His temptations real? (Hebrews 2:18; 4:15)
   B. Why must He pass the test? (Hebrews 4:16; 2:10)
   C. Can God be tempted by Satan? (James 1:13)
VI. Questionnaires and Answers

• • •

All hail to Jesus Christ, the blessed and only Potentate, the Lord of glory, the Son of the living God, the noble Prince Charming of perfection, purity and peace, the great and powerful High Priest of our profession, the appointed Savior out of the world of God's elect, the sacrificial Lamb, the supreme Sovereign with The Father, and the coming King of kings, the Monarch of men and angels–praise be to His Holy Name forever!

God's Time Line

Hebrews 1:1–3 (key verse): "God gave to our forefathers [antediluvians, patriarchs, monarchs, and prophets] the revelation of His Word of truth by different ways at different times [by dreams, visions and personal visitations], but has now in these last days [the sixth dispensation] spoken to us through His [darling] Son, whom He appointed heir and owner of all things. By whom also He created the universe, *as the Author and Arranger of the ages,* and the Designer of the expanses of space, He being the radiant brightness of His glory, and the flawless and exact image of His Divine nature, supporting all things by the Word of His power. When He had offered Himself in cleansing and clearing us from sin's guilt, took the most honored seat in heaven, at the right hand of the Almighty God" (Free Translation).

The invisible God, whom man has never seen, visited the world many times in the Person of His Son in the days of old. We now calculate that the human race is about 6,000 years old according to God's time line. Roughly estimating 1,000 years to be an age or dispensation, this has been the longest of any, called the Dispensation of Grace. Yet there is one more to come: the Golden Age of Peace, highlighted by the reign of King Jesus, when He rules the world in His Second Advent to the earth, when war and bloodshed shall vanish from the earth. This age shall be different from all past ages.

Matthew 24:14, "And this gospel of the kingdom shall be preached in all the world for a *witness unto all nations,* and *then* shall the end come" [the end of this age].

Jesus opened this age with His miraculous arrival to earth through the womb of a young *virgin* named Mary. During His ministry He told us everything we needed to know, and did for us guilty creatures everything He needed to do. Jesus could return at any time. The gospel has been extended to every nation. God is still calling out from the world a people for His name's sake, to make up the bride of Christ. Surely, God through His preachers and personal workers will still *call out* a few more good, honest-hearted men and women made good by the grace of God before the end, who were *chosen* in the beginning. Are you safe and secure in the Savior? Are you looking for the *"blessed hope?"* Are you expecting the soon-coming Christ from Glory? If not, it is high time to cleanse your heart and wash your robes, making them white in the blood of the Lamb. Friends, it's time to shine your shoes, pack your suitcase, and get your house in order, for the Day of the Lord is at hand, even at the door. Wake up to the reality of coming eternity!

What Might Have Been

Before we begin this tour with Christ through the Holy Land, have you ever thought *what it might have been* if Christ had not come in Bethlehem's manger? What then?

The Old Testament Scriptures would become a false theory, and the prophecies of the coming Messiah would be only a myth. The New Testament then could not have been written, because the Old Testament could no longer be trusted or true. The idea that we were created in God's image would become a laughing fable by the evolutionist and the modernist. The destiny of all men, like it is with the fallen angels, would be a hopeless hell. Evil would rage like a swelling river about to overflow its banks, destroying and drowning everything in its path. Sinful men could not stop sinning, but would grow worse and worse, plunging beneath the darkness of their doom. Mankind would destroy themselves through the violence of their depravity, which is born within them. The God of the Bible would have failed desperately in His exploits. But that could not be.

The good news of the Gospel is that Jesus did come the first time as expected, to "seek and to save" those that are lost, and "give His life a *ransom for many*," that is, all of God's elect, and none of them shall perish (Matthew 28:28; 1 Peter 3:9).

Because Jesus came, died and rose again, you can trust the Bible to be true, for He came just as God said He would, and shall return just as the angels said He will. By the way, if the term from the Bible "*God's elect*" bothers you, then "make your calling and election sure." If you doubt your salvation, ask Jesus to save you right now. If He does, you are God's elect (Titus 1:1; 2 Peter 1:10; Romans 10:13; 14:23).

Because Jesus came, men need not face a *hopeless hell*. Jesus came to spare us from the "*second death*" and the place prepared for the Devil and his angels (Matthew 15:14; Revelation 20:14).

Because Jesus came, men can, by His power, stop sinning and live a life above reproach by the grace of God through the *new birth*, and that work is of God (John 1:13; 3:3).

Because Jesus came, we can live not a perfect life here, but a *victorious life* over sin, the world, and the devil through Jesus who triumphed over the world of evil, by His suffering and death on the cross (1 Corinthians 15:57).

Because Jesus came, your *cross* might be burdensome and heavy here, but you will rejoice in time to come when you wear your *crown* of glory in heaven hereafter (Matthew 10:28; 1 Peter 5:4).

All of this is so because of one single, solitary life, the *Person* that we call Jesus. Do you really love Him for all that He did for you?

The Greatest Event

Tell me, my friend, whoever you are: What do you think was the greatest single event that ever happened on this planet? Some say it was the safe arrival of the astronauts on the moon and their return to earth. What good would it do to land on all the planets in space and miss the heavenly planet? Or build a city in space, but know not how to get to the Holy City, "whose builder and maker is God"?

Hear me now! Ponder this thought to see if it is true: The greatest single event on this earth was *the physical birth of its divine Creator*. Remarkable, fantastic, unbelievable, but so.

John 1:10, "*He came into the world,* the world that was made through Him, and the world knew Him not" (Free Translation).

1 Timothy 3:16, "And without controversy great is the mystery of godliness: *God was manifest in the flesh,* justified in the Spirit, seen of angels, preached unto the Gentiles, believed on in the world, received up into glory."

He came into the world lowly born of a virgin peasant, from the royal chambers of the headquarters of the tribunal Godhead. Before He is finished, He will turn the world upside down, when "every hill is brought low, and every crooked path made straight" [in the Millennium].

I say the most important, the most wonderful, the most miraculous and marvelous thing that ever happened in the process of time, if time had been a hundred, thousand, million, billion years, was when the author of time and eternity came and appeared here, whose given name was *Jesus.* The four Gospels *point* to Jesus. Without Him life would be pointless.

Jesus (literally) never authored a book. Arranged no system of theology. Left no philosophical standard. Gave no legislature but the law of love. Raised no armies except Christian soldiers. Established no colleges, but within "Him is hid all the treasures of wisdom and knowledge." Held no political office, but millions have voted for Him to be the King to rule on the throne of their hearts. He sought no approval from man, but we see Him as the ideal Man. He never married or raised a family, yet *He is quoted* more than any writer or philosopher in the annals of history.

His sayings are on the lips of thousands. His word has actually gone out into all the world. Millions have died for His cause and carried His Word to the ends of the globe. Thousands of languages, *out of* 5,045 to this date, have been reduced to writing in order to translate and transmit His life-giving message to others. Savage tribes have been brought into the light. Cannibals have become saved and civilized through believing in Him. Headhunters have been converted, their course altered, and their destination changed. I recall reading about a missionary that landed on an island somewhere in the Pacific, where all souls were lost. By grace, when he left, all were saved, leaving witness to the tribute of Jesus' truth.

The Living Art Gallery

Would you join me as we walk together through the art gallery of the New Testament, and behold on the walls the portrait and profile of Christ in colorful words in every divine Book written from every chosen writer.

We first recognize the portrait of Jesus in Matthew, as the appointed *Kingly Messiah* to the Jews. This is an excellent gospel to give as a gift to a Jewish friend or neighbor. This scene reveals Jesus' triumphant entry into Jerusalem as the King of the Jews: "Behold, thy *King* cometh . . ." (Matthew 21:5).

Then we notice Mark's portrait of the Master as the Miracle Worker: "Such *mighty works* are wrought by His hands" (Mark 6:2).

Next we come to Luke's Gospel, and on this portrait is written the *Friend* of the Friendless and the Helpless (Luke 15:2). The beloved physician describes the ministry of the *Greatest Physician*. In Acts, also written by the beloved (Greek) physician, Dr. Luke, Chapter 1, verse 8, is the theme of the book, which pictures Christ reaching around the world. From this passage we hear Him say to His church, "Ye shall be *witnesses* unto Me both in Jerusalem, and in all Judea, and in Samaria, and *unto the uttermost* parts of the earth." Those that heard Him speak knew that their mission was a world mission.

Taking it a step farther, we see in the Gospel of John a number of descriptions of Him. The one John uses the most is the "Son of God." John 20:31 gives us the purpose of this most popular Gospel: "But these are written that ye might believe that Jesus is the Christ, the Son of God and that believing ye might have life through His name."

We now leave the Gospel Corridor through the Acts of the Apostles, who all pointed to the beauty of Jesus as Savior, by making a turn to the right and entering (in the imagination of our minds) the large Epistle Hall that displays all kinds of portraits of our Lord. Let us take a good glance at each of them.

First we see Paul's Portraits of Christ in His Epistles, then the other Apostles' conception of Christ:

- Romans 5:1—Christ, the Giver of Peace With God to Men
- 1 Corinthians 1:30—Christ, Our Wisdom and Righteousness, Sanctification and Redemption

- 2 Corinthians 5:17—Christ, the Creator of a New Life
- Galatians 6:14—Christ, Our Crossbearer and Substitute
- Ephesians 4:13—Christ, Our Goal of Perfection
- Philippians 3:8—Christ, Our Most Excellent Gift
- Colossians 1:18—Christ, the heavenly Head of His Church Body on Earth
- 1 Thessalonians 4:16—Christ, Our Returning Lord for His Own
- 2 Thessalonians 1: 7–10—Christ, Our Divine Avenger
- 1 Timothy 6:15—Christ, the Blessed and Only Potentate (the King of kings and Lord of lords of the earth)
- 2 Timothy 4:1—Christ, the Judge of the Living and the Dead
- Titus 3:5—Christ, Our Savior
- Philemon 1:25—Christ, the Dispenser of Grace
- Hebrews 5:9—Christ, the Author of Eternal Salvation
- James 1:12—Christ, the Rewarder of the Crown of Life
- 1 Peter 2:25—Christ, the Shepherd and Bishop of Our Souls
- 2 Peter 3:9—Christ, Our Assurance (that none of the elect shall perish)
- 1 John 4:2—Christ, the Incarnate One
- 2 John 9—Christ's Indispensable Teachings
- 3 John 7—Christ, Our Example of Unselfishness (remembering what Jesus said, "It is more blessed to give, than to receive," Acts 20:35)
- Jude 1—Christ, the Preserver of the Believer (even before the holy calling)
- Revelation 17:14; 5:5—Christ, Our Victorious Lamb and Lion

God's King Is Born

Now we must look beyond the numerous portraits of Jesus from the writers of the Word, to the arrival of the Word, Christ the Messiah, the Anointed One that was to come. This was the supreme hour for which the centuries had been waiting: in the fulness of time, Jesus was virgin born.

The beginning of Christ's life on earth in the flesh opens with an unexplainable miracle. Some say that His birth is as great a miracle as His death, and I will not deny it. If we try to explain the mystery of the virgin birth, we lose our minds. If we dare to discredit and reject it, we lose our souls (1 John 4:2,3).

There are many *mysteries* surrounding God's Son. There is the mystery of the *Trinity,* how God can be One in three. There is the mystery of *two natures* found in Christ, that He is both the Son of Man and the Son of God., both human and divine. There is the mystery of both Jews and Gentiles being one in Christ. There are the mysteries of His *kingdom,* and the mystery of His *Church,* hidden in past ages and now revealed to us through His Spirit. His whole life was filled with magnificent and mysterious miracles that came forth from this wonderful One.

I need only but reverently to repeat what our title says from the Scripture, *"What manner of Man Is this?"* John's writings give the order of importance in the *incarnation.* Paul's letters drip heavy with the ruby-red blood of the *Redeemer's cross.* Think on these verses of Scripture that John tells about as to the importance of God, manifested in the flesh as a man-child, yea, even a tiny, wee, little baby, born in a barn.

John 1:14, "And the *Word was made flesh,* and dwelt among us (and we beheld His glory, the glory as of the only begotten of the Father), full of grace and truth."

John the Baptist, a cousin of Jesus, was born six months before our Lord, yet John mysteriously says, "He was before me" (John 1:30). Jesus lived before John. He lived before He was born, according to the opening salutation of John's Gospel, Chapter 1, verse 1. Also in 1 John 1:1,2, "That which was from the beginning, which we have *heard,* which we have *seen* with our eyes, which we have looked upon, and our hands have *handled,* of the Word of life; God the life was manifested and we have seen it, and bear witness, and show unto you that eternal life, which was with the Father, and was manifested unto us."

1 John 5:20, "And we know that the Son of God is come, and hath given us an understanding, that we may *know Him* that is true, and we are in Him that is true, even in His Son Jesus Christ. This is the *true God,* and eternal life."

Before time was, Jesus was. He existed with the Father from all eternity. Therefore, He can give us salvation for not a million years, but if we know Jesus in the forgiveness of sins and believe Him as He is revealed in God's Word, then we have *eternal* life.

2 John 7,9,10, "For many deceivers are entered into the world, who confess not that Jesus Christ is come in the flesh. This is a deceiver and an antichrist. Whosoever transgresseth, and abideth not in the *doctrine* of Christ, hath *not God*. He that abideth in the doctrine of Christ, he hath both the Father and the Son. If there come any unto you and bring not *this doctrine,* receive him not into your house, neither bid him God speed." That is, anyone or any church group that recognizes Him, honors Him, *worships Him as less than the Eternal God, is not of God.*

How important, dear reader, is the Doctrine of Incarnation! Many religionists are ever making mistakes about Jesus because they have not the Spirit. We know people by what they say as well as what they do. I know a dear brother who preceded us in the work of the ministry and has long been with the Lord. His name is C.H. Spurgeon. He shares exactly my sentiments, and I wish to use a part of his wise writing on this subject, the Doctrine of Christology. My preference is to quote from the Bible, and hardly ever do I quote from men, but I have no reservation or hesitation in referring to this great "Prince of Preachers."

> "Nearly all our modern errors, I might say all of them, begin with mistakes about Christ. Men do not like to be always preaching the same thing. There are Athenians in the pulpit as well as in the pew who spend their time in nothing but hearing some new thing. They are not content to tell over and over again the simple message, 'He that believeth in the Lord Jesus Christ hath everlasting life.' So they borrow novelties from literature and garnish the Word of God with words which man's wisdom teaches ... Jesus Christ ceases to be the cornerstone of their ministry. To shape the gospel to the diseased wishes and tastes of men enters more deeply into their purpose than to remold the mind and renew the heart of men that they receive the gospel as it is. There is no telling where they will go who once go back from following the Lord ... Only this you may take for certainty, they cannot be right in the rest, unless they speak rightly of Him."

God's Scenes Surrounding the Sinner's Savior

I would love to take you into some of the many familiar events that encompass the birth of Christ, such as the visit of the angel Gabriel to Mary when he announces to her that she is the virgin chosen to bear forth God's gift of love: "Behold, thou shalt conceive in thy womb, and bring forth a Son, and shalt call His name JESUS [which means Savior]" (Luke 1:31).

This is followed by *"Mary's Magnificat."* I especially like verse 47, in Chapter 1 of Luke: "And my spirit hath rejoiced in *God my Saviour.*" Here Mary knows nothing about any title that some have since conferred upon her as the "Queen of Heaven." But she knows that she is the handmaiden of God. She knows Jesus is to be *her Savior from sin* as well as her first-born Son.

Then there is the long trip that Joseph and Mary must take, more than seventy miles from Nazareth to Bethlehem. Not the Bethlehem of Zebulum, but the Bethlehem of Judea, in the City of David. This was done not only because of Cæsar Augustus' decree, but that the Scriptures written long ago might be fulfilled, because *"the Scriptures cannot be broken"* (John 10:35).

Then when it was time for Jesus' birth, the inn had *no room* for Him, just like the people of the world today. No room for Christ! Oh, but I hope today He has found room to dwell in your heart and is a welcome guest in your home!

The only beings that welcomed His birth were angels of God, Jewish shepherds, the Gentile wise men, and a couple of senior citizens who were looking for Him and were found in the temple, believing that they would see God's promise to Israel fulfilled. They did, and then died in faith under the special favor of God.

First, the heralding host of angels sang notes of praise to God with such a heavenly proclamation that exceeded Cæsar's decree: "For unto you [not angels, for they will never know God's great grace in salvation] is born this day [no one knows the day He came the first time, and no one will know the day He will return] in the City of David, a *Saviour* [the Lord God gave us just what we fallen creatures needed. Not a prophet only, not a priest only, not only a king, but He gave us more, a Savior] which is Christ the Lord."

The lowly shepherds responded. They found the Savior, as it was told them, in the manger, and returned, praising God for all that they had heard and seen.

Put yourself in one of the groups that sought the Savior. Would you fit into the class of common people like the shepherds, who believed what they were told from a heavenly source? They spent their spare time telling others about Him, as they returned to their flocks and families.

Would you perhaps be among *the wise men,* who found Him through the divine leadership of His Star from the East, and therefore giving Him the treasures of your life, after worshipping Him with a saved soul made possible by His grace?

Or would you fall in the dangerous, influential, intellectual group, as *King Herod,* with money and political power, who sought the infant Savior not to worship Him as he said, but to destroy Him as he attempted to do, yet failed in his bloody plan? He yet will suffer the severe consequence of eternal fire. God forbid that this be your destination!

How we Christians—who have seen Him by faith and believe the record God gave of His Son as told to us by someone less than heavenly beings—need to do as the shepherds and wise men did. *Praise God in Christ* for all the good that has been our inherited fortune to receive from above (John 3:27).

The Lost Son Found in the Temple

Twelve silent years passed when Joseph, as his custom was, took Mary and the family of seven—Jesus, the first-born; James; Joses; Judah; and Simon; plus at least two sisters (Mark 6:3)—and travelled along with a caravan of camels and donkeys, joined by kinfolks and acquaintances going to Jerusalem for the annual Passover Feast.

After remaining there worshipping God in festivities, the allotted time at the feast passed rapidly, and the time came that they must return home. Assuming the lad Jesus was in their company or with friends, they took their pilgrimage homeward. After a day's journey they began to look for Him among their relatives and friends, but failed to find Him. Turning back they came upon their supposedly lost Son in the temple court.

Luke 2:46, "... after three days, they *found Him in the temple,* sitting in the midst of the doctors, both hearing them and asking them questions."

Here the *young Student of Scripture is wiser than His masters.* Notice what His mother says in verse 48, "... Son, why hast Thou thus dealt with us? Behold, *thy father* [and she knew that Joseph was not Jesus' real father, as he was to the others; Jesus always had but one Father in heaven, although Joseph was socially addressed as His father] and I have sought Thee sorrowing."

Hear the way Jesus responded in verse 49: *"How is it that you sought Me?"* He was not being rude, but with a mild rebuke knew that she had it backwards. Was the Son of God lost? Did He as the Savior become lost and needed to be found? I often hear Christians say, *"I found Christ."* Was Jesus lost? I know they mean well, but the saying is theologically incorrect. Ought it not to be reversed and the glory given to God? I was found by Jesus, and that makes a great deal of difference. "No man (the Bible says) seeketh after God" (Romans 3:11). Jesus is the One that *"came to seek and save that which was lost."* All whom He seeks, He finds, and all whom He finds, He saves. At this early stage in the life of our Lord, He was already aware of His divine mission. Surely this must have been in His mind when He said what He did to Mary.

The Perfect Candidate for Baptism

After viewing the scenes that surrounded our Lord's humble birth, and hearing His words of wisdom descend on the ears of the doctors and rabbis and His own appointed earthly parents in the temple, we are now ready to witness His baptism in the fullness of manhood by *His forerunner,* John the Baptist. The time came for the young Carpenter to hang up His tools, close shop, and leave home to enter the ministry.

A popular preacher was baptizing people by the thousands in the Jordan River (which was his baptistry) as they confessed their sins (Mark 1:4,5). The murky Jordan River runs from north to south about seventy miles in a place below sea level, from the Sea of Galilee to the Dead Sea, within the tiny nation of Israel, centrally located among the nations of the world and called the cradle of civilization.

When Jesus was about 30, He left Nazareth and walked about seventy miles to Bethabara where John was baptizing. Bethabara meant "place of passage," where the main crossing of the Jordan was. It was the most direct route to Damascus. Since then it has been changed to Bethany, east of the river in the country of Peraea. Jericho was only five miles away from Jerusalem in Judea. Remember, the Gospel of John gives a lot of information that the synoptic Gospel writers have not recorded, because John was the youngest and last of the four Gospel writers, who lived to be the oldest. He fills in what the others did not witness, being a part of the inner circle of the twelve.

John 1:28,29, "These things were done in *Bethabara beyond Jordan,* where John was baptizing. The next day John seeth Jesus coming unto him, and saith, Behold the Lamb of God, which taketh away the sin of the world."

Behold is a word used in Scripture to alert the hearers that something unusual is about to happen.

I believe this was the very first meeting of the two men, even though their mothers were related. Based on Mary's visit to her cousin Elisabeth, she travelled all the way from Nazareth in Galilee to a town in Judea. She spent three months with Elisabeth, who was already six months pregnant with a baby that was to be named John, even though Elisabeth was old and past the age of having children. She remained there until Elisabeth's time to be delivered. John saw Jesus for the first time, referring to the words in verse 31, "And *I knew Him not*: but that He should be *made manifest to Israel . . .*" From here John's testimony bears out what the rest of the evangelists wrote, concerning the baptism of Jesus. Therefore, the place where Jesus was baptized seems to be clear from John 1:28.

What can we learn from the initiation of His baptism when Jesus was presented publicly to Israel by John? John, who was baptizing sinners in the River Jordan upon confession of their sins, said to Jesus when He asked to be baptized, "I have need to be baptized of Thee, and comest Thou to me?"

John in his preaching exposed every social and secret sin, as a man with a message sent from God. He told the people, the soldiers, King Herod, and the Pharisees what to do to find God's favor. John lived above reproach, and yet he acknowledges his unworthiness in the sinless presence of Christ. Nevertheless, Jesus responded, "It becometh us to fulfill all righteousness." In other words, Jesus is here setting the *example* for us to follow if we have received *His righteousness* and *follow Him* in the initiation of *water baptism.*

Baptism is the *first ordinance* of His church, a door into church membership. It is to be administered to only those who *confess* Christ as their Savior in the free forgiveness of their sin. It implies that you have already been *saved* through a personal contact with Christ. It suggests that you were *buried* with Him by baptism, your sins *have been washed away*, not by water but by blood—the blood of the Lamb. It pictures a *resurrection* from the watery grave, a new person made possible by the free grace of Christ, henceforth to *walk in newness of life*. In a word, *baptism is only for believers*. It is therefore a *meaningful* and *symbolic* reflection of salvation. It teaches that baptism does not save. It is only for the saved, not in order to be saved, otherwise salvation would be of works and not of grace.

When Jesus was baptized, it was a symbol of what Christ would do for His church in cleansing from sin those who are His, giving them the gift of eternal salvation in the new life that has come forth from Him.

We must not deviate from this by setting forth the traditions of men instead of obeying Christ's command "to go into all the world and teach (make disciples) of all nations, baptizing them in the name of the Father, the Son and the Holy Spirit . . ." Also, the church is to teach and indoctrinate the young converts that which Christ has commanded.

Notice that baptism follows the making of disciples. Surely it needs no debate as to the right mode of baptism. The instruction from the Word is clear as to *immersion*. Any other form destroys its teaching of a death, burial, and resurrection. Hear Paul as he gives us his advice in the Spirit on this matter from Romans 6:3–5: "Know ye not, that so many of us as were baptized into Jesus Christ were baptized into *His death*? Therefore, we are *buried* with Him by baptism into death: that like as Christ was *raised* up from the dead by the glory of the Father, even so we also should *walk* in newness of life. For *if* we have been planted together in the likeness of His death, we *shall be* also in the likeness of His resurrection."

You will readily see that baptism is typical to a death, ". . . baptized [past tense] into Jesus Christ were baptized into His death." By a burial, "Buried with Him by baptism (immersion)."

Let us get our interpretations right, for no other way will suffice. If you have experienced the first step, you most surely will the last step.

Lastly, baptism pictures a resurrection, ". . . planted together in the likeness of His death, we *shall* (future tense) be also in the likeness of His resurrection." A new life in Christ began here and is perfected hereafter.

Dear friend, you must judge yourself on this matter. If you are right you shall not be judged. I would help you if I could, by God's grace, not to continue in the error which many have allowed, if so be that you have strayed from Bible baptism; it would not hurt your conscience as a Christian to become *Scripturally baptized,* if for nothing more than having the *peace of mind* that you are not following the *"traditions of men"* but the *"command of God."*

Permit me another important thought that comes out of the baptism of Jesus. Let us notice the clear-cut recognition of the *Trinity* that is revealed to us here. Jesus, God's Son, was the center of attention as John the Baptist officiated at the place of passage, when our Lord was endorsed by heavenly authority in the ministry that would soon follow.

God the Father's voice was heard from above, stating His approval in the words, "This is *My beloved Son,* in whom I am *well pleased."* If God is well pleased with Him, we most certainly should be. The Holy Spirit, or the Spirit of God, is acknowledged "descending like a dove, and lighting upon Him."

Matthew 3:13-17, "Then cometh Jesus from Galilee to Jordan unto John, to be baptized of him. But John forbid Him, saying, I have need to be baptized of Thee, and comest Thou to me? And Jesus answering said unto him, Suffer it to be so now: for thus it becometh *us* to fulfill all righteousness. Then he suffered Him. And Jesus, when He was baptized, went up straightway out of the water: and, lo, the heavens were opened unto Him, and He saw the *Spirit of God* descending like a dove, and lighting upon Him; and lo a voice from heaven, saying, This is *My* beloved *Son,* in whom I am well pleased."

Acts 10:38, "How *God* anointed *Jesus* of Nazareth with the *Holy Spirit and with power:* who went about doing good, and healing all that were oppressed of the devil; for God was with Him."

Baptism, as the first ordinance of the church, if administered right, need never be repeated. However, in some cases it is necessary, such as when Paul rebaptized some disciples of John the Baptist, in the name of the Trinity.

Matthew 28:19, "Go ye therefore, and teach all nations, baptizing them in the name of the *Father,* and of the *Son* and of the *Holy Spirit."*

Acts 19:5, "When they heard this, they were baptized [rebaptized] in the name of the Lord Jesus [as the central Person of the Godhead]."

They henceforth were disciples and followers of Jesus, not of John the Baptist. Although John was a great man, we are not to follow men, but to *be followers of Christ*. Our preference always must be based on the Bible, not on the creed of our denomination or our devotion to a person like John.

The *Lord's Supper,* as the *second ordinance* of the church, should be administered repeatedly, "*as often* as you do it *in remembrance of Me*" (1 Corinthians 11:24–26). This ordinance will be discussed at the close of our Lord's earthly ministry. There are only two ordinances that our Lord instituted: baptism at the beginning, and the Lord's Supper at the end of His great ministry.

Temptation in the Wilderness

Following the Father's approval of Christ's baptism, which opened the way to His public ministry plus the descending Spirit of power to perform His life's work, came the brutal attacks in the wilderness from the Devil's ministry of pain, power, destruction and domination.

For a better understanding of the temptation (testing) of Christ, you should have a Scriptural background in mind, taken from any or all of the Synoptic Gospels (Matthew 4:1–11; Mark 1:12,13; Luke 4:1–13).

Before Jesus enters upon His public ministry, He must first be severely tested and tried to prove Himself a fit *Advocate* to plead our case as sinners.

For the next *forty days and nights,* He must be satanically tempted and undergo the worst temptations known to man, The place chosen for this life-and-death struggle was the dismal desert in the wild wilderness of Judea. His opponent and competitor in this far-reaching world contest and crisis was against the *worst person* who ever lived, as opposed to the *best Person* who ever lived. This event was to be blacked out to all human eyes. The only strange gallery that was permitted to view the scene were the angels of God on one hand and the evil spirits of Satan on the other.

What would be the consequence of this deadly duel?

If Satan won over the Son of God, it would be the worst defeat in the annals of history, including all the holy wars that have ever been fought. *Jesus is the representative of things that are good and right, Satan the representative and the champion of evil, and the darkness of sin and death.* If Jesus were to lose, heaven would be emptied, and hell would be full. Satan then would finally rule as the victorious god of this world,

VIEWING THE LONG-LOOKED-FOR MESSIAH

a seat he has sought since his fall. But this could not be if God be God. His promises and prophecies must not, *cannot fail.* Isaiah 42:4 says, *"He shall not fail."* He did not fail at the point in time to come from heaven to earth and be made manifest to men as promised. He did not fail at the point in time to still the storm at sea and strengthen the faith of His disciples. He did not fail at the point in time to heal all manner of diseases and show mercy on the afflicted. He did not fail at the point in time to raise the dead to prove His power over death. He does not fail at the appointed time to impart salvation to the comfortless and sinful. Neither will He fail at this battle royal to defeat the Devil, even though *He fasted for forty days and nights,* thus giving Satan the advantage in this deadly duel.

Mark tells us that Jesus was "tempted for forty days of Satan, and He was with the wild beasts." Mark says nothing as to the nature of the temptations, only when it was over. The angels ministered to Him as Matthew reported. Mark says, "The Spirit driveth Him into the wilderness." Both Matthew and Luke record that He was "led of the Spirit." Both are correct, for a person can be led to do what he dreads doing as a matter of necessity. Both accounts of Matthew and Luke are essentially the same, with the exception of the way Luke closes the conflict.

The difference Luke writes about is, "And when the devil had completed *every temptation* [which implies a lot more than three], he departed from Him for a season." This expression seems to say that Satan continued plaguing Jesus in various ways throughout His ministry.

Hebrews 4:15, "For we have not an High Priest which cannot be touched with the feeling of our infirmities; but was in *all points* tempted like as we are, *yet without sin.*"

Satan's assault on the Son represents *three stages of struggles* man has with the Devil, which takes place upon the *body,* the *mind,* and the human *spirit:*

- First, spare self. Do not suffer, if it is not necessary.
- Second, gratify sign seekers. Win the applause of men.
- Third, gain power and popularity by sacrificing principles of truth. Better to compromise rather than be persecuted.

Now let us face a few fantastic facts:

Satan was no match for the Savior. Jesus never yielded to any of his subtle temptations, because Christ was the only perfect Person on earth.

His divine side cannot be tempted with sin. The Bible says in James 1:13, "God cannot be tempted with evil . . ." Jesus, remember, is God. In Christ there was nothing that could be appealed to except in His flesh; but Jesus, unlike us, was born without sin. Jesus showed His mastery over sin and Satan by yielding not to his temptations. Nevertheless, Jesus did suffer in the wilderness from Satan, and on other occasions as well, especially at the cross.

Hebrews 2:18, "For in that He Himself hath *suffered* being tempted, He is able to succor (aid, help, relieve) them that are tempted."

The Scriptures suggest two reasons why Jesus must be tempted:

1. To prove His power over Satan, that he had no part in Him.

2. To comfort, console, help, and relieve those that are tempted.

Thus Jesus proved in all His power and purity He was more than a match for Satan's subtlety.

Regarding Satan's attack on us, we can resist him as Jesus did when He set the example for us to follow by *using the Word*. Every time Jesus was tempted, He quoted the Scriptures as the Sword of the Spirit against the enemy, and so must we. But you are first to know the Scriptures and the power of God to do this. Memorize Scripture; it is your weapon against this enemy and evil.

To conclude this section, I will do as I have done, and ask questions on both baptism and the temptations of Christ.

• • •

Questionnaire on Baptism (According to the Bible)

1. Did John or our Lord's apostles baptize any infants, or were they that were baptized old enough to be accountable?
2. Was John's mode of baptism by sprinkling, pouring, or immersion?
3. Did John baptize in or alongside the River Jordan?
4. Did Jesus have more disciples than John? John 4:1
5. Does baptism save, or is it a symbol of salvation?
6. Does a member of a church need to be rebaptized if he discovers he was saved after he was baptized?
7. Would you agree that baptism is only for believers?

8. Was the penitent thief on the cross ever baptized?
9. Who has the authority to baptize today, the church or freelance preachers?
10. Does a person need baptizing again if he fell away from the church for a few years, even though he was baptized right the first time and wants to be reinstated?

• • •

Answers to Questions on Baptism
1. No, infants were never baptized, only accountable persons.
2. Immersion
3. In Jordan River
4. Yes
5. It is a symbol of salvation.
6. Yes, his baptism was not valid, not being saved.
7. Yes
8. No
9. Church only given authority to fit candidates.
10. No, he need only repent to be accepted into fellowship of the church. If records were lost from former church, he may come by statement.

• • •

Questionnaire on Chapter 6
1. Approximately how long is God's time line from the creation of man to the present?
2. What dispensation are we now living in?
3. What was the greatest event in human history?
4. What one Person, above all others, fills the pages of the New Testament?
5. Can the birth of Christ be accepted as a miracle?
6. When Jesus as a boy was thought lost, where did His parents find Him?
7. Who baptized Jesus?
8. Was Jesus' baptism by sprinkling or immersion?

9. Why must Jesus pass the test of temptation?
10. How many times was Jesus tempted in the wilderness? Give one of the temptations.

• • •

Answers to Questions on Chapter 6

1. 6,000 years
2. Grace
3. The birth of God's Son in the world.
4. Christ
5. Yes
6. Temple
7. John the Baptist
8. Immersion
9. To prove His sinlessness, or to be a creditable Messiah to the Jews, and a Savior who could resist the Devil's temptations.
10. Three times. Temptation with bread; temptation with performing a miracle by jumping from the temple; temptation to fall down and worship Satan to have the world's power.

• • •

Questionnaire on the Temptations

1. Are the temptations of Christ in only one or in each of the Synoptic Gospels?
2. What preceded His temptations with Satan?
3. How long was Jesus tempted at this time?
4. What would the results be if Jesus yielded to the Devil?
5. Did the Devil stop after the three temptations, or does the Word imply that Jesus was tempted at others times as well?
6. Can God be tempted with evil?
7. Since Jesus was both God and man, in what side did Satan launch his attack?
8. Were the temptations of Christ real?

9. How did Jesus set the example of resisting the Devil?
10. Since Jesus was tempted, can we expect to be?

• • •

Answers to Questions on the Temptations
1. All
2. Baptism
3. Forty days and nights
4. He would have become a sinner and forfeit the purpose for which He came.
5. "Devil left Him for a season," implies that the Devil continued to try Jesus.
6. No
7. On the human side
8. Yes
9. By using the Word
10. Yes

Chapter 7

Journeying With Jesus on Soul-Winning Tours and Evangelical Crusades
-or-
Christ, the Prophet of Redemption: His Work in the Soul (Salvation)

Thought

They that are born twice must needs die but once. They that are born once must needs die twice.

• • •

I. His prophetic and redemptive work in performing miracles within the soul of man
   A. God's divine order—*doing* before *teaching* (Acts 1:1; James 1:22; 2:26)
   B. His work on the soul before the body (John 1:36,37)
      1. Four methods successfully used in soul-winning
         a. Preaching Christ—John and Andrew (John 1:36)
         b. Personal work—Peter (John 1:40–42)
         c. Precious word—Philip (John 1:43,44)
         d. Principle of prayer—Nathaniel (John 1:46–51)
      2. Enrolling for eternity—first priority
   C. Matthew is later called by Jesus (Luke 5:27–32)
   D. Other people saved in addition to the appointed Apostles
      1. Individuals saved—listing some personal cases
      2. Groups that believed—some questionable, others genuine
II. Questionnaire and Answers

• • •

In opening this important chapter as to Jesus' prophetic work, we need to recall from the Old Testament all that the prophets wrote about Him in many ways. For example:

Deuteronomy 18:15 (as the Messianic Prophet), "The Lord thy God will raise up unto thee a *Prophet* from the midst of thee, of thy brethren, like unto me: *unto Him ye shall harken.*"

Jesus was recognized as the Prophet that would come, as they believed the prophets: "Then those men, when they had seen the miracle that Jesus did, said, This is of a truth *that Prophet* that should come into the world" (John 6:14).

His meaningful and mighty ministry introduces His *threefold office* as Prophet, Priest, and King. A prophet was to represent God to the people. He would be one that would not only foretell future events, but also interpret the Divine will by telling forth past events. Who could be better fitted for the task than Jesus? He is the fulfillment of all prophecies. Jesus, as God's *Perfect Prophet*, takes the incomplete and progressive revelation and makes it complete and final. He continued to work with His Apostles to complete the incomplete revelation, even after His personal work on earth was finished.

He spoke with *authority* and not as the scribes when He said in Matthew 5:28,29, "Ye have heard that it was said by them of old time . . . *But I say* unto you . . ."

His Redemptive Work

The Old Testament prophets foresaw by faith the mission of this Messianic Prophet, and so stated His purpose.

Isaiah 7:14, "Therefore the Lord Himself shall give you a sign [meaning the birth of Jesus was a *miracle,* being born of a virgin]. Behold, a (the) virgin shall conceive, and bear a son (Son of God), and shall call His name Immanuel (God with us)."

Notice the first part of Isaiah 9:6, "For unto us a child (Child, Christ) is born, unto us a son (Son, Jesus) is given . . ."

Matthew 1:21–23 is perfectly fulfilled: "And she shall bring forth a Son, and thou shalt call his name *JESUS*: for He shall save His people from their sins. Now all this was done, that it might be fulfilled which was spoken of the Lord by the prophet, saying, Behold, a virgin shall be with Child, and shall bring forth a Son, and they shall call His name

Emmanuel, which being interpreted is, God with us."

How accurate is the Word! His redemptive mission was "to save *His people* from their sins."

God's Divine Order

Acts 1:1, "The former treatise have I made, O Theophilus, of all that Jesus began both to *do* and teach."

Doing comes before the teaching ministry. It is a pattern to ponder, that we must be *followers* before we can be *leaders*. His practice is a principle we are to apply from His personal example, as *guidelines* for the teacher of His Word, and a preacher of His gospel.

Once again, to reiterate this important point, let us listen to what Jesus said about it:

Matthew 7:24, "Therefore, whosoever heareth these sayings of mine, and doeth them, I will liken him unto a *wise man*, which built his house upon a Rock."

According to my reckoning, the *"Rock"* is Christ the Redeemer. The process to follow, based on this Instructor, is when a person hears the truth from a reliable source, he is to act upon *"these sayings of Mine (Jesus)."* If the sinner does what Jesus requires, he will repent of his sins, and believe that Jesus is God's anointed Savior, sent to redeem the souls of men that were given by the Father to the Son. The foundation is then laid by our Lord for the *believer to build upon Christ our Rock.*

As we are taught in the light of the Great Commission, "making disciples among *all nations*," and after this "teaching them to observe *all things* whatsoever I have commanded..." When the young believer "adorns the doctrine of *God our Savior* (Jesus) in all things," then he is ready to *"teach* others also." He has done wisely as the Lord required; come hades from beneath or high waters from above, his life in Christ will not fall or fail.

We shall now see, by the help of the Holy Spirit, that Christ is the *Founder* of Christianity, that He laid the ground work for the establishment of *His church* before the foundation of the world.

In Matthew 16:18, Jesus said, "Upon this *Rock* I will build My church, and the gates of hell shall not prevail against it (or shall not overcome it)."

Ephesians 2:19–22, "Now therefore ye are no more strangers and foreigners, but fellow citizens with the saints, and of the household of

God; and are built upon the foundation of the apostles and prophets, *Jesus Christ* Himself being the *Chief corner stone*; in whom all the building fitly framed together growth unto an *holy temple in the Lord."*

1 Corinthians 3:11 also tells us, "For other foundations can no man lay than that is laid, which is Jesus Christ."

Since the Bible says that this *"Foundation of God* stands sure," we have assurance and confidence in Christ as our Savior, who formally called us out of darkness into His marvelous light (2 Timothy 2:19).

Can you remember when you were saved? I did not say that you must know the day and hour, but you should be able to recall that wonderful conversion experience when you met the Master of men. Be it a few days, some months, or several years ago, you must recall a time when God gave you peace of mind.

Four of the Master's Methods

The greatest Person who ever lived in the world was Jesus.

The greatest Power in the world is Prayer.

The greatest Book in the world is the Bible.

The greatest Work in the world is *soul winning*.

We are now about to witness our Lord's first work regarding the *miracle of grace in salvation* before His miracles of mercy in service.

Method No. 1: Preaching

John, the *beloved apostle* of five books in the Bible, gives us this record in the Gospel that bears his name. He includes himself in the first of the four methods of salvation.

Hear *John the Baptist* as he briefly preached an effective message that day, which led to the conversion of two of our Lord's disciples: "Again the next day after John stood, and two of his disciples; and looking upon Jesus as he walked, he saith, *Behold the Lamb of God!* And the two disciples heard him speak, and *they followed Jesus"* (John 1:35–37).

This Baptist preacher was not a member of the Baptist Church as such, but he delivered a message that most preachers find hard to top, even though it had only five words. "Behold, the Lamb of God." A good message is measured by *depth, not length.* This was a sermon about the *Savior.*

It was a sermon deep into the heart of the Gospel.

It was a sermon on the despised cross.

It was a sermon, not about sacrificing animals, but the royal-red blood of Christ, the "Lamb of God."

It was a sermon that pointed to the work of atonement for man's sins forever.

It was a sermon that lifts from earth to heaven, from the place called Calvary to the place called Paradise, from the cross to the throne, from the throne to the crown.

This is God's first and *best* approach in the salvation of souls.

1 Corinthians 1:18,21, "For the *preaching of the cross* is to them that perish foolishness; but unto us which are saved it is the power of God. For after that in the wisdom of God the world by wisdom knew not God, it pleased God by the foolishness of preaching to save them that believe."

One time after a church service, I was shaking hands with my members when a big man said to me, "Preacher, you stepped on my toes today." My reply was, "I'm sorry, Brother, I missed. I was aiming at your heart."

This fellow-preacher, John the Baptizer, stood head and shoulders above the world's preachers. Jesus said after John was beheaded, "Among them *born of woman* there hath not risen a greater than John the Baptist." Only his successor was before him and above him.

That day became the spiritual birthday of two first charter members of the church. *Andrew and John* grew to be great men of God who *preached* the unsearchable riches of Christ.

Method No. 2: Personal Soul-Winning

The second method is extremely important to the life of the church: eyeball to eyeball, one-on-one, *personal witnessing*. Jesus not only told His disciples to fish for men, *He set the example* several times going out as the Good Shepherd to find His lost sheep.

In this approach we read in John 1:40–42, "One of the two which heard John speak, and followed him, was Andrew, Simon Peter's brother. He *first* findeth his own brother Simon, and saith unto him, We have found the Messiah, which is, being interpreted, the Christ. And he *brought* him to Jesus. And when Jesus beheld him, he said, Thou art

Simon the son of Jona: thou shalt be called Cephas, which is by interpretation, A stone."

Shortly after Andrew was saved he got a burden to see his brother Peter saved. Have you ever tried to witness to some member of your family, as Andrew brought Peter to the Lord? Happily, may I say that I was saved the same way. My oldest brother was used of the Lord to bring the youngest brother to salvation in Christ. That was me. In turn and in time the Lord was able to use me to bring my parents to the Lord. What a happy day that was! There is no greater joy than to be used of the Lord to win souls to Christ. Jesus said in Matthew 4:19, "Follow Me and I will make you *fishers of men.*" If we would follow not far off, but closely in His steps, others would see Jesus and know the joy of salvation.

Sometimes we may not realize that we brought a soul to Jesus, as a friend in school, a neighbor across the street, a partner in business, or a member of the family. Wouldn't you be happy to learn that a person you introduced to Christ became a missionary, an evangelist, a pastor, a much-needed Christian statesman, or simply a faithful, devoted wife, mother, or father, saved through your prayers and efforts?

Method No. 3: The Power of the Piercing Word

Let us look unto Jesus, the Master Soul-Winner.

John 1:43, "The day following Jesus would go forth into Galilee, and findeth Philip, and saith unto him, *Follow Me.*"

Here we can learn a lot from this conversion also. When there is no preacher or personal worker available, the Lord will visit that person He is seeking to save. For whom He seeks, He finds, and whom He finds, He saves. For it is the Father's will that none of His lost sheep shall perish, but all shall come to repentance, and to the Redeemer.

Following is a case that was stated above. No preacher or personal worker, but "Jesus only." The *Scripture and the Word* from the personal Savior are inseparable. You cannot have one without the other. Both are one and the same. "Jesus findeth Philip . . . and saith unto him, Follow Me." The word of Christ must be applied as a *means* in saving sinners. Jesus still speaks today through His Word.

I think the Spirit would have us see that Jesus called Philip by name. It was a personal call. "The Lord knows those that are His." Their names were recorded before the foundation of the world in the Lamb's Book of Life. Such preaching today can hinder a person from understanding the truth, instead of helping him. *Some get the idea* that when a soul is saved, at that time the recording angel writes his name in the Book of Life. Oh my, what a mistaken view that is!

You may remember the verse that I used in Chapter 2, "Tracing Our Family Tree to the Heart of God's Love." *The names of all of God's children were written down, numbering all of God's elect from A to Z before the foundation of the world.* Somebody must be wrong! Jesus called Philip personally. It was a heavenly calling, an effectual calling, and an irresistible calling, for thus saith the Scripture, "Whom He did *predestinate, them He also called*" (Romans 8:29,30).

We preachers extend a *general call.* Jesus issues an effectual, irresistible call. "God's people shall be willing in the day of His power" exerted within them, and they shall come in response to Christ, as Philip did (see Psalm 110:3).

Notice, please, that *Jesus findeth Philip.* He did not find Jesus. I touched on this in the opening of the New Testament as to the boy Jesus in the Temple, when Jesus said in response to His mother's rebuke, "How is it that *you sought Me?*" Jesus does the seeking, the finding, and the saving.

The *Christian world of apostasy* has it backward today. I hear so often a testimony given by some well-meaning church member say, "When *I* found Jesus . . ." or "When *I* accepted Christ . . ." To me this seems to be bragging on what *they* did, rather than what *Jesus did.*

I have a dear young brother preacher that told me the other day, "If I ever get to heaven, it will be on *my* faith, and nothing else." If he only knew that faith is a gift from the Lord, according to Ephesians 2:8! *Salvation, I say, is all of grace.* If God foresaw that we manufactured faith, then it was not God-given. Grace would not be unmerited favor. So if a person is trusting in what *he can do* in the flesh to get to heaven, apart from God in Christ, I'm afraid he will be one day sadly mistaken.

I would prefer to say simply that, *"Jesus found me. Jesus saved me."* A chorus of a hymn tells it like it is:

> *"Since the Savior found me, took away my sins,*
> *I have had the sunlight of His love within."*

I hope you can endure the word of exhortation from God's revelation. For such is the office of a preacher, *"to reprove, rebuke, and exhort with all longsuffering and doctrine."* Let us do what Hebrews 12:2 says, "Looking unto Jesus, the *Author* and Finisher of our faith."

What I have been led to say in a testimony service puts the credit and the glory where it belongs—not on me, but on *my Master*. "Beloved, once I was lost, but Jesus found me. I was blind until He gave me sight. I was a beggar, and now, thank God, I'm rich in 'the faith once for all delivered unto the saints.' I was in bondage, now I'm a free man. I once was a child of the Devil's kingdom of darkness; now, by His grace, I am a child of the King and a member of His kingdom of heaven. But most of all, I once was *dead* in trespasses and sins; now I live through the quickening, regenerating power of Jesus Christ *my Lord* (John 5:21), who loved me and gave Himself for me. I once was a hell-bound sinner, but now, thank God, I'm a heaven-bound saint. Not of what I have done will I boast, but of what Jesus has done for me at Calvary. Praise *His* holy name!"

May God have mercy on us poor, forgetful creatures like Philip. With good intentions his feeble effort was rewarded. Philip even as a babe in Christ tells his friend Nathanael, *"We* have found Him, of whom Moses in the law, and the prophets, did write, Jesus of Nazareth, the *Son of Joseph."*

Let us see where he was right first, and then we must point out a few misconceptions, or errors, in his early view of theology. After all, when *we* first became a Christian, there was a lot of things we needed to get straightened out through proper teaching. I have had to unlearn a lot in order to grow in grace.

Philip was acquainted with the writings of Moses, and Jesus did say on another occasion, *"Moses wrote of Me."* Also, he was aware that the prophets wrote about Christ as the coming Messiah. He read the Old Testament Scriptures, and this was commendable. As a *young Christian* he was eager to tell others about Christ, and this was great. That is what many of us need to do. Some professing Christians have never told a soul about Him. I would hate to think that some of you may go to heaven empty-handed. Wouldn't you, as never having brought a single lost soul to Christ for salvation? This is the greatest need of the church: to tell people about Jesus, and *bring* them to the place where they can be saved, as the Word of God is used by the Spirit.

When Philip was talking to Nathanael, his choice of words was not theologically sound, but do not think too hard of him. He said, "We have found Him." He must have already met the other three that were saved, as they were residents of the same town, and they all sounded like *Arminians*. However, after spending some time with Jesus, they discovered that it was *Jesus that found them,* because He chose them (John 1:43). Therefore, they embrace this persuasion after maturing in grace and glory, like many of us after studying the Word. Enlightening verse from 1 Peter 1:2; Acts 9:15; 2 Timothy 1:9.

Rarely does one go to the Arminian theology having once embraced the spirit of Calvinism. Most often a Christian starts as an Arminian; and when he hears the deeper truths of the *Doctrines of Grace,* which God shows them, it will thrill their soul and cause them to rejoice in the fuller revelation from the Spirit. He will never go back into the old camp again.

Method No. 4: Principle of Prayer

Nathanael is our example. He was witnessed to by his saved friend, as we must do. Being led as all potential candidates for salvation, he called upon the Lord while alone under the fig tree. (The promise is in Romans 10:9,10.) This desire was honored when, in response to Nathanael's question of "Whence knowest Thou me?" (John 1:48), Jesus said, "Before that Philip called thee, when thou wast under the fig tree . . ." [while he was in prayer].

Next, Nathanael makes his open declaration of faith (verse 49): "Rabbi (Master, Teacher), Thou art the Son of God; Thou art the King of Israel." In addition to this, please read some great passages on the principle of prayer in Jeremiah 33:3, Matthew 6:6, and Luke 18:7,8.

The individuals who were saved throughout the Gospels are legion. In more cases than we might know, one often led many to salvation. God saves us because He wants to. I'm so thankful that He not only foreknew me, but for some unknown reason that I may never know, He loved me and called me with an holy calling, not according to my goodness, because I have none, but according to His own good pleasure and purpose, which was given me in Christ Jesus before the world began. Bless God for His so great salvation!

Therefore, let me point out a few precious souls that Jesus saved in those short three and a half years while He walked among men, in addition to His Apostles. Some rich, but many poor. Some Gentiles as well as Jews. Some cultured, the most respected in their community. But many were outcasts, unworthy, unclean, and unwanted. Please read 1 Corinthians 1:27–29.

When Jesus was born and first taken to the temple on the eighth day to be circumcised, there was an old man named Simeon residing in Jerusalem, who was just and devout. The Holy Spirit gave him the assurance that he would not see death until he saw the Lord's Christ: "For mine eyes have seen Thy salvation" (Luke 2:25–35). Shortly after seeing Him as the source of salvation, he died.

Then there was one Anna, a prophetess, who grew to a great age. She was a widow of 84, who served God by fasting and praying (Luke 2:36–38). She too spoke of Jesus as the Redeemer.

Mary, the mother of Jesus, was saved when she believed the good tidings of the angel Gabriel. She overflowed with unspeakable joy when she spoke through the Spirit in Luke 1:47, "And my spirit hath rejoiced in *God my Savior.*" She believed that God had *chosen* her to bring forth His Son, along with Joseph, who also was a believer. Just a word of caution to remember: the Lord God Almighty is a jealous God. He only, in His triune Person as Father, Son, and Holy Spirit, is worthy of worship. Prayer is to be offered in the name of Jesus alone (1 Timothy 2:5).

A further look reveals other saved women who loved Jesus and showed their love in many ways. Two of these were Mary and Martha (John 11:1–44). (Their brother Lazarus, whom Jesus loved, can also be numbered among the saved.)

Then there was the woman taken in the act of adultery. Jesus said to her, "Neither do I condemn thee; go, and sin no more" (John 8:10,11).

Surely we must not forget the remarkable and *benevolent widow* who gave all to Jesus (Luke 21:1–4), or the *persistent widow* who would not give up or give in to her adversaries (Luke 18:1–8). Mark 16:9 tells about Mary Magdalene, one whom Jesus saved from demons.

How about the *depressed soul* that spent all her living on quack doctors and got no better, but only grew worse. She touched the hem of His garment and was brought to confess Christ openly (Matthew 9:20–22).

We admire the courage and unconquerable faith of the *Canaanite woman,* a Gentile who would not take "no" for an answer. She prevailed in her cause to win the favor of Jesus and His power to restore her demon-possessed daughter (Matthew 15:27,28).

I must not overlook the unnamed but well-known *woman of Samaria*. Her unforgettable experience brought her to see her sins as well as the Savior. We might think of her as the founder of the "Woman's Home Missionary Society." She was not only saved, but her influence brought many precious souls to the "light" in that city. She was avoided by the Jews, but not Jesus, for He said, "*I must* needs go through Samaria" (John 4:4,39).

God help us to drink deep into the well of water that springs up into everlasting life given by Him who said, "If any man (person) thirst, let him come unto Me, and drink. He that believeth on Me, as the Scripture hath said, out of his belly (inner most being) shall flow rivers of living water" (John 7:37,38).

Are we soul-winners like this woman at the well? May God put the desire in our hearts to witness and win our neighborhood, our town, and city to the Savior.

I'm always impressed with the Gentile *Centurion from Capernaum*, who went to Jesus for the hurt, torment, and suffering, not of himself, but of another, his lowly servant whom he loved and was greatly concerned about (Matthew 8:5–13). Jesus never turns anyone down, be he sinner or saint, who comes to Him for help. He is the *Helper of the helpless*.

Simon, the rich leper, and the *sinful woman* who anointed Jesus in the home of the well-to-do Pharisee, were both forgiven of their sins (Luke 7:40–43).

The *man called Legion,* who makes for a great missionary message, was insane in sin. After Jesus deals with him, we see him saved in soul, sound in mind, and clothed in body, on his way to tell his friends "what great things the Lord hath done for him" (Mark 5:1–20).

Then one of the *ten lepers* who were cleansed (healed) came back to the Healer, fell on his face at Jesus' feet, and gave Him thanks (Luke 17:15–19).

I love the conversion experience of *Zacchaeus,* the tax collector (Luke 19:1–10). I cannot hesitate to ask: Has Jesus come into your house as a welcomed guest? Has He saved you and your family?

Can you say, "Christ is the Head of this house, the unseen Guest at every meal, the silent Listener to every conversation?" I said years ago, taking my stand with Joshua, "As for me and my house, we will serve the Lord." God honored my stand, and what Brother Paul said to the *Philippian jailer,* is also true with me. Thank God! "Believe on the Lord Jesus Christ, and thou shalt be saved, and *thy house*" (Acts 16:31).

I would love to tell you about some lasting lessons we might share as we observe the *Centurion* in charge of Christ's execution. When *at the cross,* he cried, after seeing and hearing the things that Jesus said and did for others. Being moved by the death of this middle Malefactor, he said, "Certainly this was a righteous Man" (Luke 23:47). "Truly, this Man was the Son of God" (Mark 15:39).

I am compelled to say something, though it might be but one brief word about the *thief on the cross.* He defended Jesus and admitted his guilt, thus asking to be remembered by Jesus. The Lord, whether on the cross or on the throne, does more than we ask or think. While sin's debt was being paid, Jesus spoke in pain, "*Today* shalt *thou* be *with Me in Paradise*" (Luke 23:43).

Thank God for the living testimonies of these souls; though they be dead, yet they still speak.

Hark! There stands Joseph of Arimethaea, one of the Sanhedrins, who, being a disciple of Jesus, did not consent to His death. He loaned Him his own tomb (Matthew 27:57).

Join the two discouraged men going to Emmaus, when they were given a new vision of the resurrected Christ (Luke 24:13–32).

What do you believe about this line-up of character witnesses who expressed their convictions about the Lord Jesus Christ? I believe I will meet every one in that day, when we all gather round the throne in Glory.

I am persuaded that these men and women I have referred to, some who were mental cases, thieves, or adulterers, and others with their afflictions and infirmities, were all saved from their illnesses and transgressions.

John 2:23, "Now when He was in Jerusalem at the Passover, in the feast day, many believed in His name, when they saw the miracles which He did."

John 12:37, "But though He had done so many miracles before them, yet they believed not on Him."

We are not to seek for miracles accompanying salvation, which are often allowed by God, but we should and must seek the *Man of miracles*, who is able and willing to grant a miracle of salvation, if we appeal for His help and ask according to His will. Every believer is a walking miracle. Even though miracles cannot save, yet they were many times used as aids to faith.

Groups That Believed

In John's Gospel alone, the phrase "many believed on Him" appears eight times. A close observation of the different groups of people mentioned will show that some of these groups were *questionable* or doubtful (indicated by Q), others were *possible*, but probably lost (P), and others seemed to be *genuine* (G):

- Many believed because of His miracles—John 2:23. (P)
- Many in Samaria believed because of the woman, and many believed in Christ's Word—John 4:39,41,42. (G)
- Many believed because of the miracles—John 7:31. (P)
- Many believed, but had mixed views concerning Christ's Person—John 7:40–43. (Some Q, others G)
- Many believed at first, but later, when questioned by Christ, they were questionable—John 8:30. (Q)
- Many believed because of what John the Baptist preached and what was said about Jesus—John 10:41,42. (G)
- Many believed because of witnessing the raising of Lazarus—John 11:45; 12:11. (G)
- Many leaders believed, but did not confess Him openly, fearing excommunication—John 12:42,43. (Q)

• • •

Twelve Apostles (Matthew 10:2–4)

NAME	MEANING	MANNER OF DEATH
1. Simon Peter— also Cephas, son of Jonas (John)	Stone	Crucified upside down, feeling unworthy to be crucified like Jesus

#	Apostle	Meaning	Death
2.	Andrew, brother of Peter and son of Jonas	"Manly"	Crucified on what was later called St. Andrew's cross.
3.	James the Elder, brother of John	"Supplanter"	Beheaded by Herod in 44 A.D.
4.	John, the beloved disciple, called along with his brother James (the sons of Thunder)—parents: Zebedee and Salome	"God is gracious"	Banished on Patmos, later freed and died a natural death
5.	Philip	"Lover of horses"	Died a martyr in Italy
6.	Bartholomew or Nathanael	"Gift of God"	Flayed to death (skinned alive)
7.	Thomas, or Didymus (the doubter)	"Twin"	Died a martyr in India on what was later called Mt. Thomas
8.	Matthew, author of the first Gospel (also called Levi)	"Gift"	Died a martyr in Ethiopia
9.	James the Less, son of Alphaeus	"Supplanter"	Was crucified in Egypt
10.	Jude, also called Thaddaeus	"Man of heart"	Died a martyr in Persia
11.	Simon the Canaanite (Zealot)	"Hearing"	Crucified
12.	Judas Iscariot, son of Simon	"Traitor"	Committed suicide by hanging himself

NOTE: The manner of death of these apostles may not be reckoned historical, but traditional.

Questionnaire

1. What is the main theme of Chapter 7?
2. What is our Lord's divine order, doing before teaching, or teaching before doing?
3. Which is more important, the work on the body or the work on the soul?
4. Name the four methods given in soul winning.
5. Name a person *personally* won by Jesus' contact.
6. Who brought Peter to Jesus?
7. Which apostle is the last known to us that Jesus personally called?

Answers

1. Salvation
2. Doing before teaching
3. Work on the soul
4. (a) Preaching method, (b) personal witnessing method, (c) precious Word method, (d) principle of prayer
5. Philip
6. His brother Andrew
7. Matthew

Chapter 8

Journeying With Jesus in Healing Campaigns Both on the Masses and Individuals
-or-
Christ, the Prophet, Restoring Health to the Body: His Work (Miracles)

Thought

One proven preventative is better than a dozen possible remedies.

• • •

I. His prophetic and restoring work in performing *miracles on the bodies* of men (Isaiah 53:4; Matthew 8:16,17)

   A. *Definition and classification of miracles* in the New Testament

   B. Disposition of the first miracle over nature

   1. Place—Cana of Galilee (John 2:1–11)

   2. Purpose—To reveal His transforming power (John 2:11)

   C. *Description of the Greatest Physician* (Luke 5:31,32)

   D. Deliverance for the multitudes in seven campaigns (Matthew only)

   E. Difficulties from a paralytic case (Luke 5:17–26)

   1. First obstacle—door blocked

   2. Second obstacle—impossible case

   3. Third obstacle—doubters deny His deity

   F. *Dealing with the dead—three examples* (Matthew 5:22; Luke 7:11; John 11:38)

   G. Deliberations on the contents and conclusions

II. Questionnaire and Answers

• • •

Think on this: Blessed are your eyes for they see, and your ears for they hear, and your hands for they hold, and your head for it understands, and your mouth for it speaks, and your heart for it loves, and your soul for it lives, all because of what Jesus is to you. He is a Healer not for hire, but through prayer.

Looking at the Bible as a whole, we know that it was necessary to have the New Testament depend upon the Old Testament, otherwise it would not be complete. The Old predicts the New, and the New fulfills the Old. One cannot live without the two. Both complement each other. If we desire a full knowledge of the Word of God, we must study *both Covenants*, otherwise our understanding would be incomplete and inadequate in perceiving the truth.

In the ministry of Christ, His work was threefold: *preaching, teaching, and healing.* As we follow Jesus in His healing campaigns, we think: Shouldn't it be important, since this division of His work occupied so much of His time, that some of His healing ministry be found in the Old Testament, to give prudence and credibility to His Person? So we will begin to search out some Scriptures on this topic in the Old Testament.

As we said before, a person needs to have some knowledge of the Old in order to have a better understanding of the New. In Exodus 15:26, the latter part of the verse, God says, "*I will put none of these diseases upon thee,* which I have brought upon the Egyptians: for *I Am* the Lord that *healeth* thee."

In the divisions of clergymen you find one branch that says, "It is Satan that puts diseases on man and it is the Devil that makes a person sick, not God." In essence that is what they say. In short, they feel that the Devil makes you sick and it is never God's will for a person to be sick. Therefore, they go about to heal people that Satan made sick.

Do you see! Our verse above says differently. God permitted the Israelites during the wilderness wandering to be healthy, but on the other hand God put various diseases on the Egyptians. God did it! Hear this verse in Deuteronomy 32:39, "*I kill, I make alive. I wound, and I heal.*"

God does both, because He is sovereign. God is God. He does *what* He pleases, *when* He pleases and *as* He pleases. If He wants to punish a person for His sins, He is just in doing so. If He wants to show mercy on someone, He will show mercy. As Paul put it, in referring to God, "*I will have mercy on whom I will have mercy, and I will have compassion on whom I will have compassion*" (Romans 9:15; Exodus 33:19). Therefore, He wounds, He kills, He heals, He gives life. Believe me, *this is not the God that is preached today*. We need to get a mental grip and a spiritual hold on the sovereignty of the Almighty as revealed in the Bible.

In Exodus, which we read above, we found the significant, far-reaching words "*I Am.*" Doesn't that remind you of Christ, the great "I Am" of the New Testament?

You, along with me, have seen Christ in the Old Testament in symbols, types, and visitations to men in various ways. Now we see Him as the Healer of the Old Testament: "I will put none of these diseases upon thee. *I Am* the Lord (Christ) that healeth thee."

We go now to the prophet Isaiah, who, I suppose, wrote most about our Lord's redemptive work. But what did he have to say about healing?

Isaiah 53:4, "Surely He hath borne our griefs, and carried our sorrows: yet we did esteem *Him* stricken, smitten of God, and afflicted."

Most of this chapter carries the *theme of redemption from sin*. But I see in verse 4 a reflection of our Lord's ministry of healing that we had in mind, that led us to turn back and bring this passage forward, which I believe supports the part of the Savior's healing works.

"Surely He (Christ) hath borne (carried away) our griefs (infirmities, sicknesses) and carried (away) our sorrows (punishment or pains)" (Free Translation). This passage was fulfilled according to Matthew 8:16,17, "When the even was come, they brought unto Him many that were possessed with devils (really demons): and He cast out the spirits with His word, and healed all that were sick: that it might be *fulfilled* which was spoken by Esaias (Isaiah) the prophet, saying, *Himself took our infirmities, and bare our sicknesses.*"

It was the purpose of Jesus to heal all manner of diseases, but not His purpose that we *live forever here* in this body.

Explanation: 1. *Sickness* is an impairment to health.
2. *Disease* is a kind of sickness, *i.e.,* cancer.

I believe you can see two views here, and both are correct if properly treated.

View One—Jesus came and died to remove our sicknesses, diseases, weaknesses, infirmities, sorrows, pains, and punishment. He also carried these maladies all away to the cross and nailed them there on the tree.

I fully agree with this first view. For in heaven we shall know no sickness of any kind.

View Two—When it is within God's will to heal a person, He will honor the *means* to healing, such as faith, prayer, medicine, etc, as long as it is in keeping with His will.

If a person is not healed through any of these means, and if the person is a believer, he must say as Paul and others that had infirmities, that "*His grace is sufficient for me.*" He has a reason for everything that He does. Accept it and believe that "*all things work together for good*, if you are called *according to His purpose.*"

Some of us or most of us must needs wait upon the Lord to deliver us from such diseases when He comes. Others may be given healing on some occasion, but all believers will die of some disease or accident before the Lord comes.

So what I am saying is, do not trust some "divine healer" who says, "If you have enough faith, you can be healed any time, any place, from any condition." Then, when you are not healed, you will be discouraged and feel that God has forsaken you. This is impossible for those who are His. Please include "*If it be Thy will*" in your prayer of deliverance. This position is not well accepted today, but what truths are? There is a great deficiency in the thinking of most professing Christians on the nature of man. Is he *totally* or *partially* depraved?

The salvation of God: Is it all of God, or partly by God and partly by man? On and on we might go, but let us prayerfully study a matter through, and trust God and the Spirit to give light on the subject and reveal His will. His Word has no deficiency in it, but we do. For none but One is perfect, and that is God. Hopefully, what I said will be proven helpful.

We now shall resume our study of healing in the light of our Lord's miracles.

What Is a Miracle?

A miracle goes beyond the known laws of nature.

A miracle is an act of God, sponsored or allowed by God.

A miracle is a marvel, a wonder, something amazing, extending above the established order of the universe.

A miracle is the intervention and exertion of divine power.

A miracle is a supernatural and extraordinary event manifesting God in Christ, and thus giving creditability to His ministry and mission.

Classification of Miracles

Nicodemus, as ruler of the Senate of Sanhedrins, which was over the nation of Israel, spoke as a representative of the Jews when he said, "Rabbi, *we know* that thou art a *teacher* come from God, for no man can do these *miracles* that thou doest, except God be with him" (John 3:2).

Classification of New Testament Miracles

There are recorded some forty miracles connected with Christ's life.

Cosmic Miracles

To show His power over the realm of nature (cosmic world)
- Water changed to wine
- Feeding at one time 4,000, and another 5,000 men, plus women and children
- Stilling the storm at sea
- Jesus walking on the water
- Fig tree cursed

Demoniac Miracles

His proven power over the demonic world (demonology).
- Dumb demoniac healed
- Blind and dumb demoniac healed
- A demon possesses a man in the synagogue and was cast out
- Demoniac spirits enter swine
- Demoniac spirit cast out of an epileptic boy
- Demoniac spirit cast out of the daughter of a Syrophoenician woman

Anatomic Miracles

His power over all the operations and functions of the body (anatomy).
- Blind man cured (Bartimaeus)

- Two blind men cured
- Deaf and dumb cured
- Woman with an infirmity cured (osteoporosis)
- Man with dropsy cured
- Ten lepers cured
- Servant's ear cured
- Centurian's servant cured
- Invalid man cured
- Leprosy cured
- Mother-in-law cured
- Woman cured from hemorrhaging
- Man's withered hand cured

Neurotic Miracles

His power over the mind (neurology)
- Epilepsy, temporary insanity
- Insane Legion (lunatic)

Mortific Miracles

His divine power over the dead—the resurrection of the body (mortician)
- Twelve-year-old daughter of Jairus, dead a few hours
- Only son of a widow, deceased almost a day
- Lazarus, dead four days

Coincidental Miracles

His power over knowledge in activities of people and things (psyche)
- Shekel in mouth of fish
- Great catch of fish
- Catch of 153 fish

Christolic Miracles

His power to set forth miraculous activities, relegated to His body (Christology)
- Incarnation in body
- Two natures fused together as God and Man

- Transfiguration
- Disguising and Disappearing
- Bodily resurrection and ascension

Soteriac Miracles

His power to impart salvation (soteriology).
- His chosen disciples plus others, except Judas (as the son of perdition) that the Scriptures might be fulfilled
- From dead souls to life

Inspirational Miracles

His power of unity, plus prophecies by verbal imputation, equals the miracle of inspiration (linguistic).
- The Holy Bible is a miracle

Bequeathed Miracles

His assigned miraculous and spiritual gifts to the early church, in addition to the gift of eternal life (beneficiary)
- Gift, the word of wisdom.
- Gift, the word of knowledge.
- Gift, both common and special faith.
- Gift, the healing.
- Gift, the working of miracles.
- Gift, the prophecy.
- Gift, the discerning of spirits.
- Gift, the speaking of different languages.
- Gift, the interpreting of different languages.

Spurious Miracles (Satanic)

Satan, that old devil, is a fraud, a forger, and a counterfeiter. He takes great pleasure in trying to imitate Christ. Sometimes he can fool the best of us if we do not watch. Look with me into the next Scripture that exposes him for what he is.

"*Even him* [the lawless one, the incarnation of the man of sin] *whose coming is after the working of Satan with all power (satanic, evil power) and signs and lying wonders* [counterfeit miracles as in Revelation, accomplishing acts of healing, and miraculous signs of lying wonders, not of God]" (2 Thessalonians 2:9; Revelation 13:3,13,14).

Many miracles of healing were repeated, not on the same person, but on different people having the same difficulty.

In this array of miracles related to Jesus' life, we see proof of the sovereignty of the Son, in that He had supreme command and control over nature, for He was the Creator of all things visible and invisible. The wind and the waves obeyed His will, because He was and is the *Lord of the universe*. The dead responded to His call and touch, because He is the Lord over death, and the *Lord of life*. The infirmed, deformed, afflicted, and diseased bodies of men reacted in the presence and power of Christ, because He is the Maker of the body, fearfully and wonderfully made. The mental disorder and insanity of the mind returned to soundness, because He is the *Master over the mind*.

He saved people simply because He was their *Savior*, giving divine creditability to all His claims. He was all that He said He was. He did all that He was to do, that the Scriptures might be fulfilled. He was worthy to be called the Son of God, as well as the Son of Man. Herein is the saying true, "Jesus is Lord of all," and "Worthy is the Lamb."

The First Recorded Miracle

Next we need to travel to a little place called "Cana of Galilee," for we would see Jesus in the presence of friends and loved ones. Here He put His blessings upon a couple about to enter into holy matrimony. To my limited knowledge, I cannot recall any home that Jesus visited and was not blessed by Him in some way. He not only blessed many homes with salvation and the healing of certain individuals, but He blessed them with joy and gladness which they never forgot.

Now to get more than I can offer out of this wedding, we must be brief and come right to the point. You would first do well to review the story, filled with excitement and expectation, in John 2:1–11.

I shall not give you an expository lecture on this timely event as to the steps that developed from start to finish, but just zero in on the *miracle* and *its significance*.

It stands to reason that the *first* things said in the Bible are always of the utmost importance. Because of necessity, we must pass by these thoughts as to the benefits of Christ in the home, the words His mother said to the servants. The secrecy of the miracle of the new supply of wine replacing the old, and the only ones that knew about the miracle Christ performed, were the servants, His mother, and His disciples. Also, how we can be used of the Lord in preparing the way for miracles from above, as God saves the best for the last.

Purpose: To Reflect God's Future Glory in Christ

Two things I would most like to say something about:
1. Will we take part in the marriage of the King's Son in heaven?
2. The purpose of the miracle was twofold (verse 11):
   a. His glory was manifested.
   b. His disciples were strengthened in their faith.

In reply to the above question.

When Jesus returns to bring us into the Father's House, we will be centered around the *Bridegroom rejoicing as His Bride,* the Church.

Revelation 19:7,8,9, "Let us be glad and rejoice, and give honour to him: for the marriage of the Lamb is come, and his wife hath made herself ready. And to her was granted that she should be arrayed in fine linen, clean and white: for the fine linen is the righteousness of saints. And He saith unto me, Write, Blessed are they which are called unto the marriage supper of the Lamb. And he saith unto me, These are the true sayings of God."

It will be a time of rejoicing. It will be a time when the Bridegroom consummates this holy union with His Bride. It will be a time when the Bride has "made herself *ready.*"

The church is to preach the Gospel in all the earth, and all God's elect will be gathered in. The commission is complete when the last soul is saved; then the Lord will be ready to return.

It will be a time when God greatly blesses those who are called to the marriage supper, the royal reception of the Lamb.

The Bride wears white as a symbol of purity. The Church is made up of holy people, worldwide, representing God's chosen ones. The friends of the Bride could be all their angels, sent as messengers to the heirs of salvation (Hebrews 1:14).

The Bride and the Bridegroom have this in common: *His righteousness is her righteousness.* Will you be there?

Significance of the Miracle

This first of our Lord's signs (miracles, wonder works) was in some respect more important than all the rest. This extraordinary sign was to reveal our Lord's power and mission in *transforming grace*. It manifests His glory in every soul He saved, in every life He healed. His transforming power was a symbol of His work. His work was in the home. His work was in the synagogue and temple. His work was on the cross.

Only by His blood-bought grace are we transformed from a sinner into a saint. Alleluia! *"For the Lord God omnipotent reigneth"* (Revelation 19:16). If this isn't something to get excited about, I don't know what is!

Moreover, His disciples were new on the job. They had nothing more to go on than His call and claims. They needed to have their *faith lifted*, and cast off all doubt. They now were fortified with unfeigned faith in order to be steadfast and unmovable, always to abound in their Lord's work of mercy and love.

They now believed He was, without question, the Father's Son, the Messiah, the King of Israel.

• • •

DESCRIPTION OF THE GREATEST PHYSICIAN
(Prepared as a Get-Well Card by the Author)

The Greatest Physician
Luke 5:31, 32

Of all the doctors who ever lived, one stands out from all the rest that ever reached a place of prominence. This Surgeon's practice was unparalleled in every respect. The wonder of this Man's ministry to the infirmed was in a word "fantastic," because He dispensed no pills, wrote no prescriptions, had no office calls and charged no fees. Mysteriously enough, He never had a license; He never went to medical school; He had no credentials except His healing power. Those who heard of Him came for help, others were carried to Him by friends. This Physician healed more diseases and cured more cases than any other doctor in the history of the world.

In dealing with multiplied thousands, He was always optimistic, and He never found a person too sick that was beyond His ability to heal.

JOURNEYING WITH JESUS IN HEALING CAMPAIGNS 139

Many were brought to Him half dead, or dying with a terminal, incurable disease. He never considered any person an impossible case. He never turned anyone away for any reason. He never lost a single patient out of the thousands He served, even though other doctors had to give up on some as hopeless. All His patients experienced one hundred percent recovery. Moreover, He gladly made house calls on the request of any that asked for His help, regardless of the distance, and He traveled on foot.

The one thing all His patients had in common was that everyone was healed instantaneously, in a moment, at the touch of His hand or the sound of His voice. There was no convalescing period with them. It was nothing short of a miracle. He never interfered with the practice of other physicians. He only stepped in when asked to help, as a second opinion.

Amazingly enough, in addition to His general practice He went a step farther. After life was gone, when the deadly disease did its designed damage, He still came and restored the life. It was widely reported that a daughter, a son, and a friend were restored to life by Him after death.

Although this remarkable Doctor of whom I speak lived and died at the age of 33, an untimely and unjust death nearly two millenniums ago, He is by no means dead, but He is very much alive today. If the truth were known, many of you reading these lines have been patients of His. You too would testify that He still heals today, because you are the living proof of His healing power.

In this modern time He had enlarged the outreach of this healing ministry through skillful surgeons, up-to-date hospitals, and medical research in which He grants the cures to patients who in the recent past were considered incurable, thus unlocking the secrets of His healing power on the mass multitudes of the sick with compassion, as it was in the days of His flesh. The great difference now is that His healing process is gradual, not immediate. However, He reserves the right in keeping with His sovereign will, to heal people still without use of means. To manifest His present power to the praise of His glorious grace, so that men again may marvel.

This divine Person knows more about the body than any and all men, because He created the body and put within it all the parts from the ground up, both seen and unseen. Therefore, when the body breaks down and needs repair, we would do well to consult our Maker, for He alone is the Master-Builder of our being. He knows the functions, systems, organs, and operations of every fiber. This marvelous Man of men is not only the Greatest Physician, but the Lord of life, the Master of minds, and the Savior of souls. Now He is in His heavenly office to represent you before the Father, as the only Mediator. He intercedes in your behalf, being the Great High Priest of paradise.

May God be praised for this Omnipotent One who stands by to receive your emergency call, if you have need of His help, which is presently available regardless of your condition, whether the problem be in the body, mind, or soul. His policy covers a multitude of miseries because of His mercy. All these benefits are free that He has arranged for you, credited to His unmerited grace. You can call toll free from earth to heaven, and make your appeal to this Prince of life, the Landlord of glory, this soon-coming King of kings.

If your case is urgent, call just now, who knows what He can do for you. Those of us who love Him and adore Him call Him by His given name - Jesus.

"Casting all your cares upon Him; for He careth for you" (1 Peter 5:7).

(The Library of Congress has a copyright of this card.)

• • •

DELIVERANCE FOR THE MULTITUDES

In this section, visualize attending these seven campaigns and compare, if you will, the contrast of the Divine Healer to the professed religious healers today.

Dr. Jesus followed no rigid set of rules. He healed all who came or were brought to Him whether they had faith or not. They were all healed, and each one completely. Those He cured stayed cured. Those He healed stayed healthy of that particular disease. Now and then, one individual is singled out as a special case that we may become more acquainted with the difficulties that existed in His day. Without hospitals or medicine, Jesus single-handedly took on the world of the sick.

First Healing Campaign

Matthew 4:23–25, "And Jesus went about all Galilee, teaching in their synagogues, and preaching the gospel of the kingdom, and *healing all manner of sickness and all manner of disease among the people. And His fame went throughout all Syria: and they brought unto Him all sick people that were taken with divers diseases and torments (afflictions) and those which were possessed with demons, and those which were lunatic, and those that had the palsy; and he healed them. And there followed Him great multitudes of people from Galilee, and from Decapolis and from Jerusalem, and from Judaea, and from beyond Jordan (in Peraea)."*

You will observe that Jesus had no credentials but His healing power. Large crowds gathered to Him, enabling Him to preach for awhile, and then set aside an interval to heal.

Four large regions were moved by the news which spread throughout the whole country, that a man called Jesus was healing every sick person from Syria, as well as great crowds from Galilee, Decapolis, Jerusalem, Judaea and the area east across the Jordan.

A summary of the most severe victims will be identified. Those with various diseases, who were suffering great pain. Those who were demon possessed. Those who were paralytics and epileptics. And the good news was that He healed them all.

Second Healing Campaign

Matthew 8:16, "When the even was come, they brought unto Him *many* that were possessed with devils (demons): and He cast out the spirits with His word, and healed *all* that were sick."

The demon-possessed souls seemed to be the most common. Jesus had declared war against the demons of the underworld. He drove the evil spirits out with His word.

Did you notice as you read the Scripture, that all this was ordained, foreseen and decreed by God according to Old Testament prophecy from Isaiah 53:4? Everybody that Jesus touched, every demon that was cast out, every soul that was saved, every town and city He entered, every Roman province He reached through His healing and preaching ministry was the *fulfillment of Scripture.* For He said, "I came not to do My own will, but the *will* of Him that sent Me" (John 6:38).

His itinerary was fully known to Him in as far as the places He must go, the synagogues He was to visit, the lessons He was to teach, and the sermons He was to preach.

Can you imagine the world of good that Jesus did for those poor, painful people, who could not help themselves? I hear a person say, *"God helps those who help themselves."* These people could not help themselves. The greatest truth is that *God helps those who cannot help themselves.*

Third Healing Campaign

Matthew 9:35, "And Jesus went about *all* the cities and villages, teaching in their synagogues, and preaching the gospel of the kingdom, and healing *every sickness and every disease* among the people."

It seems that His healing and preaching ministry went hand in hand. He would *preach* to the crowds, and then *heal* the sick that were brought to Him.

Fourth Healing Campaign

Matthew 11:4,5, "Jesus answered and said unto them, Go and shew John again those things which ye do hear and see: the blind receive their sight, and the lame walk, the lepers are cleansed, and the deaf hear, the dead are raised up, and the *poor* have the *gospel preached to them.*"

This healing display was especially for the imprisoned John and his disciples to encourage their minds, and bring comfort to their hearts, that Jesus was the *One that should come.*

Fifth Healing Campaign

Matthew 12:15,17,18, "But when Jesus knew it, he withdrew himself from thence: and great *multitudes* followed Him, and *He healed them all*; that it might be *fulfilled* (from Isaiah 42:1) which was spoken by Esaias the prophet, saying, Behold My servant, whom I have chosen; My beloved, in whom My soul is well pleased: I will put My Spirit upon Him, and He shall shew judgment to the Gentiles (nations)."

Jesus had withdrawn to avoid the bloodthirsty Pharisees who had plotted to kill Him. What a contrast! The *leading religionist seeking Him to put Him to death. Jesus is seeking the lost and the helpless that He might make them whole.* All this, too, was in fulfillment of Scripture.

Sixth Healing Campaign

Matthew 14:35,36, "And when the men of that place had knowledge of Him, they sent out into all that country round about, and brought unto Him *all* that were diseased; and besought Him that they might only touch the hem of His garment: and *as many as touched* were made *perfectly whole.*"

In this marvelous meeting in the area of Gennesaret, the sick were too many for Him to heal and give each one individual attention. One company of sick would be in a single file, dragging and hobbling along with their crutches, canes and litters. As they merely went by the presence of Jesus, they reached out to touch His garment and were healed without a word, only a touch. Lines would be as far as the eye could see, insomuch that Jesus was compelled to counsel those that He healed not to tell any more people about His healing power. It appears they could not hold their tongue. They must tell others about Jesus and His great compassion, or explode in trying to hold it in. For they never met anyone like Him.

Seventh Healing Campaign

Matthew 15:30,31, "And *great multitudes* came unto Him, having with them those that were lame, blind, dumb, maimed, and many others, and cast them down at Jesus' feet; and *He healed them*: insomuch that the multitude wondered, when they saw the dumb to speak, the maimed to be whole, the lame to walk, and the blind to see: and they glorified the God of Israel."

The people who were healed and the eyewitnesses of our Lord's great restoring, healing ministry, praised the God of Israel. How do you suppose they praised Him? Why, they did what others had done before. They fell down at His blessed feet and worshipped this worthy One who was deserving of their praise.

We Gentiles ought to praise the God of Israel and the God of heaven for giving to us this *mighty Deliverer*. For He is not only the God of the Jews, but of the Gentiles. His great love, grace, and power is not restricted to one nation, but *extends to all nations. Not only to the sick in body*, but the *sick in soul*. Can't you hear the Savior say, "They that be whole have no need of a Physician, but they that are sick?"

He tells us for whom He did not come. "Not the righteous [or *self-righteous*], but for sinners to repent." Therefore, the only ones eligible to be made whole are sinners. Are you a saved or a lost sinner?

The *title* "physician" that Christ applied to Himself, is found *seven times* in the New Testament. Once in Matthew 9:12, repeated in Mark 2:17, and also in Mark 5:26, but this reference is used for physicians of no value that could not heal the hemorrhaging woman. Luke, who in Colossians 4:14 is called the beloved physician, addressed Jesus with this title more than any other, as you might suppose (Luke 4:23, 5:31, 8:43).

• • •

DIFFICULTIES FROM A PARALYTIC CASE
Luke 5:17–26 (Please read.)

First Obstacle: Door Blocked

Thank God for the faith of these four men that exhibited their love and devotion for a helpless, dying man they brought to Him, the *Helper of the helpless*. Their faith was strong in the face of barriers that we often encounter when attempting to bring a person to Christ. Their problem, like ours many times, was people. They were standing in the way. They were *blocking the door*. The four are determined, after carrying their friend for no telling how many miles, not to turn back by saying it was *"impossible."* I like to think that this faithful four got their heads turned in the right direction, as one of them could have said, "Let us pray about it." Then God gave them the solution.

Agreeing together, they settled on a plan that was not only dangerous but could be expensive. They refused to fail, even though their reputation was at stake by being called roof-breaking fanatics. They proceeded in this awkward task of completing what they started, regardless of the insurmountable odds and obstacles that the Devil put in their path.

The Devil's work, in brief, is twofold:

1. To keep people lost as long as he can.

2. To keep the saved from serving the Savior as long as he can.

Second Obstacle: The Case Impossible

When they succeeded, by God's help, to bring this poor invalid to Jesus, their faith in Him did not go unrewarded. *"When He saw their faith"* means not only the faith of the four, but the *palsied man's faith* as well.

He couldn't walk, but he could talk. No doubt his four friends must have told him about Jesus. He was in the most advanced stage of paralysis, and was desirous for them to bring him to the One who healed all manner of disease.

Dr. Luke rightly used the term "palsy" according to his day, which was slightly different from a paralytic who was partially paralyzed. Whereas palsy was a complete loss of motion insofar as this man was tormented by uncontrollable tremors. He was as bad as he could be without being dead.

When Jesus said to the palsied man, "Cheer up, son (Matthew and Mark)," or "man (Luke)," "thy sins be forgiven thee." All three usages are acceptable. He was given hope by Christ in the words "Cheer up, son," (as the son of Abraham), and in "man" (as the son of Adam), granting remittance of his sins, "thy sins are forgiven you."

His unseen sins were pardoned before Jesus made the healing of his body manifested, that he was healed of this merciless malady. The man was soon to discover that Jesus had given him *double deliverance*. Personally, I believe this was one of many cases of our Lord's anatomic miracles. This healed palsied man was the first to receive light as to what happened to many of those who were cured. They had double deliverance. It is not difficult for me to believe that Jesus healed as well as saved as many as possible. I believe that both go together, which Jesus is bringing out in this truth. Can a person, healed of a crippling or deadly and painful disease, not believe in Him?

Third Obstacle: Doubters Deny His Deity

This act of authority to forgive sin immediately brought opposition from the doctors of law, Pharisees, and Scribes that were present. The religionists of that day murmured, saying among themselves, *"Who can forgive sins but God?"* (verse 21). They were right, you know, in believing that God alone could forgive sins. Anything short of this would be blasphemy and rapidly brought such victims before the Sanhedrins involving the death penalty for blaspheming against God. That was all they were looking for. They had the witnesses. Jesus knew their *hearts* and brought out this question: "Whether is it easier, to say, *Thy sins be forgiven thee; or to say, Rise up and walk?"* (verses 22 and 23).

They were asking for evidence, whether He was God, and He gave them the proof. If a person can dispel this kind of palsy, it must be an act of God, which is equivalent to forgiveness. Since Jesus is God, He can do both. He has the authority of being God. What could they further say when he told the palsied man to "get up, take your mat, go home." He did so in front of them all.

This amazing display of mercy and grace caused many to praise God, being filled with awe and fear. Countless souls saved will be in that Gloryland, where there will be no sickness, sin, or separation, no obstacles, opposition, or oppression, thanks to His saving, healing, and forgiving power.

• • •

DEALING WITH THE DEAD

This discussion shall not delay us long, yet it is very important to set forth the significance of the three Scriptural cases Christ dealt with to properly understand the past, present, and future.

First Resurrection: A Departed Damsel of Twelve

Please read Mark 5:22, 23, 35–43. Compare Matthew 9:18; Luke 8:41.

Without going into detail, I shall briefly tell the story, and give what I believe is the meaning of the Lord's mind when He raised this damsel from the dead a short time after her death.

Her father, Jairus, a ruler of the synagogue, was looking for Jesus. When he found Him, Jesus was told about his daughter who was at the point of death, and was asked to come and heal her. When they were close to the house, two men brought the bad news to Jairus, "Your daughter is dead; why bother the Master (Teacher) anymore?" In spite of this, Jesus said, "Don't be afraid; just believe." Upon their arrival they heard a lot of commotion of weeping and wailing. Jesus told them, "The child is not dead, but asleep." Then the Lord of life put them all out, taking only her parents with Peter, James and John to the bedside. He said to the damsel who had reached the tender age of twelve, taking her by the hand, *"Talitha, Koumi,"* (meaning, *"O maiden, I say arise."*) *Immediately she stood up and walked.* Jesus gave strict instructions to tell no one of this.

What can we surmise from this amazing story? I believe Jesus teaches us these principles and ideas that come out of this *first resurrection* during His ministry.

From birth to about twelve, children are not accountable for their sins, even though born in sin. Should they die during this period they are not held responsible, but are under the grace of God and the blood of Christ. In the same sense, idiots or imbeciles are not chargeable for their sins, being in this same state of innocence. A child of twelve, depending on his background, can know his sins, *be responsive to the*

Gospel and become a believer. This was the age I was saved, raised to spiritual life from a spiritual state of sleep. I believe this is the lesson our Lord, the Teacher, would have us see within the life cycle of our earthly existence.

Some preachers teach that if an infant should die after birth, and if they are *not elected* they would go to hell. What!? Is there no mercy with God? Jesus said, *"Even so it is not the will of your Father which is in heaven that one of these little ones should perish"* (Matthew 18:14). Let us thank God for the teaching of Jesus that *not one* of these little *ones shall perish.*

Second Resurrection: A Dead Son of a Widow From Nain

Please read Luke 7:11–17 (verse 13 below, Free Translation).

Jesus and His disciples were being followed by a large crowd. As they approached the city gate of Nain, they converged with another large crowd that was coming out of the city in a funeral procession. A widow had lost her only son earlier the same day or the previous night. In that climate it is proper to have the burial as soon as possible, because decay and rapid change will set into the body and it will begin to swell and smell. I believe it was near the close of the day when this all occurred. The young man was to be buried in the cemetery outside the gates of the city.

Jesus stepped up and said to the mother, *"Don't cry, Madam,"* and touched the coffin. Immediately her son *arose* and *talked*, as He gave him back to his mother. What can we learn from our Lord in this second person that He restored to life?

When in the midst of activities we pursue our ambitions, by the providence of God we may be brought by a friend to a church, perhaps during a revival, or the preacher as a man of God that is used by the Spirit and preaches Christ to the people.

A young man, under the influence of the *Holy Spirit*, is brought under conviction. His soul is *touched*, and his heart, being heavy in sin, begins to fear God for the first time. The invitation is given. The song as well as the sermon strikes home. He must go forward, feeling the weight and burden of sins against God. He repents and believes. At the first step he senses an awareness and nearness to God. He confesses in faith, now newly born in Jesus. He is accepted into the fellowship and ministry of this Bible Church for baptism. He is now happier than he has ever been.

Why? Because Christ came into his heart, washed his sins away, and he is now a subject of the King of glory. Snatched from the Devil's darkness and domain, he steps out into the light of a new life. What happened? He, by the mercy of God, was regenerated, quenched, raised to a new life in Christ. That is exactly right!

Notice what Jesus said, "Verily, verily, I say unto you, The hour is coming, and *now is*, when the dead shall hear the voice of the Son of God: and they that hear shall live" (John 5:25). Christ, the Great Physician, touches the dead organ of the inner ear spiritually, then they accept the truth.

"The hour is coming, and now is," refers to the present time in this Dispensation of Grace, during this church age, when a sinner has the opportunity to hear the Gospel. Every elect person must be called forth by Christ through the Gospel. This is the effectual calling in Romans 8:28, "Called according to His purpose," while "dead in trespasses (transgressions) and sins" (Ephesians 2:1). Only Christ, through sound preaching, will awaken the dead. The sinner who is spiritually dead is awakened and starts talking a new language. The language of Zion is the tongue of the newborn, crying out in response to God's call, "What must I do to be saved?" (Acts 16:30). The preacher has given the answer, the Scriptures contain the answer, and Christ is still the answer. The sinner comes to Christ. He is saved on His terms, follows the leading of the Spirit with joy unspeakable and full of glory, with the assurance that Jesus has come to live within and will never forsake him.

The first resurrection that we spoke about speaks of the new life in Christ when a child, reaching the age of accountability.

The second resurrection as Jesus dealt with the dead, speaks of a spiritual resurrection, such as those in the midst of life, coming in contact with Christ and His Word, sometime before physical death.

Third Resurrection: The Raising of Lazarus From the Grave

Please read John 11:38–44.

The third person in our Lord's dealing with those who have died concerns not the spiritual, as in the first two cases. Here our Lord teaches the truth of the *resurrection of the bodies of believers*, whom *He loves*. The resurrection of the rest of the dead comes later, which we will discuss in the last chapter about "The Great White Throne Judgment."

DELIBERATIONS

While you reflect upon the issues in the development of this chapter, we hope that your conclusions will be beneficial to your spiritual growth in Christ as the healing Physician and saving Prophet. Ponder the problem of healing today. Should we expect healing for our bodies without the use of means, if the means are what God has given to medical science? This without controversy has been given and provided through surgery and medication at this present time.

Were not the miracles, clustered during intervals of Old Testament times and throughout the New, to give impetus to Jesus as Lord who proved Himself more than a match for incurable diseases? Not that He could put forth His power to heal all manner of sicknesses today as in other days, but that *He can,* if He wills to do so.

My preference would favor the position that He can today, if it was necessary to establish His power over diseases; but is it necessary? Yes, "He is the same yesterday, today and forever," unchanging and immutable, but that does not mean that He must prove Himself again in salvation or divine healing, since it has already been manifested that He can.

The greater of the two works in this realm of His power should be unquestionably the *saving of souls* over the *healing of bodies.* Therefore, let us rest our case by concluding that the "*greater work*" that we are to do is spreading "the Gospel into all the world in obedience to His command, and then shall the end come."

My closing remarks on this issue are to be weighed carefully. The Apostles were given the power to do both, as they started out on the great commission to heal as well as to save, through preaching. It seems to be our lot, at the end of the days of Grace in this same dispensation, to concentrate on what is most important, and not deny God's ability in the latter according to His will and purpose.

John's last words sealed the four Gospels about the miracles of Jesus. He implies that the signs of miracles recorded therein are just a sample, a small percentage of all the miracles He performed. Most are unknown to us, but known to them upon whom He touched, healed, saved and imparted His eternal love.

John 20:30,31, "And *many other signs truly* did Jesus in the presence of his disciples, which are not written in this book: but these are written, that ye might *believe* that Jesus is the Christ, the Son of God; and that believing ye might have life through His name."

John 21:25, "And there are also *many other things* which Jesus did, the which, if they should be written every one, I suppose that even the world itself could not contain the *books* that should be written. Amen."

• • •

Questionnaire

1. How would you define a miracle?
2. Observing the beginning of the Lord's ministry, which did He concentrate on first, healing bodies or saving souls?
3. What was the first miracle mentioned in the Gospels that Jesus performed?
4. Name seven *different* areas of miracles.
5. What kind of miracles was it, when Jesus stilled the storm?
6. In the Lord's healing ministry, which group *best* represents the number healed at that time? Choose one: (a) 100–1,000; (b) 1,000–50,000; (c) 50,000–1,000,000.
7. How many cases did Jesus find that were beyond His healing power? Choose one: (a) 0; (b) 3; (c) 7.
8. About how many miracles recorded in the Gospels are attributed to Jesus? Choose one: (a) 10; (b) 40; (c) 100.
9. What were the three obstacles in the case of the paralytic?
10. Name the three cases that describe Jesus' power to raise the dead.
11. What individual was healed of his disease and forgiven of his sin at the same time?

• • •

Answers

1. An act of God transcending the laws of nature
2. Saving souls—John's Gospel, Chapter 1, verses 35–51
3. Changing water into wine
4. (a) Cosmic; (b) Demoniac; (c) Anatomic; (d) Neurotic; (e) Mortific (dead); (f) Christolic (example: virgin birth); (g) Soteriac (salvation)

JOURNEYING WITH JESUS IN HEALING CAMPAIGNS

5. Over nature (cosmic)
6. 1,000–50,000 during earthly ministry
7. 0
8. 40
9. (a) Door blocked; (b) impossible case; (c) Christ's deity denied
10. (a) Jairus' daughter of twelve years; (b) widow's son, in funeral procession; (c) Lazarus, brother of Mary and Martha
11. The paralytic (saved and healed at the same time)

Chapter 9

Journeying With Jesus on His Preaching/Teaching Crusades
-or-
Christ, the Preaching Prophet:
His Word in the Heart (Doctrine)

Thought

Napoleon was known to have said, "I conquer empires with the sword. Christ is the greater Conqueror, for He conquers kingdoms with His love." The pen (written word) is more powerful than the sword.

• • •

I. The sermons Jesus preached
   A. In the temple (John 2:13–16)
   B. On the mountainside (Matthew, Chapters 5–7)
   C. Within the synagogue (Luke 4:16–30)

II. The parables Jesus taught (Matthew 13:10–11)
   A. Mysteries revealed—to the disciples
   B. Mysteries concealed—from the crowd
   C. Arrangement of parables (in order)

III. The prophecies Jesus made
   A. To the Jewish nation (Matthew 24:21; Romans 11:25,26; Revelation 7:4–8)
   B. To the Church of believers (Matthew 24:14; 26:29; 28:19)
   C. About the world of the wicked (Matthew 8:12; 25:41–46; Revelation 20:11–15)

IV. The prayers Jesus offered
   A. Private prayers (John 17)
   B. Public (Mark 1:35, 6:46; Luke 5:16; 6:12; 22:41; John 11:41,42)

JOURNEYING WITH JESUS—PREACHING/TEACHING

V. The death Jesus died

For whom Jesus died—our High Priest gives His life for ours (Hebrews 13:20)

VI. The resurrection power Jesus exhibited

Proofs of the resurrection (John 20:17; 1 Corinthians 15:20,57)

VII. Questionnaire and Answers

• • •

Thought

The truths of Jesus need to be heard, for His supreme message is more important than the tongues of men can ever tell.

• • •

The Sermons Jesus Preached

Wise were the officers who answered the chief priest and Pharisees, *"Never man spake like this man"* (John 7:46).

I could almost say to the officers what Jesus said to Peter after he offered this public confession concerning Christ, "Thou are the Christ, the Son of the Living God." Jesus immediately responded, lest Peter might think these choice words came from himself, *"Flesh and blood hath not revealed it unto thee, but My Father which is in heaven"* (Matthew 16:16,17).

This wonderful statement that Peter is credited with, and which God was the author of, could also be said of the reporting officers sent out to apprehend Jesus.

Would you happen to know the very first official declaration of Jesus in the opening phase of His public ministry? Here is where we need to compare Scripture with Scripture. The harmony of the Gospels would prove helpful at this point.

Mark 1:14,15, "Now *after* that *John was put in prison,* Jesus came into Galilee, preaching the gospel of the kingdom of God, and saying, The time is fulfilled, and the kingdom of God is at hand: repent ye and believe the gospel."

One might suppose that this was the place where Jesus began His public ministry. But this could not be, since it was at the time when John was cast into prison. John was cast into prison sometime after our Lord's ministry had begun. In John 3:22–24, both Jesus and John were baptizing at the same time. Once again in Luke 4:21, some might assume that this was the day Jesus started in His hometown synagogue, but this could not be, since He was at that time *already famous*.

So you see we have given concrete evidence from John that Mark 1:14,15 and Luke 4:21 could not have been the scene of His opening Words in our Lord's public ministry. Rather, it was the first Passover after baptism following the first miracle at Cana of Galilee, which was not a public demonstration of His power, because the miracle was not known by the guests. He is next seen in the temple, cleansing it from merchants and profiteers.

John 2:13-16, "And the Jews' passover was at hand, and Jesus went up to Jerusalem, and found in the temple those that sold oxen and sheep and doves, and the changers of money sitting: and when He had made a scourge of small cords, He drove them *all* out of the temple, and the sheep, and the oxen; and poured out the changers' money, and overthrew the tables; and said unto them that sold doves, Take these things hence; make not my Father's house an house of merchandise."

Here we see Jesus alone performing the *first mighty act* and speaking the actual first meaningful words of His opening public ministry. This cleansing was an inward description of the outward corruption and depravity of the Jewish nation. We shall describe the need of cleansing the church today.

The Cleansing of the Temple

In following the Scriptural order of events, you will notice Christ cleansed the *temple twice*. It was the opening and close of His public ministry, separated by the space of about three years. Each of the Synoptic writers record the general view of the first three Gospels, the last visit to the temple. John only records the first.

Here Jesus became filled with righteous indignation, highly offended and downright angry because they were using the House of God for a market place.

The church should be used for worship by preaching, teaching, healing, praying, praising and giving. Whatsoever is more than this will come to evil. Yet we hear of bingo games with prizes awarded, supper sales, cake walks, bazaars, and rummage sales in the auditorium and vestibule. They build gymnasiums for their youth and fellowship halls for the adults to be entertained with the things and people of the world.

Is not *history repeating itself*? Can you see your church in the middle? What would Jesus do and say if He returned next Sunday in some revival promotion or missionary conference, or just casually dropped into your worship service? Would He like what He saw and heard? What would He do? He would do what He did then in the temple, *drive both buyer and seller,* clergy and laity, and every accountable person out of *His Holy House.* Would Jesus say what He did in the first cleansing, "Make not My Father's House a house of merchandise?"

Moreover, He would do what He said in the second cleansing, "Is it not written, My house shall be called of all nations the *house of prayer?* but you have made it a *den of thieves* [better, robbers]" (Mark 11:17).

Again, the unsaved world of unscrupulous businessmen, who have moved into the church without love for Christ or love for souls or love for His House, have abandoned the true Gospel, bordering on apostasy, as many churches have already reached that stage, as the Word predicted (1 Timothy 4:1; 2 Timothy 3:1-5).

What should God's people do who have been deceived by this brand of thieves, and stampeded by this herd of devilish robbers in the church, who refuse to tithe, allowing robbers to rob the Lord's treasury with a lust of greed, and longing for a life of ease? They twist and wrest the Word to suit themselves and to please certain ones in their *zeal* for *worldly gain* and *fleshly amusements, building enormous and luxurious estates, robbing the poor with their golden tongues of persuasion,* begging for money as *if they had none,* when they do not know how to spend the millions from their ill-gotten gain.

How many congregations have undershepherds and pastors who preach in such a way as to keep back the floodgates of evil from flowing into their churches, while preaching in such a manner that poor lost sinners would weep their way to Jesus, touched by the Holy Spirit because of their bitter sins being exposed! They would cry out, *"Brethren, what must we do?"* as they did on the Day of Pentecost when the infant church experienced so *great a revival.* God have mercy on us preachers who are sponsoring this worldly crowd!

We are to use the method Jesus supported in *tithes and offerings,* which are to be brought into the House of God. Jesus said, referring to the tithe, *"These things ought you to have done* and not to leave the other undone" (Matthew 23:23).

There is no better means in spreading the Gospel to every land and tongue than through the *local church*—not leaving it up to some big-time evangelist to do our work as a church.

As participants in the house of worship, we who are members of the body of Christ should *cry out to God for cleansing within our churches*. Then the *Holy Spirit* may fall fresh upon us, if we meet *God's terms*.

Follow Him into the temple as He cleanses it from all impurities, unsound practices of merchandising, and everything contrary to the Word of God.

We are to pray for cleansing in the church, and to restore the wheels of prayer that can once again turn a vacant prayer meeting into a place filled with the tear-stained faces of the saints.

If we would follow our Lord in love, we must *cast out of our bodies*, as sanctified by the Holy Spirit, everything that defiles and displeases God. Our problems may be solved on the promises of a prayer-answering Lord.

A Mountainside Sermon

Matthew 5–7; Luke 6:20–49

You will observe in Matthew 5:1,2 that "His disciples came to Him, and He opened His mouth and *taught them*..." that they in turn might teach the multitudes.

In Luke 6:20 somewhat the same is stated: "He lifted up His eyes on His disciples and said..."

Also, you can readily see that the Sermon on the Mount is much longer than the sermon in Luke, which is taken from the same source. This self-same sermon is really a summary of all the main and central truths that Jesus taught His disciples, and is to be passed on. It is not an evangelical series of sermons, but mostly a *doctrinal display to be addressed to believers*. Here we see the King addressing the King's men, as a Magna Charta or manifesto, which was to be instilled within those who are being installed in the kingdom. To put it another way, this "Sermon on the Mount" is the *decrees* of the *King* to the members of *His Kingdom*. This masterpiece of a message introduces to the candidates the character and conduct of a Christian who is endowed with blessings from above. Notice now the eight steps in the Beatitudes.

It was suitable that such elevated ethics be taught from a mountain.

JOURNEYING WITH JESUS—PREACHING/TEACHING

When *Jesus opens His mouth, let us open our ears.* You will remember that the Old Testament ended with a curse. With Christ, the New Testament opens with a blessing or blessings. "Blessed" is another way of saying "happy." This prelude is the basis of the Christian's experience.

Are you a poor sinner, bankrupt of God's righteousness in your own eyes? Then you have met the first qualification of the kingdom man, the *first step* upward *(verse 3):* "Blessed are the *poor in spirit:* for theirs is the kingdom of God."

Our *second step* as a *mourner* seems to be worse off than the poor in spirit. They are brokenhearted over their sins they have discovered and committed against God. But soon they are to be comforted in the Spirit of Christ. The sorrowing shall sing *(verse 4),* "Blessed are they that mourn: for they shall be comforted."

The next characteristic of the kingdom man, or the Christian, is the *third step* to *meekness,* following poverty in soul and mourning over sin. In meekness they have the same nature of the King, for He is "meek and lowly in heart." The best is reserved for the meek *(verse 5),* "Blessed are the meek: for they shall inherit the earth."

The next attribute for the character of a Christian is the *fourth step* to *spiritual hunger.* He has none of his own. Nothing on earth can satisfy. The blood-bought must hunger and thirst after God's righteousness *(verse 6),* "Blessed are they that do hunger and thirst after righteousness: for they shall be filled." They taste of *God's satisfying Grace.*

The *fifth step* on the ladder of Christian character is *merciful.* They help the needy and shall be helped in their need. They forgive others and shall be forgiven themselves. What we are to others, God will be to us *(verse 7):* "Blessed are the merciful: for they shall obtain mercy." This mercy is from God. If we are to *find mercy from the Lord in that day, we must show mercy in this day.*

Up to *step six* in the climb to a godly character: we must receive a *pure heart.* There are no naturally pure hearts on earth. God's grace must make them so, for every thought and imagination of our fleshly heart is only evil continually *(verse 8),* "Blessed are the pure in heart: for they shall see God."

Step seven in the course of renewed character is the *peacemaker—not troublemakers or peacebreakers,* but peacemakers. Some cry, "Peace, peace," when they have no peace from Christ, the *Prince of*

Peace. He says, "My peace I give unto you..." *(verse 9),* "Blessed are the peacemakers: for they shall be called the children of God."

The *eighth step* stands highest on the standard of excellence as the last of the Christian virtues mentioned here by our Lord. *Persecution* from the lip is more common than the sting of the whip, yet both will yield a *rich reward (verse 10),* "Blessed are they that are persecuted for righteousness' sake: for theirs is the kingdom of heaven."

These are particular blessings to the elect of God who are called according to His unmeasurable grace. Did you notice the word "blessed" occurs nine times in eight Beatitudes? The last one is repeated, showing its need and importance.

Doctrinal Statements from the Sermon

The Doctrine of Christology includes many branches of truth most vital in embracing the Christian standard and influence (Scripture references are all from the Book of Matthew):

- Salt that preserves the truth (5:13)
- Light that reflects the truth (5:14–16)
- Law referring to the Decalogue (Ten Commandments) (5:17–26)
- Immorality (5:27–28; 31–32)
- Separation from evil (5:29–30)
- Profanity and oaths (5:33–37)
- Unlimited service (5:38–40)
- Christian love (5:43–47)
- Goal—perfection (5:48)
- Benevolence and giving (6:1–4)
- Direction on communion with God (6:5–15)
- Discipline of fasting (6:16–18)
- Heavenly investments (6:19–24)
- Modest apparel and daily food (6:25–32)
- Divine providence (6:32–34)
- Judgment forbidden and promises answered (7:1–6;7–11)
- "Golden Rule" (7:12)
- Two paths of men (7:13,14)
- Testing the fruit (7:15–23)
- The firm and faulty foundation (7:24–29)

The word "doctrine" scares some folks. It simply means *teaching*, or a system of beliefs. The list above is the doctrine of Christ. I have chosen two passages of Scripture in the Epistles, one from Paul, the other from John:

Titus 2:10, "... that they (believers) may adorn the *doctrine* of God our Savior in all things."

2 John 9, "Whosoever transgresseth and abideth not in the *doctrine* of Christ, hath not God. He that abideth in the *doctrine* of Christ, he hath both the Father and the Son."

Christ Rejected in His Hometown Synagogue

Luke 4:16–30 (compare Matthew 13:54–58 and Mark 6:1–6). Outline based on Luke.

Before us is one of the few *sermons* recorded that must carry a great deal of importance. It was chosen by the Holy Spirit to be shared from perhaps thousands that Jesus preached and taught in all the synagogues, *daily teaching in the temple,* as well as preaching on the mountainside, the roadside, the seaside, and in the streets of the cities. No man ever preached such sermons and taught such lessons as Jesus.

Because of the magnitude of this chapter, I must condense rather than enlarge, even though I would love to say a lot about the sermon before us.

Let us title it, *"Seven Sins in the Synagogue of Nazareth."* Carefully now consider these *seven steps.* You may fill in the body muscles from the backbone of this message once delivered by the greatest Orator, Lecturer, Expositor, Teacher, and Preacher of all time.

Introduction: What did the people in this synagogue believe that is typical to churches today?

I. They believed in *worshipping their way,* not God's way (Luke 4:16).
   A. It was their custom, as *Sabbath Day* worshippers, to meet on that day (the Law).
   B. True worshippers worship as Jesus taught on the *Lord's Day* (John 4:22–24; Luke 24:1; 1 Corinthians 16:2).

II. They *believed the Bible* as God's Word, *but not all* (verses 18–21).
   A. *Accepted* (Isaiah 61:1,2). Verse 22, "The gracious words ... His mouth" (literally, *"words of grace"*).

B. *Rejected* (1 Kings 17:8–15, Elijah; 2 Kings 5:1–14, Elisha). Verse 28, "When they *heard* . . . were filled with *wrath*." (Check verses 25–27.)
III. They *believed in Jesus as* ". . . *Joseph's Son*" (verse 22) *but not as the Son of God* (John 1:49).
   A. They believed in *His humanity*.
   B. They did not believe in *His Deity*.
IV. They *believed a traditional proverb*, but *not the promises of God* (verse 23). They thought Jesus was a "Physician of no value" (Romans 4:14–16), and thought that *He must heal Himself before others*.
V. They believed Jesus was a *Prophet* (verse 24), but *refused His message*. Jesus stated, "A prophet is not without honour but in his own country (town)" (Mark 6:4, same occasion).
VI. They believed in *works rather than faith* (verse 28). Jesus marveled because of *their unbelief* (Mark 6:6). He on different occasions marveled because of *great faith*, but only here for *no faith*.
VII. They believed in *taking vengeance* in their own hands (verses 29–30). They were filled with hate rather than love, and *tried to kill Him* before His time.

Note: Some churches would kill their pastor, if they could, for preaching the truth in Jesus' stead. Some countries kill true preachers today.

Note the likeness of a *synagogue to a church:*

1. Both have a spiritual leader, here a ruler, the other a pastor.
2. Both sing praises in psalms and hymns to God.
3. Both have the Bible taught and preached.
4. Both have ritual or ordinance for acceptance: circumcision versus believers' baptism.
5. Both meet at stated times to worship: one on the Sabbath, the other on the Lord's Day.
6. Both have periods of prayer in the service.

Parables Jesus Taught

"*I (Christ) will* open My mouth in parable(s), I will utter dark sayings of old" (Psalms 78:2).

A parable is something like an *allegory*, but slightly different. A parable, somebody said, is an "earthly story with a heavenly meaning." This I have heard nearly all my life, and it is still hard to beat.

Being a little sophisticated, the difference between an allegory and a parable is that an allegory is speaking *figuratively and symbolically* with emblems as expressions, while a parable usually compares or *illustrates the real moral attitude* or describes a *religious principle*.

Looking into the Word regarding parables in Mark, we have the *key* to them all:

Mark 4:2,10–13, "And He taught them many things by parables, and said unto them in His doctrine, . . . And when He was alone, they that were about Him with the twelve asked of Him the parable. And He said unto them, *Unto you it is given to know the mystery of the kingdom* of God: but unto them that are *without,* all these things are done in parables: that seeing they may see, and not perceive; and hearing they may hear, and not understand; lest at any time they should be *converted,* and their sins should be forgiven them. And He said unto them, *Know ye not this parable?* and how then will ye know *all parables?*"

Here we discern that parables are to be understood by *only believers,* for it is *given to them* to know the *mysteries* of the kingdom of heaven, but to the crowds or multitudes it was *not given.* Here the Sovereign God exerts His authority. The Lord of glory chooses to work this way. It is His good pleasure to reveal the great truths of His Word to *His people.* To the rest that hear, they do not understand, and they that say they see do not perceive. In God's purpose it is concealed to them just as the Bible is to unbelievers. It cannot be comprehended from the mind of the natural man (1 Corinthians 2:14).

The Mystery of the Parable of the Sower (Matthew 13:1–11)

"The same day went Jesus out of the house, and sat by the sea side. And great multitudes were gathered together unto Him, so that He went into a ship, and sat; and the whole multitude stood on the shore. And He spake many things unto them in parables, saying, Behold, a sower went forth to sow; and when he sowed, some seeds fell by the *way side,* and the fowls came and devoured them up: some fell upon *stony places,* where they had not much earth: and forthwith they sprung up, because they had no deepness of earth: and when the sun was up, they were scorched; and because they had no root, they withered away. And some fell among *thorns*; and the thorns sprung up, and choked them: but other fell into *good ground*, and brought forth fruit, some an hundredfold, some sixtyfold, some thirtyfold. Who hath ears to hear, let him hear. And the disciples came, and said unto Him, Why speakest thou unto them in parables? He answered and said unto them, Because it is given unto you to know the mysteries of the kingdom of heaven, but to them it is not given." This is God's right as Sovereign Lord.

The Interpretation Thereof (Matthew 13:16–23)

"But *blessed are your eyes,* for they see: and your *ears, for they hear.* For verily I say unto you, That many prophets and righteous men have desired to see those things which ye see, and have not seen them; and to hear those things which ye hear, and have not heard them. Hear ye therefore the parable of the sower.

"When any one heareth the word of the kingdom, and understandeth it not, then cometh the wicked one, and catcheth away that which was sown in his heart. This is he which received seed by the *way side.* But he that received the seed into *stony places,* the same is he that heareth the Word, and anon with joy receiveth it; yet hath he not root in himself, but dureth for a while: for when tribulation or persecution ariseth because of the Word, by and by he is offended. He also that received seed among the *thorns* is he that heareth the Word; and the care of this world and deceitfulness of riches, choke the Word, and he becometh unfruitful. *But* he that received seed into the *good ground* is he that heareth the Word, and understandeth it; which also beareth fruit, and bringeth forth, some an hundredfold, some sixty, some thirty."

I need not attempt to improve on our Lord's interpretation. It is there for all to read, but believers to understand by the Spirit given to them.

Parables

As we previously listed the miracles of our Lord, we shall now list our Lord's parables as they were given within all the Gospel writers, in order.

Part I—Parables found in Matthew

	Matthew
1. Tares Among Wheat	13:24–30
2. The Hidden Treasure	13:44

3. The Pearl of Great Price	13:45,46
4. The Net	13:47–50
5. Old and New Treasures	13:52
6. Unmerciful Servant	18:23–34
7. Laborers in the Vineyard	20:1–16
8. Father and two Sons	21:28–32
9. Marriage of the King's Son	22:1–14
10. Wise and Foolish Virgins	25:1–13
11. Ten Talents	25:14–30
12. Sheep and Goats	25:31–46

Part II—Parables found in Mark

	Mark
13. Growth of Seed of Grain	4:26–29
14. Watchful Porter	13:34–36

Part III—Parables found in Luke

	Luke
15. Two Debtors	7:41–50
16. Good Samaritan	10:30–37
17. Friend at Midnight	11:5–8
18. Rich Fool	12:16–21
19. Waiting Servants	12:35–40
20. Faithful and Wise Steward	12:42–48
21. Barren Fig Tree	13:6–9
22. The Shut Door	13:25–27
23. Place of Honor	14:7–11
24. Great Supper	14:16–24
25. Tower of Warring King	14:28–33
26. Lost Coin	15:8–10
27. Prodigal Son	15:11–32
28. Dishonest Steward	16:1–8
29. Rich Man and Lazarus	16:19–31
30. Farmer and His Servant	17:7–10
31. Unrighteous Judge	18:1–8
32. Pharisee and Publican	18:9–14
33. Nobleman and the Pounds	19:12–27

Part IV—Parables found in both Matthew and Luke

	Matthew	Luke
34. House on Rock and Sand	7:24–27	6:48–49
35. The Leaven	13:33	13:20,21
36. Lost Sheep	18:12–14	15:4–7
37. Mote and Beam	7:3–5	6:41–42
38. Children at Play	11:16,17	7:31,32
39. Seven Unclean Spirits	12:43–45	11:24–26

Part V—Parables found in John

40. The Bread of Life	6:26–58	
41. Shepherd and Sheep	10:1–38	
42. Vine and Branches	15:1–27	

Part VI—Parables found in all three Synoptic Gospels (must be more important)

	Matthew	Mark	Luke
43. Lamp Under a Bushel	5:14–16	4:21–23	8:16–18
44. New and Old Garments and Wineskins	9:16,17	2:21–22	5:36–39
45. The Sower	13:18–23	4:3–9	8:5–8
46. Mustard Seed	13:31,32	4:31,32	13:18,19
47. Vineyard and Husbandman	21:33–41	12:1–11	20:9–16
48. Tender Leaves of Fig Tree	24:32	13:28	21:29,30

Note: No one parable is found in all four Gospels.

The Prophecies Jesus Made

There are multitudes of prophecies about Jesus in the Old Testament that were fulfilled in the New. Jesus Himself gave several predictions about the future. However, much of His timely teaching and crowning subjects were *left up to the Apostles* to expound in a more detailed account the end of this age and the events to come.

Nevertheless, our Lord was not silent on this matter, and it seems fitting to share with you some *of His great prophecies in three areas:* first, to the *church;* second, to the *Jewish nation;* third, to the *wicked world.*

To His Church of Gentiles Mostly

Part I—Concerning her extensive work

Matthew 10:41,42, "He that receiveth a *prophet* in the name of a prophet shall receive a prophet's reward; and he that receiveth a *righteous man* in the name of a righteous man shall receive a righteous man's reward. And whosoever shall give to drink unto one of these little ones a cup of cold water only in the *name of a disciple,* verily I say unto you, he shall in no wise lose his reward."

Matthew 24:14, "And this gospel of the kingdom shall be preached in all the world for a witness unto all nations: and *then* shall the end come."

Matthew 28:19, "Go ye therefore, and teach all nations, *baptizing* them in the name of the Father, and of the Son, and of the Holy Ghost."

Mark 16:15, "And he said unto them, Go ye into all the world, and *preach* the gospel to *every creature.*"

Luke 24:47, "And that repentance and remission of sins should be preached in His name among all nations, *beginning at Jerusalem.*"

Acts 1:8, "But ye shall *receive power,* after that the Holy Ghost is come upon you: and ye shall be *witnesses* unto Me both in Jerusalem, and in all Judaea, and in Samaria, and unto the uttermost part of the earth."

Part II—Concerning her heavenly home

Matthew 13:43, "Then shall the righteous shine forth as the sun *in the kingdom of their Father.* Who hath ears to hear, let him hear."

Matthew 26:29, "But I say unto you, I will not drink henceforth of this fruit of the vine, until that day when I drink it new with you in *My Father's kingdom.*"

John 14:2,3, "In my Father's house are *many mansions:* if it were not so I would have told you. I go to *prepare a place* for you. And if I go and prepare a place for you, *I will come again,* and receive you unto myself; that where I am, there ye may be also."

John 17:24, "Father, I will that they also, whom *thou hast given Me,* be with Me where I am; that they may behold my glory, which thou hast given Me: for thou lovedst Me before the foundation of the world."

Part III—Concerning His imminent coming

Matthew 24:27,36,39,42,44, "For as the *lightning* cometh out of the east, and shineth even unto the west; so shall also the coming of the Son of man be. But of *that day* and hour *knoweth no man,* no, not the angels of heaven, but my Father only. And knew not until the flood came, and took them all away; *so shall also* the coming of the Son of man be. *Watch* therefore; for ye know not what hour your Lord doth come. Therefore be ye also *ready:* for in such an hour as ye think not the Son of man cometh."

Mark 13:29,32,33,35–37, "So ye in like manner, when ye shall *see these things* come to pass, know that it is *nigh, even at the doors.* But of that day and that hour knoweth no man, no, not the angels which are in heaven... Take ye heed, watch and pray: for ye know not when the time is. Watch ye therefore: for ye know not *when the master of the house cometh,* at *even,* or at *midnight,* or at the *cockcrowing,* or in the *morning:* lest coming suddenly he find you *sleeping.* And what I say unto you I say unto all, *Watch.*"

Luke 21:34–36, "And take heed to yourselves, lest at any time your hearts be overcharged with surfeiting, and drunkenness, and cares of this life, and so that day come upon you unawares. For as a snare shall it come on all them that dwell on the face of the whole earth. Watch ye therefore, and pray always, that ye may be accounted worthy to *escape* all these things that shall come to pass, and to stand before the Son of man."

To His Own People, But Considering the Jews Mostly

Concerning the 144,000 Jews, and the survivors in the Tribulation

Revelation 7:3,4, "Hurt not the earth, neither the sea, nor the trees, till we have sealed the servants of our God in their foreheads. And I heard the number of them which were sealed; and there were sealed an hundred and forty and four thousand of all the tribes of the children of Israel."

Matthew 24:30,31, "And *then* shall appear the *sign* of the Son of man in Heaven: and then shall all the tribes of the earth mourn, and they shall *see the Son of man* coming in the clouds of heaven with power and great glory. And He shall send *His angels* with a great sound of a trumpet, and they shall gather together *His elect* from the four winds, from one end of heaven to the other."

Matthew 25:34, "Then shall the King say unto them on His right hand, *Come, ye blessed of my Father,* inherit the kingdom prepared for you from the foundation of the world."

Luke 21:27,28, "And *then* shall *they* see the Son of man coming in a cloud with power and great glory. And when these things begin to come to pass, then look up, and lift up your heads; for *your redemption draweth nigh.*"

To the Wicked World

Concerning their judgment and punishment (in brief)

Matthew 8:12, "*But the children of the kingdom shall be cast out* into outer darkness: there shall be weeping and gnashing of teeth."

Matthew 10:28, "And fear not them which kill the body, but are not able to kill the soul: but *rather fear Him which is able to destroy both soul and body in hell.*"

Matthew 24:51, "And shall cut him asunder, and *appoint him* his portion with the *hypocrites:* there shall be *weeping and gnashing of teeth.*"

Matthew 25:41,46, "Then shall He say also unto them on the *left hand,* Depart from me, ye *cursed,* into *everlasting fire,* prepared for the devil and his angels. And these shall go away into *everlasting punishment:* but the righteous into life eternal."

Note: I have only given you some of the Scriptures on this theme to consider. We will deal more fully at the completion of the book on its all-consuming and climactic conclusion.

The Prayers Jesus Offered

The *prayer life of Jesus* is unequaled and unsurpassed. May we see in the following verses that our Lord from heaven set a bright and shining example that will help us in our communion with God our Father, as we pray in His precious Name, "The Lord Jesus Christ."

The Private Prayers of Jesus

It appears Jesus adopted a praying pattern, to open and close each day, when possible, with prayer.

Morning devotion, Mark 1:35: "And in the morning, rising up a great while before day, He went out, and departed into a solitary place, and there prayed."

Evening devotion, Mark 6:46: "And when He had sent them away, He departed into a mountain to pray."

In solitary communion, Luke 5:16: "And He withdrew Himself into the wilderness, and prayed."

All night in prayer, Luke 6:12: "And it came to pass in those days, that He went out into a mountain to pray, and continued all night in prayer to God."

In the Garden of Gethsemane, Luke 22:41: "And He was withdrawn from them about a stone's cast, and kneeled down, and prayed."

Remember this master key in prayer: "Not my will but Thine be done."

Please read the most significant supplication for all saints in John 17, and notice the repetition of the word "*given.*"

One more word of encouragement on private prayer: "But thou when thou prayest, enter into thy closet, and when thou hast shut thy door, pray to thy Father which is *in secret;* and thy Father which seeth in secret shall *reward thee openly*" (Matthew 6:6).

Lord, help us to pray and faint not.

The Public Prayers of Jesus

The first glimpse of Jesus praying in public was at His baptism. It was in the presence of John the Immerser, an eyewitness, when Jesus Himself entered the waters of Jordan, to which *three doors* were opened: the *door to His public ministry on earth, the door of the Father's house in heaven* (from which was heard a voice saying, "Thou art My beloved Son, in Thee I am well pleased"), and *the door to believers by way of baptism* (figuratively), which extends the privileges, rights, blessings, and the right hand of Christian fellowship, given within the church body.

Notice also in Luke 3:21, "... that Jesus also being baptized [at the supposed age of 30] and praying, the heaven was opened." Here Jesus uttered a few unknown but public words to His Father in the light that His mighty ministry would entail.

The sacred record brings us next to Matthew 11:25,26, when Jesus prayed, saying, "I thank thee, O Father, Lord of heaven and earth, because Thou hast *hid* these things from the *wise and prudent,* and hast *revealed them unto babes* (babies in the faith). Even so, Father: for so it seemed good in Thy sight."

This verbal public prayer of Christ shows the blindness of the Jews and the mercy of God that was extended to people who had known nothing of God's providence. *It is only by the grace of God that eyes have been opened to see the truths that we embrace.*

Three other public prayers I shall point out, which were like that at His baptism—not recording the actual prayer, but just indicating that prayer was made, in the words addressing the 5,000 (plus women and children) and the 4,000 (plus women and children):

Matthew 14:19, "He blessed and brake . . ."

Matthew 15:36, "He gave thanks, and brake . . ."

At the Lord's Supper, Jesus did likewise (Luke 22:19), "He took the bread and gave thanks . . ."

The following unforgettable public prayer, approaching the close of His meaningful ministry, was at the *graveside of Lazarus:*

John 11:41–44, "And Jesus lifted up His eyes, and said, Father, I thank Thee that Thou hast heard Me. And I knew that Thou hearest Me always: but because of the people which stand by I said it, *that they may believe* that Thou hast sent Me. And when He thus had spoken, he cried with a loud voice, Lazarus, come forth. And he that was dead came forth, bound hand and foot with graveclothes: and his face was bound about with a napkin. Jesus saith unto them, Loose him, and let him go."

What a paramount picture of His spiritual work of *raising the dead* in trespasses and sins! Compare John 5:24, ". . . passed from death unto life," and verse 25, ". . . the hour is coming and *now* is, when the dead shall hear the voice of the Son of God (He is the resurrection and the life): and they that *hear* shall live." (Check also on Ephesians 2:1–5.)

We will recall that many believed on Jesus in that cemetery service, which was equivalent to being raised from *spiritual death to new life in Christ.*

Regarding this list from the public prayer life of Jesus, we must now gather round the cross. There we see *three malefactors*. The One in the middle was the Prince of Life. Harken to the prayer of this life-giving One, which was heard by His persecutors:

Luke 23:34, "Then said Jesus, Father *forgive them;* for they know not what they do . . ."

I believe all of God's elect were included in this prayer, to forgive those around the cross and around the world for whom Jesus was dying, many of which were saved, *one on that day* and *others after the Day of Pentecost*, not forgetting all those *Old Testament saints* who died in faith, believing that their Messiah would come and save them.

Several of them heard Peter later, who stood at the foot of the cross: "Him being delivered by the determinate counsel and foreknowledge of God, ye have taken, and by wicked hands have crucified and slain" (Acts 2:23).

At the conclusion of this sermon, *3,000 were forgiven by Jesus,* including those in His intercessory prayer on the cross.

A few days later in Acts 3, Peter preached to another crowd, saying in substance (verses 14 and 15), You denied the Holy One and desired a murderer to be granted a release under Pilate's authority. You killed the Prince of Life whom God raised up. *This led to 5,000 more being saved and pardoned in that prayer* of Jesus. Acts 4:4 is only a preview of all God's people included in this prayer of forgiveness.

Then the heart-rending outburst of Christ crying to God in that unexpressable and unfathomable tormenting plea (Matthew 26:46), "Eli, Eli, lama sabachthani? that is to say, *My God, my God, why hast Thou forsaken Me?*" Jesus at this point bore the sin of *all* the children of God as He died as a *Substitute* forever. It was God the Son offering a perfect sacrifice for our atonement, for none but a perfect One could die such a death as Jesus did.

Our Lord's last public utterance in prayer just before He died is seen in Luke 23:46, "And when Jesus had cried with a loud voice He said, Father, into thy hands I commend My spirit, and having said thus, He gave up the ghost."

Thank God for Jesus! His death on the cross means the death of all our sins.

The Death Jesus Died

Let's come right to the point in asking this far-reaching question: *For whom did Jesus die?* Or did Jesus suffer the punishment of sin under the wrath of God for *all* or *some*? The *majority* say, "*All* the sins of *all* men." The *minority* say, "*All* the sins of *some* men." *Which is Scriptural and which is false?* They both certainly cannot be so. One must be eliminated. Which? Would you give place if you should happen to hold the wrong view? I appeal to logic, and to the living Word.

Proposition I: If the first is true, that Jesus died for *all* the sins of *all* men, then He must have died in vain for most men. The majority of mankind have already gone to hell in unbelief. But someone says, "It was unbelief that sent them to hell, even though Jesus died for all the sins of all men." I reply, "*Is not unbelief counted as sin*? Therefore, it must needs be covered if Jesus died for all the sins of all men."

But this is ridiculous, because all men are not being saved. Did Jesus waste His blood on those in the world who died in their own sins? Absolutely not! So this theory cannot be proven true. All such Christians must abandon this view, which would charge Christ with being the most colossal and stupendous failure in the annals of human history. If he said *that He died for the sins of all men,* then He failed in the attempt. Thus God would receive a *double payment* for which His Son paid on the cross and the sinner pays in hell. Let us cast aside this first and most popular view as unscriptural.

Proposition II: Our declaration must stand. Jesus died for *all* the sins of *some. Those who believe are the chosen ones.* They are God's elect, God's choice, not under works but through grace.

Scriptural statements *from* the Savior and *about* the Savior are more than sufficient to rest our case. Please read these important verses: Matthew 1:21; Matthew 20:28; Matthew 26:28; John 6:37,39; John 10:11,16,28,29; John 17:2,9,22; Ephesians 5:25. One day you may thank me for writing these truths to you.

If Jesus died for all men without exception, then the words "*ordained* to eternal life, the *faith of God's elect, chosen in Him* (Christ) before the foundation of the world, died for *many,* died for the *sheep,* died for the *church,*" have no meaning.

But where it says "Jesus died for all," etc., it most certainly means all men *without distinction*—the young and old, rich and poor, sick and healthy, learned and unlearned, black and white, etc.

May God help you to see the only position that honors God and brings glory to the Christ of the cross, who died in pain but did not die in vain.

Christ, the High Priest

We have said in previous pages that Jesus was to occupy a threefold office as Prophet, Priest and King. Take a moment to reflect on some

Scriptures that prove *Christ to be our present High Priest*—also that He was to give His life as a human sacrifice for the *sins of God's people*, thereby *making atonement for their souls* (please read!): John 11:49–50; John 18:12–14; Hebrews 4:14–16; 6:20; 7:3,15–17,27; 9:14–15, 24–28; 13:20–21.

The Resurrection Power Jesus Exhibited

We believe that the Doctrine of *Christ's Resurrection* distinguishes the Christian religion from all other religions in the world.

A follower of Buddha visited my church one time. We talked! He praised the self-denying Buddha as a very good man, like Christ. I said, "Jesus not only lived a perfect life, died a sacrificial death for the sins of His people, but rose triumphantly over death, which is a proven fact." I went on, "Do you have such a convincing claim concerning the founder of Buddhism?" He had to say, "No."

Jesus gave *"many infallible proofs"* of His resurrection. He appeared at least *twelve times during His forty-day post-resurrection period.*

The fact of the matter is, Jesus really was not killed by the Jews and the governor. Pontius Pilate did sentence Him to death because of the decision of the Jews as they cried, "His blood be upon us and our children." (This is true till this day.) Nevertheless, these astounding words are found in John 10:18, *"No man taketh it from Me, but I lay it down of Myself.* I have power to lay it down, and I have power to take it up again . . ."

As Paul cried out once, "If Christ be not risen, then is our preaching vain, and your faith is also vain, and we are yet in our sins." But the bottom line is, *"But now is Christ risen* from the dead, and become the firstfruits of them that slept" (1 Corinthians 15:20). "But thanks be to God, which giveth us the *victory through our Lord Jesus Christ"* (1 Corinthians 15:57).

In Christ we have *victory over sin, victory over death, and victory over hell.*

Oh, what a *wonderful Champion and Conqueror is Christ our Lord,* for our God is not the God of the dead, but of the living (Matthew 22:32)! Amen.

• • •

Questionnaire

1. What did the threefold ministry of Christ consist of?
2. What was the first official act in the Lord's public ministry?
3. Did the Lord cleanse the temple once or twice?
4. Name two other places where our Lord preached.
5. What was the text Jesus used in His hometown (church), and what were the results from a human standpoint?
6. Define a parable.
7. What is the purpose of a parable?
8. About how many parables are recorded in the New Testament: 30, 40, or 50?
9. What is the Master Key Parable?
10. What three areas do our Lord's prophecies deal with?
11. True or false: Jesus prayed long prayers in public and short prayers in private.
12. What was the pattern of Jesus' prayer life?
13. True or false: Jesus prayed often, but never wearied His body by spending all night in prayer.
14. Complete this well-known prayer of Jesus: "My Father, if it be possible, let this cup pass from Me: nevertheless . . ."
15. Which is true: Jesus died for all the sins of some men, or some of the sins of all men, or all the sins of all men?
16. Did Jesus die for the sin of unbelief in those who became believers, or the unbelieving world? Underline one.
17. Does the death of Christ involve the doctrine of election? Yes or No.
18. Did Jesus die for the sins of the world from Adam to the last man, or did Jesus die for only God's elect? Underline one.
19. Was the everlasting covenant (Hebrews 13:20) regarding the death of God's High Priest for all God's sheep or for all the world of mankind?
20. Give the one living religion in the world, and give the reason why.

• • •

Answers

1. Preaching, teaching, and healing.
2. Cleansing the temple.
3. Twice, at the first and last of His public ministry.
4. Synagogue, mountainside, and home.
5. Isaiah 61:1,2. Rejected (failed).
6. Earthly story with a heavenly meaning.
7. To conceal the truth from the unsaved, except God's elect, and reveal the truth to such believers, saved by the grace of God.
8. 50.
9. Sower.
10. The Jews, the Church and the World.
11. False.
12. Morning and evening, as well as frequently throughout the day.
13. False.
14. Not my will, but Thine be done.
15. Jesus died for all the sins of some men.
16. Sin of unbelief in those that became believers.
17. Yes.
18. Jesus died for only God's elect.
19. For all God's sheep.
20. Christianity, because Christ arose.

Chapter 10

Ascending to Meet Our Lord in the Air: The Heavenly Homecoming
-or-
Christ's Judgment Seat to Reward the Works of the Righteous (His Church)

Thought

"What a wonderful day it will be, when my Savior I shall see."

• • •

I. *The heavenly homecoming* (2 Timothy 4:8)

   A. Some of the elite company (Hebrews 11:4,5,7,8,23)

   B. Celestial seats (Matthew 8:11; Ephesians 2:6)

   C. Renewing old acquaintances (1 Corinthians 13:12)

II. The first stage of Christ's coming—*The rapture of His saints* (1 Corinthians 15:23; 1 Thessalonians 4:16,17)

   A. Conclusive proofs of the Rapture

      1. One taken, the other left (Luke 17:34–37)

      2. Examples: Noah and Lot (Luke 17:26,27,28–30)

      3. Illustrations: Two Churches, Philadelphia and Laodicea (Revelation 3:7–13,14–21)

      4. Christ calls, "Come up here" (Revelation 4:11)

         a. The voice of the past—postmillennialism

         b. The voices of the present—amillennialism and premillennialism

   B. Church, both living and dead, translated and raised before the Tribulation (Matthew 24:27,30)

III. *The Judgment Seat of Christ* (Romans 14:10; 2 Corinthians 5:10)
   A. General or special judgment
      1. Where: Some designated heavenly place—air (1 Thessalonians 4:17)
      2. When: The day the last soul is saved that completes the church (Matthew 24:14)
      3. Who: Those who are members of Christ's body (Ephesians 5:23,30)
      4. Why: To reward His servants (1 Corinthians 3:8; Revelation 22:12)
   B. Admonition to work (Matthew 24:42; Luke 6:23,35; Revelation 3:11)
IV. "The Marriage of the King's Son": The eschatological parable (Matthew 22:1–14)
   A. Present at the banquet
      1. His Kingly Father, God (Matthew 22:2)
      2. His Father's royal Son, the Bridegroom (Revelation 19:6–9; 21:9)
      3. His chosen bride, the Church, verse 9 (Revelation 17:14)
      4. His honored guests, the martyrs (Revelation 6:9–11; 7:14; 20:4)
   B. Completing "the resurrection of the just" (Luke 14:13,14; John 5:28,29; Acts 24:15; Revelation 20:4–6)
   C. Preparing for the second stage of His return—the revelation with His saints (Acts 1:10,11; Titus 2:13; Revelation 17:14; 19:11,16,19)
   D. Gleanings from the harvest must include Old Testament saints and Tribulation saints (Daniel 12:2; Revelation 7:14,15; 14:13–15; 20:4–6)
V. Questionnaire and Answers

• • •

Thought

There is no sweeter word in the English language to a pilgrim, than the word "home."

I've wandered far away from God,
Now I'm coming home;
The paths of sin too long I've trod,
Lord, I'm coming home.
Coming home, coming home,
Never more to roam,
Open wide Thine arms of love,
Lord, I'm coming home.

The Heavenly Homecoming

To give up our loved ones for a time grieves our hearts and forms a longing in our souls; yet take courage, battered and beaten, tormented and troubled pilgrim; God assures us of His precious promise in the "blessed hope" that we will meet them again, if it is well with our soul.

2 Timothy 4:8, "Henceforth there is laid up for me a *crown of righteousness,* which the Lord, the righteous Judge, shall give me at that day: and not to me only, but unto *all them also that love his appearing.*"

In that homeland we will unite again and remain forever with the Lord in whom we love and owe everything. The songs about heaven fill our hearts with joy. A more sure satisfaction is to fix our faith on Christ and His Holy Book. There we shall see *"Him who loved us and gave Himself for us."* There we will embrace our long-departed friends and loved ones within the circle of our acquaintances. There we will meet new friends that we have never seen but only read about in the sacred pages of Scripture. There we will "sit down with Abraham, Isaac and Jacob," the Old Testament saints in the Kingdom, and with Peter, Paul, James and John, the New Testament saints around the throne of Glory (Matthew 8:11).

Look at some of that elite company we will meet for the first time:

Brother *Abel,* the first martyr, because "he obtained witness that he was righteous, God testifying of his gifts . . ."

The first prophet, *Enoch,* who was the first of the translated saints that points to the living church, which will be translated when Jesus comes.

Elder *Noah,* the old "preacher of righteousness," when being warned of God, listened to Him and built as the first skilled carpenter, a refuge for his wife and children to the new world, being "heirs of the righteousness that is by faith."

Friendly *Abraham,* when called, obeyed and became the first spiritual father of all the possessors of faith. "He was looking for the celestial city with foundations, whose builder and maker is God."

Mighty *Moses,* the law giver, by faith refused the Egyptian throne for a seat with His reigning future King of kings, because he counted the "Christ" of God, a Person whom he wrote about, to have "greater riches" than any reward of this world. Although he was not permitted to enter the promised land with his fellow Hebrews, yet he was found "faithful in all his house" and will be seen in the heavenly promised land of all the world's redeemed family, to sing "the song of Moses and the Lamb."

What a silver cloud, lined with *cheering spectators* to welcome us home (Hebrews 12:1)!

The First Stage of His Coming, the Rapture of His Saints

1 Corinthians 15:23; 1 Thessalonians 4:16,17; Matthew 24:40,41; Luke 17:34–37

Conclusive Evidence

The simple explanation on this subject is stimulating to the saints. First, bear in mind that the rapture will be *universal,* not *geographical.* In Luke 17:34,35 we are told about the outreach and magnitude of the rapture:

". . . in that night there shall be *two men in one bed,* the one [saved Gentile] shall be taken, and the other [lost] shall be left." On the other side of the globe, "Two women shall be grinding together [*daytime labor*] at the mill, the one shall be taken, [*Where? To heaven,* taken up to meet and forever be with the Lord] and the other left." Left to face divine judgment and God's woes.

In verse 37 of Luke, the evangelist presents a picture of *vultures or eagles;* both of these birds feed on the carcasses of dead bodies in Palestine. The dead bodies here symbolize both immoral, *corrupt men and women that are dead spiritually beyond hope, as their habit is feasting on filth.* God's divine vengeance is about to fall on that which is termed *"the great tribulation,"* following the removal of His redeemed ones.

We have a great *example of this from Noah's days* (Luke 17:26,27; 2 Peter 2:5). God separated the eight saved in the ark from the "world of the ungodly" before judgment fell. *Likewise, in Lot's day* (Luke 17:25–30) Sodom was so corrupt its sins were piled up sky-high with lust, *sodomy and homosexuality,* which brought down the wrath of God in consuming fire upon those wicked offenders. They were so *diseased* with such open evil practices, God had to destroy them all. History is being repeated with the dreaded AIDS epidemic worldwide.

Now before the fire fell, an angel of God was sent to bring that *righteous man* Lot and his family out of the cursed and condemned city. We must be taken out and then up, before God's just judgment explodes like a time bomb.

One Taken and One Left

At the close of this church age we see in Revelation the two last churches illustrated, which are suggested in *Matthew 24:36:* "Two men shall be in the field (the field is the world): one shall be taken and the other left."

What a feast of theology and Bible-teaching is found here in this short verse from the Master Teacher! "Taken" is to be understood literally. If we are to believe anything, then we are to accept Jesus and His Word in everything. If we spiritualize the plain truth, we will be afloat on the seven seas in a canoe without a paddle.

I need not tell you of the *schism, isms,* and *divisions* within Christianity, which is the Devil's work, for he is a professional in imitating Christ (2 Corinthians 11:13–15).

When Jesus, the Sower, sowed the seed (the word) in a field, it was later discovered that somebody had secretly planted tares among the wheat (Matthew 13:25). This is the church world we live in. You would do well to ask yourself, "Does my creed correspond to Christ's charter?" If not, we are but building on drifting sand and destined for a rude awakening. It will be the fall of a lifetime. Isn't eternity worth your investigation to *determine the false from the true view?* Compare Scripture with Scripture (John 7:17).

In Revelation 3:7–13 and 14–21, we need to see, in the light of the seven churches, the *last two,* the "Church in Philadelphia" and the "Church of the Laodiceans."

The Philadelphia Church

This Philadelphia Church has an *open door* to receive her true believers in Christ. They kept and preserved the truth of the Word. They had not denied their Lord's name. They were the ones loved of the Lord, because they kept the word of His patience. He promised to keep them "from (*out of*) the *hour of temptation* that will come (not on them, but) upon all the world."

The hour of temptation is an expression revealing the time when the Devil will have a heyday doing his thing and having his own way without being restrained. Paul tells us in 2 Thessalonians 2:7 about the removing of the Holy Spirit, which makes way for the revelation of the wicked one [Satan's right-hand man, the Antichrist] referred to in verse 8. This *"Brotherly Love Church"* (for so is its meaning) shall be *exempt* from and escape the "great tribulation," which will be unprecedented as the worst woes and wrath from God in judgment on the world, *not the church.*

The Lost, Last, Left Laodecian Church

In contrast, this last church out of the seven, called the *"lukewarm church"* (Revelation 3:16), thought themselves *rich, but not in grace.* They felt independent of God, needing nothing. They knew it all and had it all. A closer look reveals they needed everything. They were naked, needing God's white raiment of righteousness because of their worldliness. They had not the Spirit, and needed Him to anoint them to see the truth of Christ. They needed God's love, instead of their love for material gain. They needed to go to work for the Lord and be zealous, for *they were trusting in their riches, not God's righteousness.* They needed to repent of all their sins to be saved. However, as far as we know, they never repented, never got their eyes opened, never embraced God's grace. Therefore, from all appearances, this materially rich, spiritually dead and blind, lukewarm, worldly church was "left"— left to face God's awful judgment.

Thank God, the true church will not go into the tribulation, because we have this God-given faith that was once and for all delivered unto the saints, therefore being *"delivered from the wrath to come"* in the great tribulation.

In addition to these two churches, the one taken and the last one left, I see another important point taken from Revelation.

The Heavenly Elders of the Church Age (Revelation 4:1-11)

Just after the messages delivered to the seven churches, given through Christ by the Spirit, the first verse of the chapter says, "*After this . . .*"—that is, the heavenly message to each earthly church for different periods of the Church Age. We see a door swing open in heaven and hear a voice (*Christ*) like a trumpet at the close of this Church Age. He calls us out of the world, "*Come up here.*" This is that One that is seated on His throne. All attention is focused on Him. To compare Scripture with Scripture, let us turn to 1 Thessalonians and see how it ties into this vision in Revelation. Look now and study with me.

Paul's Account of the Rapture

1 Thessalonians 4:14-18, "For if we *believe* that Jesus died and rose again, even so *them also which sleep in Jesus will God* [Christ] *bring with Him*. For this we say unto you by the word of the Lord, that we which are *alive* and remain unto the coming of the Lord shall not prevent (precede) them which are asleep. For the Lord Himself shall descend from heaven with a shout, with the voice of the archangel, and with the trump of God: and the dead in Christ shall rise first: *then* we which are *alive* and remain shall be caught up together with them in the clouds, to *meet the Lord in the air:* and so shall we ever be with the Lord. Wherefore comfort one another with these words."

It seems clear in the doctrine of Christ's coming for *His own* that some very distinct truths cannot be denied. His Voice is like a trumpet call. The dead in Christ, members of His body, rise first and reunite with their *souls* that were *in heaven with Him*. The bodies of believers are raised, not only from (out of) the dead, but *from the earth,* in like manner as the Lord ascended after His work was finished in the flesh.

Acts 1:10,11, "And while they looked steadfastly toward heaven as He went up, behold, two men stood by them in white apparel; which also said, Ye men of Galilee, why stand ye gazing up into heaven? This same Jesus, which is taken up from you into heaven, shall so come in like manner as ye have seen Him go into heaven."

Those living believers like Enoch are translated and "caught up." Both the living and the dead are clothed in their *glorified bodies*. Don't you see the truth of the rapture in the phrase "*caught up*?" We meet our Lord, our loved ones, and our friends known and unknown. The place is not on earth, but some designated location in the heavenlies.

Ephesians 2:6, "And hath raised us up together, and made us *sit together* in heavenly places in Christ Jesus."

Whatever is to be done from that point in heaven or later on earth, the fact will remain that we shall ever be *with the Lord.* Herein lies our comfort (1 Thessalonians 4:18).

Three Views on Christ's Return

Before we proceed to the "Judgment Seat of Christ," we must first say something about the *three positions* regarding the Doctrine of Eschatology, a study of last things. Then a brief comment on three views held on the great tribulation: pre-tribulation, mid-tribulation, and post-tribulation.

Postmillenialism

This system of thought almost became extinct after dominating the scene for centuries. The main feature of this theory is that the millennium (or one thousand years) would *come before Christ returned* as a result of a golden age of spiritual progress of preaching the Gospel in all the world. This teaches that the world will grow better through social reform, thus setting the stage for Christ's return. Many are the Scriptures that renounce this theological theory.

Read what Peter, John, and Paul said about this subject in a few choice passages, that the world was not to grow better prior to the Second Coming but rather worse (2 Peter 2:1–3; 1 John 4:1–3; 1 Timothy 4:1–3).

Objection

Postmillenialists ignore the bodily presence of Christ on earth during the millennium: "... and *they* (believers) *lived and reigned with Christ a thousand years*" (Revelation 20:4).

Postmillenialists are against the literal interpretation of Scripture and speak of the millennium as being merely "a long time," as well as the binding of Satan.

Revelation 20:5, "But the *rest of the dead lived not again* [following the first resurrection of the just or righteous] *until the thousand years were finished.*" (The "rest of the dead" means all the wicked that will be resurrected in "the resurrection of damnation," Acts 24:15; John 5:29.) Postmillenialists hold also to one general judgment.

Amillennialism

We now will give conclusive evidence that this false view, as well as the one mentioned above, is unscriptural, and its teaching falls far short of the truth. It teaches that all the promises to Israel are to be fulfilled in the Church Age. This position in general supposes that both Jews and Gentiles make up the new Israel. Amillennialists apply the principle of *spiritualizing* the main body of prophecies regarding the Jews and the church in the future reign of Christ on the earth, while *disregarding the thousand years* of Revelation 20 (where it is found six times). They do not believe in any millennium as such.

It is dangerous to spiritualize Scripture, which takes away the plain, literal interpretation that was used by the Apostles in referring to Old Testament passages.

Someone may ask at this point, "But brother, don't you believe that some Scriptures are figurative, while others are allegorical and still others symbolic?" Yes, I certainly believe and teach that they do have a place in the Scriptures, but generally Scriptures should be interpreted literally. The Holy Spirit is given to us to discern truth from error.

When Jesus said in Revelation, "These words are true and faithful," He meant just that. Read for example Romans 11:25-27. I believe these verses point to Israel's future, when their "sins shall be taken away."

Moreover, this unstable position of amillennialism holds to one general judgment, whereas the New Testament clearly sets forth four main judgments:

- When our sins were judged at the cross.
- The Judgment Seat of Christ—believers only.
- The judgment of the living nations when Jesus returns to earth with His saints.
- The Great White Throne Judgment—unbelievers only.

Premillenialism

This theological system supports the whole Bible, based on its reasonable and literal interpretations. When we fail to take God's Word at face value and accept the plain truth as it is, we step off in the wrong direction. The "pre" view has not only the acceptance of all the apostles, but the church fathers even after the close of the Apostolic Era.

The following is a transcript taken from a book authored by yours truly, titled *Bible Beliefs*. Under one of the twenty-five doctrines, I mention "The Premillennial Return of Christ." It is reprinted below to give you the ideas, based on Scripture, that the "pre" would be accepted as factual.

The Premillennial Return of Christ

"We believe in the *imminent, literal, visible* return of Christ for *His own* as He has promised. We believe that His coming consists of two *crowning events* separated by a period of seven years. *The first stage of His Second Coming will be to welcome and receive His saints in a great aerial homecoming.* All the members of the body, the church, who parted this life with faith in Christ shall then be raised up, called the '*first resurrection*' or the 'resurrection of the just,' when their bodies reunite with their souls that have been with Christ in Paradise. Then the living, remaining saints on earth will be *translated,* called the '*Rapture of the Church,*' as represented in Revelation as the Church of Philadelphia, when they are caught up in the clouds to meet the Lord in the air to ever be with Him. This multitude will then *receive their rewards* from the hand of Christ the Lord at *His judgment seat.* This will be followed by the *marriage of the Lamb,* the Bridegroom being Christ, and the Bride His Church represented by His body on earth during the Church Age or this Dispensation of Grace.

"The guests or friends of the Bridegroom, representing the Old Testament saints that are resurrected near the close of this period, along with the slain saints from the tribulation, rejoice as they celebrate the marriage supper of the Lamb with His Bride in the heavenly honeymoon. At the same time on earth, the Antichrist will be in control, and he will bring in a 'time of trouble,' the '*great tribulation,*' followed by the 'distress of nations.' The Gospel of the Kingdom will again be preached by the believing remnant of the Jews, which will result in massive persecution. Then Christ will be revealed from heaven and return with all His saints to the earth, accompanied by His Holy angels. The Antichrist is destroyed. The living nations are then judged, and the sheep separated from the goats. *Satan is bound* in the bottomless pit for *a thousand years. Jesus, the King of kings,* establishes His millennial kingdom and the *saints reign* with Him, both *Jews and Gentiles,* over all the earth from the seat of His throne in Jerusalem.

"After the millennium, *Satan* will be *loosed* for a little season, and will launch his last attack on the Holy City. *Satan* and his forces are devoured by fire from heaven, and then *cast into Hell,* the lake of fire *where the beast* and the *false prophet* are, and shall be tormented day and night forever and ever. After the final defeat of our arch enemy, the devil, comes the *Great White Throne Judgment,* which will result in all the *wicked dead* being raised in the *resurrection of damnation,* judged and cast forever into the lake of fire. The *kingdom of Christ* will be then *given* by the Son to the Father, when it shall *merge* into His everlasting *heavenly Kingdom,* without end."

His Church, Both Living and Dead, Translated and Raised Before Tribulation (Matthew 24:27,30)

Our Lord in the above passages is speaking of the secret rapture. He says in verse 27, "For as the *lightning* cometh out of the *East,* and shineth even unto the *West:* so shall also the *coming* of the Son of Man be." Lightning is accompanied by dark clouds, indicating a storm is approaching. No man knows or can know the day or hour when Jesus will come. This time is *classified* and sealed, in a safety deposit box in the burglar-proof bank in glory. Yet, the Lord warns us to know when the end is drawing near. Jesus gives the *parable of the fig tree* and all the trees (Luke 21:29-31). In the spring season when new growth occurs and shoots are seen, you know that the next season of summer is near at hand. Then Jesus says, "So *likewise* ye, when ye see these things come to pass, know ye that the kingdom of God is nigh *at hand*" (Luke 21:31).

Therefore, we cannot know when *that Day* will come, but we can see the *clouds gathering* and the storm shaping in heaven, that soon a judgment will fall on the earth. The *storm* that we can see speaks of the prevailing conditions before the Lord comes for His own. The lightning, which we cannot see before it flashes across the sky, speaks of the suddenness of the secret rapture. The Lord warns us to be *ready.* The only safe way to be ready *then* is to be ready *now.* "Watch ye therefore, and pray always, that you may be counted worthy to *escape* all these things that shall come to pass, and to *stand* before the Son of God" (verse 36). This verse speaks of the rapture.

Matthew 24:27, which we referred to above, shows the extent of the rapture, from East to West, circling the earth. In verse 30 of Matthew 24 we have the revelation of the Lord as He returns to earth with his saints.

Compare 1 Thessalonians 5:2 and 1 Thessalonians 4:13–17, which view the rapture like a thief in the night coming to remove His jewels, with 2 Thessalonians 1:7–10, which speaks of the *revelation of Christ with His saints* and fits with Matthew.

Inserted between Matthew 24:27, the *rapture,* and verse 30, the *revelation,* is verse 29, the *tribulation,* sandwiched between the *first* and *second* stages of our Lord's Second Coming. Thank the Lord for sparing us that awful event!

Post-, Mid- and Pre-Tribulation Rapturists

Now one church group says, "I believe the church will go through the tribulation." These are called *Post-Tribulation Rapturists.* Another group says, "I believe that the church will be *taken in the middle* of the tribulation." These are called *Mid-* or *Partial-Tribulation Rapturists. Pre-Tribulation Rapturists,* which I stand with, say, "We believe that the Lord, who died for our sins and was punished on our behalf, will deliver us from the wrath to come in the tribulation period that will follow the rapture of the church." As Jesus said, we the church shall "be counted worthy to *escape* all these things..." and then "to stand before the Son of God," at the soon-coming "Judgment Seat of Christ."

We have already referred to some of the major and main judgments in God's Word. Therefore, we must discount the view of the amillennialists that only subscribe to one *general judgment* when Jesus comes. To drop off the others, such as the judgment upon Israel, judgment of rewards for the church, judgment of the nations, and the judgment of the wicked dead, we feel is doing injustice to the Word of God and His program of the judgments. The fact of the matter is, these various judgments take place at different *intervals of time and place.*

Now, let us sincerely set forth this all-important judgment, applied only to the church. At this point in time the church is resurrected and translated as one body indivisible, a complete church of the living God founded by Christ, ready to account for their life on earth. The place is not on earth but some unknown place in the air. To clarify the scene, read 1 Thessalonians 4:17. In the clouds and in the air is a beautiful throne, upon which Christ is seated. This is described in Revelation 4:1–4. The *"crowns"* imply *rewards* given to the twenty-four elders, *representing the church.* Moreover, there are two very clear Scriptures that unquestionably bring this judgment to light (Romans 14:10). This verse first condemns judgment by the brethren, because their judgment cannot possibly be accurate, due to their inability to know all about the case considered. The Lord who is the Judge in all these great judgments cannot be anything less than just, knowing the heart and the motive behind each individual believer. So then all judgment as such needs to be deferred until that day, "for *we* shall all stand before the judgment seat of Christ."

The second Scripture on this timely subject that is crystal clear is found in 2 Corinthians 5:10. Hear Paul as he says, "For *we* [believers] must *all* appear before the judgment seat of Christ, that every one may *receive* the things done in his body, according to that he hath done, whether it be good or bad." What shall we receive?

Crowns of Honor

Various crowns shall be awarded to special believers:
- Incorruptible Crowns—1 Corinthians 9:25
- Crown of Rejoicing—1 Thessalonians 2:19
- Crown of Righteousness—2 Timothy 4:8
- Crown of Life—James 1:12
- Crown of Glory—1 Peter 5:4

If I interpret this scene right from Revelation 4:10,11, it shows that the elders around the throne acknowledge the *crown rights* of our Redeemer. They cast their crowns before the throne, and praise the Lord for His love shown to them in just being there (Revelation 19:12).

Nevertheless, there is more on this matter of rewards that shows we will be able to keep them through eternity, based on 1 Corinthians 3:11–15, "For other foundation can no man lay than that is laid, which is Jesus Christ. Now if any man build upon this foundation gold, silver, precious stones, wood, hay, stubble; every man's work shall be made manifest: for the day shall declare it, because it shall be revealed by fire; and the fire shall try every man's work of what sort it is. If any man's work abide which he hath built thereupon, he shall receive a reward. If any man's work shall be burned, he shall suffer loss: but he himself shall be saved; yet so as by fire." And 1 Corinthians 4:5, "Therefore judge nothing before the time, until the Lord come, who both will bring to light the hidden things of darkness, and will make manifest the counsels of the hearts: and then shall every man have praise of God."

The Foundation for Salvation

Let me interpret the principle thoughts in the above verses under consideration. The first grand thought that attracts our attention is that Jesus Christ is the one and only *Foundation* for believers. We are founded on Him, this Rock of Ages that stands every test of time: "This Foundation of God stands sure (firm) having this seal, the Lord knows them that are His (elect)."

Only believers can build on this firm Foundation. Since all judgment is committed to Christ, He is the merciful and just Judge of this judgment, for so says the Scripture: "The judgment seat of Christ" (2 Corinthians 5:10).

Who then are the subjects judged? They are all believers who have confessed His name as Lord and Savior. The day Jesus will judge the saints must be when the last member of His body that is to be saved is brought into salvation.

So often 2 Peter 3:9 is misquoted, which says, "The Lord is not slack concerning His promise *[promise to return]*, as some men count slackness, but is longsuffering to *usward [the elect to be saved before He comes]*, not willing that *any* should perish, but that all should come to repentance."

Now think a moment. Don't you believe that God is sovereign and all-powerful? He will not save all men as is usually explained. God does not take pleasure in seeing sinners die in sin and be cast into hell. However, this verse *does not mean the whole world would be saved,* for in John 17:9 He says, "I pray not for the world," and "The Lord knows *them* that are His" (2 Timothy 2:19). Surely 2 Peter 3:9 would be a contradiction if the Lord intended to save all, and that none should perish. Therefore, it is *God's will that none of His own elect, whom He has chosen, will perish.* Jesus will return the moment the *last elect* one is brought into the household of faith, through the preaching of the Gospel.

Now then, Christ as the Judge of every believer is present at this judgment, "for *we* must *all* appear" before Him. None who believe in him are left. None are present that have not been saved. I say again, *it is a judgment that believers only are to account to Him,* based on their life on earth, whether good or bad. Remember, none are saved by works, but by grace only. This work for Christ will yield a reward.

Works Tested by Fire

Grouping the works of believers that remain when tested by fire, against the wasted lives of mediocre Christians who see their works go up in smoke, with the consecrated, dedicated *believers that are "steadfast and unmovable, always abounding in the work of the Lord,"* will *rejoice in that day.* They realize that the gifts to the Lord and to the poor, shall not go unrewarded. The good deeds to the sick and needy were recorded by the Lord, and even a drink of cold water given in the name of a prophet or disciple shall not pass unnoticed by the all-seeing God.

The rich rewards of the righteous shall abound from *motives of love* and *unselfish deeds, issuing from faith.* The Lord says in His Word, and notice especially verse 12 in 1 Corinthians 3, which is a key passage, "Now if any man (person) build upon *this foundation* (Christ) *gold, silver, precious stones,"* that is, the imperishable works, whereby the believer will be rewarded (verse 14). The rest of verse 12 implies the weak and worldly Christians that are saved by grace, but have no works to show for their labor. No doubt this is in the flesh and not in the Spirit. The results will be *"wood, hay, stubble."* What a shame to live as a saved person and not go beyond the perishable! Such have their works burned up and "shall suffer *loss,* but he himself shall be *saved,* yet so as by fire." It can be said here that *nothing done for the Lord is in vain.*

Much of our works, if we will be honest, are motivated by such phrases as *"to be seen by men,"* or *"in the flesh."* Also for prestige, power, and selfish ends, but not for the Savior. All these works will go up in a puff of smoke when God lights a match to your life's work that must stand for eternity. Pause and think on this!

I hope you who may be presently classified as one who is saved "so as by fire" will see your true standing and do something about it now. Today and for the rest of your life may you plan and pray, say and do things that will *win the "well done"* from the Judge, who is the just One in that day.

Matthew 6: 20,21 should be motivating, *"For where your treasure is,* there will your *heart* be also." Banks are safe to a certain degree, but some are robbed and others collapse. Why not invest in heaven's bank?

Let the Lord admonish and motivate you by reading the verses in the chapter outline that you may reap a full reward. Meditate on Revelation 3:11, "Behold I come quickly: *hold that fast which thou hast; that no man take thy crown."*

Marriage Made in Heaven

When I have married a marvelously matched couple in holy matrimony, they say that it was *"a marriage made in heaven."* This, of course, is saying that the match is a perfect pair; but the Lord reserves the best for last. The royal wedding *between the Bridegroom and the bride* will be the most glorious ever witnessed in heaven or on earth, whether the match previously was prince or pauper. Observe this holy occasion *witnessed by, I believe, angels and martyrs.*

Marriage of the King's Son (Matthew 22:1-14)

Officiating at this high and holy wedding is God the Father Himself. He brings together by divine choice a bride that shall be united in holy matrimony to His Royal Son (Matthew 22:2). It was God that brought, in the beginning, *Eve to Adam* and *united* them as husband and wife. He must do that also with *His chosen bride,* uniting them as one with His Son, the *Second Adam,* at the end of this age.

"The kingdom of heaven is like unto a certain King which made a marriage for His Son." Here God is presented as the Father of Jesus, which is only natural. He is the *"certain King* which made a marriage for His Son." Of course the Son is rightly suited as the Bridegroom. For a better understanding of this parable, the parable of *The Ten Virgins* will help to increase and enlighten your minds and hearts on this fabulous honeymoon in heaven.

With the ten virgins in Matthew 25:1-12, we learn that *fifty percent* of the professed church, represented as virgins, are *disqualified,* because they have not the oil, typical to the third Person, the Holy Spirit. Dear reader, will you be among those that are ready, identified as *wise* when the Bridegroom comes, and be wise in the Word?

In the parable of The Marriage of the King's Son, we see also a large number that are *invited* but do not respond. Their excuse eliminates them from the reception. Verses 9 and 10 show the true character of those that responded to the servant's invitation from the King. Take note of the expression *"as many."* This phrase applies generally to God's people. Let me point out a few passages:

John 1:12, "But *as many* as received Him, to them gave he power to become the sons of God, even to them that believe on His name."

John 17:2, "As Thou hast given him power over all flesh, that He should give eternal life to *as many* as thou hast given Him."

Acts 13:48, "And when the Gentiles heard this, they were glad, and glorified the Word of the Lord: and *as many* as were ordained to eternal life believed."

Once again, in verse 9 of Matthew 22 we see that the servants who were sent out were told, ". . . *as many* as you shall find, bid to the marriage." Verse 10, "So those servants went out into the highways, and gathered together *(irresistible call)* all *as many* as were found. . ." The elect were found by God's servants.

In the last analysis, out of the many called, some are not genuine. They prove deficient in salvation as was Demas, a helper to the apostle Paul who later went back into the world. "Many are called, but few are chosen" (verse 14). Some that are called will be revealed in due time to be counterfeit, but none of God's *chosen* will fail. They endure to the end, and will be present around the throne.

The most impressive passages on this heavenly wedding is Revelation 19:6–9. Here is the bride, the church, as she is "arrayed in fine linen, clean and white; for the fine linen is the righteousness of the saints." She is called "His wife." A similar Scripture is found in 21:9, "Come here, I will show you the bride, the Lamb's wife." We are His bride, or as it says in Revelation 17:14 ". . . they that are with Him (Christ) are *called, and chosen, and faithful.*"

The Invited Guest

John 3:29, "He that hath the bride is the bridegroom: but the friends of the Bridegroom, which standeth and heareth him, rejoiceth greatly because of the Bridegroom's voice: this my joy therefore is fulfilled."

John the Baptist is speaking and refers to himself as "the *friend* of the *Bridegroom.*" John represents the guest at the marriage in the position of the Old Testament saints, not as a member of the church. When he was beheaded as a martyr, he portrayed those in the *tribulation* that were welcomed as *martyrs into the heavenly host* and the marriage supper of the Lamb.

Revelation 6:9–11, "And when he had opened the fifth seal, I saw under the altar, the souls of them that were slain for the word of God, and for the testimony which they held; and they cried with a loud voice, saying, How long, O Lord, holy and true, dost Thou not judge and avenge our blood on them that dwell on the earth? And white robes were given unto every one of them; and it was said unto them, that they should rest yet for a little season, until their fellow servants also and their brethren, that should be killed as they were, should be fulfilled."

These all are martyred that come out of the tribulation period and join the heavenly host.

Then Revelation 7:13,14 says, "And one of the elders answered, saying unto me, What are these which are arrayed in white robes? and whence came they? And I said unto him, Sir, thou knowest. And he said to me, These are they which came out of *great tribulation,* and have washed their robes, and made them white in the blood of the Lamb."

It is clear also where these came from, who appeared at the Great Supper celebration. This can be compared with Matthew 24:21,22: "For then shall be great tribulation, such as was not since the beginning of the world to this time, no, nor ever shall be. And except those days should be shortened, there should no flesh be saved: but for the elect's sake those days shall be shortened."

Lastly, in Revelation 20:4 we see, "And I saw thrones, and they sat upon them, and judgment was given unto them: and I saw the souls of them that were beheaded for the witness of Jesus, and for the word of God, and which had not worshipped the beast, neither his image, neither had received his mark upon their foreheads, or in their hands; and *they lived and reigned with Christ a thousand years.*"

These martyrs accompany the rest in heaven out of the tribulation, those that refused to worship the beast and his image.

The Last Step in the First Resurrection

Regarding the martyrs, this fourth verse says, "*they lived* and reigned with Christ..." They were resurrected after being decapitated. They are the welcomed guests and friends of the Bridegroom and the bride, on this auspicious occasion.

The Final Part of the Harvest

The last phase of the "resurrection of the just" deals with the Jews, taken from Daniel 12:2, "And many of them that sleep in the dust of the earth shall awake, *some to everlasting life,* and some to shame and everlasting contempt."

This resurrection completes the first resurrection, as the gleanings of the *harvest*.

Revelation 20:6, "Blessed and holy is he that hath part in the first resurrection: on such the second death hath no power."

Revelation of Christ With His Saints

As we prepare for the second stage of His glorious return, just a few closing but well-chosen comments from Scripture before ending this exciting study in God's time line of momentous events.

Here in the following passages let us see our Lord Jesus, now ready to appear as the *"King of kings"* with His saints, to descend upon the earth.

Titus 2:13, "Looking for that blessed hope, and the glorious appearing of the great God and our Savior Jesus Christ."

With Christ we have the "blessed hope." Without Him, life is a hopeless end.

Revelation 1:7, "Behold, He cometh with clouds; *and every eye shall see Him,* and they also which pierced Him: and *all kindreds of the earth* shall wail because of Him. Even so, Amen."

This verse reveals largely a Christ-rejected world upon His return, for they "wail because of Him."

Revelation 5:10, "And hast made us unto our God kings and priests: and we shall reign on the earth."

Believers are to be given positions of authority, as they will reign with Him on the *earth "as kings and priests."* Look at these words written by Henry Smart,

> *Lead on, O King Eternal,*
> *The day of march has come;*
> *Henceforth in fields of conquest*
> *Thy tents shall be our home;*
> *Through days of preparation*
> *Thy grace has made us strong,*
> *And now, O King Eternal,*
> *We lift our battle song.*

The next thrilling scene takes us from the marriage supper of the Lamb to the great and final Battle of Armageddon, that ends the wars of the world. After facing this global confrontation and defeat of satanic world power, we will see the judgment of the nations separated, as a shepherd divides His sheep from the goats.

Then the last dispensation comes into full view in the millennial reign, where we will learn war no more under the Prince of Peace, *as our Lord sets up His theocratic kingdom on earth in fulfillment of God's yet unfulfilled prophecy.*

• • •

Questionnaire

1. What is another Scriptural name taken from the Bible regarding the Second Coming?
2. Name two of the most important people among the saints of the Old Testament.
3. What are the two stages in the Second Coming called?
4. Give an example from Scripture of the rapture.
5. Name the church in Revelation among the seven that will be taken.
6. Name the church that will be left.
7. Is there any mention of the church or bride on earth between Revelation 4 and Revelation 18?
8. Give your position regarding the three views of the Lord's coming, and support it by a few Scriptures.
9. Give your position regarding the church going into the tribulation or being spared from it.
10. Which comes first, the resurrection of the bodies of believers in Christ or the translated saints?
11. Can the Judgment Seat of Christ, based on Romans 14:10 and 2 Corinthians 5:10, be applied to the term "general judgment" or "special judgment"? Underline one.
12. Does the Judgment Seat of Christ refer to only the church and all believers, or both the saved and lost?
13. What is the purpose of this judgment?
14. Where does The Marriage of the King's Son take place?
15. Where do the guests come from?
16. What does "eschatalogical" mean?
17. Why are people martyred in the tribulation?
18. Are any people saved during the tribulation? Who?

ASCENDING TO MEET OUR LORD IN THE AIR

19. What kind of people will be considered in the gleanings of the harvest?
20. Name the two resurrections and what separates them.

● ● ●

Answers

1. Blessed hope
2. Abraham and Moses
3. The rapture of Christ for His saints and the revelation of Christ with His saints.
4. Noah; Lot; or one taken and the other left.
5. Philadelphia
6. Laodicia
7. No.
8. Premillennial — Thessalonians 4:17; Revelation 20.
9. The whole church raised before tribulation in the resurrection of the just.
10. Resurrection of bodies
11. Special judgment
12. The church and all believers
13. To reward the righteous
14. In heaven
15. The martyrs in the tribulation
16. Last days
17. They refuse to receive the mark of the beast.
18. Yes—144,000 plus Gentiles
19. Old Testament saints. (The gleanings of the harvest represent the completion of the "resurrection of the just.")
20. Resurrection of the righteous and the resurrection of damnation, separated by the millennium.

Chapter 11

Descending With Our Lord on Earth to Reign With Our Ruling King in the Last World Community
-or-
Christ's Judgment of the Living Nations With a Loving Eye on Israel in the Millennial Age

Thought
God once again will send His Son, not to serve, but to rule.

• • •

I. The indescribable coronation of Christ [a young Prince takes the Crown of Diadem]
   A. Scenes of the saints before the throne proclaiming Him King
   B. Scriptural description (Isaiah 32:1; Revelation 4:4,10; 5:9–14; 7:9–12; 11:15–17; 14:3–5; 15:3,4; 19:1,4–6; Psalm 72:8–11; Isaiah 45:23; Romans 14:11; Daniel 7:13,14)
   C. *The King appoints positions* to the faithful in the millennial kingdom
      1. To the apostles (Luke 22:28–30; Matthew 19:28)
      2. To the Church (Luke 19:17,19; 1 Corinthians 15:40–42; 6:2, 3; 9:25; Revelation 1:6; 2:26,27; 5:10)
      3. To other saints (Daniel 7:18,27; 12:3; Revelation 5:9,10; 20:4)
II. *The most colorful royal wedding ever witnessed*
   A. The Son takes a wife given by the Father in the former Dispensation of Grace (Ephesians 1:4; 5:25; John 3:29; Revelation 21:9; 22:17)
   B. Scriptural description (Revelation 19:7–9; Isaiah 61:10; 62:5; Jeremiah 33:11)

III. *The descent of the Unconquerable One* with His armies to the earth (Revelation 14:14,15; 17:14; 19:11,13-16,19,20; Isaiah 9:6-7; Zechariah 6:12,13; 14:1-4)
   A. Three indestructible companies
      1. The holy angels (2 Thessalonians 1:7-10)
      2. The New Testament saints as the Church (Revelation 19:8,11,14)
      3. The Old Testament and Tribulation saints (Daniel 12:1,2; Revelation 18:24; 20:4,5)
   B. *The Battle of Armageddon* (Revelation 17:14; 19:15,19; Psalm 2:2-6; 45:2-5; Revelation 16:14,16)
      1. The fowls feast on the fallen (Revelation 19:17,18,21)
      2. The beast and false prophet captured and cast alive into perdition (Revelation 19:20)
      3. The beast and false prophet—their work of deception through spurious miracles (Revelation 13:14; 16:14)
      4. The old Devil seized and imprisoned for a thousand years (Revelation 20:2)

IV. *The divine division of the living nations* (Matthew 25:31-45)
   A. The Shepherd King divides the sheep from the goats (Matthew 25:32)
   B. Three world groups
      1. The sheep—believers (Matthew 25:33,34,40)
      2. The goats—unbelievers (Matthew 25:41,46)
      3. The brethren—Jews (Matthew 25:40)

V. *The world under a new Ruler* (Daniel 7:13,14,27)
   A. Conditions in the millennium
      1. A time of peace (Isaiah 2:4, 9:6,7; Zechariah 9:10)
      2. A time of comfort (Isaiah 40:1,2; 51:3)
      3. A time of health (Isaiah 33:24; Jeremiah 30:17)
      4. A time of prosperity (Isaiah 65:21-23)
      5. A time of harmony among animals (Isaiah 11:6-9)

6. A time of unity of language (Zephaniah 3:9)

7. A time of universal, unified worship (Isaiah 45:23; Zechariah 14:16; Malachi 1:11, Revelation 5:9,10)

B. *Satan's last stand* and final work of deception (Revelation 20:7–10)

VI. Questionnaire and Answers

• • •

This eleventh chapter immediately reminds me of the great clock in God's program of time that is about to strike. The events in God's calendar may take place within the course of our lives, which is encompassed in this chapter. Are you ready for what lies ahead, as we deal with a number of exciting events that believers will soon experience? It is generally conceded by students of the Bible that the end is very near. In our last chapter, we left you in glory with our Lord around the throne.

The Coronation of Christ

By the help of the Holy Spirit, we shall now see *scenes of the saints* in the presence of God, as attention of all the holy residents of heaven fix their eyes on Christ, the climax and consummation of all things.

As we develop this thrilling chapter, we shall merely introduce you to one of the many Scriptures on this crowning corner of the truth. We believe that the Holy Spirit is able to reveal the truth, once set forth from the source of all truth, the Bible.

Isaiah 32:1, "Behold [something of great importance], a King (Christ) *shall* reign in righteousness..." *Shall* denotes it is yet future. As we proceed to look in chronological order at God's last book, *Revelation,* we shall see the saints around the throne proclaiming Him King. God wrote but one Book, and in it He speaks with a tongue that is never false, writes words that are always true, and works with a hand that never fails.

Scene 1: The Reception of the Whole Church

Revelation 4:4,10,11, "And round about the throne were four and twenty seats: and upon the seats I saw four and twenty elders sitting, clothed in white raiment; and they had on their heads crowns of gold. The four and twenty elders fall down before Him that sat on the throne, and *worship Him* that liveth for ever and ever, and cast their crowns before the throne..."

These verses speak of the church being raptured as previously referred to. In this initial scene, the church is called up and is not seen again on earth till she returns with her Lord. The twenty-four elders who represent the complete church receive their rewards and cast their crowns before the Redeemer, who sits upon the throne. They proclaim Him worthy to receive glory, honor, and power, because He is the Creator. For His pleasure were all things created.

Scene II: Songs of Praise Given by the Saints to the Lamb

Revelation 5:9,10, "And they sung a new song, saying, Thou art worthy to take the book, and to open the seals thereof: for thou wast slain, and hast redeemed us to God by thy blood out of every kindred, and tongue, and people, and nation; and hast *made us unto our God kings and priests: and we shall reign on the earth.*"

"The four beasts" in verse 11 can be translated "the four living creatures." The crescendo of praise swells in volume (verse 12) that exceeds the first halleluia with the words, "Worthy is the Lamb that was slain (not only to receive glory, honor, and power, but now *angels blend their voices with the saints in this coronation chorus,* by adding that the Lamb is worthy) to receive . . . riches, and wisdom, and strength, and . . . blessing (praise).''

Scene III: The Great Multitude Increases to a Numberless Number

Revelation 7:9–12, "After this I beheld, and, lo, a *great multitude, which no man could number,* of all nations, and kindreds, and people, and tongues, stood before the throne, and before the Lamb, clothed with white robes, and palms in their hands: and cried with a loud voice, saying, Salvation to our God which sitteth upon the throne, and unto the Lamb. And all the *angels* stood round about the throne, and about the *elders,* and the four beasts, and fell before the throne on their faces, *and worshipped God,* saying, Amen: Blessing, and glory, and wisdom, and thanksgiving, and honour, and power, and might, be unto our God for ever and ever. Amen."

The praise of this exceeding great multitude now appearing before the throne centers their song in salvation, saying, "Salvation to *our God* which sitteth upon the throne, and to *the Lamb.*"

Scene IV: Solemn Worship to God in Christ Because of a Transfer of World Power

Revelation 11:15-17, "And the seventh angel sounded: and there were great voices in heaven, saying, The kingdoms of this world are become the kingdoms of our Lord, and of His Christ; and He shall reign for ever and ever. And the four and twenty elders, which sat before God on their seats, fell upon their faces and worshipped God, saying, We give Thee thanks, O Lord God Almighty, which art, and wast, and art to come; because Thou hast taken to Thee Thy great power, and hast reigned."

The time is rapidly approaching when the kingdoms of this world will become the kingdom of our Lord. *He will never relinquish the power* of the throne again to sinful men or to the one behind the scene, Satan.

Scene V: A Song Only the Firstfruits of God's Redeemed Can Sing

Revelation 14:3-5, "And they sung as it were a new song before the throne and before the four beasts, and the elders; and no man could learn that song but the *hundred and forty and four thousand,* which were redeemed from the earth. These are they which were not defiled with women; for they are virgins. These are they which follow the Lamb whithersoever He goeth. These were redeemed from among men, being the *firstfruits* unto God and to the Lamb. And in their mouth was found no guile; for they are without fault before the throne of God."

Herein is that saying true, "The first shall be last . . ." The Jews were the firstfruits. "To the Jew first, then to the Gentile." What the Jewish apostles started in the beginning, the 144,000 evangelists will finish as they preach the *everlasting Gospel* to every nation at the end, to complete the Great Tribulation period on earth. Check out also verse 6 in this chapter.

Scene VI: Both Jews and Gentiles Proclaim Jesus King of Saints

Revelation 15:3,4, "And *they* sing the *song of Moses the servant of God, and the song of the Lamb,* saying, Great and marvelous are Thy works, Lord God Almighty; just and true are Thy ways, Thou King of saints. Who shall not fear thee, O Lord, and glorify thy name? For Thou only art holy: *for all nations shall come and worship before Thee;* for thy judgments are made manifest."

Here we get a glimpse of the reign of Christ on earth in that 1,000 year generation, when all nations shall come and worship Him. This too is an unquestionable, irreversible argument that our Lord Jesus Christ will yet come to earth and reign, according to Scripture.

Scene VII: The Last Note of Praise Before the Descension

Revelation 19:1,4–6, "And after these things I heard a great voice of much people in heaven, saying, Alleluia; salvation, and glory, and honour, and power, unto the Lord our God: and the four and twenty elders and the four beasts fell down and worshipped God that sat on the throne, saying, Amen; Alleluia. And a voice came out of the throne, saying, Praise our God, all ye his servants, and ye that fear Him, *both small and great.* And I heard as it were the voice of a *great multitude,* and as the voice of many waters, and as the voice of mighty thunderings, saying, *Alleluia: for the Lord God omnipotent reigneth.*" Pause, and think on this.

Let us practice up on this "halleluia chorus," whether we be small or great, to be in harmony as part of that great throng, saying, "Halleluia (meaning *Praise Jehovah, Jesus*), for the Lord God omnipotent *reigneth* (Christ)." The other Scriptures given in the outline form can be compared to this particular time also.

During the interludes of praise, the King appoints positions of honor and authority to the faithful throughout the millennium, prior to the descent upon earth.

Positions of Honor

To the Apostles

Luke 22:28–30, "Ye are they which have continued with me in my temptations. And *I appoint unto you a kingdom,* as my Father hath appointed unto Me: that ye may eat and drink at my table in My kingdom, and *sit on thrones* judging the *twelve tribes* of Israel."

Notice the last verse, especially where the apostles, who have been appointed by Christ, "will sit on thrones judging the twelve tribes of Israel."

The Scriptures from Luke are repeated in Matthew 19:28–30 as well, to give greater potency to the passage.

To the Church

Luke 19:17–19, "And He said unto him, Well, thou good servant:

because thou hast been faithful in a very little, have thou *authority over ten cities*. And the second came, saying, Lord, thy pound hath gained five pounds. And He said likewise to him, Be thou also over five cities."

It seems to me that our gracious Lord will go above and beyond our worth to Him, in suggesting those faithful in a *"very little"* will receive His authority to rule over as many as ten cities. I think the greater our faithfulness in this life, the more power and authority will be given us to rule with Him on this terrestrial globe. Astounding! Amazing, but true!

1 Corinthians 15:40–42, "There are also celestial bodies, and bodies terrestrial: but the glory of the celestial is one, and the glory of the terrestrial is another. There is one glory of the sun, and another glory of the moon, and another glory of the stars: for one star differeth from another star in glory. *So also is the resurrection of the dead* [believers]. It is sown in corruption; it is raised in *incorruption*."

Brother Paul points out, especially in verse 41, that there shall be given degrees of authority similar to the heavenly bodies in the brightness of their glory, reflecting even the *Sun* of glory, as the Son of God. Malachi 4:2, "*Sun* of righteousness (Christ)." It is certain there shall be degrees of rewards, as there will be degrees of punishments (Luke 12:47,48).

1 Corinthians 6:2,3, "*Do ye not know that the saints shall judge the world?* and if the world shall be judged by you, are ye unworthy to judge the smallest matter? Know ye not that we shall judge angels? how much more things that pertain to this life?"

Our discretion of judgment will extend beyond this life to the millennium.

1 Corinthians 9:25, "And every man that striveth for the mastery is temperate in all things. Now they do it to obtain a corruptible crown; but *we an incorruptible*."

We shall reign as *kings* with Him being given incorruptible crowns for identification in the millennium.

Revelation 1:6, "And hath made us kings and priests unto God and his Father; to Him be glory and dominion for ever and ever. Amen."

Some translators translate this verse "*a kingdom of priests*." Such would do away with the thought of reigning with Christ as kings over cities and even nations. Nevertheless, the testimony of Jesus stands in favor of kings rather than "a kingdom," for the same is true in Revelation 5:10 [praise God!]. Compare with the above. Only here we are told where their assigned realm will be, and it is definitely stated "on the earth."

For further confirmation, see Revelation 2:26,27, where Jesus speaks with the authority of God:

"And he that overcometh, and keepeth my works unto the end, *to him will I give power over the nations:* and *he* shall rule them with a rod of iron; as the vessels of a potter shall they be broken to shivers: even as I received of my Father."

Now in verse 27 the phrase "*he* shall rule" does not refer to Christ but to the kingship of royal *believers.* In the same way that Jesus received His authority from the Father, Jesus will honor believers with the same divine authority.

Notice also Proverbs 29:2: "When the righteous are in authority, the people rejoice; but when the wicked beareth rule, the people mourn."

To Other Saints of the Old Testament and Those That Came Out of the Great Tribulation

Daniel 7:18,27 (Old Testament saints), "But the saints of the most High shall take the kingdom, and possess the kingdom for ever, even for ever and ever. And the kingdom and dominion, and the greatness of the kingdom under the whole heaven, shall be given to the people of the saints of the most High, whose kingdom is an everlasting kingdom, and all dominions shall serve and obey him."

Daniel 12:3, "And they that be wise shall shine as the brightness of the firmament; and they that turn many to righteousness as the stars for ever and ever."

Are you doing what *you* can now under the leading of the Holy Spirit, to turn many to righteousness through personal witnessing, teaching and preaching? If so, you will never regret it, and neither shall those won ever regret being told about Jesus, their only Savior from sin, death and hell.

Revelation 5:9,10 (tribulation saints), "And *they* sung a new song, saying, Thou art worthy to take the book, and to open the seals thereof: for thou wast slain, and hast redeemed us to God by thy blood out of every kindred, and tongue, and people, and nation: and hast made us unto our God kings and priests: and *we* shall reign on the earth."

Revelation 20:4 (tribulation saints), "And I saw *thrones,* and they sat upon them, and judgment was given unto them: and I saw the souls of them that were beheaded for the witness of Jesus, and for the word of God, and which *had not worshipped the beast,* neither his image, neither had received his mark upon their foreheads, or in their hands; and *they lived and reigned with Christ a thousand years.*"

The Lord sometimes holds His best for last.

We now come to visualize the royal wedding in this great heavenly reception, which is the *last taste of the old heaven.* This is to be remembered as something of splendor and glory, before joining our Lord in His descent to the earth. At this time we have all received our eternal rewards and glorified bodies, along with our earthly assignments.

Now, in the Spirit, accompanied with the aid of Holy Scripture, let us see this most colorful event.

The Royal Wedding

Revelation 19:7–9, "Let us be glad and rejoice, and give honor to Him: for the *marriage of the Lamb* is come, and His wife hath made herself ready. And to her was granted that she should be arrayed in fine linen, clean and white: for the *fine linen is the righteousness of saints.* And He saith unto me, Write, Blessed are they which are called unto the marriage supper of the Lamb. And He saith unto me, These are the true sayings of God."

Also read Ephesians 1:4; 5:25; John 3:29; Revelation 21:9 and 22:17 for extra help.

To whom does our Lord address these weighty words? It is to the *bride,* His church, now to become "His wife." His wife is also translated "His bride," which I believe is more accurate here, because she is in the process of becoming His wife. "The fine linen clean and white" stands for the acts of the righteous. Moreover, this garment of white is the attire of all the saints, splendidly decorated as to their ranks arranged by the King. Now with them He is ready to display His force and power, followed by His armies that are mounted on white horses. Surely this revelation will make a fearful appearance to the godless world below, who had been given room to repent.

For a further beautiful and personal description of the bride, read Isaiah 61:10, combined with Isaiah 62:5 and Jeremiah 33:11. We must say from Isaiah 62:5 that the bride in this relation is being used not as one person but many in the term, "so shall Thy *sons* marry Thee (Christ): and as the bridegroom rejoiceth over the bride, so shall Thy God rejoice over you (collective)."

Bear in mind that this divine bride of Christ was given by the Father to the Son, in the narrative of our earlier study of the Old Testament. *Abraham, typifying God; Isaac, Christ;* and *Rebecca as the bride* brought to Christ by the (oldest or chief) servant of Abraham named *Eliezer,* resembling the *work of the Holy Spirit* (Genesis 24:2; 15:2). Then of course she was chosen by God the Father before the foundation of the world, as previously announced in Ephesians 1:4: "According as He hath chosen us in Him before the foundation of the world, that we should be holy and without blame before Him in love."

The Return Of Christ

Revelation 14:14,15, "I looked, and behold a white cloud, and upon the cloud one sat like unto the Son of man, having on His head a golden crown, and in His hand a sharp sickle. And another angel came out of the temple, crying with a loud voice to Him that sat on the cloud, Thrust in thy sickle, and reap; for the time is come for thee to reap; for the harvest of the earth is ripe." Compare Daniel 7:13,14 and Zechariah 14:3,4.

Revelation 17:14, "These shall make war with the Lamb, and the Lamb shall overcome them: for He is Lord of lords, and King of kings: and they that are with Him are *called, and chosen, and faithful.*"

Revelation 19:11,13–16,19,20, "And I saw heaven opened, and behold a white horse; and He that sat upon him was called Faithful and True, and in righteousness He doth judge and make war. And He was clothed with a vesture dipped in blood: and His name is called The Word of God. And the armies which were in heaven followed Him upon white horses clothed in fine linen, white and clean. And out of His mouth goeth a sharp sword, that with it he should smite the nations: and He shall rule them with a rod of iron: and He treadeth the winepress of the fierceness and wrath of Almighty God. And He hath on His vesture and on His thigh a name written, *KING OF KINGS, AND LORD OF LORDS.* And I saw an angel standing in the sun: and he cried with a loud voice, saying to all the fowls that fly in the midst of heaven. Come and gather yourselves together unto the supper of the great God; *and I saw the beast, and the kings of the earth, and their armies, gathered together to make war against Him that sat on the horse, and against His army.* And the *beast* was taken, and with him the *false prophet* that wrought *miracles* before him, with which he *deceived* them that had received the mark of the beast, and them that worshipped his image. These both were *cast alive into a lake of fire* burning with brimstone"

Isaiah 9:6,7, "For unto us a child is born, unto us a son is given: and the *government shall be upon His shoulder:* and *His name* shall be *called Wonderful Counsellor, The mighty God, The everlasting Father, The Prince of Peace.* Of the increase of His government and peace there shall be no end, upon the *throne of David,* and upon His kingdom, to order it, and to establish it with judgment and with justice from henceforth even for ever. The zeal of the Lord of hosts will perform this."

Considerations of the Above Interpretations

First Consideration: The Twofold Harvest (Revelation 14:14,15)

For the full picture, read the rest of the chapter.

Here you will see a twofold harvest. First, representing Christ, previewing what He will do by coming out of a *white cloud* (Acts 1:9), a cloud receives Jesus up as He ascended. In verse 11, the eyewitnesses say that "this same Jesus which is taken up . . . into heaven, shall so come. . ."

The Lord is seated on this white cloud, which could resemble a white horse, as He also is said to resemble the Son of Man, having on His head a golden crown. *Not the victor's crown,* but the *diadem of gold,* signifying His regal crown of gold, speaking of royalty and dignity. He also is seen with a sickle, sharpened for the harvesting of God's elect ones before the wrath of God falls on the wicked. For a great companion Scripture to this, you must read for a clearer understanding "The Parable of the Wheat and Tares" in Matthew 13:30, and the interpretation in verses 38–43. This coincides with the verses above.

Second Consideration: The Crowned Conqueror

Revelation 17:14, "These," the earthly enemies that band together against the Lamb as a world confederation, are dealt with speedily with the sword of His mouth. Revelation 19:15 connects with 2 Thessalonians 2:8.

Furthermore, from verse 14 above, the word *"they"* is different from the first word *"these,"* speaking of His fierce foe. Following the King of kings we see a huge heavenly host on white horses, representing the "called, chosen and faithful." It appears that this endless column of armies in royal splendor had little to do in the campaign against the wicked world. As usual, God in Christ was their commander and fought for them, for *"the battle is the Lord's,"* so says the Scripture. They were the eyewitnesses of this present evil world destruction, when our Great Commander and Chief smites the nations with His sword (Revelation 19:15).

Third Consideration: The Names of the Rider on the White Horse (Revelation 19:11)

Here again we have no doubt as to the One on the white horse. Verse 13 reveals His identity being none other than "The Word of God." This is that special name that John represents Him as, when introducing his Gospel. The rest of the chapter is like a puzzle nearly finished, yet it just falls into place.

Verse 14, "The armies of heaven." Compare Joel 2:11 with Daniel 4:35.

I cannot refrain from saying that these are great passages of Scripture enforcing the truth that unfolds before us. Don't miss the blessing by not looking them up.

Verse 16, *"King of kings* and *Lord of lords."*

There are none more powerful than He. From verse 13, His original name is given with a vesture (garment) dipped in blood. Here is a twofold application: His own blood shed for the elect, and now the blood of the unbelievers shed worldwide, who rejected the Christ of the cross and now receive their just deserts. This is what we might call God's "reign of terror" upon the wicked. This final momentous battle is first fought in the Holy Land. It is the day of vengeance and divine retribution, locally and geographically.

Verse 19: The two forces from heaven and on earth collide. The international armies of evil declare war against Christ and His armies of righteousness. With Christ on our side there is *"no contest."* The flashing sword of Christ strikes the first and last blow, and consumes His and our enemies from the field of battle.

Verse 20. The *"beast"* representing the world's political head is taken along with the "false prophet." This antichrist has satanic power to perform miracles. Now their day in the sun has gone down. Both of these political and religious leaders are against Christ, seized alive and cast headlong into the "lake of fire." These two are the first to be "cast alive" into God's *new* permanent penitentiary. The Devil later (Revelation 20:10) will join them that make up the false trinity in the Devil's religious work of deception.

In Chapter 20 of Revelation, John, under the power of the Holy Spirit, introduces the millennium.

Fourth Consideration: The Millennial King

Isaiah 7:14; 9:6,7. These passages give us the background work of Isaiah, the prophet, as he in the same Spirit describes the Kingly reign of the Redeemer. Isaiah strikingly unfolds the future upon which we now write. The Christ of the Old and New Testament becomes in a manifold way the fulfillment of prophecy, revealing the Christ of the millennium.

Lesson 1—His Virgin Birth

This miraculously-born Son of a virgin is given the government of the world. This same view was shared by the Jewish nation when Christ came the first time. They thought He would crush the Roman yoke and take the reins of government upon His shoulders at that time. Isaiah 7:14, "Behold, a virgin shall conceive..."

Lesson 2—His Political or Theocratical Reign

His name "Emmanuel" (Matthew 1:23), meaning "God with us," is seen in what He was to be called (Isaiah 7:14), "Wonderful Counsellor, mighty God, everlasting Father, and Prince of Peace." This all must yet be fulfilled in the future, when Jesus rules the world under His theocratic reign (Isaiah 9:6,7).

Lesson 3—His Prophetical Reign Fulfilled

His government replaces the Davidic government. This millennial kingdom is established in judgment and justice. That long but temporary kingdom will be absorbed in the eternal kingdom.

Luke 1:32,33, "He shall be great, and shall be called the Son of the Highest: and the Lord God shall give unto Him the throne of His father David. And He shall reign over the house of Jacob for ever; and of His kingdom there shall be no end."

Fifth Consideration: The Twofold Nature of This New Ruler (Zechariah 6:13)

This perfect Person is here called "The Branch." He has a twofold relationship as *Priest.* He shall minister through the temple also as *King* and shall rule worldwide. Christ Jesus has both the qualities of the perfect High Priest and that of a Kingly Prince, to reign both in the millennium and in eternity. For so it shall be.

Sixth Consideration: An Old Testament Preview of the Judgment of the Living Nations

I am in this particular area using the order of the books in the Bible, rather than the order of events.

This can be followed from Joel 3:12 as well as Matthew 25:31–46. In this Old Testament prophecy, we are told *where Christ shall reign,* and as you can well imagine, it will be in the Holy City, Jerusalem (Joel 3:17,20).

The Battle of Armageddon

See with me, through the eye of faith, three indestructible companies:

1. The Holy Angels

2 Thessalonians 1:7–10, "And to you who are troubled rest with us, when the Lord Jesus shall be revealed from heaven with *His mighty angels,* in flaming fire taking vengeance on them that know not God, and that obey not the gospel of our Lord Jesus Christ: who shall be punished with everlasting destruction from the presence of the Lord, and from the glory of His power: when He shall come to be glorified in His saints, and to be admired in *all them that believe* (because our testimony among you was believed) in that day."

2. The New Testament Saints as the Church.

Revelation 19:8,11,14, "And to *her* was granted that she should be arrayed in fine linen, clean and white: for the fine linen is the righteousness of saints. And I saw heaven opened, and behold a white horse; and He that sat upon him was called Faithful and True, and in righteousness He doth judge and make war. And the *armies which were in heaven* followed Him upon white horses, clothed in fine linen, white and clean."

3. The Other Saints From the Old Testament and From the Tribulation

Daniel 12:1,2, "And at that time shall Michael stand up, the great Prince which standeth for the children of Thy people: and there shall be a time of trouble, such as never was since there was a nation even to that same time: and at that time Thy people shall be delivered, every one that shall be found written in the Book. And many of them that sleep in the dust of the earth shall awake, *some to everlasting life,* and some to shame and everlasting contempt."

Revelation 18:24, "And in her was found *the blood of prophets, and of saints,* and of all that were slain upon the earth." Revelation 20:4,5, "And I saw thrones, and they sat upon them, and judgment was given unto them: and I saw the souls of them that were beheaded for the witness of Jesus, and for the Word of God, and which had not worshipped the beast, neither his image, neither had received his mark upon their foreheads or in their hands; and *they lived and reigned* with Christ a thousand years. But the *rest of the dead* lived not again until the thousand years were finished. *This is the first resurrection.*"

Psalm 2:2–6, "The kings of the earth set themselves, and the rulers take counsel together, *against the Lord, and against His anointed,* saying, Let us break their bands asunder, and cast away their cords from us. He that sitteth in the heavens shall laugh: *the Lord shall have them in derision.* Then shall He speak unto them in *His wrath,* and vex them in His sore displeasure. Yet have I set my *King* upon my holy hill of Zion."

From Revelation 19:17,18 and 21, "And I saw an angel standing in the sun: and he cried with a loud voice, saying to all the fowls that fly in the midst of heaven, Come and gather yourselves together unto the supper of the great God; that ye may eat the flesh of kings, and the flesh of captains, and the flesh of mighty men, and the flesh of horses, and to them that sit on them, and the flesh of all men, both free and bond, both small and great. And the remnant were slain with the sword of Him that sat upon the horse, which sword proceeded out of His mouth: and all the fowls were filled with their flesh." We understand that the *fowls feast to their full on the fallen masses of men, destroyed by the Christ of warfare.* Herein is that saying true. It is "the war that ends all wars."

Living Nations Judged

It must be invariably true in the devastation when the Lord returns to earth, that many out of the surviving nations will be subjected to the judgment of Christ, as to who will be saved and who will be lost, *who will enter the millennial kingdom, and who will not.*

Before the Gentile nations are judged, however, God has promised

DESCENDING WITH OUR LORD TO REIGN

to save at the end the nation of Israel. They are judged first, after our Lord's arrival to earth—those who have endured the tribulation period and therefore punished for their national rejection of Christ when Pilate offered Him to that nation. (Compare Ezekiel 20:37 with Romans 11:26,27.)

Paul uses the expression *"as it is written,"* but he does not tell us where. If you will notice what Isaiah 59:20 has to say, you will have the place Paul had in mind, but where the King James Version says "Redeemer," it should perhaps be preferred *"Deliverer,"* for so it will be. (Compare Jeremiah 31:34 with Hebrews 8:10–12, the fulfillment.)

Notice now in the Gospel of Matthew, Chapter 25, verses 31 and 32: "When the Son of man shall come in His glory, and all the holy angels with Him, then shall He sit upon the throne of His glory: and before Him shall be gathered *all nations:* and He shall separate them one from another, as a shepherd divideth his sheep from the goats." Notice this judgment of the living Gentiles is *not in heaven,* but on earth. This takes place following His glorious return to earth, His Second Advent.

It is said in Revelation 1:7, "Behold, He cometh with clouds; and *every eye* shall see Him." Visualize this possibility if you can—the civilized world watching television, when all of a sudden He appears. We have described His coming from Scripture, when "every eye shall [then] see Him, and they also which pierced Him: and all kindreds of the *earth* shall wail because of Him. Even so, Amen." This we have continually affirmed as the *Revelation* of Jesus Christ to the earth with His saints.

The Divine Division

See now three world groups:

1. The sheep as believers.

Matthew 25:33,34,40, "And He shall set *the sheep* on His right hand, but *the goats* on the left. Then shall the King say unto them on His right hand, Come, ye blessed of My Father, inherit the kingdom prepared for you from the foundation of the world: and the King shall answer and say unto them, Verily I say unto you, Inasmuch as ye have done it unto one of the least of these *My brethren,* ye have done it unto Me."

Notice the sheep are placed on His right hand, the position of honor. The sheep have always been referred to as God's people. Christ certainly fits the beloved title, "The Good Shepherd," who laid down His life for the sheep. He says in John 10:16, "And other sheep I have, which are not of this fold: them also I must bring, and *they shall hear My voice;* and there shall be one fold, and one Shepherd." These are also His sheep that must be added to *the rest of the fold.*

In verse 37 of Matthew 25, they are called *"the righteous."* When did they become righteous? Well, it was during the tribulation when they heard the everlasting *Gospel* preached by the 144,000. These Gentiles befriended the Jews. They believed, by the grace of God, their message.

Some have falsified this judgment with two fallacies of discrepancies:

First, there are those who claim that this judgment must be *based on works as doing good* to the Jews, who are the preachers (Isaiah 66:19), and who witness to the world during the tribulation. The heart of the Gospel is Christ, which certainly includes the *blood* of His cross and the *resurrection* to the throne. Thus, those who gave help to the Jewish evangelists because of their persecution, they went without food and drink; were taken in as strangers for protection; clothed them that were stripped naked; offered medical aid to the sick and abused; and the many imprisoned that rendered aid to foster their escape. Such works are backed up by *faith.*

What says the Scripture on this matter of faith and works? *"By faith the harlot Rahab* perished not with them that believed not, when she had received the spies with peace" (Hebrews 11:31).

It will be noted that *Rahab* knew the storm of judgment was about to fall on Jericho. She knew what Israel's God had done to other nations in destroying them. She asked the spies, in faith, to be remembered and spared when the time of invasion came, and "she perished not with them that believed not." James reminds us of this same truth in Chapter 2, verse 25, and concludes the thought by saying in verse 26, "For as the body without the spirit is dead, so *faith without works* is dead also." Who is to say that the works of love to the Jews, termed "His brethren," were not based originally on *faith in Christ,* that produced protection and provisions for these brethren?

Therefore, to say that this judgment is based on works for salvation, or acceptance into the kingdom, is contrary to all Scripture. It is only by the *wonder of His grace* that any of us are saved. They who will believe will be saved as well as we at that day.

Second, the next erroneous view regarding this judgment is really ridiculous. It affirms emphatically that He (Christ) shall set the sheep *nations* on His right hand and the goat *nations* on His left, and say to the sheep nations, "Come, ye blessed of My Father, inherit the kingdom prepared for you form the foundation of the world." This interpretation must be wrong. Nations are made up of individuals. *Only those individuals who believe the messengers and receive the Lord Jesus Christ are saved.* This too is a standard rule of the Bible. Those nations that favor Israel will be blessed, and other nations, as well as individuals, will be cursed, based on Genesis 12:3.

Does that mean they were saved nations, and as a whole? Example: America favors the Israelites and are friendly to them, but that is no reason to suppose that all Americans will be saved.

The rest of the parable of the sheep and goat nations is self-explanatory. The parable gives conclusive evidence that they who represent the goats as unbelievers are told by the Judge, "Depart ye cursed into everlasting fire."

One might argue that the 144,000, that represents the Jewish nation, would all be saved. True, but that number shall be the remnant that God calls out from the 12 tribes of the whole nation, individually. Romans 9:27; Revelation 7:4-8.

Think with me on the bottom line of Matthew 25:46 (which by the way is one of the strongest verses in the Bible for the saved and the lost) as to our individual destinations and duration: "And these shall go away [not nations, but individually judged people] into everlasting punishment: but the righteous [be they Jew or Gentile, on an individual basis] into life eternal." In verse 46 you cannot fail to see that each person will be judged individually and not nationally. What you do and how you act in relation to a personal faith in Christ and His teaching still stands with Matthew 7:24-29 and 12:50. Would you agree? May the Lord so instruct us to be more than hears or readers, but also *doers* of His indestructible Word.

Prevailing conditions in the Millennium (Daniel 7:27)

Let me test your memory. Would you remember the number of dispensations in God's time line? Did I hear you say seven? That is right! Seven dispensations in like manner of the days of creation.

Exodus 20:11, "For in six days the Lord made heaven and earth...and rested the seventh day."

Do you recall that each day represents a dispensation? Note: *The last dispensation is somewhat like the first, in that men lived nearly a thousand years* (Genesis 5:27).

Would you perhaps be able to restate them? Let me jog your memory. The first day of creation represents the first Age of Innocence, with Adam and Eve. The second day, the Age of Conscience, as in the days of Noah. The third day, the Age of Human Government, with the three sons of Noah in repopulating the world. The fourth day, the Age of Promise with Abraham, Isaac and Jacob. The fifth day, the Age of Law, with Moses and the Hebrew pilgrimage to the promised land. The sixth day, the Age of Grace with Jesus, the Head of a church building program. The seventh day, the Age of Rest, with Jesus as the Kingly Prince of peace, which will be the most hallowed and sanctified of all the ages. This leads me to preview with you the *conditions of life* within the final dispensation, which prepares the way for the Everlasting Kingdom.

I will only mention *seven things* which are believed to be the most important in the millennium.

First, let me say it will be a time of peace and rest.

Isaiah 2:4, "And He shall judge among the nations, and shall rebuke many people: and they shall beat their swords into plowshares, and their spears into pruninghooks: nation shall not lift up sword against nation, *neither shall they learn war any more.*"

Isaiah 9:6,7, "For unto us a Child is born, unto us a Son is given; and the *government shall be upon His shoulder:* and His name shall be called Wonderful Counsellor, The mighty God, The everlasting Father, *The Prince of Peace.*"

Zechariah 9:10, "And I will cut off the chariot from Ephraim, and the horse from Jerusalem, and the battle bow shall be cut off: and *He shall speak peace* unto the heathen: and His dominion shall be from sea even to sea, and from the river even to the ends of the earth."

Second, it will be a time of comfort and joy.

Isaiah 40:1,2, "*Comfort ye, comfort ye, My people,* saith your God. Speak ye comfortably to Jerusalem, and cry unto her, that her warfare is accomplished, that her iniquity is pardoned: for she hath received of the Lord's hand double for all her sins."

Isaiah 51:3, "For the Lord shall comfort Zion: He will comfort all her waste places; and He will make her wilderness like Eden, and her desert like the garden of the Lord; *joy and gladness shall be found therein,* thanksgiving, and the voice of melody."

Third, it will be a time of health and happiness.

Isaiah 33:24, "*And the inhabitant shall not say, I am sick:* the people that dwell therein shall be forgiven their iniquity."

Jeremiah 30:17, "*For I will restore health* unto thee, and *I will heal* thee of thy wounds, saith the Lord; because they called thee an outcast, saying, This is Zion, whom no man seeketh after."

Fourth, it will be a time of prosperity and plenty.

Isaiah 65:21–23, "And they shall *build* houses, and inhabit them; and they shall plant vineyards, and eat the fruit of them. They shall not build and another inhabit; they shall not plant, and another eat: for as the days of a tree are the days of my people, and *Mine elect shall long enjoy the work of their hands.* They shall not labour in vain, nor bring forth for trouble; for they are the seed of the blessed of the Lord, and their offspring with them."

Fifth, it will be a time when *wild animals will be domesticated* and live at peace.

Isaiah 11:6–9, "*The wolf also shall dwell with the lamb,* and the leopard shall lie down with the kid; and the calf and the young lion and the fatling together; and a little child shall lead them. And the cow and the bear shall feed; their young ones shall lie down together and the lion shall eat straw like the ox. And the sucking child shall play on the hole of the asp, and the weaned child shall put his hand on the cockatrice' den. They shall not hurt nor destroy in all my holy mountain: for the earth shall be full of the knowledge of the Lord, as the waters cover the sea."

Sixth, it will be a time of unity of one language.

Zephaniah 3:9, "For then will I turn to the people *a pure language, that they may all call upon the name of the Lord,* to serve Him with one consent."

Seventh, a *time of universal unified worship, no false worship.*

Isaiah 45:23, "I have sworn by myself, the word is gone out of my mouth in righteousness, and shall not return, that unto *Me every knee shall bow, every tongue shall swear.*"

Malachi 1:11, "For from the rising of the sun even unto the going down of the same *My name shall be great among the Gentiles.*"

Revelation 5:9,10, "And they sung a new song, saying, Thou art worthy to take the book, and to open the seals thereof; for thou wast slain, and hast *redeemed us to God by Thy blood out of every kindred, and tongue, and people, and nation;* and hast *made us unto our God kings and priests: and we shall reign on the earth.*"

The Concluding Question

In the light of God's Word, the millennium will be a happy time for God's beloved people, the saints, both Jews and Gentiles. However, there yet remains a puzzling question that might be asked, which I will try to answer according to the grace and measure of wisdom which God through His Spirit has given me in writing this book.

Question: If those who enter the millennial kingdom are *all saved* people, and Satan is shut up in prison for a thousand years and then released, *where* do the multitudes of people come from that the Devil gathers out of the nations, in leading them to fight against the saints?

The answer is longer than the question. The heavenly saints who, in their glorified bodies, return with the Lord to the earth and reign with Him are one massive number. They will have no power of reproduction. Those saved ones singled out by our Lord from the Gentile nations as sheep, *remain in their natural bodies until the end.* They are given the ability to reproduce children. The children *born to them* are born in sin, as has always been the case.

Incidentally, you may think it strange to live in the millennium with those saints in their glorified bodies and those other saints still in their natural bodies. Well, life will be different there. When Jesus arose in *His glorified body,* the disciples thought it strange because of some new things He did, but they accepted it anyway. Therefore, from this new generation of a thousand-year life span must come *those the Devil is able to deceive,* not saved ones that were born in the millennium. With this number "as the sand of the sea," Satan attempts to overthrow the saints in their fortified camp of protection. I believe God's purpose in permitting the Devil to do this in the last dispensation, as in all dispensations, even from the beginning of the human race, is to show that all men born in sin develop an uncontrollable desire to sin. *Their depraved nature* cannot be stopped apart from the power and grace of God. Satan knows this and therefore is allowed to incite this final rebellion against the people of God. It will be divinely quenched and proved for all time, and to all creatures, that our God is Sovereign, that Christ is truly the King over all kings, including the king of the kingdom of darkness, even the Devil.

May God be praised for imparting His righteousness to us and saving us from the Devil's powers by the matchless grace of Jesus!

This Millennial Age is something to look forward to, for it will be the next best thing until we finally arrive in our eternal home.

• • •

Questionnaire

1. After reading the chapter, what part of this theme on "Christ's Return" impressed you the most? (Select one of the five headings.)
2. From Roman Numeral I (see outline), which appealed to you most, the coronation or the faithful in the millennium? Give your reason.
3. Whom do the twenty-four elders around the throne represent?
4. Who appears to be the central figure around the throne?
5. Does the church appear to be the only one group before the throne? Yes or No (circle one).
6. If your answer to the above questions is No, who else might be seen there?
7. Give one verse of Scripture that proves the fact that Christ will return as King to reign on the earth.
8. Give one verse of Scripture that proves some of the saints will reign with Christ as subordinate kings.
9. What is the name taken from Scripture (Revelation 16:14,16) of a great battle between the armies of earth and heaven, that ends at the return of Christ?
10. Who are captured and cast into the lake of fire at the conclusion of that battle?
11. What are three groups that are in view during the judgment of the living nations? (Use Scriptural terms.)
12. What are five of the conditions that will prevail in the millennium?
13. What powerful person will be imprisoned during the millennium?

14. What will he be charged with?
15. What age in time resembles the length of the millennium?

• • •

Answers

1. Select one of the five headings (see outline).
2. Give reasons for your answer.
3. The church
4. The lamb
5. No
6. (1) The four living creatures (beast)
   (2) Those identified as Old Testament saints
   (3) Those identified as tribulation saints
   (4) The holy angels
7. Revelation 19:15,16, and others
8. Revelation 1:6, and others
9. Armageddon
10. Beast and false prophet
11. (1) Sheep; (2) Goats; (3) Brethren—Jews
12. Peace, comfort, health, prosperity, animals tamed, one language, one form of worship
13. Satan
14. Deception (Revelation 20:3,8)
15. The Diluvian Age, or the time period before the great flood (The Great Deluge)

Chapter 12

Assisting Our Lord in the Final Judgment of the World's Wicked Dead—Eternal Woe
-and-
Christ Appoints the Righteous Their Place in the Father's Everlasting Kingdom—Eternal Bliss

---

I. The judgment of all the *fallen angels* – the reality of hell (1 Corinthians 6:3)

   A. A judgment first of *Satan* (Genesis 3:15; Isaiah 14:12–15; Ezekiel 28:12–17; Revelation 20:10)

   B. A judgment of the angels that *sinned* (2 Peter 2:4—Tartarus, Jude 6)

   C. A judgment assisted by the *saints* (1 Corinthians 6:3)

   D. A judgment whereby men and angels are cast into hell and eternally *separated* (Revelation 19:20; 20:10)

II. The judgment of all the *world's wicked dead*—the reality of hell (Revelation 20:10–15; Daniel 7:9,10)

   A. The final judgment in God's program (Daniel 7:13,14,22,27)

   1. *Contrary* to public opinion, dealing with the lost only (Revelation 20:12)

   2. *Consists* of an examination of the resurrected wicked only (Revelation 20:13)

   3. *Constitutes* a review of evil works only (Revelation 20:12,13)

   4. *Commits* all to the "lake of fire" as unbelievers only (Revelation 20:14)

   B. Their fatal destination (Daniel 12:2; Luke 16:19–31; Matthew 25:46; Revelation 20:10,14,15)

    C. Ten *phrases on hell* from the mouth of the Master only (Christ originally created hell for the Devil and his angels—Matthew 25:41)

    (Note: The Greek word *Hades* is the holding place of all the wicked dead before their judgment. *Gehenna,* also a Greek word, expresses the eternal abode of the wicked after their judgment)

    D. *Life after death* for the unsaved as well as the saved (Matthew 25:46)

III. The predicted and final reality of all *the righteous*—heaven (Isaiah 66:22; Acts 15:18; 2 Peter 3:13; Revelation 21:1)

    A. A tour through *the celestial city* (John 14:2, Revelation 21:2,6,10–15; 22:1–3)

        1. Viewing heaven's size, walls, gates, angels, streets, mansions, foundations, stones, trees, fountains, river, light and throne

        2. The residents of the heavenly city (Revelation 21:7,9,27)

            a. Its register —The Lamb's Book of Life (Revelation 21:27; 22:4)

            b. Its lifestyle—perfect health, happiness and holiness (Revelation 21:4; 22:3,5,11)

            c. Its unity—made one in Christ and like Christ (1 John 3:2; Revelation 21:3; John 17:21–23)

    B. The excluded, in Revelation 21:8,27; 22:15

    C. The seven "no mores" in Revelation 7:16; 21:1,4

    D. *The Lord's last invitation* (Revelation 22:12,13,14,17)

    E. The last Word about Christ, that bears the title of this book, *What Manner of Man Is This?* (Psalms 89:9; Matthew 8:23–27)

IV. Questionnaire and Answers

• • •

Poetic Thought

We will begin this final chapter with the following poem by J.W. Green:

ASSISTING OUR LORD IN THE FINAL JUDGMENT

The Judgment of Jesus

When the great busy plants of our cities
Shall have turned out their last finished work;
When the merchants have sold their last order,
And dismissed their last tired clerk;
When our banks have raked in their last dollar,
And have paid out their last dividend;
When the Judge of the earth wants a hearing—
And asks for a balance—What then?

When the choir has sung its last anthem,
And the preacher has voiced his last prayer;
When the people have heard their last sermon,
And the sound has died out in the air . . .
When the Bible lies closed on the altar,
And the pews are all empty of men . . .
When each one stands facing his record,
And the Great Book is opened—What then?

When the actors have played their last drama,
And the mimic has made his last fun;
When the movies have flashed their last picture,
And the billboards displayed their last run . . .
When the crowd seeking pleasure has vanished
And gone out into the darkness again . . .
When the trumpet of ages has sounded—
And we stand before Him—What then?

When the bugle call sinks into silence,
And the long marching columns stand still;
When the captain repeats his last orders,
And they've captured the last fort and hill;
When the flag has been hauled down forever—
And the wounded afield have checked in . . .
When the world that rejected its Saviour
Is asked for a reason—What then?

—J.W. Green

• • •

In the two previous chapters, we thought about the subject of judgment: "The Judgment Seat of Christ" and "The Judgment of the Living Nations." Now we will consider first, "The Judgment of the Fallen Angels," and then last, "The Great White Throne Judgment." Thank God, this ends God's judgment program!

Have you learned this highly controversial but essential truth, that there are several judgments in God's Word? Do not settle for the one promoted in error today known by the expression, "The General Judgment." This view, held by amillennialists (as mentioned earlier), does violence to the Holy Scripture by doing away with the dispensations in God's Word. It also does away with the last one that is referred to in Scripture as the millennium, the thousand year reign of Christ on earth.

Consider the rest of God's judgment program dealing with His first creatures created, now referred to as the fallen angels that became demons.

The Judgment of the Evil Angels

We will, as we have from the beginning, support this and every position we hold by Holy Writ, as I trust *you* do now. It is not a disgrace to be caught up in false doctrine, but when the *truth is revealed and then rejected,* it is a serious offense against the Spirit. He takes the things of Christ and reveals them to us (John 16:13,14).

1 Corinthians 6:3, "Know ye not that *we* (believers) shall judge angels?"

Remember that *all judgment* is committed to the judicial Judge, Jesus. He will invite us to share in most of these judgments as His aides and witnesses to the fact.

Satan's Doom

Genesis 3:15 implies that God predicted to bruise the head of Satan through *the seed* of a woman, and that seed, from the virgin Mary, was Christ. One of the reasons why Christ came was to "destroy the works of the Devil" (1 John 3:8).

From Isaiah 14:12–15 we learn that the Devil was first an angelic being called *Lucifer,* "son of the morning," but was cut down to the ground. Jesus said in Luke 10:18, "I saw Satan as lightning fall from heaven."

He was not allowed in the same abode as God, for what agreement has God in Christ with the Devil? He has *weakened* all nations. He attempted in *pride* to rebel against God and occupy His throne. He *determined* to be like God, but became the *god of this world*, until God in heaven will cast him in the "lake of fire" that was made for him and his fallen angels. These took sides with the Devil and were dismissed from heaven, for Isaiah says, "Thou *shalt* be brought down to hell."

Ezekiel 28:12–17 is another interesting portion of Scripture that has Satan's number. Here the Devil is *like* the king of Tyrus, Ezekiel 27:3. He said he was *perfect in beauty and full of wisdom*. He was the one that tempted Adam and Eve in Eden, the garden of God. He was made as perfect as Adam and perhaps with more wisdom and beauty, but for some mysterious reason, iniquity was found in him when he plotted against God. Bear in mind that the Devil still has the powers of attraction and at times "transforms [himself] into an angel of light" (2 Corinthians 11:14). Revelation 20:10 spells out his doom.

Now we will look at the first followers of Satan and see what some Scriptures say about them.

2 Peter 2:4 reveals that as soon as they (the wicked angels) were found out to have sinned, God spared them not. He put them in a place designated as their hell to be as by bond reserved for the time of their judgment *similar* to fallen man that awaits the final judgment of God.

Jude 6 tells us further that they had been given an estate, a home with great authority under God, but through sin they lost it all. *There is no forgiveness for fallen angels* as there is for sinful man. Thank God He made a way of escape for us through His Son!

In Hebrews 2:14,15 we have the remedy in Christ from His first advent to destroy the Devil and his demonic powers. We have the fear of death now removed, being once ourselves held under satanic powers and influence. Through Christ, Satan and his evil spirits are subjected to us and will flee from us when we but utter the Devil-destroying name of Jesus and draw near to God (James 4:7).

In Revelation 20:10 we discover that both man and the Devil are together in hell. However, from 2 Peter 2:4, when the word *hell* is used, it is not *Hades* or *Gehenna,* but *Tartarus.* This must be a separate compartment in the lake of fire for the Devil and the fallen angels (evil spirits). They will be separated from doing any more damage even in hell, which is divided, and kept apart from the human beings that will wind up there, those who have rejected the mercies of God. In a similar way, the *beast* and *false prophet,* which were the firstfruits or the forerunners of the rest of the human race, will have their eternal abode there.

The Judgment of the Wicked

Please read carefully with me about this final and horrible judgment from Revelation 20:10-15, "And *the Devil that deceived* them was *cast* into the lake of fire and brimstone, where the beast and the false prophet are, and shall be *tormented day and night for ever and ever.* And I saw a *great white throne,* and He that sat on it, from whose face the earth and the heaven fled away; and there was *found no place for them.* And I saw the *dead,* small and great, stand before God; and the *books* were opened: and *another* book was opened, which is the *book of life:* and the dead was judged out of *those things* which were written in the *books,* according to *their works.* And the *sea* gave up the dead which were in it; and death and *hell* delivered up the dead which were in them: and they were judged every man according to their works. And death and hell were cast into the lake of fire. This is the *second death.* And whosoever was not found written in the Book of Life was cast into the lake of fire." (Please read also Daniel 7:9,10,22,27.)

First, it is made clear from verse 13 that these people are *lost,* because they came not only from the hidden surface of the earth, like the sea, where the bodies are resurrected in the "resurrection of damnation" (John 5:29).

This is such an awful term that most Bibles do not carry it in their concordance. Nevertheless, the Bible states it a number of times, as "some will receive the *greater damnation.*" These souls all ascend to appear before the great Judge to determine their *degrees of punishment,* based on what they have done. Yes, they all come out of hell (Hades).

Believe me, beloved, you will not find one single saint in hell. No mistake in paperwork or angelic records in the books of heaven are possible. For in this judgment, God's recording secretaries are all His chosen, *elect angels* that would not go along with the Devil's foolish ambush for the throne (1 Timothy 5:21).

These are all lost that are released from hell (Hades). Perish the thought of a "General Judgment" here, where some will be saved and others lost. This judgment consists of the *wicked of this world,* not only the extremely violent, but the people that were rich in this world, *like* the "rich young ruler." He *was* trusting in his morality and good works to obtain the gift of eternal life. Sad will be that day for millions of church folk who played church. They make a lot of claims, but their life does not back up their words.

Matthew 7:21-23, "Not everyone that saith unto Me, *Lord, Lord,* shall enter into the kingdom of heaven; but he that doeth the will of My Father which is in heaven. Many will say to Me in that day, Lord, Lord, have we not *prophesied in Thy Name?* and in Thy Name have *cast out devils?* and in Thy Name done *many wonderful works?* And then will I profess unto *them, I never knew you:* depart from Me, ye that *work iniquity.*"

Notice carefully these words from the Master who reads hearts. People cannot fool God. He knows those that are His, and they that are children of the Devil. Do not miss the bottom line here. These people were never saved, never born again, never washed in the blood, never quickened by God's Spirit. Jesus says to such after listening to their appeal, "Then will I profess . . . *I never knew you:* depart from Me, ye that work iniquity." They were in some ways as wise as the old serpent, but as guilty as the Devil. Take heed, this judgment constitutes a review of every lost man and his works. They will be judged, both small and great, as they stand before the God of all creation.

Their particular *"book of life"* contains all their deeds done in the body. Their names are not written in the Lamb's Book of Life. Their recording angel was not guilty of any miscarriage in justice. It will be a just judgment, for all will receive their just punishment without any higher court to appeal to or parole board to let them off on good behavior. None will be released even after a hundred thousand million years. Brother, you say that is hard to take. Indeed it is! What is written is written, and no king or president can alter it. The result of this judgment is that the condemned will be committed to the lake of fire.

The Fatal Destination

Daniel 12:2. We apply the latter part of the verse, ". . . and some to shame and everlasting contempt."

Sad to say, none shall escape from God's penitentiary. Without spiritualizing, how would you treat Luke 16:19-31? It is not a parable.

Christ Himself pulls back the curtain of time that we might look down into the eternal hell.

Matthew 25:46 is to me the strongest verse in the Bible that cannot be explained away, as is the case today with so many preachers and expositors.

Revelation 20:10,14. Both verses spell out the destination of the damned. One may argue that a loving God will not cast a single soul into hell. Yet we know what God's Word teaches, and what Jesus had to say about it. If a person will not listen to the prophets and apostles, I wonder if they would hear what Jesus had to say. Would you weigh His Words carefully?

Phrases on Hell From the Greatest of All Theologians, Christ

- Matthew 5:22, "... danger of hell fire" (Gehenna)
- Matthew 5:29, "... whole body should be cast into hell" (Gehenna)
- Matthew 10:28, "... destroy both soul and body in hell" (Gehenna)
- Matthew 11:23, "... shalt be brought down to hell" (Hades)
- Matthew 16:18, "... gates of hell" (Hades) (powers of the forces of hell)
- Matthew 23:15, "... child of hell" (Gehenna)
- Matthew 23:33, "How can you escape the damnation of hell ..." (Gehenna)
- Luke 12:5, "... fear Him, which after He hath killed hath power to cast into hell" (Gehenna)
- Luke 16:23, "... in hell he lifted up his eyes, being in torments" (Hades)
- Revelation 1:18, "... keys of hell" (Hades)

Dear Friend, as a lost church member who doubts your acceptance before God, "make your calling and election sure." If you feel the burden of unforgiven sin, cry to God for mercy and ask Him to save your soul for Jesus' sake, and He will.

Heaven for People Made Holy

As we passed over the horrors of hell as quickly as possible, we finally arrive at what was predicted by Isaiah 66:22: "For as the *new heavens* and the *new earth,* which I will make, shall remain before Me, saith the Lord, so shall your seed and your name remain."

God knows the end from the beginning, for He is all-wise and all-knowing. What is decreed and ordained by God, puny man has no right to challenge.

2 Peter 3:13 says it all under divine inspiration: "Nevertheless, we, according to His promise, look for a new heaven and a new earth, wherein dwelleth righteousness."

See how God first shared His supreme plan with the prophet Isaiah, then with the apostle Peter. Soon this prophecy and promise will be a reality. There we will see with our eyes, hold with our hands, and be face to face before Him, who is the object of our love. Then we will realize in full how He will lavish *His great love* upon us.

Revelation 21:1, "And I saw a new heaven and a new earth: for the first heaven and the first earth were *passed away;* and there was no more sea."

Dearly beloved, the first creation of God, which was the heaven and earth, will vanish as in Revelation 20:11. God will not, as so many teach, renovate and restore the old world. God will not patch up the old burned, black, sinful world, but rather create a brand-new heaven and earth that has never been contaminated by sin. When God in Christ makes our eternal home, it will not be second-hand, but all new from bottom to top. God's utopia!

We are about to see one of the grandest scenes ever witnessed on this side of time. Regardless of how advanced we may think man has become, we haven't seen anything yet. Paul wrote about this dream when he said in 1 Corinthians 2:9, which was taken from Isaiah 64:4,

"For since the beginning of the world men have not heard, nor perceived by the ear, neither hath the eye seen, O God, *beside Thee,* what *He* hath prepared for him that waiteth for Him."

1 Corinthians 2:9, "But it is *written,* Eye hath not seen, nor ear heard, neither have entered into the heart of man, *the things which God hath prepared for them that love Him.*"

Without any further delay, let us see the splendor and magnificence of this "beloved city," whose "builder and maker is God (Christ)." (Reconsider here John 1:3 and Colossians 1:16,17.)

As your guide for this day in viewing the holy city, I want you to be especially aware of the *size* of this huge, handsome structure, which is unequalled in all ages, world without end. Also notice its *pearly gates*, its garnished wall of *strongest stones*, polished with all the brilliance in colors of the rainbow. We may visualize stopping periodically to eat the delicious fruit and drink the sweet living water from the *fountains* we have access to.

In addition to all that's mentioned, notice its *spacious halls* and the splendor of its *twelve foundations* made of the best and most costly stones, known and unknown to us. Lastly, before we complete the tour of our *heavenly city*, you will be amazed at the *rays of light* that grow brighter as we approach the *throne room* of our great God and His Christ, for its radiant rays light all of *heaven and earth*.

Well now, do we have any dropouts that want to go some place else more important? I hope not, so let us begin.

God's Description of the Capital City of Heaven, Where God in Christ Reigns With His Subjects Forever (Revelation 22:3–5)

In the *eternal city* of the *saved*, you will see that it has the shape of a *tetragon*—four sides, plus the top and bottom.

The City

Revelation 21:16, "And the city lieth foursquare, and the length is as large as the breadth: and he measured the city with the reed, twelve thousand furlongs. The length and the breadth and the height of it are equal."

A cubit measures eighteen inches. It is from a man's elbow to the tip of his middle finger. The angel used this measurement of man to measure the city. This translates to about *1,500 miles in each direction*. That would be approximately half way across the United States, going east to west. Can you imagine a city that tremendous? It blows our imagination to think that this *holy city* is built with the *purest of gold* (Revelation 21:18).

The Walls and Foundations

Revelation 21:18. Its *walls* are of jasper, and its *foundations* (21:19) are a remarkable work of art, because it has all of the most beautiful precious stones in it. These twelve foundations are a reminder of our

Redeemer, having all the *attributes of our God.* Christ is our foundation on every level of life.

Revelation 21:18–20 speaks of the precious gems, which we list from the first to the twelfth foundation, each *about 125 miles high:*

1. Jasper—green stone of ancient time, like a diamond
2. Sapphire—blue stone, hard like a diamond
3. Chalcedony—agate of white, polished like a pearl
4. Emerald—green and considered most valuable
5. Sardonyx—onyx of orange-red, transparent
6. Sardius—worn on breastplate—same as a ruby
7. Chrysolite—topaz-colored, yellow like gold
8. Beryl—blue-green, translucent gem
9. Topaz—crystal of different-colored quartz
10. Chrysoprase—yellow-gold, formation of gems
11. Jacinth—reddish-orange gem
12. Amethyst—deep-purple crystallized jewel

The Gates

Revelation 21:12,13,21,25. The *twelve gates remain always open,* never to be shut, signifying we are never again to fear thieves or robbers, murderers or rapists. We see three gates (each made of one solid pearl) to the north, south, east and west.

The Angels

Revelation 21:12. These *holy angels* of God are not guards to keep certain ones out, but rather to *welcome visitors* in, and those who make inquiry about the whereabouts of its citizens. Refer to Revelation 21:24–26.

The Streets

Revelation 21:21. The main street is pure gold, as are all streets, and the *central boulevard leads to the throne.*

The River

Revelation 22:1. This pure living water has various fountains distributed throughout the metropolis—notice, as clear as crystal. *This water is life-giving from its source, the throne of God.* The fountains are fountains of living water to *impart eternal youth.*

The Trees

Revelation 22:2,14. These trees, like the water, impart and sustain life. The tree of life seems to be planted on both sides of the flowing river of life.

Sorry, no hamburgers in heaven, which would mean meat, and meat would mean death to some animal; but these fruit trees bear *twelve kinds of fruit.* They never need spraying for insects, bugs or worms, for they never decay. It may be that they will need pruning like in the first Paradise. *The harvest is monthly,* having healing power. Every *citizen* and *saint* has right to this "tree of life."

The Mansions

John 14:2. The Lord not only is preparing a city beyond expression for us, but along the countless streets and lanes we will behold residential homes, lo, even *mansions* to dwell in. *Nothing but the best* from the Lover of our souls, in the *"great city"* of our Lord.

The Light

Revelation 21:23,25; 22:5. We are told about the lighting system of the city in verse 23: *"The glory of God did lighten it,* and the *Lamb* is the light thereof." There shall be *no night* there, no need of the sun or moon. Jesus was, is, and will yet be our light forever.

The Throne

Revelation 21:5; 22:3,4. You no doubt have observed that *no temple* can be found within its high and lofty walls; but the *center* of this imperishable, indestructible city is the *throne.* Scheduled throngs will gather before this *rainbowed, ivory* throne of beauty beyond comprehension. Here is where we will *sing* "unto Him that loved us and washed us in His own blood" the *"song of Moses and the Lamb,"* to the eternal praise of our great and glorious God. Churches are temples of worship. Who is it that we then will worship, but *God* face to face (verse 4).

The Citizens of the Heavenly City

The residents of the heavenly city have a well-protected *census book,* registering all of God's holy family. We call it by its beloved name, "The Lamb's Book of Life." Enclosed is written a lengthy list of the redeemed.

Revelation 21:7,9,27; 22:4. Each verse is a thrill to read, because our names and the names of our loved ones are written there. Luke 10:20, "... rejoice because your names are written in heaven." Jesus said this because He has memorized all the names from A to Z, as the Alpha and Omega. He says, "I know My sheep . . ." The residents are the "overcomers" spoken of in verse 7 of Chapter 21.

We are also called the Bride, the Lamb's wife. See Revelation 19:7–9. Also notice Psalm 45:8,9, where the queen (Church) is identified as wife of the King (Christ). This, as we have said, is a high honor representing the church, who is married to Christ.

Romans 7:4, "... that you should be married to another, even to Him that is raised from the dead, that we should bring forth fruit unto God."

I repeat! Those eligible to enter must be enrolled (Revelation 21:27): "... but they which are *written* in the Lamb's book of life." Just a reminder of God's electing grace: this book was completed before "the foundation of the world" (Revelation 14:8; 17:8).

Perfect People

Some say, "Nobody is perfect here." True, but there *everybody* will be perfect.

The lifestyle of heaven is enviable to earth dwellers. Here we suffer infirmities, there perfect health. Here we sorrow because of many things upsetting us, there perfect happiness. Here we groan, being plagued by our own sin and that of others, there perfect holiness, glorified bodies.

Saved Gentile Nations

The Bride seems to be the closest to the throne because of her relation to the Bridegroom, the Lord Jesus, her head of the household of heaven.

Then we know that the twelve tribes of Israel as a nation are honored by having their names written on the twelve gates. The twelve apostles have their names inscribed on the twelve foundations. There is more: "The *nations* (Revelation 21:24) that are *saved* shall walk in the light of it, and the kings of the earth do bring their glory and honor into it." Here is a whole new world of the saved.

Revelation 21:4; 22:3,5,11. Verse 4 in Chapter 21 reveals eyes with tears that must be wiped away, as our Lord promised.

Verse 3 in Chapter 22 speaks of the dignity of labor, especially when we are employed and given our assignments by God. We shall work and not grow weary. We shall walk and not faint; because the city has no night, we shall need no sleep. We shall be like God (1 John 3:2)—think on that!

Verse 5 in the same chapter inspires us, telling us that we *"shall reign forever and forever."*

Chapter 22, verse 11, warns us all to watch, because when He comes suddenly, He will find us according to our true lifestyle: unjust and filthy, or righteous and holy. The second group was made that way by the miracle of the new birth. We must be *partakers of His holy nature,* being born again, if we are to enter that holy place (2 Peter 1:4).

Oneness With God

One of the best things I can think of that we will experience in heaven, will be no separation, no barriers there.

Now our Christian circles are divided, there united in Christ. Every wall of separation will be broken down. Now it is said in Scripture "that the Jews have no dealings with the Samaritans." The same can be said of many nationalities, but there we will be *one in Christ's love.*

Hear Jesus as He offers this great petition as High Priest (John 17):

Verse 21, "That they all may be one . . ."

Verse 22, ". . . that they may be one, even as we (God and Christ) are one."

Verse 23, "I in them, and Thou in Me, that they may be made perfect in one."

Verse 26, ". . . the *love* wherewith Thou hast loved me may be in them."

The Excluded

What a hateful word to describe the condition of many of us Christians, because of our stand for Christ—excluded here, but not there (Revelation 21:8,27; 22:15).

Verse 8 gives us a glimpse of this company which is a menace to society. Let me list them for you: "Fearful and murderers, and whoremongers and sorcerers [this means not only they that practice magic arts, but do drugs] and idolaters and all liars." Their destiny is the "lake of fire" who make a practice of these things. Watch out, that you may receive a full reward (2 John 8).

The last phrase in this verse is the *"second death."* These people were born in sin, dead spiritually, then died physically and went to Hades, there to await their trial of many offenses. After the judgment in hell (Gehenna), he will die the second death, which never means ceasing to exist.

Verse 27, "There shall in no wise enter" those that defile themselves, others with dishonest practices and detestable abominations. They that have never been washed God's way are filthy still.

Verse 15 of Chapter 22. The list goes on again in a loving warning for sinners to forsake such immoral falsehoods. When a person says to me, "I won't be alone there," that should be of no consolation to the wicked and evil to be thrown into such a wicked, ungodly world as this.

The Seven "No Mores" of Revelation

1. Revelation 7:16—no more hunger or thirst
2. Revelation 21:1—no more sea
3. Revelation 21:4—no more death
4. Revelation 21:4—no more sorrow
5. Revelation 21:4—no more crying
6. Revelation 21:4—no more pain
7. Revelation 21:4—no more curse

What a catalog of comfort lies in these lines. Summing them up briefly, we undergo a delightful change from separation to unity, from sorrow to happiness, from weeping to rejoicing, from pain to perfect health, from the curse of sin to blessing eternal. This is grounds to praise forever our wonderful God.

The Lord's Last Invitation

Revelation 22:12,13,14,17. Notice, these are all in the last chapter and should all be written in large red letters to warn the weary in sin to *turn* now or *burn* later. He is the first and the last letter of all languages. His Word should be translated in all the world, which has more than 5,000 tongues.

Jesus wishes to bless those that honor His Word of truth, with the ever-bearing "tree of life." "And the Spirit and the bride (Church) say, *COME.*" The world may not understand the word propitiation, or reconciliation, or even justification, but they can understand the warm and loving word, COME (to Christ). He says, "I will give you rest." [Soul-rest, as you rest on the finished work of Christ.] Continuing the verse, "... let him that heareth say, COME." [Everyone who hears this good news of the Gospel, should receive Christ as Savior, and tell others what He has done.] "And whosoever will, let him take the water of life freely."

You may say, "I do not know if I am one of God's chosen." Well, *"Come and see."* That is what the first disciples did when John pointed them to Jesus. Come and see if He is not all and much more of what we have said.

Remember the *Queen of Sheba,* who heard about Solomon and came to Him, reporting later with the words, *"Behold, the half was not told me."*

You would say, "If I come freely and drink deeply in Christ and His truth, I shall never be disappointed." He says in John, "If any man thirst, let him come unto Me and drink."

Do not think of what you're to give up, but what you will gain. You give up sin and get the free gift of salvation. You give up the Devil's crowd and transfer to the members of the family of God. You give up hell and get heaven, not for a passing moment, but for all eternity. Do not tell me it does not pay to serve Jesus, for I have served Him for nearly 60 years, and it becomes better with the passing of time in this abundance of the life that "now is, and that which is to come." What He is asking is, in a word, give up your will and accept His will.

My last word about Christ: I hope and pray as you have read this book, *What Manner of Man Is This?*, that you will know more than ever before what kind of Man He is, for He is the Son of Man and God.

If you have put off coming by faith to Him, and have not yet repented of your sins, I beseech you, yea, I beg you to ask Him just now to open your heart and do for you what He once did for Lydia of old (Acts 16:14), and do in some way what He has done for countless others who have passed through this quickening, unforgettable experience.

Romans 10:13, "Whosoever shall call on the name of the Lord shall be saved."

Do it today, and do it now without delay. God bless you as you believe Him to be your victory over sin, death and hell (1 Corinthians 15:54–58).

Stilling the Storm

Psalm 89:9, "Thou rulest the raging of the sea: when the waves thereof arise, Thou stillest them."

Psalm 107:29,30, "He maketh the storm a calm, so that the waves thereof are still. Then are they glad because they be quiet; so He bringeth them to their *desired haven*."

As a battle-worn soldier of the cross, I end where I began five years ago, looking back to Matthew 8:23–27, and forward in all that the text holds in Christ. The Lord has taken me through many raging storms of life, but each time He has stilled the stressful sea in my tossed and driven soul when I looked to Him. He has brought me to my desired haven of rest as a pilgrim. So will it be to all the saints who put their trust in the One who never fails.

Remember, dear friend, Christ rules the raging sea and stills the storms of life. He brings calmness and comfort to the heart that relies ever upon Him.

Praise be to His worthy and wonderful Name. May the Lord be pleased to save by His "great grace" many who read this book, and cause you to be fruitful and reap a full reward as you continue to behold Him of whom the first disciples said, *"What Manner of Man Is This?"*

• • •

Questionnaire

1. In this last chapter, what two large world groups are judged?
2. Do the angels that sinned go to hell together with man, or are they separated?
3. Do you believe the Bible teaches eternal punishment of the wicked?
4. What are the two Greek words in the text that refer to hell?
5. Is the old heaven and earth to be restored or to be dissolved and made to vanish?
6. Give seven things that will be found in heaven.
7. Give four things people will experience there.
8. Give five kinds of people that will not enter heaven.
9. Give three of the seven "no mores" mentioned in Revelation.
10. Optional: Restate the last invitation or warning of Christ.

Answers

1. The visible world of the wicked dead. The unseen world of Satan and his demons.
2. Separated (Tartarus and Gehenna)
3. Matthew 25:46, and others
4. *Hades* and *Gehenna*
5. Pass away
6. Gates, walls, foundations, stones, streets, fountains, (angels), mansions, light, throne.
7. Health, happiness, holiness, perfection, worship, unity.
8. Fearful, unbelievers, murders, whoremongers, abominable, sorcerers, idolaters and liars.
9. No more hunger or thirst, death, sorrow, tears, curse, pain, sea.
10. Revelation 17 or 18 and 19

We Shall See the King Some Day

*Tho' the way we journey may be often drear,
On that blessed morning clouds will disappear;
After pain and anguish, after toil and care,
Thro' the endless ages joy and blessing share,
After foes are conquered, after battles won,
After strife is over, after set of sun,
There with all the loved ones who have gone before,
Sorrow past forever, on that peaceful shore.*

*We shall see the King some day,
We shall shout and sing some day;
Gathered 'round the throne,
When He shall call His own,
We shall see the King some day.*

—*L. E. Jones*

Subject Index

(From A to W)

Key words are in all capital letters.

Christ, first ADVENT of 93–110
    Greatest event, God's King is virgin born 96–97, 99–101
    Scenes surrounding His birth 101–103
    Lost son found in the temple 103–104
    One perfect Person for baptism 104–108
    Devil attempts to tempt God's Son 108–110
Christ, second ADVENT of (Part 1) 175–194
    Rapture of His saints 175, 177–179
    Illustrated by one taken, the other left 179–180
    (Philadelphian and Laodicean Church)
    Examples: Noah and Lot 179
    Three views of Christ's return in regard to the Millennium .. 182–186
    Three positions regarding the Church and the Tribulation 186–187
    Judgment Seat of Christ 187–189
    Marriage of the King's Son 190–194
Christ, second ADVENT of (Part 2) 197–217
    Scenes of the saints before the throne 175, 198–201
    Descending with our Lord to the earth 205–210
    Battle of Armageddon 193, 197, 209–210

Dividing the living nations 197, 210–213

World under a new Ruler, Christ, our sovereign King 197–198,
200, 202, 213–217

Christ, "The ANGEL of the Lord" is 51, 63–71

Appearance to Hagar, Abraham, Jacob, Moses, Joshua, Gideon,
Samson's parents

Christ, ANGELS created by 34–35, 40–41, 202

Questionnaire on angels 38–40

Christ, APPEALS to men in fifty-four ways 1–3

Christ, CHURCH of

Body 28, 35, 175–176, 177–182, 184–187, 201–202, 209

Bride 10, 35, 61, 137, 176, 190–191, 196–199, 201–202,
204–205, 209, 231–232

Builder 35, 116, 165–166, 214

Christ, unconditional COVENANT of Grace made sure to His elect by

Since the conditional convenants given to men failed by them 21,
25–32

Christ, CREATOR of all things in the invisible and visible world 34–38,
40–41, 42–44

Christ, DATA on the twelve apostles of 126–127

Christ, DEITY of 21, 24, 75–76, 100-101, 145-146, 160

Christ, DIED for many or all? 170–172

Proposition I: He died for every man's sin

Proposition II: He died for those chosen ones
God had given Him (correct position)

Christ, DISCIPLES of 14, 83, 117–127

Christ, ELECTION of the chosen in 15, 27–32

Christ, FAITH that saves is centered in 9, 10, 17–18, 32, 187, 225

Christ, FALSE faith rebuked by .... *x, xii*, 13, 17, 22

Christ, HEALING power in 16, 129, 140–144

Christ, HEAVENLY people of 226–232
    Because of God's unmerited favor 230–231
    Their holy city described 228–232
    They shall reign with God in Christ forever 232
    Seven "no mores" 233

Christ, HELL described by 222–226

Christ, HUMANITY of 22, 96–97, 100
    The only perfect Man

Christ, INCARNATION of 9, 21, 23, 76–77, 97, 99–100, 208

Christ, INVITATION given in and through
    General 9, 11–12, 16, 28, 32, 44, 71, 91–92, 191
    Special 233–234

Christ, the Supreme JUDGE of all men and angels ... 21, 25, 74, 87, 91, 222

Christ, future JUDGMENTS of
    Each special judgment is committed to the Son by the Father
        When our sins were judged at the cross 183
        The judgment seat of Christ 25, 176, 187–189
        The judgment of angels 219, 222–224
        The judgment of the Great White Throne 25, 90, 219,
                                                                       224–225, 232–233

Christ, God's appointed KING of kings 54, 79–80, 98–99, 178,
                                        190–194, 196–198, 200, 205, 207, 217

Christ, LORDSHIP of 11, 12, 18
    To the saved He must be Lord as well as Savior

Christ, LOVE of God declared and demonstrated in 28–29, 148,
    152–153, 156, 211–213, 227, 230–232

Christ, MILLENNIAL reign of 197–198
    The Age of Peace as the last dispensation
    The final fulfillments on the old earth: peace, joy, health, prosperity,
        wild animals tamed, one language, unified worship 214–217

Christ, MIRACLES of 126, 129–138
    Definition, classification, performance, purpose

Christ, His given NAME is Jesus 10–11, 58, 76, 96–97, 101–103

Christ, NATURE controlled by 9, 12
    Example: Stilling the storms of life

Christ, NEW CREATION of 35, 44–46
    "If any man be in Christ, he is a new creature (creation)"

Christ, NEW HEAVEN and New Earth prepared by 35, 47
    Residence of saved people only 226–228

Christ, Teacher of PARABLES for only God's people is
    Not for the natural man 160–162
    Arrangement of parables 162–164

Christ, PHYSICIAN of no equal is 129, 138–140
    The Doctor who served thousands without wages and never lost a case

Christ, Man of PRAYER
    Private 167–168
    Public 168–170

Christ, our great High PRIEST is 171–172
    "One Mediator between God and man"

Christ, PROPHECIES relating to 51, 74–79, 115–122
   About Him, Old Testament prophecies 73–74
   From Him, New Testament prophecies 152, 164–168

Christ, Prince of PROPHETS is 78–79, 114–115, 129, 152
   "Never man spake like this Man"; "Hear Him"
      A discussion from the Old Testament on healing
      The healing Prophet in the New Testament

Christ, Jews REJECTED their 15, 16, 159–160
   "We have no king but Caesar"

Christ, RESURRECTION power of..152, 172
   Spiritual 147–148
   Physical 146–150
   "I am the resurrection and the life."

Christ, World's greatest SERMONS by 9, 16, 152–160
   In the temple 152–156
   On the mountainside 156–158
   Within His own hometown synagogue 159–160

Christ, SYMBOLS of 50, 53–56
   Scepter, manna, rock, serpent, star, ark

Christ, TEMPTATIONS endured by..108–110

Christ, one member of the Godhead in the TRINITY 21, 23–25, 26, 100
   Three in One, and One in Three, and the One in the middle died for me.

Christ, TYPOLOGY found in 50–51
   Adam, Melchizedec, Isaac 57–62

Christ, in Daniel's VISIONS 74, 89–92

Christ, living and eternal WORD is 21, 23, 98–100
   A survey through the New Testament
   He was with God and was God and is God

Index of Scriptures

OLD TESTAMENT

GENESIS
1:1,2 .... 34, 37, 42, 49
1:26 .... 34, 37, 43
1:28 57
2:1,2 42
2:7 .... 34, 43, 50, 57
3:15 .... 73, 75, 92, 219, 222
5:27 214
7:1 .... 50, 56
7:7,16 56
12:1,2 .... 21, 27
12:3 .... 21, 27, 64, 213
14:18 .... 51, 58
14:19 .... 51, 58
14:20 .... 51, 58, 59
15:2 205
16:7–11 .... 51, 63
16:12 63
17:17 59
21:1 59
21:2 59
Chapter 22 51
22:1–14 59
22:2 59
22:5 60
22:11 .... 51, 63, 64
22:12 .... 51, 64
22:13 .... 51, 60
22:14 51
22:15–18 .... 51, 64
Chapter 24 61
24:2 205
28:12 .... 51, 63, 64, 65
28:13 .... 51, 65
28:14,15 51
31:11–13 65
32:24–30 66
35:1,2,9 67
48:16 .... 62, 78
49:10 .... 50, 54

EXODUS
2:2–10 68
3:2 .... 51, 63, 67
3:3,4 .... 51, 67
3:5 .... 51, 67, 69
3:6 .... 51, 67

7:11	68
12:14	69
14:21	68
15:26	130
16:4	50, 54
16:15	68
17:6	50, 55
19:5	21, 27
20:11	213
33:19	136
34:28	68

NUMBERS

12:6	74, 84
21:8	50, 55
22:22–35	63
24:4, 16	85
24:17	50, 55

DEUTERONOMY

18:15	73, 79, 115
32:39	130

JOSHUA

5:13–15	51, 69

JUDGES

2:4, 6	63
6:11–14	51, 69
6:11–22	63
13:13–17	51
13:13–18	70
13:13–21	63
13:18	71

1 SAMUEL

3:1	85

1 KINGS

17:8–15	160

2 KINGS

1:3	63
5:1–14	160

1 CHRONICLES

21:16, 20	63

JOB

35:10	2

PSALMS

2:2–6	197, 210
16:10	74, 83
Chapter 22	75
22:1	74, 82
22:7, 8	74, 81
22:16	82
Chapter 24	75
27:1	3
33:6, 9	34, 38
33:9	34, 38
34:7	71
35:11	74, 81
45:1	10, 19
45:2	1
45:2–5	197
45:8, 9	231

51:10	45
62:2	1
68:18	83
69:21	74, 82
72:8–11	196
78:2	160
89:9	220, 235
89:19	85
90:2	26
104:30	37
107:29, 30	9, 235
109:3, 4	74, 82
110:3	32, 120
110:4	73, 80
118:22	3
119:89	26
127:1	1

PROVERBS

18:24	2
29:2	203
29:18	74, 84

ECCLESIASTES

3:11	42
12:12	xv
7:29	34, 43

SONG OF SOLOMON

2:1	2
5:16	1

ISAIAH

2:4	197, 214
4:2	9, 11, 73, 76, 115, 208
8:14	89
9:1	78
9:2	73, 78
9:6	1, 3, 58, 71, 115
9:6, 7	9, 11, 197, 206, 208, 214
11:6–9	197, 215
14:12–15	219, 248
29:11	85
32:1	196, 198
33:22	2
33:24	197, 215
37:36	63
40:1, 2	197, 214
40:3, 4	73, 78
40:5	73
42:1	142
42:4	108
42:9	35, 47
43:2	86
45:18	42
45:23	196, 198, 215
50:6	74, 81
51:3	197, 215
52:14	82
53:4	129, 131, 141
53:9	74, 83
53:12	82
53:1–12	73, 74, 80
59:20	211
61:1, 2	73, 78, 159, 174
61:10	3, 196, 205
62:5	196, 205
63:9	51, 62
64:4	227
65:17	35, 47
65:21–23	197, 215
66:19	212
66:22	220, 226

JEREMIAH
6:16	50, 51
30:17	197, 215
31:3	22
31:15	73, 77
31:31–33	27
31:34	211
33:3	122
33:11	196, 205
33:31, 32, 33	21

LAMENTATIONS
3:22, 23	18

EZEKIEL
1:1	84
20:37	211
27:3	223
28:12–17	219, 223

DANIEL
2:19	84
2:28	74, 86
2:31–34	88
2:32	74, 88
2:32–45, 47	74, 86
2:33–45	74, 88
2:35	88
2:38, 39	88
2:40–43	88
2:44, 45	88, 89
3:15–30	86
4:3	86, 87
4:5	85
4:35	207
6:22	86
6:26, 27	87
7:9	50, 74, 87, 90, 219, 224
7:10	50, 74, 90, 219, 224
7:11–14	74, 87, 196, 197, 244
7:13	196, 205, 219
7:14	205, 219
7:18	196, 203
7:22	87, 197, 219, 224, 244, 249
7:27	87, 196, 197, 203, 213, 219, 224
8:25	87
10:5, 6	90
10:5–8	87, 94
10:8	91
10:9	87
12:1	197, 209
12:2	176, 192, 197, 209, 219, 225
12:3	196, 203

HOSEA
11:1	77
12:4	65
12:10	84

JOEL
2:11	207
2:28	84
3:12, 17, 20	209

JONAH
2:9	29

MICAH
5:2	9, 11, 73, 76

ZEPHANIAH
3:9 .... 198, 215

HAGGAI
2:7 2

ZECHARIAH
4:6 9
6:12 .... 2, 197
6:13 .... 197, 209
9:9 .... 74, 80
9:10 .... 197, 214
11:12 .... 74, 81
12:8–10 63
14:1–4 197
14:3–4 203
14:16 .... 198, 240

MALACHI
1:11 .... 198, 216
3:1 77
4:2 .... 1, 202

NEW TESTAMENT

MATTHEW
1:21 .... 9, 11, 20, 171
1:21–23 .... 93, 115
1:23 .... 77, 208
2:2 55
2:14, 15 .... 68, 77
2:16–18 77
3:13–17 .... 94, 107
4:1 68
4:2 68
4:1–11 .... 94, 108
4:13–16 78
4:19 119
4:23 2
4:23–25 140
Chapters 5–7 .... 152, 156
5:1, 2 156
5:3–6 157
5:5 3
5:7–8 157
5:9–10 158
5:13, 14–40 158
5:14–16 164
5:22 .... 129, 226
5:28 115
5:29 .... 115, 226
5:43–48 158
6:1–34 158
6:6 .... 122, 168
6:20, 21 189
6:26–58 164
7:1–29 158
7:3–5 164
7:15 17
7:21–23 .... 17, 225
7:24 116
7:24–27 164
7:24–29 213
7:28 .... 10, 17
7:29 17
8:5–13 124
8:11 .... 175, 177
8:12 .... 152, 167
8:16 .... 129, 131, 141
8:17 .... 129, 131
8:23–27 .... 220, 235
8:26 68
8:27 .... *iii*, 9, 12, 20, 21

8:34	17
9:8	9, 16
9:12	143
9:16, 17	164
9:18	146
9:20–22	123
9:33	9, 16
9:35	142
10:1–38	164
10:28	96, 167, 226
10:41, 42	165
11:4, 5	142
11:10, 11	78
11:16, 17	164
11:23	226
11:25	31, 168
11:26	168
11:27	xi
11:28	10, 18
11:29	2, 18
12:15, 17, 18	142
12:43–45	164
12:50	213
13:1–9	161
13:10, 11	152, 161
13:16–30	162
13:18–23	164
13:25	179
13:30, 38–43	206
13:31, 32	164
13:33	164
13:37	2
13:43	165
13:44	162
13:45–50	163
13:46	2
13:52	163
13:54–58	159
14:19	169
14:20, 21	68
14:35, 36	142
15:1–27	164
15:14	96
15:27, 28	124
15:30, 31	143
15:36	169
16:16, 17	153
16:18	55, 93, 116, 226
17:3	69
18:12–14	164
18:14	147
18:23–34	163
19:28	196, 201
19:29, 30	201
20:1–16	163
20:28	171
21:5	98
21:28–32	163
21:33–41	164
21:42	3
21:44	89
22:1–14	163, 176, 190
22:2	176, 190
22:9, 10, 14	191
22:32	172
23:15	226
23:23	59, 155
23:33	226
24:11	22
24:14	93, 95, 152, 165, 176
24:21	152, 192
24:22	192
24:27	166, 175, 185, 186
24:29	186
24:30	166, 175, 185, 186
24:31	166
24:32	164
24:36	166, 179

24:39	166	1:35	152, 167
24:40, 41	178	2:17	143
24:42	166, 176	2:21, 22	164
24:44	166	4:2	161
24:51	167	4:3–9	164
25:1–12	163, 190	4:10–13	161
25:13–30	163	4:21–23	164
25:31	211	4:26–29	163
25:31–45	197	4:31, 32	164
25:31–46	163, 209	4:41	*iii*, 9,12,20
25:32	197, 211	5:1–20	124
25:33	197, 211	5:22, 23	146
25:34	167, 197, 211	5:26	143
25:37	212	5:35–43	146
25:40	197, 211	6:1–6	159
25:41	34, 40, 167, 197, 220	6:2	98
25:41–46	152	6:3	103
25:46	91, 167, 197, 213, 219, 220, 226, 236	6:4	160
		6:6	160
26:15	81	6:46	152, 168
26:28	93, 171	10:17	3
26:29	152, 165	11:15, 16	78
26:46	170	11:17	78, 155
26:53	41	12:1–11	164
26:67	81	13:28	164
27:26	81	13:29, 32, 33	166
27:34	82	13:34	163
27:46	82, 185	13:35	163, 166
27:57	83, 125	13:36	163, 166
27:58–60	83	13:37	166
28:19	21, 24, 107, 152, 165	14:57	81
28:28	96	14:65	81
		15:39	125
		16:9	123
		16:15	165

MARK

1:4, 5	104
1:9–11	94
1:12, 13	108
1:14, 15	153, 154

LUKE

1:8	98

1:26	19
1:27	76
1:28	20
1:31	9, 11, 19, 77, 86, 102
1:32	86, 208
1:33	20, 86, 208
1:47	24, 102, 123
1:76	78
2:4, 5	20, 76
2:6	76
2:10	3
2:25–35	123
2:26	20
2:36–38	123
2:46, 47	93, 103
2:48	93, 103
2:49	104
3:21	168
3:21–23	94
4:1–13	94, 108
4:16	159
4:15–30	152, 159
4:18, 19	79
4:21	154
4:22	160
4:23	3, 144, 160
4:24, 26, 28–30	160
5:16	152, 168
5:17–26	129, 144
5:21–23	145
5:27–32	114
5:31	144
5:31, 32	129, 138
5:36–39	164
6:12	152, 168
6:20–49	156
6:23, 35	176
7:11	129
7:11–17	147
7:40–43	124
7:41–50	163
8:5–8, 16–18	164
8:25	*iii*, 9, 12, 20
8:41	146
8:43	144
9:23	9, 13
10:18	222
10:20	231
10:30–37	163
11:5–8	163
12:5	226
12:16–20	163
12:21, 35–40, 42–48	163
12:47, 48	202
13:6–9	163
13:18, 19	164
13:25–27	163
14:7–11	163
14:13, 14	176
14:16–24	163
14:28–33	163
15:2	98
15:8–10	163
15:11–32	163
16:1–8	163
16:19–31	163, 219, 225
16:23	226
16:26	83
17:7–10	163
17:15–19	124
17:25–30, 37	179
17:26, 27	175, 179
17:28–30	175
17:34–37	175, 178
18:1–8	123, 163
18:7, 8	122
18:9–14	163
19:1–10	124

19:10	3
19:12–27	163
19:17, 19	196
19:17–19	201
20:9–16	164
21:1–4	123
21:27, 28	167
21:29, 30	164, 185
21:34–36	166
21:31	185
21:36	185
22:15–20	58
22:19	69, 169
22:28–30	196, 201
22:41	152, 168
23:34	82, 169
23:35	81
23:43, 47	125
23:46	170
24:1	159
24:13–32	125
24:25–27	53
24:27	50
24:47	20, 165

JOHN

1:1	21, 23, 58, 100
1:3	34, 37, 227
1:4	21, 34, 37
1:10	97
1:12	190
1:13	30, 35, 45, 96
1:14	21, 23, 93, 100
1:16	18
1:23	78
1:28	105, 112
1:29	1, 57, 60, 105
1:30	94, 100
1:31	94, 105
1:32–34	94
1:35	117, 150
1:36, 37	114, 117, 150
1:38	2
1:38–51	150
1:40–42	114, 118
1:41	2
1:43	114, 119, 122
1:44	114
1:45	92
1:46–51	114
1:48	122
1:49	122, 160
1:51	65
2:1–11	129, 136
2:13–16	152, 154
2:23	9, 15, 125
2:24	9, 15
3:1–21	13
3:2	133
3:3	20, 35, 59, 96
3:5	35
3:7	35, 59
3:12	9, 14, 20
3:14, 15	55
3:16	59
3:23	126
3:22–24	153
3:27	103
3:29	191, 196
3:31	1
4:4	124
4:22–24	159
4:39	124, 126
4:41, 42	126
5:21	121
5:22	21, 87

5:24	169
5:25	148, 169
5:28	176
5:29	176, 182, 224
5:39	16
6:14	115
6:37	10, 18, 22, 30, 171
6:38	141
6:39	171
6:44	9, 15
6:45	9
6:48	1
6:48, 49, 50	54
6:55	2
6:65	15
6:66	9, 15, 20
7:17	179
7:31	126
7:37, 38	124
7:40–43	126
7:46	153
8:10, 11	123
8:12	1
8:30	126
8:56	60
10:3	29
10:10	57
10:11	3, 171
10:13	29
10:16	171, 212
10:18	172
10:28, 29	171
10:29	1
10:35	102
10:41, 42	126
11:1–44	123
11:25	2
11:38	129, 148
11:39–44	148
11:41–44	169
11:41, 42	152
11:45	126
11:49, 50	172
12:11	126
12:14, 16	80
12:20–22	52
12:37	126
12:42, 43	126
14:2	2, 165, 230
14:3	93, 165
14:16	3
14:26	62
15:4, 5	56
16:13, 14	222
Chapter 17	152, 168
17:2	171, 190
17:9	171, 188
17:21–23	121, 220, 232
17:24	165
17:26	232
18:12–14	172
18:36	3
19:38	9, 14
19:39	9
19:28–30	82
20:17	153
20:25	82
20:27	82
20:28	21, 24
20:30	20, 150
20:31	11, 20, 98, 150
21:25	11, 20, 93, 150

ACTS

1:1	114, 116
1:3	69
1:8	165

1:9	206
1:10	176, 181
1:11	176, 181, 206
2:17, 18	84
2:23	170
2:27, 31	83
3:14, 15	170
3:20–23	79
4:4	170
9:10	88
9:15	122
10:3, 17	88
10:36	1
10:38	107
13:48	22, 31, 191
15:14	62
15:18	220
16:14	234
16:30	148
16:31	1, 20, 125
19:5	107
20:35	59, 99
24:15	176, 182
26:19	85

ROMANS

3:11	30, 104
4:14–16	160
4:17–25	59
5:1	91, 98
5:12	57
5:14	54
6:3–5	106
6:23	55
7:4	231
8:1	56, 91
8:9	22
8:28	148
8:29, 30	120
8:32	60
9:5	1
9:7–9	59
9:15	131
9:21–24	89
10:9, 10	20, 122
10:13	32, 96, 234
11:25	152, 183
11:26	152, 183, 211
11:27	183, 211
11:33	9
14:10	21, 25, 176, 187, 194
14:11	196
14:23	96
15:4	51

1 CORINTHIANS

1:18, 21	118
1:24	3
1:27–29	3, 31, 123
1:30	98
2:9	227
2:14	23, 161
3:8	176
3:11	2, 117, 187
3:12–14	187, 189
3:15	187
4:5	187
6:2	196, 202
6:3	34, 41, 196, 202, 219, 222
9:25	187, 202
10:4	55
11:24–26	108
13:12	175
15:20	153, 172
15:22	57

15:23	178, 193
15:40–42	196, 202
15:45	50, 57
15:47	57
15:49	57
15:54–56	234
15:57	96, 153, 172, 234
15:58	234
16:2	159

2 CORINTHIANS

4:4	3
5:10	176, 187, 188, 194
5:17	35, 45, 57, 99
8:9	83
11:13–15	179
11:14	223
13:14	21, 24

GALATIANS

3:8, 16	61
3:28	46
4:4	76
6:14	99

EPHESIANS

1:4	22, 29, 31, 196, 204, 205
1:4–13	61
1:9, 10	46
2:1	148
2:1–5	169
2:6	175, 182
2:8	14, 120
2:9	14
2:10	35, 45

2:19–22	116
3:8–10	45
3:9	34, 37
4:8	83
4:13	99
4:24	35, 46
5:23, 30	176
5:25	171, 196, 204

PHILIPPIANS

2:8	60
2:10, 11	90
3:8	99

COLOSSIANS

1:16	34, 37, 40, 41, 227
1:17	1, 34, 37, 227
1:18	1, 2, 99
1:27	77
2:2, 3	12
2:3	1
3:10	35, 46
4:14	144

1 THESSALONIANS

1:10	71
2:19	187
4:13–17	186
14:14–18	181
4:16	99, 175, 178
4:17	175, 176, 178, 186, 195
4:18	182
5:2	186
5:21	22
5:23	35, 43

2 THESSALONIANS

1:7–10	99, 186, 197, 209
2:7	180
2:8	180, 206
2:9	136
2:13	30

1 TIMOTHY

1:17	24
2:5	123
3:16	21, 23, 97
4:1	155
4:1–3	182
5:21	40, 224
6:15	99
6:19	2

2 TIMOTHY

1:9	22, 31, 122
2:19	117, 188
3:1–5	155
4:1	2, 99
4:8	175, 177, 187
4:17	87

TITUS

1:1	96
1:2	22, 28
2:5	3
2:10	159
2:13	176, 193
3:5	99

PHILEMON

1:25	99

HEBREWS

1:1, 2	34, 38
1:1–3	93, 94
1:2	3
1:6, 7, 10	34, 40
1:8	54
1:14	137
2:9	52
2:10	3, 94
2:14, 15	223
2:18	94, 110
3:2	68
4:12	3
4:14–16	172
4:15	94, 109
4:16	94
5:5, 6	80
5:9	3, 99
6:20	172
7:2	58
7:3	58, 172
7:4	59
7:15	58, 172
7:16, 17, 27	172
8:6	27
8:10–12	211
9:14, 15, 24–28	172
10:20	2
10:28, 29, 31, 37	91
11:4, 5, 7, 8	175
11:17	59
11:18	59, 61
11:19	60
11:23	175
11:24–27	68
11:31	212
12:1	178
12:2	121

13:20 .... 21, 25, 28, 153, 172, 173
13:21 172

JAMES
1:12 .... 99, 187
1:13 .... 94, 109
1:22 114
2:25 212
2:26 .... 114, 212
4:7 223

1 PETER
1:2 122
1:10, 11 .... 73, 75, 92
2:7, 8 89
2:25 99
3:9 96
3:19 83
3:22 63
5:4 .... 3, 96, 187
5:7 140

2 PETER
1:4 232
1:10 96
2:1 .... *xi*
2:1–3 182
2:4 .... 219, 223
2:5 179
3:9 .... 93, 99, 188
3:13 .... 35, 47, 220, 227

1 JOHN
1:1 100

1:2, 4, 30 100
2:19 15
3:2 .... 220, 232
3:8 222
4:1–3 182
4:2 .... 58, 99, 100
4:3 100
4:5 .... *xi*
4:5, 6 23
5:10 13
5:11 .... 13, 20
5:20 100

2 JOHN
7 .... *xi*, 101
8 232
9 .... 99, 101, 159
10 101

3 JOHN
7 99

JUDE
1 99
6 .... 219, 223

REVELATION
1:5 .... 22, 29
1:6 .... 91, 196, 202, 218
1:7 .... 193, 211
1:8 2
1:13 91
1:13–15 .... 87, 90
1:14–16 91

1:18	90, 226
2:18	91
2:26, 27	196, 203
Chapters 3–18	194
3:7–13	175, 179
3:11	176, 189
3:14–21	175, 179
3:16	180
3:21	90
4:1–4	186
4:1–11	181
4:4	196, 198
4:10	187, 196, 198
4:11	175, 187, 198
5:5	1, 99
5:9	196, 199, 203, 216
5:9–14	196
5:10	90, 193, 196, 198, 199, 203, 216
5:11–12	199
6:9–11	176, 191
7:3, 4	166
7:4–8	152
7:9, 10	22, 29
7:9–12	196, 199
7:13	192
7:14	176, 192
7:15	176
7:16	2, 233
7:17	3
11:15–17	196, 200
13:3, 13	136
13:8	22, 29
13:14	136, 197
14:3–5	196, 200
14:8	231
14:13–15	176
14:14, 15	197, 205, 206
15:3, 4	196, 200
16:14, 16	197, 217
17:8	22, 29, 258
Chapters 17–19	236
17:8	2, 231
17:14	99, 176, 191, 197, 205, 206
18:24	197, 210
19:1, 4–6	196, 200
19:8	197, 209
19:6–9	176, 191
19:7–9	137, 196, 204, 231
19:10	51
19:11	176, 197, 205, 207, 209
19:12	91, 187
19:13, 14	207
19:13–16	197, 205
19:14	197, 209
19:15	197, 206, 207, 218
19:16	138, 176, 207, 218
19:17, 18	197, 210
19:19	87, 176, 197, 205, 207
19:20	87, 197, 205, 207, 219
19:21	197, 210
Chapter 20	183, 195, 208
20:2, 7–10	197, 198
20:3, 8	218
20:4	176, 182, 192, 196, 197, 204, 210
20:4–6	176
20:5	182, 197, 210
20:6	193
20:10	207, 219, 223, 226
20:10–15	219, 224
20:11	21, 25, 227
20:11–15	90, 152
20:12–15	219
20:14	96, 226
21:1	35, 47, 220, 227, 233
21:2	1, 220
21:3	220

21:4	220, 231, 233
21:5	2, 230
21:6	220
21:7	220, 230, 231
21:8	40, 232
21:9	1, 176, 191, 196, 204, 220, 230
21:10–15	220
21:11–27	35, 47
21:12, 13	229
21:16, 18, 19	228
21:20	229
21:21	229
21:23	230
21:24	231
21:24–26	229
21:25	229, 230
21:27	220, 230, 231, 232, 233
22:1	229
22:1–3	220
22:1–5	35, 47
22:2	230
22:3	220, 231
22:3–5	228, 230
22:4	220, 230
22:5	220, 230, 231
22:11	220, 231, 232
22:12	176, 202, 233
22:13	2, 202, 233
22:14	202, 230, 233
22:15	232, 233
22:16	1, 55
22:17	196, 202, 204, 233
22:23	230

Note

This unique book of less than 300 pages, has nearly 1,700 Scripture references that directly or indirectly point to Christ.

May each reader find full satisfaction for the soul, and fulfillment for the life that can be used for the Lord.

OUTSTANDING BOOKS
BY C. H. SPURGEON

*

MATTHEW: THE GOSPEL OF THE KINGDOM

SWORD AND TROWEL - SPURGEON'S WORKS IN HIS MAGAZINE

SERMONS ON UNUSUAL OCCASIONS

LECTURES TO MY STUDENTS

C. H. SPURGEON'S PRAYERS

METROPOLITAN TABERNACLE — ITS HISTORY AND WORK

THE BEATITUDES

THE COVENANT OF GRACE

WORDS OF CHRIST FROM THE CROSS

AN ALL-ROUND MINISTRY

ALL OF GRACE

"COME YE CHILDREN"

ONLY A PRAYER MEETING

THE SOUL WINNER

THE TEACHINGS OF NATURE IN THE KINGDOM OF GRACE

"TILL HE COME"

THE SALT CELLARS

WORDS OF WISDOM FOR DAILY LIFE

FARM SERMONS

ABLE TO THE UTTERMOST

THE TREASURY OF DAVID

NEW PARK STREET PULPIT

METROPOLITAN TABERNACLE PULPIT

These great books and many more by the late C. H. Spurgeon have been reprinted from the original editions by Pilgrim Publications. P.O. Box 66,

ELIHU BURRITT LIBRARY
CENTRAL CONNECTICUT STATE UNIVERSITY
NEW BRITAIN, CONNECTICUT 06050

REFERENCE

NOT TO BE TAKEN
FROM LIBRARY

DIRECTORY OF UNPUBLISHED EXPERIMENTAL MENTAL MEASURES

■ VOLUME 5

DIRECTORY OF UNPUBLISHED EXPERIMENTAL MENTAL MEASURES

BERT ARTHUR GOLDMAN, Ed.D.
Professor of Education
University of North Carolina at Greensboro

DAVID F. MITCHELL, Ph.D.
Assistant Professor of Sociology
University of North Carolina at Greensboro

SERIES EDITOR
Bert Arthur Goldman, Ed.D.

WCB Wm. C. Brown Publishers

Copyright © 1990 by Wm. C. Brown Publishers. All rights reserved

Library of Congress Catalog Card Number: 73-17342

ISBN 0-697-11490-2

No part of this publication may be reproduced, stored in a retrieval system, or transmitted in any form or by any means, electronic, mechanical, photocopying, recording, or otherwise, without prior written permission of the publisher.

Printed in United States of America by Wm. C. Brown Publishers, 2460 Kerper Boulevard, Dubuque, IA 52001

10 9 8 7 6 5 4 3 2 1

To our families

B.G.
D.F.M.

CONTENTS

Preface	ix
Achievement	1
Adjustment-Educational	13
Adjustment-Psychological	27
Adjustment-Social	76
Adjustment-Vocational	106
Aptitude	130
Attitude	136
Behavior	180
Communication	220
Concept Meaning	233
Creativity	239
Development	241
Family	250
Institutional Information	287
Motivation	319
Perception	331

Personality	411
Preference	431
Problem-Solving and Reasoning	444
Status	455
Trait Measurement	458
Values	487
Vocational Evaluation	504
Vocational Interest	527
Author Index	551
Subject Index	579

PREFACE

Purpose: This *Directory of Unpublished Experimental Mental Measures* Vol. 5, marks the fifth in a series of publications designed to fill a need for reference tools in behavioral and social science research. The authors recognized the need for the publication of a directory to experimental test instruments, i.e., tests that are not currently marketed commercially. It is intended that this reference provide researchers with ready access to sources of information about recently developed experimental measurement devices. The instruments are not evaluated, however it is anticipated that the directory stimulate further research of these experimental instruments. In essence, this directory provides references to nonstandardized, experimental mental measures currently undergoing development. The directory is not intended to provide evaluation of the instruments, nor is it intended to provide all necessary information for the researcher contemplating the use of a particular instrument; rather it should serve as a reference to enable the reader to identify potentially useful measures and to identify sources from which technical information concerning the instruments can be obtained.

Development: Thirty-seven relevant professional journals available to the authors were examined. The following list includes those journals which, in the judgment of the authors, contained research involving instruments of value to researchers in education, psychology, and sociology. Foreign journals were not surveyed for use in this directory. Measures identified in dissertations were excluded as a matter of expediency and because the microfilm abstracts generally contain minimal information.

American Journal of Sociology
Career Development Quarterly
Child Development
Child Study Journal
College Teaching
Comparative Social Research
Educational and Psychological Measurement
Educational Research Quarterly
Gifted Child Quarterly
Journal of Applied Psychology
Journal of College Student Personnel
Journal of Consulting and Clinical Psychology
Journal of Counseling Psychology
Journal of Creative Behavior
Journal of Educational Measurement
Journal of Educational Psychology

Journal of Educational Research
Journal of Experimental Education
Journal of General Education
Journal of Marriage and the Family
Journal of Occupational Psychology
Journal of Personality Assessment
Journal of Psychopathology and Behavioral Assessment
Journal of Reading
Journal of School Psychology
Journal of Social Psychology
Journal of Vocational Behavior
Measurement and Evaluation in Counseling and Development
Perceptual and Motor Skills
Personnel Psychology
Psychological Reports
Reading Research Quarterly
Social Psychology Quarterly
Sociological Methods and Research
Sociology and Social Research
Sociology of Education
The School Counselor

This directory lists tests described in the 1981-85 issues of the previously cited journals. An attempt was made to omit commercially published standardized tests, task-type activities such as memory word lists used in serial learning research and achievement tests developed for a single, isolated course of study. The reader should not assume that the instruments described herein form a representative sample of the universe of unpublished experimental mental measures.

Organization: This volume incorporates an additional category not found in the previous volumes, i.e., Adjustment--Vocational. Following is a brief description of each of the twenty-four categories under which the authors grouped the measures of Volume 5:

Achievement: Measure learning and/or comprehension in specific areas. Also include tests of memory and tests of drug knowledge.

Adjustment--Educational: Measure academic satisfaction. Also include tests of school anxiety.

Adjustment--Psychological: Evaluate conditions and levels of adjustment along the psychological dimension including, for example, tests of mood, fear of death, anxiety, depression, etc.

Adjustment--Social: Evaluate aspects of interactions with others. Also include tests of alienation, conformity, need for social approval, social desirability, instruments for assessing interpersonal attraction and sensitivity.

Adjustment--Vocational: Identify burnout, vocational maturity, job-related stress, job frustration, job satisfaction, etc.

Aptitude: Predict success in given activities.

Attitude: Measure reaction to a variety of experiences and objects.

Behavior: Measure general and specific types of activities such as classroom behavior and drug-use behavior.

Communication: Evaluate information exchange. Also include tests of self-disclosure and counselor/client interaction.

Concept Meaning: Test one's understanding of words and other concepts. Also include tests of conceptual structure, style, and information processing.

Creativity: Measure ability to reorganize data or information into unique configurations. Also include tests of divergent thinking.

Development: Measure emerging characteristics, primarily for preschool ages. Also include tests of cognitive and moral development.

Family: Measure intrafamily relations. Also include tests of marital satisfaction, nurturance, parental interest, and warmth.

Institutional Information: Evaluate institutions and their functioning.

Motivation: Measure goal strength. Also include measures of curiosity.

Perception: Determine how one sees self and other objects. Also include tests dealing with empathy, imagery, locus of control, self-concept, and time.

Personality: Measure general personal attributes. Also include biographical information and defense mechanisms.

Preference: Identify choices. Also include tests of preference for objects, taste preference, and sex-role preference.

Problem-Solving and Reasoning: Measure general ability to reason through a number of alternative solutions, to generate such solutions to problems, etc.

Status: Identify a hierarchy of acceptability.

Trait Measurement: Identify and evaluate unitary traits. Also include tests of anger, anxiety, authoritarianism, blame, and cheating.

Values: Measure worth one ascribes to an object or activity. Include tests of moral, philosophical, political, and religious values.

Vocational Evaluation: Evaluate a person for a specific position.

Vocational Interest: Measure interest in specific occupations and vocations as well as interest in general categories of activity.

The choice of the category under which each test was grouped was determined by the purpose of the test and/or its apparent content. The authors attempted to include the following facts regarding each test, however, in many cases not all of these facts were provided in the journal article:

Test Name

Purpose

Description

> Number of items
>
> Time required
>
> Format

Statistics

> Reliability (In most cases the particular design used to assess consistency is specified)
>
> Validity (Includes correlation with other tests and group difference information which help to define the characteristic being measured by the test)

Source

> Author
>
> Title
>
> Journal (Includes date of publication, volume, and page number)

Related Research

> Information identifying publications related to the source.
>
> Volume 5 contains only those tests for which the journal article presented as a minimum: Test Name, Purpose, Source, and at least four facts from either Description, Statistics, and Related Research.

The reader is alerted to the fact that the numbers within the Index refer to test numbers rather than to page numbers as was the case with Volume 1.

As a convenience to the reader, the authors have incorporated the indices from the four previous volumes in this Index and in so doing they converted all page numbers to test numbers. Thus, numbers 1 through 339 refer to tests of Volume 1, numbers 340 through 1034 refer to tests of Volume 2, numbers 1035 through 1595 refer to tests of Volume 3, numbers 1596 through 2369 refer to tests of Volume 4, and numbers 2370 through 3665 refer to tests of Volume 5. As was the case with Volume 4, a noncumulative author index is included.

The authors express their appreciation to Elizabeth House for typing the manuscript with assistance from Anita Hawkins. Additional thanks is extended to Ms. Katherine Poole and Deetra Thompson for their help in preparing the indices. Finally, the authors wish to thank the William C. Brown Publishers for taking over the publication of the directories.

Bert Arthur Goldman

David F. Mitchell

ACHIEVEMENT

2370
Test name: ANAPHORA TEST

Purpose: To measure understanding of anaphoric relations.

Number of items: 50

Format: Sample item presented.

Reliability: .87.

Author: Johnson, B. and Johnson, D.

Article: Elementary student's comprehension of anaphora in well-formed stories.

Journal: *Journal of Educational Research,* March/April 1985, *78*(4), 221-223.

Related research: Halliday, M.A. and Hasan, R. *Cohesion in English.* London: Longman, 1976.

2371
Test name: BASIC MATHEMATICS TEST

Purpose: To measure basic mathematics skills.

Number of items: 36

Format: Multiple-choice.

Reliability: Alpha of .89.

Validity: Correlations with Statistical Attitude Survey were .27 and .37.

Author: Roberts, D.M. and Saxe, J.E.

Article: Validity of a statistics attitude survey: A follow-up study.

Journal: *Educational and Psychological Measurement,* autumn 1982, *42*(3), 907-912.

2372
Test name: BASIC STATISTICS TEST

Purpose: To measure basic statistics.

Number of items: 20

Format: Covers descriptive statistics from frequency distributions to correlation.

Reliability: Alpha of .63 (pretest) and alpha of .55 (posttest).

Validity: Correlations with Statistical Attitude Survey ranged from .25 to .42.

Author: Roberts, D.M. and Saxe, J.E.

Article: Validity of a statistics attitude survey: A follow-up study.

Journal: *Educational and Psychological Measurement,* Autumn 1982, *42*(3), 907-912.

2373
Test name: CHILDREN'S HANDWRITING SCALE

Purpose: To measure rate and quality of penmanship (grades 3-8).

Number of items: 1 paragraph of 197 letters (except x and z) is evaluated on 5 characteristics.

Format: Children read paragraph, then copy it as well as they can. Progress in the first two minutes is marked. Characteristics rated are: form, slant, rhythm, space, and general appearance.

Reliability: For single rater .64 to .82.

Validity: Significant relationship found between males and females on letter per minute rate.

Author: Phelps, J. et al.

Article: The Children's Handwriting Scale

Journal: *Journal of Educational Research,* Sept./Oct. 1985, *79*(1), 46-50.

2374
Test name: COUNSELING INFORMATION SCALE

Purpose: To measure knowledge about counseling.

Number of items: 8

Format: Multiple-choice.

Reliability: Split-half = .67.

Validity: Counselors scored higher than students ($p < .001$).

Author: Davidshofer, C.O. and Richardson, G.G.

Article: Effects of precounseling training.

Journal: *Journal of College Student Personnel,* Nov. 1981, *22*(6), 522-527.

2375
Test name: DIAGNOSTIC INVENTORY

Purpose: To measure and evaluate manuscript and cursive writing.

Number of items: 7

Format: Trained raters rate writing on a three-point scale.

Reliability: Inter-rater reliability = .43 or above on global score and .18 or above on separate facets of writing.

Author: Armitage, D. and Ratzlaff, H.

2376
Test name: HANDWRITING LEGIBILITY

Purpose: To measure legibility of handwriting.

Number of items: 6 letters.

Format: Letters presented two at a time on worksheets and evaluated by a plastic overlay.

Reliability: Inter-scorer agreement = 96%.

Author: Sims, E.V., Jr. and Weisberg, P.

Article: Effects of page prompts on beginning handwriting legibility.

Journal: *Journal of Educational Research*, July/Aug. 1984, 77(6), 360-365.

Related research: Helwig, J. et al., 1976. The measurement of manuscript letter strokes. *Journal of Applied Behavior Analysis*, 9, 231-236.

2377
Test name: HEBREW VISUAL DISCRIMINATION TEST

Purpose: To measure nonverbal visual discrimination.

Number of items: 50

Format: Match-to-model task employing Hebrew letter script with sets of items for letters, syllables, words, phrases, and a total score.

Reliability: KR-20 internal-consistency reliability estimate for the total was .91.

Validity: Correlations with other variables ranged from -.13 to .57.

Author: Morrison, J.A. and Michael, W.B.

Article: Validity of measures reflecting visual discrimination and linguistic constructs for a sample of second-grade Hispanic children receiving reading instruction in Spanish.

Journal: *Educational and Psychological Measurement*, summer 1984, 44(2), 333-351.

Related research: Velluntino, F.R. et al., 1973. Visual recall in poor and normal readers as a function of

---

Article: The non-correlation of writing and print skills.

Journal: *Journal of Educational Research*, Jan./Feb. 1985, 78(3), 174-177.

Related research: Herrick, V.E. and Erlenbacher, A., 1963. The Evolution of Legibility in Handwriting, in V.E. Herrick (Ed.), *New Horizons for Research in Handwriting*. Madison, WI: University of Wisconsin Press.

orthographic-linguistic familiarity. *Cortex, 9*, 368-384.

2378
Test name: HUMOR PERCEPTIVENESS TEST—REVISED

Purpose: To measure humor comprehension.

Number of items: 32

Format: Items are in the form of joke completions. All items are presented.

Reliability: Reliability coefficients (split-half, Kuder-Richardson, alternate form) ranged from .84 to .93.

Validity: Correlation with WAISI Q was .58.

Author: Feingold, A.

Article: Measuring humor ability: Revision and construct validation of the Humor Perceptiveness Test.

Journal: *Perceptual and Motor Skills,* Feb. 1983, *56*(1), 159-166.

Related research: Feingold, A., 1982. Measuring humor: A pilot study. *Perceptual and Motor Skills, 54,* 986.

2379
Test name: JOBS-CAREER KEY

Purpose: To measure general occupational knowledge.

Number of items: 147

Format: Multiple-choice items measuring three areas: education-training requirements, job conditions and characteristics, and worker relationships.

Reliability: Coefficient alphas were .79 and .83. Test-retest reliability was r = .62 (2 weeks).

Author: Taylor, M.S.

Article: The roles of occupational knowledge and vocational self-concept crystallization in students' school-to-work transition.

Journal: *Journal of Counseling Psychology,* Oct. 1985, *32*(4), 539-550.

Related research: Blank, J.R., 1979. Jobs-Career Key: A test of occupational information. *Vocational Guidance Quarterly, 26,* 9-17.

2380
Test name: JOB KNOWLEDGE SURVEY

Purpose: To assess knowledge.

Number of items: 48

Format: Each item is evaluated as having a high, medium, or low involvement with data, people, and things.

Reliability: Test-retest reliabilities ranged from .44 to .80.

Validity: Correlations with Work Values Inventory ranged from -.39 to .37.

Author: Sampson, J.P. and Loesch, L.C.

Article: Relationships among work values and job knowledge.

Journal: *Vocational Guidance Quarterly*, March, 1981, *29*(3), 229-235.

Related research: Loesch, L.C. et al., 1978. A field test of an instrument for assessing job knowledge. *Measurement and Evaluation in Guidance*, *11*, 26-33.

2381
Test name: KINDERGARTEN PERFORMANCE PROFILE

Purpose: To measure and rate kindergarten children's performance.

Number of items: 8 (4 classroom work skills and 4 classroom social skills).

Reliability: Test-retest = .70-.84 for work skills; .69-.77 for social skills. Inter-rater reliability = .67-.77 for work skills; .45-.65 for social skills. Cronbach's alpha = .80-.82 for composite scores.

Author: Swartz, J.P. and Walker, D.K.

Article: The relationship between teacher ratings of kindergarten classroom skills and second grade achievement scores: An analysis of gender differences.

Journal: *Journal of School Psychology*, 1984, *22*(2), 209-217.

Related research: DiNola, A.J. et al., 1970. *Preschool and primary performance profile*. Ridgefield, N.J.: Educational Performance Associates.

2382
Test name: KNOWLEDGE OF BEHAVIORAL PRINCIPLES AS APPLIED TO CHILDREN SCALE

Purpose: To measure knowledge parents have of behavioral principles for child-management.

Number of items: 50

Format: Multiple-choice. Sample item presented.

Reliability: Split-half ranged from .76 to .88. KR-20 ranged from .59 to .88.

Author: McLoughlin, C.S.

Article: Utility and efficacy of knowledge of behavioral principles as applied to children.

Journal: *Psychological Reports,* April 1985, 56(2), 463-467.

Related research: O'Dell, S.L. et al., 1979. An instrument to measure knowledge of behavioral principles as applied to children. *Journal of Behavior Therapy and Experimental Psychiatry, 10,* 29-34.

2383
Test name: MATHEMATICS ACHIEVEMENT TEST

Purpose: To measure achievement in mathematics.

Number of items: 70

Format: Test-type questions covering concepts in skills. Sample items presented in English, Japanese, and Chinese.

Reliability: Cronbach's alpha ranged from .93 to .95 across grades and countries.

Validity: United States students scored significantly lower than Japanese and Taiwanese students ($p < .05$).

Author: Stigler, J.W. et al.

Article: Curriculum and achievement in mathematics: A study of elementary school children in Japan, Taiwan and the United States.

Journal: *Journal of Educational Psychology,* April 1982, 74(2), 315-322.

2384
Test name: MEMORY ASSESSMENT QUESTIONNAIRE

Purpose: To assess six aspects of a memory.

Number of items: 7

Format: All but two items were in Likert-scale form. All items are presented.

Reliability: Inter-judge reliability for each item ranged from .23 to .93.

Author: Ireland, M.S. and Kernan-Schloss, L.

Article: Pattern analysis of recorded daydreams, memories, and personality type.

Journal: *Perceptual and Motor Skills,* Feb. 1983, 56(1), 119-125.

Related research: Starker, S., 1973. Aspects of inner experience, autokinesis, daydreaming, dream recall and cognitive style. *Perceptual and Motor Skills, 36,* 663-673.

2385
Test name: MEMORY CHECK

Purpose: To measure mental status.

Number of items: 15

Format: Instrument is administered directly to the person being evaluated. All items are presented.

Validity: Correlations with: Competence Index was -.67; Impairment Index was -.69; Functional Behavior Survey was .71.

Author: Tobacyk, J. et al.

Article: Two brief measures for assessing mental competence in the elderly.

Journal: *Journal of Personality Assessment*, Dec. 1983, 47(6), 648-655.

Related research: Dixon, J.C., 1965. Cognitive structure in senile conditions with some suggestions for developing a brief screening test of mental status. *Journal of Gerontology*, 20, 41-49.

2386
Test name: MEMORY IMPAIRMENT SCALE

Purpose: To measure memory impairment.

Number of items: 10

Format: Observation rating scale. All items presented. Observers use a 6-point frequency scale (always to not at all).

Reliability: Item-remainder correlations ranged from .60 to .93. Inter-rater reliability (two raters) = .86. Generalizability coefficients ranged from .69 to .96.

Validity: Correlation with assorted memory tasks ranged from .48 to .86 ($p < .05$) and with Wechsler Memory Scale = .68 ($p < .01$).

Author: Knight, R.G. and Godfrey, H.P.D.

Article: Reliability and validity of a scale for rating memory impairment in hospitalized amnesiacs.

Journal: *Journal of Consulting and Clinical Psychology*, Oct. 1984, 52(5), 769-773.

2387
Test name: MORPHOGRAPHIC TRANSFER TEST

Purpose: To measure the ability to apply morphographic knowledge.

Number of items: 15 (Test A).

Format: Mulitple-choice. Sample item presented.

Reliability: Cronbach's alpha = .81.

Author: Jacka, B.

Article: The teaching of defined concepts: A test of Gragne and Briggs' model of instructional design.

Journal: *Journal of Educational Research*, March/April 1985, *78*(4), 224-227.

Related research: Gragne, R.M. and Briggs, L.J., 1974. *Principles of instructional design.* New York: Holt, Rinehart and Winston.

2388

Test name: ORAL READING AND RECALL EVALUATION SCALE

Purpose: To measure reading comprehension ability.

Number of items: 20

Format: 6-step scale from highly ineffective to highly effective.

Reliability: Alpha = .89.

Validity: Correlations with Reading Miscue Inventory ("moderately effective" RMI subjects yielded moderate scores on this scale).

Author: Taylor, J.B.

Article: Influence of speech variety on teachers' evaluation of reading comprehension.

Journal: *Journal of Educational Psychology*, Oct. 1983, *73*(5), 662-667.

2389

Test name: PERCEPTIVE LISTENING TEST

Purpose: To measure musical knowledge.

Number of items: 20

Format: 9 multiple-choice definition questions; 11 musical excerpts on audiotape. Sample items presented.

Reliability: Cronbach's alpha = .83.

Validity: Correlated .45 with IQ.

Author: Bledsoe, J.C.

Article: Efficacy of popular music in learning music concepts in seventh grade general music classes.

Journal: *Psychological Reports*, April 1984, *51*(2), 381-382.

2390

Test name: PRINT AWARENESS TEST

Purpose: To measure prereaders understanding of the function of print.

Number of items: 15

Format: Questions asked of child with pictures illustrating possible answers.

Reliability: Internal consistency = .85.

Validity: Correlations between print awareness scale and other measures of general ability and prereading skills ranged from -.05 to .77.

Author: Huba, M.E. and Kontos, S.

Article: Measuring print awareness in young children.

Journal: *Journal of Educational Research*, May/June 1985, 78(5), 272-279.

2391
Test name: READING MISCUE INVENTORY

Purpose: To measure comprehension effectiveness of oral reading by assessing how reader processes information being read.

Number of items: Varies.

Format: Takes into account deviations made by readers while reading and how the deviations affect intended meaning and ability to recall information. Sample items given.

Reliability: Ranged from .89 to .95.

Author: Taylor, J.B.

Article: Influence of speech variety on teachers' evaluations of reading comprehension.

Journal: *Journal of Educational Psychology,* Oct. 1983, 75(5), 662-667.

Related research: Goodman, Y. and Burke, C., 1972. *Reading miscue inventory manual: Procedures for diagnosis and evaluation.* New York: Macmillan.

2392
Test name: READING SPAN TEST

Purpose: To measure ability to store and process information in working memory.

Number of items: 6 (sets of unrelated sentences -- with 2-5 sentences preset).

Format: Sample item presented. Sentences presented on screens for 8 seconds, and then respondent asked to write down the last word in each. Scores were percent of final words recalled.

Validity: Correlates .53 ($p < .01$) with Nelson-Denny Reading Test.

Author: Masson, M.E.J. and Miller, J.A.

Article: Working memory and individual differences in comprehension and memory of text.

Journal: *Journal of Educational Psychology*, April 1983, 75(2), 314-318.

Related research: Daneman, M. and Carpenter, P.A., 1980. Individual differences in working memory and reading. *Journal of Verbal Learning and Verbal Behavior, 19*, 450-466.

2393
Test name: SEX INFORMATION QUESTIONNAIRE

Purpose: To measure knowledge about human sexual functioning.

Number of items: 30

Format: Multiple-choice format. Examples are presented.

Reliability: Test-retest reliability was .67.

Author: Alyn, J.H. and Becker, L.A.

Article: Feminist therapy with chronically and profoundly disturbed women.

Journal: *Journal of Counseling Psychology*, April 1984, *31*(2), 202-208.

Related research: McDermott, L., 1980. *Sex Information Questionnaire.* Unpublished manuscript, University of Colorado, Colorado Springs.

2394
Test name: SPANISH VISUAL DISCRIMINATION TEST

Purpose: To measure second graders' verbally based Spanish visual discrimination.

Number of items: 59

Format: Match-to-model task including sets of items for letters, syllables, words, phrases, and a total score.

Reliability: KR-20 internal-consistency reliability coefficients were .82 and .85.

Validity: Correlations with other variables ranged from -.11 to .57.

Author: Morrison, J.A. and Michael, W.B.

Article: Validity of measures reflecting visual discrimination and linguistic constructs for a sample of second-grade Hispanic children receiving reading instruction in Spanish.

Journal: *Educational and Psychological Measurement*, summer 1984, *44*(3), 333-351.

Related research: Ransom, G.A., 1978. *Preparing to teach reading.* Boston: Little, Brown.

2395
Test name: TEACHER RATING SCALE

Purpose: To obtain ratings of students by teachers on students' reading level.

Number of items: 7

Format: Teachers choose the one item that best describes a student. All items presented.

Reliability: Correlation between two raters was r = .58 (p < .001).

Validity: Correlates from .64 to .66 with California Achievement Test Reading Scores.

Author: Powers, S. and De La Garza, J.

Article: Stability and predictive validity of the Teacher Rating Scale.

Journal: *Psychological Reports,* Oct. 1985, *52*(2), 543-546.

Related research: Slaughter, H.B., 1980. *Teacher Rating Scale.* (Unpublished manuscript, Tucson Unified School District, E.C.I.A. Chapter 1 project, Tucson, Ariz.)

2396
Test name: TEST ON ECONOMIC DECISION-MAKING (TED)

Purpose: To assess the ability to apply and use economic principles.

Number of items: 30

Format: Multiple-choice (4-choices per question).

Reliability: Guttman split-half = .84.

Author: Kourilsky, M.

Article: Economic socialization of children: Attitude toward the distribution of rewards.

Journal: *Journal of Social Psychology,* Oct. 1981, *115*(first half), 45-57.

2397
Test name: VISUAL MEMORY TEST

Purpose: To measure the ability to remember pictures.

Number of items: 14

Format: Multiple-choice.

Reliability: KR = .49.

Author: Shaw, G.A.

Article: The use of imagery by intelligent and by creative school children.

Journal: *Journal of General Psychology,* April 1985, *112*(2), 153-171.

Related research: Marks, D.F., 1973. Visual imagery differences in the recall of pictures. *British Journal of Psychology, 61,* 17-24.

2398
Test name: WORD READING TASK MEASURE

Purpose: To measure phonics achievement of learning disabled children.

Number of items: 64 words.

Time required: 6 seconds per word.

Format: Children presented words on index cards and responses recorded on tape and evaluated by trained examiners. Sample items presented.

Reliability: Posttest split-half reliabilities ranged from .74 to .92.

Validity: Pretest scores were very low. IQ, age, and sex not strongly related to posttest scores (.13 was maximum correlation).

Author: Fayne, H.R. and Bryant, N.D.

Article: Relative effects of various words synthesis strategies on the phonics achievement of learning disabled youngsters.

Journal: *Journal of Educational Psychology*, Oct. 1981. 73(5), 616-623.

ADJUSTMENT-
EDUCATIONAL

2399
Test name: ACADEMIC AND SOCIAL INTEGRATION INSTRUMENT

Purpose: To measure the academic and social integration of students in their colleges.

Number of items: 32

Format: Multiple-choice and Likert-format agreement scales.

Reliability: Alphas ranged from .46 to .64 across the two subscales.

Author: Pascarella, E.T. and Terenzini, P.T.

Article: Predicting voluntary freshmen year persistence/withdrawal behavior in a residential university: A path analytic validation of Tinto's Model.

Journal: *Journal of Educational Psychology*, April 1983, *75*(2), 215-226.

Related research: Tinto, V., 1975. Dropout from higher education: A theoretical synthesis of recent research. *Review of Educational Research, 45*, 89-125.

2400
Test name: ADJUSTMENT TO COLLEGE SCALE

Purpose: To measure adjustment to college.

Number of items: 67

Format: Students respond to each item on a 9-point scale. Includes four subscales: academic adjustment, social adjustment, personal/emotional, goal commitment/institutional attachment and the full scale. Some examples are presented.

Reliability: Coefficient alphas ranged from .78 to .95.

Author: Baker, R.W. et al.

Article: Expectation and reality in freshmen adjustment to college.

Journal: *Journal of Counseling Psychology*, Jan. 1985, *32*(1), 94-103.

Related research: Baker, R.W. and Siryk, B., (1984). Measuring adjustment to college. *Journal of Counseling Psychology, 31*, 179-189.

2401
Test name: ADJUSTMENT TO COLLEGE SCALE

Purpose: To measure adjustment to college.

Number of items: 52

Format: Includes four subscales: academic, social, personal-emotional, general. Examples are provided.

Reliability: Cronbach's alpha ranged from .82 to .88 for the subscales and from .92 to .94 for the full scale.

Validity: Point-biserial correlations with attrition after 1 year ranged from -.02 to -.43 (N's ranged from 172 to 233). Point-biserial correlations with freshman year grade point average ranged from -.14 to .32 (N's ranged from 171 to 229).

Author: Baker, R.W. and Siryk, B.

Article: Measuring adjustment to college.

Journal: *Journal of Counseling Psychology,* April 1984, *31*(2), 179-189.

2402
Test name: CHECKLIST OF POSITIVE AND NEGATIVE THOUGHTS

Purpose: To measure positive and negative thoughts affecting concentration and performance on tests.

Number of items: 37

Format: Checklist. All items presented.

Reliability: Alpha = .77 (positive thoughts) and .79 (negative thoughts).

Author: Gralassi, J.P. et al.

Article: Behavior of high, moderate and low test-anxious students during an actual test situation.

Journal: *Journal of Consulting and Clinical Psychology,* Feb. 1985, *49*(1), 51-62.

Related research: Sarason, I.G. et al., 1978. The test anxiety scale: Concept and research. In C.D. Spielberger and I.G. Sarason (Eds.), *Stress and Anxiety, 5.* Washington, D.C.: Hemisphere.

2403
Test name: CHECKLIST OF POSITIVE AND NEGATIVE THOUGHTS—MODIFIED

Purpose: To enable students to provide data on the frequency of positive and negative thoughts outside of an actual testing situation and to assess frequency of control over negative thoughts.

Number of items: 56

Format: Part one: Subjects rate each of 37 positive and negative thoughts on a 5-point scale, indicating how often each thought occurred to them while taking exams (1 = never, 5 = very often). Part two: Subjects rate each of the 19 negative thoughts on a 6-point scale indicating how often they can control each type of thought (0 = never had a thought like this, 1 = can never stop this type of thought, 5 = can stop this type of thought very often).

Reliability: Cronbach's alphas ranged from .86 to .94.

Author: Brown, S.D. and Nelson, T.L.

Article: Beyond the uniformity myth: A comparison of academically successful and unsuccessful test-anxious college students.

Journal: *Journal of Consulting Psychology*, July 1983, *30*(3), 367-374.

Related research: Galassi, J.P. et al., 1981. Behavior of high, moderate, and low test-anxious students during an actual test situation. *Journal of Consulting and Clinical Psychology*, *49*, 51-62.

2404

Test name: CHILDREN'S ACADEMIC ANXIETY INVENTORY

Purpose: To measure academic anxieties.

Number of items: 12 (3 per 4 subject areas).

Format: 5-point Likert categories. Sample items presented.

Reliability: Test-retest = .70 to .85 (seventh graders); Test-retest = .50 to .65 (fourth graders). Alphas ranged from .50 to .65 across areas (all children).

Validity: Correlations with Otis-Lennon Mental Ability test ranged from -.20 to -.43.

Author: Gottfried, A.E.

Article: Relationships between academic intrinsic motivation and anxiety in children and young adolescents.

Journal: *Journal of School Psychology*, 1982, *20*(3), 205-215.

2405

Test name: CHILDREN'S COGNITIVE ASSESSMENT QUESTIONNAIRE

Purpose: To measure perceived negative evaluations, off-task thoughts, positive evaluations, and on-task thoughts.

Number of items: 40

Format: Yes-no. All items presented.

Reliability: Alphas ranged from .67 to .82 across subscales. Test-retest ranged from .63 to .71.

Validity: Discriminated between low, moderate, and highly anxious children (canonical correlation = .60, p < .01).

Author: Zatz, S. and Chassin, L.

Article: Cognitions of test-anxious children.

Journal: *Journal of Consulting and Clinical Psychology*, Aug. 1983, *51*(4), 526-534.

2406
Test name: CLASSROOM ADJUSTMENT SCALE

Purpose: To measure children's classroom adjustment.

Number of items: 41

Format: Includes three factors of acting-out, moodiness, and learning.

Reliability: Test-retest reliability was .92.

Author: Jason, L.A. et al.

Article: Establishing supervising behaviors in eighth graders and peer-tutoring behaviors in first graders.

Journal: *Child Study Journal*, 1981, *11*(4), 201-219.

Related research: Lorion, R.P. et al., 1975. Normative and parametric analysis of school maladjustment. *American Journal of Community Psychology*, 3, 291-301.

2407
Test name: COLLEGE DESCRIPTIVE INDEX

Purpose: To measure a student's satisfaction with their college experience.

Number of items: 129

Format: Includes the following scales: teachers, administrators, self, courses, parents, other students, noncourse activities, and finances. All adjectives comprising the items are included.

Reliability: Alphas ranged from .73 to .91.

Validity: Correlations with variables ranged from .10 to .53.

Author: Reed, J.G. et al.

Article: Development of the college descriptive index: A measure of student satisfaction.

Journal: *Measurement and Evaluation in Counseling and Development,* July 1984, *17*(2), 67-82.

Related research: Downey, R.G. et al., 1980. Development and validation of a set of university involvement scales. *Measurement and Evaluation in Guidance, 13,* 158-168.

2408
Test name: COLLEGE OPTIMISM SCALE

Purpose: To measure optimism about college life.

Number of items: 15

Format: 4-point rating scale. All items presented.

Reliability: Alphas = .85.

Validity: Correlates -.26 with Taylor Manifest Anxiety Scale; -.44 with Zung Depression Inventory; and -.22 with Neuroticism.

Author: Prola, M.

Article: A scale to measure optimism about college life.

Journal: *Psychological Reports,* April 1984, 54(2), 555-557.

2409
Test name: COMPETENCE INVENTORY FOR COLLEGE STUDENTS

Purpose: To assess degree of competence students express in dealing with interpersonal and academic life while at college.

Number of items: 52

Format: Raters evaluate subjects' role-played response on a 5-point continuum of competence.

Reliability: Alpha = .90 (all items); .85 (interpersonal items); .79 (academic items).

Validity: Correlates with GPA (.32, $p < .01$), but not with the Beck's Depression Inventory (-.09, $p > .05$).

Author: Fisher-Beckfield, D. and McFall, R.M.

Article: Development of a competence inventory for college men and evaluation of relationships between competence and depression.

Journal: *Journal of Consulting and Clinical Psychology,* Oct. 1982, 50(5), 697-705.

Related research: Goldfried, M.R. and D'Zurilla, T.J. A behavioral analytic model for assessing competence. In C.D. Spielberger (Ed.), *Current topics in clinical and community psychology, 1.* New York: Academic Press, 1969.

2410
Test name: FEAR OF CONSEQUENCE OF SUCCESS SCALE

Purpose: To measure degree of fear if one were successful in academic work.

Number of items: 18

Format: 7-point agree-disagree response categories. All items presented.

Reliability: Test-retest (8-week interval) ranged from .54 to .57 over subscales. Cronbach's alpha ranged from .83 to .88 over subscales.

Validity: Correlates significantly (.60 or higher) with Fear of Success (Good and Good, 1973), with (.24 or higher) Adult Audience Sensitivity Inventory (Pavio, 1957, 1958).

Author: Ishiyama, F.I. and Chabassol, D.J.

Article: Fear of success consequence scale: Measure of fear of social consequences of academic success.

Journal: *Psychological Reports*, April 1984, 54(2), 499-504.

2411
Test name: FEAR OF SUCCESS QUESTIONNAIRE

Purpose: To identify people who fear academic success.

Number of items: 83

Format: Yes-no responses are made to questions that specifically describe situations. Examples are provided.

Reliability: Kuder-Richardson Formula 20 reliability was .90.

Validity: Correlations with debilitating anxiety = .57; with internal-external control = .24; self-esteem = .47; need to fail scale = .77.

Author: Pappo, M.

Article: Fear of success: The construction and validation of a measuring instrument.

Journal: *Journal of Personality Assessment*, Feb. 1983, 47(1), 36-41.

2412
Test name: FEAR OF SUCCESS SCALE

Purpose: To measure success avoidance of college students.

Number of items: 27

Format: A paper-and-pencil objective test with scores ranging from 27 to 189. High scores indicate high success avoidance.

Reliability: Coefficient alphas were estimated to be .69 (males) and .73 (females).

Validity: Correlation with the: Intellectual Achievement Responsibility Questionnaire ranged from -.67 to .81 (N's ranged from 12 to 404); BEM sex-role inventory ranged from -.37 to .33. (N's ranged from 12 to 404.)

Author: Ireland-Galman, M.M. and Michael, W.B.

Article: The relationship of a measure of the fear of success construct to scales representing the locus of control and sex-role orientation constructs for a community college sample.

Journal: *Educational and Psychological Measurement*, winter 1983, *43*(4), 1217-1225.

Related research: Zuckerman, M. and Allison, S., 1976. An objective measure of fear of success: Construction and validation. *Journal of Personality Assessment*, 82, 932-946.

2413
Test name: FIRST GRADE ADJUSTMENT SCALE

Purpose: To measure student adjustment to first grade as perceived by their teachers in two dimensions: academic ability and social adjustment.

Number of items: 21

Time required: 1 to 3 minutes per child.

Format: Teacher responds to 21 multiple-choice type questions (example given).

Reliability: Hoyt reliabilities: academic ability (.92); social adjustment (.89).

Author: McClinton, S.L. and Topping, C.

Article: Extended day kindergartens: Are the effects tangible?

Journal: *Journal of Educational Research*, Sept./Oct. 1981, *75*(1), 39-40.

2414
Test name: HEALTH RESOURCES INVENTORY

Purpose: Measures teachers' profiles of childrens' school-related competences.

Number of items: 54

Format: 5-point rating scales.

Reliability: Test-retest ranged from .72 to .91 across subscales.

Author: Weissberg, R.P. et al.

Article: The primary mental health project: Seven consecutive years of program outcome research.

Journal: *Journal of Consulting and Clinical Psychology*, Oct. 1983, *51*(1), 100-107.

Related research: Gesten, E.L., 1976. A health resources inventory: The development of a measure of the personal and social competence of primary grade children. *Journal of Consulting and Clinical Psychology*, 44, 775-786.

2415

Test name: HOUSTON STRESS SCALE

Purpose: To measure student stress at the college level. (In four domains -- academic, financial, family, and personal.)

Number of items: Revision of College Environmental Stress Index (see Munoz and Garcia-Bahne).

Format: 7-point Likert response categories.

Reliability: Cronbach's alpha's ranged from .78 to .84 over domains.

Author: Pliner, J.E. and Brown, D.

Article: Projections of reactions to stress and preference for helpers among students from four ethnic groups.

Journal: *Journal of College Student Personnel*, March 1985, *26*(2), 147-151.

Related research: Munoz, D. and Garcia-Bahne, B. *A study of the Chicano experience in higher education.* (Final report for the Center for Minority Group Mental Health programs and the National Insitute of Mental Health, Contract No. NN24597-01. San Diego: University of California.)

2416

Test name: INVENTORY OF TEACHER-STUDENT RELATIONSHIPS

Purpose: To measure teacher-student relationships.

Number of items: 17

Format: Rating scale format.

Reliability: Alpha ranged from .54 to .79 across subscales.

Author: Howell, F.M. and McBroom, L.W.

Article: Social relations at home and at school: An analysis of the correspondence principle.

Journal: *Sociology of Education*, Jan. 1982, *55*(1), 40-52.

Related research: Bachman, J.G. et al., 1972. Blueprint for a longitudinal study of adolescent boys. Youth in Transition, *1*. Ann Arbor, Mich.: Institute for Social Research.

2417

Test name: MATHEMATICS ANXIETY RATING SCALE—REVISED

Purpose: To provide an index of mathematics course anxiety.

Number of items: 24

Reliability: Coefficient alpha reliability .97.

Validity: Correlations with: mathematics achievement was -.44; with achievement anxiety test was -.29 (facilitating) and .54 (debilitating); with state anxiety was .52; with trait anxiety was .52.

Author: Plake, B.S. et al.

Article: A validity investigation of the achievement anxiety test.

Journal: *Educational and Psychological Measurement*, winter 1981, *41*(4), 1215-1222.

Related research: Suinn, R.M. et al., 1972. The MARS, a measure of mathematics anxiety: Psychosomatic data. *Journal of Clinical Psychology*, 28, 373-375.

2418
Test name: MATHEMATICS ANXIETY SCALE (COLLEGE)

Purpose: To measure mathematics anxiety among college students.

Number of items: 10

Format: Likert format.

Reliability: Split-half = .88.

Author: Bander, R.S. et al.

Article: A comparison of cue-controlled relaxation and study skills counseling in the treatment of mathematics anxiety.

Journal: *Journal of Educational Psychology*, Feb. 1982, *74*(1), 96-103.

Related research: Betz, N.E., 1977. Math anxiety: What is it? Paper presented at the 85th annual convention of the American Psychological Association, San Francisco.

2419
Test name: MEDICAL SCHOOL ENVIRONMENTAL STRESS INVENTORY

Purpose: To measure stress in terms of students' perceptions of significant problems in their learning environment.

Number of items: 75

Format: Each statement described a situation which students rated as problematic on a 7-point Likert scale which ranged from 1 (not at all a problem) to 4 (a moderate problem) through 7 (extremely problematic). The first 62 items pertained to all students and the remainder to either ethnic, minority, or female.

Reliability: Internal consistency reliability of the first 62 items was .94.

Author: Arnold, L. and Jensen, T.B.

Article: Students' perception of stress in a baccalaurate-MD degree program.

Journal: *Perceptual and Motor Skills,* April 1984, *52*(2), 651-662.

Related research: Huebner, L.A. et al., 1981. The assessment and remediation of dysfunctional stress in medical schools. *Journal of Medical Education,* 56, 547.

2420
Test name: MEIER BURNOUT ASSESSMENT SCALE

Purpose: To measure student burnout.

Number of items: 27

Format: All items presented.

Reliability: Cronbach's alpha = .82.

Author: Meier, S.T. and Schmeck, R.R.

Article: The burned-out college student: A descriptive profile.

Journal: *Journal of College Student Personnel,* Jan. 1985, *26*(1), 63-69.

Related research: Meier, S., 1983. Toward a theory of burnout. *Human Relations,* 36, 899-910.

2421
Test name: NEED FOR ACADEMIC COMPETENCE SCALE

Purpose: To measure competency needs in the academic realm.

Number of items: 40

Format: True-false.

Reliability: KR-20 = .80 (males) and .83 (females).

Author: Jordan, T.J.

Article: Self-concepts, motivations and academic achievement of black adolescents.

Journal: *Journal of Educational Psychology,* Aug. 1981, *73*(4), 509-517.

Related research: Jordan, T.J., 1978. *Cognitive and personality factors related to academic achievement of inner-city junior high school students.* (Doctoral dissertation) New York University.

2422
Test name: RATING SCALE FOR KINDERGARTEN ADJUSTMENT

Purpose: To measure adjustment to nursery school.

Number of items: 18

Format: Includes 3 factors: adjustment to learning tasks, emotional adjustment, and social adjustment. For each item the teacher identifies which of five sentences best describes the child.

Reliability: Alphas ranged from .69 to .88.

Author: Levy-Shiff, R.

Article: Adaptation and competence in early childhood: Communally raised kibbitz children versus family-raised children in the city.

Journal: *Child Development,* Dec. 1983, *54*(6), 1606-1614.

Related research: Smilanski, S. and Shephatia, L., 1976. Manual for kindergarten teachers (Research Rep. No. 181, Publication No. 534). Jerusalem: Szolel Institute. [In Hebrew.]

2423
Test name: SOCIAL READJUSTMENT RATING SCALE—STRESSFUL LIFE EVENTS

Purpose: To measure student stress.

Number of items: 15

Format: Yes-no. Sample items presented.

Reliability: Cronbach's alpha = .87.

Author: Carson, N.D. and Johnson, R.E.

Article: Suicidal thoughts and problem solving preparation among college students.

Journal: *Journal of College Student Personnel,* Nov. 1985, *26*(6), 484-487.

Related research: Holmes, T.H. and Rahe, R.H., 1967. The social readjustment rating scale. *Journal of Psychosomatic Research, 11,* 213-218.

2424
Test name: STRESSFUL LIFE EVENT SCALE

Purpose: To measure the perceived stress of events as experienced by students.

Number of Items: 20 events.

Format: Each event rated for stress on a 7-point continuum.

Validity: Correlations between stress ratings by two different ethnic groups was .93; with social standing (popularity) .81 or higher.

Author: Yamamoto, K. and Byrnes, D.A.

Article: Classroom social status, ethnicity and ratings of stressful events.

Journal: *Journal of Educational Research*, May/June 1984, 77(5), 283-286.

Related research: Yamamoto, K., 1979. Children's ratings of the stressfulness of experience. *Developmental Psychology, 116,* 163-171.

2425
Test name: STRESS IN MEDICAL SCHOOL SCALE (SIMS)

Purpose: To measure stress in medical students.

Number of items: 31

Format: 0-9 scale ranging from no stress to extreme stress.

Reliability: Ranged from .77 to .98.

Validity: Of 7 stress factors, 2 decreased over 3 months (as students changed major clerkship rotations).

Author: Linn, B.S. and Zeppa, R.

Article: Dimensions of stress in junior medical students.

Journal: *Psychological Reports*, June 1984, 54(3), 964-966.

2426
Test name: STUDENT SUPPORT AND ROLE CONGRUENCE QUESTIONNAIRE

Purpose: To measure harmony of student roles and perceived faculty and peer support of female doctoral students.

Number of items: 30

Format: 4-point Likert format. Sample items presented.

Reliability: Test-retest: Role congruence = .82; faculty support = .88; peer support = .60.

Validity: Content validity established by a panel of judges.

Author: Hite, L.M.

Article: Female doctoral students: Their perceptions and concerns.

Journal: *Journal of College Student Personnel*, Jan. 1985, 26(1), 18-22.

2427
Test name: SUINN TEST ANXIETY BEHAVIOR SCALE

Purpose: To measure test anxiety.

Number of items: 50

Format: Respondents rate themselves on amount of anxiety they experience in a wide range of academic situations.

Reliability: Test-retest = .73 for graduate students (6 weeks); test-retest = .74 for undergraduates (6 weeks).

Validity: Females report greater anxiety than males (t = 3.87; df = 151).

Author: Ginter, E.J. et al.

Article: Suinn Test Anxiety Behavior Scale: Normative data for graduate students in education.

Journal: *Psychological Reports*, 1983, *50*(3) Part II, 1116-1118.

Related research: Suinn, R.M., 1971. *Suinn Test Anxiety Behavior Scale (STABS): Information for users.* Fort Collins, CO: Rocky Mountain Behavioral Science Institute.

2428
Test name: SURVEY OF FEELINGS ABOUT TESTS

Purpose: To measure test anxiety.

Number of items: 15

Format: Subjects respond by either "yes" or "no" to each question. The higher the score, the greater the expressed anxiety about test-taking. Some examples are presented.

Reliability: Cronbach's alpha was .73 (4th grade) and .80 (8th grade).

Validity: Correlations with science achievement test scores ranged from -.42 to .39.

Author: Payne, B.D. et al.

Article: Sex and ethnic differences in relationships of test anxiety to performance in science examinations by fourth and eighth grade students: Implications for valid interpretations of achievement test scores.

Journal: *Educational and Psychological Measurement*, spring 1983, *43*(1), 267-270.

Related research: Harnisch, D.L. et al., 1980. Development of a shorter, more reliable and more valid measure of test motivation. Paper presented at the annual meeting of the National Council on Measurement in Education, Boston.

2429
Test name: TEST ANXIETY INVENTORY

Purpose: To assess test anxiety.

Number of items: 16

Format: Included Likert-scaled items.

Reliability: Test-retest reliability was .79 (N = 34).

Author: Shaha, S.H.

Article: Matching-tests: Reduced anxiety and increased test effectiveness.

Journal: *Educational and Psychological Measurement*, winter 1984, *44*(4), 869-881.

Related research: Osterhouse, R.A., 1972. Desensitization and study-skills training as treatment for two types of test-anxious students. *Journal of Counseling Psychology, 19*, 301-307.

2430
Test name: TEST ANXIETY SCALE

Purpose: To measure general debilitative test anxiety.

Number of items: 21

Format: True-false.

Reliability: Split-half = .91; Test-retest = .82 (6 week interval).

Author: Bander, R.S. et al.

Article: A comparison of cue-controlled relaxation and study skills counseling in the treatment of mathematics anxiety.

Journal: *Journal of Educational Psychology*, Feb. 1982, *74*(1), 96-103.

Related research: Sarason, S.B. and Mandler, G., 1952. Some correlates of test anxiety. *Journal of Abnormal and Social Psychology, 47*, 561-565.

2431
Test name: WRITING APPREHENSION INSTRUMENT

Purpose: To measure writing apprehension.

Number of items: 26

Reliability: Internal consistency estimate = .94.

Validity: High apprehensives score lower on tests of writing skills than low apprehensives.

Author: Faigley, L. et al.

Article: The role of writing apprehension in writing performance and competence.

Journal: *Journal of Educational Research*, Sept./Oct. 1981, *75*(1), 16-21.

Related research: Daly, J.A. and Miller, M.D., 1975. The empirical development of an instrument to measure writing apprehension. *Research in the Teaching of English, 13*, 242-249.

ADJUSTMENT-PSYCHOLOGICAL

2432

Test name: ACCEPTANCE OF ILLNESS SCALE

Purpose: To measure subject's success in feeling valuable in spite of disease.

Number of items: 8

Format: 5-point agree-disagree format. Sample items presented, drawn from Linkowski (1971).

Reliability: Alpha = .83.

Author: Felton, B.J. and Revenson, T.A.

Article: Coping with chronic illness: A study of illness controllability and the influence of coping strategies on psychological adjustment.

Journal: *Journal of Consulting and Clinical Psychology*, June 1984, *52*(3), 343-353.

Related research: Linkowski, D.S., 1971. A scale to measure acceptance of disability. *Rehabilitation Counseling Bulletin*, *14*, 236-244.

2433

Test name: ACHIEVEMENT ANXIETY TEST SCALE—REVISED

Purpose: To determine the extent to which one's anxiety either facilitates or debilitates one's performance.

Number of items: 19

Format: Includes two scales: facilitating and debilitating. Examples are presented.

Reliability: Test-retest reliability = .80 (facilitating) and .42 (debilitating).

Validity: Correlations with other variables ranged from -.64 to .24.

Author: Sweeney, G.A. and Horan, J.J.

Article: Separate and combined effects of cue-controlled relaxation and cognitive restructuring in the treatment of musical performance anxiety.

Journal: *Journal of Counseling Psychology*, Sept. 1982, *29*(5), 486-497.

Related research: Alpert, R. and Haber, R.N., 1960. Anxiety in academic achievement situations. *Journal of Abnormal and Social Psychology, 61,* 207-215.

2434
Test name: ACTIVATION-DEACTIVATION ADJECTIVE CHECKLIST

Purpose: To provide a measure of subjective level of stress.

Number of items: 34

Format: Includes two factors: positive and negative arousal.

Reliability: Test-retest reliability was .75.

Author: Robbins, E.S. and Haase, R.F.

Article: Power of nonverbal cues in counseling interactions: Availability, vividness or salience?

Journal: *Journal of Counseling Psychology,* Oct. 1985, *32*(4), 502-513.

Related research: Thayer, R.E., 1967. Measurement of activation through self-report. *Psychological Reports, 20,* 663-678.

2435
Test name: ADOLESCENT PERCEIVED STRESS SCALE

Purpose: To measure perceived stress.

Number of items: 12

Format: 5-point Likert format.

Reliability: Split-half = .70.

Validity: Nonsmokers score lower on the scale than smokers (boys $p < .05$; girls $p < .05$).

Author: Mitic, W.R. et al.

Article: Perceived stress and adolescents' cigarette use.

Journal: *Psychological Reports,* Dec. 1985, *53*(3-II), 1043-1048.

2436
Test name: AFFECT BALANCE SCALE

Purpose: To measure balance of positive and negative feelings and their rate of occurrence.

Number of items: 11

Format: Agree-disagree. Sample items presented.

Reliability: Alpha ranged from .73 to .77.

Author: Hanson, S.L. and Spanier, G.B.

Article: Family development and adjustment to marital separation.

Journal: *Sociology and Social Research*, Oct. 1983, *68*(1), 19-40.

Related research: Bradburn, N. and Caplovitz, D., 1965. *Reports on Happiness*. Chicago: University of Chicago.

2437
Test name: AGGRESSION-ANXIETY SCALE

Purpose: To provide a projective measure of aggression-anxiety for five-year-old boys.

Number of items: 24

Format: Includes high to low hostility value picture cards and four categories of behavior.

Reliability: Inter-scorer reliability was .92.

Validity: Biserial correlation coefficient with teacher ratings of aggression-anxiety was .59.

Author: Henry, R.M.

Article: Validation of a projective measure of aggression-anxiety for five-year-old boys.

Journal: *Journal of Personality Assessment*, Aug. 1981, *45*(4), 359-369.

Related research: Lesser, G.S., 1958. Conflict analysis of fantasy aggression. *Journal of Personality*, *26*, 29-41.

2438
Test name: AGORAPHOBIC COGNITIONS QUESTIONNAIRE

Purpose: To assess panic attack and fear of its occurrence.

Number of items: 14

Format: 5-point frequency of occurrence scale.

Reliability: Item-total correlations ranged from .27 to .61 among agoraphobic sample and from -.08 to .70 in a normal sample.

Validity: Correlates .67 with Body Sensations Questionnaire; .38 with Beck Depression Inventory; .35 with Trait Anxiety-STAT; .43 with Eysenck Neuroticism.

Author: Chambliss, D.L. et al.

Article: Assessment of fear in agoraphobics: The body sensations questionnaire and the agoraphobics cognitions questionnaire.

Journal: *Journal of Consulting and Clinical Psychology*, Dec. 1984, *52*(6), 1090-1097.

2439
Test name: ALPERT-HABER ACHIEVEMENT ANXIETY TEST

Purpose: To measure achievement anxiety.

Number of items: 28

Format: Multiple-choice.

Reliability: Ranged from .59 to .88 across subscales, by method of responding to items that subject must use, whether or not buffer items are included.

Validity: Correlates with the self-rating scale vary by item format, but not by presence of buffer items. There was no item-format-buffer interaction.

Author: Tuck, J.P.

Article: Will the real achievement anxiety test please stand up: Effects of removing buffer items and altering item format of the Alpert-Haber Achievement Anxiety Test.

Journal: *Psychological Reports*, 1982, *51*(2), 471-478.

Related research: Huck, S.W. and Jacko, E.J., 1974. Effects of varying the response format of the Alpert-Haber Achievement Anxiety Test. *Journal of Counseling Psychology*, *21*, 159-163.

2440
Test name: ANXIETY DIFFERENTIAL

Purpose: To measure state of anxiety related to the emotional-autonomic domain.

Number of items: 18

Format: A semantic differential format.

Reliability: Test-retest reliability = .41.

Validity: Correlations with other variables ranged from -.18 to .62.

Author: Sweeney, G.A. and Horan, J.

Article: Separate and combined effects of cue-controlled relaxation and cognitive restructuring in the treatment of musical performance anxiety.

Journal: *Journal of Counseling Psychology*, Sept. 1982, *29*(5), 486-497.

Related research: Husek, T.R. and Alexander S., 1963. The effectiveness of the anxiety differential in examination stress situations. *Educational and Psychological Measurement*, *23*, 309-318.

2441
Test name: ANXIETY SYMPTOM CHECKLIST

Purpose: To measure symptoms of anxiety.

Number of items: 40 common physiological symptoms.

Format: 5-point scales indicating the frequency, intensity, and interference in life of each symptom.

Reliability: Test-retest (in past research) = .85.

Validity: Correlates .58 to .73 with measures of general anxiety (in past research).

Author: Deffenbacher, J.L. and Craun, A.M.

Article: Anxiety management training with stressed student gynecology patients: A collaborative approach.

Journal: *Journal of College Student Personnel*, Nov. 1985, *26*(6), 513-518.

Related research: Edie, C.A., 1973. Uses of AMT in treating trait anxiety. *Dissertation abstracts international*, *33*, 393-413. (University microfilms No. 73-2789,256.)

2442
Test name: AUTOMATIC THOUGHTS QUESTIONNAIRE

Purpose: To measure occurrence of automatic negative thoughts associated with depression.

Number of items: 30

Format: 5-point frequency scale.

Reliability: Alpha = .98; Split-half = .96; Item total ranged from .56 to .91.

Validity: Correlates .85 with MMPI-D; Correlates .87 with Beck Depression Inventory.

Author: Harrell, T.H. and Ryan, N.B.

Article: Cognitive-behavioral assessment of depression: Clinical validation of the automatic thoughts questionnaire.

Journal: *Journal of Consulting and Clinical Psychology*, Oct. 1983, *51*(5), 721-725.

Related research: Hollon, S.D. and Kendall, P.C., 1980. Cognitive self-statements in depression: Development of an automatic thoughts questionnaire. *Cognitive Therapy and Research*, *4*, 383-395.

2443
Test name: AVOIDANCE OF EXISTENTIAL CONFRONTATION SCALE

Purpose: To measure failure, meaninglessness, uncertainty, frustration, and suffering.

Number of items: 36

Format: 7-point semantic differential rating scale. All items presented.

Reliability: Ranged between .62 and .73 (odd-even). Test-retest = .75 (2 weeks interval).

Author: Thauberger, C.P. et al.

Article: Avoidance of existential-ontological confrontation: A review of research.

Journal: *Psychological Reports*, 1981, *49*(3), 747-764.

Related research: Thauberger, P.C., 1969. The relationship between an avoidance of existential confrontation and neuroticism and changes resulting from the basic encounter group learning experience. Unpublished Master's thesis, University of Saskatchewan, Saskatoon.

2444
Test name: AVOIDANCE OF THE ONTOLOGICAL CONFRONTATION OF DEATH SCALE

Purpose: To measure avoidance of the harsh reality of death.

Number of items: 20

Format: True-false. All items presented for forms A, B, and C.

Reliability: KR-20 ranged from .82 to .96 across forms A, B, and C. Odd-even ranged from .82 to .89 across forms A, B, and C. Test-retest ranged from .76 to .91 across forms A, B, and C.

Validity: Does not correlate with Jackson's Social Desirability Scale (correlations -.04, .04, .07 across forms). Does correlate significantly with blood pressure. Correlates .37 with Eysenck's Neuroticism Scale.

Author: Thauberger, P.C. et al.

Article: Avoidance of existential-ontological confrontation: A review of research.

Journal: *Psychological Reports*, 1981, *49*(3), 747-764.

Related research: Thauberger, P.C., 1979. The avoidance of ontological confrontation of death: A psychometric research scale. *Essence*, *3*, 9-12.

2445
Test name: BECK DEPRESSION INVENTORY

Purpose: To measure subjects' negative emotions.

Number of items: 21

Format: Each item inquires about a specific symptom cluster with four levels of severity ranging from 0 to 3.

Reliability: Split-half reliability was .93.

Validity: Correlation with clinical judgements of depression was r = .65.

Author: Kraft, R.G. et al.

Article: Effects of positive reframing and paradoxical directives in counseling for negative emotions.

Journal: *Journal of Counseling Psychology*, Oct. 1985, *32*(4), 617-621.

Related research: Beck, A.T., 1967. *Depression: Causes and treatments.* Philadelphia: University of Pennsylvania Press.

2446
Test name: BECK DEPRESSION INVENTORY—ABRIDGED

Purpose: To serve as a depression screening device.

Number of items: 13

Format: A self-report inventory whereby for each item the examinee selects from among four statements arranged in order of increasing level of depression the one statement which bests describes the examinee's current feelings.

Reliability: Cronbach's alpha was .90.

Validity: Correlation with MMPI ranged from -.39 to .63.

Author: Scott, N.A. et al.

Article: Assessment of depression among incarcerated females.

Journal: *Journal of Personality Assessment*, Aug. 1982, *46*(4), 372-379.

Related research: Beck, A.T. and Beamesderfer, A., 1974. Assessment of depression: The depression inventory. In P. Pichot (Ed.), *Psychological measurements in psychopharmacology*, 7. Paris: Karger-Basel.

2447
Test name: BOYAR'S FEAR OF DEATH SCALE

Purpose: To measure death anxiety.

Number of items: 18

Format: 6-point Likert format. Sample items presented.

Reliability: Split-half = .83; Test-rest (10-day interval) = .79.

Author: Downey, A.M.

Article: Relationship of religiosity to death anxiety of middle-aged males.

Journal: *Psychological Reports*, June 1984, *54*(3), 811-822.

Related research: Boyar, J. I., 1964. The construction and partial validation of a scale for the measurement of the fear of death. *Dissertation Abstracts International, 25,* 2041.

2448
Test name: BRIEF SYMPTOM INVENTORY

Purpose: To measure psychopathology.

Number of items: 53

Time required: 10 minutes.

Validity: Correlates .92 to .99 with symptom checklist-90.

Author: Hale, W.D. et al.

Article: Norms for the elderly on the brief symptom inventory.

Journal: *Journal of Consulting and Clinical Psychology,* April 1984, *52*(2), 321-322.

Related research: Derogatis, L.R., 1977. *The SCL-90 Manual I: Scoring, administration and procedures for the SCL-90.* Baltimore, MD: Johns Hopkins University School of Medicine, Clinical Psychometrics Unit.

2449
Test name: CENTER FOR EPIDEMIOLOGIC STUDIES DEPRESSION SCALE

Purpose: To assess depression.

Number of items: 20

Format: Subjects respond to each item on a 4-point scale indicating how often they feel the way described by the item. The scale runs from 0 (rarely) to 3 (most). Examples are presented.

Reliability: Cronbach's alphas were .90 (college students); and .86 (elderly women).

Validity: Correlations with loneliness scores ranged from .12 to .51.

Author: Schmitt, J.P. and Kurdek, L.A.

Article: Age and gender differences in and personality correlates of loneliness in different relationships.

Journal: *Journal of Personality Assessment,* Oct. 1985, *49*(5), 485-496.

Related research: Radloff, L.S., 1977. The CES-D scale: A self-report depression scale for research in the general population. *Applied Psychological Measurement, 1,* 385-401.

2450
Test name: CHILDREN'S DEPRESSION INVENTORY

Purpose: To measure depression in children.

Number of items: 27

Time required: 10-20 minutes.

Format: 3-point frequency scales that best describe behavior over the past two weeks (children's self-reports).

Reliability: Test-retest ranged from .38 to .59; Split-half ranged from .57 to .74; KR ranged from .80 to .94.

Validity: Normal group scored lower than hospitalized group (t = 2.48, p<.02); correlation with Piers-Harris = -.64 (p<.001); correlation with Kestan = .46 (p<.05). Other validity data reported.

Author: Saylor, C.F. et al.

Article: The children's depression inventory: A systematic evaluation of psychometric properties.

Journal: *Journal of Consulting and Clinical Psychology*, Dec. 1984, 52(6), 955-967.

Related research: Kovacs, M., 1982. *The children's depression inventory: A self-rated depression scale for school-aged youngsters.* Unpublished manuscript, University of Pittsburgh.
   Saylor, C.F. et al., 1984. Construct validity for measures of childhood depression: Application of multitrait-multimethod Methodology. *Journal of Consulting and Clinical Psychology*, 52, 977-985.

2451
Test name: CLIENT FEARS QUESTIONNAIRE

Purpose: To measure fears clients have of psychotherapy.

Number of items: 15

Format: 5-point concern scale. All items presented.

Reliability: Alpha ranged from .84 to .92 across two factors.

Validity: Individuals not seeking therapy had greater fears than clients (p<.001).

Author: Pipes, R.B. et al.

Article: Measuring client fears.

Journal: *Journal of Consulting and Clinical Psychology*, Dec. 1985, 53(6), 933-934.

2452
Test name: CLINICAL ASSESSMENT INVENTORY

Purpose: To measure psychiatric patients' progress.

Number of items: 50 sub-categories of behavior.

Format: Patients observed twice daily on regular nursing rounds. Major behavior categories presented.

Reliability: Agreements between pairs of observers ranged from 88.4% to 88.6%. Reliability = .85. Correlation of observations over one day interval = .945 (100 patients).

Validity: Correlates .77 with the Short Clinical Rating Scale.

Author: Brown, R.A. and Moss, G.R.

Article: Reliability and validation of a psychiatric assessment instrument for the hospital treatment of adults.

Journal: *Psychological Reports*, 1982, *51*(1), 142.

2453
Test name: COLLETT-LESTER FEAR OF DEATH SCALE

Purpose: To assess fear of death.

Number of items: 36

Format: Likert-type format with 4 scales: fear of death of self, fear of death of others, fear of dying of self, fear of dying of others.

Reliability: Subscale internal consistency reliability coefficients (alphas) ranged from .59 to .76.

Validity: Correlations with: Marlowe-Crowne Social Desirability Scale were .14 or less; Death Anxiety Scale ranged from .31 to .78.

Author: Wass, H. and Forfar, C.S.

Article: Assessment of attitudes toward death: Techniques and instruments for use with older persons.

Journal: *Measurement and Evaluation in Guidance*, Oct. 1982. *15*(3), 210-220.

Related research: Collett, L.J. and Lester, D., 1969. The fear of death and dying. *Journal of Psychology*, 72, 179-181.

2454
Test name: COMBAT-RELATED POSTTRAUMATIC STRESS DISORDER SUBSCALE

Purpose: To assess combat-related posttraumatic stress.

Number of items: 9

Format: Items taken from MMPI, Form R. Item numbers presented.

Validity: Correctly classified 82% of validation and cross-validation samples, compared to 74% with standard clinical scale rules.

Author: Keane, T.M. et al.

Article: Empirical development of an MMPI subscale for the assessment of combat-related posttraumatic stress disorder.

Journal: *Journal of Consulting and Clinical Psychology*, Oct. 1984, 52(5), 888-891.

Related research: Fairbank, J.A. et al., 1983. Some preliminary data of the psychological characteristics of Vietnam veterans with posttraumatic stress disorders. *Journal of Consulting and Clinical Psychology*, 51, 912-919.

2455
Test name: CONCERN OVER THE NEGATIVE CONSEQUENCES OF SUCCESS SCALE

Purpose: To measure concern about negative consequences of success.

Number of items: 27

Format: 4-point agreement scale.

Reliability: Alpha ranged from .46 to .78 across subscales and by sex.

Author: Hong, S. and Caust, C.D.

Article: A factor analytic evaluation of the concern over negative consequences of success scale.

Journal: *Psychological Reports*, Feb. 1985, 56(1), 331-338.

Related research: Ho, R. and Zemaitis, R., 1981. Concern over the negative consequences of success. *Australian Journal of Psychology*, 33, 19-28.

2456
Test name: CUE COUNT

Purpose: To assess behavioral anxiety.

Number of items: 7

Format: Includes verbal speech disruption and nonverbal voice characteristics items. Responses are rated by trained raters.

Reliability: Inter-rater reliability was r = .94.

Author: Strohmer, D.C. et al.

Article: Cognitive style and synchrony in measures of anxiety.

Journal: *Measurement and Evaluation in Guidance*, April 1983, 16(1), 13-17.

Related research: Dibner, A.S., 1956. Cue counting: A measure of anxiety in interviews. *Journal of Consulting Psychology*, 20, 475-478.

2457
Test name: CURRENT MOOD STATE SCALE

Purpose: To assess current mood state.

Number of items: 9

Format: Subjects rate on a 5-point scale emotions felt during past three months, as well as questions concerning their marriage and current life concerns.

Reliability: Cronbach's alpha was .926.

Author: Berman, W.H. and Turk, D.C.

Article: Adaptation to divorce: Problems and coping strategies.

Journal: *Journal of Marriage and the Family*, Feb. 1981, *43*(1), 179-189.

Related research: Pearlin, L.I. and Schooler, C., 1978. The structure of coping. *Journal of Health and Social Behavior*, *19*, 2-21.

2458
Test name: DEATH ACCEPTANCE SCALE

Purpose: To measure death acceptance.

Number of items: 7

Format: Likert-type scale.

Reliability: Internal consistency reliabilities (alpha) were .58, .70.

Validity: Correlation with death anxiety was -.26.

Author: Wass, H. and Forfar, C.S.

Article: Assessment of attitude toward death: Techniques and instruments for use with older persons.

Journal: *Measurement and Evaluation in Guidance*, Oct. 1982, *15*(3), 210-220.

Related research: Ray, J.J. and Najman, J., 1974. Death anxiety and acceptance: A preliminary approach. *Omega*, *5*, 311-315.

2459
Test name: DEATH ANXIETY SCALE

Purpose: To measure death anxiety.

Number of items: 15

Format: Personal death-related questions answered true or false.

Reliability: Test-retest reliability (3 weeks) was .83. Internal consistency reliability coefficient (alpha) was .73.

Validity: Correlations with: Manifest Anxiety Scale was .39; with Marlowe-Crowne Social Desirability Scale was .03, .21. A projective word association task was .25.

Author: Wass, H. and Forfar, C.S.

Article: Assessment of attitudes toward death: Techniques and instruments for use with older persons.

Journal: *Measurement and Evaluation in Guidance*, Oct. 1982, *15*(3), 210-220.

Related research: Templar, D.I., 1970. The construction and validation of a death anxiety scale. *Journal of General Psychology*, 82, 165-177.

2460
Test name: DEATH CONCERN SCALE

Purpose: To measure concern for death.

Number of items: 30

Format: Likert-type scale assessing conscious contemplation of death and negative evaluation of death.

Reliability: Split-half reliabilities for four administrations were above .85. Test-retest reliability (8 weeks) was .87.

Validity: Correlation with: State and Trait Anxiety Inventory were .01, .16 (males), .48, .75 (females); with Marlowe-Crowne Social Desirability Scale was .40; with Death Anxiety Scale was .56; with Collett-Lester Fear of Death Scale was .38.

Author: Wass, H. and Forfar, C.S.

Article: Assessment and attitudes toward death: Techniques and instruments for use with older persons.

Journal: *Measurement and Evaluation in Guidance*, Oct. 1982, *15*(3), 210-220.

Related research: Dickstein, L.S., 1972. Death concern: Measurement and correlates. *Psychological Reports*, 30, 563-571.

2461
Test name: DEPRESSION EXPERIENCES QUESTIONNAIRE

Purpose: To measure the subjective experiences of depression.

Number of items: 66

Format: Agree-disagree format. Sample items presented.

Reliability: Alpha ranged from .72 to .81 across subscales.

Author: Blatt, S.J. et al.

Article: Dependency and self-criticism: Psychological dimensions of depression.

Journal: *Journal of Consulting and Clinical Psychology*, Feb. 1982, *50*(1), 113-124.

Related research: Blatt, S.J. et al., 1976. *Depressive experiences questionnaire*. New Haven, Conn.: Yale University.

2462

Test name: DEPRESSION PRONENESS RATING SCALE

Purpose: To measure proneness to depression.

Number of items: Scale 3-3 items; Scale 11-11 items.

Format: Scale 3: Descriptor items followed by a nine-point scale (all items presented); Scale 11: Symptom (items) followed by a 5-point rating scale (all items presented).

Reliability: Test-retest (Scale 3) = .76; Test-retest (Scale 11) = .57.

Validity: Both scales correlate significantly with Scale 11, with Beck's Depression Inventory (short form), and with other's reports of depression. Correlations ranged from .29 to .91.

Author: Zemore, R.

Article: Development of a self-report measure of depression-proneness.

Journal: *Psychological Reports*, 1983, *52*(1), 211-216.

Related research: Zemore, R. and Bretell, D., 1983. Depression-proneness, low self-esteem, unhappy outlook, and narcissistic vulnerability. *Psychological Reports*, 52, 223-230.

2463

Test name: DEPRESSION SCALE

Purpose: To measure depression.

Number of items: 11

Format: Responses are made on a 5-point frequency scale from "never" (1) to "very often" (5).

Reliability: Coefficient alpha was .78.

Validity: Correlation with employment characteristics ranged from r = .26 to r = .14 (husbands' depression) and r = -.35 to r = .15 (wives' depression).

Author: Keith, P.M. and Schafer, R.B.

Article: Employment characteristics of both spouses and depression in two-job families.

Journal: *Journal of Marriage and the Family*, Nov. 1983, *45*(4), 877-884.

Related research: Pearlin, L. and Johnson, J., 1977. Marital status, life-strains, and depression. *American Sociological Review, 42,* 704-715.

2464

Test name: DEPRESSION SCALE

Purpose: To measure how "blue," "lonely," and "fearful" persons feel.

Number of items: 6

Format: 7-point response categories.

Reliability: Alpha = .79.

Author: Ross, C. and Mirowsky, J.

Article: Men who cry.

Journal: *Social Psychological Quarterly*, June 1984, *47*(2), 138-146.

Related research: Radloff, L.S., 1977. The CES-D scale: A self-report depression scale for research in the general population. *Applied Psychological Research*, *1*, 385-401.

2465
Test name: DEPRESSION: SELF-RATING SCALE (Children's version)

Purpose: To measure depression in children.

Number of items: 21

Format: 0-2 scale (always, sometimes, never present).

Reliability: Alpha = .76 ($p < .01$); Split-half = .67.

Validity: Depressed children score higher than non-depressed children ($p < .002$). Sensitivity = 51%; homogeneity = 91%; specificity = 95%; overall correct classifications = 74%. Correlates .81 with Child Depression Inventory.

Author: Asarnow, J.R. and Carlson, G.A.

Article: Depression self-rating scale: Utility with child psychiatric inpatients.

Journal: *Journal of Consulting and Clinical Psychology*, Aug. 1985, *53*(4), 491-499.

Related research: Birleson, A.T., 1981. The validity of depressive disorders and the development of a self-rating scale: A research report. *Journal of Child Psychiatry and Psychology*, *22*, 73-88.

2466
Test name: DISTRESS SCALE

Purpose: To measure feelings of distress and negative affect.

Number of items: 22

Format: Responses are made on a 7-point scale. Sample items are presented.

Reliability: Alpha = .89.

Validity: Correlations with other variables ranged from -.67 to .49 ($N = 120$).

Author: Bhagat, R.S. et al.

Article: Total life stress: A multimethod validation of the construct and its effects on organizationally valued outcomes and withdrawal behaviors.

Journal: *Journal of Applied Psychology*, Feb. 1985, *70*(1), 202-204.

Related research: Bradburn, N.M., 1969. *The structure of psychological well-being*. Chicago: Aldine.

2467
Test name: DYING AND DEATH SCALE

Purpose: To measure fear and beliefs about dying.

Number of items: 12

Format: 5-point Likert response categories ranging from strongly agree to strongly disagree. All items presented.

Reliability: Test-retest (48 hours) = .80.

Validity: Age groups differed significantly.

Author: Westman, A.S. et al.

Article: Denial of fear of dying or of death in young and elderly populations.

Journal: *Psychological Reports*, Oct. 1984, *55*(2), 413-444.

2468
Test name: FEAR OF DEATH SCALE

Purpose: To measure fear of death.

Number of items: 36

Format: 6-point Likert response categories.

Validity: Cluster and factor analysis suggest that 4 or 5 subscales exist.

Author: Liveh, H.

Article: Brief note on the structure of the Collett-Lester Fear of Death Scale.

Journal: *Psychological Reports*, Feb. 1985, *56*(1), 136-138.

Related research: Collett, L. and Lester, D., 1969. The fear of death and the fear of dying. *Journal of Psychology*, 72, 179-181.

2469
Test name: FEAR OF DEATH SCALE

Purpose: To measure one's fear of death.

Number of items: 21

Format: Thurstone-type scale.

Reliability: Parallel form correlation of .58; Internal consistency reliability coefficient (alpha) of .34.

Validity: Correlation with: Marlowe-Crowne Social Desirability Scale = .10; with Collett-Lester Death of Self Subscale = .78.

Author: Wass, H. and Forfar, C.S.

Article: Assessment of attitudes toward death: Techniques and instruments for use with older persons.

Journal: *Measurement and Evaluation in Guidance.* Oct. 1982, *15*(3), 210-220.

Related research: Durlak, J.A., 1972. Measurement of the fear of death: An examination of some existing scales. *Journal of Clinical Psychology, 28,* 545-547.

2470
Test name: FEAR OF SUCCCESS AND FEAR OF APPEARING INCOMPETENT SCALES

Purpose: To measure fear of success and appearing incompetent.

Number of items: 36 (incompetent), 29 (success).

Format: True-false.

Reliability: KR-20 = .89 (incompetent) and .81 (success).

Author: Brenner, O.C. and Tomkiewicz, J.

Article: Sex differences among business graduates on fear of success and fear of appearing incompetent as measured by objective instruments.

Journal: *Psychological Reports,* 1982, *51*(1), 179-182.

Related research: Good, L.R. and Good, K.C., 1973. An objective measure of the motive to avoid appearing incompetent. *Psychological Reports, 33,* 1075-1078. An objective measure of the motive to avoid success. *Psychological Reports, 33,* 1009-1010.

2471
Test name: FEAR OF SUCCESS SCALE

Purpose: To assess individual difference in the motive to avoid success.

Number of items: 27

Format: 7-point Likert response scales.

Reliability: Alpha = .68 reported for college juniors and seniors.

Author: Taylor, K.M.

Article: An investigation of vocational indecision in college students: Correlates and Moderators.

Journal: *Journal of Vocational Behavior*, Dec. 1982, *21*(3), 318-329.

Related research: Zuckerman, M. and Allison, S.N., 1976. An objective measure of fear of success: Construction and validation. *Journal of Personality Assessment, 40,* 422-430.

2472
Test name: FRUSTRATION SCALES

Purpose: To measure frustration.

Number of items: 3

Format: Responses were made on a 7-point Likert scale. High scores represented greater frustration.

Reliability: Coefficient alphas were .76 and .68.

Validity: Correlations with other variables ranged from -.42 to .36.

Author: O'Conner, E.J. et al.

Article: Situational constraint effects on performance, affective reactions and turnover: A field replication and extension.

Journal: *Journal of Applied Psychology*, Nov. 1984, *69*(4), 663-672.

Related research: Peters, L.H. and O'Connor, E.J., 1980. Situational constraints and work outcomes: The influence of a frequently overlooked construct. *Academy of Management Review, 5,* 391-397.

2473
Test name: GENERAL ANXIETY SCALE

Purpose: To measure general anxiety.

Number of items: 17

Format: True-false format.

Reliability: Internal consistency coefficient was .75.

Validity: Correlations with other variables ranged from -.43 to .50.

Author: Llabre, M.M. and Suarez, E.

Article: Predicting math anxiety and course performance in college women and men.

Journal: *Journal of Counseling Psychology*, April 1985, *32*(2), 283-287.

Related research: Sarason, I.G., 1978. The test anxiety scale: Concept and research. In C.D. Spielberger and I.G. Sarason (Eds.), *Stress and anxiety,* 5, 193-216. Washington, D.C.: Hemisphere.

2474
Test name: GENERAL WELL-BEING SCALE

Purpose: To measure subjective well-being and distress.

Number of items: 18

Format: 14 items have 6-point responses that vary by item content. 4 items have an 11-point response format.

Reliability: Alpha = .92.

Author: Himmelfarb, S.

Article: Age and sex differences in the mental health of older persons.

Journal: *Journal of Consulting and Clinical Psychology*, Oct. 1984, *52*(5), 844-856.

Related research: Fazio, A.F., 1977. *A concurrent validation study of the NCHS general well being schedule.* (U.S. Public Health Service, Vital and Health Statistics, Series 2, No. 73.) Washington, D.C.: U.S. Government Printing Office.

2475
Test name: GERIATRIC DEPRESSION SCALE

Purpose: To assess depression in the elderly.

Number of items: 30

Format: Items refer to affective, cognitive, and behavioral symptoms of depression. Examples are presented.

Validity: Correlations with other variables ranged from -.39 to .49.

Author: Fry, P.S.

Article: Development of a geriatric scale of hopelessness: Implications for counseling and intervention with the depressed elderly.

Journal: *Journal of Counseling Psychology*, July 1984, *31*(3), 322-331.

Related research: Brink, T.L. et al., 1982. Screening test for geriatric depression. *Clinical Gerontologist*, *1*, 37-43.

2476
Test name: GERIATRIC HOPELESSNESS SCALE

Purpose: To assess hopelessness in nonpsychiatric, nonpatient, and subclinically depressed elderly.

Number of items: 30

Format: Items are answered either "true" or "false." All items are presented.

Reliability: Cronbach's coefficient alpha was .69; Spearman-Brown split-half coefficient was .73.

Validity: Correlations with other variables ranged from -.55 to .49.

Author: Fry, P.S.

Article: Development of a geriatric scale of hopelessness: Implication for counseling and intervention with the depressed elderly.

Journal: *Journal of Counseling Psychology*, July 1984, *31*(3), 322-331.

Related research: Beck, A.T. et al., 1974. The measurement of pessimism: The hopelessness scale. *Journal of Consulting and Clinical Psychology*, 42, 861-865.

2477

Test name: GOLDFARB FEAR OF FAT SCALE

Purpose: To identify individual at high risk for developing eating disorders.

Number of items: 10

Format: Responses to each item are made on a 4-point Likert scale from 1 (very untrue) to 4 (very true). All items presented.

Reliability: Test-retest (1 week) reliability was r = .88 (N = 23).

Validity: Correlations with other variables ranged from -.64 to .65.

Author: Goldfarb, L.A. et al.

Article: The Goldfarb fear of fat scale.

Journal: *Journal of Personality Assessment*, June 1985, *49*(3), 329-332.

2478

Test name: GOOD AND GOOD FEAR OF SUCCESS SCALE

Purpose: To assess fear of success.

Number of items: 29

Format: True-false.

Reliability: KR-20 = .81.

Validity: Correlates positively with Zuckerman and Allison and Pappo scales, except on the Zuckerman and Allison scales negatively for males.

Author: Chabassol, D.J. and Ishiyama, F.I.

Article: Correlations among three measures of fear of success.

Journal: *Psychological Reports*, 1983, *52*(1), 55-58.

Related research: Good, L.R. and Good, K.C., 1973. An objective measure of the motive to avoid success. *Psychological Reports*, 33, 1009-1010.

2479

Test name: HAMILTON PSYCHIATRIC RATING SCALE FOR DEPRESSION

Purpose: To measure depression.

Number of items: 17

Format: Items presented by interviewer in a semi-structured interview. Items scored 0 to 2 or 0 to 4 to reflect increasing severity of symptom.

Reliability: Inter-rater reliability ranged from .80 to .90.

Author: Atkeson, B.M. et al.

Article: Victims of rape: Repeated assessment of depressive symptoms.

Journal: *Journal of Consulting and Clinical Psychology*, Feb. 1982, *50*(1), 96-102.

Related research: Hamilton, M., 1960. A rating scale for depression. *Journal of Neurology, Neurosurgery and Psychiatry*, 23, 56-62.

2480
Test name: HEALTH OPINION SURVEY

Purpose: To provide a general index of neurotic symptomatology focusing on psychosomatic complaints.

Number of items: 18

Format: Subject responds to each symptom by indicating "always," "sometimes," or "never."

Validity: Correlations with other variables ranged from -.22 to .25.

Author: Ronchi, D. and Sparacino, J.

Article: Density of dormitory living and stress: Mediating effects of sex, self-monitoring and environmental affective qualities.

Journal: *Perceptual and Motor Skills*, Dec. 1982, *55*(3, Pt. 1), 759-770.

Related research: Leighton, D.C. et al., 1963. *The character of danger*. New York: Basic Books.

2481
Test name: HIGH SCHOOL SOCIAL READJUSTMENT SCALE

Purpose: To measure stress.

Number of items: 52

Format: Yes-no.

Reliability: Test-retest ranged from .40 to .63 (6-month interval).

Validity: Correlation with Epidemiological Studies Stress Scale ranged from .25 to .27 ($p < .02$) for girls but not significant ($r = .04$) for boys.

Author: Tolor, A. and Murphy, V.M.

Article: Stress and depression in high school students.

Journal: *Psychological Reports*, Oct. 1985, 57(2), 535-541.

Related research: Tolor, A. et al., 1983. The high school social readjustment scale: An attempt to quantify stressful events in young people. *Research Communications in Psychology, Psychiatry and Behavior*, 8, 85-111.

Holmes, T.H. and Rahe, R.H., 1967. The social readjustment scale. *Journal of Psychosomatic Research*, 11, 213-218.

2482

Test name: HOPELESSNESS SCALE FOR CHILDREN

Purpose: To measure hopelessness in children. Patterned on Beck et al., Hopelessness Scale.

Number of items: 17

Format: True-not true format. All items presented.

Reliability: Item-total correlation ranged from .19 to .71 (all significant at p<.05); Alpha = .75; Split-half = .70.

Validity: Correlates .49 (p<.001) with Children's Depression Inventory; Correlates .22 (p<.05) with Depression Symptom Checklist.

Author: Kazdin, A.E. et al.

Article: Hopelessness, depression, and suicidal intent among psychiatrically disturbed inpatient children.

Journal: *Journal of Consulting and Clinical Psychology*, Aug. 1983, 51(4), 504-510.

Related research: Beck, A.T. et al., 1974. The measurement of pessimism: The hopelessness scale. *Journal of Consulting and Clinical Psychology*, 42, 861-865.

2483

Test name: HOPELESSNESS SCALE

Purpose: To measure pessimism.

Number of items: 20

Format: True-false. Sample items presented.

Reliability: Alpha = .93.

Author: Wolf, F.M. and Savickas, M.L.

Article: Time perspective and causal attributions for achievement.

Journal: *Journal of Educational Psychology*, Aug. 1985, 77(4), 471-480.

Related research: Beck, A.T. et al., 1974. The measurement of pessimism: The hopelessness scale. *Journal of Consulting and Clinical Psychology*, 42, 861-865.

2484
Test name: IMPACT OF EVENT SCALE

Purpose: To measure subjective stress.

Number of items: 15

Format: 4-point frequency of occurrence response scale (not at all to often). All items presented.

Reliability: Alpha = .79 to .92.

Validity: Discriminates patient and field subject samples in expected direction.

Author: Zilberg, N.J. et al.

Article: Impact of event scale: A cross-validation study and some empirical evidence supporting a conceptual model of stress response syndromes.

Journal: *Journal of Consulting and Clinical Psychology*, June 1982, *50*(3), 407-414.

Related research: Horowitz, M.J., 1979. Impact of event scale: A measure of subjective stress. *Psychosomatic Medicine, 41,* 209-218.

2485
Test name: INDEX OF POTENTIAL SUICIDE—CLINICAL SCALE

Purpose: To predict future suicidal behavior in hospitalized attempted suicides over a 6-month period.

Number of items: 50

Format: Includes six subscales: depression, emotional status, anxiety, alcoholism, suicidal behavior, and general health.

Reliability: Cronbach's alphas ranged from .38 to .75 for the subscales and was .84 for the total scale.

Validity: Correlations with other variables ranged from -.01 to .42.

Author: Petrie, K. and Chamberlain, K.

Article: The predictive validity of the Zung index of potential suicide.

Journal: *Journal of Personality Assessment*, Feb. 1985, *49*(1), 100-102.

Related research: Zung, W.W.K., 1974. Index of potential suicide. In A.T. Beck et al. (Eds.), *The prediction of suicide*. Maryland: Charles Press.

2486
Test name: INTENSE AMBIVALENCE SCALE

Purpose: To measure tendency to endow diverse psychisms with a positive and negative indicator at the same time.

Number of items: 45

Format: True-false.

Reliability: Test-retest (10-12 weeks) = .81. Alpha ranged from .86 to .88.

Validity: Correlates .18 (depressed subjects) and .52 (schizophrenic subjects) with Beck Depression Inventory. Correlates .04 with Phillips Premorbid Adjustment Scale. Other validity data presented.

Author: Raulin, M.L.

Article: Development of a scale to measure intense ambivalence.

Journal: *Journal of Consulting and Clinical Psychology*, Feb. 1984. 52(1), 63-72.

2487

Test name: LEVY OPTIMISM-PESSIMISM SCALE

Purpose: To measure optimism-pessimism.

Number of items: 16

Format: Multiple-choice. Sample items presented.

Reliability: Cronbach's alpha = .94.

Validity: Differentiates "morning" and "evening" persons (t = 2.30, p<.025), and thus may be associated with circadian rhythms.

Author: Levy, D.A.

Article: Optimism and pessimism: Relationships to circadian rhythms.

Journal: *Psychological Reports*, Dec. 1985, 57(3-II), 1123-1126.

2488

Test name: LIFE EVENTS CHECKLIST

Purpose: To measure total life stress.

Number of items: 83

Format: Subjects use a 7-point scale from -3 to +3 to rate the degree of positive or negative impact that each event had on their life. Examples are presented.

Reliability: Cronbach's alpha ranged from .53 to .77 (N = 282).

Author: Bhagat, R.S. et al.

Article: Total life stress: A multimethod validation of the construct and its effects on organizationally valued outcomes and withdrawal behaviors.

Journal: *Journal of Applied Psychology*, Feb. 1985, 70(1), 202-214.

Related research: Dehrenwend, B.S. et al., 1978. Exemplification of a method for scaling life events:

The PERI life events scale. *Journal of Health and Social Behavior, 19,* 205-229.

2489
Test name: LIFE EXPERIENCES SURVEY

Purpose: To measure life stress.

Number of items: 57

Format: Subjects indicate events experienced during the previous year. Negative and positive stress scores represent the sum of ratings (4-point scale) of negative and positive events.

Reliability: Test-retest (5 or 6 weeks) = .56 to .88.

Author: Heilbrun, A.B., Jr.

Article: Cognitive defenses and life stress: An information-processing analysis.

Journal: *Psychological Reports,* Feb. 1984, *54*(1), 3-17.

Related research: Johnson, J.H. and Sarason, I.G., 1979. Recent developments in research on life stress. In Hamilton, V. and Warburton, D.M. (Eds.), *Human stress and cognition: An information processing approach.* New York: McGraw-Hill, 205-233.

2490
Test name: LOUISVILLE FEAR SURVEY FOR CHILDREN

Purpose: To measure fear in children.

Number of items: 104

Format: Mothers rate children on a 5-point fear severity scale.

Reliability: Alphas ranged from .51 to .89 on subscales. Mean alpha = .76.

Validity: Correlations between child and mothers' reports ranged from -.13 to .86 (of 48 correlations 27 are significant (p<.05, .01 or .001), and in correct direction).

Author: Dollinger, S.J. et al.

Article: Lightening-strike disaster: Effects of childrens' fears and worries.

Journal: *Journal of Consulting and Clinical Psychology,* Dec. 1984, *52*(6), 1028-1038.

Related research: Staley, A.A. and O'Donnell, J.P., 1984. A developmental analysis of mothers' reports of normal children's fears. *Journal of Genetic Psychology, 144,* 165-178.

2491
Test name: MAINE SCALE OF PARANOID AND NONPARANOID SCHIZOPHRENIA

Purpose: To measure schizophrenia.

Number of items: 10

Format: Multiple-choice. All items presented.

Reliability: Test-retest ranged from .73 to .89 (4-day interval).

Validity: Correlations with other measures of schizophrenia ranged from .43 to .76. Correlations with expanded similarities test ranged from .02 to .26.

Author: Magaro, P.A. et al.

Article: The Maine scale of paranoid and nonparanoid schizophrenia.

Journal: *Journal of Consulting and Clinical Psychology*, June 1981, *49*(3), 438-447.

Related research: Vojtisek, J.E., 1976. Signal detection and size estimation in schizophrenia. Doctoral dissertation, University of Maine (1975), *Dissertation Abstracts International*, *36*, 5290B-5291B. University microfilms No. 76-7445.

2492
Test name: MALADJUSTMENT SCALE

Purpose: To measure maladjustment.

Number of items: 9

Format: Include interpersonal, intrapersonal, and somatic problems. A 5-point Likert scale ranging from 1 (not at all) to 5 (extremely) was used to rate each problem.

Reliability: Coefficient alphas were .88 (200 clients) and .91 (200 counselors).

Author: Turner, C.J. and Schwartzbach, H.

Article: A construct validation study of the counseling expectation inventory.

Journal: *Measurement and Evaluation in Guidance*, April 1983, *16*(1), 18-24.

Related research: Robinson, A., 1972. *Development and evaluation of a brief problem checklist for use in college counseling centers.* Unpublished doctoral dissertation, University of Tennessee.

2493
Test name: MENTAL HEALTH INVENTORY

Purpose: To measure psychological distress and well-being in general populations.

Number of items: 38

Format: Summated rating format.

Reliability: Internal consistency ranged from .83 to .91 across subscales. Stability ranged from .56 to .64.

Author: Veit, C.T. and Ware, J.E., Jr.

Article: The structure of psychological distress and well-being in general populations.

Journal: *Journal of Consulting and Clinical Psychology*, Oct. 1983, *51*(5), 730-742.

Related research: Dupuy, H.J., 1979. *A brief description of the research edition of the general psychological well-being schedule.* National Center for Health Statistics, Fairfax, Va.

2494
Test name: MOOD QUESTIONNAIRE

Purpose: To assess mood.

Number of items: 71

Format: Includes 6 mood dimensions: pleasantness, activation, calmness, extraversion, social orientation, and confidence.

Validity: Correlations with goals ranged from .04 to .56.

Author: Sjöberg, L. et al.

Article: Cathectic orientation, goal setting and mood.

Journal: *Journal of Personality Assessment*, June 1983, *47*(3), 307-313.

Related research: Sjöberg, I. et al., 1979. The measurement of mood. *Scandinavian Journal of Psychology*, *20*, 1-18.

2495
Test name: MORALE SCALE

Purpose: To measure morale.

Number of items: 6

Format: Responses to each item are made on a 4-point scale from "strongly agree" to "strongly disagree." All items are presented.

Reliability: Cronbach's alpha was .85 (males) and .866 (females).

Validity: Correlations with other variables ranged from -.166 to .368.

Author: Lee, G.R. and Ellithorpe, E.

Article: Intergenerational exchange and subjective well-being among the elderly.

Journal: *Journal of Marriage and the Family*, Feb. 1982, *44*(1), 217-224.

Related research: Lee, G.R. and Ihinger-Tallman, M., 1980. Sibling interaction and morale: The effects of family relations on older people. *Research on Aging*, 2, 367-391.

2496
Test name: MORALE SCALE

Purpose: To measure morale.

Number of items: 14

Format: 3-category response scale: "high," "depends," "low." All items presented.

Reliability: Alpha = .82.

Author: Dowd, J.J. and LaRossa, R.

Article: Primary group contact and elderly morale: An exchange/power analysis.

Journal: *Sociology and Social Research*, Jan. 1982, *66*(2), 184-197.

Related research: Lawton, M.P., 1975. The Philadelphia geriatric morale scale: A revision. *Journal of Gerontology*, 30, 85-89.

2497
Test name: MULTIDIMENSIONAL FEAR OF DEATH SCALE

Purpose: To measure fear of death.

Number of items: 42

Format: Includes 8 dimensions: fear of dying process, fear of the dead, fear of being destroyed, fear for significant others, fear of the unknown, fear of conscious death, fear for the body after death, and fear of premature death.

Validity: Correlation of fear of the unknown subscale with a measure of religious orthodoxy was -.64.

Author: Wass, H. and Forfar, C.S.

Article: Assessment of attitude toward death: Techniques and instruments for use with older persons.

Journal: *Measurement and Evaluation in Guidance*, Oct. 1982, *15*(3), 210-220.

Related research: Hoelter, J., 1979. Multidimensional treatment of the fear of death. *Journal of Consulting and Clinical Psychology*, 47, 996-999.

2498
Test name: MULTISCORE DEPRESSION INVENTORY—SHORT FORM

Purpose: To measure severity of depression and depressive features.

Number of items: 47

Format: Includes 9 subscales: sad mood, guilt, instrumental helplessness, low energy level, social introversion, irritability, pessimism, cognitive difficulty, and low self-esteem.

Reliability: Test-retest reliabilities: immediate (N = 108) ranged from .83 to .95 and 3 week (N = 108) ranged from .41 to .90. Coefficient alphas ranged from .71 to .92 (N = 133) and from .67 to .88 (N = 108).

Author: Berndt, D.J. et al.

Article: Multidimensional assessment of depression.

Journal: *Journal of Personality Assessment*, Oct. 1984, 48(5), 489-494.

Related research: Berndt, D.J. et al., 1983. Readability of self-report depression inventories. *Journal of Consulting and Clinical Psychology*, 51, 627-628.

2499
Test name: NEGATIVE WELL-BEING SCALE

Purpose: To measure negative well-being.

Number of items: 32

Format: Five-point rating scale.

Reliability: Alpha = .88.

Author: Litt, M.D. and Turk, D.C.

Article: Sources of stress and dissatisfaction in experienced high school teachers.

Journal: *Journal of Educational Research*, Jan./Feb. 1985, 78(3), 178-185.

Related research: Zalezik, A. et al., 1977. Stress reactions in organizations: Syndromes, causes and consequences. *Behavior Science*, 22, 151-162.

2500
Test name: PAPPO FEAR OF SUCCESS SCALE

Purpose: To measure self-doubt, preoccupation with competition, preoccupation with evaluation, repudiation of competence, and self-sabotage behavior.

Number of items: 83

Format: Yes-no.

Reliability: .90.

Validity: Correlations with Good and Good, and Zuckerman and Allison scales are generally positive, except for a negative correlation among males with Zuckerman and Allison.

Author: Chabassol, D.J. and Ishiyama, F.I.

Article: Correlations among three measures of fear of success.

Journal: *Psychological Reports*, 1983, 52(1), 55-58.

Related research: Pappo, M., 1972. *Fear of success: An empirical and theoretical analysis.* Unpublished doctoral dissertation: Teacher's College, Columbia University.

2501

Test name: PERCEIVED STRESS SCALE

Purpose: To measure perceived stress.

Number of items: 4

Format: Frequency rating scale. Sample items presented.

Reliability: Alpha = .72. Test-retest (over 2 months) = .55.

Author: Glasgow, R.E. et al.

Article: Quitting smoking: Strategies used and variables associated with success in a stop-smoking contest.

Journal: *Journal of Consulting and Clinical Psychology*, Dec. 1985, 53(6), 905-912.

Related research: Cohen, S. et al., 1983. A global measure of perceived stress. *Journal of Health and Social Behavior*, 24, 385-396.

2502

Test name: PEER NOMINATION INVENTORY OF DEPRESSION (PNID)

Purpose: To assess depression.

Number of items: 13

Format: Nomination format. Sample items presented. Children nominate (choose) other children who they believe "looks sad," "smiles," and so on.

Reliability: Reliability = .95.

Author: Lefkowitz, M.M. and Tesiny, E.P.

Article: Depression in children: Prevalence and correlates.

Journal: *Journal of Consulting and Clinical Psychology*, Oct. 1985, 53(5), 647-656.

Related research: Lefkowitz, M.M. and Tesiny, E.P., 1980. Assessment of childhood depression. *Journal of Consulting and Clinical Psychology*, 48, 43-50.

Cantwell, D.P., 1983. Assessment of childhood depression: An overview. In D.P. Cantwell and G.A. Carlson (Eds.), *Affective disorders in childhood and adolescents -- An update.* New York: Spectrum.

2503

Test name: PEER RATING DEPRESSION SCALE

Purpose: To measure depression.

Number of items: 9

Format: 4-point frequency scale.

Reliability: Alpha = .76

Validity: Correlates .44 with Beck Depression Inventory; Correlates .39 with POMS-D scores.

Author: Malouff, J.

Article: Development and validation of a behavioral peer-rating measured depression.

Journal: *Journal of Consulting and Clinical Psychology*, Nov. 1984, 52(6), 1108-1109.

2504
Test name: PERSONAL LIFE SATISFACTION SCALE

Purpose: To measure personal life satisfaction.

Number of items: 10

Format: Responses are made on a 7-point scale. Sample items are presented.

Reliability: Alpha = .83.

Validity: Correlation with other variables ranged from -.67 to .66.

Author: Bhagat, R.S. et al.

Article: Total life stress: A multimethod validation of the construct and its effects on organizationally valued outcomes and withdrawal behaviors.

Journal: *Journal of Applied Psychology*, Feb. 1985, 70(1), 202-214.

Related research: Kornhauser, A., 1965. *Mental health of the industrial worker.* New York: Wiley.

2505
Test name: PERSONALITY DATA FORM

Purpose: To measure irrational ideas, beliefs, and attitudes of individuals requesting psychotherapy.

Number of items: 50

Format: Subjects indicate the frequency with which they experience the reactions and thoughts described in the items.

Reliability: Cronbach's alpha = .91.

Validity: Correlates -.60 with Rational Behavior Inventory (Shorkey and Whiteman, 1977); .66 with Trait Anxiety Inventory (Spielberger et al., 1970); and .56 with symptom checklist (Sutton-Simon and Shorkey, unpublished).

Author: Shorkey, C.T. and Sutton-Simon, K.

Article: Personality data form: Internal reliability and validity.

Journal: *Psychological Reports*, June 1983, 52(3), 879-883.

2506
Test name: PHILADELPHIA GERIATRIC CENTER MORALE SCALE

Purpose: To measure morale of the elderly.

Number of items: 17

Format: Yes-no and satisfied-not satisfied response categories. All items presented.

Reliability: Agitation factor is most robust.

Validity: Four factors extracted from a factor analysis confirm four dimensions identified in other studies.

Author: Mancini, J.A. et al.

Article: Measuring morale: Note on use of factor scores.

Journal: *Psychological Reports*, Feb. 1985, 56(1), 139-144.

Related research: Lawton, M.P., 1975. The Philadelphia geriatric center morale scale: A revision. *Journal of Gerontology*, 30, 85-89.

2507
Test name: PHYSICAL ANHEDONIA SCALE

Purpose: To measure the lowered ability to experience pleasure.

Number of items: 61

Format: True-false. Sample items presented.

Reliability: Alpha = .83 (males) and .78 (females).

Author: Chapman, L.J. et al.

Article: Reliabilities and intercorrelations of eight measures of proneness to psychosis.

Journal: *Journal of Consulting and Clinical Psychology*, April 1982, 50(2), 187-195.

Related research: Chapman, L.J. and Chapman, L.P., 1978. *Revised Psychical anhedonia scale*. Unpublished text.
   Chapman, L.J. et al., 1976. Scales for physical and social anhedonia. *Journal of Abnormal Psychology*, 85, 374-392.

2508
Test name: PIANO PERFORMANCE ANXIETY SCALE

Purpose: To provide a self-report state-anxiety measure.

Number of items: 24

Format: Includes two subscales: cognitive-attentional, emotional-autonomic. Employs a true-false format. Examples are presented.

Reliability: Test-retest reliability = .49 (cognitive-attentional) and .27 (emotional-autonomic).

Validity: Correlation with other variables ranged from -.19 to .70.

Author: Sweeney, G.A. and Horan, J.J.

Article: Separate and combined effects of cue-controlled relaxation and cognitive restructuring in the treatment of musical performance anxiety.

Journal: *Journal of Counseling Psychology*, Sept. 1982, *29*(5), 486-497.

Related research: Sarason, I.G., 1978. The test anxiety scale: Concept and research. In C.D. Spielberger and I.G. Sarason (Eds.), *Stress and Anxiety*, 5. Washington, D.C.: Hemisphere.

2509
Test name: PRESCHOOL OBSERVATIONAL SCALE OF ANXIETY

Purpose: To assess anxiety of children too young to accurately report their internal states.

Number of items: 30

Format: Frequency of each behavior observed was recorded by observers. Examples are given.

Reliability: Inter-rater reliability was .93.

Author: Robinson, S.L. et al.

Article: Eye classification, sex, and math anxiety in learning disabled children: Behavioral observations on conservation of volume.

Journal: *Perceptual and Motor Skills*, Dec. 1985, *61*(3 Pt. 2), 1311-1321.

Related research: Glennon, B. and Weisz, J.B., 1978. An observational approach to the assessment of anxiety in young children. *Journal of Consulting and Clinical Psychology*, 46, 1246-1257.

2510
Test name: PRIVATE SELF-CONSCIOUSNESS SCALE

Purpose: To measure private preoccupation with one's own characteristics.

Number of items: 5

Format: 3-category multiple-choice. All items presented.

Reliability: Alpha = .603.

Author: Elliott, G.C. et al.

Article: Transient depersonalization in youth.

Journal: *Social Psychology Quarterly*, June 1984, *47*(2), 115-129.

Related research: Fenigstein, A.M. et al., 1975. Public and private self-consciousness: Assessment and theory. *Journal of Counseling and Clinical Psychology*, *43*, 522-527.

2511
Test name: PROCESSES OF CHANGE TEST

Purpose: To measure 10 processes of change (examples are consciousness raising, self-liberation, and self-reevaluation).

Number of items: 40

Format: 5-point Likert format. Sample items presented for each of the 10 processes.

Reliability: Alpha ranged from .75 to .91 across processes.

Author: Prochaska, J.O. and DiClemente, C.C.

Article: Stages of processes of self-change of smoking: Toward an integrative model of change.

Journal: *Journal of Consulting and Clinical Psychology*, June 1983, *51*(3), 390-395.

Related research: Prochaska, J.O. et al., 1981. Measuring processes of change. Paper presented at the annual meeting of the International Council of Psychologists, Los Angeles, CA.

2512
Test name: PROBLEM AND ROLE PROJECTION SCALES

Purpose: To measure to what extent subjects project their problems and themselves into movies, plays, books, or television shows.

Number of items: 5

Format: Multiple-choice. Sample items presented.

Reliability: Alpha (problem) = .76; Alpha (role) = .78.

Author: Hirschman, E.C.

Article: Predictors of self-projection, fantasy, fulfillment, and escapism.

Journal: *Journal of Social Psychology*, June 1983, *120*(first half), 63-76.

Related research: Hirschman, E.C. and Holbrook, M.B., 1982. Hedonic consumption: Emerging concepts, methods, propositions. *J. Market*, *46*, 92-101.

2513

Test name: PRONENESS TO DISORGANIZATION UNDER STRESS RATING

Purpose: To measure proneness to disorganization.

Number of items: 1

Format: 9-point rating scale.

Reliability: Inter-rater = .95.

Author: Morgan, K.C. and Hock, E.

Article: A longitudinal study of the psychosocial variables affecting the career patterns of women with young children.

Journal: *Journal of Marriage and the Family*, May 1984, *46*(2), 383-390.

Related research: Moss, H., 1971. *Manual for global variables -- postpartum interview for determinants of maternal contract.* Unpublished manuscript. National Institutes of Mental Health, Washington, D.C.

2514

Test name: PSYCHIATRIC EVALUATION FORM

Purpose: To quantify pathology described in diagnostic interviews and structured interviews.

Number of items: 19

Format: Six-point clinical scales.

Reliability: Inter-rater reliability ranged from .50 to .91.

Validity: Correlation of clinical impairment and cluster scores ranged from .32 to .50.

Author: Green, B.L. et al.

Article: Use of the psychiatric evaluation form to quantify children's interview data.

Journal: *Journal of Consulting and Clinical Psychology*, June 1983, *51*(3), 353-359.

Related research: Endicott, J. and Spitzer, R.L., 1972. What! Another rating scale? The psychiatric evaluation form. *Journal of Nervous and Mental Disease*, *154*, 88-104.

2515

Test name: PSYCHIATRIC STATUS SCHEDULE

Purpose: To assess psychiatric symptomatology.

Number of items: 321 (symptoms).

Format: Rating form completed by trained interviewers during a structured interview.

Reliability: Inter-rater reliability ranged from .91 to 1.00; Internal consistency ranged from .19 to .72

(reflecting low average covariance of symptom syndromes in normal populations).

Author: Kavanaugh, M.J. et al.

Article: The relationship between job satisfaction and psychiatric health symptoms for air traffic controllers.

Journal: *Personnel Psychology*, winter 1981, *34*(4), 691-707.

Related research: Spitzer, R.I. et al., 1967. Instruments and recording forms for evaluating psychiatric status and history: Rationale, method of development and description. *Comprehensive Psychiatry*, *8*, 321-943.

2516

Test name: PSYCHOSOMATIC COMPLAINTS SCALE

Purpose: To identify psychosomatic complaints.

Number of items: 9

Format: Employs a 5-point scale. A sample question is presented.

Reliability: Cronbach's alpha = .84.

Author: Frese, M. and Okonek, K.

Article: Reasons to leave shiftwork and psychological and psychosomatic complaints of former shiftworkers.

Journal: *Journal of Applied Psychology*, Aug. 1984, *69*(3), 509-514.

Related research: Mohr, G., 1984. *Measuring psychological well-being in blue collar workers*. Unpublished manuscript, Freie Universitaet, Department of Psychology, Berlin.
   Caplan, R.D. et al., 1975. Job demands and worker health. Washington, D.C.: National Institute for Occupational Safety and Health, U.S. Department of Health, Education and Welfare.

2517

Test name: PSYCHOLOGICAL STRESS SCALE

Purpose: To measure psychological stress.

Number of items: 6

Format: Employs a 5-point answer scale. A sample question is presented.

Reliability: Cronbach's alpha = .80.

Author: Frese, M. and Okonek, K.

Article: Reasons to leave shiftwork and psychological and psychosomatic complaints of former shiftworkers.

Journal: *Journal of Applied Psychology*, Aug. 1984, *69*(3), 509-514.

Related research: Semmer, N., 1982. Stress at work, stress in private life, and psychological well-being. In W. Bachmann, et al. (Eds.), *Mental load and stress in activity: European approaches.* Berlin: Deutscher Verlag der Wissenschaften, and Amsterdam: North Holland.

2518
Test name: PSYCHOPATHY IN CRIMINAL POPULATIONS CHECKLIST

Purpose: To measure psychopathy in criminal populations.

Number of items: 22

Format: Checklist format. 3-point scale (0 = does not apply, 1 = uncertainty, 2 = certain it does apply).

Reliability: Inter-rater reliability ranged from .88 to .93. Generalizability coefficient ranged from .85 to .90; Alpha ranged from .82 to .90.

Validity: Multiple correlation between checklist items and ratings of psychopathy was .86. 75% to 96% of cases correctly classified in discriminant analyses.

Author: Schroeder, M.L. et al.

Article: Generalizability of a checklist for assessment of psychopathy.

Journal: *Journal of Consulting and Clinical Psychology*, Aug. 1983, *51*(4), 511-516.

Related research: Hare, R.D., 1980. A research scale for the assessment of psychopathy in criminal populations. *Personality and Individual Differences, 1,* 111-119.

2519
Test name: PSYCHOTHERAPY PROBLEM CHECKLIST

Purpose: To measure difficult-to-change problems by self-report.

Number of items: 21

Format: 21 items include these problems: headaches, anxiety, suicide intent, disturbed sleep, etc.

Reliability: $r = .81$.

Author: Morrison, J.K. and Heeder, R.

Article: Follow-up study of the effectiveness of emotive-reconstructive therapy.

Journal: *Psychological Reports*, Feb. 1984, *54*(1), 149-150.

Related research: Morrison, J.K., and Teta, D.C., 1978. Simplified use of the semantic differential to measure psychotherapy outcome. *Journal of Clinical Psychology, 34,* 751-753.

2520

Test name: RATINGS OF BEHAVIORAL DEPRESSION

Purpose: To assess behavioral symptoms of depression.

Number of items: 30

Format: Involves a semistructured interview procedure.

Validity: Correlations with other variables ranged from -.33 to .31.

Author: Fry, P.S.

Article: Development of a geriatric scale of hopelessness: Implications for counseling and intervention with the depressed elderly.

Journal: *Journal of Counseling Psychology*, July 1984, *31*(3), 322-331.

Related research: Weinberg, J., 1975. Geriatric psychiatry. In A.M. Freeman, H.I. Kaplan, and B.J. Sadock (Eds.), *Comprehensive textbook of psychiatry*, 2, 2405-2420. Baltimore, MD: Williams & Wilkins.

2521

Test name: REASONS FOR LIVING INVENTORY

Purpose: To measure range of belief potentially important as reasons for not committing suicide.

Number of items: 48

Format: 6-point Likert scale.

Reliability: Alpha ranged from .72 to .89 across subscales.

Validity: Correlations with suicidal behaviors questionnaire generally confirm the validity of the inventory. Numerous F-tests and correlations presented.

Author: Linehan, M.M. et al.

Article: Reasons for staying alive when you are thinking of killing yourself: A reasons for living inventory.

Journal: *Journal of Consulting and Clinical Psychology*, April 1983, *51*(2), 276-286.

2522

Test name: RECENT LIFE CHANGES QUESTIONNAIRE

Purpose: To provide a method of measuring life change.

Number of items: 76

Format: Includes 5 categories: health, work, home and family, personal-social, and financial.

Reliability: Reliability was r = .84 (1 month interval).

Validity: Correlation with the schedule of recent experiences was r = .67.

Author: Pearson, J.E. and Long, T.J.

Article: Life change measurement: Scoring, reliability and subjective estimate of adjustment.

Journal: *Measurement and Evaluation in Counseling and Development,* July 1985, *18*(2), 72-80.

Related research: Rahe, R.H., 1975. Epidemiological studies of life change and illness. *International Journal of Psychiatry in Medicine, 6,* 133-146.

2523
Test name: REVISED WORRY-EMOTIONALITY SCALE

Purpose: To measure cognitive and emotional components of anxiety.

Number of items: 10

Format: 5-category multiple-choice (From "does not describe my present condition" to "describes my present condition very well"). All items presented.

Reliability: Internal consistency = .81 (worry) and .86 (emotionality).

Author: Morris, L.W. et al.

Article: Cognitive and emotional components of anxiety: Literature review and a revised worry-emotionality scale.

Journal: *Journal of Educational Psychology,* Aug. 1981, *73*(4), 541-555.

Related research: Liebert, R.M. and Morris, L.W., 1967. Cognitive and emotional components of test anxiety: A distinction and some initial data. *Psychological Reports, 20,* 975-978.

2524
Test name: REVISED CHILDREN'S MANIFEST ANXIETY SCALE

Purpose: To measure chronic anxiety.

Number of items: 37

Format: A self-report questionnaire. Includes 9 items to measure social desirability or lie scale.

Reliability: Internal consistency reliabilities were in the mid .80s.

Author: Reynolds, C.R.

Article: Long-term stability of scores on the revised Children's Manifest Anxiety Scale.

Journal: *Perceptual and Motor Skills,* Dec. 1981, *53*(3), 702.

Related research: Reynolds, C.R. and Richmond, B.O., 1978. What I think and feel: A revised measure of children's manifest anxiety.

Journal of Abnormal Child Psychology, 6, 271-280.

2525
Test name: ROLE AMBIGUITY SCALE

Purpose: To indicate role stress.

Number of items: 6

Reliability: Cronbach's alpha was .84.

Validity: Correlation with other variables ranged from -.56 to .47.

Author: Chacko, T.I.

Article: Women and equal employment opportunity: Some unintended effects.

Journal: *Journal of Applied Psychology*, Feb. 1982, *67*(1), 119-123.

Related research: Rizzo, J.R. et al., 1970. Role conflict and ambiguity in complex organizations. *Administrative Science Quarterly, 15*, 150-163.

2526
Test name: ROLE CONFLICT SCALE

Purpose: To indicate role stress.

Number of items: 8

Reliability: Cronbach's alpha was .73.

Validity: Correlation with other variables ranged from -.56 to -.07.

Author: Chacko, T.I.

Article: Women and equal employment opportunity: Some unintended effects.

Journal: *Journal of Applied Psychology*, Feb. 1982, *67*(1), 119-123.

Related research: Rizzo, J.R. et al., 1970. Role conflict and ambiguity in complex organizations. *Administrative Science Quarterly, 15*, 150-163.

2527
Test name: ROLE STRESS SCALE

Purpose: To measure role stress.

Number of items: 16

Format: 5-point Likert format.

Reliability: Alphas ranged from .70 to .88 across subscales.

Author: Keenan, A. and Newton, T.J.

Article: Frustration in organizations: Relationships to role stress, climate and psychological strain.

Journal: *Journal of Occupational Psychology*, March 1984, *57*(1), 57-65.

Related research: Rizzo, J.R. et al., 1970. Role conflict and ambiguity in complex organizations. *Administrative Science Quarterly*, *15*, 150-163.

2528
Test name: ROSENZWEIG PICTURE-FRUSTRATION STUDY

Purpose: To assess typical modes of reaction to frustration.

Number of items: 24

Format: Subjects write in what they think an anonymous person would say who is pictured to the right of each of 24 cartoon-like pictures depicting an everyday, interpersonally frustrating situation. Provides six scores: extraggression, intraggresion, imaggression, obstacle-dominance, ego-defense, and need-persistence.

Reliability: Correlations between raters ranged from .50 to .90.

Author: Graybill, D. et al.

Article: Effects of playing violent versus nonviolent video games on the aggressive ideation of aggressive and non-aggressive children.

Journal: *Child Study Journal*, 1985, *15*(3), 199-205.

Related research: Rosenzweig, S., 1978. Aggressive behavior and the Rosenzweig Picture Frustration Study. New York: Praeger.

2529
Test name: SATISFACTION WITH LIFE SCALE

Purpose: To measure global life satisfaction.

Number of items: 5

Format: Responses to each item are made on a scale from 1 (strongly disagree) to 7 (strongly agree).

Reliability: Test-retest (2 months) correlation coefficient was .82. Coefficient alpha was .87.

Validity: Correlations with other variables ranged from -.37 to .68 (N = 176) and from -.32 to .66 (N = 163).

Author: Diener, E. et al.

Article: The satisfaction with life scale.

Journal: *Journal of Personality Assessment*, Feb. 1985, *49*(1), 71-75.

2530
Test name: SCALE FOR SUICIDE IDEATORS

Purpose: To assess and quantify degree of suicide intent in suicide ideators.

Number of items: 19

Format: Interviewer rated format.

Validity: Self-report form correlates .90 with interviewer form.

Author: Schotte, D.E. and Clum, G.A.

Article: Suicide ideation in a college population: A test of a model.

Journal: *Journal of Consulting and Clinical Psychology*, Oct. 1982, 50(5), 690-696.

Related research: Beck, A. et al., 1979. Assessment of suicidal ideation: The scale for suicide ideators. *Journal of Consulting and Clinical Psychology*, 47, 343-352.

2531
Test name: SCHEDULE OF RECENT EVENTS

Purpose: To measure the amount of stress experienced from readjustment to life events.

Number of items: 43

Format: Life events included are: work, family, personal, and financial.

Reliability: Cronbach's alpha was .83 (N = 120).

Validity: Correlations with: Ego-permissiveness was r = .57 (N = 120); with Field-dependent perception was r = -.73 (N = 120).

Author: Daly, E.B.

Article: Relationship of stress and ego energy to field-dependent perception in older adults.

Journal: *Perceptual and Motor Skills*, Dec. 1984, 59(3), 919-926.

Related research: Holmes, T.H. and Masuda, M., 1973. Life change and illness susceptibility. In J.P. Scott and E.C. Senay (Eds.), *Separation and depression: Clinical and research aspects*. Symposium presented at the Chicago meeting of the American Association of the Advancement of Science (Dec. 27, 1970). Washington, D.C.: American Association for the Advancement for Science, 161-186.

2532
Test name: SCHEDULE OF RECENT EXPERIENCES

Purpose: To provide a tool for recording and studying the impact of life changes on stress-related illness.

Number of items: 42

Format: Items are weighted according to seriousness of impact and degree of adjustment required.

Reliability: Test-retest reliability ranged from .87 to .90 (1 week interval); and from .55 to .70 (6 to 9 month intervals).

Validity: Correlation with the Recent Life Changes Questionnaire was .67 (N = 109).

Author: Pearson, J.E. and Long, T.J.

Article: Life change measurement: scoring, reliability, and subjective estimates of adjustment.

Journal: *Measurement and Evaluation in Counseling and Development*, July 1985, *18*(2), 72-80.

Related research: Rahe, R.H., 1972. Epidemiological studies of life change and illness. *International Journal of Psychiatry in Medicine*, 6, 133-146.

2533
Test name: SCHEDULE OF RECENT EXPERIENCES (SRE)

Purpose: To measure stressful life events.

Number of items: 43

Format: Items (events) are checked if they have occurred in the last 12 months. A score is obtained by summing the weight of each checked item.

Validity: Correlated .40 with Organizational Readjustment Rating Scale (Naismith, 1975).

Author: Weiss, H.M. et al.

Article: Effects of life and job stress on information search behaviors of organizational members.

Journal: *Journal of Applied Psychology*, Feb. 1982, *67*(1), 60-66.

Related research: Holmes, T.H. and Rahe, R.H., 1967. The social readjustment rating scale. *Journal of Psychosomatic Research*, *11*, 213-218.

2534
Test name: SHORT FORM MULTISCORE DEPRESSION INVENTORY

Purpose: To assess severity of depressive symptoms.

Number of items: 47

Reliability: KR = .92.

Validity: Correlated .63 with Beck Depression Inventory.

Author: Berndt, D.J.

Article: Evaluation of a short form of the multiscore depression inventory.

Journal: *Journal of Consulting and Clinical Psychology*, Oct. 1983, *51*(5), 790-791.

Related research: Berndt, D.J. et al., 1980. Development and initial evaluation of a multiscore depression inventory. *Journal of Personality Assessment, 44*, 396-404.

2535
Test name: STRESS ASSESSMENT PACKAGE

Purpose: To measure stress-related variables.

Number of items: 160

Format: Includes 20 factors and 12 single item variables.

Reliability: Coefficient alphas for the 20 factors ranged from .67 to .94.

Author: Hendrix, W.H. et al.

Article: Behavioral and physiological consequences of stress and its antecedent factors.

Journal: *Journal of Applied Psychology*, Feb. 1985, *70*(1), 188-201.

Related research: Fye, S.P and Staton, C.W., 1981. Individual and organizational variables relationship to coronary heart disease. (Report No. LSSR 3-81.) Wright-Patterson AFB, OH: Air Force Institute of Technology.

Martin, W.H. and Simard, L.C., 1982. Stress and coronary heart disease in organizational, extraorganizational and individual environments. (Report No. LSSR8-82.) Wright-Patterson AFB, OH: Air Force Institute of Technology.

2536
Test name: STRESS RESPONSE SCALE

Purpose: To assess the behavioral pattern that the child is likely to adopt in response to stress.

Number of items: 40

Format: The scale is completed by the person perceiving the child's problematic behavior. Included is a total score and subscale scores for each of five response patterns: impulsive (acting out), passive-aggressive, impulsive (overactive), repressed, and dependent. A six-point rating scale is employed ranging from "never" (0) to "always" (5).

Reliability: Test-retest (1 month) reliability coefficient was r = .86 (N = 25). Coefficient alpha was .94.

Author: Chandler, L.A. and Shermis, M.D.

Article: Assessing behavioral responses to stress.

Journal: *Educational and Psychological Measurement*, winter 1985, *45*(4), 825-844.

Related research: Chandler, L.A., 1983. The Stress Response Scale: An instrument for use in assessing emotional adjustment reactions. *School Psychology Review, 12,* 260-265.

2537
Test name: STRESS SCALE

Purpose: To measure affective states indicative of psychological strain and stress.

Number of items: 19

Format: Includes three subscales: depression, anxiety, and irritation.

Reliability: Internal consistency, alpha = .89.

Author: Colarelli, S.M.

Article: Methods of communication and mediating processes in realistic job previews.

Journal: *Journal of Applied Psychology*, Nov. 1984, *69*(4), 633-642.

Related research: Caplan, R.D. et al., 1975. Job demands and worker health. Washington, DC: U.S. Government Printing Offices.

2538
Test name: SUICIDAL TENDENCIES TESTING PROCEDURE

Purpose: To assess suicidal tendencies.

Number of items: 4

Time required: 15-25 minutes.

Format: Four stories are followed by a question to which a child responds by indicating on a color-coded ruler his response. All stories presented.

Reliability: Test-retest ranged from .23 to .78 (7 of 8 statistically significant, p<.05).

Validity: Subscales correlate with themselves at two different times more strongly than with each other.

Author: Orbach, I. et al.

Article: Attraction and repulsion by life and death in suicidal and normal children.

Journal: *Journal of Consulting and Clinical Psychology*, Oct. 1983, *51*(5), 661-670.

2539
Test name: SYMPTOM CHECKLIST-90

Purpose: To measure psychiatric symptoms by self-report.

Number of items: 90

Format: 5-point scale of distress.

Reliability: Alpha ranged from .56 to .96 across 9 subscales.

Validity: Most variance accounted for by first unrotated factor. Scale may measure mainly general discomfort, not specific dimensions of symptomatology.

Author: Holcomb, W.R. et al.

Article: Factor structure of the symptom checklist-90 with acute psychiatric inpatients.

Journal: *Journal of Consulting and Clinical Psychology*, Aug. 1983, *51*(4), 535-538.

Related research: Derogatis, L.R. and Cleary, P.A., 1977. Confirmation of the dimensional structure of the SCL-90: A study in construct validation. *Journal of Clinical Psychology*, *33*, 981-989.

2540
Test name: TEDIUM MEASURE

Purpose: To measure physical, mental, and emotional exhaustion.

Number of items: 21

Format: 7-point scale (never to always).

Reliability: Alpha ranged between .91 and .93. Test-retest (1 month) = .89.

Validity: Significant correlation with job satisfaction and health problems.

Author: Stout, J.K. and Posner, J.L.

Article: Stress, role ambiguity and role conflict.

Journal: *Psychological Reports*, Dec. 1984, *55*(3), 747-753.

Related research: Pines, A.M. et al., 1981. *Burnout: From tedium to personal growth*. New York: The Free Press.
    Stout, J.K. and Williams, J.M., 1983. A comparison of two measures of burnout. *Psychological Reports*, *53*, 283-289.

2541
Test name: TEMPLAR DEATH ANXIETY SCALE

Purpose: To measure the degree of acceptance of death.

Number of items: 15

Format: True-false.

Reliability: Test-retest = .83; Split-half ranged from .43 to .83; Spearman-Brown Formula = .60.

Author: Schell, B.H. and Zinger, J.T.

Article: Death anxiety scale means and standard deviations for Ontario undergraduates and funeral directors.

Journal: *Psychological Reports*, April 1984, *54*(2), 439-446.

Related research: Templar, D.I., 1970. The construction and validation of a death anxiety scale. *Journal of General Psychology*, *82*, 165-177.

2542
Test name: TENSION INDEX

Purpose: To measure tension.

Number of items: 9

Format: Responses were made on a 5-point scale from "never" to "nearly all the time."

Reliability: Alpha was .86.

Validity: Zero-order correlations with role ambiguity was .41 and with role conflict was .69.

Author: Bedeian, A.G. et al.

Article: The relationship between role stress and job-related, interpersonal and organizational climate factors.

Journal: *Journal of Social Psychology*, April 1981, *113*(second half), 247-260.

Related research: Lyons, T.F., 1971. Role clarity, need for clarity, satisfaction, tension and withdrawal. *Organizational Behavior and Human Performance*, *6*, 99-110.

2543
Test name: TOTAL LIFE STRESS SCALE

Purpose: To measure stress.

Number of items: 83

Format: Checklist format for occurrence; 7-point Likert format (-3 to 3) to assess positive or negative impact.

Reliability: Alpha ranged from .53 to .77 across subscales.

Validity: All correlations between subscales and six validation scales were significant (r's ranged from .23 to .67 in absolute value) and were in predicted directions.

Author: Bhagat, R.S. et al.

Article: Total life stress: A multimethod validation of the construct and its effects on organizationally valued outcomes and withdrawal behaviors.

Journal: *Journal of Applied Psychology*, Feb. 1985, *70*(1), 202-214.

Related research: Dohrenwend, B.S. et al., 1978. Exemplification of a method for scaling life events:

The PERI life events scale. *Journal of Health and Social Behavior, 19,* 205-229.

Johnson, J.H. and Sarason, I.G., 1979. Recent developments in research on life stress. In V. Hamilton and D.M. Warburton (Eds.), *Human stress and cognition: An information processing approach.* New York: Wiley, 205-236.

2544
Test name: WELL-BEING SCALE

Purpose: To measure psychological and physical well-being.

Number of items: 18

Format: Forced choice format. All items presented.

Reliability: Item-scale correlations ranged from .30 to .63.

Validity: Correlated .44 (p<.01) with seeing a doctor in last 6 months, and .35 with number of days sick in last 6 months.

Author: Davidson, W.B. and Cotter, P.

Article: Adjustment to aging and relationship with offspring.

Journal: *Psychological Reports,* 1982, *50*(3, Part I), 731-738.

Related research: Pfeiffer, E., 1976. *Multidimensional functional assessment: The OARS methodology -- A manual.* Durham, NC: Center for the Study of Aging and Human Development.

2545
Test name: ZUCKERMAN AND ALLISON FEAR OF SUCCESS SCALE

Purpose: To measure fear of success.

Number of items: 27

Format: 7-point Likert scale.

Validity: Correlated positively with Pappo and Good and Good scales, except among males where correlation was negative.

Author: Chabassol, D.J. and Ishiyama, F.I.

Article: Correlations among three measures of fear of success.

Journal: *Psychological Reports,* 1983, *52*(1), 55-58.

Related research: Zuckerman, M. and Allison, S.N., 1976. An objective measure of fear of success: Construction and validation. *Journal of Personality Assessment, 40,* 422-430.

2546
Test name: ZUNG SELF-RATING DEPRESSION SCALE

Purpose: To assess behavioral changes, cognitive processes, and affective concomitants of depression.

Number of items: 20

Format: 4-point Likert type categories ("most of the time" to "none or little of the time").

Reliability: Cronbach's alpha ranged from .88 to .93 across criterion groups.

Validity: Discriminated between depressed and nondepressed clients ($p < .001$).

Author: Gabrys, J.B. and Peters, K.

Article: Reliability, discriminant, and predictive validity of the Zung Self-Rating Depression Scale.

Journal: *Psychological Reports*, Dec. 1985, *57*(3-II), 1091-1096.

Related research: Zung, W.K., 1965. A self-rating depression scale. *Archives of General Psychiatry, 12*, 63-70.

ADJUSTMENT-SOCIAL

2547
Test name: ACCULTURATION RATING SCALE FOR MEXICAN-AMERICANS

Purpose: To measure degree of acculturation.

Number of items: 20

Format: Likert format (1-Mexican/Spanish to 5-Anglo/English).

Reliability: Alpha = .88; Test-retest = .72.

Author: Franco, J.N. et al.

Article: Ethnic and acculturation differences in self-disclosure.

Journal: *Journal of Social Psychology*, Feb. 1984, *122*(first half), 21-32.

Related research: Cuellar, I. et al., 1980. An acculturation scale for Mexican American normal and clinical populations. *Hispanic Journal of Behavioral Science*, 2(3), 199-217.

2548
Test name: ACQUAINTANCE DESCRIPTION FORM

Purpose: To measure different aspects of the strength and rewardingness of an interpersonal relationship.

Number of items: 80

Format: Responses to each item are made on a 7-point scale from 0 to 6 indicating to what extent the item applies to the subject's relationship with a designated person. Includes seven scales.

Reliability: Test-retest correlations for the scales ranged from .70 to .93. Split-half reliabilities ranged from .79 to .94.

Author: Wright, P.H. and Keple, T.W.

Article: Friends and parents of a sample of high school juniors: An exploratory study of relationship intensity and interpersonal rewards.

Journal: *Journal of Marriage and the Family*, Aug. 1981, *43*(3), 559-570.

Related research: Wright, P.H., 1974. The delineation and measurement of some key variables in the study of friendship. *Representative Research in Social Psychology*, 5, 93-96.

2549
Test name: ADOLESCENT ALIENATION SCALE

Purpose: To measure adolescent alienation.

Number of items: 41

Format: 4-point agree-disagree response categories.

Reliability: Alpha ranged from .67 to .80 across subscales.

Author: James, N.L. and Johnson, D.W.

Article: The relationship between attitudes toward social interdependence and psychological health within three criminal populations.

Journal: *Journal of Social Psychology*, Oct. 1983, *121*(first half), 131-143.

Related research: Mackey, J. and Ahlgren, A., 1977. A dimension of adolescent alienation. *Applied Psychological Measurement*, *1*(2), 219-232.

2550
Test name: ADULT ORIENTATION TO CHILD AUTONOMY SCALE

Purpose: To assess adults' orientations to control or autonomy in interactions with children.

Number of items: 32

Format: Four vignettes followed by 4 items that can be rated as appropriate or not on a 7-point scale. Sample items presented.

Reliability: Cronbach's alpha ranged from .63 to .80 across subscales.

Validity: Correlated positively and significantly with intrinsic motivation and self-esteem. Correlations ranged from .27 to .56. Did not correlate with perceived physical competence.

Author: Deci, E.L. et al.

Article: An instrument to access adults' orientations toward control versus autonomy with children: Reflections on intrinsic motivation and perceived competence.

Journal: *Journal of Educational Psychology*, Oct. 1981, *73*(5), 642-650.

2551
Test name: AUDIENCE ANXIOUSNESS SCALE

Purpose: To measure audience anxiousness independent of specific social behaviors.

Number of items: 12

Format: Subjects respond to each item on a 5-point scale to identify the degree to which the item is true. The scale ranged from "not at all" to "extremely characteristic." All items are presented.

Reliability: Cronbach's alphas were .88 and .91.

Validity: Correlations with other variables ranged from -.24 to .84.

Author: Leary, M.R.

Article: Social anxiousness: The construct and its measurement.

Journal: *Journal of Personality Assessment*, Feb. 1983, *47*(1), 66-75.

2552

Test name: AVOIDANCE OF THE ONTOLOGICAL CONFRONTATION OF LONELINESS SCALE

Purpose: To measure the avoidance of the harsh reality of loneliness.

Number of items: 40

Format: True-false. All items presented.

Reliability: Cronbach's alpha = .81; Odd-even = .78.

Validity: Correlated .37 with Jackson's Social Desirability Scale. Did not correlate with Eysenck's Neuroticism Scale.

Author: Thauberger, P.C.

Article: Avoidance of existential-ontological confrontations: A review of research.

Journal: *Psychological Reports*, 1981, *49*(3), 747-764.

Related research: Thauberger, P. and Cleland, J., 1979. Measuring the abyss: Avoidance of the ontological confrontations of loneliness. Paper presented at the UCLA Research Conference on Loneliness.

2553

Test name: BRADLEY LONELINESS SCALE—MODIFIED

Purpose: To measure loneliness.

Number of items: 37

Format: 6-point Likert format (rarely true to always true).

Reliability: Internal consistency = .92.

Author: Ponzetti, J.J. and Cate, R.M.

Article: Sex differences in the relationship between loneliness and academic performance.

Journal: *Psychological Reports*, June 1981, *48*(3), 758.

Related research: Bradley, R., 1969. Measuring loneliness. Unpublished doctoral dissertation, Washington State University. *Dissertation Abstract International*, *30*, 3382B; University microfilms No. 70-1048.

2554

Test name: CHILDREN'S LONELINESS SCALE

Purpose: To measure loneliness.

Number of items: 16

Format: 5-point truth scale ("always true" to "not true at all"). All items presented.

Reliability: Alpha = .90.

Validity: Correlated -.39 with play rating of same-sex peer; -.37 with positive nomination of same-sex peer; .37 to negative nomination of same-sex peer. All correlations p<.001.

Author: Asher, S.R. and Wheeler, V.A.

Article: Children's loneliness: A comparison of rejected and neglected peer status.

Journal: *Journal of Consulting and Clinical Psychology*, Aug. 1985, 53(4), 500-505.

Related research: Asher, S.R. et al., 1984. Loneliness in children. *Child Development*, 55, 1457-1464.

2555

Test name: COGNITION OF BEHAVIORAL UNITS

Purpose: To measure social intelligence.

Number of items: 34

Format: For the first 16 items, the subject selects one of four pictures which best illustrates the feelings described in a verbal statement read to the examinees. For the remaining 18 items, the subject selects one of four facial pictures that best corresponds to a picture of a face.

Reliability: Test-retest reliability was .40.

Validity: Correlations with CIRCUS ranged from .22 to .46 (N ranged from 69 to 74).

Author: Snyder, S.D. and Michael, W.B.

Article: The relationship of performance on standardized tests in mathematics and reading to two measures of social intelligence and one of academic self-esteem for two samples of primary school children.

Journal: *Educational and Psychological Measurement*, winter 1983, 43(4), 1141-1148.

Related research: Favero, J., 1979. *Tests of SOI behavior skills and classroom activities for improving behavioral skills*. Unpublished manuscript. Glendora, Calif: Glendora Unified School District.

2556

Test name: COLLEGE PEER RATING SYSTEM

Purpose: To measure peer ratings on task orientation, classroom behavior, and social acceptance.

Number of items: 3

Format: Each child rates all others on each sociometric item. Items presented along with 5-point response categories.

Reliability: Test-retest over 4 months ranged from .64 to .78.

Validity: Correlations between ratings were significant and in expected direction.

Author: Bailey, D.B., Jr. et al.

Article: Generalized effects of a highly structured time-on-task intervention.

Journal: *Psychological Reports*, April 1984, 54(2), 483-490.

2557

Test name: COMPREHENSIVE SOCIAL DESIRABILITY SCALE FOR CHILDREN

Purpose: To assess social desirability.

Number of items: 27

Format: True-false.

Reliability: Correlation between alternate forms = .92; Alpha (internal consistency) = .57.

Validity: Correlation of .36 with Crandall, Crandall, and Katkovsky Social Desirability Scale (1965).

Author: Malizio, A.G. et al.

Article: Relationship of social desirability, age, and sex with task persistence and contingent self-reinforcement.

Journal: *Psychological Reports*, 1982, 50(1), 39-47.

2558

Test name: CONCERN FOR APPROPRIATENESS SCALE

Purpose: To measure the tendency to adopt protective self-presentation styles.

Number of items: 20

Format: Includes two subscales: cross-situational variability and attention to social comparison.

Reliability: Coefficient alpha ranged from .82 to .89. Test-retest (3 weeks) r = .84.

Validity: Correlations with other variables ranged from -.08 to .41.

Author: Cutler, B.L. and Wolfe, R.N.

Article: Construct validity of the concern for appropriateness scale.

Journal: *Journal of Personality Assessment*, June 1985, *49*(3), 318-323.

Related research: Lennox, R.D. and Wolfe, R.N., 1984. Revision of the self-monitoring scale. *Journal of Personality and Social Psychology*, *46*, 1349-1364.

2559
Test name: COUPLES THERAPY ALLIANCE SCALE

Purpose: To measure client's view of therapeutic relationship.

Number of items: 28

Format: 5-point Likert format.

Reliability: Internal consistency = .96 (total test); consistency ranged from .85 to .92 across subscales.

Author: Johnson, S.M. and Greenberg, L.S.

Article: Differential effects of experiential and problem-solving interventions in resolving marital conflict.

Journal: *Journal of Consulting and Clinical Psychology*, April 1985, *53*(2), 175-184.

Related research: Pinsof, W. and Catherall, D., 1983. *The couples' therapy alliance scale manual.* Chicago, IL: The Chicago Center for Family Studies, Northwestern University.

2560
Test name: CULTURAL MISTRUST INVENTORY

Purpose: To measure cultural mistrust among blacks.

Number of items: 48

Format: Responses are made to each item on a 7-point Likert-type scale which ranged from "strongly agree" to "strongly disagree."

Reliability: Test-retest (2 weeks) reliability estimate was .82.

Author: Terrell, F. and Terrell, S.

Article: Race of counselor, client sex, cultural mistrust level and premature termination from counseling among black clients.

Journal: *Journal of Counseling Psychology*, July 1984, *31*(3), 371-375.

Related research: Terrell, F. and Terrell, S.L., 1981. An inventory to measure cultural mistrust among blacks. *Western Journal of Black Studies*, *5*, 180-184.

2561
Test name: DIFFERENTIAL LONELINESS SCALE

Purpose: To assess dissatisfaction with four types of relationships.

Number of items: 60

Format: Subjects respond by answering "true" or "false" to items regarding the quality and quantity of interaction in relationships. Includes four scales: family, larger groups, friendship, and romantic/sexual.

Reliability: Cronbach's alpha ranged from .46 to .89.

Validity: Correlations with other variables ranged from -.89 to .54.

Author: Schmitt, J.P and Kurdek, L.A.

Article: Age and gender differences in and personality correlates of loneliness in different relationships.

Journal: *Journal of Personality Assessment*, Oct. 1985, *49*(5), 485-496.

Related research: Schmidt, N. and Sermat, V., 1983. Measuring loneliness in different relationships. *Journal of Personality and Social Psychology*, *44*, 1038-1047.

2562
Test name: DYADIC TRUST SCALE

Purpose: To measure trust between two people.

Number of items: 8

Format: 7-point Likert format. Sample items presented.

Reliability: Alpha = .85.

Author: Hansen, G.

Article: Perceived threats and marital jealousy.

Journal: *Social Psychology Quarterly*, Sept. 1985, *48*(3), 262-268.

Related research: Larzelere, R.E. and Huston, T.L., 1980. The dyadic trust scale: Toward understanding interpersonal trust in close relationships. *Journal of Marriage and the Family*, *42*, 595-604.

2563
Test name: ENLARGED ANOMIA SCALE

Purpose: To measure anomia.

Number of items: 9

Format: Agree-disagree response categories. All items presented.

Reliability: Part-whole correlations .91, .89, and .89 in each of three consecutive years. Test-retest reliability ranged from .41 to .56 from 1st to 2nd year, 2nd to 3rd year, and 1st to 3rd year.

Author: Poresky, R.H. et al.

Article: Anomia in rural women: A longitudinal comparison of two measures.

Journal: *Psychological Reports*, 1981, 49(2), 480-482.

Related research: Robinson, J.P and Shover, P.R., 1973. *Measures of psychological attitudes*. Ann Arbor, MI: Survey Research Center, University of Michigan.

2564
Test name: EVALUATION OF BEHAVIORAL IMPLICATIONS

Purpose: To measure social intelligence.

Number of items: 20

Format: Each item contains a verbal stem describing a social dilemma, followed by four alternative pictures from which the examinee selects the one that depicts the most appropriate resolution of the dilemma.

Reliability: Test-retest reliability was .55.

Validity: Correlations with CIRCUS ranged from .11 to .46 (N ranged from 69 to 74).

Author: Snyder, S.D. and Michael, W.B.

Article: The relationship of performance on standardized tests in mathematics and reading to two measures of social intelligence and one of academic self-esteem for two samples of primary school children.

Journal: *Educational and Psychological Measurement*, winter 1983, 43(4), 1141-1148.

Related research: Favero, J., 1979. Tests of SOI behavioral skills and classroom activities for improving behavioral skills. Unpublished manual, Glendora, CA: Glendora Unified School District.

2565
Test name: FRIENDLINESS QUESTIONNAIRE

Purpose: To assess the components of friendliness.

Number of items: 40

Format: Includes four components: self-concept, accessibility, rewardingness, and alienation.

Reliability: Test-retest correlations from .73 to .81 (N = 66), (3 to 4 week interval).

Author: Reisman, J.M.

Article: SACRAL: Toward the meaning and measuring of friendliness.

Journal: *Journal of Personality Assessment*, Aug. 1983, 47(4), 405-413.

Related research: Dean, D.G., 1969, Alienation: Its meaning and measurements. D.G. Dean (Ed.), *Dynamic Social Psychology*. New York: Random House.

Wright, P.H., 1969. A model and a technique for the studies of friendship. *Journal of Experimental Social Psychology*, 5, 295-309.

2566
Test name: GERIATRIC EVALUATION BY RELATIVE'S RATING INSTRUMENT

Purpose: To measure cognitive and social functioning, mood, and somatic functioning of elderly outpatients.

Number of items: 49

Format: 5-point frequency scale follows each specific and behavioral item ("almost all of the time" to "almost never").

Reliability: Inter-rater reliability = .96 for total score and ranged between .63 and .96 across subscales. Cronbach's alpha ranged from .66 to .96.

Validity: Differentiates between three groups of elderly outpatients who differ in severity of global deterioration (Reisberg, 1982).

Author: Schwartz, G.E.

Article: Development and validation of the geriatric evaluation by relatives rating instrument (GERRI).

Journal: *Psychological Reports*, Oct. 1983, 53(2), 479-488.

2567
Test name: GREENWOOD'S POSITIVE SOCIAL BEHAVIOR SCALE

Purpose: To enable teachers to evaluate kindergarten children's social competence.

Number of items: 9

Format: Includes only social behaviors of a positive nature. Teachers respond to each item on a 7-point Likert-type scale from accurate (7) to false (1) description of the child's behavior. Some examples are provided.

Validity: Correlations with other social competence scales ranged from -.67 to .57.

Author: Begin, G.

Article: Convergent validity of four instruments for teachers' assessing social competence of kindergarten children.

Journal: *Perceptual and Motor Skills*, Dec. 1983, 57(3-Part 1), 1007-1012.

Related research: Greenwood, C.R. et al., 1978. *Social assessment manual for preschool level*.

(SAMPLE). Eugene: Center at Oregon for Research in the Behavioral Education of the Handicapped.

2568
Test name: GROUP ATMOSPHERE SCALE

Purpose: To provide a description of group atmosphere.

Number of items: 10

Format: Includes an 8-point semantic differential for each item. Examples are provided.

Reliability: Median alpha = .91.

Validity: Correlations with the Job Descriptive Index Co-worker and Supervision subscales ranged from .38 to .68.

Author: Vecchio, R.P.

Article: A further test of leadership effects due to between-group variation and within-group variation.

Journal: *Journal of Applied Psychology*, April 1982, *67*(2), 200-208.

Related research: Fiedler, F.E., 1967. *A theory of leadership effectiveness.* New York: McGraw-Hill.

2569
Test name: GROUP COHESIVENESS INDEX

Purpose: To measure group cohesiveness.

Number of items: 4

Format: 4-point scale. All items presented.

Reliability: Alpha = .85.

Author: O'Reilly, C.A. III. and Caldwell, D.F.

Article: The impact of normative social influence and cohesiveness on task perceptions and attitudes: A social information processing approach.

Journal: *Journal of Occupational Psychology*, Sept. 1985, *58*(3), 193-206.

Related research: Seashore, S., 1954. Group cohesiveness in the industrial work group. Institute for Social Research, University of Michigan.

2570
Test name: HETEROSOCIAL ASSESSMENT INVENTORY FOR WOMEN

Purpose: To evaluate five dimensions that may influence performance in 12 heterosocial situations.

Number of items: 60

Format: Five questions are presented for each of 12 heterosocial situations to provide a self-assessment. An example is presented.

Reliability: Split-half reliabilities ranged from .74 to .94. Cronbach's alphas ranged from .88 to .96. Test-retest (3 weeks) reliability coefficients (N = 31) ranged from .80 to .87.

Validity: Correlations with other variables ranged from -.43 to .78 (Study I) and from -.75 to .86 (Study II).

Author: Kolko, D.J.

Article: The heterosocial assessment inventory for women: A psychometric and behavioral evaluation.

Journal: *Journal of Psychopathy and Behavioral Assessment*, March 1985, 7(1), 49-64.

Related research: Klaus, D. et al., 1977. Survey of dating habits of male and female college students: A necessary precursor to measurement and modification. *Journal of Clinical Psychology*, 33, 369-375.

2571

Test name: INDIVIDUALISM - SOCIAL DETERMINISM SCALE

Purpose: To measure individualist and social determinist beliefs.

Number of items: 11

Format: Matched-pair format. All items presented.

Reliability: Alpha = .66. Item-total correlations ranged from .38 to .55.

Validity: Did not correlate with Rosenberg Self-Esteem Scale or Srole Anomie Scale or the F-Scale. Correlated .00 to .15 across three dimensions of locus of control. Additional discriminant and construct validation presented.

Author: Zeitz, G. and Lincoln, J.R.

Article: Individualism-social determinism: A belief component in the formation of sociopolitical attitudes.

Journal: *Sociology and Social Research*, April 1981, 65(3), 283-298.

2572

Test name: INTERACTION ANXIOUSNESS SCALE

Purpose: To measure interaction anxiousness independent of specific social behaviors.

Number of items: 15

Format: Subjects respond to each item on a 5-point scale to identify the degree to which the item is true. The scale ranged from "not at all" to "extremely characteristic." All items are presented.

Reliability: Cronbach's alphas were .88 and .89.

Validity: Correlations with other variables ranged from -.33 to .87.

Author: Leary, M.R.

Article: Social anxiousness: The construct and its measurement.

Journal: *Journal of Personality Assessment*, Feb. 1983, *47*(1), 66-75.

2573
Test name: INTERPERSONAL CONFLICT RESPONSE INVENTORY

Purpose: To measure how accurately individuals classify responses to conflict situations into assertive, nonassertive and aggressive behavior.

Number of items: 36

Time required: 15 minutes.

Format: Situations are described, response is described and respondent asked to choose the best description of the response. All items presented.

Author: Warehime, R.G. and Lowe, D.R.

Article: Assessing assertiveness in work settings: A discrimination measure.

Journal: *Psychological Reports*, Dec. 1983, *53*(3-Pt. 1), 1007-1012.

Related research: Lange, A.J. and Jakubowski, P., 1976. *Responsible assertive behavior: Cognitive/behavioral procedures for trainers*. Champaign, IL: Research Press.

2574
Test name: INTERPERSONAL DEPENDENCY INVENTORY

Purpose: To assess three components of interpersonal dependency in adults.

Number of items: 48

Format: Includes three components: emotional reliance on another, lack of social self-confidence, and assertion of autonomy.

Reliability: Internal consistency reliabilities for the three components ranged from .72 to .91.

Author: Brown, S.D. and Reimer, D.A.

Article: Assessing attachment following divorce: Development and psychometric evaluation of the divorce reaction inventory.

Journal: *Journal of Counseling Psychology*, Oct. 1984, *31*(4), 520-531.

Related research: Hirschfield, R.M.A. et al., 1977. A measure of interpersonal dependency. *Journal of Personality Assessment, 41*, 610-618.

2575

Test name: INTERPERSONAL JEALOUSY SCALE

Purpose: To measure interpersonal jealousy.

Number of items: 28

Format: Subjects respond to each item on a nine-point scale ranging from (1) "absolutely false, disagree completely" to (9) "absolutely true, agree completely." Some examples are presented.

Reliability: Estimate of internal consistency reliability was .92.

Validity: Correlations with: threat level was .44 (men) and .51 (women); with degree of affirmation in answer (reflecting possessiveness) were -.40 (men) and -.37 (women).

Author: Mathes, E.W. et al.

Article: Behavioral correlates of the Interpersonal Jealousy Scale.

Journal: *Educational and Psychological Measurement*, winter 1982, *42*(4), 1227-1231.

Related research: Mathes, E.W. and Severa, N., 1981. Jealousy, romantic love and liking: Theoretical considerations and preliminary scale development. *Psychological Reports, 49*, 23-31.

2576

Test name: INTERPERSONAL PROBLEM-SOLVING ASSESSMENT TECHNIQUE

Purpose: To provide a free response test of interpersonal effectiveness.

Number of items: 46

Format: Each item is a problematic interpersonal situation in which the respondent imagines being present at the moment. Respondents write alternative ways of handling each situation and which solution they would choose. Includes 6 classes of interpersonal situations.

Reliability: Average reliability among four scores ranged from .82 to .99

Validity: Correlations with: College Self-Expression Scale ranged from -.42 to .29; Edwards Personal Preference Schedule ranged from -.42 to .36; Psychological Screening Inventory ranged from -.29 to .25.

Author: Getter, H. and Nowinski, J.K.

Article: A free response test of interpersonal effectiveness.

Journal: *Journal of Personality Assessment*, June 1981, *45*(3), 301-308.

2577
Test name: INTERPERSONAL RELATIONS SCALE

Purpose: To measure openness of interpersonal relations in schools.

Number of items: 4

Format: Multiple-choice. All items presented.

Reliability: Alpha = .87.

Validity: Correlates significantly ($p < .05$) with teacher leadership behavior and teachers' assessment of students (r's = .17 and .20, respectively).

Author: Peterson, M.F. and Cooke, R.A.

Article: Attitudinal and contextual variables explaining teachers' leadership behavior.

Journal: *Journal of Educational Psychology*, Feb. 1983, *75*(1), 50-62.

2578
Test name: INTERPERSONAL SUPPORT EVALUATION LIST

Purpose: To assess general social support.

Number of items: 10

Format: Sample items presented. Response categories not presented.

Reliability: Alpha ranged from .70 to .92. Test-retest ranged from .87 (4 weeks) to .60 (6 months).

Author: Glasgow, R.E. et al.

Article: Quitting smoking: Strategies used and variables associated with success in a stop-smoking contest.

Journal: *Journal of Consulting and Clinical Psychology*, Dec. 1985, *53*(6), 905-912.

Related research: Cohen, S. et al. Measuring the functional components of social support. In I.G. Sarason and B. Sarason (Eds.), 1983, *Social support: Theory, research and applications*. The Hague, Holland: Martines Hiijhoff.

2579
Test name: INTIMACY ATTITUDE SCALE—REVISED

Purpose: To measure intimacy attitudes.

Number of items: 50

2580
Test name: INTIMACY SCALE

Purpose: To measure intimacy.

Number of items: 42

Format: Each items is rated on a 5-point scale (strongly disagree, mildly disagree, agree/disagree equally, and strongly agree).

Reliability: Cronbach's alphas ranged from .78 to .87 (N's ranged from 15 to 217). Test-retest reliability was .57 (N = 29) for an interval of 30 days.

Author: Amidon, E. et al.

Article: Measurement of intimacy attitudes: The Intimacy Attitude Scale-Revised.

Journal: *Journal of Personality Assessment*, Dec. 1983, 47(6), 635-639.

Related research: Treadwell, T.W., 1981. *Intimacy Attitude Scale: Its structure, reliability, and validity.* Unpublished doctoral dissertation, Temple University.

2580
Test name: INTIMACY SCALE

Purpose: To measure intimacy.

Number of items: 42

Format: Includes 6 dimensions: ease of communication, confidence sharing, egocentrism, empathy, voluntary interdependence and person as unique other. Responses to each item are made on a 6-point scale ranging from "strong disagreement" to "strong agreement."

Reliability: Alphas ranged from r = .63 to r = .84.

Author: Devlin, P.K. and Cowan, G.A.

Article: Homophobia, perceived fathering and male intimate relationships.

Journal: *Journal of Personality Assessment*, Oct. 1985, 49(5), 467-473.

Related research: Fischer, J.L., 1981. Transitions in relationship style from adolescence to young adulthood. *Journal of Youth and Adolescence, 10,* 11-23.

2581
Test name: LIFE EVENTS QUESTIONNAIRE

Purpose: To measure the number of events that require a wide range of social readjustment (for college students).

Number of items: 65

Format: Checklist format.

Reliability: Split-half = .76.

Author: Miller, A. and Cooley, E.

Article: Moderator variables for the relationship between life cycle change and disorders.

Journal: *Journal of General Psychology*, April 1981, *104*(second half), 223-233.

Related research: Cooley, E. et al., 1979. Self-report assessment of life change and disorders. *Psychological Reports*, *44*, 1079-1086.

2582
Test name: LIKING PEOPLE SCALE

Purpose: To measure interpersonal orientation.

Number of items: 15

Format: A 5-point Likert scale was used from strongly agree to strongly disagree. All items are presented.

Reliability: Coefficient alpha was .85 (N = 140) and .75 (N = 73).

Validity: Correlations with: Social Anxiety Scale was r = -.18; with Misanthropy Scale was r = .38; with Social Self-Esteem was r = .49; with Judgmental Ability was r = .31; with Social Desirability was r = .10.

Author: Filsinger, E.E.

Article: A measure of interpersonal orientation: The Liking People Scale.

Journal: *Journal of Personality Assessment*, June 1981, *45*(3), 295-300.

2583
Test name: LONELINESS AND SOCIAL DISSATISFACTION MEASURE

Purpose: To assess children's feelings of loneliness and social dissatisfaction.

Number of items: 16

Format: Items focus on children's feelings of loneliness. All items are presented.

Reliability: Cronbach's alpha was .90; Split-half correlation between forms = .83; Spearman-Brown reliability coefficient = .91; Guttman split-half reliability coefficient = .91.

Validity: Correlations with sociometric status ranged from -.19 to -.37.

Author: Asher, S.R. et al.

Article: Loneliness in children.

Journal: *Child Development*, Aug. 1984, *55*(4), 1456-1464.

2584
Test name: LOVE ADDICTION SCALE

Purpose: To measure love "addiction," "mania," and "possessiveness."

Number of items: 20

Time required: 15 minutes.

Format: 5-point Likert agreement scale. Sample items presented.

Reliability: Test-retest = .99 (2 week interval).

Author: Hunter, M.S. et al.

Article: A scale to measure love addiction.

Journal: *Psychological Reports*, April 1981, *48*(2), 582.

2585
Test name: MARLOWE-CROWNE SOCIAL DESIRABILITY SCALE

Purpose: To provide a measure of social desirability.

Number of items: 33

Format: Measures social desirability in terms of the need of subjects to respond in culturally sanctioned ways.

Reliability: Internal consistency Kuder-Richardson formula 20 reliability was .88 (N = 39). Test-retest reliability was .89 (one month interval).

Author: Caillet, K.C. and Michael, W.B.

Article: The construct validity of three self-report instruments hypothesized to measure the degree of resolution for each of the first six stage crises in Erikson's developmental theory of personality.

Journal: *Educational and Psychological Measurement*, spring 1983, *43*(1), 197-209.

Related research: Crowne, D.P and Marlowe, D., 1960. A new scale of social desirability independent of psychotherapy. *Journal of Consulting Psychology*, 24, 349-354.

2586
Test name: MARTIN-LARSEN APPROVAL MOTIVATION SCALE

Purpose: To measure need for social approval.

Number of items: 20

Format: Subjects respond to each item on a 5-point scale from disagree strongly (1) to agree strongly (5). All items are presented.

Reliability: Cronbach's alpha ranged from .64 to .75 (N's ranged from 129 to 185).

Validity: Correlations with other variables ranged from -.50 to .61.

Author: Martin, H.J.

Article: A revised measure of approval motivation and its relationship to social desirability.

Journal: *Journal of Personality Assessment*, Oct. 1984, *48*(5), 508-519.

Related research: Larsen, K.S. et al., 1976. Approval seeking, social cost and aggression: A scale and some dynamics. *Journal of Psychology*, *94*, 3-11.

2587
Test name: MILLER SOCIAL INTIMACY SCALE

Purpose: To provide a measure of the maximum level of intimacy currently experienced.

Number of items: 17

Format: Six items require an answer indicating frequency on a 10-point scale. Eleven items require an answer indicating intensity on a 10-point scale. All items are presented.

Reliability: Cronbach's alphas were .91 (N = 45) and .86 (N = 39). Test-retest reliability was r = .96 (2-month interval) and r = .84 (1-month interval).

Validity: Correlations with: IRS was r = .71 (N = 45); with UCLA Loneliness Scale was r = -.65 (N = 59); with Tennessee Self-Concept Scale was r = .48 (N = 45).

Author: Miller, R.S. and Lefcourt, H.M.

Article: The assessment of social intimacy.

Journal: *Journal of Personality Assessment*, Oct. 1982, *46*(5), 514-518.

2588
Test name: MINES-JENSEN INTERPERSONAL RELATIONSHIP INVENTORY

Purpose: To measure tolerance level and quality of relationships.

Number of items: 42

Format: 4-point response scale. Sample items provided.

Reliability: Kuder-Richardson reliabilities were in the .65-.70 range.

Author: Riahinejad, A.R. and Hood, A.B.

Article: The development of interpersonal relationships in college.

Journal: *Journal of College Student Personnel*, Nov. 1984, *25*(6), 498-502.

Related research: Mines, R.A. *Change in college students along Chickering's vector of freeing of interpersonal relationships.* Iowa Student Development Project, Technical Report No. 26. Unpublished manuscript, The University of Iowa.

2589
Test name: NETWORK ORIENTATION SCALE

Purpose: To measure degree to which personal network is useless in time of need.

Number of items: 20

Format: 4-point agree-disagree scale. All items presented.

Validity: 3 factors presented: advisability/independence, history, mistrust.

Author: Vaux, A.

Article: Factor structure of the network orientation scale.

Journal: *Psychological Reports*, Dec. 1985, *57*(3-II), 1181-1182.

Related research: Tolsdorf, C., 1976. Social networks, support and coping: An exploratory study. *Family Process*, *15*, 407-417.

2590
Test name: PEER GROUP ROLE AND STUDENT ROLE SCALES (FROM ABIC)

Purpose: To measure behavior in peer group and student roles.

Number of items: 70

Format: 5-point SOMPA rating categories.

Reliability: Inter-rater reliability high. Comparison of rating categories revealed no difference between interviewers (z = .69, not significant).

Validity: Mothers give more and higher scoring ratings than teachers.

Author: Wall, S.M. and Paradise, L.V.

Article: A comparison of parent and teacher reports of selected adoptive behaviors of children.

Journal: *Journal of School Psychology*, 1981, *19*(1), 73-77.

Related research: Goodman, J.F., 1979. Is tissue the issue?: A critique of SOMPA's models and tests. *School Psychology Digest*, *8*, 47-62.

2591
Test name: PEER NETWORK FUNCTIONS SCALE

Purpose: To measure the functions of peer networks.

Number of items: 24

Format: Yes-no format.

Reliability: Alpha ranged from .60 to .82 across subscales.

Validity: No differences reported by sex and ambition, but one was found between ethnic and non-ethnic respondents.

Author: Burke, R.J.

Article: Relationships in and around organizations: It's both who you know and what you know that counts.

Journal: *Psychological Reports*, Aug. 1984, 55(1), 299-307.

2592
Test name: PERSONAL ASSESSMENT OF INTIMACY IN RELATIONSHIPS INVENTORY

Purpose: To measure intimacy in relationships.

Number of items: 36

Format: 5-point disagree-agree Likert format.

Reliability: Total = .70. Subscales ranged from .57 to .79.

Author: Johnson, S.M. and Greenberg, L.S.

Article: Differential effects of experiential and problem-solving interventions in resolving marital conflict.

Journal: *Journal of Consulting and Clinical Psychology*, April 1985, 53(2), 175-188.

Related research: Schaefer, M.T. and Olson, D.H., 1981. Assessing intimacy: The PAIR Inventory. *Journal of Marital and Family Therapy*, 1, 47-60.

2593
Test name: PICTORIAL SCALE OF PERCEIVED COMPETENCE AND SOCIAL ACCEPTANCE FOR YOUNG CHILDREN

Purpose: To assess perceived competence and social acceptance in young children, ages 4-7.

Number of items: 24

Format: Two versions: one for preschool-kindergarten; one for first-second grade. Includes two factors, each defined by two subscales. General competence - includes cognitive and physical competence subscales. Social acceptance - includes peer and maternal acceptance subscales.

Reliability: Reliabilities ranged from .50 to .89.

Author: Harter, S. and Pike, R.

Article: The pictorial scale of perceived competence and social acceptance for young children.

Journal: *Child Development*, Dec. 1984, 55(6), 1969-1982.

Related research: Harter, S., 1982. The perceived competence scale for children. *Child Development*, 53, 87-97.

2594
Test name: PREMORBID SOCIAL COMPETENCE SCALE

Purpose: To measure social competence before schizophrenia.

Number of items: 5

Format: Multiple-choice. All items and responses presented.

Reliability: Agreement in categorizing patients from records is 99%.

Validity: Factor structure of items differs by gender and by type of hospital.

Author: Zigler, E. and Levine, J.

Article: Premorbid competence in schizophrenia: What is being measured?

Journal: *Journal of Consulting and Clinical Psychology*, Feb. 1981, 49(1), 96-105.

Related research: Zigler, E. and Levine, J., 1973. Premorbid adjustment and paranoid-nonparanoid status in schizophrenia: A further investigation. *Journal of Abnormal Psychology*, 82, 189-199.

2595

Test name: PROBLEM INVENTORY FOR ADOLESCENT GIRLS (MULTIPLE-CHOICE VERSION)

Purpose: To assess social competence in adolescent girls.

Number of items: 52

Format: Subjects select a response on a 5-point scale that expresses what they would do in a situation being described.

Validity: 51 of 52 items showed significant differences (p<.05) with delinquent and nondelinquent girls. Correlated .52 with IQ and .32 with SES. Correlated -.83 with delinquent behavior checklist.

Author: Gaffney, L.R.

Article: A multiple-choice test to measure social skills in delinquent and nondelinquent adolescent girls.

Journal: *Journal of Consulting and Clinical Psychology*, Oct. 1984, 52(5), 911-912.

Related research: Graffney, L.R. and McFall, R.M., 1981. A comparison of social skills in delinquent and nondelinquent adolescent girls using a behavioral role-playing inventory. *Journal of Consulting and Clinical Psychology*, 49, 959-967.

2596

Test name: PURSUING-DISTANCING SCALE

Purpose: To measure interpersonal pursuing and distancing.

Number of items: 92

Format: Half the items reflect distancing; the other half reflect tendencies to pursue. Includes 6 domains: cognitive style, emotionality, social style, communication style, sensation seeking, and reflecting anality. All items are presented.

Reliability: Type reliability ranged from r = .23 to r = .70; Item reliability ranged from r = .07 to r = .50.

Author: Bernstein, D.M et al.

Article: Pursuing and distancing: The construct and its measurement.

Journal: *Journal of Personality Assessment*, June 1985, *49*(3), 273-281.

Related research: Fogarty, R., 1976. Marital crisis. In P. Guerin, Jr., (Ed.), *Family Therapy*. New York: Gardner Press.

2597

Test name: RELATIONSHIP EVENTS SCALE

Purpose: To provide a self-report measure of courtship progress.

Number of items: 13

Format: A Guttman scale. All items are presented.

Reliability: Correlation between scores of male and female members of couples was r = .81 (N = 55).

Validity: Correlations with other variables ranged from r = .16 to r = .59.

Author: King, C.E. and Christensen, A.

Article: The relationship events scale: A Guttman scaling of progress in courtship.

Journal: *Journal of Marriage and the Family*, Aug. 1983, *45*(3), 671-678.

Related research: Christensen, A. and King, C.E. The Relationship Events Scale (item pool and final scale), available from the authors. Department of Psychology, University of California, Los Angeles, CA., 90024.

2598

Test name: REWARD LEVEL SCALE

Purpose: To measure reward levels in six resource areas (love, status, services, goods, money, information and sexuality).

Number of items: 7

Format: 9-point Likert format.

Reliability: Alpha = .90.

Author: Lloyd, S.A. et al.

Article: Predicting premarital relationship stability: A methodological refinement.

Journal: *Journal of Marriage and the Family*, Feb. 1984, *46*(1), 71-76.

Related research: Foa, U.G. and Foa, E.G., 1974. *Societal structures of the mind.* Springfield, IL: Charles C. Thomas.

2599
Test name: ROMANTIC LOVE SYMPTOM CHECKLIST

Purpose: To measure feelings of romantic love.

Number of items: 76

Format: Respondents check any of the 76 feelings that are elicited by the thought of their beloved.

Reliability: Internal consistency = .95.

Author: Mathes, E.W.

Article: Mystical experience, romantic love and hypnotic susceptibility.

Journal: *Psychological Reports*, 1982, *50*(3 Pt. 1), 701-702.

Related research: Rubin, Z., 1974. Measurement of romantic love. *Journal of Personality and Social Psychology*, *83*, 268-277.

2600
Test name: ROMANTIC LOVE SYMPTOM CHECKLIST

Purpose: To measure feelings of romantic love.

Number of items: 35

Format: Subjects check or do not check items. Sample items presented.

Reliability: Internal consistency = .92 (men) and .91 (women).

Validity: Correlated .37 (men) and .48 (women) with Rubin's Romantic Love Scale.

Author: Mathes, E.W. and Wise, P.S.

Article: Romantic love and ravages of time.

Journal: *Psychological Reports*, Dec. 1983, *53*(3 Pt. 1), 839-846.

Related research: Mathes, E.W., 1982. Mystical experiences, romantic love and hypnotic susceptibility. *Psychological Reports*, *50*, 701-702.

2601
Test name: SELLS AND ROFF SCALE OF PEER RELATIONS

Purpose: To evaluate the degree to which a child is accepted or rejected by peers.

Format: A teacher rating form.

Reliability: Ranged from .58 to .75.

Validity: Correlations with the Battelle Developmental Inventory ranged from .16 to .56 (N = 50). Correlations with the Wide Range Achievement Test ranged from .00 to .22 (N = 50).

Author: Guidubaldi, J. and Perry, J.D.

Article: Concurrent and predictive validity of the Battelle Development Inventory at the first grade level.

Journal: *Educational and Psychological Measurement*, winter 1984, *44*(4), 977-985.

Related research: Sells, S. and Roff, M., 1967. Peer acceptance-rejection and personality development in children. Washington, D.C.: Government Printing Office.

2602
Test name: SIMULATED SOCIAL INTERACTION TEST

Purpose: To assess social skills.

Number of items: 8

Format: Consists of 8 social simulations in which subjects are asked to role play. All items are presented.

Reliability: Reliability coefficients ranged from r = .76 to r = .82.

Author: Steinberg, S.L. et al.

Article: The effects of confederate prompt delivery style in a standardized social simulation test.

Journal: *Journal of Behavioral Assessment*, Sept. 1982, *4*(3), 263-272.

Related research: Curran, J.P., 1982. A procedure for the assessment of social skills: *The Simulated Social Interaction Test*. In J.P. Curran and P.M. Monti (Eds.), *Social skills training: A practical handbook for assessment and treatment*. New York: Guilford Press.

2603
Test name: SOCIAL ACTIVITY QUESTIONNAIRE

Purpose: To measure dating experience.

Number of items: 7

Format: Evaluates dating frequency, comfort, and skill and satisfaction with present dating situation.

Validity: Correlations with Heterosocial Assessment Inventory for Women ranged from .06 to .32.

Author: Kolko, D.J.

Article: The Heterosocial Assessment Inventory for Women: A psychometric and behavioral evaluation.

Journal: *Journal of Psychopathology and Behavioral Assessment*, March 1985, 7(1), 49-64.

Related research: Christensen, A. and Arkowitz, H., 1974. Preliminary report on practice dating and feedback as treatment for college dating problems. *Journal of Counseling Psychology, 21*, 92-95.

2604
Test name: SOCIAL ANXIETY SCALE

Purpose: To measure social anxiety.

Number of items: 28

Format: True-false questions concerning how one feels in a variety of social contexts and what situations one tends to avoid.

Reliability: Test-retest (1 month) reliability coefficient was .68.

Author: Oppenheimer, B.T.

Article: Short-term small group intervention for college freshmen.

Journal: *Journal of Counseling Psychology*, Jan. 1984, *31*(1), 45-53.

Related research: Watson, D. and Friend, R., 1969. Measurement of social-evaluative anxiety. *Journal of Consulting and Clinical Psychology, 33*, 448-457.

2605
Test name: SOCIAL ANXIETY SUBSCALE OF THE SELF-CONSCIOUSNESS SCALE

Purpose: To assess social anxiety.

Number of items: 6

Format: Subjects respond to each item on a 5-point scale indicating how well the item describes them. The scale ranges from 0 (extremely not like me) to 4 (extremely like me). An example is presented.

Reliability: Test-retest (2 weeks) correlation was .73.

Validity: Correlations with other variables ranged from -.45 to .63.

Author: Schmidt, J.P. and Kurdek, L.A.

Article: Correlates of social anxiety in college students and homosexuals.

Journal: *Journal of Personality Assessment*, Aug. 1984, *48*(4), 403-409.

Related research: Fenigstein, A. et al., 1975. Public and private self-consciousness: Assessment and theory. *Journal of Consulting and Clinical Psychology, 43*, 522-527.

2606
Test name: SOCIAL COMPETENCE OBSERVATION MEASURE

Purpose: To assess children's behavior with peers, with teacher, and when alone.

Number of items: 28

Format: Time-sampling format in which observers record incidences of 28 behaviors at 5-second intervals. All items presented.

Reliability: Inter-rater ranged from .92 to .98.

Validity: Factor 1 items correlated .64 ($p<.01$) with Factor 1 of KPI (males only) and .71 ($p<.01$) with Factor 2 of KPI (females only).

Author: Ali Khan, N. and Hoge, R.D.

Article: A teacher-judgement measure of social competence: Validity data.

Journal: *Journal of Consulting and Clinical Psychology*, Dec. 1983, 51(6), 809-814.

Related research: Connolly, J. and Doyle, A., 1981. Assessment of social competence in preschoolers: Teachers vs. peers. *Developmental Psychology, 17*, 454-462.

2607
Test name: SOCIAL FUNCTIONING INDEX

Purpose: To measure energy, self-control, hygiene practices, communication, and awareness of environment's structure.

Number of items: 51

Format: Raters indicate on a 5-point adequacy scale the behavior of patients on each of the 51 items. All items presented.

Reliability: Inter-rater reliability ranged from .19 to .94 across items. Total score reliability across raters = .85.

Validity: Three rehabilitation consultants verified content validity, following determination that related scales were not valid for the purpose of the present scale.

Author: Peterson, L.

Article: Social functioning assessment of aftercare psychiatric patients in socialization therapy.

Journal: *Psychological Reports*, Dec. 1983, 53(3 Pt. II), 1123-1130.

2608
Test name: SOCIAL PERFORMANCE SURVEY SCHEDULE

Purpose: To measure range of behaviors that contribute to social skill.

Number of items: 50 positive behaviors.

Format: 5-point frequency response scale for each of the 50 behaviors indicating how often each respondent demonstrates it.

Reliability: Cronbach's alpha = .94.

Validity: Correlated -.40 with Beck Depression Inventory; -.59 with MMPI Depression; .59 with Social Activity; .64 with Social Skills; -.54 with MMPI Social Introversion; .55 with MMPI Social Desirability. p<.01 for all correlations.

Author: Lowe, M.R.

Article: Validity of the positive behavior subscale of the Social Performance Survey Schedule in a psychiatric population.

Journal: *Psychological Reports*, 1982, *50*(1), 83-87.

2609

Test name: SOCIAL PERFORMANCE SURVEY SCHEDULE

Purpose: To measure social skill.

Number of items: 100

Format: Includes positive and negative subscales and seven factors.

Reliability: Coefficient alpha was .94. Test-retest reliability was r = .87.

Author: Lowe, M.R. and D'Illio, V.

Article: Factor analysis of the Social Performance Survey Scale.

Journal: *Journal of Psychopathology and Behavioral Assessment*, March 1985, *7*(1), 13-22.

Related research: Lowe, M.R. and Cautela, J.R., 1978. A self-report measure of social skill. *Behavior Therapy*, *9*, 535-544.

2610

Test name: SOCIAL PERFORMANCE SURVEY SCHEDULE—REVISED

Purpose: To measure social skills.

Number of items: 31

Format: The items describe various behaviors and respondents indicate how frequently they emit such behaviors.

Reliability: Inter-rater reliability coefficients ranged from .47 to .76. Alpha coefficients ranged from .83 to .86.

Author: Wessberg, H.W. et al.

Article: Evidence for the external validity of a social simulation measure of social skills.

Journal: *Journal of Behavioral Assessment*, Sept. 1981, 3(3), 209-220.

Related research: Lowe, M.R. and Cautela, J.R., 1978. A self-report measure of social skill. *Behavior Therapy*, 9, 535-544.

2611
Test name: SOCIAL PROPENSITY SCALE

Purpose: To measure social propensity.

Number of items: 50

Format: 19 asterisk continuum. (Applies very closely at one end. Doesn't apply to me at all at other end.)

Reliability: Cronbach's alpha = .94, .95, and .92 over 3 years of testing.

Validity: Correlations with social adjustment ranged from .29 to .45. Correlates .33 with campus activities. Correlates -.25 with attrition.

Author: Baker, R.W. and Siryk, B.

Article: Social propensity and college adjustment.

Journal: *Journal of College Student Personnel*, July 1983, 24(4), 331-336.

2612
Test name: SOCIAL ANOMIA SCALE

Purpose: To examine comparative feelings of anomia among married women.

Number of items: 9

Format: Response to each item is either disagree (0) or agree (1). All items are presented.

Reliability: Coefficient alpha is .73.

Author: Lovell-Troy, L.A.

Article: Anomia among employed wives and housewives: An exploratory analysis.

Journal: *Journal of Marriage and the Family*, May 1983, 45(2), 301-310.

Related research: Srole, L. et al., 1962. *Mental health in the metropolis: The midtown Manhattan study*. New York: McGraw-Hill.

2613
Test name: TAXONOMY OF PROBLEMATIC SOCIAL SITUATIONS FOR CHILDREN

Purpose: To identify and classify problematic social situations.

Number of items: 44

Format: 1-5 scale on which teachers indicated how much of a problem the item (situation) was for the child.

Reliability: Alphas ranged from .89 to .97 (p<.001) across subscales. Total alpha = .96. Test-retest ranged from .57 to .72 (total = .79).

Validity: Teachers rated situations more problematic for rejected children than for adaptive children (p<.001).

Author: Dodge, K.A. et al.

Article: Situational approach to the assessment of social competence in children.

Journal: *Journal of Consulting and Clinical Psychology*, June 1985, 53(3), 344-353.

2614
Test name: TEXAS SOCIAL BEHAVIOR INDEX

Purpose: To measure personal worth and social interaction.

Number of items: 32

Format: Likert format.

Reliability: Alternate forms = .89.

Validity: Correlated .50-.52 with self-esteem scale of California Personality Inventory.

Author: McIntire, S.A. and Levine, E.L.

Article: An empirical investigation of self-esteem as a composite construct.

Journal: *Journal of Vocational Behavior*, Dec. 1984, 25(3), 290-303.

Related research: Helmreich, R. and Stapp, J., 1974. Short forms of the Texas Social Behavior Inventory (TSBI), an objective measure of self-esteem. *Bulletin of the Psychonomic Society*, 4(5A), 473-475.

2615
Test name: UCLA REVISED LONELINESS SCALE

Purpose: To measure loneliness.

Number of items: 20

Format: Ten positively and ten negatively worded statements followed by 4-point (never to often) response categories. Sample items presented.

Validity: Correlated significantly (r = .41, p<.001) with time spent alone, and with a self-labeling loneliness scale (r = .71).

Author: Booth, R.

Article: An examination of college GPA, composite ACT scores, IQs, and gender in relation to loneliness of college students.

Journal: *Psychological Reports*, Oct. 1983, 53(2), 347-352.

Related research: Russell, D. et al., 1980. The revised UCLA Loneliness Scale, concurrent and discriminant validity evidence. *Journal of Personality and Social Psychology, 39*, 472-480.

2616
Test name: VANDERBILT PSYCHOTHERAPY PROCESS SCALE

Purpose: To measure patient characteristics, therapist characteristics, and their interaction.

Number of items: 80

Format: 5-point Likert scales. Judges rate patient, therapist, and their interaction. All items presented.

Reliability: Inter-rater reliability = .90 (experienced raters). Alpha ranged from .82 to .96 across subscales.

Author: O'Malley, S.S. et al.

Article: The Vanderbilt Psychotherapy Process Scale: A report on the scale development and process-outcome study.

Journal: *Journal of Consulting and Clinical Psychology*, Aug. 1983, *51*(4), 581-586.

Related research: Strupp, H.H. et al., 1981. *Vanderbilt Psychotherapy Process Scale*, Vanderbilt University.

ADJUSTMENT-VOCATIONAL

2617
Test name: ADMINISTRATIVE STRESS INDEX

Purpose: To measure perceived job-related stress for administrators.

Number of items: 25

Format: 5-point Likert format. All items presented.

Reliability: Alphas exceeded .70.

Validity: Four subscales identified by factor analysis. Role-based stress correlated -.02 with age, -.01 with years of administrative experience, and -.11 (p<.01) with position. Correlated, respectively, -.10,-.10 (p<.01) and -.02. Boundary-Spanning Stress correlated, respectively, are .11 (p<.01), .23 (p<.001) and .23 (p<.001). Conflict-Mediating Stress correlated, respectively, are -.05 (p<.05), -.10 (p<.01) and -.38 (p<.001).

Author: Koch, J.L. et al.

Article: Job stress among school administrators: Factorial dimensions and differential effects.

Journal: *Journal of Applied Psychology*, Aug. 1982, 67(4), 493-499.

Related research: Indik, B. et al., 1964. Demographic correlates of psychological strain. *Journal of Abnormal and Social Psychology*, 69, 26-38.

2618
Test name: ADULT VOCATIONAL MATURITY ASSESSMENT INTERVIEW

Purpose: To assess an individual's ability to cope with tasks associated with choosing, preparing for, and entering an occupation.

Number of items: 120

Format: Includes eight scales: orientation to work, orientation to education, concern with choice, self-appraisal: interests and abilities, self-appraisal: personality characteristics, self-appraisal: values, exploring occupations, and using resources.

Reliability: Internal consistency reliability estimates ranged from .52 to .91.

Validity: Correlations with other variables ranged from -.25 to .75 (N = 20).

Author: Manuele, C.A.

Article: Modifying vocational maturity in adults with delayed career development: A life skills approach.

Journal: *Vocational Guidance Quarterly*, Dec. 1984, *33*(2), 101-112.

Related research: Manuele, C., 1983. The development of a measure of vocational maturity for adults with delayed career development. *Journal of Vocational Behavior*, *23*, 45-63.

2619
Test name: BURNOUT MEASURE

Purpose: To measure burnout.

Number of items: 21

Format: Includes three components: physical exhaustion, emotional exhaustion, and mental exhaustion. Responses are recorded on a 7-point scale.

Reliability: Cronbach's alpha = .89.

Author: Etzion, D.

Article: Moderating effect of social support on the stress-burnout relationship.

Journal: *Journal of Applied Psychology*, Nov. 1984, *69*(4), 615-622.

Related research: Pines, A. et al., 1981. *Burnout: From tedium to personal growth*. New York: Free Press.

2620
Test name: COUNSELOR OCCUPATIONAL STRESS INVENTORY (COSI)

Purpose: To measure occupational stress among school counselors.

Number of items: 50

Format: Likert format.

Reliability: Alpha ranged from .81 to .95 across subscales.

Author: Moracco, J.C. et al.

Article: Measuring stress in school counselors: Some research findings and implications.

Journal: *The School Counselor*, Nov. 1984, *32*(2), 110-118.

Related research: Moracco, J.C. and Gray, P., 1983. The COSI: Development of an instrument to assess stress in counselors. Paper presented at the annual convention of the American Personnel and Guidance Association, Washington, D.C.

2621

Test name: DEPRESSION AND IRRITATION SCALES

Purpose: To measure job-related stress and irritation.

Number of items: 9

Format: 4-point response scales. Sample items presented.

Reliability: Alpha (depression) = .81; Alpha (irritation) = .80.

Author: Ganster, D.C. et al.

Article: Managing organizational stress: A field experiment.

Journal: *Journal of Applied Psychology*, Oct. 1982, *67*(5), 533-542.

Related research: Cobb, S., 1970. *A variable from the Card Sort Test: A study of people changing jobs*. (Project analysis memo No. 12.) Ann Arbor, MI: University of Michigan, ISR.

2622

Test name: EMPLOYEE ATTITUDE SURVEY

Purpose: To assess employee attitudes including satisfaction with pay, staffing, and performance appraisal.

Number of items: 31

Format: 5-point Likert format. All items presented.

Reliability: Alphas ranged from .70 to .95 across subscales.

Author: Gomez-Mejia, L.R.

Article: Dimensions and correlates of the personnel audit as an organizational assessment tool.

Journal: *Personnel Psychology*, summer 1985, *38*(2), 293-308.

Related research: Gomez-Mejia, L.R, 1983. Sex differences during political socialization. *Academy of Management Journal*, 26, 492-499.

2623

Test name: FRUSTRATION SCALE

Purpose: To measure job frustration.

Number of items: 3

Format: 7-point Likert format.

Reliability: Alpha ranged from .68 to .76.

Author: O'Connor, E.J. et al.

Article: Situational constraint effects on performance, affective reactions, and turnover: A field replication and extension.

Journal: *Journal of Applied Psychology*, Nov. 1984, 69(4), 663-672.

Related research: Peters, L.H. and O'Connor, E.J., 1980. Situational constraints and work outcomes: The influence of a frequently overlooked construct. *Academy of Management Review*, 5, 391-397.

2624
Test name: HOPPOCK JOB SATISFACTION BLANK—SHORT FORM

Purpose: To measure overall job satisfaction.

Number of items: 4

Format: The items measure affect, duration, social comparison, and behavioral intention.

Reliability: Cronbach's alphas were .79 and .81; Test-retest (6 months) = .73.

Author: Scandura, T.A. and Graen, G.B.

Article: Moderating effects of initial leader-member exchange status on the effects of a leadership intervention.

Journal: *Journal of Applied Psychology*, Aug. 1984, 69(3), 428-436.

Related research: Hoppock, R. (1935). *Job satisfaction*. New York: Harper.

2625
Test name: INDEX OF JOB SATISFACTION

Purpose: To measure general job satisfaction.

Number of items: 18

Format: Each item was rated on a 5-point Likert scale from minimum to maximum job satisfaction.

Reliability: Odd-even reliability corrected by Spearman-Brown formula was .87 (N = 231). Cronbach's alpha was .94.

Author: Rahim, A.

Article: Demographic variables in general job satisfaction in a hospital: A multivariate study.

Journal: *Perceptual and Motor Skills*, Dec. 1982, 55(3 Pt. I), 711-719.

Related research: Brayfield, A.H. and Rothe, H.F., 1951. An index of job satisfaction. *Journal of Applied Psychology*, 35, 307-311.

2626
Test name: INFLUENCE SCALE

Purpose: To measure perceived influence at work.

Number of items: 4

Format: 5-point scale (never true to always true). All items presented taken from Vroom's influence scale.

Reliability: Alpha = .83.

Author: Jackson, S.E.

Article: Participation in decision making as a strategy for reducing job-related stress.

Journal: *Journal of Applied Psychology*, Feb. 1983, *69*(1), 3-19.

Related research: Vroom, V.H., 1959. Some personality determinants of the effects of participation. *Journal of Abnormal and Social Psychology*, 59, 322-327.

2627
Test name: IRRITATION/STRAIN SCALE

Purpose: To measure irritation/strain from work.

Number of items: 4

Format: Employs a 5-point scale. A sample question is presented.

Reliability: Cronbach's alpha = .88.

Author: Frese, M. and Okonek, K.

Article: Reasons to leave shiftwork and psychological and psychosomatic complaints of former shiftworkers.

Journal: *Journal of Applied Psychology*, Aug. 1984, *69*(3), 509-514.

Related research: Mohr, G., 1984. *Measuring psychological well-being in blue collar workers*. Unpublished manuscript. Freie Universitaet, Department of Psychology, Berlin.

2628
Test name: JOB BURNOUT INVENTORY

Purpose: To measure job burnout.

Number of items: 15

Format: 7-point Likert response categories. All items presented.

Reliability: Cronbach's alpha ranged from .67 to .82 across subscales.

Validity: Correlated non-significantly with health symptoms, episodic stress and chronic job stress, but significantly (p<.05) with sick days taken.

Author: Ford, D.L., Jr. and Murphy, C.J.

Article: Exploratory development and validation of a perceptual job burnout inventory: Comparison of corporate sector and human services professionals.

Journal: *Psychological Reports*, June 1983, *52*(3), 995-1006.

2629
Test name: JOB DESCRIPTIVE INDEX

Purpose: To measure job satisfaction.

Format: Includes the following: pay, promotions, work, co-workers, and supervision.

Reliability: Coefficient alpha ranged from .15 to .90.

Validity: Correlation with absenteeism ranged from -.49 to .23.

Author: Teborg, J.R. et al.

Article: Extension of the Schmidt and Hunter validity generalization procedure to the prediction of absenteeism behavior from knowledge of job satisfaction and organizational commitment.

Journal: *Journal of Applied Psychology*, Aug. 1982, *67*(4), 440-449.

Related research: Smith, P.C. et al., 1969. *The measurement of satisfaction in work and retirement.* Chicago: Rand McNally.
  Johnson, S.M. et al., 1982. Response format of the Job Descriptive Index: Assessment of reliability and validity by the multitrait-multimethod matrix.
Journal of Applied Psychology, *67*(4), 500-505.

2630
Test name: JOB DESCRIPTIVE INDEX —MODIFIED

Purpose: To measure job satisfaction.

Number of items: 70

Format: Includes separate scores to measure satisfaction with: the work itself, promotion, supervision, co-workers, and pay. Utilizes a 5-point Likert scale.

Reliability: Coefficient alphas for separate scores ranged from .81 to .98.

Validity: Correlations with other measures ranged from -.82 to .74.

Author: Adler, S. and Golan, J.

Article: Lateness as a withdrawal behavior.

Journal: *Journal of Applied Psychology*, Oct. 1981, *66*(5), 544-554.

Related research: Smith, P.C. et al., 1969. *The measurement of satisfaction in work and retirement.* Chicago: Rand McNally.

2631
Test name: JOB DIAGNOSTIC SURVEY

Purpose: To measure the apprentices' general job satisfaction.

Number of items: 5

Format: A 7-point scale format is employed.

Reliability: Alpha coefficient = .89 (N = 166).

Validity: Correlations with other variables ranged from .09 to .52.

Author: Tharenou, P. and Harker, P.

Article: Moderating influence of self-esteem on relationships between job complexity, performance and satisfaction.

Journal: *Journal of Applied Psychology*, Nov. 1984, 69(4), 623-632.

Related research: Hackman, J.R. and Oldham, G.R. (1974). The Job Diagnostic Survey: An instrument for the diagnosis of jobs and the evaluation of redesign projects. (Tech Rep. No. 4) New Haven, CT: Yale University, Department of Administrative Sciences.

2632
Test name: JOB INVOLVEMENT QUESTIONNAIRE

Purpose: To measure job satisfaction.

Number of items: 6

Format: 7-point scale.

Reliability: Test-retest = .65.

Author: Barling, J. and Van Bart, D.

Article: Mothers' subjective employment experiences and the behavior of their nursery school children.

Journal: *Journal of Occupational Psychology*, March 1983, 57(1), 49-56.

Related research: Warr, P. et al., 1979. Scales for the measurement of some attitudes as aspects of psychological well-being. *Journal of Occupational Psychology*, 52, 129-148.

2633
Test name: JOB PERCEPTION SCALES

Purpose: To measure satisfaction with job.

Number of items: 21

Format: Semantic differential scales modified to five anchor points.

Reliability: Test-retest (3 week interval) ranged from .64 to .80.

Validity: Principal components factor analysis revealed the five hypothesized dimensions initially expected: work, pay, promotions, supervision, and co-workers. Significant multitrait-multimethod procedures indicate convergent and discriminant validity.

Author: Hatfield, J.D. et al.

Article: An empirical evaluation of a test for assessing job satisfaction.

Journal: *Psychological Reports*, Feb. 1985, 56(1), 39-45.

2634
Test name: JOB SATISFACTION SCALE

Purpose: To measure job satisfaction.

Number of items: 18

Format: Likert format.

Reliability: Alpha = .83.

Author: Jamal, M.

Article: Shiftwork related to job attitudes, social participation and withdrawal behavior: A study of nurses and industrial workers.

Journal: *Personnel Psychology*, autumn 1981, 34(3), 535-547.

Related research: Brayfield, A.H. and Rathe, F.H., 1951. An index of job satisfaction. *Journal of Applied Psychology*, 35, 307-311.

2635
Test name: JOB SATISFACTION SCALE

Purpose: To measure job satisfaction.

Number of items: 13

Format: 7-point rating scale.

Reliability: Alpha = .85.

Author: Litt, M.D. and Turk, D.C.

Article: Sources of stress and dissatisfaction in experienced high school teachers.

Journal: *Journal of Educational Research*, Jan./Feb. 1985, 78(3), 178-185.

Related research: Hackman, J.R. and Oldham, G.R. (1974). The Job Diagnostic Survey: An instrument for the diagnosis of jobs and the evaluation of job redesign projects. (Tech Rep. No. 4) New Haven, CT: Yale University, Department of Administrative Sciences.

2636
Test name: JOB SATISFACTION SCALE

Purpose: To measure job satisfaction.

Number of items: 2

Format: 5 and 7-point response scales. Both items presented.

Reliability: Alpha = .86.

Author: Louis, M.R. et al.

Article: The availability and helpfulness of socialization practices.

Journal: *Personnel Psychology*, winter 1983, *36*(4), 857-866.

Related research: O'Reilly, C. and Caldwell, D.F., 1980. Job choice: The impact of intrinsic and extrinsic factors on subsequent satisfaction and commitment. *Journal of Applied Psychology*, *65*, 559-565.

2637

Test name: JOB SATISFACTION SCALE

Purpose: To measure job satisfaction as a chronic mood state.

Number of items: 20

Format: Items are bipolar adjectives separated by a 7-point scale. A few examples are presented.

Reliability: Coefficient alpha was .84.

Validity: Correlations with other variables ranged from -.21 to .31.

Author: Smith, C.A. et al.

Article: Organizational citizenship behavior: Its nature and antecedents.

Journal: *Journal of Applied Psychology*, Nov. 1983, *68*(4), 653-663.

Related research: Scott, W.E., Jr., 1967. The development of semantic differential scales as measures of "morale." *Personnel Psychology, 20,* 179-198.

2638

Test name: JOB-RELATED TENSION INDEX

Purpose: To provide an overall measure of perceived psychological tension or strain associated with stresses at work.

Number of items: 15

Format: Likert-type scale.

Reliability: Reported internal consistency ranged from .73 to .87.

Author: Abush, R. and Burkhead, E.J.

Article: Job stress in midlife working women: Relationships among personality type, job characteristics and job tension.

Journal: *Journal of Counseling Psychology*, Jan. 1984, *31*(1), 36-44.

Related research: Kahn, R.L. et al., 1964. *Organizational stress: Studies* *in role conflict and role ambiguity.* New York: Wiley.

2639
Test name: JOB-RELATED TENSION INDEX

Purpose: To measure organizational stress.

Number of items: 14

Format: Likert-type items.

Reliability: Test-retest reliability coefficient was .724.

Author: West, D.J., Jr. et al.

Article: Component analysis of occupational stress inoculation applied to registered nurses in an acute care hospital setting.

Journal: *Journal of Counseling Psychology*, April 1984, *31*(2), 209-218.

Related research: Kahn, R.L. et al., 1964. *Organizational stress: Studies in role conflict and role ambiguity.* New York: Wiley.

2640
Test name: JOB-RELATED TENSION INDEX

Purpose: To measure job-related tension.

Number of items: 9

Format: 5-point Likert response categories. Sample items presented.

Reliability: Median item intercorrelation = .27. Split-half reliability = .69.

Author: Wright, D., and Thomas, J.

Article: Role strain among psychologists in the midwest.

Journal: *Journal of School Psychology*, 1982, *20*(2), 96-102.

Related research: Lyons, T.F., 1971. Role clarity, need for clarity, satisfaction, tension and withdrawal. *Organizational Behavior and Human Performance*, 6, 99-110.

2641
Test name: JOB STRESS QUESTIONNAIRE

Purpose: To measure role conflict, role ambiguity, organizational conflict, and workgroup cooperation.

Number of items: 36

Format: 5-point Likert format. Sample items presented.

Reliability: Alpha ranged from .55 to .84 across subscales.

Author: Burr, R.G.

Article: Smoking among U.S. Navy enlisted men: Some contributing factors.

Journal: *Psychological Reports*, Feb. 1984, 54(1), 287-294.

Related research: Butler, M.C. and Burr, R.G., 1980. Utility of a multidimensional locus of control scale in predicting health and job related outcomes in military environments. *Psychological Reports, 47*, 719-728.

2642
Test name: JOB STRESS SCALES

Purpose: To measure environmental and psychological stress.

Number of items: 16 (10 environmental, 6 psychological).

Format: 5-point answering scale. Sample items presented.

Reliability: Alpha = .84 (environmental); Alpha = .80 (psychological).

Author: Frese, M. and Okonek, K.

Article: Reasons to leave shiftwork and psychological and psychosomatic complaints of former shiftworkers.

Journal: *Journal of Applied Psychology*, Aug. 1984, 69(3), 509-514.

Related research: Semmer, N., 1982. Stress at work, stress in private life, and psychological well-being. In W. Bachmann et al., (Eds.), *Mental load and stress in activity: European approaches*. Berlin: Deutscher Verlag der Wissenschaften.

2643
Test name: JOB TEDIUM SCALE

Purpose: To measure physical, emotional, and mental exhaustion.

Number of items: 21

Format: 7-point scale (1 = never, 7 = always).

Reliability: Test-retest (1 month) = .89; (2 months) = .76; (6 months) = .66. Alpha (internal consistency) ranged from .91 to .93.

Validity: Significant (p<.05) correlations in expected direction with job satisfaction, desire to leave job and negative attitude toward clients, and Maslach Burnout Scale.

Author: Stout, J.K. and Williams, J.M.

Article: Comparison of two measures of burnout.

Journal: *Psychological Reports*, Aug. 1983, 53(1), 283-289.

Related research: Pines, A.M. et al., 1981. *Burnout: From tedium to personal growth*. New York: Free Press.

2644
Test name: JOB TIME-DEMANDS SCALE

Purpose: To measure job time-demands experienced by people who have family and employment responsibilities.

Number of items: 15

Format: 4-point Likert response categories ("almost never" to "almost always") to each item which describe time-demand situations. All items presented.

Reliability: Cronbach's alpha on composite scale = .80. Alpha ranged from .66 to .82 on three subscales derived by factor analysis.

Validity: People who reported job-family difficulties scored higher on the Job Time-Demand Scale (t = 9.61, p<.001).

Author: Johnson, P.

Article: Development of a measure of job-time demands.

Journal: *Psychological Reports*, Dec. 1982, *51*(3 Pt. 2), 1087-1094.

2645
Test name: MARKET DISSATISFACTION SCALE

Purpose: To measure how secure and well-paid a respondent's job is.

Number of items: 7

Format: 5-point Likert format. All items presented.

Reliability: Alpha ranged from .51 to .55.

Validity: Correlated with potential grievance (r = .25 and .30, p<.01).

Author: Blyton, P. et al.

Article: Job status and white-collar members' union activities.

Journal: *Journal of Occupational Psychology*, March 1981, *54*(1), 33-45.

2646
Test name: MEIER BURNOUT ASSESSMENT

Purpose: To measure cognitions and expectations related to burnout.

Number of items: 23

Format: True-false.

Reliability: Alpha = .79.

Validity: Correlated .58 with Maslach Burnout Inventory.

Author: Meier, S.T.

Article: The construct validity of burnout.

Journal: *Journal of Occupational Psychology*, Sept. 1984, *57*(3), 211-219.

Related research: Meier, S., 1983. Toward a theory of burnout. *Human Relations, 36,* 899-910.

2647
Test name: NEED FOR CLARITY INDEX

Purpose: To measure respondent need for clear assessment of job performance.

Number of items: 4

Format: 5-point Likert response categories.

Reliabilities: Median item intercorrelation = .40. Split-half reliability = .65.

Author: Wright, D. and Thomas, J.

Article: Role strain among psychologists in the midwest.

Journal: *Journal of School Psychology,* 1982, *20*(2), 96-102.

Related research: Lyons, T.F., 1971. Role clarity, need for clarity, satisfaction, tension and withdrawal. *Organizational Behavior and Human Performance, 6,* 99-110.

2648
Test name: NURSING STRESS SCALE

Purpose: To measure the frequency with which certain nursing situations are perceived as stressful by nurses.

Number of items: 34

Format: Subjects respond to each item on a scale from 0 (never) to 3 (very frequently). Includes 7 factors: death and dying, conflict with physicians, inadequate preparation, lack of support, conflict with other nurses, work load, and uncertainty concerning treatment. All items are presented.

Reliability: Test-retest reliability ranged from .42 to .86. Spearman-Brown coefficients ranged from .57 to .84. Guttman split-half coefficients ranged from .46 to .79. Coefficient alphas ranged from .64 to .89. Standardized item alphas ranged from .65 to .89.

Validity: Correlations with other variables ranged from -.15 to .39.

Author: Gray-Toft, P. and Anderson, J.G.

Article: The Nursing Stress Scale: Development of an instrument.

Journal: *Journal of Behavioral Assessment,* March 1981, *3*(1), 11-23.

2649
Test name: OCCUPATIONAL STRESS SCALE

Purpose: To measure occupational stress.

Number of items: 34

Format: True-false-undecided response categories. Sample items presented.

Reliability: Split-half and test-retest reliabilities ranged from .60 to .87.

Author: Petrie, K. and Rotherham, M.J.

Article: Insulators against stress: Self-esteem and assertiveness.

Journal: *Psychological Reports*, 1982, *50*(3, Pt. 1), 963-966.

Related research: Weyer, G. and Hodapp, V., 1974. Development of a questionnaire for measuring perceived stress. *Archiv für Psychologie*, *127*, 161-188.

2650
Test name: ORGANIZATIONAL READJUSTMENT RATING SCALE

Purpose: To measure stressful events on the job.

Number of items: 31

Format: 31 events are checked if they have occurred in the last 12 months. Sum of item weights yields a stress score.

Validity: Correlated .40 with Holmes and Rahe Schedule of Recent Experiences Scale.

Author: Weiss, H.M. et al.

Article: Effects of life and job stress on information search behaviors of organizational members.

Journal: *Journal of Applied Psychology*, Feb. 1982, *67*(1), 60-66.

Related research: Naismith, D.C., 1975. *Stress among managers as a function of organizational change.* Doctoral dissertation. George Washington University.

2651
Test name: PAY INCREASE SCALE

Purpose: To measure meaningfulness of pay increases.

Number of items: 16

Format: Paired comparison. Money-oriented responses paired with recognition-oriented responses.

Reliability: Internal consistency = .96.

Author: Frzystofiak, F. et al.

Article: Pay, meaning, satisfaction and size of a meaningful pay increase.

Journal: *Psychological Reports*, 1982, *51*(2), 660-662.

Related research: Krefting, L.A. and Mahoney, T.A., 1977. Determining the size of meaningful pay increase. *Industrial Relations, 16,* 89-93.

2652
Test name: PAY SATISFACTION SCALE

Purpose: To measure satisfaction with pay.

Number of items: 7

Format: Four items were concerned with perceived fairness of pay and three items were concerned with satisfaction of pay.

Reliability: Cronbach's alpha was .89.

Validity: Correlations with other variables ranged from -.39 to .51.

Author: Motowidlo, S.J.

Article: Predicting sales turnover from pay satisfaction and expectation.

Journal: *Journal of Applied Psychology,* Aug. 1983, *68*(3), 484-489.

Related research: Motowidlo, S.J., 1982. Relationship between self-rated performance and pay satisfaction among sales representatives. *Journal of Applied Psychology, 67,* 209-213.

2653
Test name: PERCEIVED INFLUENCE SCALE

Purpose: To measure how much influence respondent would like to have at work.

Number of items: 4

Format: 9-point Likert format.

Reliability: Alpha = .86.

Author: Rafaeli, A.

Article: Quality circles and employee attitudes.

Journal: *Personnel Psychology,* autumn 1985, *38*(3), 603-615.

Related research: Hackman, J.R. and Lawler, E.E., 1971. Employee reactions to job characteristics. *Journal of Applied Psychology, 55,* 259-286.

2654
Test name: PHYSICAL AND PSYCHOLOGICAL STRESS SCALES

Purpose: To measure stress at work.

Number of items: 15

Format: Varies. All items presented.

Reliability: Ranged from .64 to .90 across component subscales.

Author: Frese, M.

Article: Stress at work and psychosomatic complaints: A causal interpretation.

Journal: *Journal of Applied Psychology*, May 1985, *70*(2), 314-328.

Related research: Zapf, D. et al. Scale documentation of the research project -- Psychological stress at work: Factors promoting and impeding humane working conditions. Institut Fuer Psychologie, Freie Universitaet Berlin, 1000 Berlin 33, Federal Republic of Germany.

2655
Test name: POTENTIAL AND ACTUAL STRESSORS SCALES

Purpose: To measure teacher stress.

Number of items: 9 separate scales contain from 3 to 7 items each.

Format: Multiple-choice. Sample items presented.

Reliability: Alpha ranged from .58 to .94 across scales.

Author: Tellenback, S. et al.

Article: Teacher stress: Exploratory model building.

Journal: *Journal of Occupational Psychology*, March 1983, *56*(1), 19-33.

Related research: Tellenback, S. et al. Teacher stress: A structural-comparative analysis. *Pedagogical Reports, 14.* Lund: Department of Education.

2656
Test name: POTENTIAL GRIEVANCE SCALE

Purpose: To measure how much a respondent might want his union to help with job problems.

Number of items: 5

Format: 5-point Likert format. All items presented.

Reliability: Alpha ranged from .71 to .73.

Validity: Correlated with market dissatisfaction ($r = .25$ and .30, $p < .01$).

Author: Blyton, P. et al.

Article: Job status and white-collar members' union activity.

Journal: *Journal of Occupational Psychology*, March 1981, *54*(1), 33-45.

2657
Test name: PROPENSITY TO LEAVE SCALE

Purpose: To assess likelihood of leaving an organization.

Number of items: 3

Format: 5-point multiple-choice.

Reliability: Alpha = .83.

Author: Bedeian, A.G.

Article: The relationship between role stress and job-related interpersonal and organizational climate factors.

Journal: *Journal of Social Psychology*, April 1981, *113*(second half), 247-260.

Related research: Lyons, T.F., 1971. Role clarity, need for clarity, satisfaction, tension and withdrawal. *Organizational Behavior and Human Performance, 6,* 99-110.

2658
Test name: PSYCHOLOGICAL STRESS AT WORK SCALE

Purpose: To measure psychological stress at work.

Number of items: 14

Format: Includes items relating to: uncertainty in the job, organizational problems, environmental stress, danger of accidents, and intensity.

Reliability: Coefficient alphas ranged from .52 to .79.

Validity: Correlations with physical stress ranged from -.22 to .42.

Source: Frese, M.

Article: Stress at work and psychosomatic complaints: A causal interpretation.

Journal: *Journal of Applied Psychology*, May 1985, *70*(2), 314-328.

2659
Test name: SATISFACTION SCALE

Purpose: To measure overall satisfaction with work, salary, research and teaching support, colleagues, and the power and decision-making structure within the university.

Number of items: 16

Format: Responses were made on a 5-point scale ranging from very dissatisfied to very satisfied.

Reliability: Internal consistency reliability was .91.

Validity: Correlations with other variables ranged from -.53 to .87.

Author: Zalesny, M.D.

Article: Comparison of economic and noneconomic factors in predicting faculty vote preference in a union representation election.

Journal: *Journal of Applied Psychology*, May 1985, *70*(2), 243-256.

Related research: Terborg, J.R. et al., 1982, August. University faculty dispositions toward unionization: A test of Triandis' model. Paper presented at the American Psychological Association's Meeting, Washington, D.C.

2660
Test name: SATISFACTION WITH 3/38 WORK SCHEDULE SCALE

Purpose: To measure satisfaction with working 38 hours in 3 work days.

Number of items: 7

Format: 7-point Likert format. All items presented.

Reliability: Alpha = .93.

Validity: A group actually on a 3-day / 38-hour schedule scored higher than a group on a 5-day / 40-hour schedule.

Author: Latack, J.C. and Foster, L.W.

Article: Implementation of compressed work schedules: Participation and job design as critical factors for employee acceptance.

Journal: *Personnel Psychology*, spring 1985, *38*(1), 75-92.

2661
Test name: SATISFACTION WITH THE NAVY SCALE

Purpose: To measure satisfaction with the Navy.

Number of items: 6

Format: Likert format.

Reliability: Alpha = .80.

Author: James, L.R. et al.

Article: Perceptions of psychological influence: A cognitive information processing approach for explaining moderated relationships.

Journal: *Personnel Psychology*, autumn 1981, *34*(3), 453-475.

Related research: Jones, A.P. et al., 1977. Black-white differences in job satisfaction and its correlates. *Personnel Psychology*, *30*, 5-16.

2662
Test name: SCHOOL PSYCHOLOGIST STRESS INVENTORY

Purpose: To identify and measure sources of stress among school psychologists.

Number of items: 35 job-related events.

Format: Respondents indicate how stressful each event is on a scale of 1 to 9.

Validity: Factor analysis yielded 9 factors with eigenvalues greater than one. Statistically significant differences by gender reported on 6 factors, significant differences by age on 5 factors, significant differences by salary on 4 factors.

Author: Wise, P.S.

Article: School psychologists' rankings of stressful events.

Journal: *Journal of School Psychology*, 1985, 23(1), 31-41.

2663
Test name: TASK SATISFACTION SCALE

Purpose: To measure subjects' overall task satisfaction.

Number of items: 7

Format: Responses are made on a 7-point Likert scale. Sample items are presented.

Reliability: Coefficient alpha was .85.

Validity: Correlation with performance was r = .21.

Author: Phillips, J.S. and Freedman, S.M.

Article: Contingent pay and intrinsic task interest: Moderating effects of work values.

Journal: *Journal of Applied Psychology*, May 1985, 70(2), 306-313.

2664
Test name: TEACHER BURNOUT SURVEY

Purpose: To measure and assess burnout.

Number of items: 65

Format: Likert.

Reliability: Spearman-Brown split-half = .88.

Author: Farber, B.A.

Article: Stress and burnout in suburban teachers.

Journal: *Journal of Educational Research*, July/Aug. 1984, 77(6), 325-331.

Related research: Maslach, C. and Jackson, S., 1981. The measure of experienced burnout. *Journal of Occupational Behavior*, 2, 1-15.

2665

Test name: TEACHER OCCUPATIONAL STRESS FACTOR QUESTIONNAIRE

Purpose: To identify the perceived occupational stress factors of teachers.

Number of items: 30

Format: Responses are made on a scale from not stressful to extremely stressful. Includes four factors: Relationships with teachers, work and compensation, working with students, perceptions of respect from others. All items are presented.

Reliability: Cronbach's alpha coefficients ranged from .79 to .92. Overall reliability was .93.

Author: Foxworth, M.D. et al.

Article: The factorial validity of the Teacher Occupational Stress Factor Questionnaire for the teacher of the gifted.

Journal: *Educational and Psychological Measurement,* summer 1984, *44*(2), 527-532.

Related research: Clark, E.H., 1980. *An analysis of occupational stress factors as perceived by public school teachers.* Unpublished doctoral dissertation, Auburn University.
  Halpin, G. et al., 1985. Teacher stress as related to locus of control, sex and age. *Journal of Experimental Education,* *53*(3), 136-140.
  Harris, K. et al., 1985. Teacher characteristics and stress. *Journal of Educational Research,* *78*(6), 346-350.

2666

Test name: TEACHER STRESS INVENTORY

Purpose: To measure occupational stress in teachers.

Number of items: 38

Format: Likert. (2 responses per item - one for strength and one for frequency of stress.)

Reliability: Alpha ranged from .62 to .95 across subscales and across samples of respondents.

Validity: Items factored similarly in different samples (types) of teachers (regular and special education).

Author: Fimian, M.J.

Article: The development of an instrument to measure occupational stress in teachers: The Teacher Stress Inventory.

Journal: *Journal of Occupational Psychology,* Dec. 1984, *57*(4), 277-293.

2667

Test name: TENSION SCALE

Purpose: To measure feelings of being bothered by work-related factors.

Number of items: 9

Format: 5-category multiple-choice.

Reliability: Alpha = .86.

Author: Bedeian, A.G. et al.

Article: The relationship between role stress and job-related interpersonal and organizational climate factors.

Journal: *Journal of Social Psychology*, April 1981, *113*(second half), 247-260.

Related research: Kahn, R.L. et al., 1964. *Organizational stress: Studies in role conflict and role ambiguity.* New York: Wiley.

2668
Test name: TRIPLE AUDIT OPINION SURVEY (TAOS)

Purpose: To measure job satisfaction.

Number of items: 104

Format: 5-point Likert format.

Reliability: Ranged from .74 to .95.

Author: Lee, R. et al.

Article: Sex, wage-earner status, occupational level and job satisfaction.

Journal: *Journal of Vocational Behavior*, June 1981, *18*(3), 362-373.

Related research: The TAOS is a variation of the Minnesota Satisfaction Questionnaire.

2669
Test name: UNION INSTRUMENTALITY SCALE

Purpose: To measure how much nurses perceive joining a union as leading to various outcomes.

Number of items: 13

Format: 5-point scale (never to always).

Reliability: Alphas ranged from .72 to .82 for extrinsic and intrinsic items.

Validity: Does not correlate significantly (r = .11) with locus of control (Rotter, 1966), or pro-Strike attitudes (R = .19). Does correlate significantly with intention to join a union (r = .34).

Author: Beutell, N.J. and Biggs, D.L.

Article: Behavioral intentions to join a union: Instrumentality X valence, locus of control and strike attitudes.

2670
Test name: WARR JOB SATISFACTION QUESTIONNAIRE

Purpose: To measure satisfaction with intrinsic and extrinsic job factors.

Number of items: 15

Format: 7-point Likert format.

Reliability: Test-retest = .63.

Author: Barling, J. and Van Bart, D.

Article: Mothers' subjective employment experience and the behavior of their nursery school children.

Journal: *Journal of Occupational Psychology*, March 1984, 57(1), 49-56.

Related research: Warr, P. et al., 1979. Scales for the measurement of some attitudes as aspects of psychological well-being. *Journal of Occupational Psychology*, 52, 129-148.

2671
Test name: WORK ALIENATION-INVOLVEMENT SCALE

Purpose: To measure work alienation-involvement.

Number of items: 15

Format: 5-point Likert agreement scales.

Reliability: Alpha = .89.

Author: Lefkowitz, J. et al.

Article: The role of need level and/or need salience as moderators of the relationship between need satisfaction and work alienation-involvement.

Journal: *Journal of Vocational Behavior*, April 1984, 24(2), 142-158.

Related research: Lefkowitz, J. and Somers, M., 1982. Work alienation-involvement: Scale construction, validation, and a developmental model. American Psychological Association Convention, Division 14, Poster Session I, Washington, D.C.

2672
Test name: WORK ROLE CENTRALITY SCALE

Purpose: To determine the degree to which the work role dominates the attention and interests of the employee relative to nonorganizational roles.

Number of items: 5

Journal: *Psychological Reports*, Aug. 1984, 55(1), 215-222.

Format: A 5-point format was employed.

Reliability: Coefficient alpha was .74.

Author: Drasgow, F. and Miller, H.E.

Article: Psychometric and substantive issues in scale construction and validation.

Journal: *Journal of Applied Psychology*, June 1982, *67*(3), 268-279.

Related research: Dubin, R., 1956. Industrial workers' worlds: A study of the "central life interests" of industrial workers. *Social Problems*, 131-140.

2673
Test name: WORK SATISFACTION SCALE

Purpose: To measure degree to which respondent obtained specific rewards from work.

Number of items: 25

Format: 5-point rating scales. Sample items presented.

Reliability: Alpha = .94.

Author: Pistrang, N.

Article: Women's work involvement and experience of new motherhood.

Journal: *Journal of Marriage and the Family*, May 1984, *46*(2), 433-447.

Related research: Robinson, J.P. et al., 1974. *Measures of occupational attitudes and occupational characteristics*. Ann Arbor, MI: Survey Research Center of the Institute for Social Research.

2674
Test name: WORK TEDIUM QUESTIONNAIRE

Purpose: To measure work tedium.

Number of items: 21

Format: Subjects indicate their frequency of experiencing mental, emotional, and physical exhaustion at work on a 7-point frequency scale.

Reliability: Coefficient alpha was .79.

Validity: Correlations with other variables ranged from -.10 to -.82.

Author: Adler, S. and Golan, J.

Article: Lateness as a withdrawal behavior.

Journal: *Journal of Applied Psychology*, Oct. 1981, *66*(5), 544-554.

Related research: Kafry, D. and Pines, A., 1980. The experience of tedium in life and work. *Human Relations*, 33, 477-503.

2675
Test name: WORKER OPINION SURVEY

Purpose: To measure shop-floor job satisfaction.

Number of items: 48

Time required: 6-8 minutes.

Reliability: KR = .71 to .86.

Validity: Multitrait-multimethod validity with Job Descriptive Index met all Campbell and Fiske criteria.

Author: Soutar, G.N. and Weaver, J.R.

Article: The measurement of shop-floor job satisfaction: The convergent and discriminant validity of the worker opinion survey.

Journal: *Journal of Occupational Psychology*, March 1982, 55(1), 27-33.

Related research: Cross, D., 1973. The worker opinion survey: A measure of shop-floor satisfaction. *Occupational Psychology*, 47, 193-208.

2676
Test name: WORK ORIENTATION SCALE

Purpose: To measure orientation to work.

Number of items: 10

Format: Yes-no, or frequency (i.e., never to often). Sample items presented.

Reliability: Cronbach's alpha = .63.

Validity: Correlated significantly with burnout (-.16 to -.19).

Author: Nagy, S.

Article: Burnout and selected variables as components of occupational stress.

Journal: *Psychological Reports*, Feb. 1985, 56(1), 195-200.

APTITUDE

2677
Test name: CHILD'S LEARNING ABILITY RATING SCALE

Purpose: To measure child's learning.

Number of items: 16

Time required: 4 seconds per item.

Format: Children asked to match geometric design with eight concrete and eight abstract nouns.

Reliability: Split-half (Spearman-Brown) = .85. Inter-rater = .71.

Author: Dean, R.S. and Kundert, D.K.

Article: Intelligence and teachers' ratings as predictors of abstract and concrete learning.

Journal: *Journal of School Psychology*, 1981, *19*(1), 78-85.

2678
Test name: COGNITIVE TASKS

Purpose: To measure cognitive ability of elementary school children in Japan, China, and the United States.

Number of items: Ranged from 138 (1st graders) to 149 (5th graders).

Format: Includes 10 tasks: coding, spatial relations, perceptual speed, auditory memory, verbal-spatial, serial memory (words), serial memory (numbers), verbal memory, vocabulary, general information.

Reliability: Cronbach's alpha ranged from .47 to .98.

Author: Stevenson, H.W. et al.

Article: Cognitive performance and academic achievement of Japanese, Chinese, and American children.

Journal: *Child Development*, June 1985, *56*(3), 718-734.

Related research: Stigler, J.W. et al., 1982. Curriculum and achievement in mathematics: A study of elementary school children in Japan, Taiwan, and the United States. *Journal of Educational Psychology*, *74*, 315-322.

2679
Test name: COMPUTER SCIENCE SUCCESS PREDICTOR TEST

Purpose: To measure level of success in beginning computer science courses.

Number of items: 30

Time required: 1 class period.

Format: Questions on logic, reading comprehension, alphabetic and numeric sequences, algorithmic execution, and alphanumeric translation.

Reliability: KR-20 = .76.

Validity: R^2 = .25 with final examination.

Author: Wileman, S. et al.

Article: Factors influencing success in beginning computer science courses.

Journal: *Journal of Educational Research*, March/April 1987, *74*(4), 223-226.

2680
Test name: HUMOR PERCEPTIVENESS TEST

Purpose: To measure humor aptitude.

Number of items: 18

Format: Each item is a sentence-completion item taken from a fairly common joke. A few examples are presented.

Reliability: Corrected split-half reliability was .75 (n = 56).

Validity: Correlation with the Humor Achievement Test was .66 (N = 45). Correlation with GPA was r = -.24 (n = 35).

Author: Feingold, A.

Article: Measuring humor: A pilot study.

Journal: *Perceptual and Motor Skills*, June 1982, *54*(3, Pt. 1), 986.

2681
Test name: LATERALITY INDEX

Purpose: To assess cognitive impairment resulting from unilateral hemispheric damage to the brain using the WAIS-R.

Format: The Index is devised from Factor 2 of the WAIS-R (Worksheet provided).

Reliability: Split-half = .78. Retest = .79.

Validity: An LI that is more extreme than 10th or 90th percentile is indicative of probable damage.

Author: Lawson, J.S. et al.

Article: A laterality index of cognitive impairment devised from a principal-components analysis of the WAIS-R.

Journal: *Journal of Consulting and Clinical Psychology*, Dec. 1983, *51*(6), 841-847.

Related research: Lawson, J.S. and Inglis, J., 1983. A laterality index of cognitive impairment after hemispheric damage: A measure devised from a principal-components analysis of the Wechsler Adult Intelligence Scale. *Journal of Consulting and Clinical Psychology*, 51, 832-840.

2682
Test name: LEADERSHIP OPINION QUESTIONNAIRE

Purpose: To measure leadership potential in college students.

Number of items: 40

Format: Multiple-choice.

Validity: Significant expected differences between known leaders and non-leaders on the consideration and structure dimensions.

Author: DeJulio, S.S. et al.

Article: The measurement of leadership potential in college students.

Journal: *Journal of College Student Personnel*, May 1981, 22(3), 202-213.

Related research: Fleishman, E.A., 1957. A leader behavior description for industry. In R.M. Stogdill and A.E. Coons (Eds.), *Leader behavior: Its description and measurement*. Columbus, Ohio: Bureau of Business Research.

2683
Test name: MULTIVARIATE ACHIEVEMENT PREDICTOR TEST

Purpose: To predict academic achievement.

Number of items: 64

Time required: Less than one class period.

Reliability: Alphas ranged from .56 to .86.

Author: Foshay, W.R. and Misanchuk, E.R.

Article: Toward the multivariate modeling of achievement, aptitude, and personality.

Journal: *Journal of Educational Research*, May/June 1981, 74(5), 352-357.

Related research: Misanchuk, E.R., 1977. A model-based prediction of scholastic achievement. *Journal of Educational Research*, 71, 30-35.

2684
Test name: NON-COGNITIVE QUESTIONNAIRE

Purpose: To predict academic success by race.

Number of items: 21

Format: Includes 18 Likert-type items and 3 open-ended questions dealing with present goals, past accomplishments, group memberships, and offices held.

Reliability: Test-retest reliability (2 weeks, N = 18) on the Likert-type items ranged from .70 to .94.

Author: Tracey, T.S. and Sedlacek, W.E.

Article: Non-cognitive variables in predicting academic success by race.

Journal: *Measurement and Evaluation in Guidance*, Jan. 1984, *16*(4), 171-178.

Related research: Sedlacek, W.E. and Brooks, G.C., Jr., 1976. *Racism in American education: A model for change*. Chicago: Nelson-Hall.

2685
Test name: PERCEPTUAL ACUITY TEST

Purpose: To assess non-transformational intellectual functions.

Number of items: 30

Time required: 20 minutes.

Format: 5 geometric figures are presented to subjects on a screen. Subjects are asked to choose 1 that meets specified criteria.

Validity: Correlates .21 to .33 with age. Correlates .38 with Gollschaldt Hidden Figures Test, .28 with Cane-Ruch Spatial Relations Test, and -.41 with Witkin's rod-and-frame test.

Author: Gough, H.G. and Weiss, D.S.

Article: A nontransformational test of intellectual competence.

Journal: *Journal of Applied Psychology*, Feb. 1981, *66*(1), 102-110.

Related research: Gough, H.G. and McGurk, E.A., 1967. A group test of perceptual acuity. *Perceptual and Motor Skills*, *24*, 1107-1115.

2686
Test name: REAL ESTATE CAREER SCALE

Purpose: To measure, with biographical data, a person's probable success in the career of real estate agent.

Number of items: 85

Format: Multiple-choice. Scoring done by the England "weighted application blank" (WAB) method.

Reliability: Test-retest (1 week) = .84 (n = 13).

Validity: Using obtaining a real estate license as a criterion, 60 to 62 percent of "failures" were eliminated and 69 to 80 percent of "successes" were retained.

Author: Mitchell, T.W. and Klimoski, R.J.

Article: Is it rational to be empirical? A test of methods for scoring biographical data.

Journal: *Journal of Applied Psychology*, Aug. 1982, *67*(4), 411-418.

Related research: England, G.W., 1971. *Development and use of weighted application blanks.* (Rev.) Minneapolis: University of Minnesota, Industrial Relations Center.

2687
Test name: RIGHT HEMISPHERE ORIENTATION SCALE

Purpose: To measure hemispheric orientation.

Number of items: 7

Format: 7 pairs of metaphoric characteristics said to typify hemispheric (left-right) orientation presented to subjects at the ends of a 7-point scale. All items presented.

Reliability: Internal consistency = .82.

Author: Hirschman, E.C.

Article: Psychological sexual identity and hemispheric orientation.

Journal: *Journal of General Psychology*, April 1983, *108*(second half), 153-168.

Related research: Springer, S.P. and Deutsch, G., 1981. *Left brain/right brain.* San Francisco: W.H. Freeman.

2688
Test name: SIMON-DOLE LISTENING COMPREHENSION TEST

Purpose: To measure listening comprehension as a predictor of reading comprehension.

Number of items: 38

Format: For each item, the child places an X on one of three pictures that best answers a question. Also included are 19 short passages.

Reliability: Kuder-Richardson Formula 20 estimated reliability was .84.

Validity: Correlations with the Boehm Test of Basic Concepts was .42, .62. Correlation with the Comprehensive Test of Basic Skills was .34.

Author: Dole, J.A. et al.

Article: The development and validation of a listening comprehension test as a predictor of reading comprehension: Preliminary results.

Journal: *Educational Research Quarterly*, 1984-1985, 9(4), 40-46.

2689
Test name: THUMIN TEST OF MENTAL DEXTERITY

Purpose: To measure intelligence.

Number of items: 100

Time required: 60 minutes.

Format: Multiple-choice.

Validity: Product-moment correlation with WAIS full scale was .84.

Author: Thumin, F.J. et al.

Article: Relationship between the Thumin Test of Mental Dexterity and the WAIS.

Journal: *Perceptual and Motor Skills*, Oct. 1983, 57(2), 599-603.

Related research: Thumin, F.J. and Stern, A., 1977. Two construct validity studies of the Thumin Test of Mental Dexterity. *Psychological Reports*, 40, 884-886.

2690
Test name: YOUR STYLE OF LEARNING AND THINKING— FORM C-A

Purpose: To determine hemispheric preferences.

Number of items: 36

Format: Respondents select one of three choices which represent left, right, or the integrative capacity of right and left hemispheres. Examples are presented.

Reliability: Reliability coefficients ranged from .58 to .97.

Author: Shannon, M. and Rice, D.R.

Article: A comparison of hemispheric preference between high ability and low ability elementary children.

Journal: *Educational Research Quarterly*, fall 1983, 7(3), 7-15.

Related research: Kalsounis, B., 1979. Evidence for the validity of the scale. Your style of learning and thinking. *Perceptual and Motor Skills*, 48, 177-178.

ATTITUDE

2691
Test name: ATTITUDES OF ELEMENTARY TEACHERS QUESTIONNAIRE

Purpose: To measure teachers' attitudes about students and teaching.

Number of items: 30

Format: 5-point agreement-disagreement scale. Sample item presented.

Reliability: Alphas ranged from .54 to .84 over subscales. Alpha for total scale was .694.

Author: Mitman, A.L.

Article: Teachers' differential behavior toward higher and lower achieving students and its relation to selected teacher characteristics.

Journal: *Journal of Educational Psychology*, April 1985, 77(2), 149-161.

Related research: Mitman, A.L. Effects of teachers' naturally occurring expectations and a feedback treatment on teachers and students. *Dissertation Abstracts International*, 42, 618-A. (University microfilms No. 8115812.)

2692
Test name: ATTITUDE TOWARD COLLEGE INVENTORY

Purpose: To measure attitudes toward college.

Number of items: 12

Format: 5-point Likert scale. Sample item presented.

Reliability: Cronbach's alpha = .68 (pretest), .68 (posttest). Test-retest = .63 (10 day interval).

Validity: Significant correlation (p<.01) with interest in college, perceived affordability, perceived difficulty, and perceived intelligence.

Author: Johanson, R.P. and Vopava, J.R.

Article: Attitude assessment and prediction of college attendance among economically disadvantaged students.

Journal: *Journal of College Student Personnel*, July 1985, 26(4), 339-342.

2693
Test name: ATTITUDES TOWARD DISABLED PERSONS SCALE

Purpose: To measure attitudes toward disabled persons.

Number of items: 20

Format: Likert format. (6-point scale.)

Reliability: Median stability coefficient = .73. Split-half reliability = .75 to .85.

Author: Antonak, R.F.

Article: Prediction of attitudes toward disabled persons: A multivariate analysis.

Journal: *Journal of General Psychology*, Jan. 1981, *104*(first half), 119-123.

Related research: Yuker, H.E. et al., 1966. A scale to measure attitudes toward disabled persons. Human Resources Study No. 5. Albertson, NY: Human Resources Center.

2694
Test name: ATTITUDES TOWARD MAINSTREAMING SCALE

Purpose: To measure teacher attitudes toward mainstreaming individuals with different handicaps.

Number of items: 18

Format: Includes three dimensions: learning capabilities, general mainstreaming, and traditional limiting disabilities.

Reliability: Internal consistency reliabilities for the three subscales ranged from .78 to .88 and .91 for the total scale.

Author: Green, K. and Harvey, D.

Article: Cross-cultural validation of the attitudes toward mainstreaming scale.

Journal: *Educational and Psychological Measurement*, winter 1983, *43*(4), 1255-1261.

Related research: Berryman, J.D. and Neal, W.R., 1980. The cross validation of the Attitudes Toward Mainstreaming Scale (ATMS). *Educational and Psychological Measurement*, 40, 469-474.

2695
Test name: ATTITUDES TOWARD NUCLEAR DISARMAMENT SCALE (AND)

Purpose: To measure attitudes toward nuclear disarmament.

Number of items: 21

Format: Likert format.

Reliability: Split-half = .84 ($p < .01$).

Validity: ROTC respondents differed significantly from nuclear freeze proponents (t = 10.59, $p < .001$) in predicted direction. Correlated .51 with negative Soviet Union attitudes ($p < .01$).

Author: Larsen, K.S.

Article: Attitudes toward nuclear disarmament and their correlates.

Journal: *Journal of Social Psychology*, Feb. 1985, *125*(1), 17-21.

2696

Test name: ATTITUDES TOWARD NURSES SCALE

Purpose: To measure attitudes toward nurses.

Number of items: 20

Format: 4-point Likert-type format. All items presented.

Reliability: Alpha ranged from .80 to .84.

Validity: Participants in a summer program with nurses scored higher than nonparticipants and those who did not apply (F = 3.73, p<.05) (DF = 2,64).

Author: Hojat, M. and Herman, M.W.

Article: Developing an instrument to measure attitudes toward nurses: Preliminary psychometric findings.

Journal: *Psychological Reports*, April 1985, *56*(2), 571-579.

2697

Test name: ATTITUDES TOWARD OLD PEOPLE

Purpose: To measure attitudes toward older persons.

Number of items: 137

Format: Includes 13 categories: conservatism, activities and interests, financial, physical, family, personality traits, attitude toward the future, best time of life, insecurity, mental deterioration, sex, interference, and cleanliness.

Reliability: Test-retest ranged from .36 to .62.

Author: Finnerty-Fried, P.

Article: Instruments for the assessment of attitudes toward older persons.

Journal: *Measurement and Evaluation in Guidance*, Oct. 1982, *15*(3), 201-209.

Related research: Tuckman, J. and Lorge, I., 1953. Attitudes toward old people. *Journal of Social Psychology*, *37*, 249-260.

2698

Test name: ATTITUDES TOWARD SEEKING PROFESSIONAL PSYCHOLOGICAL HELP SCALE

Purpose: To identify attitudes toward using professional counseling services.

Number of items: 29

Format: Includes four subscales: stigma, need, openness, and confidence.

Reliability: Test-retest reliability was .83.

Author: Sanchez, A.R. and Atkinson, D.R.

Article: Mexican-American cultural commitment, preference for counselor ethnicity, and willingness to use counseling.

Journal: *Journal of Counseling Psychology*, April 1983, *30*(2), 215-220.

Related research: Fischer, E.H. and Turner, J.L., 1970. Orientations to seeking help: Development and research utility of an attitude scale. *Journal of Consulting and Clinical Psychology*, *35*, 79-90.

2699

Test name: ATTITUDES TOWARD SEX ROLES SCALE

Purpose: To measure perceptions of sex-appropriate attitudes and behaviors, with emphasis on those that may influence career development directly or indirectly.

Number of items: 35

Format: Low scores indicate responses toward an androgynous end of a scale (no differentiation made between the sexes) as opposed to high scores which indicate responses toward a dichotomous end of the scale (roles divided into male and female categories).

Reliability: Alpha coefficients ranged from .80 to .92.

Validity: Correlations with other variables ranged from .18 to .36.

Author: Hawley, P. and Even, B.

Article: Work and sex-role attitudes in relation to education and other characteristics.

Journal: *Vocational Guidance Quarterly*, Dec. 1982, *31*(2), 101-108.

Related research: Goldman, R.D. et al., 1973. Sex differences in the relationship of attitudes toward technology to choice of field of study. *Journal of Counseling Psychology*, *20*, 412-418.

2700

Test name: ATTITUDES TOWARD OCCUPATIONS SCALE

Purpose: To measure attitudes about traditional and nontraditional occupations.

Number of items: 16

Format: Semi-projective. Students must complete each of 16 sentences. Sample items presented.

Reliability: Inter-rater reliability = .95.

Author: Haring, M.J. and Beyard-Tyler, K.C.

Article: Career development: Counseling with women: The challenge of nontraditional careers.

Journal: *The School Counselor*, March 1984, *31*(4), 301-309.

Related research: Getzels, J.W. and Walsh, J.J., 1958. The method of paired direct and projective questionnaires in the study of attitude structure and socialization. *Psychological Monographs*, 72 (1, Whole No. 454).

2701
Test name: ATTITUDES TOWARD STATISTICS

Purpose: To measure attitude change in introductory statistics students.

Number of items: 29

Format: Includes two subscales: Attitude toward field of statistics and attitude toward course. Employs a Likert-type format with a 5-point response scale from "strongly disagree" to "strongly agree."

Reliability: Coefficient alphas were .92 (for field) and .90 (for course). Test-retest reliabilities (2 weeks) were .82 (field) and .91 (course).

Validity: Correlation of grade with course subscale was r = .27; with field subscale was r = -.04.

Author: Wise, S.L.

Article: The development and validation of a scale measuring attitudes toward statistics.

Journal: *Educational and Psychological Measurement*, summer 1985, *45*(2), 401-405.

2702
Test name: ATTITUDES TOWARD THE HANDICAPPED SCALE

Purpose: To measure attitudes of third graders toward the handicapped.

Number of items: 12

Format: Employed a Likert-type scale ranging from "very happy" to "very unhappy." An example is presented. Five items involved the handicapped, five did not.

Reliability: Coefficient alpha for the questions that involved the handicapped was .77. Coefficient alpha for the questions that did not involve the handicapped was .79.

Author: Beardsley, D.A.

Article: Using books to change attitudes toward the handicapped among third graders.

Journal: *Journal of Experimental Education*, winter 1981/1982, *50*(2), 52-55.

Related research: Yuker, H.E. et al., 1966. The measurement of attitudes toward disabled persons. Human Resources Study No. 7. Albertson, NY: Human Resources Center. Reprint ed., Albertson, N.Y.: Insurance Company of North America, 1970.

2703
Test name: ATTITUDES TOWARD WOMEN SCALE

Purpose: To measure attitudes toward women's roles.

Number of items: 25

Format: The items depict various roles women may enact. The higher the score, the greater the pro-feminist attitude.

Reliability: Alpha was .90 (women) and .89 (men).

Author: Beutell, N.J. and Greenhaus, J.H.

Article: Integration of home and nonhome roles: Women's conflict and coping behavior.

Journal: *Journal of Applied Psychology*, Feb. 1973, *68*(1), 43-48.

Related research: Spence, J.T. et al., 1973. A short version of the Attitudes Toward Women Scale. *Bulletin of the Psychometric Society*, 2, 219-220.

2704
Test name: ATTITUDES TOWARD WOMEN SCALE—ADAPTED

Purpose: To measure attitudes toward the appropriate roles of women in society.

Number of items: 15

Format: Subjects respond to each item on a 4-point scale ranging from agree strongly to disagree strongly.

Reliability: Internal consistency coefficients were .89 and .86.

Validity: Correlations with other variables ranged from -.27 to .35.

Author: Stafford, I.P.

Article: Relation of attitudes toward women's roles and occupational behavior to women's self-esteem.

Journal: *Journal of Counseling Psychology*, July 1984, *31*(3), 332-338.

Related research: Spence, J.T. and Helmreich, R.L., 1978. Masculinity and femininity: Their psychological dimensions, correlates, and antecedents. Austin: University of Texas Press.

McHale, S.M. and Huston, T.L., 1984. Men and women as parents: sex role orientations, employment, and parental roles with infants. *Child Development*, 55(4), 1349-1361.

2705
Test name: ATTITUDES TOWARD WORKING MOTHERS SCALE

Purpose: To measure educators' attitudes toward working mothers.

Number of items: 32

Format: 7-point Likert format (strongly agree to strongly disagree).

Reliability: Cronbach's alpha ranged from .94 to .95 for males and females.

Author: Tetenbaum, T.J. et al.

Article: Educators' attitudes toward working mothers.

Journal: *Journal of Educational Psychology*, June 1981, 73(3), 369-375.

Related research: Tetenbaum, T.J. et al., 1983. The construct validation of an attitudes toward working mothers scale. *Psychology of Women Quarterly*, 8(1), 69-78.

2706
Test name: ATTITUDE TOWARD AGGRESSION SCALE

Purpose: To measure attitudes toward aggression.

Number of items: 4

Format: 5-point response categories (almost always true to never true). All items presented.

Reliability: Alpha = .70.

Author: Liska, A.E. et al.

Article: Estimating attitude-behavior reciprocal effects within a theoretical specification.

Journal: *Social Psychology Quarterly*, March 1984, 47(1), 15-23.

Related research: Backman, J. et al., 1967. *Youth in transition*, 1, Ann Arbor, MI: Survey Research Center.

2707
Test name: ATTITUDE TOWARD CONTROVERSY SCALE

Purpose: To measure attitudes toward controversy.

Number of items: 5

Format: 5-point Likert format. All items presented.

Reliability: Alpha = .94.

Author: Smith, K.A. et al.

Article: Effects of controversy on learning in cooperative groups.

Journal: *Journal of Social Psychology*, April 1984, *122*(second half), 199-209.

Related research: Johnson, D.W. et al., 1978. The effects of cooperative and individualized instruction on student attitudes and achievement. *Journal of Social Psychology*, *104*, 207-216.

2708
Test name: ATTITUDE TOWARD COUNSELING SCALE

Purpose: To measure attitudes toward counseling.

Number of items: 32

Format: 5-point Likert items.

Reliability: Split-half = .76.

Validity: Counselors (and counseling graduate students) differed significantly from a group of former clients who gave negative evaluations of services.

Author: Davidshafter, C.O. and Richardson, G.G.

Article: Effects of precounseling training.

Journal: *Journal of College Student Personnel*, Nov. 1981, *22*(6), 522-527.

2709
Test name: ATTITUDE TOWARD DREAMS SCALE

Purpose: To measure attitudes toward dreams.

Number of items: 17

Format: The first item was not scored. Three subscales were formed by the remaining 16 items: person's own attitude toward dreams; person's perceptions of attitudes of significant others toward dreams; and the person's perception of attitudes of other people in general toward dreams or toward individuals who publicly discuss dreams. All items are presented.

Reliability: Cronbach's alpha coefficients of internal consistency ranged from .66 to .76 for the subscales and .69 for the 16 items scored.

Validity: Correlation of the 16 items with dream recall frequency was r = .31.

Author: Cernovsky, Z.Z.

Article: Dream recall and attitude toward dreams.

Journal: *Perceptual and Motor Skills*, June 1984, *58*(3), 911-914.

2710
Test name: ATTITUDE TOWARD EDUCATIONAL INQUIRY

Purpose: To measure attitude toward educational research.

Number of items: 38

Format: Subject responds to each item on a 5-point scale from "very unfavorable" (1) to "very favorable" (5).

Reliability: Gulliksen estimate of reliability was .79.

Validity: Correlations with perceived confidence in competencies was .14, with perceived importance of competencies was .48.

Author: Stauffer, A.J.

Article: The validity of selected measures to predict success on a non-traditional criterion development for an educational research program.

Journal: *Educational and Psychological Measurement*, spring 1983, *43*(1), 237-241.

Related research: Stauffer, A.J., 1974. An investigation of the procedures for developing and validating the classroom attitude toward educational inquiry. *Educational and Psychological Measurement*, *34*, 893-898.

2711
Test name: ATTITUDE TOWARD EVANGELISM SCALE

Purpose: To measure attitudes toward evangelism.

Number of items: 21

Format: 5-point Likert format. Sample items presented.

Reliability: Split-half = .83.

Validity: Correlates .76 with fanaticism. Evangelism scores higher for Protestants than non-Protestants (t = 3.00, p<.001). No difference by age or sex.

Author: Seyfarth, L.H. et al.

Article: Attitude toward evangelism: Scale development and validity.

Journal: *Journal of Social Psychology*, June 1984, *123*(first half), 55-61.

2712
Test name: ATTITUDE TOWARD INSTRUCTION SCALE

Purpose: To measure positive or negative affect toward experimental instructional treatments.

Number of items: 10

Format: 7-point bipolar adjective scales. All scales presented.

Reliability: Spearman-Brown = .92.

Author: Alesandrini, K.L.

Article: Pictorial-verbal and analytic-holistic learning strategies in science learning.

Journal: *Journal of Educational Psychology*, June 1981, *73*(3), 358-368.

Related research: Snow, R.E., 1974. Representative and quasi-representative designs for research on teaching. *Review of Educational Research*, *44*, 265-291.

2713
Test name: ATTITUDE TOWARD MALE HOMOSEXUALITY SCALE

Purpose: To measure homophobia.

Number of items: 28

Format: Responses to each item are made on a 9-point scale ranging from "strongly disagree" to "strongly agree." Scores ranged from 28 to 252.

Reliability: Internal consistency was .934.

Validity: Correlations with other variables ranged from r = -.26 to r = .24.

Author: Devlin, P.K. and Cowan, G.A.

Article: Homophobia, perceived fathering, and male intimate relationships.

Journal: *Journal of Personality Assessment*, Oct. 1985, *49*(5), 467-473.

Related research: MacDonald, A.P., Jr. and Games, R.G., 1974. Some characteristics of those who hold positive and negative attitudes toward homosexuals. *Journal of Homosexuality*, *1*, 9-27.

2714
Test name: ATTITUDE TOWARD SELF-CONTROL SCALE

Purpose: To measure attitude toward self-control.

Number of items: 6

Format: 6 response categories. (very good to very bad). All items presented.

Reliability: Alpha ranged between .74 and .78.

Author: Liska, A.E. et al.

Article: Estimating attitude-behavior reciprocal effects within a theoretical specification.

Journal: *Social Psychology Quarterly*, March 1984, *47*(1), 15-23.

Related research: Backman, J. et al., 1967. *Youth in transition*, *1*, Ann Arbor, MI: Survey Research Center.

2715
Test name: ATTITUDES TOWARD MATHEMATICS SCALE

Purpose: To measure attitudes toward mathematics and its teaching.

Number of items: 11

Format: Each of 11 concepts is measured with 10, 7-point bipolar scales.

Reliability: Alpha = .94 (mathematics) and .88 (the teacher when teaching mathematics).

Author: Schofield, H.L.

Article: Teacher effects on cognitive and affective pupil outcomes in elementary school mathematics.

Journal: *Journal of Educational Psychology*, Aug. 1981, *73*(4), 462-471.

Related research: Schofield, H.L. and Start, K.B., 1978. Mathematics attitude and achievement among student teachers. *Australian Journal of Education*, *22*(1), 72-82.

2716
Test name: ATTITUDE TOWARD TEACHING SCALE

Purpose: To measure general attitude toward career.

Number of items: 11

Format: Six response Likert-type scale.

Reliability: Split-half reliability was .71. Test-retest coefficient was .79.

Validity: Correlations with other variables ranged from -.24 to .69.

Author: Thomas, R.G. and Bruning, C.R.

Article: Validities and reliabilities of minor modifications of the Central Life Interests and Career Salience Questionnaire.

Journal: *Measurement and Evaluation in Guidance*, Oct. 1981, *14*(3), 128-135.

Related research: Merwin, J.C. and DiVesta, F.J., 1959. A study of need and theory and career choice. *Journal of Counseling Psychology*, *6*, 302-308.

2717
Test name: ATTITUDE TOWARD TREATMENT OF DISABLED STUDENTS SCALE

Purpose: To measure attitude toward disabled students.

Number of items: 32

Format: Likert-type items.

Reliability: Cronbach's alpha = .88.

Validity: Correlations of .32 with Attitude Toward Disabled Persons Scale.

Author: Fonosch, G.G. and Schwab, L.O.

Article: Attitudes of selected university faculty members towards disabled students.

Journal: *Journal of College Student Personnel*, May 1981, 22(3), 229-235.

2718
Test name: ATTITUDINAL TEST

Purpose: To measure students' attitudes toward achievement tests.

Number of items: 12

Format: Responses to each item are made on a scale from 0 (strongly disagree) to 7 (strongly agree). All items are presented.

Reliability: Test-retest reliability was .87 (N = 45).

Validity: Correlations with achievement scores ranged from r = -.18 to r = .45.

Author: Karmos, A.H. and Karmos, J.S.

Article: Attitudes toward standardized achievement tests and their relation to achievement test performance.

Journal: *Measurement and Evaluation in Counseling and Development*, July 1984, 17(2), 56-66.

2719
Test name: BARGAINING OF JOB-RELATED ISSUES SCALE

Purpose: To measure approval of union-management cooperation.

Number of items: 14

Format: 3-point rating scale. Sample items presented.

Reliability: Alpha ranged from .65 to .71 across subscales.

Author: Holley, W.H. et al.

Article: Negotiating quality of worklife, productivity and traditional issues: Union members preferred roles of their union.

Journal: *Personnel Psychology*, summer 1981, 34(2), 309-328.

Related research: Dyer, L. et al., 1977. Union attitudes toward management cooperation. *Industrial Relations*, 16, 163-172.

2720

Test name: BIAS IN ATTITUDE SURVEY SCALE

Purpose: To assess attitudes and beliefs about sex roles.

Number of items: 35

Format: The items are declarative statements dealing with the facts and beliefs about men and women and their personalities. A five-point Likert scale from strongly agree to strongly disagree is used.

Reliability: Coefficient alphas ranged from .85 to .94.

Author: Phifer, S.J. and Plake, B.S.

Article: The factorial validity of the Bias in Attitude Survey Scale.

Journal: *Educational and Psychological Measurement*, autumn 1983, *43*(3), 887-891.

Related research: Jean, P.J. and Reynolds, C.R., 1980. Development of the Bias in Attitude Survey: A sex-role questionnaire. *The Journal of Psychology*, *104*, 269-277.

2721

Test name: CALCULATOR ATTITUDE SCALE

Purpose: To measure attitudes about calculators.

Number of items: 20

Format: Likert-type scale.

Reliability: Alpha of .82 (pretest) and alpha of .85 (posttest).

Validity: Correlations with Statistical Attitude Survey ranged from -.04 to .17.

Author: Roberts, D.M. and Saxe, J.E.

Article: Validity of a statistics attitude survey: A follow-up study.

Journal: *Educational and Psychological Measurement*, autumn 1982, *42*(3), 907-912.

Related research: Geisinger, K.F. and Roberts, D.M., 1978. Individual differences in calculator attitudes and performance in a statistics course. Paper presented at American Educational Research Association, Toronto.

2722

Test name: CHILDREN'S ATTITUDES TOWARD TELEVISION COMMERCIALS

Purpose: To measure children's attitudes toward T.V. commercials.

Number of items: 7

Format: 4-point agreement scale. All items presented.

Reliability: Alpha = .57. Test-retest = .34 to .80.

Validity: Items do not always form one factor.

Author: Macklin, M.C.

Article: Psychometric investigation of Rossiter's short test measuring children's attitudes toward T.V. commercials.

Journal: *Psychological Reports*, April 1984, *54*(2), 623-627.

Related research: Rossiter, J.R., 1977. Reliability of a short test measuring children's attitudes toward T.V. commercials. *Journal of Consumer Research*, *3*, 179-184.

2723
Test name: CHILDREN'S ATTITUDE TOWARD AUTHORITY SCALE

Purpose: To measure attitude toward authority among children in grades 7 to 11.

Number of items: 28

Format: Likert format. All items presented.

Reliability: Alpha = .86.

Validity: Correlates .65 with authoritarian personality.

Author: Ray, J.J. and Jones, J.M.

Article: Attitude to authority and authoritarianism among schoolchildren.

Journal: *Journal of Social Psychology*, April 1983, *119*(second half), 199-203.

2724
Test name: COGNITIVE AND AFFECTIVE COMPUTER ATTITUDE SCALES

Purpose: To measure computer attitudes.

Number of items: 14

Format: Includes two subscales: cognitive and affective. Responses are made on a 5-point Likert scale ranging from "strongly agree" (0) to "strongly disagree" (4). All items are presented.

Reliability: Alpha coefficients were .929 for cognitive items and .896 for affective items.

Author: Bannon, S.H. et al.

Article: Cognitive and affective computer attitude scales: A validity study.

Journal: *Educational and Psychological Measurement*, autumn 1985, *45*(3), 679-681.

Related research: Ahl, D., 1976. Survey of public attitudes toward computers in society. In D.H. Ahl (Ed.), *The best of creative computering* (Vol. 1). Morristown, New Jersey: Creative Computing Press.

2725
Test name: COMMUNITY DENTAL HEALTH IDEOLOGY SCALE

Purpose: To measure a student's attitude and attitude change with respect to community dental health care and private practice.

Number of items: 23

Format: Students indicate level of agreement with each item from 1 (low) to 4 (high). Includes two factors. Most items are presented.

Reliability: Coefficient alpha for factor 1 was .70 and for factor 2 was .55.

Author: Stein, M.I. et al.

Article: Factor analytic study of the Kurtzman Community Dental Health Ideology Scale.

Journal: *Perceptual and Motor Skills*, Feb. 1983, 56(1), 79-82.

Related research: Kurtzman, C., 1977. A scale of community dental health ideology: Establishing a valid means of measurement for evaluation. *Journal of Public Health Dentistry*, 37, 275-280.

2726
Test name: COMPUTER ATTITUDE SCALE

Purpose: To measure attitudes about computers.

Number of items: 20

Format: 5-point Likert format. All items presented.

Reliability: Alpha ranged from .79 to .84.

Validity: Correlates negatively with computer aptitude (-.22, $p < .001$).

Author: Dambrot, F.H. et al.

Article: Correlates of sex differences in attitudes toward and involvement with computers.

Journal: *Journal of Vocational Behavior*, Aug. 1985, 27(1), 71-86.

2727
Test name: COMPUTER ATTITUDE SCALE

Purpose: To measure teachers' attitudes toward computers.

Number of items: 40

Format: Includes four subscales: computer anxiety, computer confidence, computer liking, and computer usefulness. Examples are presented.

Reliability: Coefficient alphas for the four subscales ranged from .82 to .90. Coefficient alpha for the total score was .95.

Author: Loyd, B.H. and Loyd, D.E.

Article: The reliability and validity of an instrument for the assessment of computer attitudes.

Journal: *Educational and Psychological Measurement*, winter 1985, *45*(4), 903-908.

Related research: Loyd, B.H. and Gressard, C., 1984. Reliability and factorial validity of computer attitude scales. *Educational and Psychological Measurement, 44,* 501-505.

2728
Test name:
COMPUTER-RELATED ATTITUDES SCALE

Purpose: To assess computer-related attitudes.

Number of items: 10

Format: 7-point Likert response format.

Reliability: Alpha = .85.

Validity: Correlated .83 with computer beliefs.

Author: Stone, D.L. et al.

Article: Relationship between rigidity, self-esteem, and attitudes about computer-based information systems.

Journal: *Psychological Reports*, Dec. 1984, *55*(3), 991-998.

2729
Test name:
COMPUTER-RELATED BELIEFS SCALE

Purpose: To assess computer-related beliefs on 4 dimensions.

Number of items: 21

Format: 7-point Likert response format.

Reliability: Alpha = .86.

Validity: Correlates -.63 with rigidity ($p < .01$) and .02 with self-esteem ($p < .05$).

Author: Stone, D.L. et al.

Article: Relationship between rigidity, self-esteem and attitudes about computer-based information systems.

Journal: *Psychological Reports*, Dec. 1984, *55*(3), 991-998.

2730
Test name: CONSEQUENCES OF WORKING AND NOT WORKING SCALE

Purpose: To measure attitudes toward consequence of working and not working.

Number of items: 29

Format: Each item responded to on 3, 5-point Likert scales: (1)

Desirability in general, (2) desirability if working, and (3) desirability if not working. Difference between 2 and 3 yielded a single score. All items presented.

Reliability: Alpha = .88.

Author: Granrose, C.S.

Article: A Fishbein-Ajzen model of intention to work following childbirth.

Journal: *Journal of Vocational Behavior*, Dec. 1984, *25*(3), 359-372.

Related research: Fishbein, M. and Ajzen, I., 1975. *Belief, attitude, intention and behavior.* Reading, MA: Addison-Wesley.

2731

Test name: CONSERVATISM SCALE

Purpose: To measure conservatism of American public opinion.

Number of items: 22

Format: Likert format. All items presented.

Reliability: Alpha = .85. Correlation between positively and negatively scored halves = .45.

Author: Ray, J.J.

Article: A scale to measure conservatism of American public opinion.

Journal: *Journal of Social Psychology*, April 1983, *119*(second half), 293-294.

Related research: Ray, J.J., 1982. Authoritarianism/libertarianism as the second dimension of social attitudes. *Journal of Social Psychology*, *117*, 33-34.

2732

Test name: CONSERVATISM SCALE FOR URBAN AFRIKANERS

Purpose: To measure conservatism.

Number of items: 14

Format: Likert format. (Subset of items from Ray Conservatism Scale used in California.)

Reliability: Alpha = .73.

Author: Ray, J.J. and Heavan, P.C.L.

Article: Conservatism and Authoritarianism among urban Afrikaners.

Journal: *Journal of Social Psychology*, April 1984, *122*(second half), 163-170.

Related research: Ray, J.J., 1983. A scale to measure conservatism of American public opinion. *Journal of Social Psychology*, *119*, 293-294.

2733
Test name: CONTROVERSY ATTITUDE SCALE

Purpose: To measure attitudes toward controversy.

Number of items: 5

Format: Likert format.

Reliability: Cronbach's alpha reliability was .94.

Author: Lowry, N. and Johnson, D.W.

Article: Effects of controversy on epistemic curiosity, achievement and attitudes.

Journal: *Journal of Social Psychology*, Oct. 1981, *115*(first half), 31-43.

Related research: Johnson, D.W. et al., 1978. The effects of cooperative and individualized instruction on student attitudes and achievement. *Journal of Social Psychology, 104*, 207-216.

2734
Test name: CONVENTIONALITY SCALE

Purpose: To measure conventional attitudes.

Number of items: 7

Format: Guttman. Five items from Nettler.

Reliability: Reproducibility = .87 for 74 undergraduates.

Author: Raden, D.

Article: Dogmatism and conventionality.

Journal: *Psychological Reports*, 1982, *50*(3), 1020-1022.

Related research: Nettler, G., 1957. A measure of alienation. *American Sociological Review, 22*, 670-677.

2735
Test name: COURSE STRUCTURE INVENTORY

Purpose: To identify student attitudes toward course structure.

Number of items: 66

Format: Includes two subscales: attitude toward course structure and attitude toward course difficulty.

Reliability: Coefficient alpha reliabilities for the two subscales were .74 and .76.

Validity: Correlation of the subscales with three personality measures of arousal, dogmatism and achievement motivation, and with grade point average ranged from -.37 to .26.

Author: Strom, B. et al.

Article: The course structure inventory: Discriminant and construct validity.

Journal: *Educational and Psychological Measurement*, Winter 1982, *42*(4), 1125-1133.

2736
Test name: CREECH MENTAL ILLNESS QUESTIONNAIRE

Purpose: To measure opinions and attitudes about mental illness.

Number of items: 64

Format: 6-point Likert format.

Reliability: Pretest reliability was .81 (Hoyt).

Author: Napoletano, M.A.

Article: Correlates of changes in attitudes towards mental illness among vocational nursing students.

Journal: *Psychological Reports*, 1981, *49*(1), 147-150.

Related research: Creech, S., 1977. Changes in attitudes about mental illness among nursing students following a psychiatric practicum. *Journal of Psychiatric Nursing and Mental Health Services*, 15, 9-14.

2737
Test name: DREAM QUESTIONNAIRE

Purpose: To measure attitudes to and experience of dreaming.

Number of items: 17

Format: Subjects respond to each item on a four-point scale from "never" to "always." All items are presented.

Validity: Correlation with the Harvard Group Scale of Hypnotic Susceptibility was .50.

Author: Gibson, H.B.

Article: Dreaming and hypnotic susceptibility: A pilot study.

Journal: *Perceptual and Motor Skills*, April 1985, *60*(2), 387-394.

Related research: Arkin, A.M. et al., (Ed.), 1978. *The mind in sleep: Psychology and Psychophysiology.* Hillside, N.J.: Erlbaum.
    Cohen, D.B., 1979. *Sleep and dreaming: Origins, nature and functions*. Oxford: Pergamon.
    Wolman, B.B. (Ed.), 1979. *Handbook on dreams*. New York: Van Nostrand.

2738
Test name: EDUCATIONAL ATTITUDES INVENTORY

Purpose: To identify the general content of teacher attitudes relative to the educational process.

Number of items: 34

Format: Responses from agree to disagree to each item were made on a 5-point scale. Includes four factors: affective, cognitive, directive, and interpretive.

Reliability: Split-half reliability coefficients ranged from .73 to .89.

Author: Bunting, C.E.

Article: Dimensionality of teacher education beliefs: An exploratory study.

Journal: *Journal of Experimental Education*, summer 1984, 52(4), 195-198.

Related research: Bunting, C.E., 1981. The development and validation of the educational attitudes inventory. *Educational and Psychological Measurement, 41,* 559-565.

2739
Test name: EDUCATION SCALE VII

Purpose: To measure traditional and progressive educational attitudes.

Number of items: 30

Format: 7-point agreement scale.

Reliability: Alpha ranged from .65 to .87.

Author: Borko, H. and Cadwell, J.

Article: Individual differences in teachers' decision strategies: An investigation of classroom organization and management decisions.

Journal: *Journal of Educational Psychology*, Aug. 1982, 74(4), 598-610.

Related research: Kerlinger, F.N. and Pedhazur, E.J., 1968. Educational attitudes and perceptions of desirable traits of teachers. *American Educational Research Journal*, 5, 543-559.

2740
Test name: ENJOYMENT OF MATHEMATICS SCALE

Purpose: To measure attitude toward mathematics.

Number of items: 11

Format: Employs a 5-point Likert-style format from 0 (strongly disagree) to 4 (strongly agree). All items are presented.

Reliability: Coefficient alpha was .88.

Validity: Correlations with other variables ranged from -.246 to .566.

Author: Watson, J.M.

Article: The Aiken attitude to mathematics scales: Psychometric data on reliability and discriminant validity.

Journal: *Educational and Psychological Measurement*, winter 1983, *43*(4), 1247-1253.

Related research: Aiken, L.R., 1974. Two scales of attitude toward mathematics. *Journal for Research in Mathematics Education*, 5, 67-71.

2741
Test name: ESTES READING ATTITUDE SCALE

Purpose: To measure attitudes toward reading.

Number of items: 20

Format: Likert-type items whereby students respond on a five-point scale ranging from strongly disagree to strongly agree.

Reliability: Coefficient alpha reliability indices ranged from .78 to .93.

Author: Plake, B.S. et al.

Article: The relationship of ethnic group membership to the measurement and meaning of attitudes towards reading: Implications for validity of test score interpretations.

Journal: *Educational and Psychological Measurement*, winter 1982, *42*(4), 1259-1267.

Related research: Estes, T.H., 1971. A scale to measure attitudes towards reading. *Journal of Reading*, *15*, 135-138.

2742
Test name: FEMALE ROLES QUESTIONNAIRE

Purpose: To measure attitudes toward female roles.

Number of items: 25

Format: 4-point Likert response categories. All items presented.

Reliability: Great Britain: Split-half = .92. Test-retest = .94. 20-item Dutch version: Test-retest = .92 (10 days).

Validity: Women in traditional occupations score lower than women in non-traditional occupations ($p < .04$). Discriminates between men and women with high school and elementary school educations (p ranged from .03 to .04).

Author: Hubbard, F.O.A et al.

Article: Validation of a questionnaire measuring attitudes toward females' social roles for a Dutch population.

Journal: *Psychological Reports*, 1982, *51*(2), 491-498.

Related research: Slade, P. and Jenner, F.A., 1978. Questionnaire measuring attitudes to female social roles. *Psychological Reports*, *43*, 351-354.

2743
Test name: FISCHER PRO-CON ATTITUDE SCALE

Purpose: To assess attitudes about seeking psychological help.

Format: 5-point Likert format.

Reliability: Test-retest range from .73 to .89 over 2 week to 2 month interval. Internal consistency = .86.

Validity: Seekers of help and non-seekers of help differ significantly (p < .001).

Author: Hall, L.E. and Tucker, C.M.

Article: Relationships between ethnicity, conceptions of mental illness, and attitudes associated with seeking psychological help.

Journal: *Psychological Reports*, Dec. 1985, *57*(3, I), 907-916.

Related research: Fischer, E.H. and Turner, J.L., 1972. Orientations to seeking professional psychological help. *Journal of Consulting and Clinical Psychology*, *30*, 70-74.

2744
Test name: FOREIGN LANGUAGE ATTITUDE SCALE

Purpose: To measure attitude toward foreign language.

Number of items: 22

Format: Subjects respond to items on a 5-point Likert scale. Examples are provided.

Reliability: Internal consistency reliability was approximately .90.

Validity: Correlations with other variables ranged from -.07 to .47.

Author: Raymond, M.R. and Roberts, D.M.

Article: Development and validation of a foreign language attitude scale.

Journal: *Educational and Psychological Measurement*, winter 1983, *43*(4), 1239-1246.

2745
Test name: GABLE-ROBERTS ATTITUDES TOWARD SCHOOL SUBJECTS

Purpose: To measure attitudes toward specified school subjects.

Number of items: 23

Format: Likert-type items responded to on a 5-point scale from "strongly agree" to "strongly disagree." Eleven items were written in a negative direction. All items are presented.

Reliability: Alpha reliabilities ranged from .59 to .94.

Author: Gable, R.K. and Roberts, A.D.

Article: An instrument to measure attitude toward school subjects.

Journal: *Educational and Psychological Measurement*, spring 1983, *43*(1), 289-293.

Related research: Remmers, H.H. (Ed.), 1960. *A scale to measure attitude toward any school subject.* Lafayette, Ind.: Purdue Research Foundation.

2746
Test name: GENDER ROLE ORIENTATION

Purpose: To measure traditional and nontraditional gender role attitudes.

Number of items: 10

Format: 7-point Likert format. Sample items presented.

Reliability: Alpha = .89.

Author: Hansen, G.

Article: Perceived threats and marital jealousy.

Journal: *Social Psychology Quarterly*, Sept. 1985, *48*(3), 262-268.

Related research: Brogan, D. and Kutner, N.G., 1976. Measuring sex-role orientation. *Journal of Marriage and the Family, 38*, 31-40.

2747
Test name: GENERAL ATTITUDE TO INSTITUTIONAL AUTHORITY SCALE (GAIAS)

Purpose: To measure attitude toward institutional authority.

Number of items: 16 (short form).

Format: Same format as 32-item full scale.

Reliability: Alpha = .89. Subscale alphas ranged from .62 to .82.

Validity: Correlates negatively with age (-.54) and positively with The Authority Behavior Inventory (.76). Not correlated with Ray's Directiveness Scale (.03).

Author: Rigby, K.

Article: Acceptance of authority and directiveness as indicators of authoritarianism: A new framework.

Journal: *Journal of Social Psychology*, April 1984, *122*(second half), 171-180.

2748
Test name: HETEROSEXUAL ATTITUDES TOWARD HOMOSEXUALITY SCALE

Purpose: To measure attitudes toward homosexuality.

Number of items: 20

Format: Likert format. Sample items presented.

Reliability: Item-total correlations ranged between .57 and .74. Split-half = .92.

Author: Nevid, J.S.

Article: Exposure to homoerotic stimuli: Effects on attitudes and affects of heterosexual viewers.

Journal: *Journal of Social Psychology*, April 1983, *119*(second half), 249-255.

Related research: Larsen, K.S. et al., 1980. Attitudes of heterosexuals toward homosexuality: A Likert-type scale and construct validity. *Journal of Sex Research, 16*, 245-257.

2749
Test name: HOMOSEXISM SCALE

Purpose: To measure prejudicial attitudes toward homosexuals.

Number of items: 53 (long form); 15 (short form).

Format: 5-point Likert format. Sample items presented.

Reliability: Alpha = .98 (long); Alpha = .96 (short).

Validity: Males score higher than females ($t = 1.85$, $p < .05$). Subjects who knew homosexuals score lower than those who did not ($t = 5.44$, $p < .001$).

Author: Hansen, G.L.

Article: Measuring prejudice against homosexuality (homosexism) among college students: A new scale.

Journal: *Journal of Social Psychology*, Aug. 1982, *117*(second half), 233-236.

2750
Test name: HOMOSEXISM SCALE—SHORT FORM

Purpose: To measure prejudicial attitudes towards homosexuals.

Number of items: 15

Format: Subjects respond on a 5-point scale from strongly agree to strongly disagree.

Reliability: Alpha reliability coefficient was .96.

Author: Hansen, G.L.

Article: Measuring prejudice against homosexuality

(homosexism) among college students: A new scale.

Journal: *Journal of Social Psychology*, Aug. 1982, *117*(second half), 233-236.

Related research: Lumby, M.E., 1976. Homophobia: The quest for a valid scale. *Journal of Homosexuality*, 2, 39-47.

2751
Test name: INFORMATION-PRIVACY VALUES, BELIEFS, AND ATTITUDES INTERVIEW SCHEDULE

Purpose: To obtain data concerning information-privacy values, information-privacy beliefs, information-privacy attitudes, information experiences, future intentions concerning information control activities, and demographic characteristics.

Number of items: 69 plus several demographic items.

Format: Generally responses were made on either a 7-point scale where 1=strongly disagree to 7=strongly agree, or on a "yes", "no" basis. Sample items are presented.

Reliability: Coefficient alphas ranged from .68 to .93.

Author: Stone, E.F. et al.

Article: A field experiment comparing information-privacy values, beliefs, and attitudes across several types of organizations.

Journal: *Journal of Applied Psychology*, Aug. 1983, *68*(3), 459-468.

Related research: Stone, E.F. et al., 1980. *Development of a measure to assess individuals' values, beliefs, and attitudes concerning control over personal information.* Unpublished manuscript, Purdue University.

2752
Test name: INVASION OF PRIVACY SCALE

Purpose: To measure attitudes toward invasion of privacy in employment situations.

Number of items: 5

Format: 5-point Likert format (strongly agree to strongly disagree).

Reliability: Alpha = .87.

Author: Tolchinsky, P.D. et al.

Article: Employee perceptions of invasion of privacy: A field simulation experiment.

Journal: *Journal of Applied Psychology*, June 1981, *66*(3), 308-313.

Related research: Ganster, D.C. et al., 1979. Information privacy in organizations: An examination of employee perceptions and attitudes. Proceedings of the 39th Annual Conference of the National Academy of Management, 262-266.

2753
Test name: INVENTORY OF CAREER ATTITUDES

Purpose: To measure perceived realism of career-planning beliefs.

Number of items: 28

Format: 5-point agreement scale.

Reliability: Alpha = .76.

Author: Pinkney, J.W. and Ramirez, M.

Article: Career-planning myths of Chicano students.

Journal: *Journal of College Student Personnel*, July 1985, 26(4), 300-305.

Related research: Woodrick, C.P., 1979. *The development and standardization of an attitude scale designed to measure myths held by college students.* Unpublished doctoral dissertation. Texas A&M University, Galveston.

2754
Test name: JOB ATTITUDE SURVEY

Purpose: To measure attitude towards supervisor, general management, work group, working conditions, pay, and locus of control.

Number of items: 47

Format: Likert-type format.

Reliability: Alpha = .84 (split-half).

Author: Kasperson, C.J.

Article: Locus of control and job satisfaction.

Journal: *Psychological Reports*, 1982, 50(3, part I), 823-826.

Related research: Smith, P. et al., 1969. *The measurement of satisfaction in work and retirement.* Chicago: Rand-McNally.

2755
Test name: KOGAN'S ATTITUDES TOWARD OLD PEOPLE SCALE

Purpose: To identify sentiments toward older persons.

Number of items: 17

Format: Items are matched positive-negative pairs of statements. Items include: residence, homogeneity, intergenerational relations, dependence, cognitive style, personal appearance, and power.

Reliability: Odd-even reliability coefficients ranged from .66 to .85.

Author: Finnerty-Fried, P.

Article: Instruments for the assessment of attitudes toward older persons.

Journal: *Measurement and Evaluation in Guidance*, Oct. 1982, *15*(3), 201-209.

Related research: Kogan, N.A., 1961. Attitudes toward old people: The development of a scale and an examination of correlates. *Journal of Abnormal and Social Psychology*, *62*, 44-54.

2756
Test name: LANGUAGE ATTITUDE SCALE

Purpose: To measure teachers' attitudes toward black English.

Number of items: 25

Format: 5-point Likert format.

Reliability: Alpha = .95. Item-total correlations ranged from .42 to .82.

Author: Taylor, J.B.

Article: Influence of speech variety on teachers' evaluation of reading comprehension.

Journal: *Journal of Educational Psychology*, Oct. 1983, *75*(5), 662-667.

Related research: Taylor, O., 1962. Teachers' attitudes toward black and nonstandard English as measured by the Language Attitude Scale. In R. Shuy and R. Fasold (Eds.), *Language attitudes: Current trends and prospects*. Washington, D.C.: Georgetown University Press.

2757
Test name: LEARNING ORIENTATION / GRADE ORIENTATION SCALE

Purpose: To measure learning and grade orientation in college students.

Number of items: 20

Format: Forced choice.

Reliability: Test-retest = .71 ($p < .001$).

Author: Meredith, G.M.

Article: Course- and instructor-related correlates of student's orientation toward grades and learning.

Journal: *Psychological Reports*, 1981, *49*(3), 794.

Related research: Eison, J.A., 1981. A new instrument for assessing student's orientations towards grades and learning. *Psychological Reports*, *48*, 919-924.

2758
Test name: LIBRARY ATTITUDE SCALE

Purpose: To indicate student attitudes toward the school library/librarian.

Number of items: 16

Format: Responses are made anonymously on a three-option scale (Yes, ?, No).

Reliability: Hoyt reliability index was .92.

Author: Schon, I. et al.

Article: A special motivational intervention program and junior high school students' library use and attitudes.

Journal: *Journal of Experimental Education*, winter 1984-1985, *53*(2), 97-101.

Related research: Schon, I. et al., 1984. The effects of a special school library program on elementary students' library use and attitudes. *School Library Media Quarterly*, *12*(3), 227-231.
    Davies, R.A., 1979. *The school library media center: Instructional force for excellence* (3rd ed.). New York: R.R. Bowker.

2759
Test name: MACHO SCALE

Purpose: To measure masculine attitudes.

Number of items: 18

Format: 5-point Likert format.

Reliability: Alpha = .89.

Author: Brinkerhoff, M.B. and Mackle, M.

Article: Religion and gender: A comparison of Canadian and American student attitudes.

Journal: *Journal of Marriage and the Family*, May 1985, *47*(2), 415-429.

Related research: Villemez, W.J. and Touhey, J.C., 1977. A measure of individual differences in sex stereotyping and sex discrimination: The "macho" scale. *Psychological Reports*, *41*, 411-415.

2760
Test name: MALE SEX-ROLE ATTITUDE SURVEY

Purpose: To assess male sex-role attitudes.

Number of items: 29

Format: Includes two scales: one focuses on traditional attitudes, the other emphasizes liberated attitudes. Responses are made on a 7-point scale from very strongly agree to very strongly disagree.

Reliability: Test-retest (3 weeks) correlations were .85 and .92.

Author: Fiebert, M.S. and Vera, W.

Article: Test-retest reliability of a male sex-role attitude survey: The traditional liberated content scale.

Journal: *Perceptual and Motor Skills,* Feb. 1985, *60*(1), 66.

Related research: Biggs, P. and Fiebert, M.S., 1984. A factor analytic examination of American male attitudes. *Journal of Psychology, 116*, 113-116.

2761
Test name: MATHEMATICS ATTITUDE SCALE

Purpose: To measure student attitudes toward mathematics.

Number of items: 24

Reliability: Alpha ranged between .50 and .91 across subscales.

Validity: Correlates significantly with arts and sciences grades and education grades, but not business and technology grades ($p < .05$). Significant r's ranged between .28 and .49.

Author: Gadzella, B.M. et al.

Article: Mathematics course grades and attitudes in mathematics for students enrolled in three university colleges.

Journal: *Psychological Reports,* Dec. 1985, *57*(3,I), 767-772.

Related research: Aiken, L.R. Attitudes toward mathematics and science in Iranian middle schools. *School Science and Mathematics, 79*, 229-234.

2762
Test name: MATHEMATICS ATTITUDE SCALE

Purpose: To measure student self-concept as a mathematician and opinion of mathematics.

Number of items: 14

Format: Likert items. Sample items presented.

Reliability: Alpha = .25.

Validity: Significantly associated with achievement as determined by F test ($p < .05$).

Author: Tsai, S-L and Walberg, H.J.

Article: Mathematics achievement and attitude productivity in junior high students.

Journal: *Journal of Educational Research,* May/June 1983, *76*(5), 267-272.

2763
Test name: MIKULECKY BEHAVIORAL READING ATTITUDE MEASURE

Purpose: To measure secondary and postsecondary respondents' attitudes toward reading.

Number of items: 20

Format: Response to each item is made on a scale of (1) "very unlike me" to (5) "very like me."

Reliability: Coefficient alpha for the total instrument was .89 (N = 411).

Author: Hawk, J.W. et al.

Article: The factor structure of the Mikulecky Behavioral Reading Attitude Measure.

Journal: *Educational and Psychological Measurement*, winter 1984, *44*(4), 1059-1065.

Related research: Mikulecky, L.J., 1976. *The developing, field testing, and initial norming of a secondary/adult level reading attitude measure that is behaviorally oriented and based on Krathwohl's taxonomy of the affective domain.* Unpublished doctoral dissertation, University of Wisconsin-Madison.

2764
Test name: MONEY ATTITUDE SCALE

Purpose: To measure money attitudes.

Number of items: 29

Format: Includes five factors: power-prestige, retention-time, distrust, quality, and anxiety. Subjects respond to each item on a 7-point, Likert-type scale. All items are presented.

Reliability: Coefficient alphas for total score and factors ranged from .69 to .80. Test-retest reliability coefficients ranged from .87 to .95 (5 weeks).

Validity: Correlations with related measures ranged from -.33 to .48.

Author: Yamauchi, K.T. and Templer, D.I.

Article: The development of a money attitude scale.

Journal: *Journal of Personality Assessment*, Oct. 1982, *46*(5), 522-528.

2765
Test name: MOVIE ATTITUDE SCALE

Purpose: To measure attitudes about motion pictures.

Number of items: 40

Format: 5-point response categories. Sample items presented.

Validity: Factor analysis revealed several dimensions, not one overall favorable/unfavorable dimension.

Author: Austin, B.A.

Article: A factor analytic study of attitudes toward motion pictures.

Journal: *Journal of Social Psychology*, Aug. 1982, *117*(second half), 211-217.

Related research: Bannerman, J. and Lewis, J.M., 1977. College students' attitudes toward movies. *Journal of Popular Film*, 6, 126-139.

2766
Test name: MULTIRACIAL ATTITUDE QUESTIONNAIRE (MAQ)

Purpose: To measure multiracial attitudes of teachers in five dimensions.

Format: Likert-type items.

Reliability: Alpha reliability ranged from .39 to .92 across dimensions.

Validity: Intercorrelation among the five dimensions ranged from .05 to .76. Correlations presented with several other instruments suggest considerable construct validity.

Author: Giles, M.B. and Sherman, T.M.

Article: Measurement of multiracial attitudes of teacher trainees.

Journal: *Journal of Educational Research*, March/April 1982, *75*(4), 204-209.

2767
Test name: NURSES ATTITUDES TOWARDS ARTHRITIS SCALE

Purpose: To measure nurses attitudes towards arthritis.

Number of items: 25

Format: 5-point Likert format.

Reliability: Alpha = .74.

Validity: Nurses who completed a clinical rotation in rheumatology scored more favorably than nurses who did not complete the rotation (F = 6.17, p < .02, DF = 1,103).

Author: Nambayan, A. et al.

Article: Scale for assessing nurses attitudes towards arthritis.

Journal: *Psychological Reports*, Aug. 1985, *57*(1), 57.

2768
Test name: PERCEPTIONS OF MEXICAN-AMERICANS SCALE

Purpose: To measure sixth-graders' attitudes toward and perceptions of Mexican-Americans.

Number of items: 24

Format: Responses were made on a three-point scale of "Yes," "?," and "No." Some examples are presented.

Reliability: Hoyt reliability estimates ranged from .86 to .92.

Validity: Correlation with teachers' ratings was .1.

Author: Schon, I. et al.

Article: The effects of special curricular study of Mexican culture on Anglo- and Mexican-American students' perceptions of Mexican-Americans.

Journal: *Journal of Experimental Education*, summer 1982, *50*(4), 215-218.

2769
Test name: PROCRASTINATION INVENTORY

Purpose: To assess subjects' attitudes about their procrastination.

Number of items: 36

Format: Includes two subscales: controllability and expectation to change. Subjects rated all items on a 7-point scale ranging from true to false. Examples are presented.

Reliability: Cronbach's alphas were .76 and .89.

Author: Lopez, F.G. and Wambach, C.A.

Article: Effects of paradoxical and self-control directives in counseling.

Journal: *Journal of Counseling Psychology*, March 1982, *29*(2), 115-124.

Related research: Strong, S. et al., 1979. Motivational and equipping functions of interpretation in counseling. *Journal of Counseling Psychology*, *26*, 98-107.

2770
Test name: PUNITIVENESS SCALE

Purpose: To measure punitiveness towards criminals.

Number of items: 12

Format: Likert-format. Sample items presented.

Reliability: Alpha ranged from .78 to .82.

Author: Ray, J.J.

Article: The punitive personality.

Journal: *Journal of Social Psychology*, June 1985, *125*(3), 329-333.

Related research: Ray, J.J., 1982. Prison sentence and public opinion. *Australian Quarterly*, *54*, 435-443.

2771
Test name: PUPIL CONTROL IDEOLOGY SCALE

Purpose: To measure beliefs and attitudes teachers have about pupil control.

Number of items: 20

Format: 5-point Likert-type items.

Reliability: Alpha = .89.

Author: Harris, K.R. et al.

Article: Teacher characteristics and stress.

Journal: *Journal of Educational Research*, July/Aug. 1985, 78(6), 346-350.

Related research: Willower, D.J., 1975. Some comments on inquiries on schools and student control. *Teachers' College Record*, 77, 32-59.

2772
Test name: RACIAL IDENTITY ATTITUDE SCALE

Purpose: To measure racial identity attitudes.

Number of items: 24

Format: Includes 4 subscales: pre-encounter, encounter, immersion-emersion, and internalization.

Reliability: Coefficient alphas ranged from .66 to .72.

Author: Parham, T.A. and Helms, J.E.

Article: The influence of black students' racial identity attitudes on preferences for counselor's race.

Journal: *Journal of Consulting Psychology*, May 1981, 28(3), 250-257.

Related research: Hall, W.S. et al., 1972. Stages in the development of black awareness: An exploratory investigation. In R.L. Jones (Ed.), *Black psychology*. New York: Harper & Row.

2773
Test name: RACIAL IDENTITY ATTITUDE SCALE

Purpose: To measure attitudes associated with various stages of black identity development.

Number of items: 30

Format: Includes four subscales: pre-encounter, encounter, immersion-emersion, and internalization.

Reliability: Internal consistency reliability coefficients ranged from .66 to .72.

Author: Parham, T.A. and Helms, J.E.

Article: Relation of racial identity attitudes to self-actualization and affective states of black students.

Journal: *Journal of Counseling Psychology*, July 1985, *32*(3), 431-440.

Related research: Parham, T.A. and Helms, J.E., 1981. The influence of black students' racial identity attitudes on preference for counselor's race. *Journal of Counseling Psychology, 28*, 250-256.

2774
Test name: RATIONAL BEHAVIOR INVENTORY—LOW READING LEVEL

Purpose: To measure the average degree and nature of rational beliefs.

Number of items: 37

Format: Designed for assessment of adolescents with mild to moderate reading difficulties who may require special education or counseling services.

Reliability: Cronbach's alpha was .82.

Validity: Correlation with Rosenberg Self-Esteem Scale was r = .30; with Buss-Durkee Hostility Inventory-Negativism Scale was r = -.24.

Author: Shorkey, C.T. and Saski, J.

Article: A low reading-level version of the Rational Behavior Inventory.

Journal: *Measurement and Evaluation in Guidance*, July 1983, *16*(2), 95-99.

2775
Test name: READING ATTITUDE SCALE

Purpose: To indicate student attitude toward reading.

Number of items: 17

Format: Responses are made anonymously on a three-option scale (Yes, ?, No).

Reliability: Hoyt reliability was .91.

Author: Schon, I. et al.

Article: A special motivational intervention program and junior high school students' library use and attitudes.

Journal: *Journal of Experimental Education*, winter 1984-1985, *53*(2), 97-101.

Related research: Schon, I. et al., 1984. The effects of a special school library program on elementary students' library use and attitudes. *School Library Media Quarterly, 12*(3), 227-231.

2776
Test name: RISK-TAKING INVENTORY

Purpose: To measure attitudes toward situations that involve tension, risk, and adventure.

Number of items: 38

Format: Yes, Doubtful, No response categories. Sample items presented.

Reliability: Alpha = .89. Split-half = .87. Test-retest = .90.

Validity: People with risky jobs score higher than people with no-risk jobs ($p < .05$).

Author: Keinan, G. et al.

Article: Measurement of risk takers' personality.

Journal: *Psychological Reports*, Aug. 1984, 55(1), 163-167.

2777
Test name: ROMANTIC ATTITUDES SCALES

Purpose: To measure romantic attitudes of university students.

Number of items: 84

Format: 5-point Likert response categories (very romantic to very unromantic). Sample items presented.

Reliability: Exceeded .90 on each of three subscales identified by a factor analysis.

Validity: Three factors extracted: traditional romance, sexual behavior, and routine activities.

Author: Prentice, D.S. et al.

Article: Romantic attitudes of American university students.

Journal: *Psychological Reports*, Dec. 1983, 53(3, Pt. I), 815-822.

2778
Test name: SCHOOL ATTITUDE SCALE

Purpose: To measure attitudes towards school.

Number of items: 8

Format: Agree-disagree format. Sample item presented.

Reliability: Cronbach's alpha = .74.

Author: Brader, P.K. et al.

Article: Further observations on the link between learning disabilities and juvenile delinquency.

Journal: *Journal of Educational Psychology*, Dec. 1981, 73(6), 838-850.

Related research: Educational Testing Service, 1971. *Michigan Assessment of Basic Skills, Form*

UMT, Book 2. Unpublished manuscript. E.T.S., Princeton, N.J.

2779
Test name: SCHOOL SENTIMENT INVENTORY

Purpose: To measure school attitudes.

Number of items: 37

Format: Includes five subscales: attitudes toward teachers, school subjects, school structure and climate, peers, and a general estimate of school attitudes. Responses are either "yes" or "no."

Reliability: Test-retest reliability was .87.

Author: Sloan, V.J. et al.

Article: A comparison of orientation methods for elementary school transfer students.

Journal: *Child Study Journal*, 1984, *14*(1), 47-60.

Related research: Frith, S. and Narikawa, D., 1972. *Measures of self-concept, grades K-12.* Los Angeles: Instructional Objectives Exchange.

2780
Test name: SEAT BELT SCALES

Purpose: To measure reported use and beliefs about seat belt use.

Number of items: 4 (reported use) and 14 (beliefs).

Format: Use items rated on a 7-point use scale ("not at all likely to use" to "very likely"). Belief items rated on a 7-point scale. Sample items presented.

Reliability: Alpha (use) = .93; Alpha (belief) = .80.

Validity: Use scale items all load on one factor. Belief items factor into three subscales (convenience, effectiveness, comfort).

Author: Jonah, B.A.

Article: Legislation and the prediction of reported seat belt use.

Journal: *Journal of Applied Psychology*, Aug. 1984, *69*(3), 401-407.

2781
Test name: SEX KNOWLEDGE AND ATTITUDE TEST

Purpose: To collect information about sexual attitudes, knowledge, degree of experience in a variety of sexual behaviors.

Number of items: 106

Format: Knowledge portion contains 71 true-false items, the attitude portion has 35 five-alternative Likert-type items.

Reliability: Internal consistency reliability (coefficient alpha) estimates for attitude scales from .68 to .86 and .87 for the knowledge scale.

Author: Smith, P. et al.

Article: Training teachers in human sexuality: Effect on attitude and knowledge.

Journal: *Psychological Reports*, April 1981, *48*(2), 527-530.

Related research: Lief, H.I. and Reed, D.M., 1970. *Sex knowledge and attitude test*. Philadelphia: Center for the Study of Sex Education in Medicine, Department of Psychiatry, University of Pennsylvania School of Medicine.
Miller, W.R. and Lief, H.I., 1979. The sex knowledge and attitude test. *Journal of Sex and Marital Counseling*, 5, 282-287.

2782
Test name: SEX-ROLE EGALITARIANISM SCALE

Purpose: To measure attitudes toward the equality of males and females.

Number of items: 95

Format: Includes five domains of adult living: marital roles, parental roles, employment roles, social-interpersonal-heterosexual roles, and educational roles. Responses are made on a 5-point Likert-type rating scale ranging from "strongly agree" to "strongly disagree." There are two forms. Examples are presented.

Reliability: Internal consistency estimates were .97 for both forms and ranged from .84 to .89 for the domains. Equivalence coefficient for the total score was .93 and ranged from .84 to .88 for the domains. Stability coefficients ranged from .81 to .91.

Author: King, D.W. and King, L.A.

Article: Measurement precision of the Sex-Role Egalitarianism Scale: A generalizability analysis.

Journal: *Educational and Psychological Measurement*, summer 1983, *43*(2) 435-447.

Related research: King, L.A. et al., 1981. A new measure of sex-role attitudes. Paper presented at the meeting of the Midwestern Psychological Association.

2783
Test name: SEX-ROLE ORIENTATION SCALE

Purpose: To identify sex-role orientation.

Number of items: 36

Format: Responses were made on a 5-point scale from strongly agree (1) to strongly disagree (5). High scores indicate more nontraditional attitudes toward sex roles. An example is presented.

Reliability: Alpha reliability was .95.

Author: Keith, P.M.

Article: Sex-role attitudes, family plans, and career orientations: Implications for counseling.

Journal: *Vocational Guidance Quarterly*, March 1981, *29*(3), 244-252.

Related research: Brogan, D. and Kutner, N., 1976. Measuring sex-role orientation: A normative approach. *Journal of Marriage and the Family*, *38*, 31-40.

2784
Test name: SITUATIONAL ATTITUDE SCALE—HANDICAPPED

Purpose: To measure attitudes toward handicapped.

Number of items: 100 (10 situations with 10 bipolar semantic differential scales).

Format: 5-point semantic differential (situations presented).

Reliability: Split-half reliability ranged between .67 and .90 across situations.

Author: Stovall, C. and Sedlacek, W.E.

Article: Attitudes of male and female university students toward students with different physical disabilities.

Journal: *Journal of College Student Personnel*, July 1983, *24*(4), 325-330.

Related research: Sedlacek, W.E. and Brooks, G.C., 1972. *Situational attitude scale (SAS Manual)*. Chicago: Natresources.

2785
Test name: SOCIAL INTERDEPENDENCE SCALE

Purpose: To measure teenagers attitudes toward cooperative, competitive, and individualistic learning situations.

Number of items: 22

Format: 7-point response categories.

Reliability: Alphas ranged from .84 to .97 across subscales.

Author: Norem-Hebeisen, A. et al.

Article: Predictors and concomitants of changes in drug use patterns among teenagers.

Journal: *Journal of Social Psychology*, Oct. 1984, *124*(first half), 43-50.

Related research: Johnson, D.W. and Norem-Hebeisen, A., 1977. Attitudes toward interdependence among persons and psychological health. *Psychological Reports, 109*, 253-261.

2786
Test name: STATISTICS ATTITUDE SURVEY

Purpose: To measure student attitudes toward statistics.

Number of items: 34

Format: At least one third of the items measure student success in solving statistics problems or success in understanding statistics concepts.

Reliability: Coefficient alpha values were approximately .94.

Author: Wise, S.L.

Article: The development and validation of a scale measuring attitudes toward statistics.

Journal: *Educational and Psychological Measurement*, summer 1985, *45*(2), 401-405.

Related research: Roberts, D.M. and Bilderback, E.W., 1980. Reliability and validity of a statistics attitude survey.

Educational and Psychological Measurement, 40, 235-238.

2787
Test name: STEREOTYPE SURVEY

Purpose: To measure attitudes toward the roles of males and females.

Number of items: 25

Format: Subjects answer "true" or "false" to each item. All items are presented.

Reliability: Kuder-Richardson formula 21 produced a coefficient of .88.

Validity: Correlation with the Attitude Toward Women Scale was .75 (N = 100).

Author: Wilson, J. and Daniel, R.

Article: The effects of a career-option workshop on social and vocational stereotypes.

Journal: *Vocational Guidance Quarterly*, June 1981, *29*(4), 341-349.

2788
Test name: STUDENT DEVELOPMENT INVENTORY

Purpose: To document college students' present attitudes and possible changes in attitudes associated with counseling, remediation, and general educational programs.

Number of items: 70

Format: Includes the following subscales: self-confidence in mathematics, enjoyment of mathematics, smooth communication, self-confidence with superiors, self-confidence with peers, self-confidence in writing, and enjoyment of writing. Responses are made on a 5-point scale from "almost always characteristic of me" (5) to "never characteristic of me" (1).

Reliability: Coefficient alphas for the seven subscales ranged from .82 to .93.

Author: Jackson, L.M. et al.

Article: Reliability and factorial validity of the Student Development Inventory.

Journal: *Educational and Psychological Measurement*, autumn 1985, *45*(3), 671-677.

Related research: Chickering, A.W., 1972. *Education and identity.* San Francisco: Jossey-Bass Publishers.

2789
Test name: STUDENT FEES AND SERVICES QUESTIONNAIRE

Purpose: To measure student attitudes about fees and services made available by fees.

Number of items: 31

Format: 3-point rating scale of importance. 2-point use scale (yes-no). 2-point provision scale (should provide-should not provide).

Reliability: Cronbach's alphas: usage (.75), importance (.95), provision (.93).

Author: Matross, R.

Article: An analysis of student attitudes toward cocurricular services and fees.

Journal: *Journal of College Student Personnel*, Sept. 1981, *22*(5), 424-428.

Related research: Matross, R. and Barnett, R., 1978. The 1978 survey on Twin Cities Campus student service fees. *Office for Student Affairs Research Bulletin*, *18*(10).

2790
Test name: SUBSTANCE-USE SCALE

Purpose: To measure attitudes toward substance use.

Number of items: 4 vignettes.

Format: 5-point Likert scale (strongly disapprove to strongly approve). All items presented.

Reliability: Alpha = .72. Item-to-scale correlations ranged between .72 and .76.

Author: Gary, L.E. and Berry, G.L.

Article: Some determinants of attitudes toward substance use in an urban ethnic community.

Journal: *Psychological Reports*, April 1984, *54*(2), 539-545.

Related research: Giovannoni, J.M. and Becerra, R.M., 1979. *Defining child abuse.* New York: Free Press.

2791
Test name: TEST ATTITUDE SURVEY

Purpose: To identify children's attitudes toward tests and the test-taking situation.

Number of items: 12

Format: Items were answered either "yes" or "no," indicating agreement or disagreement with the statement. Examples are presented.

Reliability: Kuder-Richardson 20 was .78 and .76.

Author: Scruggs, T.E. et al.

Article: Attitudes of behaviorally disordered students toward tests.

Journal: *Perceptual and Motor Skills*, April 1985, *60*(2), 467-470.

Related research: Taylor, C. and Scruggs, T.E., 1983. Research in progress: Improving the test-taking skills of LD and BD elementary students. *Exceptional Children*, *50*, 277.

2792
Test name: TEST ATTITUDE SURVEY

Purpose: To measure students' feelings toward tests.

Number of items: 22

Format: Responses to each item were "yes" or "no." Examples are presented.

Reliability: Kuder-Richardson 20 was .75.

Author: Tolfa, D. et al.

Article: Attitudes of behaviorally disordered students toward tests: A replication.

Journal: *Perceptual and Motor Skills*, Dec. 1985, *61*(3, Pt. 1), 963-966.

Related research: Scruggs, T.E. et al., 1985. Attitudes of behaviorally disordered students toward tests. *Perceptual and Motor Skills*, 60, 467-470.

2793
Test name: TEST OF SCIENCE RELATED ATTITUDES

Purpose: To measure science related attitudes.

Number of items: 70

Format: Includes seven scales.

Reliability: Subscale reliability (Cronbach's alpha) ranged from .68 to .91. Reliability for the whole test was .95.

Author: Schibeci, R.A. and McGaw, B.

Article: Empirical validation of the conceptual structure of a test of science-related attitudes.

Journal: *Educational and Psychological Measurement*, winter 1981, 41(4), 1195-1201.

Related research: Fraser, B.J., 1978. Development of a test of science-related attitudes. *Science Education*, 62, 509-515.

2794
Test name: TUTORING ATTITUDE QUESTIONNAIRE

Purpose: To measure attitudes toward tutoring.

Number of items: 24

Format: 9-point Likert format.

Reliability: Cronbach's alpha = .93 (internal consistency was .88 or above on three subscales).

Validity: Correlations between subscales ranged from .28 to .68.

Author: Bierman, K.L. and Furman, W.

Article: Effects of role and assignment rationale on attitudes formed during peer tutoring.

Journal: *Journal of Educational Psychology*, Feb. 1981, 73(1), 33-40.

2795
Test name: VALUE OF MATHEMATICS SCALE

Purpose: To measure attitude toward mathematics.

Number of items: 10

Format: Employs a 5-point Likert-style format from 0 (strongly disagree) to 4 (strongly agree). All items are presented.

Reliability: Coefficient alpha was .68.

Validity: Correlations with other variables ranged from -.016 to .146.

Author: Watson, J.M.

Article: The Aiken attitude to mathematics scales: Psychometric data on reliability and discriminant validity.

Journal: *Educational and Psychological Measurement*, winter 1983, *43*(4), 1247-1253.

Related research: Aiken, L.R., 1974. Two scales of attitude toward mathematics. *Journal for Research in Mathematics Education*, 5, 67-71.

2796
Test name: WOMEN AS MANAGERS SCALE

Purpose: To measure attitudes towards women as managers.

Number of items: 21

Format: 7-point rating scales (strongly agree to strongly disagree). Sample item presented.

Reliability: Alpha = .90.

Author: Beutell, N.J.

Article: Correlates of attitudes toward American women as managers.

Journal: *Journal of Social Psychology*, Oct. 1984, *124*(first half), 57-63.

Related research: Peters, L.H. et al., 1974. Women as Managers Scale (WAMS): A measure of attitudes toward women in management positions. *JSAS Cat. Selec. Do. in Psychology*, 27 (MS No. 585).

2797
Test name: WORK INVOLVEMENT ATTITUDE SCALES

Purpose: To measure work involvement.

Number of items: 16

Format: 5-point Likert format. All items presented.

Reliability: Alphas ranged from .68 and .81 across subscales.

Validity: Two of three subscales discriminate between subjects who select "same" or "different" employment areas.

Author: Jans, N.A.

Article: The nature and measurement of work involvement.

Journal: *Journal of Occupational Psychology*, March 1984, *55*(1), 57-67.

Related research: Saleh, S.D. and Hosek, J., 1976. Job involvement: concepts and measurement. *Academy of Management Journal*, *19*, 213-224.

2798

Test name: WORLD MINDEDNESS SCALE

Purpose: To measure attitude toward nations and tolerance toward foreigners.

Number of items: 32

Format: Likert-type. Sample items presented.

Reliability: Odd-even = .87 (corrected Spearman-Brown = .93). Test-retest = .93 (over 28 days).

Author: Crawford, J.C. and Lamb, C.W., Jr.

Article: Effect of worldmindedness among professional buyers upon their willingness to buy foreign products.

Journal: *Psychological Reports*, 1982, *50*(3, part 1), 859-862.

Related research: Sampson, D.L. and Smith, H.P., 1957. A scale to measure worldmindedness attitudes. *Journal of Social Psychology, 45*, 99-106.

BEHAVIOR

2799
Test name: ACHENBACH CHILD BEHAVIOR CHECKLIST

Purpose: To measure problem behavior in children.

Number of items: 118

Format: Checklist format.

Reliability: Inter-parent = .84; Intraclass = .98; Test-retest (1 week) = .95.

Author: Webster-Stratton, C.

Article: Randomized trial of two-parent programs for families with conduct-disordered children.

Journal: *Journal of Consulting and Clinical Psychology*, Aug. 1984, 52(4), 666-678.

Related research: Achenbach, T.M. and Edelbrock, C.S., 1981. Behavioral problems and competencies reported by parents of normal and disturbed children aged four through sixteen. *Monographs of the Society for Research in Child Development*, 46, 1-82.

2800
Test name: AGGRESSIVE ACT REPORT

Purpose: To measure subjects' experience with aggression.

Number of items: 303

Format: Items represent specific aggressive acts designed to sample 3 types of aggression: direct active physical aggression, direct active verbal aggression, and indirect physical aggression. Examples are presented.

Reliability: Cronbach's alpha was .97.

Validity: Correlations with Buss-Durkee Hostility-Guilt Inventory was .43 (N = 45).

Author: Driscoll, J.M.

Article: Effects of perceiver's experience with aggression on attributions about aggressors.

Journal: *Perceptual and Motor Skills*, June 1985, 60(3), 815-826.

Related research: Driscoll, J.M., 1982. Perception of an aggressive interaction as a function of the perceiver's aggression. *Perceptual and Motor Skills*, 54, 1123-1154.

2801
Test name: AGGRESSION, MOODINESS, LEARNING PROBLEMS SCALE (AML)

Purpose: To measure problems of aggression, moodiness, and learning of preschoolers as perceived by teachers.

Number of items: 11

Format: 5-point adjustment scale for each item.

Reliability: Test-retest ranged between .73 and .86 across subscales and ages of children.

Author: Handal, P.J. and Hopper, S.

Article: Relationship of sex, social class, and rural/urban locale to preschoolers' AML scores.

Journal: *Psychological Reports*, Dec. 1985, 57(3, I), 707-713.

Related research: Cowen, E.L. et al., 1973. The AML: A quick screening device for early identification of school adaptation. *American Journal of Community Psychology*, *1*, 12-35.

2802
Test name: ALCOHOL ABUSE SCALE OF THE PIPS

Purpose: To identify alcohol abusers.

Number of items: 12

Format: Yes-no. Sample items presented.

Validity: Scale correctly classified 88% of women and 82% of men as alcoholics or non-alcoholics.

Author: Vincent, K.R. and Williams, W.

Article: Alcohol abuse scale of the Psychological Inventory of Personality and Symptoms: A cross-validation.

Journal: *Psychological Reports*, Dec. 1985, 57(3, II), 1077-1078.

Related research: Vincent, K.R., 1985. The Psychological Inventory of Personality and Symptoms (PIPS): A new test of psychopathology based on DSM-III. *The Journal: Houston International Hospital*, *3*, 20-27.

2803
Test name: ASSERTIVE FRIEND CARTOON TEST

Purpose: To measure the ability to refuse.

Number of items: 4

Time required: 15 minutes.

Format: 4 prompting lines paired with empty word balloons respondents fill in. Sample measure for smoking marijuana presented.

Reliability: Inter-rater reliability .90 or greater.

Author: Bobo, J.K. et al.

Article: Assessment of refusal skill in minority youth.

Journal: *Psychological Reports*, Dec. 1985, 57(3, II), 1187-1191.

2804
Test name: ATTRIBUTION INTERFERENCE CODING SYSTEM

Purpose: To measure teachers' tendency to attribute cause of problem classroom behavior to students or to situation, or to both.

Number of items: 24 vignettes.

Format: Vignettes are short descriptions of problem behavior to which teachers respond by stating strategies they would use. All vignettes presented along with coding system.

Reliability: Percent exact agreement = 76%.

Author: Brophy, J.E. and Rohrkemper, M.M.

Article: The influence of problem ownership on teachers' perceptions and strategies for coping with problem students.

Journal: *Journal of Educational Psychology*, June 1981, 73(3), 295-311.

Related research: Rohrkemper, M.M. and Brophy, J.E., 1979. *Classroom strategy study: Investigating teacher strategies with problem students.* (Research series No. 50.) Institute for Research on Teaching, Michigan State University.

2805
Test name: AUTHORITY BEHAVIOR INVENTORY (ABI)

Purpose: To measure behavior relating to acceptance of authority.

Number of items: 16

Format: Score 1 (never) to 5 (very frequently). Sample items presented.

Reliability: Alpha = .78.

Validity: Correlated .76 with General Attitude to Institutional Authority Scale. Correlated -.11 with Ray Directiveness Scale.

Author: Rigby, K.

Article: Acceptance of authority and directiveness as indicators of authoritarianism: A new framework.

Journal: *Journal of Social Psychology*, April 1984, 122(second half), 171-180.

2806
Test name: AUTONOMY-CONTROL SCALE

Purpose: To measure role autonomy-control in children and adolescents.

Number of items: 14 childhood and 16 adolescence items.

Format: Five-point scale form. Items taken from existing scales.

Reliability: Test-retest = .91 (two month, new sample, N = 41).

Validity: Significant correlations found between autonomy-control scores and separate family ratings (N = 50).

Author: DeMan, A.F.

Article: Autonomy-control variation in child-rearing and self-image disparity in young adults.

Journal: *Psychological Reports*, Dec. 1982, *51*(3, II), 1039-1044.

Related research: Koch, H.L. et al., 1934. A scale for measuring attitudes toward the question of childrens' freedom. *Child Development*, 5, 253-266.
Itkin, W., 1982. Some relationships between intra-family attitudes and pre-parental attitudes toward children. *Journal of Genetic Psychology*, *112*, 71-78.

2807
Test name: BEHAVIOR PROBLEM CHECKLIST

Purpose: To assess problem behavior.

Number of items: 55

Format: Informed observers check problems they observe in the subject.

Reliability: Test-retest ranged from .79 to .83. Inter-rater reliability ranged from .67 to .78.

Author: Szapocznik, J. et al.

Article: Conjoint versus one-person family therapy: Some evidence for the effectiveness of conducting family therapy through one person.

Journal: *Journal of Consulting and Clinical Psychology*, Dec. 1983, *51*(6), 889-899.

Related research: Quay, H.C. and Peterson, D.R., 1979. *Behavior Problem Checklist*. Graduate School of Applied and Professional Psychology, Rutgers State University.

2808
Test name: BEHAVIOR RATING INDEX FOR CHILDREN

Purpose: To provide a prothetic measure of children's behavior problems.

Number of items: 13

Format: Each item is rated on a 5-point Likert-type scale from 1 (rarely or never) to 5 (most or all of the time). All items are presented.

Reliability: Coefficient alphas ranged from .60 to .86. Test-retest reliability ranged from .50 to .89. Intraclass correlation coefficients ranged from .71 to .92.

Validity: Correlation with the Child Behavior Checklist r = .76.

Author: Stiffman, A.R. et al.

Article: A brief measure of children's behavior problems: The Behavior Rating Index for Children.

Journal: *Measurement and Evaluation in Counseling and Development*, July 1984, *17*(2), 83-90.

2809
Test name: BEHAVIORAL INDECISION SCALE

Purpose: To measure behavioral indecision.

Number of items: 22

Format: Thurstone format.

Reliability: Cronbach's alpha = .66; Test-retest = .57.

Validity: Correlates .62 with Career Decision Scale; .59 with Identity Scale; .27 with A-State Anxiety; .35 with A-Trait Anxiety; and .13 with Locus of Control.

Author: Fuqua, D.R. and Hartman, B.W.

Article: A behavioral index of career indecision for college students.

Journal: *Journal of College Student Personnel*, Nov. 1983, *24*(6), 507-512.

2810
Test name: BEHAVIORAL RATING SCALES

Purpose: To measure duration, intimacy, and nonverbal affective behavior in dyads and triads.

Number of items: 9

Format: Observer-coders rate interaction on 9 behaviors. All items presented.

Reliability: Ranged between r = .75 and r = .90 across subscales.

Author: Solano, C.H. and Dunnam, M.

Article: Two's company: Self-disclosure and reciprocity in triads versus dyads.

Journal: *Social Psychology Quarterly*, June 1985, *48*(2), 183-187.

Related research: Taylor, R.B. et al., 1979. Sharing secrets: Disclosure and discretion in dyads and triads. *Journal of Personality and Social Psychology*, 37, 1196-1203.

2811
Test name: BEHAVIORAL STYLE QUESTIONNAIRE

Purpose: To assess children's temperament or behavioral style.

Number of items: 100

Format: Parents rate their child on a 6-point scale. Includes three factors: 1) Intensity of affective expression such as intensity, mood, activity, and threshold; 2) flexibility-rigidity such as adaptability, persistence, and distractability; and 3) approach-withdrawal such as that dimension, activity, persistence, and sensory thresholds.

Validity: Correlations with neonatal noncrying movements per hour ranged from .04 to .30; Correlations with neonatal median amplitude of movements per day ranged from .01 to .09.

Author: Korner, A.F. et al.

Article: The relation between neonatal and later activity and temperament.

Journal: *Child Development*, Feb. 1985, 56(1), 38-42.

Related research: McDevitt, S.C. and Carey, W.B., 1978. The measurement of temperament in 3 to 7 year old children. *Journal of Child Psychology and Psychiatry, 19,* 245-253.

Field, T. and Greenberg, R., 1982. Temperament ratings by parents and teachers of infants, toddlers and preschool children. *Child Development, 53*(1), 160-163.

2812
Test name: BODY SENSATIONS QUESTIONNAIRE

Purpose: To measure body sensation associated with autonomic arousal.

Number of items: 17

Format: 5-point scale.

Reliability: Item-total ranged from .44 to .79 in agoraphobic sample and from -.09 to .88 in normal sample.

Validity: Correlates .36 with Beck Depression Inventory; Correlates .21 with Trait Anxiety - STAI; Correlates .67 with Agoraphobic Cognition.

Author: Chambliss, D.L. et al.

Article: Assessment of fear in agoraphobics: The Body Sensations Questionnaire and the Agoraphobic Cognitions Questionnaire.

Journal: *Journal of Consulting and Clinical Psychology*, Dec. 1984, 52(6), 1090-1097.

2813
Test name: BULIMIA TEST

Purpose: To measure symptoms of bulimia.

Number of items: 32

Format: Self-report, multiple-choice format. All items presented.

Reliability: Test-retest = .87 (p < .0001).

Validity: Correlates .82 (point-biserial) with bulimic and control group subjects; Correlates .93 with binge scale and .68 with the EAT scale (Garner and Garfinkel, 1979).

Author: Smith, M.C. and Thelen, M.H.

Article: Development and validation of a test for bulimia.

Journal: *Journal of Clinical and Consulting Psychology*, Oct. 1984, *52*(5), 863-872.

2814
Test name: CAREER ACTIVITIES SURVEY

Purpose: To assess information-seeking activities.

Number of items: 30

Format: A behavioral checklist.

Reliability: Coefficient alpha was .64.

Author: Robbins, S.B. et al.

Article: Attrition behavior before career development workshops.

Journal: *Journal of Counseling Psychology*, April 1985, *32*(2), 232-238.

Related research: Miller, M., 1982. Interest pattern structure and personality characteristics of clients who seek career information. *Vocational Guidance Quarterly*, *31*, 28-35.

2815
Test name: CHILD ABUSE POTENTIAL INVENTORY

Purpose: To screen individuals suspected of abuse.

Number of items: 160

Format: Forced-choice format.

Reliability: KR-20 ranged from .92 to .96; Test-retest = .94 (one day) and .90 (one week).

Author: Ellis, R.H. and Milner, J.S.

Article: Child abuse and locus of control.

Journal: *Psychological Reports*, April 1981, *48*(2), 507-510.

Related research: Milner, J.S. and Wimberly, R.C., 1979. An inventory for the identification of child abusers. *Journal of Clinical Psychology, 35,* 95-100.

2816
Test name: CHILD BEHAVIOR PROFILE—TEACHER VERSION

Purpose: To obtain teachers' reports of problem behavior of children.

Number of items: 118

Format: 5- and 7-point rating scales. Sample item presented.

Reliability: Test-retest = .89; 2-4 month stability ranged from .64 to .77.

Author: Edelbrock, C. and Achenbach, T.M.

Article: The teacher version of the Child Behavior Profile: I. Boys aged 6-11.

Journal: *Journal of Consulting and Clinical Psychology,* April 1984, 52(1), 207-217.

Related research: Achenbach, T.M. and Edelbrock, C., The Child Behavior Profile: II. Boys aged 12-16 and girls aged 6-11 and 12-16. *Journal of Consulting and Clinical Psychology, 47,* 223-233.

2817
Test name: CHILD TEMPERAMENT QUESTIONNAIRE

Purpose: To measure child behavior in an educational setting.

Number of items: 23

Format: 6-point Likert format.

Validity: LISREL revealed the same three temperament variables across 5 grade levels.

Author: Cadwell, J. and Pullis, M.

Article: Assessing changes in the meaning of children's behavior: Factorial invariance of teachers' temperament ratings.

Journal: *Journal of Educational Psychology,* Aug. 1983, 75(4), 553-560.

Related research: Keogh, B.K. et al., 1982. A short form of the Teacher Temperament Questionnaire. *Journal of Educational Measurement, 19,* 323-329.

2818
Test name: CHILDREN'S COERCIVE BEHAVIOR SCALE

Purpose: To measure coercive behavior in children.

Number of items: 16

Format: Observed behavior recorded as a rate per minute for child, mother, and father. All items presented are taken from Toobert, et al., MOSAIC.

Reliability: Inter-observer agreement ranged from .57 to .75.

Author: Loeber, R. and Dishion, T.J.

Article: Boys who fight at home and school: Family conditions influencing cross-setting consistency.

Journal: *Journal of Consulting and Clinical Psychology*, Oct. 1984, *52*(5), 759-768.

Related research: Toobert, D.J. et al., 1980. *Measure of social adjustment in children: MOSAIC*, Unpublished manuscript.

2819
Test name: CHILDREN'S DRUG-USE SURVEY

Purpose: To measure drug-use of children.

Number of items: 16

Format: How often, when, and where alcohol, marijuana, and inhalants are used is asked.

Reliability: Internal consistency ranged from .87 to .94.

Validity: Item clusters correlated positively.

Author: Oetting, E.R.

Article: Reliability and discriminant validity of the Children's Drug-Use Survey.

Journal: *Psychological Reports*, June 1985, *56*(3), 751-756.

2820
Test name: CLASSROOM ADJUSTMENT RATING SCALE

Purpose: To measure problem classroom behaviors.

Number of items: 41

Format: 5-point severity scale.

Validity: Test-retest exceeds .85 on all subscales.

Author: Weissberg, R.P. et al.

Article: The primary mental health project: Seven consecutive years of program outcome research.

Journal: *Journal of Consulting and Clinical Psychology*, Feb. 1983, *51*(1), 100-107.

Related research: Lorion, R.P. et al., 1975. Normative and parametric analyses of school maladjustment. *American Journal of Community Psychology*, *3*, 293-301.

2821
Test name: CLASSROOM BEHAVIOR OBSERVATION

Purpose: To measure behavior of LD children and nondisabled children in six categories: inattentive behavior, off-task verbalizations/vocalizations; nonacademic/nondisruptive behavior; impulse behavior; disruptive behavior; inappropriate location of activities.

Time required: Observations made at 10-second intervals for 6 minutes.

Reliability: Inter-observer agreements ranged from 79% to 100%. Stability coefficients ranged from .43 to 1.00.

Validity: Behaviors supplied by teachers of LD children.

Author: Gettinger, M. and Fayne, H.R.

Article: Classroom behavior during small group instruction and learning performance in learning disabled and nondisabled children.

Journal: *Journal of Educational Research*, Jan./Feb. 1982, 75(3), 182-187.

Related research: Brophy, J.E. et al., 1975. Classroom observation scales: Stability across time and context and relationships with student learning gains. *Journal of Educational Psychology, 67,* 873-881.

2822
Test name: CLASSROOM INAPPROPRIATE BEHAVIOR SCALE

Purpose: To measure inappropriate classroom behavior.

Number of items: 8

Format: Raters observe classroom in 30-minute sessions, divided into 10-second intervals. (8 seconds observation, 2 seconds recording.)

Reliability: Inter-rater reliability = 82-99% (median 94%).

Author: Witt, J.C. and Elliott, S.N.

Article: The response cost lottery: A time efficient and effective classroom intervention.

Journal: *Journal of School Psychology*, 1982, 20(2), 155-161.

Related research: Madsen, C.H. et al., 1968. Rules, praise and ignoring: Elements of elementary classroom control. *Journal of Applied Behavior Analysis, 1,* 139-150.

2823
Test name: CLASSROOM INTERACTION ANALYSIS

Purpose: To assess patterns of action in classrooms between students and teachers.

Number of items: 47

Format: The 47 items are grouped into 5 major categories (types) of interaction that trained raters observe on tapescripts. All items presented.

Reliability: Inter-rater reliability ranged from 95 to 99 percent.

Author: Thomas, E.C. and Holcomb, H.

Article: Nurturing productive thinking in able students.

Journal: *Journal of General Psychology,* Jan. 1981, *104*(first half), 67-79.

Related research: Aschner, M.J. et al., 1965. *A system for classifying thought processes in the context of classroom verbal interaction*, Unpublished manuscript, University of Illinois, Urbana.

2824
Test name: CODE FOR INSTRUCTIONAL STRUCTURE AND STUDENT ACADEMIC RESPONSE

Purpose: To measure behavior of students.

Number of items: 53 events in 6 areas.

Time required: 10 seconds for 3 areas.

Format: Behavior recorded on code sheets.

Reliability: Inter-observer agreement exceeded 85%.

Author: Thurlow, M. et al.

Article: Student reading during reading class: The lost activity in reading instruction.

Journal: *Journal of Educational Research*, May/June 1984, 77(5), 267-272.

Related research: Greenwood, C.R. et al., 1978. *Code for instructional structure and student academic response: CISSAR.* Kansas City, KS: Juniper Gardens Children's Project, Bureau of Child Research, University of Kansas.

2825
Test name: COMBAT EXPOSURE SCALE

Purpose: To measure combat involvement from hospital records of veterans' military experience.

Number of items: 7

Format: Guttman. All items presented.

Reliability: Coefficient of reproducibility = .93.

Validity: Correlated .86 with Egendorf et al., Combat Scale.

Author: Foy, D.W. et al.

Article: Etiology of post-traumatic stress disorder in Vietnam veterans: Analysis of premilitary, military and combat exposure influences.

Journal: *Journal of Consulting and Clinical Psychology*, Feb. 1984, 52(1), 79-87.

2826
Test name: COMPETITION KNOWLEDGE TEST

Purpose: To measure competitive behavior.

Number of items: 60

Format: Multiple-choice test. All items are presented.

Reliability: Internal consistency, split-half was .89 (N = 178). Test-retest was .88 (N = 130).

Author: Kildea, A.E.

Article: The Competition Knowledge Test.

Journal: *Perceptual and Motor Skills*, April 1985, 60(2), 477-478.

Related research: Kildea, A.E. and Kukulka, G., 1984. Reliability of the Competition Knowledge Test. *Psychological Reports*, 54, 957-958.

2827
Test name: CONNERS TEACHER RATING SCALE

Purpose: To screen for hyperactivity in children.

Number of items: 39

Reliability: Alphas ranged from .61 to .94 across subscales (all but one alpha was below .76).

Validity: Coefficients of congruence of factor structure ranged from .42 to .91 across studies; from .86 to .99 across whole vs. random half and across random half samples.

Author: Trites, R.L. et al.

Article: Factor analysis of the Conners Teacher Rating Scale based on a large normative sample.

Journal: *Journal of Consulting and Clinical Psychology*, Oct. 1982, 50(5), 615-623.

Related research: Conners, C.K., 1969. A teacher rating scale for use in drug studies with children. *American Journal of Psychiatry*, 126, 884-888.

2828
Test name: CONNERS TEACHER RATING SCALE—REVISED

Purpose: To enable teachers to rate pupils' classroom behavior.

Number of items: 28

Format: Includes 3 subscales: conduct problems, hyperactivity, and inattentive-passive. Also 5 miscellaneous items were included.

Reliability: Intraclass reliability coefficient was .758.

Author: Conger, A.J. et al.

Article: A generalizability study of the Conners Teacher Rating Scale—revised.

Journal: *Educational and Psychological Measurement*, winter 1983, *43*(4), 1019-1031.

Related research: Goyette, C.H. et al., 1978. Normative data on revised Conners parent and teacher rating scales. *Journal of Abnormal Child Psychology*, *6*, 221-238.

2829
Test name: CONSUMPTION EXPERIENCES SCALE

Purpose: To assess what kinds of activities are approached in terms of cause and effect, involvement, escape, or learning experience.

Number of items: 14

Format: Checklist format.

Reliability: KR-20 ranged from .71 to .77 across subscales.

Author: Hirschman, E.C.

Article: Sexual identity and the acquisition of rational, absorbing, escapist and modelling experiences.

Journal: *Journal of Social Psychology*, Feb. 1985, *125*(1), 63-73.

Related research: Swanson, G.E., 1978. Travels through inner space: Family structure and openness to absorbing experience. *American Journal of Sociology*, *83*, 890-919.

Tellegren, A. and Atkinson, B., 1974. Openness to absorbing and self-altering experiences. *Journal of Abnormal Psychology*, *38*, 268-277.

Hirschman, E.C., 1983. On the acquisition of aesthetic, escapist and agentic experiences. *Empirical Studies of the Arts*, *1*, 153-168.

2830
Test name: COPING STRATEGIES INVENTORY

Purpose: To measure cognitive and behavioral strategies people use to confront stressful situations.

Number of items: 76

Format: 5-point Likert format.

Reliability: Cronbach's alpha ranged from .76 to .93 across subscales.

Author: Ritchey, K.M. et al.

Article: Problem-solving appraisal versus hypothetical problem solving.

Journal: *Psychological Reports*, Dec. 1984, *55*(3), 815-818.

Related research: Tobin, D.L. et al., 1982. *The assessment of coping: Psychometric development of the coping strategies inventory.* Unpublished manuscript, Ohio University, Athens, OH.

2831
Test name: DAILY CHILD BEHAVIOR CHECKLIST

Purpose: To assess child behavior problems initially and to serve as a measure of change that occurs with treatment.

Number of items: 65

Format: A checklist containing pleasing and displeasing behaviors. All items are presented.

Reliability: Test-retest (2 weeks) correlations ranged from -.189 to .665.

Validity: Correlations with the Parent Attitude Test ranged from -.855 to .581.

Author: Furey, W. and Forehand, R.

Article: The Daily Child Behavior Checklist.

Journal: *Journal of Behavioral Assessment*, June 1983, *5*(2), 83-95.

2832
Test name: DELINQUENCY SCALES

Purpose: To measure delinquency through self-report.

Number of items: 31

Format: 6-point frequency scales.

Reliability: Alpha ranged from .52 to .78 across subscales.

Author: McCarthy, J.D. and Hoge, D.R.

Article: The dynamics of self-esteem and delinquency.

Journal: *American Journal of Sociology*, Sept. 1984, *90*(2), 396-400.

Related research: Short, J.F. and Nye, E.I., 1957. Reported behavior as a criterion of deviant behavior. *Social Problems*, *5*, 207-213.

2833
Test name: DISORDERED EATING TEST

Purpose: To measure disordered eating.

Number of items: 10

Format: True-false. Sample item presented.

Reliability: Cronbach's alpha = .70.

Validity: Correlated .60 with shortened version of the Eating Attitude Test.

Author: Segal, S.A. and Figley, C.R.

Article: Bulimia: Estimate of incidence and relationship to shyness.

Journal: *Journal of College Student Personnel*, May 1985, *26*(3), 240-244.

Related research: Garner, D.M. and Garfinkel, P.E., 1979. The Eating Attitude Test: An index of the symptoms of anorexia nervosa. *Psychological Medicine, 9*, 273-281.

2834
Test name: FUNCTIONAL BEHAVIOR SURVEY

Purpose: To provide a behavior rating scale of mental impairment.

Number of items: 20

Format: Instrument is completed by two independent observers. Each item is rated on a 5-point scale from 1 (hardly ever) to 5 (nearly always). All items are presented.

Validity: Correlations with: Competence Index was -.65; Impairment Index was -.78; Memory Check was .71.

Author: Tobacyk, J. et al.

Article: Two brief measures for assessing mental competence in the elderly.

Journal: *Journal of Personality Assessment*, Dec. 1983, *47*(6), 648-655.

Related research: Dixon, J.C., 1965. Cognitive structure in senile conditions with some suggestions for developing a brief screening test of mental status. *Journal of Gerontology, 20*, 41-49.

2835
Test name: HEALTH AND DAILY LIVING FORM

Purpose: To assess health status.

Number of items: 38

Format: Consists of three lists: medical conditions, physical symptoms, and medications. Subjects check whether each item in each list was experienced during the past 12 months.

Reliability: Cronbach's alphas ranged from .30 to .80.

Validity: Correlations with loneliness scores ranged from -.04 to .54.

Author: Schmitt, J.P. and Kurdek, L.A.

Article: Age and gender differences in and personality correlates of loneliness in different relationships.

Journal: *Journal of Personality Assessment*, Oct. 1985, *49*(5), 485-496.

Related research: Moos, R.H. et al., 1983. *The Health and Daily Living Form Manual*, Unpublished manuscript, Stanford University.

2836
Test name: HOLISTIC LIVING INVENTORY

Purpose: To measure frequency of activities that indicate a holistic style of life.

Number of items: 20

Format: Multiple-choice. Sample items presented.

Reliability: Split-half ranged from .08 to .91 across subscales.

Validity: Non-alcoholics score higher than alcoholics on physical scale. People without medical problems score higher than those with none and exercisers score higher than non-exercisers (all p < .01).

Author: Stoudenomice, J. et al.

Article: Validation of a Holistic Living Inventory.

Journal: *Psychological Reports*, Aug. 1985, *57*(1), 303-311.

2837
Test name: HOLT INTIMACY DEVELOPMENT INVENTORY

Purpose: To measure behaviors in closest relationships.

Number of items: 66

Format: Likert type.

Reliability: Guilford's R ranged from .67 to .84 across three subscales.

Author: Prager, K.J.

Article: Development of intimacy in young adults: A multidimensional view.

Journal: *Psychological Reports*, June 1983, *52*(3), 751-756.

Related research: Holt, M.L., 1977. *Human intimacy in young adults: An experimental development scale.* Unpublished doctoral dissertation. University of Georgia.

2838
Test name: IJR BEHAVIOR CHECKLIST FOR PARENTS, TEACHERS AND CLINICIANS

Purpose: To measure behavior syndromes for diagnostic evaluations.

Number of items: 597

Time required: One month for parent and teacher form. Single interview for clinician.

Format: Frequency rating scale for each item.

Reliability: Alpha ranged from .66 to .90 across subscales and across forms.

Author: Lessing, E.E. et al.

Article: Parallel forms of the IJR Behavior Checklist for Parents, Teachers and Clinicians.

Journal: *Journal of Consulting and Clinical Psychology*, Feb. 1981, *49*(1), 34-50.

Related research: Lessing, E.E. et al., 1973. Differentiating children's symptoms checklist items on the basis of the judged severity of psychopathology. *Genetic Psychology Monographs*, 88, 329-350.

2839
Test name: ILLNESS BEHAVIOR INVENTORY

Purpose: To provide a self-report measure of illness behavior.

Number of items: 20

Format: Responses are made to each item on a 6-point Likert scale ranging from strong agreement to strong disagreement. Includes two dimensions: work-related illness behavior and social illness behavior. All items are presented.

Reliability: Coefficient alphas were .88 and .89. Test-retest (2 weeks) reliability coefficients for each item ranged from .82 to 1.00 (N = 32).

Validity: Correlations with other illness behavior measures ranged from .32 to .48. Predictive validity coefficients ranged from .30 to .38 (N = 63).

Author: Turkat, I.D. and Pettegrew, L.S.

Article: Development and validation of the Illness Behavior Inventory.

Journal: *Journal of Behavioral Assessment*, March 1983, *5*(1), 35-47.

2840
Test name: INFANT BEHAVIOR QUESTIONNAIRE

Purpose: To provide an assessment of infant temperament.

Number of items: 87

Format: Includes 6 scales: activity level, smiling and laughter, fear, distress of limitations, soothability, duration of orienting.

Reliability: Coefficient alpha ranged from .67 to .85.

Author: Rothbart, M.K.

Article: Measurement of temperament in infancy.

Journal: *Child Development*, June 1981, 52(2), 569-578.

Related research: Thomas, A. et al., 1963. *Behavioral individuality in early childhood.* New York: New York University Press.

2841
Test name: INGRATIATION TACTICS SCALE

Purpose: To measure extent of use of ingratiating behavior by self report.

Number of items: 35

Format: 5-point response categories (completely true to completely false). Sample items presented.

Reliability: Alphas ranged from .46 to .76 across subscales.

Author: Bohra, K.A. and Pandey, J.

Article: Ingratiation toward strangers, friends, and bosses.

Journal: *Journal of Social Psychology*, April 1984, 122(second half), 217-222.

Related research: Bohra, K.A., 1981. *The effects of social power, need dimension and incentive on ingratiation.* Ph.D. Thesis, University of Allahabad, India.

2842
Test name: INITIATING STRUCTURE SCALE

Purpose: To measure a supervisor's behavior to initiate structured activity.

Number of items: 10

Format: Items given. Response categories not given, but would appear to be Likert-type scales. Items taken from the Leadership Behavior Description Questionnaire Form XII.

Reliability: .87.

Author: Markham, S.E. and Scott, K.D.

Article: A component factor analysis of the Initiating Structure Scale of the Leadership Behavior Description Questionnaire.

Journal: *Psychological Reports*, 1983, 52(1), 71-77.

Related research: Schriesheim, C. and Stogdill, R., 1975. Differences in factor structure across three versions of the Ohio State Leadership Scales. *Personnel Psychology*, 28, 189-206.

2843
Test name: LEADER BEHAVIOR DESCRIPTION SCALE

Purpose: To provide a behavior description.

Number of items: 27

Format: Response to each item is made on an 8-point scale from "very true of him" to "not at all true of him." Some examples are given.

Reliability: Cronbach's alpha was .91.

Validity: Correlations with other scales ranged from .38 to .75.

Author: Vecchio, R.P.

Article: A further test of leadership effects due to between-group variation and within-group variation.

Journal: *Journal of Applied Psychology*, April 1982, *67*(2), 200-208.

Related research: Rice, R.W. and Chemers, M.M., 1975. Personality and situational determinants of leader behavior. *Journal of Applied Psychology*, *60*, 20-27.

2844
Test name: LEADERSHIP INVENTORY

Purpose: To measure leadership characteristics of elementary and secondary gifted students.

Number of items: 19

Format: 4-point Likert categories.

Reliability: .69 when items reduced to 18 by Spearman-Brown formula. Guttman split-half = .68.

Author: Chauvin, J.C. and Karnes, F.A.

Article: Reliability of a leadership inventory used with gifted students.

Journal: *Psychological Reports*, Dec. 1982, *51*(3, I), 770.

Related research: Stacy, M., 1979. *Leadership inventory*, Yakima, WA: Yakima Public Schools.

2845
Test name: LEADERSHIP STYLE SCALE

Purpose: To measure executives' perception of their own leadership styles.

Number of items: 45

Format: 5-point Likert format. Sample items presented.

Reliability: Split-half ranged from .67 to .75 across subscales.

Validity: Authoritarian subscale correlated .27 with nurtrant task subscale and -.18 with participative subscale. Participative and nurtrant subscales correlated .88 (all p < .05).

Author: Sinha, J.B.P and Ghowdhary, G.P.

Article: Perception of subordinates as a moderator of leadership effectiveness in India.

Journal: *Journal of Social Psychology*, Feb. 1981, *113*(first half), 115-121.

2846
Test name: LIE SCALE

Purpose: To detect lying on Child Abuse Potential Inventory.

Number of items: 18

Format: Agree-disagree. All items presented.

Reliability: KR-20 ranged from .64 to .79.

Validity: No significant correlations between the lie scale and the abuse scales.

Author: Milner, J.S.

Article: Development of a lie scale for the Child Abuse Potential Inventory.

Journal: *Psychological Reports*, 1982, *50*(3, I), 871-874.

Related research: Milner, J.S., 1980. *The Child Abuse Inventory: Manual*. Webster, NC: Psytec Corp.

2847
Test name: MAZE TEST

Purpose: To measure stimulus-seeking behavior.

Number of items: 5 presentations of a maze.

Format: Paper-and-pencil maze presented five times. Contains no blind alleys and all routes are of equal distance from start to goal. Score is based upon number of different traversions from preceding traversions.

Reliability: Cronbach's alpha was .81.

Validity: Correlations with which-to-discuss test was -.06.

Author: Silverstein, A.B. et al.

Article: Psychometric properties of two measures of intrinsic motivation.

Journal: *Perceptual and Motor Skills*, Oct. 1981, *53*(2), 655-658.

Related research: Howard, K.I., 1961. A test of stimulus-seeking behavior. *Perceptual and Motor Skills*, *13*, 416.

2848
Test name: MOTION SICKNESS QUESTIONNAIRE

Purpose: To measure susceptibility to motion sickness.

Number of items: 5

Format: The entire questionnaire is presented.

Reliability: Test-retest correlations were .81 and .65.

Validity: Correlation with number of chair rotations was r = -.45.

Author: Mirabile, C.S., Jr. and Ford, M.R.

Article: A clinically useful polling technique for assessing susceptibility to motion sickness.

Journal: *Perceptual and Motor Skills*, June 1982, 54(3, I), 987-991.

2849
Test name: MULTI-ALCOHOLIC PERSONALITY INVENTORY SCALE

Purpose: To measure alcohol dependency.

Number of items: 20

Format: A paper-and-pencil, self-report questionnaire involving yes and no responses. Includes four factors: drinking pattern, psychological, stress, personality. All items are presented.

Reliability: Test-retest (2 weeks) reliability coefficients ranged from .89 to .95. Alpha coefficient was .95.

Validity: Concurrent validity established by means of the two group discriminant function in which alcoholics' overall mean was 14.29 and that of non-alcoholics was 2.10, the difference being significant beyond the 0.001 level.

Author: Kim, Y.C.

Article: Development of a behavioral scale via factor analysis.

Journal: *Journal of Experimental Education*, spring 1984, 52(3), 163-167.

2850
Test name: NOISE SENSITIVITY SCALE

Purpose: To measure general reactivity to noise among college students.

Number of items: 21

Format: Responses are made on a 6-point scale ranging from agree strongly (1) to disagree strongly (6).

Reliability: Kuder-Richardson reliability ranged from .84 to .87. Test-retest (9 weeks) reliability was .75 (N = 72). Cronbach's alpha = .76 (N = 150).

Author: Topf, M.

Article: Personal and environmental predictors of patient disturbance due to hospital noise.

Journal: *Journal of Applied Psychology*, Feb. 1985, *70*(1), 22-28.

Related research: Weinstein, N., 1978. Individual differences in reactions to noise: A longitudinal study in a college dormitory. *Journal of Applied Psychology, 63*, 458-466.

2851
Test name: ORGANIZATIONAL CITIZENSHIP BEHAVIOR SCALE

Purpose: To measure helpful but not necessarily required employee behavior.

Number of items: 16

Format: Employees are rated in 16 behaviors on a 5-point scale. All items presented.

Reliability: Alpha ranged from .85 to .88 across two subscales (factors).

Validity: Two factors, altruism and generalized compliance, identified by factor analysis (oblique rotation). Factors correlate .43.

Author: Smith, C.A. et al.

Article: Organizational citizenship behavior: Its nature and antecedents.

Journal: *Journal of Applied Psychology*, Nov. 1983, *68*(4), 653-663.

2852
Test name: OVEREXCITABILITY QUESTIONNAIRE

Purpose: To assess five forms of overexcitability.

Number of items: 21

Format: Subjects' responses to each item written at their leisure were rated independently by two raters using a scale of intensity from 0 (no overexcitability) to 3 (rich and intense expression).

Reliability: Inter-rater correlation coefficients ranged from .60 to .95.

Author: Piechowski, M.M. et al.

Article: Comparison of intellectually and artistically gifted on five dimensions of mental functioning.

Journal: *Perceptual and Motor Skills*, April 1985, *60*(2), 539-549.

Related research: Lysy, K.Z. and Piechowski, M.M., 1983. Personal growth: An empirical study using Jungian and Dabrowskian measures. *Genetic Psychology Monographs, 108*, 267-320.

2853
Test name: OZAWA BEHAVIORAL RATING SCALE

Purpose: To assess attention deficit disorder (DSM III) in learning disabled children.

Number of items: 15

Format: Employs a Likert-format whereby each item is assigned a value of 1 (optimal attentive behavior) to 5 (optimal inattentive behavior). The test provides 3 scores: impulsivity, distractability, and total score. Examples are presented.

Reliability: Coefficient alpha was .952 (N = 52).

Validity: Correlations with the WISC-R and the Matching Familiar Figures Test ranged from .18 to .50.

Author: Ozawa, J.P. and Michael, W.B.

Article: The concurrent validity of a behavioral rating scale for assessing attention deficit disorder (DSM III) in learning disabled children.

Journal: *Educational and Psychological Measurement*, summer 1983, *43*(2), 623-632.

2854
Test name: PAIN BEHAVIOR SCALE

Purpose: To provide a scale for rating pain behavior.

Number of items: 10

Format: Items include: verbal, nonverbal, downtime, grimace, posture, mobility, body language, equipment use, stationary movement, medications. Items are rated 0 (none), 1/2 (occasional), or 1 (frequent).

Reliability: 3 trained raters produced inter-rater reliabilities ranging from .94-.96. Test-retest reliability over 2 consecutive days was .89.

Author: Feuerstein, M. et al.

Article: The Pain Behavior Scale: Modification and validation for outpatient use.

Journal: *Journal of Psychopathology and Behavioral Assessment*, Dec. 1985, *7*(4), 301-305.

Related research: Richards, J.S. et al., 1982. Assessing pain behavior: The UAB pain behavior scale. *Pain*, *14*, 393-398.

2855
Test name: PARENTAL BEHAVIOR SCALE

Purpose: To assess maternal and grandmaternal child-rearing activity.

Number of items: 30

Format: Includes four parental behaviors: supporting, demanding, controlling, and punishing. Examples are presented.

Reliability: Mean internal consistency for all subscales was .63. Mean factor-score reliability was .76.

Author: Wilson, M.N.

Article: Mothers' and grandmothers' perceptions of parental behavior in three-generational black families.

Journal: *Child Development*, Aug. 1984, 55(4), 1333-1339.

Related research: Devereux, E.C. et al., 1969. Child-rearing in England and the United States: A cross-national campaign. *Journal of Marriage and Family, 31*, 257-270.

2856
Test name: PARENT CHECKLIST OF CHILD BEHAVIOR

Purpose: To rate behaviors of children during the prior month.

Number of items: 53

Format: "Never true" to "always true" response categories.

Reliability: Alphas ranged from .58 to .83 over subscales. Total alpha = .88.

Author: Hodges, W.F. et al.

Article: The cumulative effect of stress on preschool children of divorced and intact families.

Journal: *Journal of Marriage and the Family*, Aug. 1984, 46(3), 611-617.

Related research: Hodges, W.F. et al., 1983. Parent-child relationships and adjustment in preschool children in divorced and intact families. *Journal of Divorce, 7*, 43-58.

2857
Test name: PEDIATRIC PAIN QUESTIONNAIRE

Purpose: To elicit children's description of pain.

Number of items: 45

Format: All items are presented. Items include short answer responses.

Reliability: Test-retest (72-hour time span, N = 97 children grades 4 to 7) produced 70% agreement between first and second sets of responses.

Author: Tesler, M. et al.

Article: Developing an instrument for eliciting children's description of pain.

Journal: *Perceptual and Motor Skills*, Feb. 1983, 56(1), 315-321.

Related research: Melzack, R., 1975. The McGill questionnaire: Major properties and scoring methods. *Pain, 1*, 277-299.

2858

Test name: PEJORATIVE EPITHET SCALE

Purpose: To measure the aggressiveness and frequency of aggressive use of epithets.

Number of items: 316

Format: Subjects were to indicate how much aggression a word implied if used against them and how often it has been used in general (on T.V., in print media, and so on).

Reliability: Repeated words = .95 (p < .01) (correlation between first and second ratings).

Validity: Aggressiveness and frequency of use ratings correlated .59 (p < .001).

Author: Driscoll, J.M.

Article: Aggressiveness and frequency of aggressive-use ratings for pejorative epithets by Americans.

Journal: *Journal of Social Psychology*, June 1981, *114*(first half), 111-126.

2859

Test name: PERCEPTIONS OF STUDENT MISBEHAVIOR SCALE

Purpose: To measure perceived reasons for student problem behavior.

Number of items: 26

Format: Likert-type response categories for each of 26 reasons (very important to not important). All items presented.

Reliability: Inter-judge reliability of 26 reasons: 87.6%.

Author: Guttman, J.

Article: Pupils', teachers', and parents' causal attributions for problem behavior at school.

Journal: *Journal of Educational Research*, Sept./Oct. 1982, *76*(1), 14-21.

Related research: Weiner, B. (Ed.), 1974. *Achievement motivation and attribution theory.* Morristown, NJ: General Learning Press.

2860

Test name: PHYSICAL HEALTH LOG

Purpose: To measure frequency and duration of acute and chronic physical illness by self-report.

Number of items: 45

Format: Persons asked how many episodes of 28 diseases they experienced and how long they lasted (over past 12 months).

Reliability: Test-retest ranged between .66 and .91 for various items.

Validity: No sex differences in reliabilities were found.

Author: Blotcky, A.D. et al.

Article: Reliability of retrospective self-reports of physical illness.

Journal: *Psychological Reports*, Feb. 1984, *54*(1), 179-182.

2861
Test name: PLAY BEHAVIORS OBSERVATION SYSTEM

Purpose: To measure play behaviors in children.

Number of items: 8

Format: Eight cognitive play categories (all described) are rated by trained observers.

Reliability: Inter-observer agreement per 30 second time units ranged from .74 to 1.00 (mean = .90; median = .88).

Author: Rooparine, J.L.

Article: Peer play interaction in a mixed-age preschool setting.

Journal: *Journal of General Psychology*, April 1981, *101*(second half), 161-166.

Related research: Parten, M.B., 1932. Social participation among preschool children. *Journal of Abnormal and Social Psychology*, 1932, *27*, 243-269.

Smilansky, S., 1975. *The effects of sociodramatic play on disadvantaged preschool children.* New York: Wiley.

2862
Test name: PLAY REPORT

Purpose: To measure the degree of social complexity present in play choices.

Number of items: 4

Format: For each question, two play choices were requested and the children were to circle with whom they played, i.e., by themselves, with grownups, with friends, or on a team. All items are presented.

Reliability: Ranged from .43 to .88 (boys) and .24 to .77 (girls).

Validity: .75 (boys) and .64 (girls).

Author: Sleet, D.A.

Article: Differences in the social complexity of children's play choices.

Journal: *Perceptual and Motor Skills*, Feb. 1985, *60*(1), 283-287.

Related research: Seagoe, M.V., 1970. An instrument for the analysis of children's play as an index of degree of socialization. *Journal of School Psychology, 8,* 139-143.

2863
Test name: PRACTICAL TRAINING OBSERVATION SCHEDULE

Purpose: To measure behavior of instructors and trainees in the metalworking industry.

Number of items: 18 (behavior categories).

Format: Behavior coded on observation sheet in linear time structure. All items presented. Code sheet illustrated.

Reliability: Inter-observer agreement: π = .91.

Author: Jungermann, H. et al.

Article: Observation of interaction in practical training.

Journal: *Journal of Occupational Psychology,* Dec. 1981, *54*(4), 233-245.

Related research: Flanders, N.A., 1970. *Analyzing teaching behavior.* Reading, MA: Addison-Wesley.

2864
Test name: PREVENTIVE HEALTH BEHAVIOR INVENTORY

Purpose: To assess extent of preventive health care behavior.

Number of items: 41 behaviors.

Format: 5-point frequency scale (always to never).

Reliability: KR-20 = .79. Test-retest (3-day interval) = .84.

Author: Price, J.H. et al.

Article: Preventive health behaviors related to the ten leading causes of mortality of health-fair attenders and non-attenders.

Journal: *Psychological Reports,* Feb. 1985, *56*(1), 131-135.

Related research: Baur, K.G. and Wilson, R.W., 1981. The challenge of prevention: Are America's greatest health burdens avoidable? *HCFA Forum,* 5, 16-25.

2865
Test name: PROBLEM BEHAVIOR RATING SCALE

Purpose: To assess teachers' perceptions of problem classroom behavior.

Number of items: 20

Format: 5-point rating scale. All items presented.

Reliability: Alpha = .80.

Author: Safran, S.P. and Safran, J.S.

Article: Classroom context and teachers' perceptions of problem behaviors.

Journal: *Journal of Educational Psychology*, Feb. 1985, 77(1), 20-28.

Related research: Gropper, G. et al., 1968. Training teachers to recognize and manage social and emotional problems in the classroom. *Journal of Teacher Education*, 19, 477-485.

2866
Test name: PROBLEM INVENTORY FOR ADOLESCENT GIRLS

Purpose: To measure the competence of the behavior of adolescent girls.

Number of items: 52

Format: Subjects respond to 52 situations by explaining what they would do. Raters then judge the competence of the response on a 5-point scale. Sample situations presented.

Reliability: Inter-rater alphas .70 or larger.

Validity: Classified 85 percent of subjects into delinquent/non-delinquent categories.

Author: Gaffney, L.R. and McFall, R.M.

Article: A comparison of social skills in delinquent and non-delinquent girls using a behavioral role-playing inventory.

Journal: *Journal of Consulting and Clinical Psychology*, Dec. 1981, 49(6), 959-967.

2867
Test name: PROCEDURE BEHAVIOR CHECKLIST

Purpose: To assess behavioral manifestations of pain.

Number of items: 8

Format: Each behavior is rated by observers on a 1-5 scale of pain severity. All categories presented.

Reliability: Inter-rater correlations ranged from .16 to .86 across pain types and three time periods. Of 9 total correlations only one was non-significant ($p < .05$ or $p < .01$).

Author: LeBaron, S. and Zeltzer, L.

Article: Assessment of acute pain and anxiety in children and adolescents by self-reports, observer reports, and a behavior checklist.

Journal: *Journal of Consulting and Clinical Psychology*, Oct. 1984, 52(5), 729-738.

Related research: Katz, E.R. et al., 1981. Behavioral distress in children with cancer undergoing medical procedures: Developmental considerations. *Journal of Consulting and Clinical Psychology*, 49, 470-471.

2868
Test name: PROCRASTINATION LOG

Purpose: To measure clients' perceptions of their current levels of procrastination, their effort to change, and their satisfaction with those levels.

Number of items: 22

Format: Includes 4 scales: procrastination behavior, procrastination satisfaction, effort to change, and effort satisfaction. Responses were made on 7-point scales.

Reliability: Test-retest reliabilities ranged from .50 to .62. Internal consistency reliabilities ranged from .63 to .78.

Author: Claiborn, C.D. et al.

Article: Effects of congruence between counselor interpretations and client beliefs.

Journal: *Journal of Counseling Psychology*, March 1981, 28(2), 101-109.

Related research: Strong, S.R. et al., 1979. Motivational and equipping functions of interpretation in counseling. *Journal of Counseling Psychology*, 26, 98-107.

2869
Test name: PROCRASTINATION LOG

Purpose: To measure procrastination behavior and satisfaction with that behavior.

Number of items: 11

Format: Self-report form including two subscales.

Reliability: Internal consistency reliabilities were .63 and .77.

Author: Damstreegt, D.C. and Christofferson, J.

Article: Objective self-awareness as a variable in counseling process and outcome.

Journal: *Journal of Counseling Psychology*, July 1982, 29(4), 421-424.

Related research: Strong, S.R. et al., 1979. Motivational and equipping functions of interpretation in counseling. *Journal of Counseling Psychology*, 26, 98-107.

2870
Test name: PUPIL RATING FORM

Purpose: To measure behavior and personality of students by quantifying information in school records.

Time required: 15 minutes.

Format: Teachers rate 28 dimensions on a 1-to-5 rating scale.

Reliability: Test-retest ranged from .63 to .95 (median = .84). Inter-judge reliability ranged from .41 to .82 (median = .70).

Validity: Correlations with observational data ranged from .26 to .69 (median = .48).

Author: Watt, N.F. et al.

Article: Social, emotional and intellectual behavior at school among children at high risk for schizophrenia.

Journal: *Journal of Consulting and Clinical Psychology*, April 1982, 50(2), 171-181.

Related research: Watt, N.F. et al., 1970. School adjustment and behavior of children hospitalized for schizophrenia as adults. *American Journal of Orthopsychiatry*, 40, 637-657.

2871
Test name: RATIONAL BEHAVIOR INVENTORY

Purpose: To measure the rationality-irrationality continuum.

Number of items: 37

Format: Agreement or disagreement indicated on a 5-point scale.

Reliability: Correlation between pre- and posttest scores ranged between .32 and .69 (ten-week interval).

Author: Thyer, B.A. et al.

Article: Cognitive belief systems and their persistence: Test-retest reliability of the Rational Behavior Inventory.

Journal: *Psychological Reports*, Dec. 1983, 53(3, Pt. I), 915-918.

Related research: Shorkey, C. and Whiteman, V., 1977. Development of the Rational Behavior Inventory: Initial validity and reliability. *Educational and Psychological Measurement*, 37, 527-534.

2872
Test name: SCHOOL LEADERSHIP INVENTORY

Purpose: To measure leadership styles in schools.

Number of items: 20

Format: Multiple-choice.

Reliability: Split-half = .89.

Author: Cummings, O.W. and Nall, R.L.

Article: Counselor burnout and school leadership style: A connection.

Journal: *The School Counselor*, Jan. 1982, *29*(3), 190-195.

Related research: Likert, R., 1967. *The human organization: Its management and value.* New York: McGraw-Hill.

2873
Test name: SELF-CONTROL SCHEDULE

Purpose: To measure learned resourcefulness.

Number of items: 36

Format: 6-point self-rating scale.

Reliability: Test-retest (4 weeks) = .96; Alpha ranged from .78 to .86.

Author: Rosenbaum, M. and Palmon, N.

Article: Helplessness and resourcefulness in coping with epilepsy.

Journal: *Journal of Consulting and Clinical Psychology*, April 1984, *52*(2), 244-253.

Related research: Rosenbaum, M., 1980. A schedule for assessing self-control behaviors: Preliminary findings. *Behavior Therapy, 11,* 109-121.

2874
Test name: SELF REPORT DELINQUENCY SCALE

Purpose: To measure delinquency.

Number of items: 6

Format: Open-ended frequency scales. All items presented.

Reliability: Alpha = .78.

Author: Hagan, J. et al.

Article: The class structure of gender and delinquency: Toward a power-control theory of common delinquent behavior.

Journal: *American Journal of Sociology*, May 1986, *90*(3), 1151-1178.

Related research: Hirschi, T., 1969. *Causes of delinquency.* Berkeley and Los Angeles: University of California Press.

2875
Test name: SEXUAL EXPERIENCES SURVEY

Purpose: To measure sexual aggression and victimization.

Number of items: 10

Format: Yes-no format.

Reliability: Alpha = .74 (female); .89 (male). Test-retest agreement over two weeks was 93%.

Validity: Self-report correlated .73 (female) with report to an interviewer; Male correlation was .61 (both p < .01).

Author: Koss, M.P. and Gidycz, C.A.

Article: Sexual experiences survey: Reliability and validity.

Journal: *Journal of Consulting and Clinical Psychology*, June 1985, 53(3), 422-423.

Related research: Koss, M.P. and Oros, C.J., 1982. The sexual experiences survey: A research instrument for investigating sexual aggression and victimization. *Journal of Consulting and Clinical Psychology*, 50: 455-457.

2876
Test name: SEXUAL FANTASY QUESTIONNAIRE

Purpose: To measure intensity of sexual fantasies.

Number of items: 34

Format: Frequency indicated in Likert-type format: occasion of fantasy indicated by noting masturbation or intercourse. Items presented.

Reliability: Cronbach's alpha = .79; Test-retest (2-day interval) = .84.

Author: Price, J.H. and Miller, P.A.

Article: Sexual fantasies of black and of white college students.

Journal: *Psychological Reports*, June 1984, 54(3), 1007-1014.

Related research: Shanor, K., 1977. *The fantasy files.* New York: Times Books.

2877
Test name: SLEEP QUESTIONNAIRE

Purpose: To provide a subjective assessment of sleep.

Number of items: 55

Format: Includes 7 factors: depth of sleep, difficulties in waking up, quality and latency of sleep, negative-affect dreams, length of sleep, dream recall and vividness, and sleep irregularity. Responses are made on a 5-point Likert scale. Sample items are presented.

Reliability: Test-retest (10 weeks) reliability coefficients ranged from .68 to .96 (N = 45); Cronbach's alpha ranged from .53 to .88 (N = 88).

Author: Domino, G. et al.

Article: Subjective assessment of sleep by sleep questionnaire.

Journal: *Perceptual and Motor Skills*, Aug. 1984, *59*(1), 163-170.

Related research: Domino, G. and Fogl, A., 1980. Sleep patterns in college students. *Psychology*, *17*, 7-14.

2878
Test name: STONY BROOK SCALE

Purpose: To assess hyperactivity and aggression in hyperactive children.

Number of items: 92

Format: Judges use 5- or 6-point scale to rate children.

Validity: Correlations between the Stony Brook Scale and the Connors Teacher-Rating Scale and Peterson-Quay Behavior Problem Checklist confirm validity through factor structure of responses on the latter two scales.

Author: O'Leary, S. and Steen, P.L.

Article: Subcategorizing hyperactivity: The Stony Brook Scale.

Journal: *Journal of Consulting and Clinical Psychology*, June 1982, *50*(3), 426-432.

Related research: Loney, J. et al., 1978. An empirical basis for subgrouping the hyperkinetic/minimal brain dysfunction syndrome. *Journal of Abnormal Psychology*, *87*, 431-441.

2879
Test name: STUDENT ACTIVIST SCALE

Purpose: To measure activist behavior.

Number of items: 3

Format: Guttman.

Reliability: Reproducibility .90 or greater. Scalability .60 or greater.

Author: Green, J.J. et al.

Article: College activism reassessed: The development of activists and non-activists from successive cohorts.

Journal: *Journal of Social Psychology*, Oct. 1984, *124*(first half), 105-113.

2880
Test name: STUDENT BEHAVIOR OBSERVATION INSTRUMENT

Purpose: To measure types of behavior in classrooms.

Number of items: 19

Format: Behavior recorded for one student at a time for 6 minutes over 10 days. Procedure involved 5 seconds of observation and 7 seconds of recording.

Reliability: Cohen's Kappa = .91.

Author: Howe, A.C. et al.

Article: Pupil behaviors and interactions in desegregated urban junior high activity-centered science classrooms.

Journal: *Journal of Educational Psychology*, Feb. 1985, 75(1), 97-103.

Related research: Power, C.N. and Tisher, R.P., 1974. *Interaction patterns and their relationship with outcomes in Australian science education project classrooms*. Paper presented at the annual meeting of the National Association for Research in Science Teaching, Chicago, April.

2881
Test name: STUDENT BEHAVIORS QUESTIONNAIRE

Purpose: To measure desirability of student behavior as assessed by faculty members.

Number of items: 57

Format: 5-point Likert response categories. All items presented.

Reliability: Internal consistency = .81.

Author: Brozo, W.G. and Schmelzer, R.V.

Article: Faculty perceptions of student behaviors: A comparison of two universities.

Journal: *Journal of College Student Personnel*, May 1985, 26(3), 229-234.

Related research: Williams, V.G. and Winkworth, J.M., 1974. The faculty looks at student behaviors. *Journal of College Student Personnel*, 15, 305-310.

2882
Test name: STUDENT OBSERVATION FORM

Purpose: To measure observed student behavior in the classroom.

Number of items: 5 variables each with 2 to 7 categories.

Time required: 55-second observation cycles.

Format: 10 observations per subject per 55-minute class period. Coded variables are presented.

Reliability: Inter-rater reliability = .78.

Author: Seifert, E.H. and Beck, J.J., Jr.

Article: Relationships between task time and learning gains in secondary schools.

Journal: *Journal of Educational Research*, Sept./Oct. 1984, 78(1), 5-10.

2883
Test name: STUDY SKILLS QUESTIONNAIRE

Purpose: To measure time management, concentration, listening, note-taking, text-reading, and test preparation.

Number of items: 36

Format: Respondents asked to indicate how representative an item is of their behavior. Sample items presented.

Reliability: Test-retest (over 2 weeks) = .82 (N = 72).

Author: Scott, K.J. and Robbins, S.B.

Article: Goal instability: Implications for academic performance among students in learning skills courses.

Journal: *Journal of College Student Personnel*, March 1985, 26(2), 129-133.

Related research: Kochenour, E. et al., 1983. Developing a model of academic success: An empirical analysis. Paper presented at the American College Personnel Association Convention, Houston, March.

2884
Test name: SUPPORTIVE LEADERSHIP BEHAVIOR SCALE

Purpose: To measure leader supportiveness.

Number of items: 17

Format: Includes 10 items from Form XII of the Ohio State Leader Behavior Description Questionnaire and 7 items pertaining to other leader behavior dimensions.

Reliability: Coefficient alpha was .86.

Validity: Correlations with other variables ranged from -.33 to .26.

Author: Smith, C.A. et al.

Article: Organizational citizenship behavior: Its nature and antecedents.

Journal: *Journal of Applied Psychology*, Nov. 1983, 68(4), 653-663.

Related research: House, R.J. and Dressler, G., 1974. The path-goal theory of leadership: Some post hoc and a priori test. In J.G. Hunt and L.L. Larson (Eds.), *Contingency approaches to leadership*. Carbondale: Southern Illinois University Press.

2885
Test name: SURVEY OF HETEROSOCIAL INTERACTIONS

Purpose: To measure approach behavior.

Number of items: 20

Format: Taps interactive ability in specific heterosexual-social situations.

Validity: Correlations with Heterosocial Assessment Inventory for Women ranged from .51 to .78.

Author: Kolko, D.J.

Article: The Heterosocial Assessment Inventory for Women: A psychometric and behavioral evaluation.

Journal: *Journal of Psychopathology and Behavioral Assessment*, March 1985, 7(1), 49-64.

Related research: Twentyman, C.T. and McFall, R.M., 1975. Behavioral training of social skills in shy males. *Journal of Consulting and Clinical Psychology*, 43, 384-395.

2886
Test name: SUSTAINING FANTASY QUESTIONNAIRE—SHORT FORM

Purpose: To measure sustaining functions of fantasies.

Number of items: 88

Format: Includes 10 factors: aesthetics, use of God, power and revenge, admiration of self, dying and illness, withdrawal and protection, love and closeness, suffering, competition, restitution. Responses to each item are made on a 5-point Likert-scale from 1 (hardly at all) to 5 (extremely). All items are presented.

Reliability: Cronbach's alpha for each scale ranged from .67 to .90.

Validity: Correlations with MMPI scores ranged from -.33 to .52.

Author: Zelin, M.L. et al.

Article: The Sustaining Fantasy Questionnaire: Measurement of sustaining functions of fantasies in psychiatric inpatients.

Journal: *Journal of Personality Assessment*, Aug. 1983, 47(4), 427-439.

2887
Test name: TEACHER BEHAVIOR SCALE

Purpose: To measure teacher classroom behavior.

Number of items: 19

Time required: 80 minutes (10 8-minute periods).

Format: 8 minutes of observation in 10-second blocks. Examples of behavior presented for all 19 behaviors.

Reliability: Number of agreement/total agreement + disagreements = .79.

Author: Hoskins, R. et al.

Article: Teacher and student behavior in high and low ability groups.

Journal: *Journal of Educational Psychology*, Dec. 1983, *75*(6), 865-876.

2888
Test name: TEACHER CLASSROOM BEHAVIOR SCALE

Purpose: To measure anger, praise, instruction-giving, and encouragement of students.

Number of items: 17

Format: Observations done in half-day sessions using a tally-system. All 17 behaviors presented with examples.

Reliability: Ranged from .67 to 1.00 across items.

Author: Ascione, F.R. and Borg, W.R.

Article: A teacher-training program to enhance mainstreamed handicapped pupils' self-concepts.

Journal: *Journal of School Psychology*, 1983, *21*(4), 297-301.

Related research: Borg, W.F., 1977. Changing teacher and pupil performance with protocols. *Journal of Experimental Education*, *45*, 9-18.

2889
Test name: TEACHER LEADERSHIP BEHAVIOR SCALE

Purpose: To measure student perceptions of teacher leadership behavior.

Number of items: 5

Format: 5-point format from "a very little extent" to "a very great extent." All items presented.

Reliability: Alpha = .90.

Author: Peterson, M.F. and Cooke, R.A.

Article: Attitudinal and contextual variables explaining teachers' leadership behavior.

Journal: *Journal of Educational Psychology*, Feb. 1983, *75*(1), 50-62.

Related research: Taylor, J.C. and Bowers, D.G., 1972. *Survey of organizations*. Ann Arbor, MI:

Institute for Social Research, University of Michigan.

2890
Test name: TEACHER RATING SCALE

Purpose: To measure teachers' ratings of children on misbehavior and academic concentration.

Number of items: 73

Format: 5-point (always-never) scale.

Reliability: Internal consistency = .98.

Author: Forness, S.R. and MacMillan, D.L.

Article: Influences on the sociometric ratings of mildly handicapped children: A path analysis.

Journal: *Journal of Educational Psychology*, Feb. 1983, 75(1), 63-74.

Related research: Agard, J.A. et al., 1978. *Teacher Rating Scale: An Instrument of the PRIME Instrument Battery*. Unpublished manuscript: U.S. Office of Education/Bureau for Education of the Handicapped.

2891
Test name: TEACHER'S SELF-CONTROL RATING SCALE

Purpose: To enable teachers to rate children on self-control.

Number of items: 15

Format: 5-point rating scale (1 = never, 5 = very often). All items presented.

Reliability: Test-retest (2 week interval = .94) (.88 to .93 across two subscales).

Validity: 24 out of 30 correlation coefficients significant with Child Behavior Rating Scale (significant correlations ranged from .30 to .81; $p < .05$).

Author: Humphrey, L.L.

Article: Children's and teachers' perspectives on children's self-control: The development of two rating scales.

Journal: *Journal of Consulting and Clinical Psychology*, Oct. 1982, 50(5), 624-633.

Related research: Kendall, P.C. and Wilcox, L.E., 1979. Self-control in children: Development of a rating scale. *Journal of Consulting and Clinical Psychology*, 47, 1020-1029.

2892
Test name: TEACHER TREATMENT INVENTORY

Purpose: To measure teacher behavior toward high or low achieving students (both male and female).

Number of items: 43

Format: 4-category response scale (Always, often, sometimes, never). All items are presented.

Reliability: Alpha ranged from .71 to .80 across subscales.

Author: Weinstein, R.S. et al.

Article: Student perceptions of differential treatment in open and traditional classrooms.

Journal: *Journal of Educational Psychology,* Oct. 1982, 74(5), 678-692.

Related research: Weinstein, R.S. and Middlestodt, S.E., 1979. Student perceptions of teacher interactions with male high and low achievers. *Journal of Educational Psychology, 71,* 421-431.

2893
Test name: TEACHING BEHAVIOR SCALE FOR CHILD TUTORS

Purpose: To measure teaching behavior of children as tutors.

Number of items: 11

Time required: 10-minute tutoring session.

Format: Verbal transcripts coded by raters. All items presented.

Reliability: Percentage of observer agreement ranged from 88% to 96% across items.

Author: Ludeke, R.J. and Hartup, W.W.

Article: Teaching behaviors of 9- and 11-year-old girls in mixed-age and same-age dyads.

Journal: *Journal of Educational Psychology,* Dec. 1983, 75(6), 908-914.

2894
Test name: UNION MEMBERSHIP AND BEHAVIOR SCALE

Purpose: To measure extent of union membership and behavior for university faculty members.

Number of items: 6

Format: Yes/no format.

Reliability: Internal consistency = .57.

Author: Zalesny, M.D.

Article: Comparison of economic and non-economic factors in predicting faculty vote preference in a union representation election.

Journal: *Journal of Applied Psychology*, May 1985, *70*(2), 243-256.

Related research: Terborg, J.R. et al., 1982. University faculty dispositions toward unionization: A test of Triand's model. Paper presented at the American Psychological Association Meeting. Washington, D.C.

2895
Test name: VALENCE SCALE

Purpose: To assess desirability, importance, attractiveness, and influence of actions.

Number of items: 4

Format: 5-point Likert format.

Reliability: Alpha = .80.

Author: Campbell, D.J.

Article: The effects of goal-contingent payment on the performance of a complex task.

Journal: *Personnel Psychology*, spring 1984, *37*(2), 23-40.

Related research: Campbell, D.J., 1976. *A critical examination and comparison of instrumentality and social exchange theories.* Unpublished Ph.D. dissertation, Purdue University.

2896
Test name: WILE GROUP LEADERSHIP QUESTIONNAIRE

Purpose: To measure alternative leaders' behavior.

Number of items: 21 group situations are described.

Format: For each situation, 19 alternative behaviors are listed. Respondents choose which one most closely resembles their own styles.

Reliability: Ranged from .50 to .86 over the 19 scales.

Author: Gardner, K.G. et al.

Article: Toward a comprehensive assessment of leadership behavior in groups.

Journal: *Psychological Reports*, Dec. 1982, *51*(3, part I), 991-998.

Related research: Wile, D.B., 1972. Non-experimental uses of the Group Leadership Questionnaire (GTO-C). In J.W. Pfeiffer and J.E. Jones (Eds.), *The 1972 Annual Handbook for Group Facilitators*. Iowa City: University Associates, 36-67.

COMMUNICATION

2897

Test name: ADOLESCENT COMMUNICATION INVENTORY

Purpose: To elicit the child's perception of satisfaction of communication with his/her parents.

Number of items: 33

Format: Children address the questions twice: first with reference to mother and again in reference to father.

Reliability: Test-retest (2 to 3 weeks) reliability coefficients ranged from .78 to .88. Split-half reliability coefficient was .86.

Validity: Correlations with Coopersmith Self-Esteem Inventory were .74 and .14 (N = 60).

Author: Omizo, M.M. et al.

Article: The Coopersmith Self-Esteem Inventory as a predictor of feelings and communication satisfaction toward parents among learning disabled, emotionally disturbed and normal adolescents.

Journal: *Educational and Psychological Measurement*, summer 1985, *45*(2), 389-395.

Related research: Bienvenu, M.J., 1970. Measurement of marital communication. *Family Coordinator*, *18*, 26-31.

2898

Test name: ADOLESCENT GOAL ATTAINMENT SCALE

Purpose: To measure and evaluate goal attainment of individual counseling.

Number of items: Can contain one to five goals.

Format: 5-point scale ranging from best anticipated success to most likely unfavorable outcome. Ratings made independently by student and counselor.

Reliability: Weighted Kappa's averaged between .42 and .82 with all but one showing significant pupil-counselor agreement.

Validity: Correlation = .48 between goal attainment scores and teacher ratings of satisfaction with students.

Author: Maher, C.A. and Barbrack, C.R.

Article: Evaluating individual counseling of conduct problem adolescents: The goal attainment scaling method.

Journal: *Journal of School Psychology*, 1984, *22*(3), 285-297.

Related research: Kiresuk, T.J. and Sherman, R.E., 1968. Goal attainment scaling: A general method for evaluating mental health programs. *Community Mental Health Journal, 4*, 443-453.

2899
Test name:
BARRETT-LEONARD RELATIONSHIP INVENTORY

Purpose: To measure development of client-counselor relationship.

Number of items: 64

Format: Multiple-choice for positive and negative items pertaining to core therapeutic conditions.

Reliability: Test-retest = .92.

Author: Lawe, C.F. et al.

Article: Effects of pretraining procedures for clients in counseling.

Journal: *Psychological Reports*, August 1983, *53*(1), 327-334.

Related research: Lin, T., 1964. Counseling relationship as a function of counselor's self-confidence. *Journal of Counseling Psychology, 20*, 293-297.
　Hill, C.E. et al., 1981. Nonverbal communication and counseling outcome. *Journal of Counseling Psychology, 28*(3), 203-212.
　Curtis, J.M., 1981. Effect of therapist's self-disclosure on patients' impressions of empathy, competence and trust in analogue of a psychotherapeutic interaction. *Psychological Reports, 48*(1), 127-136.
　Chippaone, D. et al., 1981. Relationship of client-perceived facilitative conditions on outcome of behaviorally oriented assertive training. *Psychological Reports, 49*(1), 251-256.

2900
Test name:
BARRETT-LEONARD RELATIONSHIP INVENTORY— REVISED

Purpose: To measure the client's perception of the counselor.

Number of items: 36

Format: Includes 5 dimensions: empathic understanding, unconditionality of regard, level of regard, congruence, and resistance.

Reliability: Reliability coefficients corrected by the Spearman-Brown formula ranged from .82 to .93.

Author: Bacorn, C.N. and Dixon, D.N.

Article: The effects of touch on depressed and vocationally undecided clients.

Journal: *Journal of Counseling Psychology,* Oct. 1984, *31*(4), 488-496.

Related research: Mann, B. and Murphy, K.C., 1975. Timing of self-disclosure, reciprocity of self-disclosure and reactions to an initial interview. *Journal of Counseling Psychology, 22,* 304-308.
  Claiborn, C.D. et al., 1983. Effects of intervention discrepancy for negative emotions. *Journal of Counseling Psychology, 30*(2), 164-171.

2901
Test name: BARRETT-LEONARD RELATIONSHIP INVENTORY— REVISED

Purpose: To measure counselor effectiveness.

Number of items: 85

Format: Includes the following: empathy, genuineness, unconditionality of regard, level of regard, and resistance. Examples are presented.

Reliability: Internal consistency reliabilities ranged from .73 to .92. Test-rest (2-week to 12-month intervals) ranged from .80 to .90.

Author: Ponterotto, J.G. and Furlong, M.J.

Article: Evaluating counselor effectiveness: A critical review of rating scale instruments.

Journal: *Journal of Counseling Psychology,* Oct. 1985, *32*(4), 597-616.

Related research: Claiborn, C.D. et al., 1983. Effects of intervention discrepancy for negative emotions. *Journal of Counseling Psychology, 30*(2), 164-171.

2902
Test name: CARLETON UNIVERSITY RESPONSIVENESS TO SUGGESTION SCALE (CURSS)

Purpose: To assess responsiveness to test suggestions associated with hypnosis.

Number of items: 7

Format: Subjects rate extent to which they experience what is suggested by each item on a 4-point scale.

Reliability: Item-total correlations ranged from .43 to .98.

Validity: Coefficients of reproducibility ranged from .86 to .89 over subscales.

Author: Spanos, N.P. et al.

Article: The Carleton University Responsiveness to Suggestion

Scale: Normative data and psychometric properties.

Journal: *Psychological Reports,* Oct. 1983, *53*(2), 523-535.

Related research: Spanos, N.P. et al., 1983. The Carleton University Responsiveness to Suggestion Scale: Relationship with other measures of hypnotic susceptibility, expectancies and absorption. *Psychological Reports, 53,* 723-734.

2903
Test name: CLIENT RATING SCALE

Purpose: To measure therapists' ratings of client.

Number of items: 11

Format: 7-point scale.

Reliability: Inter-rater reliability ranged from .83 to .91 across items.

Validity: Face validity judged acceptable.

Author: Genschaft, J.L.

Article: The effects of race and role preparation on therapeutic interaction.

Journal: *Journal of College Student Personnel,* Jan. 1982, *23*(1), 33-35.

2904
Test name: COMMUNICATION SATISFACTION QUESTIONNAIRE

Purpose: To measure satisfaction with communication in organizations.

Number of items: 42

Format: 7-point Likert-type rating scale. All items presented.

Reliability: Alpha ranged between .76 and .86 across 8 subscales.

Author: Crino, M.D. and White, M.C.

Article: Satisfaction in communication: An examination of the Downs-Hazen Measure.

Journal: *Psychological Reports,* 1981, *49*(3), 831-837.

Related research: Downs, C. and Hazen, M., 1977. A factor analytic study of communication satisfaction. *Journal of Business Communication, 14,* 63-73.

2905
Test name: COMMUNICATION SCALE

Purpose: To assess accurate conveyance of thoughts and feelings and ability to transmit expectations in dyads.

Number of items: 18

Format: Responses are made on a 5-point scale from 1 (never) to 5 (always).

Reliability: Reliability coefficients were .75 (older parents) and .94 (children).

Validity: Correlations with other variables ranged from -.192 to .693.

Author: Quinn, W.H.

Article: Personal and family adjustment in later life.

Journal: *Journal of Marriage and the Family*, Feb. 1983, *45*(1), 57-73.

Related research: Bienvenu, M.J., 1970. Measurement of marital communication. *Family Coordinator, 19,* 26-31.

2906

Test name: COMPLIANCE WITH INTERVIEWER REQUESTS SCALE

Purpose: To measure importance and willingness to give information to interviewer.

Number of items: 26

Time required: 10 minutes.

Format: 5-point rating scale for willingness and importance.

Reliability: Cronbach's alpha = .70 (importance) and .75 (willingness).

Author: Siegfried, W.D., Jr. and Wood, K.

Article: Reducing college student's compliance with inappropriate interviewer requests: An educational approach.

Journal: *Journal of College Student Personnel*, Jan. 1983, *24*(1), 66-71.

2907

Test name: CONFIDENCE SCALE

Purpose: To measure information-processing confidence.

Number of items: 10

Format: Likert-type format.

Reliability: Test-retest = .69; Alpha = .43.

Author: Evans, R.H.

Article: Innovativeness and information processing confidence.

Journal: *Psychological Reports*, April 1985, *56*(2), 557-558.

Related research: Wright, P., 1975. Factors affecting cognitive resistance to advertising. *Journal of Consumer Research, 2,* 1-9.

2908

Test name: CONTEXTUAL UNCERTAINTY SCALE

Purpose: To assess agreement and disagreement with second-order outcome links.

Number of items: 5

Format: 5-point Likert format. All items presented.

Reliability: Alpha = .74.

Author: Ashford, S.J. and Cummings, L.L.

Article: Proactive feedback seeking: The instrumental use of the information environment.

Journal: *Journal of Occupational Psychology*, March 1985, *58*(1), 67-79.

Related research: Heslin, R. et al., 1972. Information search as a function of stimulus uncertainty and the importance of the response. *Journal of Personality and Social Psychology*, 23, 333-339.
    Tybout, A. and Scott, C., 1982. *When self-perception occurs: Certainty and informativeness of behaviors as mediators of processing.* Unpublished manuscript, Northwestern University.

2909
Test name: COUNSELING APPROPRIATENESS CHECKLIST

Purpose: To measure appropriateness of discussing problems with counselors.

Number of items: 66

Format: 5-point Likert-type items.

Reliability: Test-retest = .88.

Validity: 5-member panel judged items to be valid.

Author: Miles, G.B. and McDavis, R.J.

Article: Effects of four orientation approaches on disadvantaged black freshmen students' attitudes toward the counseling center.

Journal: *Journal of College Student Personnel*, Sept. 1982, *23*(5), 413-418.

Related research: Warman, R., 1969. Differential perceptions of counseling role. *Journal of Counseling Psychology*, 7, 269-274.

2910
Test name: DECISION-MAKING POLICY SCALE

Purpose: To measure perceived influence in decision-making.

Number of items: 4

Format: 5-point scale (never true to always true). Items are a subscale of Newman's PWE Scale.

Reliability: Alpha = .59.

Author: Jackson, S.E.

Article: Participation in decision-making as a strategy for reducing job-related stress.

Journal: *Journal of Applied Psychology*, Feb. 1983, *68*(1) 3-19.

Related research: Newman, J.E., 1977. Development of a measure of perceived work environment (PWE). *Academy of Management Journal, 20,* 520-534.

2911
Test name: DYADIC INTERACTION SCALE

Purpose: To measure student-teacher interaction.

Number of items: 11 categories of interaction.

Time required: 40 minutes.

Format: 3 observers record teacher-student interaction in classrooms.

Reliability: Inter-observer agreement ranged from .80 to 1.00.

Author: Irvine, J.J.

Article: Teacher communication patterns as related to the race and sex of the student.

Journal: *Journal of Educational Research*, July/August 1985, *78*(6), 338-345.

Related research: Good, T. and Brophy, J., 1978. *Looking in classrooms.* New York: Harper and Row.

2912
Test name: GROUP DECISION-MAKING SCALE

Purpose: To measure extent to which individuals perceive their work group as having decision-making responsibilities.

Number of items: 13

Format: 5-point response format. Sample items presented.

Reliability: Alpha = .82.

Author: Kemp, N.J. et al.

Article: Autonomous work groups in a Greenfield site: A comparative study.

Journal: *Journal of Occupational Psychology*, Dec. 1983, *56*(4), 271-288.

Related research: Gulowsen, J., 1972. A measure of work group autonomy. In L.E. Davis and J.C. Taylor (Eds.), *Design of Jobs.* London: Penguin.

2913

Test name: INTERACTION CODING SYSTEM

Purpose: To assess speaker and listener skills.

Number of items: 12 categories.

Format: Raters code responses that are homogeneous in content without regard to duration and syntactical structure. Sample items presented for each of the 12 categories.

Reliability: Alpha ranged from .85 to .99 (verbal codes) and from .52 to .82 (nonverbal codes).

Author: Hahlweg, K. and Revenstorf, D.

Article: Effects of behavior marital therapy in couples' communication and problem-solving skills.

Journal: *Journal of Consulting and Counseling Psychology,* Aug. 1984, 52(4), 553-566.

Related research: Wegener, C. et al., 1979. Empirical analysis of communication in distressed couples. *Behavior Analysis Modification,* 3, 178-188.

2914

Test name: INTERPERSONAL TRUST SCALE

Purpose: To measure the generalized expectancy that oral and written statements can be relied upon.

Number of items: 25

Reliability: Test-retest reliability was .58 and .68. Split-half reliability was .76. Cronbach's alpha was .79.

Validity: Correlations with other variables ranged from -.17 to .14.

Author: Cutler, B.L. and Wolfe, R.N.

Article: Construct validity of the Concern for Appropriateness Scale.

Journal: *Journal of Personality Assessment,* June 1985, 49(3), 318-323.

Related research: Rotter, J.B., 1980. Interpersonal trust, trustworthiness and gullibility. *American Psychologist,* 35, 1-7.

2915

Test name: LEADER-MEMBER EXCHANGE SCALE—REVISED

Purpose: To assess the quality of supervisor-subordinate interaction.

Number of items: 5

Format: A 1-to-5 response format was employed.

Reliability: Coefficient alpha was .83.

Validity: Correlations with: average leadership style was .68, .48; turnover was -.19, -.44.

Author: Ferris, G.R.

Article: Role of leadership in the employee withdrawal process: A constructive replication.

Journal: *Journal of Applied Psychology*, Nov. 1985, *70*(4), 777-781.

Related research: Graen, G. et al. Role of leadership in the employee withdrawal process. *Journal of Applied Psychology, 67*, 868-872.

2916
Test name: LEADER-MEMBER EXCHANGE SCALE—MEMBER FORM

Purpose: To measure the quality of exchange between supervisors and subordinates.

Number of items: 7

Format: Response to each item was made on 4-point scales. All items were presented.

Reliability: Cronbach's alphas were .86 and .84. Test-retest correlation (6 months) was .67.

Author: Scandura, T.A. and Graen, G.B.

Article: Moderating effects of initial leader-member exchange status on the effects of a leadership intervention.

Journal: *Journal of Applied Psychology*, Aug. 1984, *69*(3), 428-436.

Related research: Liden, R. and Graen, G., 1980. Generalizability of the vertical dyad linkage model of leadership. *Academy of Management Journal, 23*, 451-465.

2917
Test name: MEASURE OF ELEMENTARY COMMUNICATION APPREHENSION

Purpose: To measure communication apprehension.

Number of items: 20

Format: Likert-type statements employing smiling and frowning faces. All items are presented.

Reliability: Test-retest reliability was .80. Split-half reliabilities ranged from .64 to .77.

Author: Harris, K.R. and Brown, R.D.

Article: Cognitive behavior modification and informed teacher treatments for shy children.

Journal: *Journal of Experimental Education*, spring 1982, *50*(3), 137-143.

Related research: Garrison, J.P. and Garrison (Harris), K.R., 1979. Measurement of communication apprehension among children: A factor in the development of basic speech skills. *Communication Education*, 28, 119-128.

2918
Test name: NEGOTIATING LATITUDE SCALES

Purpose: To measure member-reported and leader-reported negotiating latitude.

Number of items: 8 (4 member and 4 leader).

Format: Likert and multiple-choice formats. All items presented.

Reliability: Cronbach's alpha ranged from .62 to .68 across scales.

Author: Rosse, J.G. and Kraut, A.I.

Article: Reconsidering the vertical dyad linkage model of leadership.

Journal: *Journal of Occupational Psychology*, March 1983, 56(1), 63-71.

Related research: Graen, G. and Schiemann, W., 1978. Leader-member agreement: A vertical dyad approach. *Journal of Applied Psychology*, 63, 206-212.

2919
Test name: ORGANIZATIONAL COMMUNICATION SCALE

Purpose: To measure frequency of communication levels of organizational personnel.

Number of items: 8

Format: 12-point frequency rating scale (daily to never). Sample items presented.

Reliability: Alpha ranged from .67 to .75 across three subscales.

Validity: Items factored into three dimensions corresponding to Hall's interpersonal, organizational, and interorganizational communication types.

Author: Hoffman, E.

Article: The effect of race-ratio composition on the frequency of organizational communication.

Journal: *Social Psychology Quarterly*, March 1985, 48(1), 17-26.

Related research: Hall, R.H., 1982. *Organizations: Structure and process*. Englewood Cliffs, NJ: Prentice-Hall.

2920
Test name: PEAK COMMUNICATIONS EXPERIENCES SCALES

Purpose: To measure "great moments" in interpersonal communication.

Number of items: 19

Format: 6-point Likert-type response categories. All items presented.

Validity: Six factors extracted. Women rated peak experiences higher than men (p < .02).

Author: Gordon, R.D.

Article: Dimensions of peak communications experiences: An exploratory study.

Journal: *Psychological Reports*, Dec. 1985, 57(3, Pt. 1), 824-826.

Related research: Gordon, R. and Dulaney, E., 1983. Peak communication experiences: Concept, structure and sex differences. ERIC Research Document No. 221931.

2921
Test name: PRIMARY COMMUNICATION INVENTORY

Purpose: To measure the frequency of both verbal and nonverbal communication.

Number of items: 50

Format: Includes 25 verbal and nonverbal communications for which couples rate the frequency of occurrence between them.

Reliability: Test-retest reliability was .73.

Author: Tucker, C.M. and Horowitz, J.E.

Article: Assessment of factors in marital adjustment.

Journal: *Journal of Behavioral Assessment*, Dec. 1981, 3(4), 243-252.

Related research: Navran, L., 1967. Communication and adjustment in marriage. *Family Process*, 6, 173-184.

2922
Test name: RATING OF ALTER-COMPETENCE

Purpose: To measure partner's communicative competence in a particular episode.

Number of items: 27

Format: Items assess the degree to which other was cooperative, trustworthy, disclosing, assertive, expressive, attentive, etc.

Reliability: Cronbach's alpha reliability coefficient was .95.

Validity: Correlations with other variables ranged from .48 to .79.

Author: Spitzberg, B.H. and Cupach, W.R.

Article: Conversational skill and locus of perception.

Journal: *Journal of Psychopathology and Behavioral Assessment*, Sept. 1985, 7(3), 207-220.

Related research: Cupach, W.R. and Spitzberg, B.H., 1981. *Relational competence: Measurement and validation.* Paper presented at the Western Speech Communication Association Convention, San Jose, CA.

2923
Test name: REFERENTIAL COMMUNICATIONS TEST

Purpose: To measure effectiveness of referential communication.

Number of items: 10 pretest, 10 posttest, and 10 follow-up items.

Format: Items are word-pairs in which one is underlined. Children must create clues about communicating which word is underlined to another child who must select between the two words. All pairs presented.

Reliability: Judges reach 80% agreement on quality of clues.

Author: Asher, S.R. and Wigfield, A.

Article: Influence and comparison training on childrens' referential communication.

Journal: *Journal of Educational Psychology*, April 1981, 73(2), 232-241.

Related research: Rosenberg, S. and Cohen, B.D., 1966. Referential processes of speakers and listeners. *Psychological Reports*, 73, 208-231.

2924
Test name: SELF-RATED COMPETENCE

Purpose: To measure self's communicative competence in a particular episode.

Format: Items assess the degree to which self was cooperative, trustworthy, disclosing, assertive, expressive, attentive, etc.

Reliability: Cronbach's alpha reliability coefficient was .84.

Validity: Correlations with other variables ranged from .51 to .65.

Author: Spitzberg, B.H. and Cupach, W.R.

Article: Conversational skill and locus of perception.

Journal: *Journal of Psychopathology and Behavioral Assessment*, Sept. 1985, 7(3), 207-220.

Related research: Cupach, W.R. and Spitzberg, B.H., 1981. *Relational competence: Measurement and validation.* Paper presented at the Western Speech Communication Association Convention, San Jose, CA.

2925

Test name: SOCIAL REINFORCEMENT ORIENTATION CHECKLIST

Purpose: To measure the extent of use of smiling and other behavior in daily interaction.

Number of items: 50

Format: 3-point response categories indicate the extent of use. All items presented.

Reliability: Test-retest ranged from .65 to .78. Split-half = .75.

Validity: Correlated .29 ($p < .05$) with extroversion and .37 ($p < .05$) with the F scale.

Author: Ibrahim, A.

Article: Social reinforcement orientation approach to personality.

Journal: *Psychological Reports*, June 1985, 56(3), 743-750.

2926

Test name: VERTICAL EXCHANGE SCALE

Purpose: To measure leader-member exchange.

Number of items: 12

Format: Included: approachability and flexibility of supervisor toward the newcomer, supervisor's willingness to use his authority to help the newcomer solve problems, clarity of the supervisor's expectations and his feedback to the newcomer, the newcomer's latitude to influence the supervisor to change his role situation, and the opportunity of newcomers to share after-hours social and leisure activities.

Reliability: Cronbach's alpha ranged from .87 to .92; Test-retest correlation coefficients ranged from .37 to .80.

Validity: Correlation with other variables ranged from -.18 to .36.

Author: Wakabayashi, M. and Graen, G.B.

Article: The Japanese career progress study: A 7-year follow-up.

Journal: *Journal of Applied Psychology*, Nov. 1984, 69(4), 603-614.

Related research: Wakabayashi, M., 1980. *Managerial career progress in a Japanese organization.* Ann Arbor, MI: UMI Research Press.

CONCEPT MEANING

2927
Test name: AUTOMATIC WORD PROCESSING TASK

Purpose: To measure the automaticity of word processing.

Number of items: 20 (line drawings).

Format: Items are line drawings of an easily pictured noun of one syllable. Time for naming pictures appearing alone is subtracted from the time of name in Stroop condition. The difference is the measure of automatic word processing.

Reliability: SB ranged from .74 to .75.

Author: DeSoto, J.L. and DeSoto, C.B.

Article: Relationship of reading achievement to verbal processing abilities.

Journal: *Journal of Educational Psychology*, Feb. 1983, 75(1), 116-127.

Related research: Rosinski, R.R. et al., 1975. Automatic semantic processing in a picture-word interference task. *Child Development*, 46, 247-253.

2928
Test name: COMPETITION KNOWLEDGE TEST

Purpose: To measure the ability to distinguish between competition and other associated constructs.

Number of items: 60

Format: Multiple-choice.

Reliability: Internal consistency ranged from .78 to .92. KR-20 = .91.

Author: Kildea, A.E. and Kukulka, G.

Article: Reliability of the Competition Knowledge Test.

Journal: *Psychological Reports*, June 1984, 54(3), 957-958.

Related research: Kildea, A.E., 1983. Competition: A model for conception. *Quest*, 35, 169-181.

2929
Test name: CONCEPT ATTAINMENT SCALE

Purpose: To measure concept attainment in science courses.

Number of items: 12 items for each of 5 concepts.

Format: Multiple-choice. Sample concepts and items presented.

Reliability: KR-20 = .89.

Validity: Validated by a panel of science educators.

Author: Rollins, M.M. et al.

Article: Attainment of selected earth science concepts by Texas high school seniors.

Journal: *Journal of Educational Research,* Nov./Dec. 1983, 77(2), 81-88.

Related research: Frayer, D.A. et al., 1969. *A schema for testing the level of concept mastery* (Working paper No. 16). Madison, WI: Wisconsin Research and Development Center for Cognitive Learning.

2930
Test name: CONCEPT DEFINITION AND APPLICATION TEST

Purpose: To measure student success at learning and applying concepts.

Number of items: 20

Format: 10 "definition" and 10 "application" questions each with 5 multiple-choice responses.

Validity: Kuder-Richardson 20 formula = .78 (N = 68).

Author: Ross, S. et al.

Article: Field experiences as meaningful contexts for learning about learning.

Journal: *Journal of Educational Research,* Nov./Dec. 1981, 75(2), 103-107.

Related research: Ross, S.M. and Bush, A.J., 1980. Effects of abstract and educationally oriented learning contexts on achievement and attitudes of preservice teachers. *Journal of Educational Research,* 74, 19-23.

2931
Test name: IDEA INVENTORY

Purpose: To measure the rationality-irrationality cognitive dimension.

Number of items: 33

Format: 3-point agree-disagree scale. Sample items presented.

Reliability: Test-retest = .81 or more over two test occasions and for males and females.

Author: Vestre, N.D.

Article: Test-retest reliability of the idea inventory.

Journal: *Psychological Reports,* June 1984, 54(3), 873-874.

Related research: Kassinove, H., et

al., 1977. Developmental trends in rational thinking: Implications for rational emotive school mental health programs. *Journal of Community Psychology*, 5, 266-274.

2932
Test name: INTERNAL SCANNING SCALE

Purpose: To measure breadth of association.

Number of items: 73

Format: Free associations obtained for each of 73 words (items) that have no popular responses. Scores obtained by averaging the normative frequencies of responses.

Reliability: Split-half = .93.

Author: Heilbrun, A.B., Jr.

Article: Cognitive defenses and life stress: An information-processing analysis.

Journal: *Psychological Reports*, Feb. 1984, 54(1), 3-17.

Related research: Heilbrun, A.B., Jr., 1972. Style of adaptation to perceived aversive maternal control and internal scanning behavior. *Journal of Consulting and Clinical Psychology*, 39, 15-21.

2933
Test name: NEGATION ELICITATION SCALE

Purpose: To measure negative language constructions.

Number of items: 24

Format: Items were objects with something missing (wheels from small cars, for example). Children are asked what is wrong with objects. All items described.

Reliability: Inter-observer agreement was 95%.

Validity: Correct constructions increase with age (3 to 6 years) for both monolingual and bilingual children.

Author: Madrid, D. and Garcia, E.E.

Article: Development of negation in bilingual Spanish/English and monolingual English speakers.

Journal: *Journal of Educational Psychology*, Oct. 1981, 73(5), 624-631.

2934
Test name: PARAGRAPH COMPLETION METHOD

Purpose: To measure the degree of integrative complexity relative to interpersonal stimuli.

Number of items: 5

Time required: 2 minutes.

Format: A semi-projective

measure, whereby subjects complete each stem by adding at least two additional sentences within a 2-minute time limit. Items are presented.

Reliability: Inter-rater reliability was r = .83.

Author: Strohmer, D.C. et al.

Article: Cognitive style and synchrony in measures of anxiety.

Journal: *Measurement and Evaluation in Guidance*, April 1983, *16*(1), 13-17.

Related research: Harvey, O.J. et al., 1961. *Conceptual systems and personality organization.* New York: Wiley.

2935
Test name: RECEPTIVE LANGUAGE MEASURE

Purpose: To measure infants' receptive language.

Number of items: 34

Format: The infant is required to correctly identify the picture in each pair labeled by the experimenter.

Author: Ungerer, J.A. and Sigman, M.

Reliability: Test-retest reliability was .87 and .94. Kuder-Richardson coefficient was .91.

Article: The relation of play and sensorimotor behavior to language in the second year.

Journal: *Child Development*, Aug. 1984, *55*(4), 1448-1455.

Related research: Beckwith, L. and Thompson, S., 1976. Recognition of verbal labels of pictured objects and events by 17-to-30 month old infants. *Journal of Speech and Hearing Research*, *19*, 690-699.

2936
Test name: RELATIONSHIP JUDGEMENT TEST

Purpose: To measure the perceived relationship between pairs of concepts.

Number of items: 20

Time required: 15 minutes.

Format: Degree of relationship indicated on a 9-point scale.

Reliability: Test-retest (10 minute interval with concept-pairs reversed) = .67. (This is the mean correlation between test and retest for all respondents.)

Validity: Individual reliability correlated significantly with a multiple-choice exam over the same material (r = .43, p < .001).

Author: Diekhoff, G.M.

Article: Testing through relationship judgements.

Journal: *Journal of Educational Psychology*, April 1983, 75(2), 227-233.

2937
Test name: SIGHT WORD VOCABULARY TEST

Purpose: To measure sight word vocabulary.

Number of items: 178 words for preprimer through second grade.

Format: List presented to students.

Reliability: Kuder-Richardson 21 = .97.

Author: Reifman, B. et al.

Article: Effects of work bank instruction on sight word acquisition: An experimental note.

Journal: *Journal of Educational Psychology*, Jan./Feb. 1981, 74(3), 175-178.

Related research: Mangieri, J., 1978. Dolch list revisited. *Reading World*, *18*, 91-95.

2938
Test name: SIMILE APPRECIATION SCALE

Purpose: To measure appreciation of figurative language usage.

Number of items: 36

Time required: 60-90 minutes.

Format: Paired-comparisons. Sample items presented. Students asked to choose the "best" of two similes.

Validity: Verbal IQ related to appreciation for sixth and third graders, while figured-fluency and originality related to appreciation for kindergartners.

Author: Malgady, R.G.

Article: Metric distance models of creativity and children's appreciation of figurative language.

Journal: *Journal of Educational Psychology*, Dec. 1981, 73(6), 866-871.

2939
Test name: TEST OF NUMBER CONCEPTS

Purpose: To assess young children's number development.

Number of items: 59

Format: Includes nine subtests: rational counting; choosing more; just after, before, and between; counting on and back; equalizing two sets of counters; identity; equivalence conservation; verbal word problems; concrete word problems.

Reliability: Coefficient alphas were .95 (pretest) and .97 (posttest).

Author: Clements, D. et al.

Article: Relationship between pretraining knowledge and learning.

Journal: *Child Study Journal*, 1985, *15*(1), 57-70.

Related research: Carpenter, T.P and Moser, J.M., 1982. The development of addition and subtraction problem solving skills. In T.P. Carpenter, et al., (Eds.), *Addition and subtraction: A cognitive perspective*. Hillsdale, NJ: Lawrence Erlbaum.

CREATIVITY

2940
Test name: CREATIVE ACTIVITIES CHECKLIST

Purpose: To identify creative activities of children.

Number of items: 65

Format: Includes seven domains of items: art, writing, science, performing arts, crafts, music, and public presentation. An example is presented.

Reliability: Coefficient alpha was .94.

Author: Runco, M.A. and Albert, R.S.

Article: The reliability and validity of ideational originality in the divergent thinking of academically gifted and nongifted children.

Journal: *Educational and Psychological Measurement*, autumn 1985, *45*(3), 483-501.

Related research: Hocevar, D., 1978. Studies in the evaluation of tests of divergent thinking. *Dissertation Abstracts International*, *35*, 4658A-4686A. (University microfilms No. 78-69.)

2941
Test name: REMOTE ASSOCIATES TEST

Purpose: To measure creativity.

Number of items: 30

Format: Respondents write a word that has something in common with three listed words.

Reliability: KR = .53.

Author: Shaw, G.A.

Article: The use of imagery by intelligent and by creative school children.

Journal: *Journal of General Psychology*, April 1985, *112*(2), 153-171.

Related research: Mednick, S.A., 1962. The associative basis of the creative process. *Psychological Review*, *69*, 220-232.

2942
Test name: TEACHER'S EVALUATION OF STUDENT'S CREATIVITY

Purpose: To enable teachers to evaluate their students' creativity.

Number of items: 25

Format: Each item is a behavioral descriptor which the teacher rates on a seven point Likert-type scale from (1) rarely to (7) extremely. An example is provided.

Reliability: Coefficient alpha was .96.

Author: Runco, M.A. and Albert, R.S.

Article: The reliability and validity of ideational originality in the divergent thinking of academically gifted and nongifted children.

Journal: *Educational and Psychological Measurement*, autumn 1985, *45*(3), 483-501.

Related research: Runco, M.A., 1984. Teachers' judgments of creativity and social validation of divergent thinking tests. *Perceptual and Motor Skills*, *59*, 711-717.

DEVELOPMENT

2943
Test name: ADULT DEVELOPMENT SCALE

Purpose: To measure the dimensions of early adult development.

Number of items: 16

Format: Raters coded interview responses to 16 items as (1) developmentally young, (3) developmentally advanced, and (2) unable to determine. Items presented.

Reliability: Inter-rater reliability ranged from .31 to .93, and averaged .68.

Validity: Significant relationships to age were found for 11 of the 16 items.

Author: Kuh, G.D. and Thomas, M.L.

Article: The use of adult development theory with graduate students.

Journal: *Journal of College Student Personnel*, Jan. 1983, 24(1), 12-19.

Related research: Thomas, M.L. and Kuh, G.D., 1982. A composite framework for understanding development during the early adult years. *Personnel and Guidance Journal*, 61, 14-17.

2944
Test name: ADULT VOCATIONAL MATURITY ASSESSMENT INTERVIEW

Purpose: To measure vocational maturity in adults with delayed career development.

Number of items: 120

Format: Numerical response scales of varying ranges, all with a definition of scoring. Sample item included.

Reliability: Alphas ranged from .52 to .82 across subscales. Total reliability = .91.

Validity: Subscales more highly related to total measure than to each other. Scales responded to career development intervention.

Author: Manuele, C.A.

Article: The development of a measure to assess vocational maturity in adults with delayed career development.

Journal: *Journal of Vocational Behavior*, Aug. 1983, 23(1), 45-63.

2945
Test name: CHILD BEHAVIOR RATING SCALE

Purpose: To evaluate children's psychosocial development.

Number of items: 28

Format: Combines items from Classroom Adjustment Rating Scale and the Health Resources Inventory.

Reliability: Test-retest ranged from .72 to .92.

Author: Humphrey, L.L.

Article: Children's and teachers' perspectives on children's self-control: The development of two rating scales.

Journal: *Journal of Consulting and Clinical Psychology*, Oct. 1982, 50(5), 624-633.

Related research: Rochester Social Problem Solving Core Group, 1980. *The Child Behavior Rating Scale.* Unpublished manuscript, University of Rochester.
    Lorion, R.P. et al., 1975. Normative and parametric analysis of school maladjustment. *American Journal of Community Psychology*, 3, 291-301.
    Gesten, E.L., 1976. A health resources inventory: The development of a measure of the personal and social competence of primary grade children. *Journal of Consulting and Clinical Psychology*, 44, 775-786.

2946
Test name: CLASSIFICATION AND SERIATION TEST

Purpose: To measure acquisition of classification and seriation as logical operations.

Number of items: 50 operations.

Format: All operations described.

Reliability: Alpha = .90 (pretest) and .92 (posttest).

Validity: Consistent, moderate and positive correlations between classification and seriation scores and scores of number concepts test. r's ranged from .07 to .69 (13 of 14 significant).

Author: Clements, D.H.

Article: Training effects on the development and generalization of Piagetian logical operations and knowledge of numbers.

Journal: *Journal of Educational Psychology*, Oct. 1984, 76(5), 766-776.

2947
Test name: CONTENT ANALYSIS SCALES OF PSYCHOSOCIAL MATURITY

Purpose: To measure positive and negative constructs used at each of Erikson's eight stages.

Number of items: 16

Format: Key self-descriptive statements for each construct are presented.

Reliability: Inter-judge reliability ranged from .80 to .95.

Author: Viney, L.L. and Tych, A.M.

Article: Content analysis scales measuring psychosocial maturity in the elderly.

Journal: *Journal of Personality Assessment*, June 1985, *49*(3), 311-317.

Related research: Viney, L.L. and Tych, A.M., 1982. *Content analysis scales to measure psychosocial maturity: A set of research tools.* Unpublished paper: The University of Wollongong.

2948
Test name: EGO DEVELOPMENT TEST (SHORT VERSION)

Purpose: To measure ego development.

Number of items: 12

Format: Sentence completion. Items from Loevinger and Wessler's 36-item scale.

Reliability: Alpha = .69; Inter-rater = .91.

Author: Hansell, S.

Article: Ego development and peer friendship networks.

Journal: *Sociology of Education*, Jan. 1981, *54*(1), 51-63.

Related research: Loevinger, J. and Wessler, R., 1970. *Measuring ego development: Volume I.* San Francisco: Jossey-Bass.

2949
Test name: EGO IDENTITY SCALE

Purpose: To reflect the degree of successful or unsuccessful resolution of each of the first six of Erikson's eight stage crises within a theory of psychosocial development.

Number of items: 72

Format: Respondents agree or disagree with each item.

Reliability: Split-half (corrected) reliability coefficients were .849 (N = 70) and .85 (N = 70).

Author: Caillet, K.C. and Michael, W.B.

Article: The construct validity of three self-report instruments hypothesized to measure the degree of resolution for each of the first six stage crises in Erikson's developmental theory of personality.

Journal: *Educational and Psychological Measurement*, spring 1983, *43*(1), 197-209.

Related research: Rasmussen, J.E., 1964. Relationship of ego identity to psychosocial effectiveness. *Psychological Reports*, *15*, 815-825.

2950
Test name: EGO IDENTITY SCALE

Purpose: To measure progress toward ego-identity achievement.

Number of items: 12

Format: Each item pairs two statements in a forced-choice format to minimize effects of social desirability. Sample items presented.

Reliability: Split-half = .68.

Validity: Correlates negatively with dogmatism and positively with internal locus of control, intimacy, personally derived values and political, moral and occupational commitment.

Author: Savickas, M.L.

Article: Identity in vocational development.

Journal: *Journal of Vocational Behavior*, Dec. 1985, *27*(3), 329-337.

Related research: Tan, A.L. et al., 1977. A short measure of Eriksonian ego identity. *Journal of Personality Assessment*, *41*, 279-284.

2951
Test name: EGO STAGE DEVELOPMENT INVENTORY

Purpose: To reflect the degree of successful or unsuccessful resolution of each of the first six of Erikson's eight stage crises within a theory of psychosocial development.

Number of items: 144

Format: Twelve items represent each of the positive resolutions and 12 items represent each of the negative resolutions for each of the first six stage crises.

Reliability: Coefficient alphas ranged from .68 to .90.

Author: Caillet, K.C. and Michael, W.B.

Article: The construct validity of three self-report instruments hypothesized to measure the degree of resolution for each of the first six stage crises in Erikson's developmental theory of personality.

Journal: *Educational and Psychological Measurement*, spring 1983, *43*(1), 197-209.

Related research: Caillet, K.C., 1980. Ego Stage Development Inventory. Unpublished self-report inventory. (Available from author,

California State University, Long Beach, CA.)

2952
Test name: EMOTIONAL MATURITY SCALE

Purpose: To measure emotional empathy.

Number of items: 33

Format: Each item is scored from +4 (very strong agreement) to -4 (very strong disagreement).

Reliability: Split-half reliability was .84.

Author: Hanson, R.A. et al.

Article: Age and gender differences in empathy and moral reasoning among adolescents.

Journal: *Child Study Journal*, 1985, *15*(3), 181-188.

Related research: Mehrabian, A. and Epstein, N., 1972. A measure of emotional empathy. *Journal of Personality*, *40*, 525-543.

2953
Test name: INTELLECTUAL/ACADEMIC DEVELOPMENT SCALE

Purpose: To measure satisfaction with intellectual/academic development of freshmen.

Number of items: 7

Format: Likert-type scale.

Reliability: Alpha = .74.

Author: Pascarella, E.T. and Terenzini, P.T.

Article: Contextual analysis as a method for assessing resident group effects.

Journal: *Journal of College Student Personnel*, March 1982, *23*(2), 108-114.

Related research: Pascarella, E.T. and Terenzini, P.T., 1980. Predicting persistence and voluntary dropout decisions from a theoretical model. *Journal of Higher Education*, *51*, 60-75.

2954
Test name: INTELLECTUAL AND PERSONAL DEVELOPMENT

Purpose: To measure intellectual and personal development.

Number of items: 11

Format: Four-point response scale.

Reliability: For intellectual development: alpha = .74; for personal development: alpha = .80.

Author: Pascarella, E.T. and Terenzini, P.T.

Article: Residence arrangement, student/faculty relationships and freshmen-year educational outcomes.

Journal: *Journal of College Student Personnel*, March 1981, 22(2), 147-156.

Related research: Pascarella, E. and Terenzini, P., 1978. Student-faculty informal relationships and freshmen-year educational outcomes. *Journal of Educational Research, 71*, 183-189.

2955
Test name: INVENTORY OF PSYCHOSOCIAL DEVELOPMENT

Purpose: To reflect the degree of successful or unsuccessful resolution of each of the first six of Erikson's eight stage crises within a theory of psychosocial development.

Number of items: 60

Format: Five items reflect successful and 5 reflect unsuccessful resolutions of each of Erikson's first six stages of psychosocial development. Subjects respond to each item on a 7-point scale from definitely most characteristic of you (7) to definitely most uncharacteristic of you (1).

Reliability: Test-retest reliability ranged from .45 to .81 (6 week interval).

Author: Caillet, K.C. and Michael, W.B.

Article: The construct validity of three self-report instruments hypothesized to measure the degree of resolution for each of the first six stage crises in Erikson's developmental theory of personality.

Journal: *Educational and Psychological Measurement*, spring 1983, 43(1), 197-209.

Related research: Constantinople, A., 1969. An Eriksonian measure of personality development in college students. *Developmental Psychology, 1*, 357-372.

2956
Test name: MENTAL DEVELOPMENT SCALES

Purpose: To assess developmental levels of children from birth to three years of age in a familiar setting.

Number of items: Six scales whose readings come from assessments of drawing, playing, object exploration, and other characteristics.

Format: Observations obtained in a semi-structured mode.

Reliability: Guttman reproducibility ranged from .938 to .997. Scalability ranged from .667 to .984.

Validity: Correlations of six scales

ranged from .508 to .954 with Bayley Scales of Infant Development and Stanford-Binet Intelligence Scale.

Author: Wagner, B.

Article: Reliability, scalability and validity of an instrument to assess developmental levels of children from birth to three years of age.

Journal: *Psychological Reports*, Feb. 1983, *52*(1), 217-218.

2957
Test name: MORAL DEVELOPMENT SCALE

Purpose: To assess overall level of children's moral reasoning within a Piagetian framework.

Number of items: 15

Format: Consists of six stories concerned with moral realism and nine concerned with justice. Stick figure cartoons depicting each story are presented while each story is read. Responses are scored on the basis of moral choice and justification for the choice. Examples are presented.

Reliability: Coefficient alpha was .83 (N = 112). Test-retest was .82 (N = 32).

Validity: Correlations with a composite measure of verbal and math reasoning ability were .31 and .29.

Author: Kurtines, W. and Pimm, J.B.

Article: The Moral Development Scale: A Piagetian measure of moral judgment.

Journal: *Educational and Psychological Measurement*, spring 1983, *43*(1), 89-105.

Related research: Kurtines, W. and Pimm, J., 1978. *The Moral Development Scale Manual.* Unpublished manuscript. (Available from William M. Kurtines, Department of Psychology, Florida International University, Miami, FL 33199.)

2958
Test name: SCALE OF INTELLECTUAL DEVELOPMENT

Purpose: To measure intellectual-ethical development in undergraduates.

Number of items: 86

Format: Four-choice Likert format. Sample items presented.

Reliability: Cronbach's alpha = .81 (dualism), .70 (relativism), .76 (commitment), .73 (empathy).

Validity: Correlations with Erwin Identity Scale generally negative, except for SID Commitment Scale, which were positive. Correlations with perceived self scale generally negative and low (a total of 48 correlations are presented).

Author: Erwin, T.D.

Article: The Scale of Intellectual Development.

Journal: *Journal of College Student Personnel,* Jan. 1983, *24*(1), 6-12.

Related research: Perry, W.G., Jr., 1970. *Forms of intellectual and ethical development in the college years.* New York: Holt, Rinehart and Winston.

2959
Test name: SENTENCE COMPLETION TEST

Purpose: To measure ego development.

Number of items: 36

Format: Items are incomplete sentences to be completed. An example is presented.

Reliability: Cronbach's alpha was .89.

Author: Browning, D.L. and Quinlan, D.M.

Article: Ego development and intelligence in a psychiatric population: Weschler subtest scores.

Journal: *Journal of Personality Assessment,* June 1985, *49*(3), 260-263.

Related research: Loevinger, J. et al., 1970. *Measuring ego development* (Vol. 2). San Francisco: Jossey-Bass.
    Swensen, C.H. et al., 1981. Stage of family life cycle, ego development and the marriage relationship. *Journal of Marriage and the Family, 43*(4), 841-853.

2960
Test name: SOCIAL SCIENCES PIAGETIAN INVENTORY

Purpose: To measure performance on a variety of concrete and formal operational tasks.

Number of items: 30

Format: Multiple-choice items: Examples are presented.

Reliability: Kuder-Richardson formula 20 reliability coefficients cluster around .80. Test-retest coefficient was .87 (N = 141 fifth through ninth graders with one week interval).

Validity: Correlation with Otis-Lennon Mental Ability Test was r = .54.

Author: Carter, K.R. and Ormrod, J.E.

Article: Acquisition of formal operations by intellectually gifted children.

Journal: *Gifted Child Quarterly*, summer 1982, *26*(3), 110-115.

2961
Test name: TESTS OF SPECIFIC COGNITIVE ABILITIES FOR 3-YEAR-OLDS

Purpose: To measure specific mental abilities in preschool children as young as three years of age.

Number of items: 60

Format: Includes 4 subtests: Vocabulary, recognition memory, form discrimination, and hidden animals.

Reliability: Test-retest reliability coefficients ranged from .57 to .82 (N = 48).

Validity: Correlation with the Stanford-Binet was .64 (N = 50).

Author: Singer, S. et al.

Article: The development and validation of a test battery to measure differentiated cognitive abilities in three-year-old children.

Journal: *Educational and Psychological Measurement*, autumn 1984, *44*(3), 703-713.

FAMILY

2962
Test name: ABBREVIATED DYADIC ADJUSTMENT SCALE

Purpose: To measure marital adjustment.

Number of items: 7

Format: All items are presented.

Reliability: Alpha reliability coefficient was .76.

Author: Sharpley, C.F. and Rogers, H.J.

Article: Preliminary validation of the abbreviated Spanier Dyadic Adjustment Scale: Some psychometric data regarding a screening test of marital adjustment.

Journal: *Educational and Psychological Measurement*, winter 1984, *44*(4), 1045-1049.

Related research: Spanier, G.B., 1976. Measuring dyadic adjustment: New scales for assessing the quality of marriage and similar dyads. *Journal of Marriage and the Family*, *38*, 15-38.
  Sharpley, C.F. and Cross, D.G., 1982. A psychometric evaluation of the Spanier Dyadic Adjustment Scale. *Journal of Marriage and the Family*, *44*, 739-741.

2963
Test name: ACCEPTANCE OF MARITAL TERMINATION SCALE

Purpose: To identify a range of feelings about marital termination.

Number of items: 11

Format: Responses are made on a 4-point scale of: not at all, slightly, somewhat, very much. All items are presented.

Reliability: Cronbach's alpha was .90.

Validity: Correlations with other variables ranged from -.50 to .28 (males) and from -.45 to .26 (females).

Author: Thompson, L. and Spanier, G.B.

Article: The end of marriage and acceptance of marital termination.

Journal: *Journal of Marriage and the Family*, Feb. 1983, *45*(1), 103-113.

Related research: Kitson, G.C., 1982. Attachment to the spouse and divorce: A scale and its application. *Journal of Marriage and the Family*, *44*, 379-393.

2964
Test name: ADOLESCENT ABUSE INVENTORY

Purpose: Measures parental attitudes toward maltreatment and the likelihood that they would act in abusive manners given provocative adolescent behavior.

Number of items: 26

Format: Items consist of hypothetical situations. A sample item is presented.

Reliability: Overall coefficient alpha reliabilities for mothers ranged from .607 to .877 and for fathers they ranged from .644 to .881.

Author: Garbarino, J. et al.

Article: Families at risk for destructive parent-child relations in adolescence.

Journal: *Child Development*, Feb. 1984, *55*(1), 174-183.

Related research: Sebes, J.M., 1983. *Determining risk for abuse in families with adolescents: The development of a criterion measure.* Unpublished doctoral dissertation, Pennsylvania State University.

2965
Test name: AFFECTIVE INTIMACY INDEX

Purpose: To measure one's perception of closeness and emotional bonding in an intimate relationship.

Number of items: 10

Format: Subjects agree or disagree with each item on a 7-point scale. Scores range from 10 (least intimate) to 70.

Reliability: Coefficient alpha = .78.

Validity: Correlations with other variables ranged from -.64 to .74.

Author: Tolstedt, B.E. and Stokes, J.P.

Article: Relation of verbal, affective and physical intimacy to marital satisfaction.

Journal: *Journal of Counseling Psychology*, Oct. 1983, *30*(4), 573-580.

Related research: Walster, E. et al., 1978. *Equity: Theory and research.* Boston: Allyn & Bacon.

2966
Test name: AREAS OF CHANGE QUESTIONNAIRE

Purpose: To measure spouse's presenting complaints in areas of marital change.

Number of items: 34

Format: Multiple-choice and 7-point Likert scales. All items presented.

Reliability: Internal consistency = .89.

Validity: Correlated -.70 with Marital Adjustment Scale. Correlated from -.02 to +.44 on subscales of Spouse Observation Checklist.

Author: Margolin, G. et al.

Article: Areas of Change Questionnaire: A practical approach to marital assessment.

Journal: *Journal of Consulting and Clinical Psychology*, Dec. 1983, *51*(6), 920-931.

Related research: Weiss, R.L. and Birchler, G.R., 1975. *Areas of Change*. Unpublished manuscript. Department of Psychology, University of Oregon, Eugene.

Witkin, S. et al., 1983. Group training in marital communication: A comparative study. *Journal of Marriage and the Family*, 45(3), 661-669.

2967
Test name: ATTITUDE TOWARD NONMATERNAL CARE RATING

Purpose: To measure degree to which a mother believes others can take care of her child.

Number of items: 1

Format: 9-point rating scale.

Reliability: Inter-rater = .88.

Author: Morgan, K.C. and Hock, E.

Article: A longitudinal study of the psychosocial variables affecting the career patterns of women with young children.

Journal: *Journal of Marriage and the Family*, May 1984, *46*(2), 383-390.

Related research: Hock, E., 1976. *Alternative approaches to child rearing and their effects on the mother-infant relationship.* (ED 122943.) Urbana, IL: Educational Resources Information Center/Early Childhood Education.

2968
Test name: BARRIERS TO MARITAL DISSOLUTION SCALE

Purpose: To measure perceptions to barriers to dissolution of marriage.

Number of items: 11

Format: 5-point Likert format.

Reliability: Alpha = .74.

Author: Sabatelli, R.M. and Cecil-Pigo, E.F.

Article: Relational interdependence and commitment in marriage.

Journal: *Journal of Marriage and the Family*, Nov. 1985, *47*(4), 931-937.

Related research: Levinger, G., 1974. A three-level approach to attraction: Toward an understanding of pair relatedness. In T.L. Huston (Ed.), *Foundations of Interpersonal Attraction*. New York: Academic Press.

2969
Test name: CALDWELL INVENTORY OF HOME STIMULATION

Purpose: To measure several dimensions of the child's environment in a structured interview.

Number of items: 45

Format: The scale is administered during a home visit. Includes 6 subscales: maternal responsiveness, avoid restriction/punishment, organization of environment, provision of play materials, maternal involvement, variety of stimulation.

Reliability: .90.

Validity: Correlations with Bayley and Reynell Scales ranged from .06 to .40.

Author: Siegal, L.S.

Article: Infant tests as predictors of cognitive and language development at two years.

Journal: *Child Development*, June 1981, *52*(2), 545-557.

Related research: Elardo, R. et al., 1975. The relation of infants' home environment to mental tests performance from six to thirty six months: A longitudinal analysis. *Child Development*, *46*, 71-76.
Dourninck, W.J. van et al., 1981. The relationship between twelve-month home stimulation and school achievement. *Child Development*, *52*(8), 1080-1083.

2970
Test name: CHANGES IN SELF-PERCEPTION SCALE

Purpose: To measure a woman's feelings about herself after having a baby.

Number of items: 17

Format: 5-point adjective rating scales. Sample items presented.

Reliability: Alpha ranged from .79 to .85 across two subscales.

Author: Pistrang, N.

Article: Women's work involvement and experience of new motherhood.

Journal: *Journal of Marriage and the Family*, May 1984, *46*(2), 433-447.

Related research: Steffensmeier, R.H., 1982. A role model of the transition to parenthood. *Journal of Marriage and the Family*, 44, 319-334.

2971
Test name: CHILD'S REPORT OF PARENTAL BEHAVIOR INVENTORY

Purpose: To assess parental child-rearing behaviors.

Number of items: 108

Format: Includes 18 subscales. Responses to each item are recorded on a 3-point scale of "like," "somewhat like," and "not like."

Reliability: The mean internal consistency was .71. The mean inter-rater agreement was .30.

Author: Schwarz, J.C. et al.

Article: Assessing child-rearing behaviors: A comparison of ratings made by mother, father, child and sibling on the CRPBI.

Journal: *Child Development*, April 1985, 56(2), 462-479.

Related research: Schludermann, E. and Schludermann, S., 1970. Replicability of factors in children's report of parent (CRPBI). *Journal of Psychology*, 76, 239-249.

2972
Test name: COMMUNICATIONS SKILLS TEST

Purpose: To measure interaction in married couples.

Format: Observation scale. Observers rate statements made by couples on a 5-point scale. Examples of the rating protocol presented.

Reliability: Inter-observer agreement averaged .82 (range .71 to .95).

Validity: Mean scores at pre-assessment comparable. Intervention increased scores, control group scores decreased slightly. Correlates .30 ($p < .01$) with communication box ratings.

Author: Floyd, F.J. and Markman, H.J.

Article: An economical observational measure of couples' communication skill.

Journal: *Journal of Consulting and Clinical Psychology*, Feb. 1984, 52(1), 97-103.

2973
Test name: CONFLICT TACTICS SCALE

Purpose: To measure marital conflict.

Number of items: 18

Format: 7-point frequency scale (never to more than 20 times per year).

Reliability: Interspousal reliability ranged from -.07 to 1.00.

Author: Jouriles, E.N. and O'Leary, K.D.

Article: Interspousal reliability of reports of marital violence.

Journal: *Journal of Consulting and Clinical Psychology*, June 1985, 53(3), 419-421.

Related research: Hornung, C.A. et al., 1981. Status relationships in marriage: Risk factors in spouse abuse. *Journal of Marriage and the Family*, 43, 675-692.
   Straus, M.A., 1979. Measuring intrafamily conflict and violence: The Conflict Tactics (CT) Scale. *Journal of Marriage and the Family*, 6, 131-149.

2974
Test name: COPING STRATEGIES AND RESOURCES INVENTORY

Purpose: To identify coping strategies and resources of wives divorced or widowed.

Number of items: 45

Format: The perceived efficacy of coping strategies was rated on a 4-point scale from "not at all helpful" to "very helpful." Six factors are included.

Reliability: Coefficient alphas ranged from .675 to .793.

Author: Berman, W.H. and Turk, D.C.

Article: Adaptation to divorce: Problems and strategies.

Journal: *Journal of Marriage and the Family*, Feb. 1981, 43(1), 179-189.

Related research: McCubbin, H.I. et al., 1976. Coping repertories of families adapting to prolonged war-induced separations. *Journal of Marriage and the Family*, 38, 461-472.

2975
Test name: COPING WITH SEPARATION INVENTORY—REVISED

Purpose: To measure wives coping behavior upon separation.

Number of items: 30

Format: 3-point helpfulness rating scale.

Reliability: Alphas ranged from .71 to .85 across subscales.

Author: Patterson, J.M. and McCubbin, H.I.

Article: Gender roles and coping.

Journal: *Journal of Marriage and the Family*, Feb. 1984, *46*(1), 95-104.

Related research: McCubbin, H. et al., 1980. Developing family invulnerability to stress: Coping patterns and strategies wives employ in managing family separations. In J. Trost (Ed.), *The Family in Change*. Västerås, Sweden: International Library.

2976
Test name: DIVORCE POTENTIAL INDEX

Purpose: To measure marital satisfaction.

Number of items: 5

Format: Respondents are asked to report specific behaviors considered indicative of potential for divorce. Scores are obtained on a scale with a mean of 50 and a standard deviation of 10.

Reliability: Coefficient alpha was .73.

Validity: Correlations with other variables ranged from -.54 to -.80.

Author: Tolstedt, B.E. and Stokes, J.P.

Article: Relation of verbal, affective and physical intimacy to marital satisfaction.

Journal: *Journal of Counseling Psychology*, Oct. 1983, *30*(4), 573-580.

2977
Test name: DIVORCE REACTION INVENTORY

Purpose: To measure post-separation attachment.

Number of items: 46

Format: A few sample items are presented.

Reliability: Cronbach's alpha was .97, .99; Split-half (odd vs. even) was .98.

Validity: Correlation with self-rated adjustment was r = -.75.

Author: Brown, S.D. and Reimer, D.A.

Article: Assessing attachment following divorce: Development and psychometric evaluation of the divorce reaction inventory.

Journal: *Journal of Counseling Psychology*, Oct. 1984, *31*(4), 521-531.

Related research: Bowlby, J., 1980. *Attachment and loss, III: Loss*. New York: Basic Books.

2978
Test name: DYADIC ADJUSTMENT SCALE

Format: Includes two scales: family ownership and family economizing.

Reliability: Coefficient alphas were: .85 (economizing) and .83 (ownership).

Validity: Correlations with other variables ranged from -.24 to .60.

Author: Fergusson, D.M. et al.

Article: The measurement of family material well-being.

Journal: *Journal of Marriage and the Family*, Aug. 1981, *43*(3), 715-725.

Related research: Department of Social Welfare, New Zealand. *Survey of persons aged 65 years and over: Report of results relating to social security benefit rates.* Wellington: New Zealand Government Printer.

2988
Test name: FAMILY RESOURCE QUESTIONNAIRE

Purpose: To measure social support after stroke.

Number of items: 17

Format: 4-point Likert-type response categories. All items presented. Items administered in an interview setting.

Reliability: Inter-rater reliability = .91.

Validity: Correlates .65 (p < .01) with Social Ties Checklist (Starr, Robinson and Price, 1983).

Author: Pomeroy, S. et al.

Article: Family Resource Questionnaire: Reliability and validity of a social support measure for families of stroke patients.

Journal: *Psychological Reports*, April 1985, *56*(2), 411-414.

2989
Test name: FAMILY VIGNETTES

Purpose: To assess probable presence and duration of maltreatment.

Number of items: 9

Format: Interviewers decide which of nine 58-62 word sample family descriptions rank ordered from severe long-term maltreatment, through more recent, less severe maltreatment to positive parenting represents the family being assessed.

Reliability: Pearson product-moment correlations among interviewer ratings ranged from .52 to .93.

Author: Garbarino, J. et al.

Article: Families at risk for destructive parent-child relations in adolescence.

Journal: *Child Development*, Feb. 1984, *55*(1), 174-183.

Related research: Sebes, J.M., 1983. *Determining risk for abuse in families with adolescents: The development of a criterion measure.* Unpublished doctoral dissertation, Pennsylvania State University.

2990
Test name: FILIAL EXPECTANCY SCALE—ADAPTED

Purpose: To measure obligation adult children feel toward their elderly parents.

Number of items: 5

Format: Subjects indicate degree of agreement with each item by responding on a 5-point scale with high scores indicating greater filial responsibility.

Reliability: Cronbach's alpha was .73.

Author: Cicirelli, V.G.

Article: Adult children's attachment and helping behavior to elderly parents: A path model.

Journal: *Journal of Marriage and the Family*, Nov. 1983, *45*(4), 815-825.

Related research: Seelbach, W. and Saver, W., 1977. Filial responsibility, expectations and morale among aged persons. *Gerontologist, 17,* 421-425.

2991
Test name: FILIAL EXPECTATIONS MEASURE

Purpose: To assess parents' expectations of their children's involvement with them across content areas.

Number of items: 10

Format: Areas covered are: contact, sentiment, caretaking, and accessibility. Responses are made on a scale from 1 (strongly disagree) to 4 (strongly agree).

Reliability: Reliability coefficient was .74.

Validity: Correlations with other variables ranged from -.198 to .082.

Author: Quinn, W.H.

Article: Personal and family adjustment in later life.

Journal: *Journal of Marriage and the Family*, Feb. 1983, *45*(1), 57-73.

Related research: Seelbach, W.C., 1978. Correlates of aged parents' filial responsibility expectations and realizations. *Family Coordinator, 27,* 341-350.

2992
Test name: FILIAL RESPONSIBILITY MEASURE

Purpose: To assess children's attitudes regarding the extent of responsibility they hold for their parents across content areas.

Number of items: 10

Format: Areas covered are: contact, sentiment, caretaking, and accessibility. Responses are made on a scale from 1 (strongly disagree) to 4 (strongly agree).

Reliability: Reliability coefficient was .88 (adult children).

Validity: Correlations with other variables ranged from -.091 to .437.

Author: Quinn, W.H.

Article: Personal and family adjustment in later life.

Journal: *Journal of Marriage and the Family*, Feb. 1983, *45*(1), 57-73.

Related research: Seelbach, W.C., 1978. Correlates of aged parents' filial responsibility expectations and realizations. *Family Coordinator*, 27, 341-350.

2993
Test name: HENDERSON ENVIRONMENTAL LEARNING PROCESS SCALE—MODIFIED

Purpose: To measure the intellectual environment of the home.

Number of items: 34

Format: 5-point (high-low) scale.

Reliability: Carmines and Zeller reliability = .80.

Author: Valencia, R.R.

Article: Family status, family constellation, and home environmental variables as predictors of cognitive performance of Mexican-American children.

Journal: *Journal of Educational Psychology*, June 1984, *77*(3), 323-331.

Related research: Henderson, R.W. et al., 1982. Development and validation of the Henderson Environmental Learning Process Scale. *Journal of Social Psychology*, 88, 185-196.

2994
Test name: HOME EDUCATIONAL ENVIRONMENT INDEX

Purpose: To evaluate the educational environment of the home.

Number of items: 39

Format: Includes four dimensions: parent's knowledge and interest in school-related activities; parent's support of academic activities; opportunities for and quality of the interaction between parent and child on school-related activities; and parent's belief in the use of schooling for the child's future.

Reliability: Coefficient alpha ranged from .71 to .80. Test-retest coefficient was .76 (4 weeks, N = 40).

Validity: Correlation with the Dave structured interview was .61. Correlations with standardized reading achievement ranged from r = .51 to r = .63.

Author: Dolan, L.

Article: The prediction of reading achievement and self-esteem from an index of home educational environment: A study of urban elementary schools.

Journal: *Measurement and Evaluation in Guidance*, July 1983, *16*(2), 86-94.

Related research: Dolan, L.J., 1980. Home, school and pupil attitudes. *Evaluation in Education: An International Review Series*, 4, 265-358.

2995
Test name: HOMEMAKERS SATISFACTION QUESTIONNAIRE

Purpose: To measure homemaker's "job" satisfaction.

Number of items: 13

Format: Items taken from 20-item Minnesota Satisfaction Questionnaire. 5-point Likert-type response categories. Items presented.

Reliability: Alpha = .83.

Author: Ivancevich, J.M. and Matteson, M.T.

Article: Occupational stress, satisfaction, physical well-being and coping: A study of homemakers.

Journal: *Psychological Reports*, 1982, *50*(3, Pt. 1), 995-1005.

Related research: Weiss, D.J. et al., 1967. *Manual for the Minnesota Satisfaction Questionnaire: Minnesota studies in vocational rehabilitation XXII*. Minneapolis: Industrial Relations Center, University of Minnesota.

2996
Test name: HOMEMAKING COMMITMENT SCALE

Purpose: To assess how much a person values family and home-related activities.

Number of items: 8

Format: Items are rated on a 5-point scale.

Reliability: Coefficient alpha was .81.

Author: Koski, L.K. and Subich, L.M.

Article: Career and homemaking choices of college preparatory and vocational education students.

Journal: *Vocational Guidance Quarterly*, Dec. 1985, *34*(2), 116-123.

Related research: Farmer, H., 1983. Career and homemaking plans for high school youth. *Journal of Counseling Psychology, 30*, 40-45.
  Super, D.E. et al., 1978. *The Work Salience Inventory*. New York: Columbia University, Teachers College (mimeographed).

2997
Test name: HOME OBSERVATION FOR MEASUREMENT OF THE ENVIRONMENT

Purpose: To provide a measure of environmental stimulation.

Number of items: 45

Format: A checklist for marking whether present or absent in the home. Includes six subscales: emotional and verbal responsivity; avoidance of restriction and punishment; organization of the environment; provision of appropriate play materials; maternal involvement with child; and opportunities for variety in daily stimulation.

Reliability: Stability for total scores over first two years of life was .79. Stability of subscales ranged from .44 to .66. Internal consistency coefficients ranged from .44 to .89.

Author: Mitchell, S.K. and Gray, C.A.

Article: Developmental generalizability of the HOME Inventory.

Journal: *Educational and Psychological Measurement*, winter 1984, *41*(4), 1001-1010.

Related research: Bradley, R.H. and Caldwell, B.M., 1976. The relation of infants' home environments to mental test performance at 54 months: A follow-up study. *Child Development, 47*, 1172-1174.

2998
Test name: HOME OBSERVATION FOR MEASUREMENT OF THE ENVIRONMENT INVENTORY

Purpose: To provide a preschool scale for assessing environmental processes of black children.

Number of items: 55

Format: Includes 8 subscales: toys, games, and reading materials;

language stimulation; physical environment; pride, affection, and warmth; stimulation of academic behavior; encouraging social maturity; variety of stimulation; and physical punishment.

Validity: Correlations with elementary school achievement tests ranged from -.03 to .50.

Author: Bradley, R.H. and Caldwell, B.M.

Article: The Home Inventory: A validation of the preschool scale for black children.

Journal: *Child Development*, June 1981, 52(2), 708-710.

Related research: Bradley, R. and Caldwell, B., 1979. Home Observation for Measurement of the Environment: A revision of the preschool scale. *American Journal of Mental Deficiency*, 84, 235-244.

2999
Test name: INDEX OF ACHIEVEMENT VALUES

Purpose: To assess the mother's general valuation of achievement and independence within the family.

Number of items: 7

Format: Employs a five-choice scale.

Validity: Correlation with Traditional Family Ideology was .54.

Author: McGowan, R.J. and Johnson, D.L.

Article: The mother-child relationship and other antecedents of childhood intelligence: A causal analysis.

Journal: *Child Development*, June 1984, 55(3), 810-820.

Related research: Strodtbeck, F., 1958. Family interaction, value, and achievement. In D.C. McClelland (Ed.), *Talent and Society*. New York: Van Nostrand.

3000
Test name: INDEX OF SPOUSE ABUSE

Purpose: To measure extent of abuse inflicted upon a women by her spouse or partner.

Number of items: 30

Format: Includes two types of abuse: physical and nonphysical. Responses are made on a 5-point scale from 1 (never) to 5 (very frequently). All items are presented.

Reliability: Coefficient alphas were .903 and .942 (physical abuse) and .912 and .969 (nonphysical abuse).

Validity: Coefficient of discriminant validity was .73 (physical abuse) and .80 (nonphysical abuse).

Author: Hudson, W.W. and McIntosh, S.R.

Article: The assessment of spouse abuse: Two quantifiable dimensions.

Journal: *Journal of Marriage and the Family*, Nov. 1981, *43*(4), 873-885.

3001
Test name: INFLUENCE ON PARENTS SCALE

Purpose: To measure the extent to which early adolescents feel they influence their parents' decision making.

Number of items: 30

Format: Includes two subscales for identifying influence on mother and on father. Responses are made on a six-point Likert scale. Examples are presented.

Reliability: Cronbach's alphas ranged from .749 to .859.

Author: Thornburg, H.D. and Shinn, J.M.

Article: Early adolescents' perceived influence on parental behavior.

Journal: *Child Study Journal*, 1982, *12*(1), 21-26.

Related research: Baranowski, M.D., 1978. Adolescents' attempted influences on parental behavior. *Adolescence*, *13*, 585-604.

3002
Test name: INTERACTION STRAIN QUESTIONNAIRE

Purpose: To measure role conflict.

Number of items: 12

Format: True - don't know - untrue response categories.

Reliability: Alpha = .75.

Author: Barling, J. and VanBart, D.

Article: Mothers' subjective employment experiences and the behavior of their nursery school children.

Journal: *Journal of Occupational Psychology*, March 1984, *57*(1), 49-56.

Related research: Parry, G. and Warr, P., 1980. The measurement of mother's work attitudes. *Journal of Occupational Psychology*, *53*, 245-252.

3003
Test name: INTERPARENTAL CONFLICT SCALES

Purpose: To assess amount of conflict in family settings.

Number of items: 37

Format: The parents and adolescents rate the amount of conflict in family settings across such domains as finances, child rearing, etc.

Reliability: Test-retest reliability was .91.

Author: Garbarino, J. et al

Article: Families at risk for destructive parent-child relations in adolescence.

Journal: *Child Development*, Feb. 1984, *55*(1), 174-183.

Related research: Schwartz, J.C. and Zuroff, D.C., 1979. Family structure and depression in female college students: Effects of parental conflict, decision-making power and inconsistency of love. *Journal of Abnormal Psychology*, *80*, 398-406.

3004
Test name: INTIMACY SCALE

Purpose: To measure general intimacy or affection of mothers and daughters.

Number of items: 17

Format: Individual scores are produced by summing and averaging the items. All items are presented.

Reliability: Cronbach's alphas ranged from .91 to .97.

Author: Walker, A.J. and Thompson, L.

Article: Intimacy and intergenerational aid and contact among mothers and daughters.

Journal: *Journal of Marriage and the Family*, *45*(4), 841-849.

Related research: Walker, A.J., 1979. *The social networks of young marrieds: distinguishing among relationship types*. Unpublished dissertation, Pennsylvania State University.

3005
Test name: INVENTORY OF FAMILY RELATIONSHIPS

Purpose: To measure parent-child interaction in the family by questioning children.

Number of items: 26

Format: Rating scale format.

Reliability: Alpha ranged from .66 to .84 across subscales.

Author: Howell, F.M. and McBroom, L.W.

Article: Social relations at home and at school: An analysis of the correspondence principle.

Journal: *Sociology of Education*, Jan. 1982, 55(1), 40-52.

Related research: Bachman, J.G., 1970. The impact of family background and intelligence on tenth grade boys. *Youth in Transition, Vol. I.* Ann Arbor: Institute for Social Research.

3006
Test name: JEALOUSY SCALE

Purpose: To measure jealousy in marriage.

Number of items: 8

Format: Subjects respond, on an 11-point scale, how they would feel about their mates' behavior in 8 situations. All items presented.

Reliability: Alpha = .65.

Author: Hansen, G.

Article: Perceived threats and marital jealousy.

Journal: *Social Psychology Quarterly*, Sept. 1985, 48(3), 262-268.

Related research: Mathes, E.W. et al., 1982. A convergent validity study of six jealousy scales. *Psychological Reports*, 50, 1143-1147.

3007
Test name: KANSAS MARITAL SATISFACTION SCALE

Purpose: To measure marital satisfaction.

Number of items: 3

Format: Items are of the "how satisfied are you with ...?" format followed by 7 numbered response categories (extremely dissatisfied to extremely satisfied).

Reliability: Alphas ranged from .93 to .98.

Validity: Correlated with marital social desirability (.41, $p < .0001$), but not with individual social desirability (.05).

Author: Schumm, W.R. et al.

Article: Characteristics of responses to the Kansas Marital Satisfaction Scale by a sample of 84 married mothers.

Journal: *Psychological Reports*, Oct. 1983, 53(2), 567-572.

Related research: Mitchell, S.E. et al., 1983. Test-retest reliability of the Kansas Marital Satisfaction Scale. *Psychological Reports*, 53(2), 545-546.
   Schumm, W.R., 1983. Characteristics of the Kansas Marital Satisfaction Scale in a sample of 79 married couples. *Psychological Reports*, 53(2), 583-588.

3008
Test name: KANSAS PARENTAL SATISFACTION SCALE

Purpose: To measure parental satisfaction with children and parenting.

Number of items: 3

Format: 7-point Likert format.

Reliability: Alpha ranged from .78 to .84.

Validity: Significantly correlated with self-esteem (.38 to .68).

Author: James, D.E. et al.

Article: Characteristics of the Kansas Parental Satisfaction Scale among two samples of married parents.

Journal: *Psychological Reports*, Aug. 1985, 57(1), 163-169.

3009
Test name: LIFE CHANGES SCALE

Purpose: To measure how much a mother's life changes after the birth of a child.

Number of items: 8

Format: 5-point response scales. Sample items presented.

Reliability: Alpha = .88.

Author: Pistrang, N.

Article: Women's work involvement and experience of new motherhood.

Journal: *Journal of Marriage and the Family*, May 1984, 46(2), 433-447.

Related research: Hoffman, L.W., 1978. Effects of the first child on the woman's role. In W.B. Miller and L.F. Newman (Eds.), *The first child and family formation*. Chapel Hill, NC: Carolina Population Center.

3010
Test name: LITTLE PARENTAL VALUING STYLES SCALE

Purpose: To evaluate attitudes and behaviors expressed by parents toward problem children.

Number of items: 52

Format: 6-point Likert format.

Reliability: Internal consistency = .50 to .79.

Author: Little, L.F. and Thompson, R.

Article: Truancy: How parents and teachers contribute.

Journal: *The School Counselor*, March 1983, 30(4), 285-291.

Related research: Little, L.F., 1980. The impact of Gestalt group psychotherapy on parents' perceptions of children identified as problematic. Doctoral dissertation, University of Kentucky. *Dissertation Abstracts International*, 1981, *42*. University microfilms No. 8116912.

3011
Test name: LOCKE WALLACE SHORT MARITAL ADJUSTMENT TEST

Purpose: To measure marital dissatisfaction.

Number of items: 14

Format: Multiple-choice items with a high score representing a high level of marital dissatisfaction.

Validity: Correlations with Ryder's Lovesickness Scale r = .54 (husbands) and r = .53 (wives). Correlations with individual locus of control r = -.03 (husbands) and r = .19 (wives).

Author: Doherty, W.J.

Article: Locus of control differences and marital dissatisfaction.

Journal: *Journal of Marriage and the Family*, May 1981, *43*(2), 369-377.

Related research: Locke, H.J. and Wallace, K.M., 1959. Short marital adjustment and prediction tests: Their reliability and validity. *Marriage and Family Living, 21*, 251-255.

3012
Test name: LOVESICKNESS SCALE

Purpose: To measure marital dissatisfaction relative to one's partner not being sufficiently loving or attentive.

Number of items: 32

Format: Responses either "true," "partly true," or "false." A sample item is presented.

Reliability: Cronbach's alpha was .89 (husbands) and .91 (wives).

Validity: Correlations with Locke Wallace Short Marital Adjustment Test r = .54 (husbands) and r = .53 (wives). Correlations with individual locus of control r = -.02 (husbands) and r = .17 (wives).

Author: Doherty, W.J.

Article: Locus of control differences and marital dissatisfaction.

Journal: *Journal of Marriage and the Family*, May 1981, *43*(2), 369-377.

Related research: Ryder, R.G., 1973. Longitudinal data relating marriage satisfaction and having a child. *Journal of Marriage and the Family*, 35, 604-608.

3013
Test name: MARITAL ACTIVITIES INVENTORY

Purpose: To discriminate between distressed and nondistressed couples.

Number of items: 85

Format: Contains an inventory of common recreational, self-enhancing, affectional, and utilitarian activities.

Reliability: Test-retest (11 weeks) reliability coefficients were r = .71 and .87 (N = 12).

Author: Stein, S.J. et al.

Article: The interrelationships and reliability of a multilevel behavior-based assessment package for distressed couples.

Journal: *Journal of Behavioral Assessment*, Dec. 1982, 4(4), 343-360.

Related research: Weiss, R.L. et al., 1973. A framework for conceptualizing marital conflict, a technology for altering it, some data for evaluating it. In L.A. Hamerlynck et al., (Eds.), *Behavior change: Methodology concepts and practice*. Champaign, IL: Research Press, pp. 309-342.

3014
Test name: MARITAL ADJUSTMENT SCALE

Purpose: To measure marital adjustment.

Number of items: 7

Format: Three agreement items, three frequency of occurrence items, and one global happiness item.

Reliability: Alpha = .77.

Author: Hansen, G.

Article: Perceived threats and marital jealousy.

Journal: *Social Psychology Quarterly*, Sept. 1985, 48(3), 262-268.

Related research: Spanier, G.B., 1976. Measuring dyadic adjustment. New scales for assessing the quality of marriage and similar dyads. *Journal of Marriage and the Family*, 38, 15-38.
   Sharpley, C.F. and Cross, D.G., 1982. A psychometric evaluation of the Spanier Dyadic Adjustment Scale, *Journal of Marriage and the Family*, 44, 39-41.

3015
Test name: MARITAL ADJUSTMENT TEST

Purpose: To provide an index of marital adjustment.

Number of items: 15

Format: A score of 100 is the cutoff between nondistressed (above 100) and distressed (below 100).

Reliability: Split-half coefficient was .90.

Author: Volkin, J.I. and Jacob, T.

Article: The impacts of spouse monitoring on target behavior and recorder satisfaction.

Journal: *Journal of Behavioral Assessment*, June 1981, *3*(2), 99-109.

Related research: Locke, H.J. and Wallace, K.M., 1957. Short marital adjustment and prediction tests: Their reliability and validity. *Marriage and Family Living, 21*, 251-255.

3016
Test name: MARITAL ALTERNATIVE SCALE

Purpose: To measure frequency of marital alternatives if separation or divorce were to occur.

Number of items: 11

Format: Possible alternatives to marriage followed by 4-point scale (impossible to certain). Sample items presented.

Reliability: Alpha = .78.

Author: Hansen, G.

Article: Perceived threats and marital jealousy.

Journal: *Social Psychology Quarterly*, Sept. 1985, *48*(3), 262-268.

Related research: Udry, J.R., 1981. Marital alternatives and marital disruption. *Journal of Marriage and the Family, 43*, 889-897.

3017
Test name: MARITAL COMMUNICATION INVENTORY

Purpose: To measure marital communication.

Number of items: 46

Format: Self-report. Items are given.

Reliability: Internal consistency reliabilities ranged from .73 to .95.

Author: Schumm, W.R. et al.

Article: Dimensionality of the Marital Communication Inventory and marital conventionalization: A third report.

Journal: *Psychological Reports*, Feb. 1981, *48*(1), 163-171.

Related research: Schumm, W.R. et al., 1979. Dimensionality of the Marital Communication Inventory:

A preliminary factor analytic study. *Psychological Reports*, *45*, 123-128.

3018
Test name: MARITAL COMPARISON LEVEL INDEX

Purpose: To measure evaluations of marital relationships.

Number of items: 32

Format: 7-point scales expressing a comparison of current experiences with current expectations.

Reliability: Alpha = .93.

Author: Sabatelli, R.M. and Cecil-Pigo, E.F.

Article: Relational interdependence and commitment in marriage.

Journal: *Journal of Marriage and the Family*, Nov. 1985, *47*(4), 931-937.

Related research: Sabatelli, R.M., 1984. The Marital Comparison Level Index: A measure for assessing outcomes relative to expectations. *Journal of Marriage and the Family*, 46, 651-662.

3019
Test name: MARITAL CONVENTIONALIZATION SCALE

Purpose: To measure marital conventionalization.

Number of items: 15

Format: There are two formats: 1) Respondents mark either "true" or "false" for each item. 2) Respondents select one statement from a pair of statements in a forced-choice format. All items are presented.

Reliability: Alpha reliability was .83 (N = 205) for true/false format and .90 (N = 160) for forced-choice format.

Validity: Correlations with marital adjustment ranged from .629 to .787.

Author: Hansen, G.L.

Article: Marital adjustment and conventionalization: A reexamination.

Journal: *Journal of Marriage and the Family*, Nov. 1981, *43*(4), 855-863.

Related research: Edmonds, V.H., 1967. Marital conventionalization: Definition and measurement. *Journal of Marriage and the Family*, 29, 681-688.

3020
Test name: MARITAL DISAFFECTION AND DISHARMONY SCALES

Purpose: To measure marital disaffection and disharmony (items from Marital Satisfaction Inventory).

Number of items: 44

Format: True-false. All items presented.

Reliability: Internal consistency ranged from .87 to .95. Test-retest ranged from .83 to .89.

Validity: 29 behavioral correlations presented (p < .05) that ranged from .22 to .41.

Author: Snyder, D.K. and Regts, J.M.

Article: Factor scales for measuring marital disharmony and disaffection.

Journal: *Journal of Consulting and Clinical Psychology*, Oct. 1982, 50(5), 736-743.

Related research: Snyder, D.K., 1979. *Marital Satisfaction Inventory*, Los Angeles, CA: Western Psychological Services.

3021
Test name: MARITAL GOAL-ORIENTATION SCALE

Purpose: To assess intentionality that couples employ to improve their marriages.

Number of items: 7

Format: Multiple-choice. (1 = once in a while to 5 = almost always.)

Reliability: Alpha ranged from .86 to .89. Test-retest ranged from .76 to .87.

Validity: Correlated .51 to .90 with marital conflict.

Author: Eggeman, K. et al.

Article: Assessing spouses' perceptions of Gottman's Temporal Form in marital conflict.

Journal: *Psychological Reports*, Aug. 1985, 57(1), 171-181.

3022
Test name: MARITAL HAPPINESS SCALE

Purpose: To measure marital happiness.

Number of items: 10

Format: Areas include: household responsibilities; occupational progress; sex; spouse independence; other marital dimensions; and general happiness. Responses made on a 10-point scale.

Reliability: Reliability coefficients ranged from .66 to .89 (N = 12).

Validity: Correlations with other variables ranged from -.30 to .78 (N = 46).

Author: Stein, S.J. et al.

Article: The interrelationships and reliability of a multilevel behavior-based assessment package for distressed couples.

Journal: *Journal of Behavioral Assessment,* Dec. 1982, *4*(4), 343-360.

Related research: Azrin, N. et al., 1973. Reciprocity counseling: A rapid learning based procedure for marital counseling. *Behavior Research Therapy, 11,* 365-382.

3023
Test name: MARITAL INSTABILITY INDEX

Purpose: To measure instability in marriage.

Number of items: 12

Format: Yes-no format.

Reliability: Internal consistency = .93.

Author: Booth, A. and Edwards, J.N.

Article: Age at marriage and marital instability.

Journal: *Journal of Marriage and the Family,* Feb. 1985, *47*(1), 67-75.

Related research: Booth, A. et al., 1983. Measuring marital instability.

Journal of Marriage and the Family, 40, 387-394.

3024
Test name: MARITAL INTERACTION CODING SYSTEM

Purpose: To measure interaction between married couples.

Number of items: 28

Format: Observers code behavior every 30 seconds in 10-minute exchanges. Sample types of behavior presented.

Reliability: Mean inter-observer correlation = .81. Point-by-point reliability ranged from .57 to .74.

Author: Margolin, G. and Wampold, B.E.

Article: Sequential analysis of conflict and accord in distressed and non-distressed marital partners.

Journal: *Journal of Consulting and Clinical Psychology,* Aug. 1981, *49*(4), 554-567.

Related research: Hops, H. et al., 1972. *Marital Interaction Coding System.* Unpublished manuscript. University of Oregon and Oregon Research Institute.

3025
Test name: MARITAL INTERACTION SATISFACTION SCALE

Purpose: To measure satisfaction with marital interaction.

Number of items: 14

Format: 7-point desired frequency scale. Sample items presented.

Reliability: Alpha averaged .73 across husbands and wives and across 3 time periods.

Author: Belsky, J. et al.

Article: Stability and change in marriage across the transition to parenthood: A second study.

Journal: *Journal of Marriage and the Family*, Nov. 1985, *47*(4), 855-865.

Related research: Huston, T., 1983. The topography of marriage: A longitudinal study of change in husband-wife relationships over the first year. Plenary address: International Conference on Personal Relationships, Madison, WI.

3026
Test name: MARITAL QUALITY SCALE

Purpose: To measure marital quality.

Number of items: 27

Format: A Likert-type scale composed of five parts.

Reliability: Cronbach's alpha was .91.

Author: Bowen, G.L. and Orthner, D.K.

Article: Sex-role congruency and marital quality.

Journal: *Journal of Marriage and the Family*, Feb. 1983, *45*(1), 223-230.

Related research: Powers, W.G. and Hutchinson, K., 1979. The measurement of communication apprehension in the marriage relationship. *Journal of Marriage and the Family*, *41*, 89-95.

3027
Test name: MARITAL SATISFACTION QUESTIONNAIRE

Purpose: To measure marital satisfaction of wives.

Number of items: 36

Format: Includes 3 parts: general issues, issues of agreement with husband, and extent of satisfaction of handling issues with husbands.

Reliability: Cronbach's alpha was .95.

Validity: Correlation with interviewer's perception of respondent's marital satisfaction provided an r = .64.

Author: Madden, M.E. and Janoff-Bulman, R.

Article: Blame, control, and marital satisfaction: Wives' attributions for conflict in marriage.

Journal: *Journal of Marriage and the Family*, Aug. 1981, *43*(3), 663-674.

Related research: Locke, H.J., 1968. *Predicting adjustment in marriage*. Westport, CT: Greenwood Press.

3028
Test name: MARITAL SATISFACTION SCALE

Purpose: To measure marital satisfaction.

Number of items: 10

Format: 5-point frequency scales. Sample items presented.

Reliability: Alpha = .80.

Author: Farrell, J. and Markides, K.S.

Article: Marriage and health: A three-generational study of Mexican-Americans.

Journal: *Journal of Marriage and the Family*, Nov. 1985, *47*(4), 1029-1036.

Related research: Gilford, R. and Bengston, V., 1979. Measuring marital satisfaction in three generations: Positive and negative dimensions. *Journal of Marriage and the Family*, *41*, 387-398.

3029
Test name: OBJECTIVE MARITAL DEPENDENCY MEASURE

Purpose: To provide an index of wives' objective dependency.

Number of items: 3

Format: Includes 3 dichotomous variables: women working, children age 5 or younger, husband earned 75% of couples' income.

Reliability: Cronbach's alpha was .598

Validity: Correlation with wives' subjective marital dependency was .147.

Author: Kalmuss, D.S. and Straus, M.A.

Article: Wife's marital dependency and wife abuse.

Journal: *Journal of Marriage and the Family*, May 1982, *44*(2), 277-286.

3030
Test name: PARENT-ADOLESCENT RELATIONSHIPS SCALE

Purpose: To measure closeness to parents.

Number of items: 21

Format: 5-point closeness response categories. Sample items presented.

Reliability: Alpha ranged from .71 to .78 across two subscales.

Author: Bell, N.J. and Avery, A.W.

Article: Family structure and parent-adolescent relationships: Does family structure really make a difference?

Journal: *Journal of Marriage and the Family*, May 1987, 47(2), 503-508.

Related research: Rundquist, E.A. and Sletto, R.F., 1936. *Personality in the Depression*. Minneapolis: University of Minnesota Press.

3031
Test name: PARENTAL ACCEPTANCE - REJECTION QUESTIONNAIRE

Purpose: To measure parental warmth.

Number of items: 60

Format: A self-report questionnaire whereby children are asked to reflect upon the warmth, hostility, neglect, and undifferentiated rejection they experienced in their families. Responses are made on a four-point Likert-type scale ranging from "almost always true" to "almost never true." Examples are presented.

Reliability: Coefficient alphas ranged from .72 to .90.

Author: Rohner, R.P. and Pattengill, S.M.

Article: Perceived parental acceptance-rejection and parental control among Korean adolescents.

Journal: *Child Development*, April 1985, 56(2), 524-528.

Related research: Rohner, R.P., 1984. *Handbook for the study of parental acceptance and rejection.* (Rev. ed.) Storrs, CT: Center for the Study of Parental Acceptance and Rejection, University of Connecticut.

3032
Test name: PARENT ATTITUDE SURVEY (PAS)

Purpose: To measure parents' child-rearing attitudes.

Number of items: 77

Format: Likert format.

Reliability: Split-half ranged from .68 to .86.

Author: Williams, R.E. et al.

Article: Effects of STEP on parental attitudes and locus of control of their learning disabled children.

Journal: *The School Counselor*, Nov. 1984, *32*(2), 126-133.

Related research: Hereford, C.F., 1963. *Changing parental attitudes through group discussion.* Austin, TX: University of Texas Press.

3033
Test name: PARENT-CHILD RELATION QUESTIONNAIRE—SHORT FORM II

Purpose: To measure adults' retrospective reports of parental behavior.

Number of items: 50

Format: 5-point response scale (very true to very untrue).

Reliability: Cronbach's alpha ranged from .64 to .90 across scales, by sex.

Author: Tzuriel, D. and Haywood, H.C.

Article: Locus of control and child-rearing practices in intrinsically motivated and extrinsically motivated children.

Journal: *Psychological Reports*, Dec. 1985, *57*(3, Pt. I), 887-894.

Related research: Roe, A. and Siegelman, M., 1963. A parent-child relation questionnaire. *Child Development*, *34*, 335-369.

3034
Test name: PARENT-CHILD RELATIONSHIP SURVEY

Purpose: To assess the quality of parent-child relationships.

Number of items: 48 (24 for mothers, 24 for fathers).

Format: Likert-type items.

Reliability: .96 for father scale and .94 for mother scale.

Author: Worley, S.M. and Shwebel, A.I.

Article: The parent-child relationship survey: An examination of its psychometric properties.

Journal: *Psychological Reports*, Aug. 1985, *57*(1), 155-161.

Related research: Fine, M.A. et al., 1983. Long-term effects of divorce on parent-child relationships. *Developmental Psychology*, *19*, 703-713.

3035
Test name: PERCEIVED MARITAL SATISFACTION INDEX

Purpose: To measure marital satisfaction.

Number of items: 5

Format: Respondents indicate the degree to which they are happy or satisfied with their marriage. Scores range from 5 to 35.

Reliability: Coefficient alpha was .88.

Validity: Correlations with other variables ranged from -.80 to .74.

Author: Tolstedt, B.E. and Stokes, J.P.

Article: Relation of verbal, affective and physical intimacy to marital satisfaction.

Journal: *Journal of Counseling Psychology*, Oct. 1983, *30*(4), 573-580.

Related research: Locke, H.J. and Wallace, K.M., 1959. Short marital adjustment and prediction tests: Their reliability and validity. *Marriage and Family Living, 21*, 251-255.

3036
Test name: PERCEIVED PATERNAL PARENTING SCALES

Purpose: To measure perceived paternal parenting.

Number of items: 19

Format: Includes four scales: nurturance, instrumental companionship, affective punishment, and sex-role enforcement.

Reliability: Internal reliability coefficients ranged from .66 to .81.

Author: Devlin, P.K. and Cowan, G.A.

Article: Homophobia, perceived fathering and male intimate relationships.

Journal: *Journal of Personality Assessment*, Oct. 1985, *49*(5), 467-473.

Related research: McDonald, M.P., 1971. Internal-external locus of control: Parental antecedents. *Journal of Consulting and Clinical Psychology, 37*, 141-147.

Spence, J. and Helmreich, R.L., 1978. *Masculinity and femininity. Their psychological dimensions, correlates and antecedents*. Austin, TX: University of Texas Press.

3037
Test name: PERCEIVED SECURITY SCALE

Purpose: To measure mothers' perceptions of childrens' fear, anxiety, and sorrow in daily separations and in unfamiliar surroundings.

Number of items: 11

Format: Four- and five-point rating scales. All items presented.

Reliability: Cronbach's alpha = .84.

Validity: When subjects are divided into A1 + A2, B1 + B2 + B3, and B4 + C groups on Ainsworth's Strange Situation (1978), the means differed significantly (F = 7.01, P < .01) with the B4 + C scoring considerably less secure than the other groups.

Author: Van Ijzendoorn, M. H. et al.

Article: How B is B4? Attachment and security of Dutch children in Ainsworth's Strange Situation and at home.

Journal: *Psychological Reports*, June 1983, 52(3), 683-691.

3038
Test name: PERSONAL HISTORY INVENTORY FOR CHILDREN

Purpose: To measure parental support systems of children as perceived by teachers.

Number of items: 14

Format: Yes-no. All items presented.

Reliability: Test-retest (one month) ranged from .80 (divorced parents) to .90 (intact families).

Validity: Correlates significantly with evaluations of self, mothers' evaluations, and fathers' evaluations (p < .05). Significant correlations ranged in magnitude from .18 to .41.

Author: Parish, T.S. and Wigle, S.E.

Article: Discerning functionality of children's support systems through use of the Personal History Inventory for children.

Journal: *Psychological Reports*, Aug. 1985, 57(1), 32-34.

3039
Test name: PHYSICAL INTIMACY MEASURE

Purpose: To measure physical intimacy.

Number of items: 15

Format: Items deal with: attractiveness of spouse, a variety of physical and sexual activities, and pleasure derived from those physical and sexual activities.

Reliability: Coefficient alpha = .89.

Validity: Correlations with other variables ranged from -.54 to .66.

Author: Tolstedt, B.E. and Stokes, J.P.

Article: Relation of verbal, affective and physical intimacy to marital satisfaction.

Journal: *Journal of Counseling Psychology*, Oct. 1983, *30*(4), 573-580.

3040
Test name: PSYCHOLOGICAL SEPARATION INVENTORY

Purpose: To measure adolescent psychological separation from parents.

Number of items: 138

Format: Includes four scales of independence: functional, emotional, conflictual, and attitudinal. Examples of each are presented. Responses are made on a 5-point Likert-type scale ranging from "not at all true of me" (0) to "very true of me" (4).

Reliability: Cronbach's coefficient alpha ranged from .84 to .92. Test-retest (2 to 3 weeks) reliability coefficients ranged from .49 to .94 for 26 males and from .70 to .96 for 28 females.

Validity: Correlations with other variables ranged from -.37 to .30 for males and from -.38 to .41 for females.

Author: Hoffman, J.A.

Article: Psychological separation of late adolescents from their parents.

Journal: *Journal of Counseling Psychology*, April 1984, *31*(2), 170-178.

Related research: Sherman, A.W., 1946. Emancipation status of college students. *The Journal of Genetic Psychology*, *68*, 171-180.

3041
Test name: REWARDINGNESS SCALE

Purpose: To measure how rewarding marriage is.

Number of items: 7

Format: Likert format.

Reliability: Alpha = .86.

Author: Hansen, G.

Article: Perceived threats and marital jealousy.

Journal: *Social Psychology Quarterly*, Sept. 1985, *48*(3), 262-268.

Related research: Cate, R.M. et al., 1982. Fairness and reward level as predictors of relationship satisfaction. *Social Psychology Quarterly*, *45*, 177-181.

3042
Test name: ROLLINS CHILD-REARING SCALE

Purpose: To measure parental behavior with children.

Number of items: 78

Format: Children rate parents on each item. Items available from B. Rollins and D. Thomas, Department of Child Development, Brigham Young University, Provo, Utah, 84602.

Reliability: Alpha ranged from .66 to .86 across subscales.

Validity: Items yielded similar factors in cross-cultural comparisons.

Author: Jenson, L. et al.

Article: Maternal behavior and the development of empathy in preschool children.

Journal: *Psychological Reports*, June 1981, *48*(3), 879-884.

Related research: Thomas, P.L., 1977. *Validity in parent-child research: A comparison of self-report and behavioral observations*. Paper presented to the annual meeting of the Council of Family Relations.

3043

Test name: SCALES FOR INVESTIGATION OF DUAL-CAREER FAMILY—REVISED

Purpose: To assess relevant information about dual-career women.

Number of items: 44

Format: Includes 6 scales: Marriage type, domestic responsibility, satisfaction, self-image, career line, and career salience. All items are presented.

Reliability: Coefficient alphas for the scales ranged from .29 to .74.

Validity: Correlations with PRF ANDRO SCALES ranged from r = -.38 to r = .43.

Author: Gaddy, C.D. et al.

Article: A study of the Scales for Investigation of the Dual-Career Family.

Journal: *Measurement and Evaluation in Counseling and Development*, Oct. 1985, *18*(3), 120-127.

Related research: Pendleton, B.F. et al., 1980. Scales for investigation of the dual-career family. *Journal of Marriage and the Family*, 42, 269-276.

3044

Test name: SIBLING RELATIONSHIP QUESTIONNAIRE

Purpose: To assess children's perceptions of the qualities of their sibling relationships.

Number of items: 51

Format: Measures the following qualities: intimacy, prosocial behavior, companionship, similarity, nurturance by sibling, nurturance of sibling, admiration by sibling, admiration of sibling, affection, dominance by sibling, dominance over sibling, quarreling, antagonism, competition, parental partiality, general relationship evaluation.

Reliability: Test-retest (10 days) reliabilities ranged from .58 to .86 (N = 84).

Validity: Mean correlation with Children's Social Desirability Questionnaire was r = .14.

Author: Furman, W. and Buhrmester, D.

Article: Children's perceptions of the qualities of sibling relationships.

Journal: *Child Development*, April 1985, *56*(2), 448-461.

3045
Test name: SPOUSE ADJECTIVE TEST

Purpose: To measure spouses' descriptions of self and partner.

Number of items: 45

Format: Spouse checks adjectives that apply to self and on identical list for those that apply to spouse. Examples are presented. Provides 4 scores.

Validity: Correlations with locus of control ranged from -.37 to .26 (husbands) and from -.48 to .32 (wives).

Author: Doherty, W.J.

Article: Locus of control differences and marital dissatisfaction.

Journal: *Journal of Marriage and the Family*, May 1981, *43*(2), 369-377.

Related research: Ryder, R.G., 1971. Dimensional structure of SPAT (The Spouse Adjective Test). *Catalog of selected documents in psychology*, *1*, 17.

3046
Test name: SUBJECTIVE MARITAL DEPENDENCY SCALE

Purpose: To assess perceptions of wives concerning who would be hurt more in each of five areas by a marriage break up.

Number of items: 5

Format: Includes 5 areas: financial, sexual, loss of friends, angry relatives, and loneliness.

Reliability: Coefficient alpha was .35

Validity: Correlation with wives' objective marital dependency was .147.

Author: Kalmuss, D.S. and Straus, M.A.

Article: Wife's marital dependency and wife abuse.

Journal: *Journal of Marriage and the Family*, May 1982, *44*(2), 277-286.

3047
Test name: TRADITIONAL FAMILY IDEOLOGY

Purpose: To measure the mother's attitude toward traditional versus modern family behavior.

Number of items: 12

Format: Employs a five-choice rating scale.

Validity: Correlation with the Index of Achievement Values was .54.

Author: McGowan, R.J. and Johnson, D.L.

Article: The mother-child relationship and other antecedents of childhood intelligence: A causal analysis.

Journal: *Child Development*, June 1984, *55*(3), 810-820.

Related research: Levinson, D. and Huffman, P., 1955. Traditional family ideology and its relation to personality. *Journal of Personality*, *23*, 251-273.

3048
Test name: TRANSITION TO PARENTHOOD MEASURE

Purpose: To measure the degree of difficulty of the transition to parenthood.

Number of items: 25

Format: Includes 3 factors: parental responsibilities and restrictions; parental gratifications; and marital intimacy and stability. All items are presented.

Reliability: Reliability coefficients for the three factors were .751, .822, and .762.

Validity: Correlations with other variables ranged from -.334 to .394.

Author: Steffensmeier, R.H.

Article: A role model of the transition to parenthood.

Journal: *Journal of Marriage and the Family*, May 1982, *44*(2), 319-334.

Related research: Steffensmeier, R.H., 1977. *A role analysis of the transition to parenthood: Research continuities and further development.* Unpublished doctoral dissertation, University of Iowa.

INSTITUTIONAL INFORMATION

3049
Test name: ADJECTIVE RATING SCALE

Purpose: To measure student expectations and perceptions of academic program and nonacademic life.

Number of items: 24 adjectives, plus 2 statements.

Format: Four-point response scale per adjective. Sample adjective presented. Statements also presented.

Reliability: Internal consistency was .83 for program and .94 for nonacademic life on a factorially derived subscale.

Author: Pascarella, E.T. and Terenzini, P.T.

Article: Residence arrangement, student/faculty relationships and freshman year educational outcomes.

Journal: *Journal of College Student Personnel*, March 1981, 22(2), 147-156.

Related research: Kelly, E. et al., 1978. The development and use of the Adjective Rating Scale: A measure of attitude toward causes and programs. *Journal of Selected Abstracts in Science*, 8, 19-20.

3050
Test name: AGENCY CLIMATE QUESTIONNAIRE

Purpose: To measure organization in six dimensions: structure, support, concern, autonomy, morale, and conflict.

Number of items: 80

Format: 5-point scale.

Reliability: Internal consistency across scales ranged from .53 to .83.

Author: Heller, R.M. et al.

Article: Convergent and discriminant validity of psychological and objective indices of organizational climate.

Journal: *Psychological Reports*, 1982, 51(1), 183-195.

Related research: Schneider, B. and Bartlett, C.J., 1968. Individual differences and organizational climate: Research plan and questionnaire development. *Personnel Psychology*, 21, 323-333.

3051

Test name: AUTONOMY SCALE

Purpose: To measure job autonomy and influence.

Number of items: 9

Format: 5-point scale (never true to always true). Taken from Moos and Insel's Work Environment Scale.

Reliability: Alpha = .62.

Author: Jackson, S.E.

Article: Participation in decision-making as a strategy for reducing job-related stress.

Journal: *Journal of Applied Psychology*, Feb. 1983, *68*(1), 3-19.

Related research: Moos, R.H. and Insel, P.M., 1984. *Work environment scale (Form R)*. Palo Alto, CA: Consulting Psychologists Press.

3052

Test name: BEHAVIOR CODES FOR JOB ENVIRONMENT

Purpose: To measure, by observation, job behavior.

Number of items: 133 behaviors.

Format: Observers enter codes on a Datamyte 900 data collector. All categories of work are presented.

Reliability: Levels of agreement (Spearman rank-order correlation) ranged from .76 to .97 after observers had been trained 6 hours per week for 18 weeks.

Author: Ruggiero, M. and Steinberg, L.D.

Article: The empirical study of teenage work: A behavioral code for the assessment of adolescent job environments.

Journal: *Journal of Vocational Behavior*, Aug. 1981, *19*(2), 163-174.

Related research: Torgerson, L., 1977. Datamyte 900. *Behavior Research Methods and Instrumentation*, *9*(5), 405-406.

3053

Test name: BOUNDARY-SPANNING ROLES QUESTIONNAIRE

Purpose: To measure the extent of boundary-spanning roles in school psychologists' jobs.

Number of items: 13

Format: 5-point Likert response categories.

Reliability: Cronbach's alpha = .89.

Author: Jerrell, J.M.

Article: Boundary-spanning functions served by rural school psychologists.

Journal: *Journal of School Psychology*, 1984, 22(3), 259-271.

Related research: Jemison, D.B., 1980. *An empirical identification of interorganizational boundary-spanning roles*. Paper presented at the Academy of Management Annual Conference, San Diego.

3054
Test name: BRANCH BANK CLIMATE FOR SERVICE SURVEY

Purpose: To measure perceptions of the service-related practices of the branch bank.

Number of items: 28

Format: Includes four climate for service dimensions: branch management, systems support, customer attention/retention, and logistics support. Examples are presented.

Reliability: Coefficient alphas ranged from .53 to .85.

Validity: Correlations with other variables ranged from -.28 to .64.

Author: Schneider, B. and Bowen, D.E.

Article: Employee and customer perceptions of service in banks: replication and extension.

Journal: *Journal of Applied Psychology*, Aug. 1985, 70(3), 423-433.

Related research: Katz, K. and Kahn, R.L., 1978. *The social psychology of organizations*. (2nd ed.) New York: Wiley.

3055
Test name: CHILDREN'S PERCEPTIONS OF EVERYDAY SCHOOLING CONVENTIONS

Purpose: To measure children's "perceived reality" at their schools.

Number of items: 35

Format: Semi-structured interview. Sample items presented.

Reliability: 98.5% agreement among raters of interview responses.

Validity: 98.1% correspondence between childrens' values and values implicit in several "value" items.

Author: Lee, P.C. et al.

Article: Elementary school children's perceptions of their actual and ideal school experience: A developmental study.

Journal: *Journal of Educational Psychology*, Dec. 1983, 75(6), 838-847.

3056

Test name: CLASSROOM BEHAVIOR SCALE

Purpose: To measure classroom context.

Number of items: 12 discreet behaviors monitored.

Time required: 15 minutes per day for 4 days per child.

Format: 10-second observation followed by 10-second recording in each 15 minute period. Behavior categories presented.

Reliability: .94 across all behaviors. Range was .60 to 1.00.

Author: Low, B.P. and Clement, P.W.

Article: Relationships of race and socioeconomic status to classroom behavior, academic achievement and referral for special education.

Journal: *Journal of School Psychology*, 1982, *20*(2), 103-112.

3057

Test name: CLASSROOM ENVIRONMENT INDEX

Purpose: To measure psychological environment or press of the classroom.

Number of items: 300

Reliability: KR-20 ranged from .32 to .80 across 30 subscales.

Validity: Differentiates between grades, subjects, classrooms, and levels.

Author: Walker, W.J. and Richman, J.

Article: Dimensions of classroom environmental press.

Journal: *Psychological Reports*, Oct. 1984, *55*(2), 555-562.

Related research: Stern, G.G., 1970. *People in context*. New York: Wiley.

3058

Test name: CLASSROOM LIFE INSTRUMENT

Purpose: To measure aspects of classroom life in 15 dimensions.

Number of items: 67

Format: 5-point truth-falsity scale.

Reliability: Alpha ranged from .51 to .85 across subscales.

Validity: Factor analysis confirms 15 factors.

Author: Johnson, D.W. and Johnson, R.T.

Article: Social interdependence and perceived academic and personal support in the classroom.

Journal: *Journal of Social Psychology*, June 1983, *120*(first half), 77-82.

3059
Test name: CLIENT SATISFACTION SCALE

Purpose: To measure satisfaction with psychiatric treatment services.

Number of items: 28

Format: Yes-no format. All items presented.

Validity: Two factors were extracted in a factor analysis: General satisfaction and satisfaction with activities and hospital environment.

Author: Distefano, M.K. et al.

Article: Factor structure of a clients' satisfaction scale with psychiatric patients.

Journal: *Psychological Reports*, Dec. 1983, *53*(3, Pt. 2), 1155-1159.

Related research: Glenn, R.N., 1978. Measuring patient opinions about hospitalization using the Client Satisfaction Scale. *Hospital and Community Psychiatry*, *29*(3), 158-161.

3060
Test name: COMMUNITY SATISFACTION SCALE—REVISED

Purpose: To measure community satisfaction.

Number of items: 34

Reliability: Cronbach's alpha = .89.

Validity: A factor analysis revealed 8 interpretable factors in which social and physical variables were intermingled.

Author: Bardo, J.W. and Bardo, D.J.

Article: A re-examination of substantive components of community satisfaction in a British new town.

Journal: *Journal of Social Psychology*, June 1983, *120*(first half), 35-45.

Related research: Bardo, J.W., 1976. Dimensions of community satisfaction in a British new town. *Multivar. Experimental Clinical Research*, *2*, 129-134.

3061
Test name: COMPREHENSIVE JOB EVALUATION TECHNIQUE

Purpose: To provide an instrument for job evaluation.

Number of items: 75

Format: Includes 15 scales of 5 items each: education, time to proficiency, previous experience, mental effort, physical effort, supervisory responsibility, financial responsibility, responsibility for the safety of others, surroundings, hazards, dexterity, monotony, visual effort, social interaction involving teaching and counseling, and social interaction involving negotiating and influencing.

Reliability: Correlations between raters equalled or exceeded .70.

Author: Doverspike, D. and Barrett, G.V.

Article: An internal bias analysis of a job evaluation instrument.

Journal: *Journal of Applied Psychology*, Nov. 1984, *69*(4), 648-662.

Related research: Treiman, D.J., 1979. *Job evaluation: An analytic review*. Washington: National Academy of Sciences.

3062
Test name: CONGREGATION SATISFACTION QUESTIONNAIRE

Purpose: To measure satisfaction with eight aspects of a religious congregation: leaders, members, facilities, services, education, rules, special programs, and clergy.

Number of items: 79

Format: Multiple-choice. Sample items presented.

Reliability: Alphas ranged from .67 to .90 across subscales. Test-retest ranged from .62 to .82 across subscales.

Validity: Multitrait-multimethod matrix of CSQ and single-item criterion measures yielded support of validity in two of three Campbell and Fiske criteria.

Author: Silverman, W.H. et al.

Article: Measuring member satisfaction with the church.

Journal: *Journal of Applied Psychology*, Nov. 1983, *68*(4), 664-677.

3063
Test name: COUNSELING EVALUATION INVENTORY

Purpose: To measure counseling climate, comfort, and satisfaction with counseling.

Number of items: 19

Format: Each item is rated on a 5-point scale.

Reliability: Test-retest reliability ranged from .62 to .83.

Validity: Correlations with congruence measures ranged from -.16 to .38.

Author: Hill, C.E. et al.

Article: Nonverbal communication and counseling outcome.

Journal: *Journal of Counseling Psychology*, May 1981, *28*(3), 203-212.

Related research: Linden, J.D. et al., 1965. Development and evaluation of an inventory for rating counselors. *Personnel and Guidance Journal, 43,* 267-276.

3064
Test name: COURSE EVALUATION SCALES

Purpose: To measure student perceptions of college courses.

Number of items: 31

Format: 7-point Likert type items with appropriate anchor adjectives.

Reliability: Cronbach's alpha ranged from .50 to .80 across subscales.

Validity: Eight factors extracted, of which three significantly discriminated between dropping or not dropping a course (they were: student performance, motivation, and impression of instructor).

Author: Reed, J.G.

Article: Dropping a college course: Factors influencing students withdrawal decisions.

Journal: *Journal of Educational Psychology*, June 1981, *73*(3), 376-385.

3065
Test name: COURSE RATING SCALE FOR ORGANIZATIONAL BEHAVIOR

Purpose: To measure importance of topics in organizational behavior courses (in 13 dimensions).

Number of items: 56

Format: 7-point scale ranging between "important topics" to "quite unimportant topics." All items presented.

Reliability: Cronbach's alpha ranged from .69 to .90 across dimensions.

Author: Rahim, A.

Article: Organizational behavior courses for graduate students in business administration: Views from the tower and battlefield.

Journal: *Psychological Reports*, 1981, *49*(2), 583-592.

3066
Test name: CUSTOMER SERVICE-RELATED PRACTICES SURVEY

Purpose: To measure attitudes about service quality provided to customers.

Number of items: 24

Format: Includes five dimensions: courtesy/competency; utility/security; adequate staff; employee morale; branch administration. Sample items are presented.

Reliability: Coefficient alphas ranged from .41 to .88

Validity: Correlations with other variables ranged from -.41 to .72.

Author: Schneider, B. and Bowen, D.E.

Article: Employee and customer perceptions of service in banks: replication and extension.

Journal: *Journal of Applied Psychology*, Aug. 1985, *70*(3), 423-433.

3067

Test name: DEPARTMENTAL QUALITY SCALE

Purpose: To measure quality of college departments.

Number of items: 11

Format: 5-point bipolar response scale. Items presented in abbreviated form.

Reliability: Horst reliability ranged from .17 to .94 across items in separate student and alumni samples.

Validity: Students scored higher than alumni on 3 instruction and classroom items. Alumni scored higher on vocational guidance item ($p < .01$).

Author: Wise, S.L. et al.

Article: Alumni ratings as an indicator of departmental quality.

Journal: *Journal of Educational Psychology*, Feb. 1981, *73*(1), 71-77.

3068

Test name: EDUCATIONAL GOALS SCALE

Purpose: To assess student and parental beliefs about how important and how well schools are meeting goals.

Number of items: 12

Format: Rating scale format. All items presented.

Reliability: Alpha ranged from .91 (parents) to .95 (students).

Author: Grandjean, B.D. and Vaughn, E.S. III.

Article: Client perceptions of school effectiveness: A reciprocal causation model for students and their parents.

Journal: *The Sociology of Education*, Oct. 1981, *54*(4), 275-290.

Related research: Grandjean, B.D. and Bernal, H.H., 1979. Sex and centralization in a semiprofession. *Sociology of Work and Occupations*, *6*, 84-102.

3069
Test name: EFFECTANCE TEST

Purpose: To measure the production of effects upon the environment.

Number of items: 80

Format: Includes three subscales: effect on self, effect on objects, and effect on people.

Reliability: Kuder-Richardson 20 reliabilities ranged from .71 to .86 (N = 609).

Validity: Correlations with other scales ranged from -.25 to .54 (N = 82 males) and from -.41 to .61 (N = 110 females).

Author: Lamont, D.J.

Article: A three-dimensional test for White's effectance motive.

Journal: *Journal of Personality Assessment*, Feb. 1983, *47*(1), 91-99.

3070
Test name: ENVIRONMENTAL CHECKLIST

Purpose: To measure geographical environments such as cities, neighborhoods, and college campuses.

Number of items: 140

Format: Respondents checked adjectives that describe a specified place.

Reliability: Phi coefficient = .82 (test-retest, 21-day interval).

Validity: Correlates .58 with number of positive urban items checked on the McKechnie's urbanity scale (1975).

Author: Domino, G.

Article: Measuring geographical environments through adjectives: The environmental checklist.

Journal: *Psychological Reports*, Aug. 1984, *55*(1), 151-160.

3071
Test name: ENVIRONMENTAL STRESS SCALE

Purpose: To measure environmental stress.

Number of items: 10

Format: Employs a 5-point answer scale. A sample question is presented.

Reliability: Cronbach's alpha = .84.

Author: Frese, M. and Okonek, K.

Article: Reasons to leave shiftwork and psychological and psychosomatic complaints of former shiftworkers.

Journal: *Journal of Applied Psychology*, Aug. 1984, *69*(3), 509-514.

Related research: Semmer, N., 1982. Stress at work, stress in private life, and psychological well-being. In W. Bachmann et al., (Eds.), *Mental load and stress in activity: European approaches*. Berlin: Deutscher Verlag der Wissenschaften, and Amsterdam: North Holland.

3072
Test name: ENVIRONMENTAL UNCERTAINTY SCALE

Purpose: To measure perceived level of environmental uncertainty.

Number of items: 12

Format: 6-point frequency scale (never to always) indicated how often respondent encountered each of 12 situations in the job.

Reliability: Alpha = .56.

Author: Anderson, T.N., Jr. and Kida, T.E.

Article: The effect of environmental uncertainty on the association of expectancy attitudes, effort and performance.

Journal: *Journal of Social Psychology*, Oct. 1985, *125*(5), 631-636.

Related research: Duncan, R.B., 1972. Characteristics of organizational environments and perceived environmental uncertainty. *Administrative Science Quarterly*, *17*, 313-327.

3073
Test name: GLOBAL JOB CLASSIFICATION SCALE

Purpose: To classify jobs by global assessments of supervisors and incumbents in place of more time-consuming and costly task approaches.

Number of items: 28

Time required: 10-15 minutes.

Format: All possible pairs of 8 jobs rated on a 7-point similarity scale.

Validity: Correlation between global and task methods = .84. Correlation between supervisor and incumbent ratings = .94.

Author: Sackett, P.R.

Article: A comparison of global judgement vs. task-oriented approaches to job classification.

Journal: *Personnel Psychology*, winter 1981, *34*(4), 791-804.

3074
Test name: GROUP ATMOSPHERE SCALE

Purpose: To measure group atmosphere.

Number of items: 10

Format: Semantic differential.

Reliability: Alpha = .91.

Author: Vecchio, R.P.

Article: A further test of leadership effects due to between-group variation and within-group variation.

Journal: *Journal of Applied Psychology*, April 1982, *67*(2), 200-208.

Related research: Fiedler, F.E., 1967. *A theory of leadership effectiveness.* New York: McGraw-Hill.

3075
Test name: HASSLES SCALE

Purpose: To measure irritants of daily living.

Number of items: 117

Format: Checklist.

Reliability: Test-retest = .68 (4-month interval).

Author: Nowack, K.M.

Article: Type A behavior, family health history and psychological distress.

Journal: *Psychological Reports*, Dec. 1985, *57*(3, Pt. 1), 799-806.

Related research: Kanner, A.D. et al., 1979. Comparison of two modes of stress measurement: Daily hassles and uplifts versus major life events. *Journal of Behavioral Medicine, 4,* 41-51.

3076
Test name: HENDERSON ENVIRONMENTAL LEARNING PROCESS SCALE

Purpose: To measure stimulation, parental guidance, modes, reinforcement, and aspiration.

Number of items: 51 (of 55 original items).

Format: All items presented. Each is a "how often" question.

Reliability: Average item inter-item correlation ranged from .14 to .22 using alternative methods.

Validity: Factors do not correspond to those extracted by Henderson.

Author: Silverstein, A.B. et al.

Article: Factor structure of the Henderson Environmental Learning Process Scale.

Journal: *Psychological Reports*, 1982, *50*(3, Pt. 1), 856-858.

Related research: Henderson, R.W., 1972. Development and validation of the Henderson Environmental Learning Process Scale. *Journal of Social Psychology*, *88*, 185-196.

3077
Test name: HUMAN RESOURCES PRACTICES SURVEY

Purpose: To measure perceptions of the organization's human resources practices.

Number of items: 40

Format: Includes five dimensions: work facilitation, supervision, organizational career facilitation, organizational status, new employee socialization. Examples are presented.

Reliability: Coefficient alphas ranged from .54 to .91.

Validity: Correlations with other variables ranged from .01 to .56.

Author: Schneider, B. and Bowen, D.E.

Article: Employee and customer perceptions of service in banks: replication and extension.

Journal: *Journal of Applied Psychology*, Aug. 1985, *70*(3), 423-433.

3078
Test name: INDIVIDUALIZED CLASSROOM ENVIRONMENT QUESTIONNAIRE

Purpose: To measure environmental perceptions of classrooms.

Number of items: 50

Format: Includes five subscales: personalization, participation, independence, investigation, and differentiation.

Reliability: Alpha reliability coefficients for the subscales ranged from .74 to .92.

Validity: Correlation with other scales ranged from .16 to .37.

Author: Fraser, B.J.

Article: Development of short forms of several classroom environment scales.

Journal: *Journal of Educational Measurement*, fall 1982, *19*(3), 221-227.

Related research: Rentoul, A.J. and Fraser, B.J., 1979. Conceptualization of enquiry-based or open classroom learning environments. *Journal of Curriculum Studies*, 11, 233-245.

3079
Test name: JOBS-CAREER KEY

Purpose: To measure four domains of job information (economic, education-training, job parts, and worker relationships).

Number of items: 157

Format: Multiple-choice.

Reliability: Internal consistency ranged from .43 to .91. Test-retest (N = 19) = .62 (4-month interval).

Author: Yanico, B.J. and Mihlbauer, T.C.

Article: Students' self-estimated and actual knowledge of gender traditional and nontraditional occupation.

Journal: *Journal of Vocational Behavior*, June 1983, 22(3), 278-287.

Related research: Blank, J.R., 1978. Job-Career Key: A test of occupational information. *Vocational Guidance Quarterly*, 27, 6-17.

3080
Test name: JOB CHARACTERISTICS INVENTORY

Purpose: To measure workers' perceptions of eight core job characteristics.

Number of items: 24

Format: Characteristics assessed include: variety, autonomy, feedback, significance, identity, challenge, dealing with others, and friendship opportunities. Employs a Likert-type scale.

Reliability: Internal consistency estimates ranged from .24 to .76.

Author: Abush, R. and Burkhead, E.J.

Article: Job stress in midlife working women: Relationships among personality type, job characteristics and job tension.

Journal: *Journal of Counseling Psychology*, Jan. 1984, 31(1), 36-44.

Related research: Sims, H.P., Jr. et al., 1976. The measurements of job characteristics. *Academy of Management Journal*, 19, 195-212.

3081
Test name: JOB COMPONENTS INVENTORY

Purpose: A job analysis technique to measure physical and perceptual requirements, mathematical requirements, communication requirements, and decision-making/responsibility requirements.

Number of items: 26 tools-use categories, 23 perceptual/physical items, 27 mathematical items, 22 communication items, 9 decision-making items.

Format: Paper and pencil and physical testing formats.

Reliability: Kendal's tau ranged between .21 and .85 across subscales for supervisor-jobholder pairing.

Validity: Scales discriminated occupational area (clerical vs. engineering) and job title (8 titles). Ten of 12 F ratios significant at $p < .001$. Discriminates between organizations less well. Three of 6 F's significant at $p < .05$.

Author: Banks, M.H.

Article: The Job Components Inventory and the analysis of jobs requiring limited skill.

Journal: *Personnel Psychology*, spring 1983, 36(1), 57-66.

3082
Test name: JOB COMPONENTS INVENTORY II

Purpose: To measure the characteristics of work.

Time required: 40 minutes to 53 minutes.

Format: Interview format.

Reliability: Inter-office correlation = .80; Inter-rater agreement = .75.

Validity: Supervisor-job holder agreement = .72.

Author: Banks, M.H. and Miller, R.L.

Article: Reliability and convergent validity of the Job Components Inventory.

Journal: *Journal of Occupational Psychology*, Sept. 1984, 57(3), 181-184.

Related research: Banks, M.H. et al., 1983. The Job Components Inventory and the analysis of jobs requiring limited skill. *Personnel Psychology*, 36, 57-66.

3083
Test name: JOB FEEDBACK SURVEY

Purpose: To assess the amount and type of feedback information available to individuals at work.

Number of items: 95

Format: Various formats. All items presented.

Reliability: Alphas ranged from .68 to .90 across 15 subscales.

Validity: 9 subscales discriminated two feedback environments (a utility and a hospital), $p \leq .05$.

Author: Herold, D.M. and Parsons, C.K.

Article: Assessing the feedback environment in work organizations: Development of the Job Feedback Survey.

Journal: *Journal of Applied Psychology*, May 1985, 70(2), 290-305.

Related research: Herold, D.M. and Greller, M.M., 1977. Feedback: The definition of a construct. *Academy of Management Journal*, 20, 142-147.

3084
Test name: JOB STRUCTURE PROFILE

Purpose: To describe the structure of jobs.

Number of items: 248

Format: Trained interviewer prompts job raters.

Reliability: Inter-rater = .95. Single-rater = .71. Retest = .76.

Author: Patrick, J. and Moore, A.K.

Article: Development and reliability of a job analysis technique.

Journal: *Journal of Occupational Psychology*, June 1985, 58(2), 149-158.

Related research: McCormick, E.K. et al., 1972. A study of characteristics and job dimensions as based on the Position Analysis Questionnaire (PAQ). *Journal of Applied Psychology*, 56, 347-368.

3085
Test name: JOB TREATMENT INDEX

Purpose: To measure perceptions of job-related sex discrimination.

Number of items: 11

Format: Men and women are asked to respond to each item by comparing their own treatment to that of the opposite sex (worse than, same as, better than).

Reliability: Alpha = .92.

Author: Graddick, M.M. and Farr, J.L.

Article: Professionals in scientific disciplines: Sex-related differences in working life commitments.

Journal: *Journal of Applied Psychology*, Nov. 1983, 68(4), 641-645.

Related research: Connolly, T. et al., 1976. *The woman professional in science and engineering: An empirical study of key decisions.* New York: National Science Foundation.

3086
Test name: LECTURE EVALUATION INSTRUMENT

Purpose: To measure qualities that make a good mathematics lecture.

Number of items: 63

Format: 5-point response categories (very poor to very good).

Reliability: Alphas ranged from .70 to .94 across subscales.

Author: Clarkson, P.C.

Article: Papua New Guinea students: Perceptions of mathematics lecturers.

Journal: *Journal of Educational Psychology*, Dec. 1984, *76*(6), 1386-1395.

Related research: Marsh, H.W., 1981. Students' evaluation of tertiary instruction: Testing the applicability of American surveys in an Australian setting. *Australian Journal of Education*, *25*, 177-193.

3087
Test name: LIVING ENVIRONMENT SCALE

Purpose: To measure living environment.

Number of items: 6

Format: Includes assessment of: satisfaction with privacy, transportation, feelings of security, housing, neighborhood, and proximity of supportive relationships. Responses are made on a scale from 1 (very dissatisfied) to 4 (very satisfied).

Reliability: Reliability coefficient was .64 (older parents).

Validity: Correlations with other variables ranged from -.070 to .210.

Author: Quinn, W.H.

Article: Personal and family adjustment in later life.

Journal: *Journal of Marriage and the Family*, Feb. 1983, *45*(1), 57-73.

Related research: Johnson, E.S., 1978. Good relationships between older mothers and their daughters: A causal model. *The Gerontologist*, *18*, 301-308.

3088
Test name: MECHANISTIC STRUCTURAL JOB CHARACTERISTICS SCALES

Purpose: To measure mechanistic structural job characteristics.

Number of items: 20

Format: Includes the following scales: job codification, job specificity, hierarchy of authority, and lack of participation. Sample items are presented.

Reliability: Coefficient alphas ranged from .62 to .83.

Author: Marino, K.E. and White, S.E.

Article: Departmental structure, locus of control and job stress: The effect of a moderator.

Journal: *Journal of Applied Psychology*, Nov. 1985, *70*(4), 782-784.

Related research: Hage, G. and Aiken, M., 1969. Routine technology, social structure, and organizational goals. *Administrative Science Quarterly, 14*, 366-376.

3089
Test name: MEDICAL SCHOOLS LEARNING ENVIRONMENT SURVEY

Purpose: To measure students' perceptions of their medical school.

Number of items: 55

Format: Includes a four-point response scale of: seldom, occasionally, fairly often, very often. Items comprised seven subscales of: flexibility, student-student interaction, emotional climate, supportiveness, meaningful learning experience, organization, and breadth of interest. Some items are presented.

Reliability: Coefficient alphas ranged from .56 to .94.

Author: Feletti, G.I. and Clark, R.M.

Article: Construct validity of a learning environment survey for medical schools.

Journal: *Educational and Psychological Measurement*, autumn 1981, *41*(3), 875-882.

Related research: Marshall, R.E., 1978. Measuring the medical school learning environment. *Journal of Medical Education, 53*, 98-104.

3090
Test name: MINNESOTA THERAPY RATING SCALE

Purpose: To identify differences between two forms of therapy used in treatment of depression.

Number of items: 48

Format: 9-point Likert format. Raters view tapes of sessions and rate them on 9-point scales. All items presented.

Reliability: Modal item reliability = .70. Reliabilities of subscales ranged from .46 to .90.

Validity: Classification of 12 sample tapes with 18 variable discriminant functions yielded perfect classification.

Author: DeRubeis, R.J. et al.

Article: Can psychotherapies for depression be discriminated? A systematic investigation of cognitive therapy and interpersonal therapy.

Journal: *Journal of Consulting and Clinical Psychology*, Oct. 1982, *50*(5), 744-756.

Related research: Young, J., 1981. *The development of the Cognitive Therapy Scale*. Unpublished manuscript, Center for Cognitive Therapy, Philadelphia.

3091
Test name: MOTIVATING POTENTIAL SCORE

Purpose: To measure job complexity.

Number of items: 15

Format: Includes five job characteristics: skill variety, autonomy, task identity, task significance, and feedback from the job itself. Five-point response scales are employed.

Reliability: Alpha coefficient = .89 (N = 166).

Validity: Correlations with other variables ranged from .04 to .45.

Author: Tharenou, P. and Harker, P.

Article: Moderating influence of self-esteem on relationship between job complexity, performance and satisfaction.

Journal: *Journal of Applied Psychology*, Nov. 1984, *69*(4), 623-632.

Related research: Hackman, J.R. and Oldham, G.R., 1974. *The Job Diagnostic Survey: An instrument for the diagnosis of jobs and the evaluation of redesign projects*. (Tech. Rep. No. 4.) New Haven, CT: Yale University, Department of Administrative Sciences.

3092
Test name: MULTIMETHOD JOB DESIGN QUESTIONNAIRE

Purpose: To permit an examination of job design.

Number of items: 70

Format: Includes four sections: motivational, mechanistic, biological, and perceptual/motor. Sample items are presented.

Reliability: Inter-rater reliabilities ranged from .89 to .93.

Validity: Correlations with theoretical job outcome composites ranged from -.77 to .54.

Author: Campion, M.A. and Thayer, P.W.

Article: Development and field evaluation of an interdisciplinary measure of job design.

Journal: *Journal of Applied Psychology*, Feb. 1983, *70*(1), 29-43.

3093
Test name: MY CLASS INVENTORY

Purpose: To measure actual classroom environment.

Number of items: 38

Format: Subjects respond to each item on a yes-no format. Includes five scales: satisfaction, friction, competitiveness, difficulty, and cohesiveness.

Reliability: Alpha reliability coefficients for the subscales ranged from .73 to .88.

Validity: Correlation with other scales ranged from .13 to .30.

Author: Fraser, B.J.

Article: Development of short forms of several classroom environment scales.

Journal: *Journal of Educational Measurement*, fall 1982, *19*(3), 221-227.

Related research: Fisher, D.L. and Fraser, B.J., 1981. Validity and use of My Class Inventory. *Science Education*, 65, 145-156.

3094
Test name: MY CLASS INVENTORY

Purpose: To measure primary classroom climate.

Number of items: 45

Format: Includes five scale dimensions: satisfaction, friction, competitiveness, difficulty, and cohesion. Employs a yes-no format.

Reliability: Scale reliabilities ranged from .54 to .77.

Validity: Correlations with sex-bias scores ranged from -.61 to .84.

Author: Prawat, R.S. and Solomon, D.J.

Article: Validation of a classroom climate inventory for use at the early elementary level.

Journal: *Educational and Psychological Measurement*, summer 1981, *41*(2), 567-573.

Related research: Anderson, G.J. and Walberg, H.J., 1974. Learning environments. In H.J. Walberg (Ed.), *Evaluating educational performance*. Berkeley, CA: McCutcheon.

3095
Test name: NARRATIVE JOB DESCRIPTION CLASSIFICATION SYSTEM

Purpose: To describe key characteristics of jobs and similarities and differences between jobs.

Number of items: 121

Format: Narrative job descriptions taken from U.S. Civil Service Commission Qualification Standards (1978).

Reliability: Intraclass correlations of PAQ Job Dimensions for 121 jobs ranged between .20 and .90. Average pairings correlations ranged from .36 to .88.

Validity: PAQ job dimensions for the 121 descriptions demonstrated multiple correlations of .51 to .85 with ability requirement estimates from the Dictionary of Occupational Titles.

Author: Jones, A.P. et al.

Article: Narrative job descriptions as potential sources of job analysis ratings.

Journal: *Personnel Psychology*, winter 1982, *35*(4), 813-828.

Related research: McCormick, E.J. et al., 1972. A study of job characteristics and job dimensions as based on the Position Analysis Questionnaire (PAQ). *Journal of Applied Psychology*, *56*, 347-368.

3096
Test name: OCCUPATION ANALYSIS INVENTORY

Purpose: To rate jobs and occupations.

Number of items: 617

Format: The items are referred to as "work elements" which are descriptions of work activities and conditions. Examples are given.

Reliability: The mean element reliability coefficient was .53.

Author: Cunningham, J.W. et al.

Article: Systematically derived work dimensions: Factor analysis of the Occupational Analysis Inventory.

Journal: *Journal of Applied Psychology*, May 1983, *68*(2), 232-251.

Related research: Cunningham, J.W. et al., 1974. The development of the Occupation Analysis Inventory: An "ergometric" approach to an educational problem. *JSAS Catalog of Selected Documents in Psychology*, *4*, 144. (Ms. No. 803.)

3097
Test name: ORGANIZATIONAL CLIMATE QUESTIONNAIRE

Purpose: To measure working conditions.

Number of items: 30

Format: 4-point agreement scales. All items presented. Items modified from Litwin and Stringer Organizational Climate Scale.

Validity: Subscales correlate significantly (p < .01) with intrinsic, extrinsic, and social job satisfaction.

Author: Schnake, M.E.

Article: An empirical assessment of the effects of affective response in the measurement of organizational climate.

Journal: *Personnel Psychology,* winter 1983, *36*(4), 791-807.

Related research: Litwin, G.H. and Stringer, R.A., 1968. *Motivation and organizational climate.* Boston: Harvard University.

3098
Test name: ORGANIZATIONAL CLIMATE QUESTIONNAIRE— REVISED

Purpose: To measure 7 dimensions of organizational climate.

Number of items: 34

Format: 7-point Likert scale. Sample items presented.

Reliability: All alphas were .69 or greater (average = .78).

Author: Mossholder, K.W. et al.

Article: An examination of intraoccupational differences: Personality, perceived work climate and outcome preferences.

Journal: *Journal of Vocational Behavior,* April, 1985, *26*(2), 164-176.

Related research: Litwin, G.H. and Stringer, R.A., 1968. *Motivation and organizational climate.* Boston: Harvard University.

3099
Test name: ORGANIZATIONAL CLIMATE SCALE

Purpose: To assess the perceptions of workers and employers regarding organizational climate.

Number of items: 18

Format: Items deal with the following climate dimensions: leadership, motivation, communication, decisions, goals, and control.

Validity: Item correlations between workers and employers ranged from -.84 to .73.

Author: Narayanan, S. and
Venkatachalam, R.

Article: Perception of
organizational climate.

Journal: *Perceptual and Motor
Skills,* Aug. 1982, 55(1), 15-18.

Related research: Likert, R., 1967.
The human organization. New
York: McGraw-Hill.

3100

Test name: ORIGIN CLIMATE
QUESTIONNAIRE

Purpose: To assess classroom
climate.

Number of items: 24

Format: A Likert-type scale which
includes measures of the students'
perceptions of teachers' behaviors
directed toward developing
goal-setting, goal-directed behavior,
accurate perceptions of reality,
internal control, personal
responsibility, and self-confidence
among students. The items are split
between positive and negative
wording.

Validity: Correlations with
attributed responsibility for: success
was .254 (grade 8) and .345 (grade
11); failure was .185 (grade 8) and
.448 (grade 11). Correlations with
grades were .204 (grade 8) and .198
(grade 11).

Author: Sadowski, C.J. and
Woodward, H.R.

Article: Relationship between
origin climate, perceived
responsibility and grades.

Journal: *Perceptual and Motor
Skills,* Aug. 1981, 53(1), 259-261.

Related research: DeCharms, R.,
1976. *Enhancing motivation:
Changes in the classroom.* New
York: Irvington.

3101

Test name: PLEASANT EVENTS
SCHEDULE

Purpose: To measure potentially
reinforcing events by behavioral
self-report.

Number of items: 320

Format: 3-point rating scale (not
happened, happened a few times,
happened often). All items
presented.

Reliability: Test-retest ranged from
.50 to .88 with 1, 2, and 3 month
intervals.

Validity: Validity ranged from .22
to .77 (Multimethod, multitrait).
Extensive validity data reported.

Author: MacPhillamy, D.J. and
Lewinsohn, P.M.

Article: The Pleasant Events Schedule: Studies on reliability, validity and scale intercorrelation.

Journal: *Journal of Consulting and Clinical Psychology*, June 1982, *50*(3), 363-380.

Related research: MacPhillamy, D.J. and Lewinsohn, P.M., 1972. *Pleasant Events Schedule.* Unpublished manuscript, University of Oregon.

3102
Test name: PREFERRED ORGANIZATIONAL CLIMATES SCALE

Purpose: To measure how well hypothetical organizations satisfy personality needs and vocational interests of individuals.

Number of items: 9 (organizational types).

Format: 9-point Likert scales. All nine organizational climates are presented.

Reliability: Alpha ranged from .89 to .95.

Author: Burke, R.J. and Deszca, E.

Article: Preferred organizational climates of type A individuals.

Journal: *Journal of Vocational Behavior*, Aug. 1982, *21*(1), 50-59.

Related research: Rothstein, M. and Rush, J.C., 1980. *Organizational choice as a means of satisfying individual needs and interests.* Unpublished working paper, School of Business Administration, University of Western Ontario, London, Ontario.

3103
Test name: PROJECT COMPLEXITY CHECKLIST

Purpose: To measure the dimensions of project complexity.

Number of items: 11

Format: Item stems followed by three to seven responses, any or all of which can be checked. All items presented in an appendix. Projects rated were validated at national or state levels and offered to schools for adoption.

Reliability: Inter-rater reliability of five raters was .96.

Validity: Content validity assessed by a panel of four experts.

Author: Humphries, J. and Newfield, J.

Article: Identifying and measuring dimensions of project complexity.

Journal: *Journal of Educational Research*, March/April 1982, *75*(4), 248-253.

Related research: Goodlad, J.I. and Klein, M.F., 1974. *Looking behind the classroom door.* Worthington, OH: Charles A. Jones.

3104
Test name: POSITION DESCRIPTION QUESTIONNAIRE—SHORT FORM

Purpose: To provide a vehicle for analyzing managerial positions.

Number of items: 54

Format: Includes nine dimensions of managerial behavior: strategic planning, product/service activities, controlling, monitoring business indicators, supervising, coordinating, customer relations/marketing, external contact, and consulting.

Reliability: Median internal consistency was .73. Median alternate form reliability coefficient was .71. Coefficient alphas ranged from .69 to .91.

Author: Colarelli, S.M. et al.

Article: Cross-validation of a short form of the position description questionnaire.

Journal: *Educational and Psychological Measurement,* winter 1982, *42*(4), 1279-1283.

Related research: Page, R.C. and Gomez, L.R., 1979. *The development and application of job evaluation and staffing systems using the Position Description Questionnaire.* Personal research report No. 162-79. Minneapolis: Control Data Corporation.

3105
Test name: PUPIL CONTROL IDEOLOGY FORM

Purpose: To measure the pupil control ideology of schools.

Number of items: 20

Format: Likert-type items with responses scored from 5 (strongly agree) to 1 (strongly disagree).

Reliability: Split-half corrected reliability coefficients were .95 (N = 170) and .91 (N = 55).

Validity: Correlations with self-concept as a learner ranged from -.29 to -.51 (for 35 students), and -.12 to -.51 (for 35 teachers).

Author: Lunenburg, F.C.

Article: Pupil control ideology and self-concept as a learner.

Journal: *Educational Research Quarterly,* 1983, *8*(3), 33-39.

Related research: Willower, D.J. et al., 1967. *The school and pupil control ideology.* University Park: Pennsylvania State University.

3106
Test name: REACTION INVENTORY

Purpose: To identify specific stimulus situations which lead to anger.

Number of items: 76

Format: Responses to each item are made on a 5-point scale ranging from "not at all" to "very much."

Reliability: Test-retest reliability coefficient was .70.

Author: Biaggio, M.K. et al.

Article: Reliability and validity of four anger scales.

Journal: *Journal of Personality Assessment*, Dec. 1981, *45*(6), 639-648.

Related research: Evans, D.R. and Strangeland, M., 1971. Development of the Reaction Inventory to measure anger. *Psychological Reports*, *29*, 412-414.

3107
Test name: ROBUSTNESS SEMANTIC DIFFERENTIAL SCALE

Purpose: To measure school principals' job robustness.

Number of items: 10

Format: Includes polar adjectives and a seven-point response scale. Examples are presented.

Reliability: Test-retest (4 weeks) reliabilities were .77 and .78.

Validity: Correlations with other variables ranged from .21 to .59.

Author: Eisenhauer, J.E. et al.

Article: Role conflict, role ambiguity and school principals' job robustness.

Journal: *Journal of Experimental Education*, winter 1984/85, *53*(2), 86-90.

Related research: Licata, J.W. and Willower, D.J., 1978. Toward an operational definition of environmental robustness. *Journal of Educational Research*, *71*, 218-222.

3108
Test name: SCHOOL CLIMATE QUESTIONNAIRE

Purpose: To measure qualities such as openness and cohesiveness of staff.

Number of items: 14

Format: Likert-type format.

Reliability: Internal consistency = .81.

Author: Nagy, S. and Davis, L.

Article: Burnout: A comparative analysis of personality and environmental variables.

Journal: *Psychological Reports*, Dec. 1985, 57(3, Pt. 2), 1319-1326.

Related research: Fielding, M., 1982. Personality and situational correlates of teacher stress and burnout. *Dissertation Abstracts International*, 43, 400-A.

3109
Test name: SCHOOL LEARNING ENVIRONMENT SCHEDULE

Purpose: To assess adolescents' perceptions of their school learning environment.

Number of items: 20

Format: Likert-type items dealing with contexts identified as: regulative, instructional, imaginative or innovative, and interpersonal. Examples are presented.

Validity: Correlations with aspirations ranged from .16 to .41.

Author: Marjoribanks, K.

Article: Families, schools and aspirations: Ethnic group differences.

Journal: *Journal of Experimental Education*, spring 1985, 53(3), 141-147.

Related research: Bernstein, B., 1977. Social class, language and socialization. In J. Karabel and A.H. Halsey (Eds.), *Power and ideology in education*. New York: Oxford University Press.

3110
Test name: SENSITIVITY TO NOISE SCALE

Purpose: To measure reactivity to noise.

Number of items: 21

Format: 6-point Likert format.

Reliability: Test-retest = .75 (N = 72). Alpha = .76 (N = 150).

Author: Topf, M.

Article: Personal and environmental predictors of patient disturbance due to hospital noise.

Journal: *Journal of Applied Psychology*, Feb. 1985, 70(1), 22-28.

Related research: Weinstein, N., 1978. Individual differences in reactions to noise: A longitudinal study in a college dormitory. *Journal of Applied Psychology*, 63, 458-466.

3111
Test name: SOUTH AFRICAN LIFE EVENT SCALE

Purpose: To measure exposure and seriousness of life events among South African whites.

Number of items: 92

Format: Multiple-choice.

Reliability: Test-retest varied between .83 and .93.

Author: Chalmers, B.

Article: Types of life events and factors influencing their seriousness rating.

Journal: *Journal of Social Psychology*, Dec. 1983, *121*(second half), 283-295.

Related research: Antononsky, A., 1974. Conceptual and methodological problems in the study of resistance resources and stressful life events. In B.S. Dohrenwend and B.P. Dohrenwend (Eds.), *Stressful life events: Their nature and effects*. New York: Wiley, pp. 245-258.
    Chalmers, B., 1981. Development of a life event scale for pregnant, white South African women. *South African Journal of Psychology, 11*, 74-79.

3112
Test name: STAFF DEVELOPMENT EVALUATION QUESTIONNAIRE

Purpose: To measure clinical staff's perceptions and valuations of in-service programs.

Number of items: 16

Format: Six-point Likert scale. (1 = strongly disagree to 6 = strongly agree.) Sample items presented.

Reliability: Cronbach's alpha = .83. Test-retest = .81.

Validity: Face validity (by experts in adult learning and continuing education).

Author: Abraham, I.L. and Hagerty, B.K.

Article: Development and internal reliability testing of an instrument to measure attitudes toward in-service programming among psychiatric hospital staff.

Journal: *Psychological Reports*, Oct. 1983, *53*(2), 589-590.

3113
Test name: STAFF DEVELOPMENT QUESTIONNAIRE

Purpose: To measure factors productive of knowledge use in staff development.

Number of items: 52

Format: Likert-type items. Sample items presented.

Reliability: Ranged from .20 to .78 on various items and scales.

Author: Walberg, H.J. and Genova, W.J.

Article: Staff, school, and workshop influences on knowledge use in educational improvement efforts.

Journal: *Journal of Educational Research*, Nov./Dec. 1982, 76(2), 69-80.

Related research: Genova, W.J. and Walberg, H.J., 1979. *Promoting student integration in city high schools: A research study and improvement guide for practitioners.* Washington, DC: NIE.

3114
Test name: STUDENT LEARNING ENVIRONMENT QUESTIONNAIRE

Purpose: To measure motivation to learn, quality of instruction, class environment, and home, peer and media environment.

Number of items: 5 to 7 items on each of seven subscales.

Format: 5-point Likert format. Sample items presented.

Reliability: Internal consistency ranged from .35 to .64 (mean = .52).

Validity: Items as measures of the subscales assessed by LISREL.

Author: Parkerson, J.A. et al.

Article: Exploring causal models of educational achievement.

Journal: *Journal of Educational Psychology*, Aug. 1984, 76(4), 638-646.

3115
Test name: TASK COMPLEXITY SCALE

Purpose: To measure complexity of tasks.

Number of items: 7

Format: Semantic differential. Sample adjective pairs presented.

Reliability: Alpha = .71.

Author: Huber, V.L.

Article: Effects of task difficulty, goal setting and strategy on performance of a heuristic task.

Journal: *Journal of Applied Psychology*, Aug. 1985, 70(3), 492-504.

Related research: Scott, W.E., 1967. Activation theory and task design. *Organizational Behavior and Human Performance, 1*, 3-30.

3116
Test name: TEACHER ASSESSMENT OF STUDENT SCALE

Purpose: To measure the qualities of a "good class."

Number of items: 3

Format: Multiple-choice. All items presented.

Reliability: Alpha = .80.

Validity: Correlates with student assessments of their own standards (r = .41, p < .01).

Author: Peterson, M.F. and Cooke, R.A.

Article: Attitudinal and contextual variables explaining teachers' leadership behavior.

Journal: *Journal of Educational Psychology*, Feb. 1983, *75*(1), 50-62.

3117
Test name: TEACHER OCCUPATIONAL STRESS FACTOR QUESTIONNAIRE

Purpose: To identify occupational stress factors perceived by public school teachers.

Number of items: 30

Format: Factors include: administration support, working with students, financial security, relationships with teachers, and task overload.

Reliability: Cronbach's alpha reliabilities ranged from .85 to .91.

Author: Moracco, J.C. et al.

Article: Comparison of perceived occupational stress between teachers who are contented and discontented in their career choices.

Journal: *Vocational Guidance Quarterly*, Sept. 1983, *32*(1), 44-51.

Related research: Moracco, J.C. et al., 1981. The factorial validity of the Teacher Occupational Stress Questionnaire. *Educational and Psychological Measurement, 42*, 275-283.

3118
Test name: UNION AS A MECHANISM FOR CHANGE SCALE

Purpose: To measure the value of union representation in the organization.

Number of items: 6

Format: A 6-point scale was used to respond to each item. All items are presented.

Reliability: Estimate of internal consistency was .80.

Validity: Correlation with other variables ranged from -.21 to .18. Correlation with direct questions about the instrumentality of the union as a mechanism for changing conditions of employment and company policy was r = .56.

Author: Hammer, T.H. et al.

Article: Absenteeism when workers have a voice: The case of employee ownership.

Journal: *Journal of Applied Psychology*, Oct. 1981, *66*(5), 561-573.

Related research: Hammer, T.H. and Stern, R.M., 1980. Employee ownership implications for the organizational distribution of power. *Academy of Management Journal*, 23, 78-100.

3119
Test name: VANDERBILT NEGATIVE INDICATORS SCALE (VNIS)

Purpose: To measure factors negatively related to therapeutic outcome.

Number of items: 42

Format: A rating scale ranging from 0 to 5 reflects judgements by raters of therapeutic interaction.

Reliability: Alpha ranged from .26 to .84 across subscales. Inter-rater reliability ranged from .73 to .93 across subscales.

Validity: Canonical correlation between VNIS and six outcome variables = .95. Subscale correlations ranged from -.34 to -.59 across outcome measures.

Author: Sachs, J.S.

Article: Negative factors in brief psychotherapy: An empirical assessment.

Journal: *Journal of Consulting and Clinical Psychology*, Aug. 1983, *51*(4), 557-564.

Related research: Strupp, H.H. et al., 1981. *Vanderbilt Negative Indicators Scale: An instrument for the identification of deterrents to progress in time-limited dynamic psychotherapy.* Unpublished manuscript, Vanderbilt University.

3120
Test name: WARD ATMOSPHERE SCALE—SHORT FORM

Purpose: To conceptualize and evaluate the psychiatric treatment environment with particular attention to the therapeutic milieux.

Number of items: 40

Format: Includes three major dimensions and ten subscales.

Reliability: Overall internal consistency was .93. Internal consistency coefficients for major dimensions ranged from .80 to .85. Subscale internal consistency coefficients ranged from .45 to .79.

Author: Abraham, I.L. and Foley, T.S.

Article: The Work Environment Scale and the Ward Atmosphere Scale (short forms): Psychometric data.

Journal: *Perceptual and Motor Skills*, Feb. 1984, 58(1), 319-322.

Related research: Moos, R.H. and Moos, B.S., (1983). Adaptation and the quality of life in work and family settings. *Journal of Community Psychology*, 11(2), 158-170.

3121
Test name: WEATHER BELIEFS INVENTORY

Purpose: To obtain ratings of the weather's influence on affective states and overt behaviors.

Number of items: 158

Format: Includes 50 preselected affective states and 108 overt behaviors. Half of the items in each category have positive value and half negative. A 5-point scale is employed.

Validity: Correlations with weather superstitiousness ranged from .26 to .35.

Author: Jorgenson, D.O.

Article: Superstition and the perceived causal influence of the weather.

Journal: *Perceptual and Motor Skills*, Feb. 1981, 52(1), 111-114.

Related research: Jorgenson, D.O., 1981. Perceived causal influence of the weather as a function of actor-observer perspective, affect-behavior locus, affect-behavior evaluation and locus of control. *Environment and Behavior*, 13(2), 239-256.

3122
Test name: WORK EXPECTATIONS SCALE

Purpose: To measure expectation for expanding work role beyond working hours.

Number of items: 4

Format: 7-point response scales. All items presented.

Reliability: Alpha = .88.

Validity: Correlates with perceived work overload ($r = .21$, $p < .01$) and with inter-role conflict ($r = .25$, $p < .01$).

Author: Cooke, R.A. and Rousseau, D.M.

Article: Stress and strain from family roles and work-role expectations.

Journal: *Journal of Applied Psychology*, May 1984, *69*(2), 252-260.

Related research: Quinn, R.P. and Staines, G.L., 1979. *The Quality of Employment Survey*. Ann Arbor, MI: Institute for Social Research.

MOTIVATION

3123
Test name: ACADEMIC MOTIVATION SCALE

Purpose: To measure academic motivation.

Number of items: 46

Format: 19-point rating scale on 38 items. Seriated responses on 4 items.

Reliability: Cronbach's alpha = .88.

Validity: Significant correlations presented with high school class rank, first semester GPA, and self-assessed academic self-adjustment.

Author: Baker, R.W. and Siryk, B.

Article: Measuring academic motivation of matriculating college freshmen.

Journal: *Journal of College Student Personnel,* Sept. 1984, *25*(5), 459-464.

Related research: Topkin, W.E., 1967. *Commitment and academic performance in college freshmen.* Unpublished doctoral dissertation, Clark University.

3124
Test name: ACHIEVEMENT MOTIVATION SCALE

Purpose: To measure achievement motivation.

Number of items: 20

Format: Ten of the items are positive and ten are negative. All items are presented.

Reliability: Reliability was .87.

Validity: Correlations with: prediction of rated actual life achievement was .405; occupation was .315; rated success-orientation was .394; rated task-orientation was .094; rated achievement orientation was .342; rated fear of failure was .254; rated need for achievement was .295.

Author: Ray, J.J.

Article: Measuring achievement motivation by immediate emotional reactions.

Journal: *Journal of Social Psychology,* Feb. 1981, *113*(first half), 85-93.

3125
Test name: ACHIEVEMENT MOTIVATION SCALE

Purpose: To measure achievement motivation.

Number of items: 6

319

Format: Items are rated on a scale from 1 (disagree) to 5 (agree).

Validity: Correlations with other variables ranged from -.05 to .39.

Author: Tepper, M.E. and Powers, S.

Article: Prediction of high school algebra achievement with attributional, motivational, and achievement measures.

Journal: *Perceptual and Motor Skills*, Aug. 1984, 59(1), 120-122.

Related research: Myers, A.E., 1965. Risk taking and academic success and their relation to an objective measure of achievement motivation. *Educational and Psychological Measurement*, 25, 355-363.

3126
Test name: ACHIEVEMENT ORIENTATION—REVISED

Purpose: To measure achievement motivation.

Number of items: 20

Reliability: Alpha was .68.

Validity: Correlation with Directiveness Scale was .021.

Author: Ray, J.J.

Article: Authoritarianism and achievement motivation in India.

Journal: *Journal of Social Psychology*, Aug. 1982, 117(second half), 171-182.

Related research: Ray, J.J., 1980. The comparative validity of Likert, projective and forced-choice indices of achievement motivation. *Journal of Social Psychology*, 111, 63-72.

3127
Test name: CHILDREN'S ACADEMIC INTRINSIC MOTIVATION INVENTORY

Purpose: To measure intrinsic motivation for school learning.

Number of items: 122

Format: 5-point Likert response categories. Sample items presented.

Reliability: Alphas ranged from .67 to .93 across subscales. Test-retest ranged from .66 to .76.

Validity: Shared variance of subscales average 15%. Factor analysis supported distinctions between subscales: reading, math, social studies, sciences, and general.

Author: Gottfried, A.E.

Article: Academic intrinsic motivation in elementary and junior high school students.

Journal: *Journal of Educational Psychology*, Oct. 1985, 77(5), 631-645.

Related research: Gottfried, A.E., 1982. Relationships between academic intrinsic motivation and anxiety in children and young adolescents. *Journal of School Psychology, 20*(3), 205-215.

3128
Test name: DATING MOTIVE SCALE

Purpose: To measure motives for dating member of the opposite sex.

Number of items: 15

Format: 7-point importance scale. Sample items presented.

Reliability: Alpha ranged from .73 to .88 across subscales.

Validity: Four-factor structure of items was similar for males and females. Factor intercorrelations similar for males and females.

Author: White, G.L.

Article: Jealousy and partner's perceived motives for attraction to a rival.

Journal: *Social Psychology Quarterly*, March 1981, *44*(1), 24-30.

3129
Test name: DESIRE FOR SOCIAL POWER SCALE

Purpose: To measure desire for social power.

Number of items: 28

Format: 6-point Likert response categories. All items presented.

Reliability: Test-retest = .88. Alpha = .89.

Author: Booth, R.Z. et al.

Article: Social power need and gender among college students.

Journal: *Psychological Reports*, Aug. 1984, *55*(1), 243-246.

Related research: Good, L.R. and Good, K.C., 1972. An objective measure of the motive to attain social power. *Psychological Reports, 30*, 247-251.

3130
Test name: DESIRE TO HAVE PAID EMPLOYMENT SCALE

Purpose: To measure desire to have paid employment.

Number of items: 6

Format: 5-point agreement scale.

Reliability: Alpha = .82.

Author: Warr, P. and Jackson, P.

Article: Men without jobs: Some correlates of age and length of employment.

Journal: *Journal of Occupational Psychology*, March 1984, 57(1), 77-85.

Related research: Warr, P. et al., 1979. Scales for the measurement of some work attitudes and aspects of psychological well-being. *Journal of Occupational Psychology*, 52, 129-148.

3131
Test name: GHISELLI SELF-DESCRIPTION INVENTORY

Purpose: To measure initiative.

Number of items: 64

Format: Forced-choice.

Validity: Multitrait-multimethod evaluation shows clear support for convergent validity.

Author: Schippman, J.S. and Prien, E.P.

Article: The Ghiselli self-description inventory: A psychosomatic appraisal.

Journal: *Psychological Reports*, Dec. 1985, 53(3, Pt. 2), 1171-1177.

Related research: Ghiselli, E.E., 1955. A scale for the measurement of initiative. *Personnel Psychology*, 8, 157-164.

3132
Test name: GOOD AND GOOD SOCIAL POWER MOTIVATION SCALE

Purpose: To measure social power motivation.

Number of items: 28

Format: True-false responses.

Reliability: KR-20 estimate for internal consistency reliability was .89.

Author: Golden, S.B., Jr. and Royal, E.G.

Article: A construct validation of the Good and Good Measure of Social Power Motivation.

Journal: *Educational and Psychological Measurement*, winter 1982, 42(4), 1219-1226.

Related research: Good, L.R. and Good, K.C., 1972. An objective measure of the motive to attain social power. *Psychological Reports*, 30, 247-251.

3133
Test name: INDEX OF NOVELTY SEEKING

Purpose: To measure internal and external cognition seeking.

Number of items: 20

Format: Self-report scales scored in a dichotomous manner.

Reliability: Internal consistency ranged from .71 to .79.

Author: Hirschman, E.

Article: Psychological sexual identity and hemispheric orientation.

Journal: *Journal of General Psychology*, April 1983, *108*(second half), 153-168.

Related research: Pearson, P., 1970. Relationships between global and specified measures of novelty seeking. *Journal of Consulting and Clinical Psychology*, *32*, 199-204.

3134
Test name: INSTRUMENT OF ALTRUISTIC MOTIVATION

Purpose: To measure altruistic motivation in two dimensions: altruism and anti-utilitarianism.

Number of items: 10

Format: Respondents indicate on a four-point scale how much ten activities are enjoyed. All items presented.

Reliability: Cronbach's alpha was .69 (altruism) and .67 (anti-utilitarianism).

Author: Yogev, A. and Ronen, R.

Article: Cross-age tutoring: Effects on tutors' attitudes.

Journal: *Journal of Educational Research*, May/June 1982, *75*(5), 261-268.

Related research: Vizeltir, V., 1974. *Evaluation of altruistic motivations as intrinsic or extrinsic by men and women*. Master's thesis, Tel Aviv University (Hebrew).

3135
Test name: INTRACEPTION SCALE

Purpose: To measure interest in and response to specific needs, motives, and experiences of others and how these social meanings are used to understand behavior.

Number of items: 30

Format: Adjective checklist.

Reliability: Alpha ranged from .77 to .79.

Author: Heilbrun, A.B., Jr.

Article: Cognitive factors in social effectiveness.

Journal: *Journal of Social Psychology*, Aug. 1983, *120*(second half), 235-243.

Related research: Gough, H.G. and Heilbrun, A.B., 1965. *Manual for the Adjective Checklist*. Palo Alto, CA: Consulting Psychologists Press.

3136

Test name: INTRINSIC MOTIVATION SCALE

Purpose: To measure intrinsic (job) motivation.

Number of items: 4

Format: 5-point Likert format.

Reliability: Internal consistency = .71.

Author: Blau, G.J.

Article: A multiple study investigation of the dimensionality of job involvement.

Journal: *Journal of Vocational Behavior*, Aug. 1985, *27*(1), 19-36.

Related research: Lawler, E. and Hall, D., 1970. Relationship of job characteristics to job involvement satisfaction and intrinsic motivation. *Journal of Applied Psychology*, 54, 305-312.

3137

Test name: INTRINSIC TASK INTEREST SCALE

Purpose: To measure intrinsic task motivation, interest, and satisfaction.

Number of items: 15

Format: 7-point Likert format. Sample items presented.

Reliability: Alphas ranged from .85 to .94 across subscales.

Author: Phillips, J.S. and Freedman, S.M.

Article: Contingent pay and intrinsic task interest: Moderating effects of work values.

Journal: *Journal of Applied Psychology*, May 1985, *70*(2), 306-313.

Related research: Mayo, R.J., 1977. The development and construct validation of a measure of intrinsic motivation. *Dissertation Abstracts International*, *37*, 5417B-5418B. (University microfilms No. 77-7491, 103.)

3138

Test name: JOB MOTIVATION SCALES

Purpose: To measure intrinsic, social, and service motivation.

Number of items: 9

Format: "How important is this reward to you?" followed by 9 work rewards. Respondents rate rewards on a 7-point importance scale.

Reliability: Alphas ranged from .69 to .77 across subscales.

Author: Pearce, J.L.

Article: Job attitude and motivation differences between volunteers and employees from comparable organizations.

Journal: *Journal of Applied Psychology*, Nov. 1983, *68*(4), 646-652.

Related research: Pearce, J.L., 1983. Participation in voluntary associations: How membership in formal organizations changes the rewards of participation. In D.H. Smith and J. Van Til (Eds.), *International Perspective on Voluntary Action Research*. Washington, DC: University Press of America.

3139
Test name: LEVEL OF MOTIVATION FOR RETRAINING SCALE

Purpose: To measure motivation for vocational retraining.

Number of items: 23 (descriptions of subject).

Format: 5-point bipolar scales ranging from "highly correct" to "highly incorrect." All items presented.

Reliability: Test-retest ranged from .68 to .74 across subscales.

Validity: Internalization subscale correlated with locus of control (.33, p < .01), and vocational maturity (.47, p < .01).

Author: Schwarzwald, J. and Shoham, M.

Article: A trilevel approach to motivators for retraining.

Journal: *Journal of Vocational Behavior*, June 1981, *18*(3), 265-276.

3140
Test name: MAYO TASK REACTION QUESTIONNAIRE— MODIFIED

Purpose: To measure intrinsic motivation.

Number of items: 8

Format: Responses are made on a 7-point Likert scale. Sample items are presented.

Reliability: Coefficient alpha was .94.

Validity: Correlation with performance was r = .32.

Author: Phillips, J.S. and Freedman, S.M.

Article: Contingent pay and intrinsic task interest: Moderating effects of work values.

Journal: *Journal of Applied Psychology*, May 1985, *70*(2), 306-313.

Related research: Mayo, R.J., 1977. The development and construct validity of a measure of intrinsic motivation. *Dissertation Abstracts International, 37,* 5417B-5418B. (University microfilms No. 77-7491, 103.)

3141

Test name: MEHRABIAN AND BANK ACHIEVEMENT QUESTIONNAIRE

Purpose: To measure achievement motivation.

Number of items: 38

Format: 9-point agreement scale for each item.

Reliability: KR-20 = .91.

Validity: Correlates .74 with Jackson's (1967) scale.

Author: Waddell, F.T.

Article: Factors affecting choice, satisfaction and success in the female self-employed.

Journal: *Journal of Vocational Behavior,* Dec. 1983, 23(3), 294-304.

Related research: Mehrabian, A. and Bank, L., 1969. A questionnaire measure of individual differences in achieving tendency. *Educational and Psychological Measurement,* 29, 445-461.

3142

Test name: NACH NAFF SCALE

Purpose: To measure achievement motivation.

Number of items: 30

Format: Forced-choice questionnaire on which the subject selects either an achievement- or an affiliation-oriented response from each pair of self-descriptive adjectives.

Reliability: Split-half corrected reliability is estimated to be .80.

Validity: Correlations with: grade-point average .27 (68 females) and .49 (30 males); psychology quiz grades .21 (106 females) and -.10 (56 males); Strong Vocational Interest Blank Scales ranged from -.24 to .37 (56 males) and -.33 to .41 (107 females); California Psychological Inventory Scales ranged from -.24 to .29 (49 males) and -.32 to .34 (86 females).

Author: Sid, A.K.W. and Lindgren, H.C.

Article: Achievement and affiliation motivation and their correlates.

Journal: *Educational and Psychological Measurement,* winter 1982, 42(4), 1213-1218.

Related research: Lindgren, H.C., 1976. Measuring need to achieve by Nach Naff Scale -- a forced-choice questionnaire. *Psychological Reports,* 39, 907-910.

3143
Test name: NEED SATISFACTION SCALE

Purpose: To measure job-derived need and fulfillment.

Number of items: 10

Format: Multiple-choice.

Reliability: Alphas ranged from .69 to .89.

Author: Lefkowitz, J. et al.

Article: The role of need level and/or need salience as moderators of the relationship between need satisfaction and work alienation-involvement.

Journal: *Journal of Vocational Behavior*, April 1984, *24*(2), 142-158.

Related research: Porter, L.W., 1961. A study in perceived need satisfaction in bottom and middle management jobs. *Journal of Applied Psychology, 45*, 1-10.

3144
Test name: REWARD LEVEL SCALE

Purpose: To assess love, status, services, goods, money, and information as rewards.

Number of items: 7

Format: 9-point Likert format.

Reliability: Alpha = .90.

Author: Cate, R.M. et al.

Article: The effect of equity, equality and reward level on the stability of students' premarital relationships.

Journal: *Journal of Social Psychology*, Dec. 1985, *125*(6), 715-721.

Related research: Foa, U.G. and Foa, E.G., 1974. *Societal structures of the mind.* Springfield, IL: Charles C. Thomas.
  Cate, R.M. et al., 1982. Fairness and reward level as predictors of relationship satisfaction. *Journal of Social Psychology, 45*(3), 177-181.

3145
Test name: SARNOFF SURVEY OF ATTITUDES TOWARD LIFE

Purpose: To measure motivation for upward mobility.

Number of items: 18

Format: 6-point agreement scales.

Reliability: Alpha = .67.

Author: Howard, A. et al.

Article: Motivation and values among Japanese and American managers.

Journal: *Personnel Psychology,* winter 1983, *36*(4), 883-898.

Related research: Bray, D.W. et al., 1979. *Formative years in business: A long-term AT&T study of managerial lives.* New York and Melbourne, FL: Robert E. Krieger Publishing Co.

3146

Test name: SENSATION SEEKING SCALE

Purpose: To measure "optimum stimulation level."

Number of items: 22

Format: Forced-choice format requires respondents to choose between two events.

Reliability: Split-half ranged from .68 to .74.

Author: Miller, A. and Cooley, E.

Article: Moderator variables for the relationship between life cycle change and disorders.

Journal: *Journal of General Psychology,* April 1981, *104*(second half), 223-233.

Related research: Zuckerman, M. et al., 1964. Development of sensation seeking scale. *Journal of Consulting Psychology, 28,* 477-482.

3147

Test name: SENSATION SEEKING SCALE FORM VI

Purpose: To measure sensation seeking.

Number of items: 128

Format: Includes four subscales: Experience-thrill and adventure seeking; Experience-disinhibition; intention-thrill and adventure seeking; intention-disinhibition.

Reliability: Coefficient alphas ranged from .62 (N = 38) to .94 (N = 38). Test-retest (7 weeks) reliability ranged from .84 to .93 (N = .49).

Author: Zuckerman, M.

Article: Experience and desire: A new format for sensation seeking scales.

Journal: *Journal of Behavioral Assessment,* June 1984, *6*(2), 101-114.

Related research: Zuckerman, M. et al., 1978. Sensation seeking in England and America: Cross-cultural, age and sex comparisons. *Journal of Consulting and Clinical Psychology, 46,* 139-149.

3148

Test name: SENTENCE COMPLETION SCALE

Purpose: To measure the motivation to manage and to predict managerial performance.

Number of items: 40

Format: Sentence completion format.

Reliability: Inter-scorer reliabilities ranged from .61 to .91 with an average of .83.

Author: Bartal, K.M. et al.

Article: Sex and ethnic effects on motivation to manage among college business students.

Journal: *Journal of Applied Psychology*, Feb. 1981, *66*(1), 40-44.

Related research: Miner, J.B., 1965. *Studies in management education.* New York: Springer.
    Miner, J.B., 1978. The Miner Sentence Completion Scale: A reappraisal. *Academy of Management Journal*, *21*, 283-294.

3149
Test name: TASK AROUSAL SCALE

Purpose: To measure task-specific arousal.

Number of items: 7

Format: Semantic differential. Sample adjective pairs presented.

Reliability: Alpha = .87.

Author: Huber, V.L.

Article: The effects of task difficulty, goal setting and strategy on performance of a heuristic task.

Journal: *Journal of Applied Psychology*, Aug. 1985, *70*(3), 492-504.

Related research: Scott, W.E. and Rowland, K.M., 1970. The generality and significance of semantic differential scales as measures of "morale." *Organizational Behavior and Human Performance*, *5*, 576-591.

3150
Test name: TEACHER EFFECTANCE MOTIVATION RATING

Purpose: To measure effectance motivation.

Number of items: 30

Format: Includes a rating checklist describing student characteristics to which the teacher responds on a 7-point scale to indicate the extent to which each student is described by the characteristic. Sample items are presented.

Reliability: Reliability coefficients (alpha) were .96 and .95.

Author: Pearlman, C.

Article: The effects of level of effectance motivation, IQ, and a penalty/reward contingency on the choice of problem difficulty.

Journal: *Child Development*, April 1984, 55(2), 537-542.

Related research: Pearlman, C., 1982. The measurement of effectance motivation. *Educational and Psychological Measurement*, 42(1), 49-56.

3151
Test name: WELLS-BLEDSOE MOTIVATION CHECKLIST

Purpose: To measure adolescents' school motivation.

Number of items: 51

Format: Includes two factors. All items are presented.

Reliability: Cronbach's alphas were .83 and .82.

Validity: Correlations with Iowa Test of Basic Skills ranged from -.17 to .30. Correlations with Otis-Lennon Quick Scoring Test ranged from -.22 to .33.

Author: Wells, G.R. and Bledsoe, J.C.

Article: Development and validation of the Wells-Bledsoe Motivation Checklist.

Journal: *Perceptual and Motor Skills*, Aug. 1984, 59(1), 243-248.

3152
Test name: WHICH-TO-DISCUSS TEST

Purpose: To measure curiosity.

Number of items: 20

Format: Each item includes a pair of geometric figures and symbols with one of each pair being more balanced than the other. Subjects indicate which one they would choose if they could hear a story about only one of them.

Reliability: Cronbach's alpha was .90.

Validity: Correlation with Maze test was -.06.

Author: Silverstein, A.B. et al.

Article: Psychometric properties of two measures of intrinsic motivation.

Journal: *Perceptual and Motor Skills*, Oct. 1981, 53(2), 655-658.

Related research: Maw, W.H. and Maw, E.W., 1961. Nonhomeostatic experiences as stimuli of children with high curiosity. *California Journal of Educational Research*, 12, 57-61.

PERCEPTION

3153
Test name: ACADEMIC SELF-CONCEPT SCALE

Purpose: To measure general academic self-concept.

Number of items: 40

Format: Subjects indicate one of four levels of agreement to each item. Examples are presented.

Reliability: Internal consistency estimate of reliability was .91.

Validity: Correlations with the Dimensions of Self-Concept measure ranged from -.37 to .34 (N = 202). Correlation with GPA was .52 (N = 589).

Author: Halote, B. and Michael, W.B.

Article: The construct and concurrent validity of two college-level academic self-concept scales for a sample of primarily Hispanic community college students.

Journal: *Educational and Psychological Measurement*, winter 1984, *44*(4), 993-1007.

Related research: Reynolds, W.M. et al., 1980. Initial development and validation of the Academic Self-Concept Scale. *Educational and Psychological Measurement*, 40, 1013-1016.

3154
Test name: ACADEMIC SELF-ESTEEM SCALE

Purpose: To measure academic self-esteem.

Number of items: 11

Format: Yes-no. Sample items presented.

Reliability: Alpha = .72.

Author: Rosenfield, D. et al.

Article: Classroom structure and prejudice in desegregated schools.

Journal: *Journal of Educational Psychology*, Feb. 1981, *73*(1), 17-26.

Related research: Vitale, M., 1974. *Evaluation of the Title III Dallas junior high school career education project: 1973-1974*. Report No. 74-291. Dallas Independent School District, Department of Research and Evaluation.

3155
Test name: ACADEMIC SELF-SCHEMA

Purpose: To measure academic self-esteem.

Number of items: 26 of 58 from Coopersmith Self-Esteem Inventory.

Format: Sample items presented.

Reliability: Pretest alpha = .73.

Author: Corno, L. and Mandinach, E.B.

Article: Using existing classroom data to explore relationships in a theoretical model of academic motivation.

Journal: *Journal of Educational Research*, Sept./Oct. 1983, 77(1), 33-42.

Related research: Coopersmith, S. (Ed.), 1967. Coopersmith Self-Esteem Inventory. *The Antecedents of Self Esteem*. San Francisco: W.H. Freeman.

3156

Test name: ACHIEVABILITY OF FUTURE GOALS SCALE

Purpose: To measure optimism.

Number of items: 8

Format: 7-point Likert scale. Sample items presented.

Reliability: Alpha = .73.

Author: Wolf, F.M. and Savickas, M.L.

Article: Time perspective and causal attributions for achievement.

Journal: *Journal of Educational Psychology*, Aug. 1985, 77(4), 471-480.

Related research: Heimberg, L., 1961. *Development and construct validation of an inventory for the measurement of future time perspectives*. Unpublished master's thesis, Vanderbilt University.
  Savickas, M.L. et al., 1984. Time perspective in vocational maturity and career decision making. *Journal of Vocational Behavior*, 25(3), 258-269.

3157

Test name: ACHIEVEMENT ATTRIBUTION SCALE

Purpose: To measure attributions for achievement (subscale of multidimensional-multiattributional causality scale).

Number of items: 24

Format: 5-point Likert scales. Sample items presented.

Reliability: Alpha ranged from .47 to .71 over subscales.

Author: Wolf, F.M. and Savickas, M.L.

Article: Time perspective and causal attributions for achievement.

Journal: *Journal of Educational Psychology*, Aug. 1985, 77(4), 471-480.

Related research: Lefcourt, H.M. et al., 1979. The Multidimensional-multiattributional Causality Scale. *Canadian Journal of Behavioral Science*, 11, 286-304.

3158
Test name: AFFECTIVE ENTRY QUESTIONNAIRE

Purpose: To measure expectations of course, instructor, and subject matter at the beginning of a semester.

Number of items: 52

Format: Likert format.

Reliability: Internal consistency = .85.

Validity: In this use of the scale large proportions of respondents (87%) reported "no basis for judgement" on 5 items. 60% made that response to all 15 questions measuring instructor characteristics.

Author: Barké, C.R. et al.

Article: Relationship between course entry attitudes and end-of-course ratings.

Journal: *Journal of Educational Psychology*, Feb. 1983, 75(1), 75-85.

3159
Test name: ALCOHOL EXPECTANCY QUESTIONNAIRE

Purpose: To measure perceived effects of alcohol consumption.

Number of items: 90

Format: Agree-disagree format.

Reliability: Alpha ranged from .28 to .95 across subscales (five of six scales had alphas of .79 or greater).

Author: Brown, S.A. et al.

Article: Do alcohol expectancies mediate drinking patterns of adults?

Journal: *Journal of Consulting and Clinical Psychology*, Aug. 1985, 53(4), 512-519.

Related research: Brown, S.A., 1985. Expectancies versus background in the prediction of college drinking patterns. *Journal of Consulting and Clinical Psychology*, 53, 123-130.

3160
Test name: ALCOHOL EXPECTANCY QUESTIONNAIRE FOR ADOLESCENTS

Purpose: To measure expectancies associated with alcohol consumption.

Number of items: 100

Format: True-false.

Reliability: Alpha = .90.

Validity: Two-factor solutions were produced at all age levels - one revealed alcohol as a positive transforming agent and one revealed alcohol to be a negative transforming agent.

Author: Christiansen, B.A. et al.

Article: Development of alcohol-related expectancies in adolescents: Separating pharmacological from social-learning influences.

Journal: *Journal of Consulting and Clinical Psychology*, June 1982, *50*(3), 336-344.

Related research: Brown, S.A. et al., 1980. Expectations of reinforcement from alcohol: Their domain and relation to drinking patterns. *Journal of Consulting and Clinical Psychology*, *48*, 419-426.

3161
Test name: AMOUNT OF INVESTED MENTAL EFFORT SCALE

Purpose: To measure the perceived effort required to understand material presented on film and in print.

Number of items: 4

Format: 4-category multiple-choice format. All items presented.

Reliability: Cronbach's alpha = .81.

Author: Soloman, G.

Article: Television is "easy" and print is "tough": The differential investment of mental effort in learning as a function of perceptions and attributions.

Journal: *Journal of Educational Psychology*, Aug. 1984, *76*(4), 647-658.

Related research: Kunkle, D., 1981. *Answering the AIME: An empirical analysis of the relationship between mental effort and learning from TV.* Unpublished manuscript, University of Southern California.

3162
Test name: APPRAISAL INTERVIEW ASSESSMENT SCALE

Purpose: To measure subordinates perceptions of the most recent appraisal interview.

Number of items: 23

Format: 7-point "very true" to "very false" response scales.

Reliability: Alphas ranged from .79 to .87 across subscales.

Author: Ivancevich, J.M.

Article: Subordinates' reactions to performance appraisal interviews: A test of feedback and goal-setting techniques.

Journal: *Journal of Applied Psychology*, Oct. 1982, *67*(5), 581-587.

Related research: Greller, M.M., 1978. The nature of subordinate participation in the appraisal interview. *Academy of Management Journal, 21*, 646-658.

3163
Test name: ARTICULATION SURVEY

Purpose: To measure importance of the problem of articulation of community college and 4-year colleges and universities.

Number of items: 41

Format: 6-point response categories, ranging from not a problem to problem of major significance.

Reliability: Intercorrelations were .71 to 1.00 (p<.05) for 38 of 41 items.

Validity: Items reviewed by a panel of expert articulation professionals.

Author: Remley, T.P., Jr. and Stripling, R.O.

Article: Perceptions of transfer problems experienced by community college graduates.

Journal: *Journal of College Student Personnel*, Jan. 1981, *24*(1), 43-50.

3164
Test name: ATTRIBUTION QUESTIONNAIRE

Purpose: To assess degree to which people believe that obtaining or not obtaining a job is due to internal or external factors.

Number of items: 12

Format: Responses to items ranged from "always true" to "never true." All items presented.

Reliability: Alpha ranged from .51 to .54. Inter-item correlations ranged from -.24 to .54.

Validity: Factor analysis revealed a general external and a general internal factor plus a situational factor.

Author: Gurney, R.M.

Article: Leaving school, facing unemployment and making attributions about the causes of unemployment.

Journal: *Journal of Vocational Behavior*, Feb. 1981, *18*(1), 79-91.

3165
Test name: ATTRIBUTIONAL STYLE QUESTIONNAIRE

Purpose: To assess the general attributional style of clients.

Number of items: 12

Format: Each item is an event with either good or bad outcomes. The subject is asked to list the major cause of the event and then to rate the internality, stability, and globality of the cause on a 7-point continuum.

Reliability: Coefficient alphas ranged from .46 to .69. Test-retest reliabilities ranged from r = .57 to r = .69.

Author: Claiborn, C.D. and Dowd, E.T.

Article: Attributional interpretations in counseling: Content versus discrepancy.

Journal: *Journal of Counseling Psychology*, April 1985, *32*(2), 197-205.

Related research: Peterson, C. et al., 1982. The Attributional Style Questionnaire. *Cognitive Therapy and Research*, 6, 188-196.

3166

Test name: ATTRIBUTIONAL TENDENCY SCALE

Purpose: To measure if attributions in the classroom represent high or low locus of control.

Number of items: 5

Format: Guttman.

Reliability: Reproducibility = .92. Scalability = .56.

Author: Oren, D.L.

Article: Evaluation systems and attributional tendencies in the classroom: A sociological approach.

Journal: *Journal of Educational Research*, May/June 1983, *76*(5), 307-312.

Related research: Massey, G.C. and Dornbusch, S.M., 1977. *Self-enhancement, self-consistency and distinctiveness of feedback in a field study of academic self-concept: Attribution processes in inner-city high schools*. Technical report No. 49. Center for Research and Development in Education, Stanford University.

3167

Test name: AUSTRALIAN SEX-ROLE SCALE

Purpose: To measure masculine and feminine characteristics.

Number of items: 30

Format: 7-point rating scale (1 = never or almost never true, 7 = always or almost always true).

Reliability: Alpha ranged from .14 to .80 over subscales on Forms A and B.

Author: Hong, S-M et al.

Article: Factor structure of the Australian Sex-Role Scale.

Journal: *Psychological Reports*, Oct. 1983, *53*(2), 499-505.

Related research: Antill, J.K. et al., 1981. An Australian Sex-Role Scale. *Australian Journal of Psychology*, *33*, 169-183.

3168
Test name: AUTONOMY-CONTROL SCALE

Purpose: To measure autonomy-control variation.

Number of items: 40

Format: 5-point response scale.

Reliability: Test-retest = .91 (N = 41, two months).

Author: DeMan, A.F.

Article: Autonomy-control variation in child-rearing and anomie in young adults.

Journal: *Psychological Reports*, 1982, *51*(1), 7-10.

Related research: DeMan, A.F., 1982. Autonomy-control variation and self-esteem: Additional findings. *Journal of Psychology*, *111*, 9-13.

3169
Test name: AUTOSTEREOTYPE-HETEROSTEREOTYPE SCALE

Purpose: To measure stereotypes among managers of different nationalities.

Number of items: 18

Format: Adjectival pairs scored from 1 to 7. All pairs (items) presented along with instructions to respondents.

Validity: Two factors identified by method of principal components. Comparability coefficient for respondents of different nationalities was .96.

Author: Stening, B.W. et al.

Article: Mutual perception of managerial performance and style in multinational subsidiaries.

Journal: *Journal of Occupational Psychology*, Dec. 1981, *54*(4), 255-263.

Related research: Triandis, H.C., 1972. *The analysis of subjective culture*. New York: Wiley.

3170
Test name: AWARENESS OF COMPREHENSION FAILURE TEST

Purpose: To measure children's ability to monitor and detect their own cognitive processes.

Number of items: 18

Format: Children are asked questions concerning their awareness that information is lacking. Sample questions presented.

Reliability: Test-retest = .73.

Author: Clements, D.H. and Gullo, D.F.

Article: Effects of computer programming on young children's cognition.

Journal: *Journal of Educational Psychology*, Dec. 1984, 76(6), 1051-1058.

Related research: Markman, E.M., 1977. Realizing you don't understand: A preliminary investigation. *Child Development*, 48, 986-992.

3171
Test name: BEHAVIOROID INTERNAL-EXTERNAL SCALE

Purpose: To measure relationships between verbalized beliefs and behavior by keying on behavioral attributes on the internal and external end of the Rotter I-E Scale.

Number of items: 26

Format: All items presented.

Reliability: Test-retest = .78. KR-20 = .83. Spearman-Brown split-half ranged from .72 to .93.

Validity: Correlated .19 with Blame Attribution and .16 with Social Desirability.

Author: Russell, G.M.

Article: Development of a behavioroid I-E locus of control scale.

Journal: *Psychological Reports*, Dec. 1982, 51(3, Pt. 2), 1095-1099.

3172
Test name: BELIEF IN LUNAR EFFECTS SCALE

Purpose: To assess beliefs in lunar effects.

Number of items: 9

Format: 3-point agreement scale. All items presented.

Reliability: Cronbach's alpha = .85.

Validity: Correlates .47 (p<.001) with reported positive influence of a full moon. Correlates significantly with logical ability (-.17) and with various paranormal scales (.19 to .39).

Author: Rotton, J. and Kelly, I.W.

Article: A scale for assessing belief in lunar effects: Reliability and concurrent validity.

Journal: *Psychological Reports*, Aug. 1985, 57(1), 239-245.

3173
Test name: BELL REALITY TESTING INVENTORY

Purpose: To assess the perceptions of reality.

Number of items: 45

Format: True-false format.

Reliability: Alphas ranged from .82 to .87. Split-half ranged from .77 to .85.

Validity: 92% correct classification with inpatient schizophrenics. Age unrelated to subscales. Other validity data presented.

Author: Bell, M.D. et al.

Article: Scale for the assessment of reliability testing: Reliability, validity and factorial invariance.

Journal: *Journal of Consulting and Clinical Psychology*, Aug. 1985, 53(4), 506-511.

Related research: Bell, M. et al., 1980. *Reality testing - object relations assessment scale: Reliability and validity studies.* Paper presented at the American Psychological Association Convention, Montreal.

3174
Test name: BLOOD DONOR SALIENCE SCALE

Purpose: To assess if donor role is part of a person's self-concept.

Number of items: 5

Format: Nine-point agreement scale. All items presented.

Reliability: Alpha = .81.

Validity: Salience of donor role ranked third behind work and religion.

Author: Callero, P.

Article: Role-identity salience.

Journal: *Social Psychology Quarterly*, June 1985, 48(3), 203-215.

Related research: Jackson, S., 1981. Measurement of commitment to role identities. *Journal of Personality and Social Psychology*, 40, 138-146.

3175
Test name: BODY CATHEXIS SCALE—MODIFIED

Purpose: To assess the degree of satisfaction or dissatisfaction felt about parts and processes of the body.

Number of items: 40

Format: Subjects evaluate body characteristics on a five-point

Likert scale ranging from 1 (strongly negative) to 5 (strongly positive).

Reliability: Test-retest reliability was .87.

Author: Tucker, L.A.

Article: Internal structure, factor satisfaction and reliability of the Body Cathexis Scale.

Journal: *Perceptual and Motor Skills*, Dec. 1981, 53(3), 891-896.

Related research: Secord, P.F. and Jourard, S.M., 1953. The appraisal of body-cathexis: body cathexis and the self. *Journal of Consulting Psychology*, 17, 343-347.

3176
Test name: BODY-ESTEEM SCALE

Purpose: To measure children's affective evaluation of their bodies.

Number of items: 24

Format: Subjects respond to each item by "yes" or "no." High esteem has an equal number of "yes" and "no" responses. All items are presented.

Reliability: Split-half reliability was .85.

Validity: Correlation with: Self-body was .67; relative weight was -.55; self-esteem was .68; self-rest was .62.

Author: Mendelson, B.K. and White, D.R.

Article: Relation between body-esteem and self-esteem of obese and normal children.

Journal: *Perceptual and Motor Skills*, June 1982, 54(3, Pt. 1), 899-905.

3177
Test name: BODY PARTS SATISFACTION SCALE

Purpose: To assess satisfaction with body.

Number of items: 24

Format: 6-point Likert satisfaction scales.

Reliability: Alpha = .89.

Author: Noles, S.W. et al.

Article: Body image, physical attractiveness and depression.

Journal: *Journal of Consulting and Clinical Psychology*, Feb. 1985, 53(1), 88-94.

Related research: Bohrnstedt, G.W., 1977. *On measuring body satisfaction*. Unpublished manuscript, Indiana University.
  Berscheid, E. et al., 1973. The happy American body: A survey

report. *Psychology Today*, November, pp. 119-131.

3178
Test name: BRIEF LOCUS OF CONTROL SCALE

Purpose: To measure locus of control.

Number of items: 6

Format: Likert-type format applied to Rotter items. All items presented.

Reliability: Alpha = .68.

Validity: Correlates .25 with life satisfaction; -.13 with perceived risk; -.32 with not coping; .22 with good health; and .19 with activity (all p<.001).

Author: Lumpkin, J.R.

Article: Validity of a brief locus of control scale for survey research.

Journal: *Psychological Reports*, Oct. 1985, *57*(2), 655-659.

3179
Test name: CANADIAN SELF-ESTEEM INVENTORY FOR ADULTS

Purpose: To measure self-esteem.

Number of items: 40

Format: Dichotomous scoring categories.

Reliability: Internal consistency coefficients ranged from .20 to .76 across subscales.

Author: Blau, G.J. and Lenihan, M.

Article: Note on internal consistency of Canadian Self-Esteem Inventory for Adults.

Journal: *Psychological Reports*, 1981, *49*(1), 81-82.

Related research: Battle, J., 1980. Relationship between self-esteem and depression among high school students. *Perceptual and Motor Skills*, *51*, 157-158.

3180
Test name: CAREER DECISION-MAKING SELF-EFFICACY SCALE

Purpose: To measure self-efficacy expectations related to a variety of tasks or behaviors associated with career decision-making.

Number of items: 50

Format: Includes five subscales. Responses to each item are made on a 10-point Likert scale.

Reliability: Average alpha for all subscales is .88.

Author: Robbins, S.B.

Article: Validity estimates for the Career Decision-Making Self-Efficacy Scale.

Journal: *Measurement and Evaluation in Counseling and Development*, July 1985, *18*(2), 64-71.

Related research: Taylor, K.M. and Betz, N.M., 1983. Application of self-efficacy theory to the understanding and treatment of career indecision. *Journal of Vocational Behavior*, 22, 63-81.

Journal: *Journal of Counseling Psychology*, Jan. 1985, *32*(1), 139-142.

Related research: Russell, D., 1982. The Causal Dimension Scale: A measure of individuals' perceived causes. *Journal of Personality and Social Psychology*, 42, 1137-1145.

Abraham, I.L., 1985. Causal attributions of depression: Reliability of the "Causal Dimension Scale" in research on clinical inference. *Psychological Reports*, 56(2), 415-418.

3181
Test name: CAUSAL DIMENSION SCALE

Purpose: To measure how individuals perceive causes.

Number of items: 9

Format: Includes three subscales, one of which is controllability: the degree to which loneliness could be altered by someone. The higher the score the greater the possibility.

Reliability: Coefficient alpha was .88 for each subscale.

Author: Conoley, C.W. and Garber, R.A.

Article: Effects of reframing and self-control directives on loneliness, depression, and controllability.

3182
Test name: CHILDREN'S LOCUS OF CONTROL SCALE

Purpose: To measure locus of control.

Number of items: 26

Format: Yes-no format.

Reliability: Test-retest = .68 (one week interval).

Author: Thomson-Rountree, P. and Woodruff, A.E.

Article: An examination of project aware: The effects on children's attitudes toward themselves, others and school.

Journal: *Journal of School Psychology*, 1982, *20*(1), 20-31.

Related research: Bradley, R.H. and Teeter, T.A., 1977. Perceptions of control over social outcomes and student behavior. *Psychology in the Schools*, 14, 230-235.

Thomson-Rountree, P. et al., 1981. An examination of the relationship between role-taking and social competence. *Child Study Journal*, 71(4), 253-264.

3183
Test name: CHILDREN'S NOWICKI-STRICKLAND INTERNAL-EXTERNAL CONTROL SCALE

Purpose: To measure generalized locus of control orientation.

Number of items: 40

Format: Yes-no format.

Reliability: Test-retest (six week interval) ranged from .63 to .71 across grade levels.

Author: Piotrowski, C., and Dunham, F.Y.

Article: Locus of control orientation and perception of "hurricane" in fifth graders.

Journal: *Journal of General Psychology*, July 1983, 109(first half), 119-127.

Related research: Nowicki, S., Jr., and Strickland, B.R., 1973. A locus of control scale for children. *Journal of Consulting and Clinical Psychology*, 40, 148-154.

3184
Test name: CHILDREN'S OWN PERCEPTIONS AND EXPERIENCES OF STRESSORS

Purpose: To measure children's perceptions of stressors in their lives and their experiences and emotional reactions to those stressors.

Number of items: 60

Format: A 5-point Likert-type scale from 1 (not upsetting at all) to 5 (extremely upsetting) is used to determine how upsetting each item is. Also the children are asked whether the event ever happened to them and if so, whether it upset or worried them. Seven factors are identified. All items are presented.

Reliability: The average coefficient alpha for the factors was .84.

Author: Colton, J.A.

Article: Childhood stress: Perceptions of children and professionals.

Journal: *Journal of Psychopathology and Behavioral Assessment*, June 1985, 17(2), 155-173.

Related research: Chandler, L.A., 1981. The source of stress inventory. *Psychology in the Schools*, 18, 164-168.

3185
Test name: CHILDREN'S PERCEIVED SELF-CONTROL SCALE

Purpose: To measure children's perception of self-control.

Number of items: 11

Format: Children respond to items either by choosing "usually yes" or "usually no." All items presented.

Reliability: Test-retest (2 week interval) = .71 (from .18 to .63 across 4 subscales).

Validity: 5 of 40 correlations with Child Behavior Rating Scale were significant (significant correlations ranged from .39 to .49, $p \leq .05$).

Author: Humphrey, L.L.

Article: Childrens' and Teachers' perspectives on children's self-control: The development of two rating scales.

Journal: *Journal of Consulting and Clinical Psychology*, Oct. 1982, 50(5), 624-633.

3186
Test name: CHILDREN'S PERSONAL ATTRIBUTES INVENTORY

Purpose: To measure evaluative-affective aspects of self-concept.

Number of items: 48

Format: Checklist format. Respondents mark the 15 adjectives on the list of 48 that best describes themselves.

Reliability: Split-half = .83.

Validity: Correlates .66 with Piers-Harris measure of self-concept.

Author: Verna, G.B. and Runion, K.B.

Article: The effects of contextual dissonance on the self-concept of youth from a high versus low socially valued group.

Journal: *Journal of Social Psychology*, Aug. 1985, *125*(4), 449-458.

Related research: Parish, T.S. and Taylor, J., 1978. The Personal Attribute Inventory for Children: A report on its validity and reliability. *Educational and Psychological Measurements*, 38, 565-569.

3187
Test name: CHILDREN'S SELF-PERCEPTION SCALE

Purpose: To measure self-perception of children.

Number of items: 17

Format: 5-point Likert response categories. Sample items presented.

Reliability: Alpha = .82.

Validity: Perceived ability correlates with grades (.11) and teacher's judgment of achievement (.10). Perceived effort and perceived conduct correlated with grades (.17) (in all cases, p<.001).

Author: Pintrich, P.R. and Blumenfeld, P.C.

Article: Classroom experience and children's self-perceptions of ability, effort and conduct.

Journal: *Journal of Educational Psychology*, Oct. 1985, 77(5), 646-657.

3188
Test name: CHILDREN'S SEX-ROLE TEST

Purpose: To measure masculinity and femininity.

Number of items: 24

Format: 4-point rating scale. All items presented.

Reliability: Split-half and test-retest were .79 or above.

Validity: Boys scored significantly higher on masculinity than girls.

Author: Moore, S.M.

Article: The Children's Sex-Role Test.

Journal: *Psychological Reports*, Oct. 1985, 57(2), 586.

3189
Test name: CLASS CONSCIOUSNESS SCALE

Purpose: To measure awareness of social class among children.

Number of items: 18 drawings.

Format: Children match drawings of upper, middle, and lower class mothers, fathers, children, houses, and automobiles into families. All drawings presented.

Reliability: Split-half = .77.

Validity: Correlates .91 with age of child.

Author: Mookherjee, H.N. and Hogan, H.W.

Article: Class consciousness among young rural children.

Journal: *Journal of Social Psychology*, June 1981, *114*(first half), 91-98.

3190
Test name: CLIENT BELIEFS INVENTORY

Purpose: To measure beliefs about problems with negative emotions and the prospects for change.

Number of items: 32

Format: Includes 4 scales: expectation to change, motivation to change, self-control, and understanding.

Reliability: Alpha coefficients ranged from .39 to .83.

Author: Claiborn, C.D. et al.

Article: Effects of intervention discrepancy in counseling for negative emotions.

Journal: *Journal of Counseling Psychology*, April 1983, *30*(2), 164-171.

Related research: Strong, S.R. et al., 1979. Motivational and equipping functions of interpretation in counseling. *Journal of Counseling Psychology*, 26, 98-107.

3191
Test name: CLIENT EXPECTANCY QUESTIONNAIRE

Purpose: To measure clients' expectations for counseling sessions.

Number of items: 14

Format: 6-point Likert format.

Reliability: Cronbach's alpha = .88.

Author: Friedlander, M.L. and Kaul, J.J.

Article: Preparing clients for counseling: Effect of role induction on counseling process and outcome.

Journal: *Journal of College Student Personnel*, 1983, *24*(3), 207-214.

Related research: Howard, K. et al., 1970. Patients' satisfactions in psychotherapy as a function of patient-therapist pairing. *Psychotherapy: Theory, Research and Practice*, 7, 130-134.
   Friedlander, M.L., 1982. Expectations and perceptions of counseling: Changes over time and in relation to verbal behavior. *Journal of College Student Personnel*, 23(5), 402-408.

3192
Test name: COGNITIVE ERROR QUESTIONNAIRE (GENERAL AND LOWER BACK PAIN VERSIONS)

Purpose: To measure cognitive error (cognitive distortion).

Number of items: 24 items in each version.

Format: Vignettes presented to subjects after which they respond to cognitions that reflect one of four cognitive errors (responses are made on a 5-point scale). Sample items presented.

Reliability: Test-retest ranged from .80 to .85. Alternate forms ranged from .76 to .82. Internal consistency ranged from .89 to .92.

Validity: Correlates .53 to .60 with Hammen and Krantz Depressed-Distorted Questionnaire.

Author: Lefebvre, M.F.

Article: Cognitive distortion and cognitive errors in depressed psychiatric and low back pain patients.

Journal: *Journal of Consulting and Clinical Psychology*, Aug. 1981, *49*(4), 517-525.

Related research: Lefebvre, M.F., 1980. *Cognitive distortion in depressed psychiatric and low back pain patients.* Doctoral dissertation, University of Vermont, 41,693 B. University Microfilms No. 80-17, 652.

3193
Test name: COGNITIVE PROCESS SURVEY

Purpose: To assess imaginal life, orientation toward imaginal life, and defensiveness.

Number of items: 30

Format: Subjects respond to each item on a 5-point scale from "strongly agree" to "strongly disagree." Examples are presented.

Reliability: Subscale coefficient alphas ranged from .72 to .78 (N = 350).

Validity: Correlations with other variables ranged from -.33 to .65 (N = 222).

Author: Martinetti, R.F.

Article: Cognitive antecedents of dream recall.

Journal: *Perceptual and Motor Skills*, April 1985, *60*(2), 395-401.

Related research: Martinetti, R.F., 1983. Dream recall, imaginal processes and short-term memory: A pilot study. *Perceptual and Motor Skills*, *57*, 718.

3194
Test name: COLLEGE STUDENT ACADEMIC LOCUS OF CONTROL SCALE

Purpose: To predict a wide range of relevant college students' behaviors.

Number of items: 28

Format: True-false response is made to each item. All items are presented.

Reliability: Test-retest (5 weeks) reliability was .92. KR-20 internal consistency was .70.

Validity: Correlations with other variables ranged from .50 to -.38.

Author: Trice, A.D.

Article: An academic locus of control scale for college students.

Journal: *Perceptual and Motor Skills*, Dec. 1985, *61*(3, Pt. 2), 1043-1046.

3195
Test name: CONNECTICUT NEEDS ASSESSMENT SURVEY

Purpose: To assess the counselor's role.

Number of items: 24

Format: 4-point Likert format. All items presented.

Reliability: Alpha ranged from .66 to .76 across subscales.

Author: Helms, B.J. and Ibrahim, F.A.

Article: A comparison of counselor and parent perceptions of the role and function of the secondary school counselor.

Journal: *The School Counselor*, March 1985, *32*(4), 266-274.

Related research: Ibrahim, F.A., 1981. *Design and methodology for the development of a model school counselor education curriculum.* Paper presented at the annual convention of the American Personnel and Guidance Association, St. Louis.

3196
Test name: CONTINGENT-NONCONTINGENT EXPECTANCY SCALE

Purpose: To measure locus of control for academic achievement by distinguishing whether one's academic success will be contingent or noncontingent with one's actions or attributes.

Number of items: 32

Format: 10-point Likert format. Sample items presented.

Reliability: Cronbach's alpha ranged from .74 to .90 over 5 subscales.

Validity: Significant correlations with ability, effort, worry, emotionality, extrinsic-intrinsic motivation, and other measures reported for various subscales were in the predicted direction.

Author: Palenzuela, D.L.

Article: Critical evaluation of locus of control: Towards a reconceptualization of the construct and its measurement.

Journal: *Psychological Reports*, June 1984, *54*(3), 683-709.

3197
Test name: COOPERSMITH SELF-ESTEEM INVENTORY

Purpose: To measure self-esteem in various contexts.

Number of items: 58

Format: True-false items with eight items constituting a "lie" scale.

Reliability: Test-retest reliability was .88 (50 items over 5 weeks) and .70 (over 3 years).

Author: Miller, L.B. and Bizzell, R.P.

Article: Long-term effects of four preschool programs: ninth- and tenth-grade results.

Journal: *Child Development,* August 1984, 55(4), 1570-1587.

Related research: Coopersmith, S., 1967. *Antecedents of self-esteem.* San Francisco: W.H. Freeman.
Halpin, G. et al., 1981. Locus of control and self-esteem among American Indians and whites: A cross-cultural comparison. *Psychological Reports,* 48(1), 91-98.

3198

Test name: COUNSELING EXPECTATION INVENTORY

Purpose: To describe possible outcomes clients might hope to accomplish through counseling.

Number of items: 14

Format: Items are rated twice: first to indicate the probability that an item can be accomplished through counseling, a 0 (not at all likely) to 10 (completely likely) scale is used; second to rate the importance of each outcome, a 1 (extremely unimportant) to 7 (extremely important) scale is used. The product of each pair of ratings is added for all items. Items are presented.

Reliability: Coefficient alphas were .93 (200 clients) and .92 (200 counselors).

Author: Turner, C.J. and Schwartzbach, H.

Article: A construct validation study of the counseling expectation inventory.

Journal: *Measurement and Evaluation in Guidance,* April 1983, 16(1), 18-24.

Related research: Schwartzbach, H., 1981. *The development and validation of the prognostic expectation inventory for use with a college counseling population.* Unpublished doctoral dissertation, Rutgers - The State University.

3199

Test name: COUNSELOR FUNCTION INVENTORY

Purpose: To provide counselors' perceptions of the role of the school counselor.

Number of items: 77

Format: Includes 7 areas of counselor service: placement, counseling, follow-up, orientation, student data, information, and miscellaneous.

Reliability: Test-retest r = .96. Odd-even, split-half r = .86.

Author: Brown, D.R. and Hartman, B.

Article: Differential effects of incentives on response error, response rate and reliability of a mailed questionnaire.

Journal: *Measurement and Evaluation in Guidance*, April 1980, *13*(1), 20-28.

Related research: Shumate, G.F. and Oelke, M.C., 1967. Counselor function inventory. *School Counselor*, 15, 130-133.

3200
Test name: COUNSELOR PERCEPTION QUESTIONNAIRE

Purpose: To measure counselor's perceptions of counseling sessions.

Number of items: 14

Format: 6-point Likert format.

Reliability: Cronbach's alpha = .94.

Author: Friedlander, M.L. and Kaul, T.J.

Article: Preparing clients for counseling: Effect of role induction on counseling process and outcome.

Journal: *Journal of College Student Personnel*, 1983, *24*(3), 207-214.

Related research: Howard, K. et al., 1970. Patients' satisfactions in psychotherapy as a function of patient-therapist pairing. *Psychotherapy: Theory, Research and Practice*, 7, 130-134.

3201
Test name: COVERT THOUGHTS QUESTIONNAIRE

Purpose: To assess self-statements.

Number of items: 26

Format: Includes an equal number of positive and negative self-statements to which subjects respond on a scale from 1 (never had the thought) to 5 (very often had the thought).

Reliability: Cronbach's alphas were .81 (positive items) and .87 (negative items).

Validity: Correlations with other variables ranged from -.47 to .53.

Author: Bruch, M.A. et al.

Article: Relationships of cognitive components of test anxiety to test performance: Implications for assessment and treatment.

Journal: *Journal of Counseling Psychology*, Oct. 1983, *30*(4), 527-536.

Related research: Galassi, J.P. et al., 1981. Behavior of high, moderate and low test-anxious students during an actual test situation. *Journal of Consulting and Clinical Psychology*, *49*, 51-62.

3202
Test name: DEVIANT ROLE/IDENTITY SCALE

Purpose: To measure role/identities of deviant individuals.

Number of items: 11 adjective pairs.

Format: Semantic differential (all adjective pairs presented).

Validity: MMPI Pd Scale: subjects with delinquent self-concepts described themselves as having more deviant feelings and behavior than subjects with disturbed or popular self-concepts.

Author: Chassin, L., et al.

Article: Identifying with a deviant label: The validation of a methodology.

Journal: *Social Psychology Quarterly*, March 1981, *44*(1), 31-36.

Related research: Burke, P. and Tully, J., 1977. The measurement of role identity. *Social Forces, 55*, 881-897.

3203
Test name: EDUCATIONAL ATTRIBUTION SCALE

Purpose: To measure role of attributional processes in educational outcomes (i.e., locus of control).

Number of items: 3

Format: 9-point rating scales. All items presented (one each for distinctiveness, consistency, and consensus).

Validity: Low scores on test are made by students who are high in external attribution.

Author: Forsyth, D.R. and McMillan, J.H.

Article: The attribution cube and reaction to educational outcomes.

Journal: *Journal of Educational Psychology*, Oct. 1981, *73*(5), 632-641.

Related research: Kelly, H.H., 1981. *Attribution in social interaction*. Morristown, NJ: General Learning Press.

3204
Test name: EFFICACY TO INFLUENCE CHANGE SCALE

Purpose: To measure perceived collective efficacy to influence change in university policy and to change the present situation.

Number of items: 18

Format: Responses were scored as indicating either positive or negative outcome.

Reliability: Internal consistency reliability was .88.

Validity: Correlations with other variables ranged from -.72 to .78.

Author: Zalesny, M.D.

Article: Comparison of economic and noneconomic factors in predicting faculty vote preference in a union representation election.

Journal: *Journal of Applied Psychology*, May 1985, 70(2), 243-256.

3205
Test name: EFFORT VERSUS ABILITY VERSUS EXTERNAL SCALE

Purpose: To assess childrens' causal attributions for academic difficulties.

Number of items: 30

Format: For each of 5 failure situations children choose one of 3 causes of failure, and for each selected cause of failure children select two of three attributions.

Reliability: Test-retest ranged from .56 to .82. Internal consistency ranged from .63 to .77.

Validity: Correlations with Intellectual Achievement Responsibility Scale (Crandall et al., 1965) ranged from .59 to .63.

Author: Licht, B.G. et al.

Article: Causal attributions of learning disabled children: Individual differences and their implications for persistence.

Journal: *Journal of Educational Psychology*, April 1985, 77(2), 208-216.

3206
Test name: EGO-STRENGTH AND SELF-ESTEEM MEASURE

Purpose: To measure levels of ego-strength and self-esteem (ability to share feelings, personal adequacy, sense of reality, alienation, loneliness, self-confidence).

Number of items: 80

Format: True-false.

Reliability: Alphas ranged from .62 to .67 across subscales.

Author: Fry, P.S. and Addington, J.

Article: Comparison of social problem solving of children from open and traditional classrooms: A two-year longitudinal study.

Journal: *Journal of Educational Psychology*, April 1984, 76(2), 318-329.

Related research: Barron, F., 1953. An ego-strength scale which predicts response to psychotherapy. *Journal of Consulting Psychology*, 17, 327-333.
  Helmreich, R. and Stapp, J., 1974. Short forms of the Texas Social Behavior Inventory (TSBI), an objective measure of self-esteem. *Bulletin of the Psychonomic Society*, 4, 473-475.

3207
Test name: ESTIMATE OF SELF-COMPETENCE SCALE

Purpose: To measure generalized expectancy of task success.

Number of items: 12

Reliability: Internal consistency reliability estimate was .78. Test-retest estimate was .86.

Validity: Correlations with other variables ranged from -.40 to .51.

Author: Motowidlo, S.J.

Article: Construct validity for a measure of generalized expectancy of task success.

Journal: *Educational and Psychological Measurement*, winter 1981, *41*, 4 963-972.

Related research: Motowidlo, S.J., 1979. Development of a measure of generalized expectancy of task success. *Educational and Psychological Measurement*, *39*, 69-80.

3208
Test name: EXPECTATIONS ABOUT COUNSELING QUESTIONNAIRE

Purpose: To measure clients' expectations about counseling prior to entering counseling.

Number of items: 35

Format: Includes 17 scales and employs a Likert format with 7 response alternatives (1 = not true to 7 = definitely true).

Reliability: Internal consistency estimates for the 17 scales ranged from .71 to .89.

Author: Heesacker, M. and Heppner, P.P.

Article: Using real client perceptions to examine psychometric properties of the Counselor Rating Form.

Journal: *Journal of Counseling Psychology*, April 1983, *30*(2), 180-187.

Related research: Heppner, P.P. and Heesacker, M., 1983. Perceived counselor characteristics, client expectations and client satisfaction with counseling. *Journal of Counseling Psychology*, 30, 31-39.

3209
Test name: EXPECTATIONS ABOUT COUNSELING—SHORT FORM

Purpose: To measure expectations about counseling.

Number of items: 53

Format: Responses to each item are made on a 7-point continuum from definitely do not expect this to be true (1) to definitely do expect this to be true (7).

Reliability: Reliabilities ranged from .69 to .81.

Author: Hardin, S.I. and Subich, L.M.

Article: A methodological note: Do students expect what clients do?

Journal: *Journal of Counseling Psychology*, Jan. 1985, 32(1), 131-134.

Related research: Tinsley, H.E.A. et al., 1980. Factor analysis of the domain of client expectancies about counseling. *Journal of Counseling Psychology*, 27, 561-570.

3210
Test name: EXPECTATIONS ABOUT COUNSELING QUESTIONNAIRE—REVISED

Purpose: To measure clients' expectations about counseling prior to entering counseling.

Number of items: 45

Format: Includes six scales: client openness, motivation, counselor acceptance, expertness, attractiveness, and trustworthiness. Likert format with 7 response alternatives.

Reliability: Internal consistency for the six scales ranged from .84 to .95.

Validity: Correlation with other variables ranged from -.33 to .35.

Author: Heppner, P.P. and Heesacker, M.

Article: Perceived counselor characteristics, client expectations and client satisfaction with counseling.

Journal: *Journal of Counseling Psychology*, Jan. 1983, 30(1), 31-39.

Related research: Tinsley, H.E.A. et al., 1980. Factor analysis of the domain of client expectancies about counseling. *Journal of Counseling Psychology*, 27, 561-570.

3211

Test name: EXTRAORDINARY BELIEF INVENTORY

Purpose: To survey belief in paranormal phenomena.

Number of items: 30

Format: 7-point Likert format. Sample items presented.

Reliability: Alpha ranged from .68 to .92 across subscales.

Validity: Mean correlation between subscales = .48.

Author: Otis, L.P. and Alcock, J.E.

Article: Factors affecting extraordinary belief.

Journal: *Journal of Social Psychology*, Oct. 1982, *118*(first half), 77-85.

3212

Test name: FEELINGS OF INADEQUACY SCALE

Purpose: To measure self-esteem.

Number of items: 19

Format: Multiple-choice. All items presented.

Reliability: Alpha ranged from .68 to .88 across subscales.

Validity: Correlated .40 to .82 with Rosenberg Self-Esteem Scale.

Author: O'Brien, E.J.

Article: Global self-esteem scales: Unidimensional or multidimensional.

Journal: *Psychological Reports*, Oct. 1985, *57*(2), 383-389.

Related research: Eagly, A.H., 1967. Involvement as a determinant of response to favorable and unfavorable information. *Journal of Personality and Social Psychology*, 7(3, Whole No. 643).

3213

Test name: FLORIDA KEY OF LEARNER SELF-CONCEPT— REVISED

Purpose: To measure self-concept.

Number of items: 22

Format: Uses behavioral ratings of student self-concept and includes factors of: relating, asserting, investing, and coping.

Reliability: Ranged from .84 to .93.

Validity: Correlation with Behavioral Academic Self-Esteem was .90.

Author: Benner, E.H. et al.

Article: A construct validation of academic self-esteem for intermediate grade-level children.

Journal: *Measurement and Evaluation in Guidance.* Oct. 1983, *16*(3), 127-134.

Related research: Purkey, W.W. et al., 1973. The Florida Key: A scale to infer learner self-concept. *Educational and Psychological Measurement, 33,* 979-984.

3214
Test name: GENDER POWER SCALES

Purpose: To measure perceived power of persons.

Number of items: 17

Format: Bipolar scales with a 7-point range. All items presented.

Reliability: Alpha on subscales ranged from .43 to .89.

Author: Molm, L.D.

Article: Gender and power use: An experimental analysis of behavior and perceptions.

Journal: *Social Psychology Quarterly,* Dec. 1985, *48*(4), 285-300.

Related research: Bovermon, I.K. et al., 1972. Sex-role stereotypes: A current appraisal. *Journal of Social Issues, 28,* 59-78.

3215
Test name: GENERALIZED EXPECTANCY OF SPORT SUCCESS SCALE

Purpose: To measure athlete's expectation of future athletic success.

Number of items: 20

Format: Bipolar adjectives rated on 5-point scale.

Reliability: Test-retest = .90. Internal consistency = .95.

Author: Horn, T.S.

Article: Coaches' feedback and changes in children's perceptions of their physical competence.

Journal: *Journal of Educational Psychology,* April 1985, *77*(2), 174-186.

Related research: Coulson, H.M. and Cobb, R., 1979. *Assessment of a scale to measure generalized expectancy of sport success.* Paper presented at the Annual Meeting of the American Alliance for Health, Physical Education and Health, New Orleans.

3216
Test name: GENERALIZED SELF-EFFICACY SCALE

Purpose: To measure one's expectations to perform across broad range of challenging activities which require effort and perseverance.

Number of items: 27

Format: Responses to each item are made on a 7-point Likert scale ranging from strongly agree to strongly disagree. Examples are provided.

Validity: Correlation with the Goal Attainment Scale was r = .37.

Author: Tipton, T.M. and Worthington, E.L., Jr.

Article: The measurement of generalized self-efficacy: A study of construct validity.

Journal: *Journal of Personality Assessment.* Oct. 1984, 48(5), 545-548.

Related research: Tipton, R.M. et al., 1980. Faith and locus of control. *Psychological Reports*, 46, 1151-1154.

3217
Test name: HEALTH LOCUS OF CONTROL SCALE

Purpose: To measure the extent to which individuals perceive themselves to be in control of their own personal health.

Number of items: 11

Format: Includes two factors: one with items worded in an internal direction, the other factor with items worded in an external direction.

Reliability: Coefficient alphas were .70 and .67 (for factors 1 and 2, respectively).

Validity: Correlations with the Marlowe-Crowne Social Desirability Scale were r = -.009 (factor 1) and r = -.13 (factor 2).

Author: Gutkin, T.B. et al.

Article: The Health Locus of Control Scale: Psychometric properties.

Journal: *Educational and Psychological Measurement*, summer 1985, 45(2), 407-409.

Related research: Wallston, B.S. et al., 1976. Development of validation of the Health Locus of Control (HLC) scale. *Journal of Consulting and Clinical Psychology*, 44, 580-585.
  Keller, R.T., 1983. Predicting absenteeism from prior absenteeism, attitudinal factors, and nonattitudinal factors. *Journal of Applied Psychology*, 68(3), 536-540.

3218
Test name: HEALTH LOCUS OF CONTROL SCALE

Purpose: To measure perceived patient control over health in a hospital setting.

Number of items: 6

Format: Two-option forced-choice items. All items presented.

Reliability: Test-retest = .81.

Validity: Medical care givers scored more highly internal than patients.

Author: Tadmor, C.S. and Hofman, J.E.

Article: Measuring locus of control in a hospital setting.

Journal: *Psychological Reports*, April 1985, 56(2), 525-526.

3219
Test name: HEART DISEASE LOCUS OF CONTROL SCALE

Purpose: To assess locus of control relating to heart disease.

Number of items: 20

Format: 6-point Likert agreement response categories.

Reliability: Test-retest = .83. Cronbach's alpha ranged from .76 to .86 across subscales.

Validity: Subscales correlated significantly with Multidimensional Health Scale subscales (significant correlations ranged from .27 to .73 in absolute value).

Author: O'Connell, J.K. and Price, J.H.

Article: Development of a heart disease locus of control scale.

Journal: *Psychological Reports*, Feb. 1985, 56(1), 159-164.

3220
Test name: ILLNESS BEHAVIOR INVENTORY

Purpose: To assess perceived illness behavior of one's mother, father, and oneself as a child.

Number of items: 20

Format: Each item is rated on a Likert scale from 1 to 6.

Reliability: Test-retest reliabilities ranged from .77 to 1.0 (2 weeks).

Author: Turkat, I.D. and Guise, B.J.

Article: Test of reliability of perception of parental and childhood illness behavior.

Journal: *Perceptual and Motor Skills*, Aug. 1983, 57(1), 101-102.

Related research: Turkat, I.D. and Pettegrew, L.S., 1983. Development and validation of the Illness Behavior Inventory. *Journal of Behavioral Assessment*, 5, 35-47.

3221
Test name: INSTRUCTIONAL OBJECTIVES EXCHANGE SELF-APPRAISAL INVENTORY

Purpose: To measure self-concept.

Number of items: 36

Format: Yes-no. Inventory is read to children who after each question respond on an answer sheet.

Reliability: Test-retest (total) = .70 (.29 to .58 across subscales). KR-20 internal consistency (total) = .37 (.50 to .60 across subscales).

Author: Soule, J.C. et al.

Article: Dimensions of self-concept for children in kindergarten and grades 1 and 2.

Journal: *Psychological Reports*, Feb. 1981, *48*(1), 83-88.

Related research: UCLA, 1972. *Measures of self-concept K-12*. Rev. ed. Instructional Objectives Exchange, University of California, Los Angeles.

3222
Test name: INTELLECTUAL ACHIEVEMENT RESPONSIBILITY SCALE

Purpose: To measure perceived locus of control in intellectual and academic activities.

Number of items: 34

Format: Forced-choice.

Reliability: Test-retest ranged from .66 to .74 over grade levels.

Author: Tzuriel, D. and Haywood, H.C.

Article: Locus of control and child-rearing practices in intrinsically motivated and extrinsically motivated children.

Journal: *Psychological Reports*, Dec. 1985, *57*(3, Pt. 1), 887-894.

Related research: Crandall, V.C. et al., 1965. Children's beliefs in their own control of reinforcements in intellectual-academic situations. *Child Development*, *36*, 90-108.

Halpin, G. et al., 1981. Locus of control and self-esteem among American Indians and whites: A cross-cultural comparison. *Psychological Reports*, *48*(1), 91-98.

Benner, E.H. et al., 1983. A construct validation of academic self-esteem for intermediate grade-level children. *Measurement and Evaluation in Guidance*, *16*(3), 127-134.

3223
Test name: INTERNAL CONTROL INDEX

Purpose: To measure locus of control in adults.

Number of items: 28

Format: Responses are made on a 5-point scale from (A) "rarely" to (E) "usually." All items are presented.

Reliability: Reliability coefficient alpha was .84 and .85.

Validity: Correlation with Mirels' Factor I of Rotter's I-E Scale was r = -.385.

Author: Duttweiler, P.C.

Article: The Internal Control Index: A newly developed measure of locus of control.

Journal: *Educational and Psychological Measurement,* summer 1984, *44*(2), 209-221.

3224
Test name: I-E SCALE

Purpose: To measure internal or external locus of control.

Number of items: 45 (including 13 buffer items).

Format: Forced-choice. Modification of Rotter I-E Scale.

Reliability: Test-retest = .76.

Author: Hood, J. et al.

Article: Locus of control as a measure of ineffectiveness in anorexia nervosa.

Journal: *Journal of Consulting and Clinical Psychology,* Feb. 1982, *50*(1), 3-13.

Related research: Ried, D.W. and Ware, E.E., 1973. Multidimensionality of internal-external control: Implications for past and future research. *Canadian Journal of Behavioral Science, 5,* 264-271.

3225
Test name: I-E LOCUS OF CONTROL SCALE

Purpose: To measure locus of control.

Number of items: 23

Format: Includes six nonreactive filler items to make it more difficult to identify the test's purpose.

Reliability: Internal consistency coefficient (Kuder-Richardson) was .70 (N = 400). Test-retest reliability coefficient was .72 (N = 60, one month), and .55 (N = 117, two months).

Validity: Correlations with Marlowe-Crowne Social Desirability Scale ranged from r = -.34 to r = -.42.

Author: Harris, R.M. and Salomone, P.R.

Article: Toward an abbreviated internal-external locus of control.

Journal: *Measurement and Evaluation in Guidance,* Jan. 1981, *13*(4), 229-234.

Related research: Rotter, J.B., 1966. Generalized expectancies for internal versus external control of reinforcement. *Psychological Monographs, 80*, 1-28. (Whole No. 609.)

3226
Test name: IRRATIONAL BELIEFS TEST

Purpose: To assess degree of irrational beliefs.

Number of items: 100

Format: 5-point Likert agreement scales.

Reliability: Test-retest ranged from .61 to .80. Alphas ranged from .35 to .73.

Author: Lohr, J.M. and Rea, R.G.

Article: A disconfirmation of the relationship between fear of public speaking and irrational beliefs.

Journal: *Psychological Reports*, June 1981, *48*(3), 795-798.

Related research: Lohr, J.M. and Bonge, D., 1980. Retest reliability of the Irrational Beliefs Test. *Psychological Reports, 47*, 1314.

3227
Test name: IRRATIONAL PERSONALITY TRAIT INVENTORY SCALE— REVISED

Purpose: To measure irrational beliefs and perceptions.

Number of items: 52

Format: Consists of clinically derived items. Examples are presented. Responses are recorded on a 5-point Likert scale. Scores ranged from 52 to 260. Higher scores reflect irrational self-thoughts.

Reliability: Cronbach's alpha = .95.

Validity: Correlations with other variables ranged from .50 to .73.

Author: Thompson, D.G. and Hudson, G.R.

Article: Values clarification and behavioral group counseling with ninth grade boys in a residential school.

Journal: *Journal of Counseling Psychology*, July 1982, *29*(4), 394-399.

Related research: Ross, G.R., 1977. *Reducing irrational personality traits, trait anxiety, and intra-interpersonal needs in high school students.* Paper presented at the annual meeting of the Florida Educational Research Association, St. Petersburg Beach.

3228
Test name: ITALIAN STEREOTYPE SCALE

Purpose: To measure respondent's involvement with a set of Italian behaviors.

Number of items: 21

Format: Respondent estimated frequency of each behavior for nine target persons on a 5-point (never-always) scale.

Reliability: Cronbach's alpha = .83.

Validity: Factor analysis revealed four interpretable factors: socio-cultural activities, family, in-group, and tradition.

Author: Caltabiano, N.J.

Article: Perceived differences in ethnic behavior: A pilot study of Italo-Australian Canberra residents.

Journal: *Psychological Reports*, Dec. 1984, *55*(3), 867-873.

3229
Test name: JANIS-FIELD FEELINGS OF INADEQUACY SCALE

Purpose: To measure self-esteem.

Number of items: 20

Format: Responses are made on a 5-point Likert scale.

Validity: Correlations with the Irrational Beliefs Test ranged from -.59 to .16 (N = 251).

Author: Daly, M.J. and Burton, R.L.

Article: Self-esteem and irrational beliefs: An exploratory investigation with implications for counseling.

Journal: *Journal of Counseling Psychology*, July 1983, *30*(3), 361-366.

Related research: Eagly, A.H., 1967. Involvement as a determinant of response to favorable and unfavorable information. *Journal of Personality and Social Psychology Monographs*, 7(3, Whole No. 643).

3230
Test name: LEVENSON LOCUS OF CONTROL QUESTIONNAIRE

Purpose: To measure locus of control.

Number of items: 24

Format: 6-point Likert rating scale.

Validity: Previously reported factor structure not found in these data from Australian high school students, although the findings indicate multidimensionality.

Author: Hong, S-M and Bartenstein, C.

Article: Dimensions of Levenson's locus of control with Australian high school students.

Journal: *Psychological Reports*, 1982, *51*(2), 395-400.

Related research: Walkey, F.H., 1979. Internal control, powerful others and chance: A confirmation of Levenson's factor structure. *Journal of Personality Assessment*, *43*, 532-535.
    Levenson, H., 1974. Activism and powerful others: Distinctions within the concept of internal-external control. *Journal of Personality Assessment*, *38*, 377-383.

3231
Test name: LINDGREN EMBEDDED FIGURES TEST

Purpose: To measure field independence.

Number of items: 20

Format: For each item, the subject finds a figure among lines in a rectangle.

Reliability: Test-retest reliability was .81.

Validity: Correlation with Group Embedded Figures Test was .61.

Author: Hicks, L.A. and Lindgren, H.C.

Article: Field dependence and ability to judge spatial coordinates.

Journal: *Perceptual and Motor Skills*, Dec. 1985, *61*(3, Pt. 1), 984-986.

3232
Test name: LIPSITT SELF-CONCEPT SCALE

Purpose: To measure positive and negative evaluations of self.

Number of items: 22

Format: Subjects rate themselves on a 5-point scale on traits such as friendly, obedient, and lazy.

Reliability: Internal reliability ranged from .84 to .85 in three separate administrations.

Validity: Significant negative relationships to Children's Manifest Anxiety and positive relationships to academic motivation.

Author: Peterson, G.W. et al.

Article: Children's self-esteem and maternal behavior in three low-income samples.

Journal: *Psychological Reports*, 1983, *52*(1), 79-86.

3233
Test name: LOCUS OF CONTROL INVENTORY FOR THREE ACHIEVEMENT DOMAINS (LOCITAD)

Purpose: To measure locus of control perceived for intellectual, physical, and social activities.

Number of items: 47

Reliability: Minimum item-total correlation = .30. KR-20 ranged between .52 and .53 (.75 total scale).

Validity: Correlates .78 with Intellectual Achievement Responsibility Scale.

Author: Williams, R.E. et al.

Article: Effects of STEP on parental attitudes and locus of control of their learning disabled children.

Journal: *The School Counselor*, Nov. 1984, *32*(2), 126-133.

Related research: Bradley, R. et al., 1977. A new scale to assess locus of control in three achievement domains, *Psychological Reports, 41*, 656-661.

3234
Test name: LOCUS OF CONTROL MEASURE

Purpose: To measure locus of control of college students.

Number of items: 4

Format: Responses to each item are made on a 5-point scale ranging from 1 (strongly agree) to 5 (strongly disagree).

Reliability: Coefficient alphas ranged from .49 to .57.

Author: Behuniak, P., Jr. and Gable, R.K.

Article: A longitudinal study of self-concept and locus of control for persisters in six college majors.

Journal: *Educational Research Quarterly*, spring 1981, *6*(1), 3-12.

Related research: Conger, A.S. et al., 1977. *National longitudinal study of high school seniors: Group profiles on self-esteem, locus of control and life goals*. (NCES 77-260: HEW), Washington, D.C.

3235
Test name: LOCUS OF CONTROL SCALE

Purpose: To measure locus of control.

Number of items: 12

Format: Likert-type scale.

Reliability: Test-retest reliability coefficient was r = .75 (one week interval).

Validity: Correlation with the Marlowe-Crowne Social Desirability Scale was r = .09.

Author: Harris, R.M. and Salomone, P.R.

Article: Toward an abbreviated internal-external locus of control scale.

Journal: *Measurement and Evaluation in Guidance*, Jan. 1981, *13*(4), 229-234.

Related research: MacDonald, A.R. and Tseng, M.S., 1976. Dimensions of internal versus external control revisited. In R.K. Gable and D.L. Thompson, (Eds.), Perception of personal control and conformity of vocational choice as correlates of vocational development. *Journal of Vocational Behavior, 8,* 259-267.

3236
Test name: LOCUS OF CONTROL SCALE

Purpose: To assess locus of control.

Number of items: 24

Format: Includes 3 scales: internal, powerful others, and chance.

Reliability: Kuder-Richardson reliabilities ranged from .67 to .82. Test-retest reliabilities ranged from r = .08 to r = .78.

Author: Harris, R.M. and Salomone, P.R.

Article: Toward an abbreviated internal-external locus of control.

Journal: *Measurement and Evaluation in Guidance*, Jan. 1981, *13*(4), 229-234.

Related research: Levenson, H., 1972. *Distinctions within the concept of internal-external control: Development of a new scale.* Proceedings of the 80th Annual Convention of the American Psychological Association, 7, 259-260.

3237
Test name: LOCUS OF CONTROL SCALE

Purpose: To measure locus of control.

Number of items: 88

Format: Likert-type scale for 46 items.

Reliability: Test-retest reliability coefficients for the 46 items ranged from .18 to .75 (N = 300).

Validity: Correlation of the 46 items with the Rotter I-E Scale was .82.

Author: Harris, R.M. and Salomone, P.R.

Article: Toward an abbreviated internal-external locus of control.

Journal: *Measurement and Evaluation in Guidance*, Jan. 1981, *13*(4), 229-234.

Related research: Collins, B.E., 1974. Form components of the Rotter Internal-External Scale. *Journal of Personality and Social Psychology, 29,* 381-391.

3238

Test name: LOCUS OF CONTROL SCALE

Purpose: To assess locus of control.

Number of items: 40

Format: High scores indicate externality.

Reliability: Alpha was .72 (American children) and .61 (Venezuelans).

Author: Prawat, R.S. et al.

Article: Attitude development in American and Venezuelan schoolchildren.

Journal: *Journal of Social Psychology*, Dec. 1981, *115*(second half), 149-158.

Related research: Nowicki, S. and Strickland, B., 1973. A locus of control scale for children. *Journal of Consulting and Clinical Psychology*, 40, 148-154.

3239

Test name: LOCUS OF CONTROL SCALE

Purpose: To measure locus of control.

Number of items: 11

Format: For each item subjects select either internal or external locus of control statement which they more strongly believe is true. Examples are presented.

Reliability: Cronbach's alpha was .60.

Validity: Correlations with loneliness scores ranged from -.02 to -.46.

Author: Schmitt, J.P. and Kurdek, L.A.

Article: Age and gender differences in and personality correlates of loneliness in different relationships.

Journal: *Journal of Personality Assessment*, Oct. 1985, *49*(5), 485-496.

Related research: Valecha, G.K. and Ostrum, T.M., 1974. An abbreviated measure of internal-external locus of control. *Journal of Personality Assessment*, 38, 369-376.

3240

Test name: LOCUS OF CONTROL SCALE

Purpose: To measure internal locus of control.

Number of items: 29

Format: Subjects choose two statements for each item: One statement reflects an external frame of reference, the other an internal frame of reference.

Reliability: Cronbach's alpha was .78.

Validity: Correlations with social anxiety were -.38 (college students) and -.31 (homosexuals).

Author: Schmitt, J.P. and Kurdek, L.A.

Article: Correlates of social anxiety in college students and homosexuals.

Journal: *Journal of Personality Assessment*, Aug. 1984, *48*(4), 403-409.

Related research: Rotter, J.B., 1966. Generalized expectancies for internal versus external control of reinforcement. *Psychological Monographs*, *80*, 1-28.
Martin, J.D. and Coley, L.A., 1984. *Educational and Psychological Measurement*, *44*(2), 517-521.

3241
Test name: LOCUS OF CONTROL SCALE FOR CHILDREN

Purpose: To measure generalized expectancy for the locus of control of reinforcement in children.

Number of items: 21

Format: Yes-no.

Reliability: Test-retest = .83. Internal consistency = .72.

Author: Lokan, J.J. et al.

Article: A study of vocational maturity during adolescence and locus of control.

Journal: *Journal of Vocational Behavior*, June 1982, *20*(3), 331-342.

Related research: Nowicki, S., Jr., and Strickland, B.R., 1973. A locus of control scale for children. *Journal of Consulting and Clinical Psychology*, *40*, 148-154.

3242
Test name: LOCUS OF CONTROL SCALE FOR CHILDREN'S PERCEPTIONS OF SOCIAL INTERACTIONS

Purpose: To measure children's perceptions of social interactions.

Number of items: 48

Format: Includes three scores: Number of items answered in the internal direction, number of positive content items answered in the internal direction, and number of negative content items answered in the internal direction. A social desirability scale is included.

Reliability: Coefficients of internal consistency ranged from .75 to .81. Test-retest correlations (10 days) ranged from .65 to .70.

Validity: Correlations with other measures ranged from .30 to .44.

Author: Dahlquist, L.M. and Ottinger, D.R.

Article: Locus of control and peer status: A scale for children's perceptions of social interactions.

Journal: *Journal of Personality Assessment*, June 1983, *47*(3), 278-287.

3243
Test name: MANAGERIAL COMPETENCE SCALE

Purpose: To measure perceptions of the competence of female managers.

Number of items: 17

Format: Likert format.

Reliability: Alphas ranged from .69 to .82 across subscales.

Author: Ezell, H.F. et al.

Article: The effects of having been supervised by a woman on perceptions of female managerial competence.

Journal: *Personnel Psychology*, summer 1981, *34*(2), 291-299.

Related research: Snyder, R.A. and Morris, J.H., 1978. Reliability of the factor structure of the Wagner and Morse Competence Index. *Psychological Reports*, *43*, 419-425.
  Wagner, F.R. and Morse, J.J., 1975. A measure of individual sense of competence. *Psychological Reports*, *36*, 451-459.

3244
Test name: MATHEMATICS ACHIEVEMENT QUESTIONNAIRE

Purpose: To assess locus of control.

Number of items: 20

Format: Includes obtaining students' views of mathematics, problem-solving, their mathematics teachers, their fellow mathematics students. Students responded to each item by choosing either an internal or an external point of view.

Reliability: KR-20 reliability coefficients ranged from .5 to .6. Also reliability coefficients ranged from .6 to .8.

Validity: Correlation with SAT was .07.

Author: McLeod, D.B. and Adams, V.M.

Article: Locus of control and mathematics instruction: Three exploratory studies.

Journal: *Journal of Experimental Education*, winter 1980/81, *49*(2), 94-99.

3245
Test name: MATHEMATICS AS A MALE DOMAIN SCALE

Purpose: To measure the extent to which subjects stereotype mathematics as being a male domain.

Number of items: 12

Format: Likert-type items. Higher scores indicate weaker stereotyping by the subjects.

Reliability: Split-half reliability coefficient was .87.

Validity: Correlation with other variables ranged from -.23 to .34.

Author: Llabre, M.M. and Suarez, E.

Article: Predicting math anxiety and course performance in college women and men.

Journal: *Journal of Counseling Psychology*, April 1985, *32*(2), 283-287.

Related research: Fennema, E. and Sherman, J., 1976. Fennema-Sherman Mathematics Attitude Scales: Instruments designed to measure attitudes toward the learning of mathematics by females and males. *JSAS Catalog of Selected Documents in Psychology*, *6*, 31.

3246
Test name: MATHEMATICS ATTRIBUTION SCALE

Purpose: To assess high school students' attributions of achievement in algebra or geometry.

Number of items: 32

Format: Consists of eight 4-item subscales.

Validity: Correlations with the Multidimensional-Multiattributional Causality Scale ranged from -.31 to .52.

Author: Powers, S. et al.

Article: Convergent validity of the Multidimensional-Multiattributional Causality Scale with the Mathematics Attribution Scale.

Journal: *Educational and Psychological Measurement*, autumn 1985, *45*(3), 689-692.

Related research: Fennema, E. et al., 1979. Mathematics Attribution Scale: An instrument designed to measure students' attributions of the causes of their successes and failures in mathematics. *Journal Abstract Service of the American Psychological Association: Catalog of Selected Documents in Psychology*, *9*(2), 26.

Douglas, P. et al., 1985. Achievement motivation and

attributions for success and failure. *Psychological Reports, 57*(3), 751-754.

3247
Test name: MATHEMATICAL SELF-CONCEPT QUESTIONNAIRE

Purpose: To measure pupils' self-concept of mathematical achievement, ability, and affect.

Number of items: 21

Format: 3-point Likert scale. One sample item presented.

Reliability: Alpha = .83.

Validity: Construct validity tested with factor analysis of items. Two achievement factors, two affective factors, and one ability factor were extracted.

Author: Mevarech, Z.R. and Rich, Y.

Article: Effects of computer-assisted mathematics instruction on disadvantaged pupils' cognitive and affective development.

Journal: *Journal of Educational Research*, Sept./Oct. 1985, *79*(1), 5-11.

3248
Test name: MATHEMATICS SELF-CONCEPT SCALE

Purpose: To measure student mathematics self-concept.

Number of items: 24

Format: Double-Q sort of mathematics student behavior and attitude descriptors, one sort for ideal student and one sort for themselves. Sample items presented.

Reliability: Test-retest = .92.

Author: Peterson, K. et al.

Article: Geometry students' role-specific self-concept: Success, teacher, and sex differences.

Journal: *Journal of Educational Research*, Nov./Dec. 1983, *77*(2), 122-126.

Related research: Peterson, K. et al., 1980. Science students' role-specific self-concept: Course, success and gender. *Science Education, 64*, 169-174.

3249
Test name: MATHEMATICS SELF-EFFICACY SCALE

Purpose: To measure math-related self-efficacy.

Number of items: 52

Format: Includes three subscales: Math tasks, math courses, and math problems.

Validity: Correlations with other variables ranged from -.25 to .66.

Author: Hackett, G.

Article: Role of mathematics self-efficacy in the choice of math-related majors of college women and men: A path analysis.

Journal: *Journal of Counseling Psychology*, Jan. 1985, 32(1), 47-56.

Related research: Betz, N.E. and Hackett, G., 1983. The relationship of mathematics self-efficacy expectations to the selection of science-based college majors. *Journal of Vocational Behavior*, 23, 329-345.

3250
Test name: ME SCALE

Purpose: To measure self-concept of gifted children.

Number of items: 40

Format: Students respond to each item by agreeing or disagreeing. All items are presented.

Reliability: KR-20 = .80.

Validity: Correlation with the Piers-Harris Self-Concept Scale was .65.

Author: Feldhusen, J.F. and Kolloff, M.B.

Article: Me: A self-concept scale for gifted children.

Journal: *Perceptual and Motor Skills*, Aug. 1981, 53(1), 319-323.

3251
Test name: MULTIDIMENSIONAL HEALTH LOCUS OF CONTROL SCALE

Purpose: To assess locus of control as a multidimensional health construct.

Number of items: 18

Format: Includes three subscales: Internal, powerful others, and chance.

Reliability: Cronbach's alpha reliabilities ranged from .59 (internal) to .76 (powerful others).

Author: Desmond, S. et al.

Article: Health locus of control and voluntary use of seat belts among high school students.

Journal: *Perceptual and Motor Skills*, Aug. 1985, 61(1), 315-319.

Related research: Wallston, K.A. et al., 1978. Development of the Multidimensional Health Locus of Control (MHLC) scales. *Health Education Monographs*, 6, 160-170.

Slenker, S.E. et al., 1985. Health locus of control of joggers and nonexercisers. *Perceptual and Motor Skills*, *61*, 323-328.

Winefield, H.R., 1982. Reliability and validity of the Health Locus of Control Scale. *Journal of Personality Assessment*, *46*(6), 614-619.

Adler, D. and Price, J.H., 1985. Relation of agoraphobics: Health locus of control orientation to severity of agoraphobia. *Psychological Reports*, *56*(2), 619-625.

3252

Test name: MULTIDIMENSIONAL MEASURE OF CHILDREN'S PERCEPTIONS OF CONTROL

Purpose: To measure children's perceived control.

Number of items: 48

Format: Represented by the items are: each source of control, within each domain, for each outcome. Responses to each item are made on a four-point Likert format. All items are presented.

Reliability: Subscale coefficient alphas ranged from .39 to .70. Test-retest reliabilities (9 months) ranged from .30 to .48; (17 months) ranged from .25 to .50.

Author: Connell, J.P.

Article: A new multidimensional measure of children's perceptions of control.

Journal: *Child Development*, Aug. 1985, *56*(4), 1018-1041.

Related research: Harter, S. and Connell, J.P., 1984. A model of the relationships among children's academic achievement and their self-perceptions of competence, control and motivational orientation. In J. Nichols (Ed.), *The development of achievement motivation*. Greenwich, CT: JAI, pp. 219-250.

3253

Test name: MULTIDIMENSIONAL-MULTIATTRIBUTIONAL CAUSALITY SCALE

Purpose: To measure attributions of general school achievement to four causal factors.

Number of items: 24

Format: Includes eight 3-item subscales.

Validity: Correlations with the Mathematics Attribution Scale ranged from -.31 to .52.

Author: Powers, S. et al.

Article: Convergent validity of the Multidimensional-Multiattributional Causality Scale with the Mathematics Attribution Scale.

Journal: *Educational and Psychological Measurement*, autumn 1985, *45*(3), 689-692.

Related research: Lefcourt, H.M. et al., 1979. The Multidimensional-Multiattributional Causality Scale: The Development of a Goal-Specific Locus of Control Scale. *Canadian Journal of Behavioral Science, 11*, 286-304.
    Powers, S. et al., 1985. Applicability and validity investigation of the Multidimensional-Multiattributional Causality Scale. *Educational and Psychological Measurement, 45*(4), 897-901.

3254
Test name: NONSEXIST PERSONAL ATTRIBUTE INVENTORY FOR CHILDREN

Purpose: To measure self-concept.

Number of items: 32

Format: Subjects indicate which 10 words on a list best describes them. All items presented.

Reliability: Test-retest correlations ranged from .35 to .74 (N's ranged from 29 to 272).

Validity: Correlations with Piers-Harris Children's Self-Concept scale ranged from .29 to .72 (N's ranged from 31 to 297).

Author: Parish, T.S. and Rankin, C.I.

Article: The Nonsexist Personal Attribute Inventory for Children: A report on its validity and reliability as a self-concept scale.

Journal: *Educational and Psychological Measurement*, spring 1982, *42*(1), 339-343.

3255
Test name: NOWICKI-STRICKLAND INTERNAL-EXTERNAL CONTROL SCALE FOR ADULTS

Purpose: To measure locus of control with simpler language than Rotter's scale.

Number of items: 40

Format: Yes-no.

Reliability: Alpha = .69.

Validity: Correlated from .48 to .68 with Rotter's scale among college students.

Author: Tiggemann, M. and Winefield, A.H.

Article: The effects of unemployment on the mood, self-esteem, locus of control and depressive affect of school-leavers.

Journal: *Journal of Occupational Psychology*, March 1984, *57*(1), 33-42.

Related research: Nowicki, S. and Duke, M.P., 1974. A locus of control scale for non-college as well as college adults. *Journal of Personality Assessment*, 38, 136-137.

3256
Test name: OCCUPATIONAL SELF-EFFICACY SCALE

Purpose: To measure occupational self-efficacy.

Number of items: 68 (4 items each for 17 different occupations).

Format: 7-point Likert response categories. All items presented.

Reliability: Test-retest ranged from .73 to .77.

Author: Wheeler, K.G.

Article: Comparisons of self-efficacy and expectancy models of occupational preferences for college males and females.

Journal: *Journal of Occupational Psychology*, March 1983, 56(1), 73-78.

Related research: Hackett G. and Betz, N.E., 1981. A self-efficacy approach to the career development of women. *Journal of Vocational Behavior*, 18, 326-339.

3257
Test name: ORIENTATION TO LITERACY TEST

Purpose: To measure the child's understanding of the purpose of literacy.

Number of items: 10 sets of four drawings.

Format: Child instructed to point to correct response in drawings.

Reliability: Cronbach internal consistency = .717.

Author: Mayfield, M.

Article: Code systems instruction and kindergarten children's perception of the nature and purpose of reading.

Journal: *Journal of Educational Research*, Jan./Feb. 1983, 76(3), 161-168.

Related research: Evanechko, P. et al., 1973. An investigation of the reading readiness domain. *Research in the Teaching of English*, 7, 61-78.

3258
Test name: PAY EXPECTATION SCALE

Purpose: To measure pay expectation in other employment situations.

Number of items: 5

Format: High scores reflect stronger expectations of earning higher pay by taking other employment.

Reliability: Cronbach's alpha was .78.

Validity: Correlations with other variables ranged from -.39 to .02.

Author: Motowidlo, S.J.

Article: Predicting sales turnover from pay satisfaction and expectation.

Journal: *Journal of Applied Psychology*, Aug. 1983, *68*(3), 484-489.

3259
Test name: PEER ROLE-TAKING QUESTIONNAIRE

Purpose: To serve as a measure of role-taking.

Number of items: 10

Format: The subject names one person from the group who is most like each of the 10 presented descriptions. All items are presented.

Reliability: Intraclass correlations representing reliability ratings ranged from .85 to .99.

Validity: Spearman correlation with the Role-Taking Task was rho = .22.

Author: Moser, R.S.

Article: The measurement of role taking in young adults.

Journal: *Journal of Personality Assessment*, Aug. 1984, *48*(4), 380-387.

3260
Test name: PERCEIVED COMPETENCE SCALE FOR CHILDREN

Purpose: To measure children's self-perception of competence.

Number of items: 28

Format: Includes three domains of perceived competence: cognitive, social, and physical as well as children's general self-esteem.

Reliability: Coefficient alphas ranged from .54 to .78.

Author: Stigler, J.W. et al.

Article: The self-perception of competence by Chinese children.

Journal: *Child Development*, Oct. 1985, *56*(5), 1259-1270.

Related research: Harter, S., 1982. The Perceived Competence Scale for Children. *Child Development*, 53, 87-97.
　　Horn, T.S.. Coaches' feedback and changes in children's perceptions of their physical competence. *Journal of Educational Psychology*, 77(2), 174-186.

3261
Test name: PERCEIVED CONFIRMATION SCALE

Purpose: To determine the degree to which the respondent perceives the partner to have confirmed and supported the respondent's identity in the interaction.

Number of items: 6

Format: The items are global judgment items.

Reliability: Coefficient alpha was .82 and .69.

Validity: Correlation with rating of alter-competence was r = .71.

Author: Spitzberg, B.H. and Cupach, W.R.

Article: Conversational skill and locus of perception.

Journal: *Journal of Psychopathology and Behavioral Assessment*, Sept. 1985, 7(3), 207-220.

Related research: Cissna, K.N., 1976. *Interpersonal confirmation: A review of current theory, measurement and research.* Paper presented at the Central States Speech Association Convention, Chicago. (ED 126 544.)

3262
Test name: PERCEIVED PARTICIPATION SCALE

Purpose: To measure perceptions faculty have of decision-making at their colleges.

Number of items: 3

Format: Multiple-choice. All items presented.

Reliability: Alpha = .76.

Validity: Correlated .68 (p<.05) with distribution of control in colleges.

Author: Peterson, M.F. and Cook, R.A.

Article: Attitudinal and contextual variables explaining teachers' leadership behavior.

Journal: *Journal of Educational Psychology*, Feb. 1983, 71(1), 50-62.

3263
Test name: PERCEIVED SOMATATYPE SCALE

Purpose: To measure perceived somatatype.

Number of items: 7 male figures - 2 questions per figure.

Format: Subject selects which figure best resembles his own body-build and the figure that best appears to be what he would like to be.

Reliability: Test-retest ranged from .94 to .96 over 2 weeks.

Validity: Significant associations between somatatype and Body Cathexis Scale (Secord and Jourard).

Author: Tucker, L.A.

Article: Relationship between perceived somatatype and body cathexis of college males.

Journal: *Psychological Reports*, 1982, *50*(3, Pt. 1), 983-989.

Related research: Secord, P.F. and Jourard, S.M., 1953. The appraisal of body-cathexis: Body-cathexis and the self. *Journal of Consulting Psychology*, *17*, 343-347.

3264
Test name: PERCEIVED UNDERSTANDING SCALE

Purpose: To measure perception of being understood or misunderstood.

Number of items: 16

Format: Items rated on a 5-point scale.

Reliability: Test-retest = .90. Cronbach's alpha = .89.

Author: Cahn, D.D.

Article: Relative importance of perceived understanding in initial interaction and development of interpersonal relationships.

Journal: *Psychological Reports*, June 1983, *52*(3), 923-929.

Related research: Cahn, D.D. and Shulman, G.M., 1982. *Measurement of the perception of being understood/misunderstood: Development and assessment.* Paper presented at the annual meeting of the Central States Speech Association, Milwaukee, WI.

3265
Test name: PERCEPTION OF CHILD PSYCHOLOGIST QUESTIONNAIRE

Purpose: To measure perception of child psychologists held by parents.

Number of items: 7

Format: 7 problem situations are presented to respondents who then choose one of nine professional occupations that might help. Child psychology is one of the nine. All problems presented.

Reliability: Test-retest yielded 85% agreement (over 8 weeks, N = 18).

Author: Murphy, G.C. et al.

Article: Perceptions of child psychologists held by parents of Australian school children.

Journal: *Psychological Reports*, 1982, *51*(1), 47-51.

Related research: Murphy, G.C. et al., 1978. Client perceptions of professional helpers. *Australian Journal of Social Issues*, 13, 207-215.

3266
Test name: PERCEPTUAL ABERRATION SCALE

Purpose: To measure transient aberrations in perception.

Number of items: 35

Format: True-false. Sample items presented.

Reliability: Alpha ranged from .88 to .90.

Validity: Correlated .70 to Perceptual Aberration (Chapman, et al., 1981).

Author: Chapman, L.J. et al.

Article: Reliabilities and intercorrelations of eight measures of proneness to psychosis.

Journal: *Journal of Consulting and Clinical Psychology*, April 1982, 50(2), 187-195.

Related research: Chapman, L.J. et al., 1978. Body-image aberration in schizophrenia. *Journal of Abnormal Psychology*, 87, 399-407.

3267
Test name: PERFORMANCE EXPECTANCY SCALE

Purpose: To measure perceptions of performance and expectancy on the job.

Number of items: 8

Format: Likert-type format. All items presented.

Reliability: Alpha = .86.

Author: Lee, C. and Schuler, R.S.

Article: A constructive replication and extension of a role and expectancy perception model of participation decision making.

Journal: *Journal of Occupational Psychology*, June 1982, 55(2), 109-118.

Related research: House, R.J. and Dessler, J., 1974. The path-goal theory of leadership: Some post hoc and a priori tests. In J.G. Hunt and L.L. Larson (Eds.), *Contingency approaches to leadership*. Carbondale, IL: Southern Illinois Press.

3268
Test name: PERFORMANCE SELF-ATTRIBUTION SCALE

Purpose: To measure attributions a child makes about his or her task performance.

Number of items: 20

Format: Number of statements circled as descriptive of child's own behavior are summed to yield a total score on each of four subscales. All statements presented.

Validity: Three independent judges classified states into four categories with 90 percent agreement.

Author: Ames, C.

Article: Achievement attributions and self-instructions under competitive and individualistic goal structures.

Journal: *Journal of Educational Psychology*, June 1984, *76*(3), 478-487.

Related research: Diener, C. and Dweck, C., 1978. An analysis of learned helplessness: Continuous changes in performance, strategy and achievement cognitions following failure. *Journal of Personality and Social Psychology*, *36*, 451-462.

3269
Test name: PERSONAL ATTRIBUTE INVENTORY

Purpose: To identify 30 adjectives that subjects believe are most descriptive of a target group.

Number of items: 100 adjectives.

Format: Half of the adjectives are positive and half are negative.

Reliability: Test-retest reliabilities ranged from .90 to .95.

Author: Eberly, C. et al.

Article: Mental health professionals' attitudes toward physically handicapped groups in attributionally ambiguous and non-ambiguous situations.

Journal: *Journal of Counseling Psychology*, May 1981, *28*(3), 276-278.

Related research: Parish, T.S. et al., 1976. The personal attribute inventory. *Perceptual and Motor Skills*, *42*, 715-720.

3270
Test name: PERSONAL ATTRIBUTE INVENTORY FOR CHILDREN

Purpose: To measure children's perceptions of self.

Number of items: 48

Format: Contains positive and negative descriptors from which the children choose 15 which best describe themselves.

Validity: Correlations with: Behavior Rating Profile, Student Scales ranged from .28 to .48 (N ranged from 276 to 628); State-Trait Anxiety Inventory for Children ranged from -.44 to -.56 (N ranged from 279 to 631).

Author: Nunn, G.D. et al.

Article: Concurrent validity of the Personal Attribute Inventory for Children with the State-Trait Anxiety Inventory for Children and the Behavior Rating Profile - Student Scales.

Journal: *Educational and Psychological Measurement*, summer 1983, *43*(2), 639-641.

Related research: Parish, T. and Taylor, J., 1978. The Personal Attribute Inventory for Children: A report on its reliability and validity as a self-concept scale. *Educational and Psychological Measurement*, 1978, *38*, 565-569.

3271
Test name: PERSONAL ATTRIBUTES QUESTIONNAIRE

Purpose: To measure sexual identity.

Number of items: 24

Format: 5-point continuum bounded by extreme adjective pairs. Sample items presented.

Reliability: Alpha = .79 (masculinity) and .84 (femininity).

Author: Hirschman, E.C.

Article: Sexual identity and the acquisition of rational, absorbing, escapist and modeling experiences.

Journal: *Journal of Social Psychology*, Feb. 1985, *125*(1), 63-73.

Related research: Spence, J.T. et al., 1975. Ratings of self and peers on sex-role attributes. *Journal of Personality and Social Psychology*, *32*, 19-39.
Arnold, S.T., 1981. Attitudes of counselors-in-training toward career goals of a male client. *Vocational Guidance Quarterly*, *29*(3), 221-228.

3272
Test name: PERSONAL CONTROL SCALE

Purpose: To measure extent to which respondents believe luck or personal control shapes events.

Number of items: 5

Format: Forced-choice paired statements.

Reliability: .52.

Author: Begley, T.M. and Alker, H.

Article: Anti-busing protest: Attitudes and actions.

Journal: *Social Psychology Quarterly*, Dec. 1983, *45*(4), 187-197.

Related research: Forward, J.P. and Williams, J.R., 1970.

Internal-external control and black militancy. *Journal of Social Issues*, 26, 75-93.

3273
Test name: PERSONAL DYNAMICS PROFILES

Purpose: To measure major aspects of self-perception.

Number of items: 60

Format: Subjects respond to each adjective on a 5-point Likert scale.

Reliability: Ranged from .704 to .938.

Validity: Predictive validity ranged from .498 to .627.

Author: Mann, J. and Houston, S.

Article: Profile of women managers.

Journal: *Colorado Journal of Educational Research*, spring 1981, 20(3), 5-6.

Related research: Houston, S.R. and Solomon, D., 1978. *Personal Dynamics Profiles Occupational Survey*. Research Methodology Monographs No. 4, University of Northern Colorado.

3274
Test name: PERSONAL REACTION SCALE

Purpose: To measure locus of control perceptions of college and non-college adults.

Number of items: 41

Format: Includes six factors: fate, social self, personal self, self-determination, luck, and powerlessness. All items are presented.

Reliability: Spearman-Brown reliability estimates for each factor ranged from .39 to .84.

Author: Galejs, I. et al.

Article: Personal reaction scale for college and non-college adults: Its development and factorial validity.

Journal: *Educational and Psychological Measurement*, summer 1984, 44(2), 383-393.

Related research: Nowicki, S. and Duke, M.P., 1974. A locus of control scale for non-college as well as college adults. *Journal of Personality Assessment*, 36, 136-137.

3275
Test name: PHYSICAL ATTRACTIVENESS SCALE

Purpose: To measure peoples' perception of their own attractiveness.

Number of items: 24

Format: 5-point Likert response categories.

Reliability: Internal consistency = .88 and .90.

Author: Starr, P.

Article: Physical attractiveness and self-esteem ratings of young adults with cleft lip and/or palate.

Journal: *Psychological Reports*, 1982, 50(2), 467-470.

Related research: Lerner R.M. et al., 1973. Relations among Physical attractiveness, body attitudes and self-conception in male and female college students. *Journal of Psychology*, 85, 119-129.

3276
Test name: PIERS-HARRIS SELF-CONCEPT SCALE

Purpose: To measure pupil self-esteem.

Number of items: 80

Time required: 15-20 minutes.

Format: True-false self-descriptive statements.

Reliability: Internal consistency = .93. Test-retest = .71.

Author: Fox, R. et al.

Article: Student evaluation of teacher as a measure of teacher behavior and teacher impact on students.

Journal: *Journal of Educational Research*, Sept./Oct. 1983, 77(1), 16-21.

Related research: Piers, E.V. and Harris, D.B., 1964. Age and other correlates of self-concept in children. *Journal of Educational Psychology*, 55, 91-95.

3277
Test name: PORTER NEEDS SATISFACTION QUESTIONNAIRE—REVISED

Purpose: To assess the level of need deficiencies perceived by educators in five need categories.

Number of items: 13

Format: Includes five subscales: security, social interaction, esteem, autonomy, and self-actualization. A 7-point rating scale is used ranging from (1) minimum to (7) maximum. All items are presented.

Reliability: Cronbach's alpha reliability coefficients were .89 (factor I) and .46 (factor II).

Author: Pierson, D. et al.

Article: A cross validation of the Porter Needs Satisfaction Questionnaire for Educators.

Journal: *Educational and Psychological Measurement*, autumn 1985, *45*(3), 683-688.

Related research: Trusty, F. and Sergiovanni, T., 1966. Perceived need deficiencies of teachers and administrators: A proposal for restructuring teacher roles. *Educational Administration Quarterly*, 2, 168-180.

3278
Test name: PRIMARY PICTORIAL SELF-ESTEEM TEST

Purpose: To measure general or global academic self-esteem.

Number of items: 26

Format: Each item consists of a statement read to the examinee who selects one of three pictures of faces perceived as reflecting the respondent's feeling relative to the statement read.

Reliability: Test-retest reliability ranged from .58 to .64

Validity: Correlations with CIRCUS ranged from .00 to .24 (N ranged from 69 to 74).

Author: Snyder, S.C. and Michael, W.B.

Article: The relationship of performance on standardized tests in mathematics and reading to two measures of social intelligence and one of academic self-esteem for two samples of primary school children.

Journal: *Educational and Psychological Measurement*, winter 1983, *43*(4), 1141-1148.

Related research: Kirkwood, W.J., 1978. *The development and validation of the Primary Pictorial Self-Esteem Test: Intellectual development.* Unpublished manual, Downey, Calif.: Downey Unified School District.

3279
Test name: PRIMARY SELF-CONCEPT INVENTORY

Purpose: To measure self-concept.

Number of items: 18

Format: Child is told a story about a picture and is asked to circle the person in the picture most like himself.

Reliability: Test-retest ranged from .51 to .91.

Author: Summerlin, M.L. et al. Article, The effect of magic circle participation on a child's self-concept.

Journal: *The School Counselor*, Sept. 1983, *31*(1), 49-52.

Related research: Muller, D.G. and Leonetti, R., 1974. *Primary self-concept inventory test manual.* Austin, Texas: Learning Concepts.

3280
Test name: PROBLEM-SOLVING INVENTORY

Purpose: To assess peoples' perceptions of their personal problem-solving behaviors and attitudes.

Number of items: 32

Format: Employs a six-point Likert scale. Low scores reflect effective problem-solving.

Reliability: Internal consistency ranged from .72 to .90 (N = 140). Test-retest (2 weeks) ranged from .83 to .89 (N = 31).

Validity: Correlations with vocational identity ranged from r = -.18 to r = -.40.

Author: Heppner, P.P. and Krieschok, T.S.

Article: An applied investigation of problem-solving appraisal, vocational identity, and career service requests, utilization, and subsequent evaluations.

Journal: *Vocational Guidance Quarterly*, June 1983, *31*(4), 240-249.

Related research: Heppner, P.P. and Petersen, C.H., 1982. The development and implications of a personal problem-solving inventory. *Journal of Counseling Psychology*, 29, 66-75.

3281
Test name: PROCRASTINATION INVENTORY

Purpose: To measure beliefs regarding the causes of procrastination and the likelihood of changing those causes.

Number of items: 40

Format: Includes 4 scales: controllability, justification, motivation to change, and expectation to change. Responses to each item are made on a 7-point scale ranging from "true" to "false."

Reliability: Test-retest reliabilities ranged from .73 to .83. Internal consistency reliabilities ranged from .37 to .84.

Author: Claiborn, C.D. et al.

Article: Effects of congruence between counselor interpretations and client beliefs.

Journal: *Journal of Counseling Psychology*, March 1981, *28*(2), 101-109.

Related research: Strong, S.R. et al., 1979. Motivational and equipping functions of interpretation in counseling. *Journal of Counseling Psychology, 26,* 98-107.

3282
Test name: PUPIL CONTROL IDEOLOGY SCALE

Purpose: To measure a respondent's pupil control orientation on a humanistic-custodial continuum.

Number of items: 20

Format: Employs a Likert-type scale from 5 (strongly agree) to 1 (strongly disagree).

Reliability: Split-half Spearman-Brown corrected coefficient was .95 (N = 170) and .91 (N = 55).

Author: Graham, S. et al.

Article: A factor analysis of the pupil control ideology scale.

Journal: *Journal of Experimental Education,* summer 1985, *53*(4), 202-206.

Related research: Willower, D.J. et al., 1967/1973. *The school and pupil control ideology.* The Pennsylvania State University Studies, Number 24. University Park: The Pennsylvania State University.
　Halpin, G. et al., 1982. Personality characteristics and self-concept of preservice teachers related to their pupil control orientation. *Journal of Experimental Education,* 50(4), 195-199.

3283
Test name: PUPIL CONTROL IDEOLOGY SCALE—REVISED

Purpose: To measure a respondent's pupil control orientation on a humanistic-custodial continuum.

Number of items: 10

Format: Responses are made on a 5-point Likert-type scale ranging from 5 (strongly agree) to 1 (strongly disagree). All items are presented.

Reliability: Coefficient alpha was .71.

Author: Graham, S. et al.

Article: An analysis of the dimensionality of the Pupil Control Ideology Scale.

Journal: *Educational and Psychological Measurement,* winter 1985, *45*(4), 889-896.

Related research: Graham, S. et al., 1985. A factor analysis of the Pupil Control Ideology Scale. *Journal of Experimental Education,* 53, 202-206.

3284
Test name: RATIONAL BEHAVIOR INVENTORY

Purpose: To assess irrational beliefs.

Number of items: 37

Format: 5-point scale (agree-disagree).

Reliability: Test-retest ranged from .71 to .82 (3 and 10-day intervals). Split-half = .73.

Author: Ray, J.B. and Friedlander, R.B.

Article: Changes in rational beliefs among treated alcoholics.

Journal: *Psychological Reports*, Dec. 1984, *55*(3), 883-886.

Related research: Sharkey, C.T. and Sutton-Simon, K., 1983. Reliability and validity of the rational behavior inventory with a clinical population. *Journal of Clinical Psychology*, *39*, 34-38.

3285
Test name: REFLECTIONS OF SELF AND ENVIRONMENT

Purpose: To measure self-actualization.

Number of items: 80

Format: Responses are recorded on a 5-point rating scale from 1 (no) to 5 (definitely). Some items are presented.

Reliability: Hoyt internal consistency coefficient was .90 (N = 31 males) and .94 (N = 85 females).

Validity: Correlations with other variables ranged from .14 to .73.

Author: Buckmaster, L.R. and Davis, G.A.

Article: ROSE: A measure of self-actualization and its relationship to creativity.

Journal: *Journal of Creative Behavior*, 1985, *19*(1), 30-37.

3286
Test name: REFLECTIONS OF SELF BY YOUTH

Purpose: To measure self-actualizing growth in preadolescents.

Number of items: 62

Format: Includes two factors: feelings and perceptions of self. All items are presented.

Reliability: Test-retest Pearson Product-Moment correlation was .84.

Author: Schatz, E.M. and Buckmaster, L.R.

Article: Development of an instrument to measure self-actualizing growth in preadolescents.

Journal: *Journal of Creative Behavior*, 1984, *18*(4), 263-272.

Related research: Buckmaster, L.R., 1980. Development of an instrument to measure self-actualization and an investigation into the relationship between self-actualization and creativity. Unpublished master's theses, University of Wisconsin.

3287
Test name: RELATIONSHIP BELIEF INVENTORY

Purpose: To assess irrational beliefs about self.

Number of items: 40

Format: Six-point "strongly true" to "strongly false" scale. Sample items presented.

Reliability: Alpha ranged from .72 to .81 across 5 subscales.

Validity: All subscales correlated positively with the Irrational Beliefs Test (r's ranged from .11 to .31, N = 200, p<.05). All subscales correlated negatively with Locke-Wallace Marital Adjustment Scale (r's ranged from -.18 to -.38, N = 200, p<.05).

Author: Eidelson, R.J. and Epstein, N.

Article: Cognition and relationship maladjustment: Development of a measure of dysfunctional relationship beliefs.

Journal: *Journal of Consulting and Clinical Psychology*, Oct. 1982, *50*(5), 715-720.

3288
Test name: ROLE AMBIGUITY SCALE

Purpose: To measure clarity of responsibilities, authority, and expectations of supervisor for jobs.

Number of items: 6

Format: 5-point Likert format.

Reliability: Alpha = .79.

Author: Ashford, S.J. and Cummings, L.L.

Article: Proactive feedback seeking: The instrumental use of the information environment.

Journal: *Journal of Occupational Psychology*, March 1985, *58*(1), 67-79.

Related research: Rizzo, J.R. et al., 1970. Role conflict and ambiguity in complex organizations. *Administrative Science Quarterly*, 15, 150-163.

Bedeian, A.G. et al., 1981. The relationship between role stress and job-related, interpersonal, and organizational climate factors. *Journal of Social Psychology, 113,* second half, 247-260.

3289
Test name: ROLE CONFLICT SCALE

Purpose: To measure role conflict of nursing staff.

Number of items: 8

Format: A 5-point response scale from "very false" to "very true" was used.

Reliability: Alpha was .89.

Validity: Zero-order correlations with variables ranged from -.48 to .69.

Author: Bedeian, A.G. et al.

Article: The relationship between role stress and job-related interpersonal and organizational climate factors.

Journal: *Journal of Social Psychology,* April 1981, *113*(second half), 247-260.

Related research: Rizzo, J.R. et al., 1970. Role conflict and ambiguity in complex organizations. *Administrative Science Quarterly, 15,* 150-163.

3290
Test name: ROLE CONFLICT AND AMBIGUITY SCALE

Purpose: To measure role conflict and role ambiguity.

Number of items: 14

Format: Includes 8 conflict items and 6 ambiguity items. Responses are made on a 5-point scale ranging from always to never. Examples are given.

Reliability: Reliabilities ranged from .78 to .82.

Validity: Correlations with other variables ranged from -.07 to .45.

Author: Eisenhauer, J.E. et al.

Article: Role conflict, role ambiguity and school principals' job robustness.

Journal: *Journal of Experimental Education,* winter 1984/1985, *53*(2), 86-90.

Related research: Rizzo, J.R. et al., 1970. Role conflict and ambiguity in complex organizations. *Administrative Science Quarterly, 15,* 150-163.
House, R.J. et al., 1983. Role conflict and ambiguity scales: Reality or artifacts? *Journal of Applied Psychology, 68*(2), 334-337.
Rosenkrantz, S.A. et al., 1983. Role conflict and ambiguity scales: an evaluation of psychometric properties and the role of social

desirability response bias.
Educational and Psychological Measurement, *43*(4), 957-970.

3291
Test name: ROLE EXPECTATIONS SCALE

Purpose: To measure managers' business view, management style, relationships to subordinates, and technical orientation.

Number of items: 15

Format: 5-point importance scales. All items presented.

Reliability: Alphas ranged from .74 to .84 across subgroups.

Validity: Four factors can be extracted from the 15 items but median reliability of the resulting subscales is only .58.

Author: Berger-Gross, V. and Kraut, A.I.

Article: Great expectations: A no-conflict explanation of role conflict.

Journal: *Journal of Applied Psychology*, May 1984, *69*(2), 261-271.

3292
Test name: ROLE QUESTIONNAIRE

Purpose: To assess one's perceived level of role conflict and role ambiguity.

Number of items: 14

Format: Includes two factors: role conflict and role ambiguity. All items are presented.

Reliability: Reliability coefficients ranged from .78 to .86.

Author: Schwab, R.L. et al.

Article: Assessing role conflict and role ambiguity: A cross validation study.

Journal: *Educational and Psychological Measurement*, summer 1983, *43*(2), 587-593.

Related research: Rizzo, J.R. et al., 1970. Role conflict and ambiguity in complex organizations. *Administrative Science Quarterly*, *15*, 150-163.

3293
Test name: ROSENBERG SELF-ESTEEM SCALE

Purpose: To provide a global measure of self-esteem.

Number of items: 10

Format: Each item is rated on a 4-point Likert scale ranging from "strongly agree" (1), to "strongly disagree" (4).

Reliability: Test-retest (2 weeks) reliability was r = .85. Coefficient alpha was .75.

Author: Robbins, S.B.

Article: Validity estimates for the Career Decision-Making Self-Efficacy Scale.

Journal: *Measurement and Evaluation in Counseling and Development*, July 1985, *18*(2), 64-71.

Related research: Rosenberg, M., 1979. *Conceiving the self*. New York: Basic Books.
Stafford, I.P., 1984. Relation of attitudes toward women's roles and occupational behavior to women's self-esteem. *Journal of Counseling Psychology*, *31*(3), 332-338.

3294
Test name: RRF ANDRO SCALES

Purpose: To measure sex-role identity and self-esteem.

Number of items: 85

Format: Includes scales measuring: masculinity, femininity, and self-esteem.

Reliability: Coefficient alphas ranged from .65 to .79.

Validity: Correlations with Scales for Investigation of the Dual-Career Family - Revised ranged from r = -.38 to r = .43.

Author: Gaddy, C.D. et al.

Article: A study of the Scales for Investigation of the Dual-Career Family.

Journal: *Measurement and Evaluation in Counseling and Development*, Oct. 1985, *18*(3), 120-127.

Related research: Berzins, J.I. et al., 1978. A new measure of psychological androgyny based on the Personality Research Form. *Journal of Consulting and Clinical Psychology*, *46*, 126-138.

3295
Test name: SCALE OF SELF-ESTEEM

Purpose: To measure self-esteem.

Format: Responses were made on a 5-point scale from strongly agree (1) to strongly disagree (5).

Reliability: Alpha reliability was .81.

Validity: Correlations with other variables ranged from r = .20 to r = .43.

Author: Keith, P.M.

Article: Sex-role attitudes, family plans, and career orientations: implications for counseling.

Journal: *Vocational Guidance Quarterly*, March 1981, *29*,(3) 244-252.

Related research: Rosenberg, M., 1965. *Society and the adolescent self-image.* Princeton, N.J.: Princeton University Press.

3296
Test name: SELF-ACCEPTANCE SCALE

Purpose: To measure self-esteem.

Number of items: 36

Format: Responses were made on a 5-point continuum.

Reliability: Alpha reliability estimate was .89.

Validity: Correlations with Interpersonal Jealousy Scale ranged from -.34 to -.40.

Author: Stewart, R.A. and Beatty, M.J.

Article: Jealousy and self-esteem.

Journal: *Perceptual and Motor Skills*, Feb. 1985, *60*(1), 153-154.

Related research: Berger, E.M., 1952. The relation between expressed acceptance of self and expressed acceptance of others. *Journal of Abnormal and Social Psychology*, *47*, 778-782.

3297
Test name: SELF-CONCEPT AND MOTIVATION INVENTORY (SCAMIN)

Purpose: To measure motivation and self-concept.

Number of items: 24

Format: Items read to children who then circle their choice of a face pictured on an answer sheet.

Reliability: Test-retest = .77 (elementary form).

Author: Soule, J.C. et al.

Article: Dimensions of self-concept for children in kindergarten and grades 1 and 2.

Journal: *Psychological Reports*, Feb. 1981, *48*(1), 83-88.

Related research: Farrah, G.A. et al., 1968. *Self-concept and motivation inventory: What face you wear*, Dearborn Heights, MI: Person-O-Metrics.

3298
Test name: SELF-CONCEPT APPRAISAL SCALES

Purpose: To measure self-concept, appraisal of spouses' self-concept and perceived appraisal by spouse.

Number of items: 21

Format: Semantic differential. All adjective-pairs presented.

Reliability: Alpha ranged between .78 and .82.

Author: Schafer, R.B.

Article: Equity/inequity and self-concept: An interactionist analysis.

Journal: *Social Psychology Quarterly*, March 1984, *47*(1), 42-49.

Related research: Sherwood, J.J., 1962. *Self-identity and self-actualization: A theory and research*. Unpublished doctoral dissertation, University of Michigan.

3299
Test name: SELF-CONCEPT AS A LEARNER SCALE

Purpose: To measure one's self-concept as a learner in the school context.

Number of items: 50

Format: Includes four subscales: motivation, task orientation, problem-solving or intellectual ability, and class membership.

Reliability: Test-retest reliability for the total score ranged from .79 to .90 (time between testing ranged from 7 days to 3 months). Coefficient alphas ranged from .88 to .91.

Author: Baldauf, R.B., Jr. et al.

Article: The reliability and factorial validity of the Self Concept as a Learner (SCAL) measure for year seven students in Australia.

Journal: *Educational and Psychological Measurement*, autumn 1985, *45*(3), 655-659.

Related research: Waetjen, W., 1972. Procedure for the analysis of the self-concept as a learner scale. Mimeo, 5 pages.
   Lunenburg, F.C., 1983. Pupil control ideology and self-concept as a learner. *Educational Research Quarterly*, *8*(3), 33-39.

3300
Test name: SELF-CONCEPT MEASURE

Purpose: To measure self-concept of college students.

Number of items: 4

Format: Responses to each item are made on a 5-point scale ranging from 1 (strongly agree) to 5 (strongly disagree).

Reliability: Coefficient alphas ranged from .66 to .79.

Author: Behuniak, P., Jr., and Gable, R.K.

Article: A longitudinal study of self-concept and locus of control for persisters in six college majors.

Journal: *Educational Research Quarterly*, spring 1981, *6*(1), 3-12.

Related research: Conger, A.S. et al., 1977. National longitudinal study of high school seniors: Group profiles on self-esteem, locus of control, and life goals. (NCES 77-260: HEW) Washington, D.C.

3301
Test name: SELF-CONCEPT OF ABILITY SCALE

Purpose: To measure academic self-concept.

Number of items: 8

Format: Employs a 5-point Likert-type scale. Students rate present school ability on five items and they rate their future academic ability on three items.

Reliability: Test-retest reliability coefficients (1 year) ranged from .69 to .77.

Author: Byrne, B.M.

Article: Investigating measures of self-concept.

Journal: *Measurement and Evaluation in Guidance*, Oct. 1983, *16*(3), 115-126.

Related research: Brookover, W.B. et al., Eds., 1967. *Self-concept of ability and school achievement III: Relationship of self-concept to achievement in high school.* (Educational Research series No. 36.) East Lansing, MI: Educational Publication Services.

3302
Test name: SELF-CONSCIOUSNESS SCALE

Purpose: To measure self-consciousness.

Number of items: 23

Format: Subjects respond to each item on a 5-point scale from 0 (extremely uncharacteristic) to 4 (extremely characteristic) as to how well each item describes them. Includes three scales: private self-consciousness, public self-consciousness, and social anxiety. Examples are presented.

Reliability: Cronbach's alphas ranged from .56 to .84.

Validity: Correlations with loneliness scores ranged from -.18 to .38.

Author: Schmitt, J.P. and Kurdek, L.A.

Article: Age and gender differences in and personality correlates of loneliness in different relationships.

Journal: *Journal of Personality Assessment*, Oct. 1985, *49*(5), 485-496.

Related research: Fenigstein, A. et al., 1975. Public and private self-consciousness: Assessment and theory. *Journal of Consulting and Clinical Psychology, 43*, 522-527.

Vleeming, R.G. and Engelse, J.A., Assessment of private and public self-consciousness: A Dutch replication. *Journal of Personality Assessment, 45*(4), 385-389.

3303
Test name: SELF-DESCRIPTION QUESTIONNAIRE

Purpose: To measure academic and non-academic self-concept.

Number of items: 72

Format: 5-point response scale from 1 (true) to 5 (false).

Reliability: Alpha ranged from .65 to .95 across subscales and grade level.

Author: Marsh, H.W. et al.

Article: Self-descriptive questionnaire: Age-sex effects in the structure and level of self-concept for preadolescent children.

Journal: *Journal of Educational Psychology*, Oct. 1984, *76*(5), 940-956.

Related research: Marsh, H.W. et al., 1983. Preadolescent self-concept: Its relation to self-concept as inferred by teachers and to academic ability. *British Journal of Educational Psychology, 53*, 60-78.

Marsh, H.W. et al., 1983. Self-concept, reliability, stability, dimensionality, validity, and the measurement of change. *Journal of Educational Psychology, 75*(5), 772-790.

3304
Test name: SELF-DESCRIPTION QUESTIONNAIRE

Purpose: To measure student self-concept (preadolescent).

Number of items: 56

Format: Multiple-choice and rating scales. Sample item descriptions presented.

Reliability: Alpha ranged from .80s to .90s over subscales.

Author: Marsh, H.W. et al.

Article: The relationship between dimensions of self-attribution and dimensions of self-concept.

Journal: *Journal of Educational Psychology*, Feb. 1984, *76*(1), 3-32.

Related Research: Marsh, H.W. et al. Preadolescent self-concept: Its relation to self-concept as inferred by teachers and to academic ability. *British Journal of Occupational Psychology,* 1983, *53,* 60-78.

3305

Test name: SELF-DESCRIPTION QUESTIONNAIRE III

Purpose: To measure university-aged respondents' self-concept.

Number of items: 136

Format: Includes 13 factors: mathematics, verbal, academic, problem-solving/creativity, physical abilities/sports, physical appearance, relations with same sex peers, relations with opposite sex peers, relations with parents, religion/spirituality, honesty/reliability, emotional stability/security, general self-concept. Students respond to each item on an 8-point scale from 1 (definitely false) to 8 (definitely true). All items are presented.

Reliability: Coefficient alphas ranged from .75 to .95.

Validity: Correlations with other criteria ranged from -.24 to .61.

Author: Marsh, H.W. and O'Neill, R.

Article: Self-Description Questionnaire III: The construct validity of multidimensional self-concept ratings by late adolescents.

Journal: *Journal of Educational Measurement*, summer 1984, *21*(2), 153-174.

Related research: Marsh, H.W. et al., 1983. Multitrait-multimethod analyses of the Self-Description Questionnaire: Student-teacher agreement on multidimensional ratings of student self-concept. *American Educational Research Journal, 20*, 333-357.

3306

Test name: SELF-EFFICACY MEASURES

Purpose: To measure four aspects of self-efficacy with respect to science and engineering field achievement.

Number of items: 15

Format: Subjects indicate whether they believe they could successfully complete the educational requirements of and job duties performed in 15 science and engineering fields. Subjects indicate their degree of confidence and their ability to complete the educational requirements and job duties. A 10-point scale was employed to indicate strength of confidence.

Reliability: Test-retest correlations for the four efficacy scales (8 week interval) ranged from .58 to .89. Coefficient alphas ranged from .79 to .89.

Validity: Correlation of level of educational requirements with PSAT was $r = .41$ and with high school rank was $r = .38$.

Correlation with strength of educational requirement with PSAT was r = .53 and with high school rank was r = .37.

Author: Lent, R.W. et al.

Article: Relation of self-efficacy expectations to academic achievement and persistence.

Journal: *Journal of Counseling Psychology*, July 1984, *31*(3), 356-362.

Related research: Betz, N.E. and Hackett, G., 1981. The relationship of career-related self-efficacy expectations to perceived career options in college women and men. *Journal of Counseling Psychology*, *28*, 399-410.

3307
Test name: SELF-EFFICACY SCALE

Purpose: To measure self-efficacy.

Format: 14-point Likert scale. All items presented.

Reliability: Alphas ranged from .71 to .86.

Validity: Correlated significantly with locus of control (Rotter), personal contact (Gurin, et al.), social desirability (Crowne and Marlowe), ego strength (Barron), interpersonal competency (Holland and Baird), and self-esteem (Rosenberg).

Author: Sherer, M. et al.

Article: The self-efficacy scale: Construction and validation.

Journal: *Psychological Reports*, 1982, *51*(2), 663-671.

3308
Test name: SELF-EFFICACY SCALE

Purpose: To measure perceived self-efficacy.

Number of items: 6

Format: Items were based on an 11-point scale ranging from 0 to 100.

Reliability: Cronbach's alpha coefficient was .87.

Author: Valerio, H.P. and Stone, G.L.

Article: Effects of behavioral, cognitive, and combined treatments for assertion as a function of differential deficits.

Journal: *Journal of Counseling Psychology*, March 1982, *29*(2), 158-168.

Related research: Bandura, A., 1977. Self-efficacy: Toward a unifying theory of behavior change. *Psychological Review*, *84*, 191-215.

3309
Test name: SELF-ESTEEM INVENTORY

Purpose: To measure self-concept.

Number of items: 58

Format: Includes a lie scale and four subscales assessing: perception of peers, parents, school, and self.

Reliability: Coefficient alpha was .86 for total test and for subscales coefficients ranged from .61 to .71.

Validity: Correlation with: Children's Self-Concept Scale r = .63. Behavioral Academic Assessment Scale r = .47. Children's Social Desirability Scale r = .17.

Author: Johnson, B.W. et al.

Article: The Coopersmith Self-Esteem Inventory: A construct validation study.

Journal: *Educational and Psychological Measurement*, autumn 1983, *43*(3), 907-913.

Related research: Coopersmith, S., 1967. *The antecedents of self-esteem*. San Francisco: Freeman.

3310
Test name: SELF-ESTEEM INVENTORY—FORM B

Purpose: To enable teachers to evaluate students' self-esteem.

Number of items: 25

Reliability: Test-retest (2 months) reliability coefficients ranged from .72 to .85.

Validity: Correlations with other variables ranged from .05 to .62.

Author: Chiu, L-H.

Article: The reliability and validity of the Coopersmith Self-Esteem Inventory - Form B.

Journal: *Educational and Psychological Measurement*, winter 1985, *45*(4), 945-949.

Related research: Coopersmith, S., 1967. *The antecedents of self-esteem*. San Francisco: Freeman.

3311
Test name: SELF-ESTEEM INVENTORY—GENERAL SELF SUBSCALE

Purpose: To measure general self-concept.

Number of items: 26

Format: Each item is answered either "like me" or "unlike me."

Reliability: Test-retest coefficients ranged from .52 to .60 (6 months).

Author: Byrne, B.M.

Article: Investigating measures of self-concept.

Journal: *Measurement and Evaluation in Guidance*, Oct. 1983, *16*(3), 115-126.

Related research: Drummond, R.J. et al., 1977. Stability and sex differences on the Coopersmith Self-Esteem Inventory for students in grades two to twelve. *Psychological Reports*, *40*, 943-946.

3312
Test name: SELF-ESTEEM SCALE

Purpose: To assess a person's general feeling toward self.

Number of items: 6

Format: Respondents asked if feelings are similar to those described on a 7-point favorableness scale.

Reliability: Coefficient of reproducibility = 90.2%.

Author: Starr, P. et al.

Article: Physical attractiveness and self-esteem ratings of young adults with cleft lip and/or palate.

Journal: *Psychological Reports*, 1982, *50*(2), 467-470.

Related research: Simmons, R.G., et al., 1973. Disturbance in the self-image at adolescence. *American Sociological Review*, *38*, 553-568.

3313
Test name: SELF-ESTEEM SCALE

Purpose: To provide a unidimensional measure of general self-concept of high school students.

Number of items: 10

Format: A Guttman scale with a 4-point Likert-scaling format ranging from "strongly agree" to "strongly disagree."

Reliability: Test-retest coefficient was .85 for 28 college students over a 2-week interval.

Author: Byrne, B.M.

Article: Investigating measures of self-concept.

Journal: *Measurement and Evaluation in Guidance*, Oct. 1983, *16*(3), 115-126.

Related research: Silber, E. and Tippett, J., 1965. Self-esteem: Clinical assessment and measurement validation. *Psychological Reports*, *16*, 1017-1071.

3314
Test name: SELF-ESTEEM SCALE

Purpose: To measure self-esteem.

Number of items: 10

Format: Respondents indicate degree of agreement to adjective list corresponding to how well each describes themselves. Seven-point response scale.

Reliability: Alpha = .79.

Author: Hansen, G.

Article: Perceived threats and marital jealousy.

Journal: *Social Psychology Quarterly*, Sept. 1985, *48*(3), 262-268.

Related research: Anderson, N.H., 1968. Likeableness ratings of 555 personality trait words. *Journal of Personality and Social Psychology*, 9, 272-279.

3315
Test name: SELF-ESTEEM SCALE

Purpose: To measure self-esteem.

Number of items: 10

Reliability: Coefficient alpha was .84.

Validity: Correlations with other variables ranged from -.22 to .27.

Author: Keller, R.T.

Article: Predicting absenteeism from prior absenteeism, attitudinal factors, and nonattitudinal factors.

Journal: *Journal of Applied Psychology*, Aug. 1983, *68*(3), 536-540.

Related research: Ellis, R.A. and Taylor, M.S., 1983. Role of self-esteem within the job search process. *Journal of Applied Psychology*, *68*, 632-640.
   Rosenberg, M., 1965. *Society and the adolescent self-image*. Princeton, N.J.: Princeton University Press.

3316
Test name: SELFISM SCALE

Purpose: To measure beliefs about how one should best construe problem situations involving a variety of needs.

Number of items: 28

Format: Responses are made on a 5-point Likert-type scale from (1) strongly agree to (5) strongly disagree. Examples are presented. Also contains 12 filler items to disguise somewhat the purpose of the scale.

Reliability: Spearman-Brown split-half reliabilities were .84 (males) and .83 (females). Test-retest reliability (7 weeks) was .61 (N = 92) and for four weeks was .91 (N = 66).

Validity: Correlations with other measures ranged from -.37 to .43.

Author: Phares, E.J. and Erskine, N.

Article: The measurement of selfism.

Journal: *Educational and Psychological Measurement*, autumn 1984, *44*(3), 597-608.

3317
Test name: SENSE OF COMPETENCE MEASURE

Purpose: To measure an individual's sense of competence resulting from mastering the work setting.

Number of items: 23

Format: A 5-point Likert scale is employed.

Reliability: Alpha coefficient = .94.

Validity: Correlations with other variables ranged from .11 to .52.

Author: Tharenou, P. and Harker, P.

Article: Moderating influence of self-esteem on relationships between job complexity, performance, and satisfaction.

Journal: *Journal of Applied Psychology*, Nov. 1984, *69*(4), 623-632.

Related research: Wagner, F.R. and Morse, J.J., 1975. A measure of individual sense of competence. *Psychological Reports*, *36*, 451-459.

3318
Test name: SEX STEREOTYPE MEASURE (KOREAN)

Purpose: To measure awareness of sex-trait stereotypes.

Number of items: 32

Format: Subjects assign each of 32 traits to male or female silhouetted figures.

Reliability: Test-retest = .69 and .70 for Korean girls and boys, respectively.

Author: Lee, J.Y. and Sugawara, A.I.

Article: Awareness of sex-trait stereotypes among Korean children.

Journal: *Journal of Social Psychology*, Aug. 1982, *117*(second half), 161-170.

Related research: Williams, J.E. et al., 1977. Sex stereotype measure II (SSM II) (Technical Rep.). Winston-Salem, NC: Department of Psychology, Wake Forest University.

3319
Test name: SEX STEREOTYPE QUESTIONNAIRE

Purpose: To assess attitudes toward gender role.

Number of items: 122

Format: Employs a modified semantic differential format. Subjects respond to the statements by first identifying their ideal male, then their ideal female, and lastly they identify those characteristics which reflect themselves.

Reliability: Reliability is reported to range from .56 to .70.

Author: Stevens, G. et al.

Article: Factor analyses of two "attitude toward gender role" questionnaires.

Journal: *Journal of Personality Assessment*, June 1984, *48*(3), 312-316.

Related research: Rosenkrantz, P. et al., 1968. Sex-role stereotypes and self-concepts in college students. *Journal of Consulting and Clinical Psychology*, 32(3), 287-297.

3320
Test name: SKILLS RATING INVENTORY

Purpose: To measure self-assessment of personal skills.

Number of items: 44

Format: Two ratings were made on each item: frequency of activity and quality of performance. Each rating was made on a 5-point rating scale.

Reliability: Alpha = .93 (number of skills) and .93 (quality of skills).

Validity: Number and quality correlated at r = .38.

Author: Prager, K.J.

Article: Educational aspirations and self-esteem in returning and traditional community college students.

Journal: *Journal of College Student Personnel*, March 1983, *24*(2), 144-147.

3321
Test name: STUDENT SELF-CONCEPT SCALE

Purpose: To measure intellectual and academic self-concept and interpersonal and social self-concept.

Number of items: 11

Format: Rating scale from above to below average.

Reliability: Intellectual and academic (5 items) alpha = .68. Interpersonal and social (6 items) alpha = .63.

Author: Pascarella, E.T.

Article: The influence of on-campus living verses commuting to college on intellectual and interpersonal self-concept.

Journal: *Journal of College Student Personnel*, July 1985, 26(4), 292-299.

Related research: Pascarella, E.T., 1984. Reassessing the effects of living on-campus versus commuting to college: A causal modelling approach. *Review of Higher Education*, 7, 247-260.

3322
Test name: STUDENT PERCEPTION SCALES

Purpose: To measure perceptions of academic preparation, university demands, institutional climate, and personal adjustment.

Number of items: 31

Format: 5-point scale.

Reliability: Cronbach's alpha ranged from .57 to .77.

Author: Holahan, C.K. et al.

Article: The formation of student performance expectancies: The relationship of student perceptions and social consequences.

Journal: *Journal of College Student Personnel*, Nov. 1982, 23(6), 497-502.

3323
Test name: STUDENT PERFORMANCE ATTRIBUTION SCALE

Purpose: To assess how students attribute cause of performance on tests.

Number of items: 22

Format: 7-point Likert format.

Reliability: Cronbach's alpha = .84; SB odd-even = .88.

Validity: Does not significantly correlate with social desirability ($r = .06$) or self-esteem ($r = .11$).

Author: Ames, R. and Lau, S.

Article: An attributional analysis of student help-seeking in academic settings.

Journal: *Journal of Educational Psychology*, June 1982, 74(3), 414-423.

3324
Test name: SUBORDINATE PERCEPTIONS SCALE

Purpose: To measure subordinates perception of psychological influence.

Number of items: 6

Format: Likert format.

Reliability: Alpha = .82.

Author: James, L.R. et al.

Article: Perceptions of psychological influence: A cognitive information processing approach for explaining moderated relationships.

Journal: *Personnel Psychology*, autumn 1981, *34*(3), 453-475.

Related research: James, L.R. et al., 1979. Correlates of psychological influence: An illustration of the psychological climate approach to work environment perceptions. *Personnel Psychology*, 32, 563-588.

3325
Test name: SUPERVISEE LEVELS QUESTIONNAIRE

Purpose: To identify counselor supervisees' perceptions of their counseling and supervision behavior.

Number of items: 24

Format: Responses to each item were made on a 7-point Likert-scale. Includes three subscales: self-awareness, dependency-autonomy, and theory/skills acquisition. Sample items are presented.

Reliability: Cronbach's alpha ranged from .55 to .76.

Author: McNeill, B.W. et al.

Article: Supervisees' perceptions of their development: A test of the counselor complexity model.

Journal: *Journal of Counseling Psychology*, Oct. 1985, *32*(4), 630-633.

Related research: Stoltenberg, C.D., 1981. Approaching supervision from a developmental perspective: The counselor complexity model. *Journal of Counseling Psychology*, 28, 59-65.

3326
Test name: SUPERVISOR'S APPLICATION OF DISCIPLINE SCALE

Purpose: To measure employees perception of their boss and the manner they use in disciplinary actions.

Number of items: 38

Format: 5-point agreement scale.

Reliability: Alpha ranged from .88 to .90 across two subscales. Inter-rater reliability ranged from .31 to .43.

Validity: Two factors extracted (style and consistency) that together explain 95% of variance.

Author: Arvey, R.D. et al.

Article: Use of discipline in an organization: A field study.

Journal: *Journal of Applied Psychology*, Aug. 1984, 69(3) 448-460.

3327
Test name: SYDNEY ATTRIBUTION SCALE

Purpose: To measure students' perception of causes of academic success and failure.

Number of items: 72

Format: 5-point response scale.

Reliability: Alphas ranged from .57 to .86 across subscales.

Author: Marsh, H.W.

Article: Relations among dimensions of self-attribution, dimensions of self-concept, and academic achievements.

Journal: *Journal of Educational Psychology*, Dec. 1984, 76(6), 1291-1308.

Related research: Marsh, H.W. et al., 1984. The relationship between dimensions of self-attribution and dimensions of self-concept. *Journal of Educational Psychology*, 76, 3-32.

3328
Test name: TASK-SPECIFIC AND SOCIAL SELF-ESTEEM SCALES

Purpose: To measure self-evaluation of ability and performance on a particular task, and self-perception of how others view ability on a particular task.

Number of items: 41

Format: 5-point Likert format. Sample items presented.

Reliability: Alphas above .80.

Validity: Academic ability and satisfaction correlated significantly (r = .81, p<.001) as did athletic ability and satisfaction (r = .84, p<.001).

Author: McIntire, S.A. and Levine, E.L.

Article: An empirical investigation of self-esteem as a composite construct.

Journal: *Journal of Vocational Behavior*, Dec. 1984, 25(3), 290-303.

3329
Test name: TASK-SPECIFIC SELF-ESTEEM SCALE

Purpose: To measure task-specific self-esteem in the job search context.

Number of items: 10

Format: Items deal with individuals' confidence in general search ability and in specific job search knowledge and skills.

Responses are made on a 5-point Likert scale. All items are presented.

Reliability: Coefficient alphas were .82 and .83.

Validity: Correlations with other variables ranged from -.40 to .54.

Author: Ellis, R.A. and Taylor M.S.

Article: Role of self-esteem within the job search process.

Journal: *Journal of Applied Psychology*, Nov. 1983, 68(4), 632-640.

3330
Test name: TEACHING EFFECTIVENESS QUESTIONNAIRE

Purpose: To measure what teachers believe to be effective teaching.

Number of items: 20

Format: 5-point Likert items. All items presented.

Reliability: Cronbach's alphas all above .84 (for pre- and posttests).

Author: Guskey, T.

Article: The effects of staff development on teachers' perceptions about effective teaching.

Journal: *Journal of Educational Research*, July/Aug. 1985, 78(6), 378-381.

Related research: Guskey, T.R., 1984. The influence of change in instructional effectiveness upon the affective characteristics of teachers. *American Educational Research Journal*, 7, 265-274.

3331
Test name: TEACHER EFFICACY SCALE

Purpose: To measure the belief that teachers can help even the most difficult or unmotivated students.

Number of items: 30

Format: Likert format. All items presented.

Validity: Convergent and discriminant validity assessed by multitrait-multimethod analysis supported use of the construct.

Author: Gibson, S. and Demba, M.H.

Article: Teacher efficacy: A construct validation.

Journal: *Journal of Educational Psychology*, Aug. 1984, 76(4), 569-582.

Related research: Gibson, S. and Brown, R., 1982. The development of teacher's personal responsibility/self-efficacy scale. Paper presented at the annual meeting of the American Educational Research Association, New York.

3332
Test name: TEACHER LOCUS OF CONTROL SCALE

Purpose: To measure teacher locus of control.

Number of items: 24

Format: Likert-type scale including 4 response choices: strongly agree, agree, disagree, strongly disagree. One half of the items are oriented toward internal locus of control and one half toward external locus of control.

Reliability: Coefficient alphas were .85 (N = 111) and .78 (N = 130).

Author: Halpin, G. et al.

Article: Teacher stress as related to locus of control, sex, and age.

Journal: *Journal of Experimental Education*, spring 1985, 53(3), 136-139.

Related research: Hall, B.W. et al., 1980. Development and validation of a teacher locus of control scale. Paper presented at the meeting of the National Council on Measurement in Education, Boston.

3333
Test name: TEACHER LOCUS OF CONTROL

Purpose: To measure teacher expectancies for internal or external control of aspects of teacher role.

Number of items: 32

Format: Each item is a contrast between an internal and external belief. Sample item presented.

Reliability: Alpha = .86. Temporal stability: = .75 (two weeks) and .62 (three weeks).

Validity: Factorial four factors were extracted (recognition, teaching/learning process, relations with teachers, attitudes of parents and society).

Author: Maes, W.R. and Anderson, D.E.

Article: A measure of teacher locus of control.

Journal: *Journal of Educational Research*, Sept./Oct. 1985, 79(1), 27-32.

3334
Test name: TEACHER LOCUS OF CONTROL SCALE

Purpose: To measure perceptions of control in the classroom.

Number of items: 28

Format: Forced-choice items.

Reliability: Kuder-Richardson formula 20 = .81 (I- subscale). Kuder-Richardson formula 20 = .71 (I+ subscale).

Validity: TCL more predictive of teacher and student behavior than E-I scale according to correlations presented.

Author: Rose, J.S. and Medway, F.J.

Article: Measurement of teachers' beliefs in their control over student outcome.

Journal: *Journal of Educational Research*, Jan./Feb. 1981, *74*(3), 185-190.

Related research: Rotter, J.B., 1966. Generalized expectancies for internal vs. external control of reinforcement. *Psychological Monographs*, *80*(1). Whole No. 609.

3335
Test name: TEMPORAL INTEGRATION SCALES

Purpose: To measure time perspective in terms of long-term personal direction and time utilization.

Number of items: 40

Format: 7-point Likert response scales. Sample items presented.

Reliability: Alpha ranged from .80 to .83.

Author: Wolf, F.M. and Savickas, M.L.

Article: Time perspective and causal attributions for achievement.

Journal: *Journal of Educational Psychology*, Aug. 1985, *77*(4), 471-488.

Related research: Wessman, A.E., 1973. Personality and the subjective experience of time. *Journal of Personality Assessment*, *37*, 103-114.

3336
Test name: THERAPIST EXPECTANCY INVENTORY

Purpose: To measure therapists' pretreatment expectancies.

Number of items: 29

Format: Likert-scale (1 = not at all expect; 8 = greatly expect). All items presented.

Reliability: Cronbach's alphas ranged from .67 to .87 on four subscales.

Validity: Four-factor solution accounted for 34% of the variance in the responses.

Author: Bernstein, B.L. et al.

Article: Therapist expectancy inventory: Development and preliminary validation.

Journal: *Psychological Reports*, April 1983, *52*(2), 479-487.

3337
Test name: UNDERSTANDING LITERACY BEHAVIOR TEST

Purpose: To measure child's recognition of reading and writing activities.

Number of items: 10 sets of four drawings.

Format: Child instructed to point to each person who is reading.

Reliability: Cronbach internal consistency = .758.

Author: Mayfield, M.

Article: Code systems instructions and kindergarten children's perception of the nature of and purpose of reading.

Journal: *Journal of Educational Research*, Jan./Feb. 1983, *76*(3), 161-168.

Related research: Evanechko, P. et al., 1973. An investigation of the reading readiness domain. *Research in the Teaching of English*, 7, 61-78.

3338
Test name: WALLACE SELF-CONCEPT SCALE

Purpose: To estimate the perception one holds toward the concept "myself as a person."

Number of items: 15

Format: Items are bipolar.

Reliability: Test-retest coefficients ranged from .72 to .81. Coefficient alpha was .81.

Validity: Convergent validity correlations ranged from .45 to .64. Discriminant validity correlation with the Crowne-Marlowe Social Desirability Scale was .23.

Author: Wallace, G.R. et al.

Article: Factorial comparison of the Wallace Self-Concept Scale between special education teachers and regular classroom teachers.

Journal: *Educational and Psychological Measurement*, summer 1984, *44*(2), 199-207.

Related research: White, G. and Chan, E., 1983. A comparison of self-concept scores of Chinese and white graduate students and professionals. *Journal of Non-White Concerns*, *11*(4), 138-141.

3339
Test name: WALLSTON HEALTH LOCUS OF CONTROL SCALE

Purpose: To measure sense of control of health.

Number of items: 9

Format: 4-point agree-disagree scale. All items presented.

Reliability: Alpha = .65.

Author: Seeman, M. et al.

Article: Social networks and health status: A longitudinal analysis.

Journal: *Social Psychology Quarterly*, Sept. 1985, *48*(3), 237-248.

Related research: Wallston, K.A. and Wallston, B.S., 1980. Health locus of control scales. Pp. 189-243 in J. Lefcourt (Ed.), *Advances and Innovation in Locus of Control Research*. New York: Academic Press.

3340
Test name: WEIGHT LOCUS OF CONTROL SCALE

Purpose: To measure locus of control with respect to weight.

Number of items: 4

Format: Employs a 6-point Likert-type format ranging from 1 (strongly disagree) to 6 (strongly agree) for the two externally worded items and reverse scoring for the two internally worded items. All items are presented.

Reliability: Test-retest reliability was .67 (N = 110). Cronbach's alpha was .58 (N = 113) and .56 (N = 112).

Validity: Correlations with other scales ranged from -.30 to .35.

Author: Saltzer, E.B.

Article: The Weight Locus of Control (WLOC) Scale: A specific measure for obesity research.

Journal: *Journal of Personality Assessment*, Dec. 1982, *46*(6), 620-628.

3341
Test name: WORK-NONWORK CONFLICT SCALE

Purpose: To measure perceived conflict between work and nonwork.

Number of items: 6

Format: 5-point response scale (completely true to completely not true). All items presented.

Reliability: Alpha = .69.

Validity: Correlates significantly with "inclusiveness" among army personnel.

Author: Shamir, B.

Article: Some antecedents of work-nonwork conflict.

Journal: *Journal of Vocational Behavior*, Aug. 1983, *23*(1), 98-111.

PERSONALITY

3342
Test name: ABBREVIATED TEMPERAMENT QUESTIONNAIRE

Purpose: To assess temperament.

Number of items: 30

Format: For children 5 to 7 years. Includes 4 components and employs a 5-point rating scale.

Reliability: 50% of item reliabilities > r = .80 (N = 15) (1 month). 80% of item reliabilities > r = .60 (N = 15) (1 month).

Author: Hubert, N.C. et al.

Article: The study of early temperament: Measurement and conceptual issues.

Journal: *Child Development*, June 1982, *53*(3), 571-600.

Related research: Garside, R.F. et al., 1975. Dimensions of temperament in infant school children. *Journal of Child Psychology and Psychiatry and Allied Disciplines*, *16*, 219-231.

3343
Test name: ACT UNISEX INTEREST INVENTORY

Purpose: To measure Holland personality types.

Number of items: 90 (6 subscales of 15 items each).

Format: Item responses are "like," "indifferent," and "dislike."

Reliability: Alpha ranged from .85 to .92 across subscales.

Author: Wolfe, L.K. and Betz, N.

Article: Traditionality of choice and sex-role identification as moderators of the congruence of occupational choice in college women.

Journal: *Journal of Vocational Behavior*, Feb. 1981, *18*(1), 43-55.

Related research: Hanson, G.R., 1974. *Assessing the interest of college youth: Summary of research and applications*. (ACT Research Report No. 67.) Iowa City, Iowa: American College Testing Program.
  Hanson, G.R., et al., 1977. *Development and validation of sex-balanced interest inventory scales*. (ACT Research Report No. 78.) Iowa City, Iowa: American College Testing Program.

3344
Test name: AGREEMENT RESPONSE SCALE—REVISED

Purpose: To measure the agreeing-response tendency.

Number of items: 15

Format: Each item reflects value or belief-oriented statements about oneself. Subjects respond on a 7-point scale from 1 (strongly disagree) to 7 (strongly agree).

Reliability: Internal consistency was .71

Validity: Correlation with satisfaction was .21

Author: Blau, G. and Katerberg, R.

Article: Agreeing response set: Statistical nuisance or meaningful personality concept?

Journal: *Perceptual and Motor Skills*, June 1982, *54*(3-I), 851-857.

Related research: Couch, A. and Keniston, K., 1961. Agreeing response set and social desirability. *Journal of Abnormal and Social Psychology*, *62*, 175-179.

3345
Test name: BABY BEHAVIOR QUESTIONNAIRE

Purpose: To assess temperament.

Number of items: 54

Format: Includes 7 factors: intensity/activity, regularity, approach/withdrawal, sensory sensitivity, attentiveness, manageability, sensitivity to new foods.

Reliability: Test-retest correlation coefficients ranged from r = .63 to r = .93 (N = 26). Alphas ranged from .51 to .72.

Author: Hubert, N.C. et al.

Article: The study of early temperament: Measurement and conceptual issues.

Journal: *Child Development*, June 1982, *53*(3), 571-600.

Related research: Bohlin, G. et al., 1981. Dimensions of infant behavior. *Infant Behavior and Development*, *4*, 83-96.

3346
Test name: BASIC PERSONALITY INVENTORY

Purpose: To measure independent components of psychopathology.

Number of items: 220

Format: True-false.

Reliability: KR-20 ranged from .47 to .83 across subscales. Item-total correlations ranged from .29 to .44.

Validity: Validity coefficients averaged .21.

Author: Holden, R.R. and Jackson, D.N.

Article: Disguise and the structured self-report assessment of psychopathology: I. An analogue investigation.

Journal: *Journal of consulting and clinical psychology*, April 1985, 53(2), 211-222.

Related research: Jackson, D.H., 1976. *The basic personality inventory*. London, Canada: Author.

3347
Test name: BEHAVIOR CHECKLIST

Purpose: To assess temperament.

Number of items: 25

Format: For children 4-14 years. Includes 5 temperament types: easy, difficult, slow warmer, environmentalist, emotionally fragile.

Reliability: Test-retest correlation coefficients (8 weeks) ranged from r = .44 to r = .82 (N = 50).

Validity: Correlation with parent ratings of behavior description items ranged from r = .27 to r = .70.

Author: Hubert, N.C. et al.

Article: The study of early temperament: Measurement and conceptual issues.

Journal: *Child Development*, June 1982, 53(3), 571-600.

3348
Test name: BEHAVIORAL STYLES QUESTIONNAIRE

Purpose: To assess temperament.

Number of items: 100

Format: For children 3-7 years. Includes 9 categories: activity level, rhythmicity, approach/withdrawal, adaptability, intensity, sensory threshold, mood, distractibility, attention span/persistence.

Reliability: Test-retest reliability coefficients (1 month) ranged from r = .67 to r = .94 (N = 53). Alphas ranged from .47 to .80 (N = 350).

Validity: Correlations with other measures ranged from r = .29 to r = .35.

Author: Hubert, N.C. et al.

Article: The study of early temperament: Measurement and conceptual issues.

Journal: *Child Development*, June 1982, 53(3), 571-600.

Related research: McDevitt, S.C. and Carey, W.B., 1978. Measurement of temperament in 3- to 7-year-old children. *Journal of Child Psychology and Psychiatry and Allied Disciplines*, 19, 245-253.

3349
Test name: BIOGRAPHICAL QUESTIONNAIRE

Purpose: To identify a variety of biographical information.

Number of items: 118

Format: Includes 15 factors for females and 13 factors for males.

Reliability: Coefficient alphas for female data ranged from .70 to .89 and coefficient alphas for male data ranged from .67 to .89.

Author: Eberhardt, B.J. and Muchinsky, P.M.

Article: Biodata determinants of vocational typology: An integration of two paradigms.

Journal: *Journal of Applied Psychology*, Dec. 1982, *67*(6), 714-727.

Related research: Owens, W.A. and Schoenfeldt, L.F., 1979. Toward a classification of persons. *Journal of Applied Psychology*, *64*, 569-607.

3350
Test name: CHILD ABUSE POTENTIAL INVENTORY

Purpose: A screening device to differentiate abusers from nonabusers.

Number of items: 160

Format: Agree-disagree format.

Reliability: KR-20 ranged from .92 to .96.

Validity: Classification rate for abusers is 94%. Eight subscales correlate between .19 and .34 with abuse (all significant, p<.05 or .01); .15 to .26 with neglect (7 of 8 significant, p<.05 or .01); and .10 to .29 with failure to thrive (3 of 8 significant p<.01).

Author: Milner, J.S. et al.

Article: Predictive validity of the child abuse potential inventory.

Journal: *Journal of Consulting and Clinical Psychology*, Oct. 1984, *52*(5), 879-884.

Related research: Milner, J.S., 1980. *The Child Abuse Potential Inventory Manual*. Webster, NC: Psytec Corporation.

3351
Test name: CHILD STIMULUS SCREENING SCALE

Purpose: To assess temperament.

Number of items: 46

Format: For children 3 months to 7 years. Employs a 9-point rating scale.

Reliability: Kuder-Richardson coefficient = .82 (N = 157).

Validity: Correlations with other measures ranged from r = -.42 to r = .54.

Author: Hubert, N.C. et al.

Article: The study of early temperament: Measurement and conceptual issues.

Journal: *Child Development*, June 1982, 53(3), 571-600.

Related research: Mehrabian, A. and Falander, C., 1978. A questionnaire measure of individual differences in child stimulus screening. *Educational and Psychological Measurement*, 38, 1119-1127.

3352

Test name: COLORADO CHILDHOOD TEMPERAMENT INVENTORY

Purpose: To assess temperament.

Number of items: 30

Format: Includes the following content: sociability, emotionality, activity, attention span-persistence, reaction to food, soothability.

Reliability: Test-retest correlation coefficients ranged from r = .43 to r = .80 (1 week) (N = 31 twins). Alphas ranged from .73 to .88.

Author: Hubert, N.C. et al.

Article: The study of early temperament: Measurement and conceptual issues.

Journal: *Child Development*, June 1982, 53(3), 571-600.

Related research: Rowe, D.C. and Plomin, R., 1977. Temperament in early childhood. *Journal of Personality Assessment*, 41, 150-156.

3353

Test name: COUNSELOR RATING FORM

Purpose: To measure the interviewer's perception of the student's persuasiveness.

Number of items: 12

Format: Includes the dimensions of: expertness, attractiveness, and trustworthiness. A semantic differential with 7-point items.

Reliability: Split-half reliabilities ranged from .84 to .90.

Author: Wild, B.K. and Kerr, B.A.

Article: Training adolescent job-seekers in persuasion skills.

Journal: *Vocational Guidance Quarterly*, Sept. 1984, 33(1), 63-69.

Related research: Barak, A. and LaCrosse, M.B., 1977. Comparative perception of practicum counselor behavior: A process and methodological investigation.

Counselor Education and Supervision, 16, 202-208.

3354
Test name: DAYDREAM ASSESSMENT QUESTIONNAIRE

Purpose: To rate daydreams.

Number of items: 7

Format: All items except two are in Likert-scale form. All items are presented.

Reliability: Inter-judge reliability for each item ranged from .36 to .91.

Author: Ireland, M.S. and Kernan-Schloss, L.

Article: Pattern analysis of recorded daydreams, memories and personality types.

Journal: *Perceptual and Motor Skills,* Feb. 1983, *56*(1), 119-125.

Related research: Starker, S., 1973. Aspects of inner experience: Autokinesis, daydreaming, dream recall and cognitive style. *Perceptual and Motor Skills, 36,* 663-673.

3355
Test name: DEFENSE MECHANISMS INVENTORY

Purpose: To determine characteristic coping mechanisms employed by individuals when faced with a series of conflict situations.

Number of items: 40

Format: Scores are derived for the relative usage of five major groups of defenses. Subjects indicate how they would respond if faced with each of the 10 conflicts.

Validity: Correlations with the percent of menstrual complaints ranged from -.350 to .487. Correlations with the sum of menstrual complaints ranged from -.220 to .168.

Author: Greenberg, R.P. and Fisher, S.

Article: Menstrual discomfort, psychological defenses and feminine identification.

Journal: *Journal of Personality Assessment,* Dec. 1984, *48*(6), 643-648.

Related research: Gleser, G.C. and Ihilevich, D., 1969. An objective instrument for measuring defense mechanisms. *Journal of Consulting and Clinical Psychology, 33,* 51-60.

3356
Test name: DIMENSIONS OF TEMPERAMENT SURVEY

Purpose: To assess the dimensions of temperamental individuality across the life span.

Number of items: 34

Format: Includes five factors: activity level, attention span/distractibility, adaptability/approach-withdrawal, rhythmicity, and reactivity.

Reliability: Test-retest reliability ranged from .60 to .93.

Author: Lerner, R.M. et al.

Article: Assessing the dimensions of temperamental individuality across the life span: The Dimensions of Temperament Survey (DOTS).

Journal: *Child Development*, Feb. 1982, 53(1), 149-159.

Related research: Thomas, A. and Chess, S. The role of temperament in the contributions of individuals to their development. In R.M. Lerner and N.A. Busch-Rossnagel (Eds.), 1981. *Individuals as producers of their development: A life-span perspective*. New York: Academic Press.

3357
Test name: EASI-I TEMPERAMENT SURVEY

Purpose: To assess temperament.

Number of items: 20

Format: For children 1-9 years. Includes the following categories: emotionality, activity, sociability, impulsivity.

Reliability: Test-retest correlation coefficients ranged from r = .75 to r = .92 (N = 20), r = .59 to .68 (21 days) (N = 27). Alphas ranged from .69 to .76 (N = 66).

Author: Hubert, N.C. et al.

Article: The study of early temperament: Measurement and conceptual issues.

Journal: *Child Development*, June 1982, 53(3), 571-600.

Related research: Buss, A.H. et al., 1973. The inheritance of temperament. *Journal of Personality*, 4, 513-524.

3358
Test name: EASI-III TEST

Purpose: To measure temperament.

Number of items: 57

Format: Includes the following scales: emotionality, activity, sociability, and impulsivity. This latter scale was further divided into a planning scale.

Reliability: Alpha reliabilities for the scales ranged from .65 to .81.

Author: Harburg, E. et al.

Article: Handedness and temperament.

Journal: *Perceptual and Motor Skills*, Feb. 1981, *52*(1), 283-290.

Related research: Buss, A.H. and Plomin, R., 1974. *A temperament theory of personality development.* New York: Wiley.

3359
Test name: EGO INVOLVEMENT SCALE

Purpose: To measure subjective relevance regarding the areas of achievement and interpersonal contact.

Number of items: 25

Format: 6-point Likert format. All items presented.

Reliability: Alpha ranged from .76 to .86 in two subscales (interpersonal contact and achievement).

Validity: Males and females do not differ ($F_{1,102}$ = .63, p<.80) and both sexes assign greater revelance to interpersonal contact than to achievement (p<.01).

Author: Krahé, B.

Article: Self-serving biases in perceived similarity and causal attributions of other people's performance.

Journal: *Social Psychology Quarterly*, Dec. 1983, *46*(4), 318-329.

3360
Test name: EGO PERMISSIVENESS QUESTIONNAIRE

Purpose: To measure the relative amount of ego energy.

Number of items: 50

Format: Includes five subscales: peak experience, dissociated experiences, openness to experience, belief in the supernatural, and intrinsic arousal. Range of scores is from 0 to 200.

Reliability: Test-retest reliability ranged from .20 to .50. Coefficient alpha was .87 (N = 120).

Validity: Correlation with TAT Expression scores was r = .40.

Author: Daly, E.B.

Article: Relationship of stress and ego energy to field-dependent perception in older adults.

Journal: *Perceptual and Motor Skills*, Dec. 1984, *59*(3), 919-926.

Related research: Taft, R., 1970. Measurement of the dimension of ego permissiveness. *Personality: An International Journal*, *1*, 163-184.

3361
Test name: EXPRESSION OF EMOTION SCALE

Purpose: To measure the extent to which each of four different types of emotions are expressed.

Number of items: 16

Format: Includes emotions of: love, hate, happiness, and sadness. Responses are made on Likert-scale from 1 (never) to 4 (very often).

Reliability: Test-retest reliability was .83 (1 week with N = 34), and .72 (6 weeks with N = 33).

Author: Dosser, D.A., Jr. et al.

Article: Situational context of emotional expressiveness.

Journal: *Journal of Counseling Psychology*, July 1983, *30*(3), 375-387.

Related research: Davidson, B. et al., 1983. Affective self-disclosure and marital adjustment: A test of equity theory. *Journal of Marriage and the Family*, 45, 93-102.

3362
Test name: INFANT BEHAVIOR QUESTIONNAIRE

Purpose: To assess temperament.

Number of items: 87

Format: For infants 3 to 12 months. Includes 6 scales: activity level, smiling and laughing, distress to limitations, fear, soothability, duration of orienting.

Reliability: Test-retest correlation coefficients ranged from r = -.02 to r = .74 (3-12 months) (N = 36-105), r = -.14 to r = .81 (3-12 months) (N = 36). Alphas ranged from .63 to .88 (N = 464).

Author: Hubert, N.C. et al.

Article: The study of early temperament: Measurement and conceptual issues.

Journal: *Child Development*, June 1982, *53*(3), 571-600.

Related research: Rothbart, M., 1981. Measure of temperament in infancy. *Child Development*, 52, 569-578.

3363
Test name: INFANT CHARACTERISTICS QUESTIONNAIRE

Purpose: To assess temperament.

Number of items: 24

Format: For infants 4-6 months. Includes the following categories: activity level, rhythmicity, approach/withdrawal, adaptability, intensity, sensory threshold, mood, distractibility, attention span/persistence, fussiness, sociability, changeability, and soothability.

Reliability: Test-retest correlation coefficients ranged from r = .47 to r = .70 (1 month) (N = 112). Alphas ranged from .39 to .79 (N = 196).

Validity: Correlations with other measures ranged from r = -.25 to r = .40.

Author: Hubert, N.C. et al.

Article: The study of early temperament: Measurement and conceptual issues.

Journal: *Child Development*, June 1982, *53*(3), 571-600.

Related research: Bates, J. et al., 1979. Measurement of infant difficultness. *Child Development, 50,* 794-803.

3364
Test name: INFANT TEMPERAMENT QUESTIONNAIRE

Purpose: To assess temperament.

Number of items: 70

Format: For infants 3 1/2 to 8 1/2 months. Includes 9 categories: activity level, rhythmicity, approach/withdrawal, adaptability, intensity, sensory threshold, mood, distractibility, attention span/persistence.

Reliability: Test-retest reliability coefficients (2 weeks to 5 months) ranged from r = .27 to r = .93 (N ranged from 20 to 151).

Validity: Correlations with: Infant Characteristics Questionnaire ranged from -.06 to .22; with Bayley mental series r = .58 (N = 12). Teacher-rated adjustment scores r = .42; with mother's mood r = .28 (N = 132).

Author: Hubert, N.C. et al.

Article: The study of early temperament: Measurement and conceptual issues.

Journal: *Child Development*, June 1982, *53*(3), 571-600.

Related research: Carey, W.B., 1970. A simplified method for measuring infant temperament. *Journal of Pediatrics, 77,* 188-194.

3365
Test name: INFANT TEMPERAMENT QUESTIONNAIRE

Purpose: To provide infant temperament ratings.

Number of items: 70

Time required: Approximately 20 minutes.

Format: Includes the following scales: activity, rhythmicity, adaptability, approach, threshold, intensity, mood, distractibility, and persistence.

Reliability: Cronbach's alphas ranged from .20 to .67.

Validity: Correlations with observed behavior ranged from -.26 to .17.

Author: Sameroff, A.J. et al.

Article: Sociocultural variability in infant temperament ratings.

Journal: *Child Development*, Feb. 1982, *53*(1), 164-173.

Related research: Carey, W.B., 1972. Measuring infant temperament. *Journal of Pediatrics*, *81*, 414.

3366
Test name: MANAGING PEOPLE INVENTORY

Purpose: To assess trust and respect.

Number of items: 26

Format: Responses to each item were either "usually true," or "not usually true." All items are presented.

Reliability: KR-20 estimates were .937 and .927.

Validity: Correlations with a criterion item were .796 and .783.

Author: Drehmer, D.E. and Grossman, J.H.

Article: Scaling managerial respect: A developmental perspective.

Journal: *Educational and Psychological Measurement*, autumn 1984, *44*(3), 763-767.

3367
Test name: NEED FOR COGNITION SCALE

Purpose: To assess individual differences in need for cognition.

Number of items: 18

Format: All items are presented.

Reliability: Theta coefficient was .90 (N = 527).

Author: Cacioppo, J.T. et al.

Article: The efficient assessment of need for cognition.

Journal: *Journal of Personality Assessment*, June 1984, *48*(3), 306-307.

Related research: Cacioppo, J.T. and Petty, R.E., 1982. The need for cognition. *Journal of Personality and Social Psychology*, *42*, 116-131.

3368
Test name: OFFICE ATTITUDE QUESTIONNAIRE

Purpose: To assess tendencies to be a "power seeker" or "politician" in the office.

Number of items: 50

Format: "Mostly true" to "mostly false" format.

Reliability: Alpha = .90. Split-half = .88.

Author: Biberman, G.

Article: Personality and characteristic work attitudes of persons with high, moderate, and low political tendencies.

Journal: *Psychological Reports*, Dec. 1985, 57(3-II), 1303-1310.

Related research: Dubrin, A.J., 1981. Winning at office politics: 50 questions to help you play like a pro. *Success*, 46, 26-28.

3369

Test name: OPEN PROCESSING STYLE SCALE

Purpose: To measure the "open processing" cognitive style.

Number of items: 24

Format: 5-point descriptive verbal anchors for each of 12 "open" and 12 "cautious" styles.

Reliability: KR-8 = .82. Test-retest = .72.

Author: Joseph, W.B.

Article: Receivers' open processing style as a moderator of communications persuasiveness.

Journal: *Psychological Reports*, June 1983, 52(3), 963-967.

Related research: Walton, J. et al., 1978. Validation of the consumer creativity scale. Proceedings of the 86th annual convention of the American Psychological Association, Division 23, pp. 47-48.

3370

Test name: PARENT TEMPERAMENT QUESTIONNAIRE

Purpose: To assess temperament.

Number of items: 72

Format: For children 3 to 7 years. Includes 9 categories: activity level, rhythmicity, approach/withdrawal, adaptability, intensity, sensory threshold, mood, distractibility, attention span/persistence.

Reliability: Estimate ranged from r = .15 to r = .74 (N = 126).

Validity: Correlations between: mother and teacher ranged from -.08 to .31; between father and teacher ranged from -.02 to .34.

Author: Hubert, N.C. et al.

Article: The study of early temperament: Measurement and conceptual issues.

Journal: *Child Development*, June 1982, 53(3), 571-600.

Related research: Thomas, A. and Chess, S., 1971. *Temperament and development*, New York: Brunner/Mazel.

3371
Test name: PERSONAL STYLE INVENTORY

Purpose: To measure Jungian personality types.

Number of items: 32

Format: Bipolar items.

Reliability: Values of -1.00 take the opposite side of each scale (multitrait-multimethod).

Validity: Validity coefficients ranged from .52 to .70.

Author: Ware, R. et al.

Article: A preliminary study to assess validity of the personal style inventory.

Journal: *Psychological Reports*, June 1985, 56(3), 903-910.

3372
Test name: PSYCHOLOGICAL INVENTORY OF PERSONALITY AND SYMPTOMS

Purpose: To assess personality and symptoms of individuals.

Number of items: 346

Format: Built from descriptors and criteria of the DSM-III.

Reliability: Test-retest (1 week) ranged from .62 to .93.

Validity: No significant differences between ratings of 3 attending clinicians.

Author: Vincent, K.R.

Article: Rated clinical utility of the Psychological Inventory of Personality and Symptoms.

Journal: *Psychological Reports*, June 1985, 56(3), 847-850.

Related research: McMurrey, A.D. and Vincent, K.R., 1985. Reliability of the Psychological Inventory of Personality and Symptoms. *Psychological Reports*, 56, 902.

3373
Test name: POST COLLEGE EXPERIENCE INVENTORY

Purpose: To measure individual life experiences 3-4 years after college graduation.

Number of items: 97

Reliability: KR-20 ranged from .50 to .85 over 12 factors (median = .64).

Validity: Four factors differentiated males (p<.01), three factors differentiated females (p<.05).

Author: Davis, K.R., Jr.

Article: A longitudinal analysis of biographical subgroups using Owens' developmental-integrative model.

Journal: *Personnel Behavior*, spring 1984, *37*(1), 1-14.

Related research: Davis, K.R., 1978. *Biographical correlates of post-college experience*. Doctoral dissertation, University of Georgia. *Dissertation Abstract International*, *38*, 3940B.

3374
Test name: PUPIL EVALUATION INVENTORY

Purpose: To provide an instrument for peer assessment.

Number of items: 35

Format: Includes 3 factors: Likeability, aggression, and withdrawal.

Reliability: Test-retest (8 weeks) reliability coefficients ranged from .70 to .93.

Validity: Correlations with other variables ranged from -.74 to .83.

Author: Vogel, J. et al.

Article: Comparability of peer-assessment measures: A multitrait-multimethod and selection analytic approach.

Journal: *Journal of Psychopathology and Behavioral Assessment*, Dec. 1985, *7*(4), 385-396.

Related research: Pekarik, E.G. et al., 1976. The pupil evaluation inventory. *Journal of Child Psychology*, *4*, 93-97.

3375
Test name: REVISED INFANT TEMPERAMENT QUESTIONNAIRE

Purpose: To assess temperament.

Number of items: 95

Format: For infants 4 to 8 months. Includes 9 categories: activity level, rhythmicity, approach/withdrawal, adaptability, intensity, sensory threshold, mood, distractibility, attention span/persistence.

Reliability: Test-retest reliability coefficients (25.1 days) ranged from r = .66 to r = .81 (N = 41).

Validity: Correlations with: Piagetian sensorimotor development r = .58 (N = 100); a variety of factors' r's ranged from -.66 to .46 (N = 29).

Author: Hubert, N.C. et al.

Article: The study of early temperament: Measurement and conceptual issues.

Journal: *Child Development*, June 1982, *53*(3), 571-600.

Related research: Carey, W.B. and McDevitt, S.C., 1978. Revision of the Infant Temperament Questionnaire. *Pediatrics, 61,* 735-739.
Field, T. and Greenberg, R., 1982. Temperament ratings by parents and teachers of infants, toddlers, and preschool children. *Child Development*, *53*(1), 160-163.

3376
Test name: SELF-CONSCIOUSNESS SCALE

Purpose: To measure self-consciousness.

Number of items: 23

Format: Includes four factors: social anxiety, public self-consciousness, self-reflectiveness, internal state awareness. Responses to each item are made on a 5-point scale from "extremely characteristic" (0) to "extremely uncharacteristic" (4). All items are presented.

Reliability: Cronbach's alphas ranged from .71 to .79.

Author: Burnkrant, R.E. and Page, T.J., Jr.

Article: A modification of the Fenigstein, Scheier, and Buss self-consciousness scales.

Journal: *Journal of Personality Assessment*, Dec. 1984, *48*(6), 629-637.

Related research: Fenigstein, A. et al., 1975. Public and private self-consciousness: Assessment and theory. *Journal of Consulting and Clinical Psychology*, *43*, 522-527.

3377
Test name: SERVICE ORIENTATION INDEX FOR NURSES AIDES

Purpose: To measure the disposition to be helpful, thoughtful, considerate, and co-operative (for nursing aides).

Number of items: 92

Reliability: Internal consistency = .81.

Validity: Correlated .42 with overall job performance; .22 with communications skills; .20 with relational skills; .23 with working under pressure.

Author: Hogan, J. et al.

Article: How to measure service orientation.

Journal: *Journal of Applied Psychology*, Feb. 1984, *69*(1), 167-173.

Related research: Hogan, R.A., socioanalytic theory of personality. In M. Page (Ed.), 1983, *Nebraska Symposium on Motivation*. Lincoln, NE: University of Nebraska Press.

3378
Test name: SWEDISH SIX-MONTH TEMPERAMENT QUESTIONNAIRE

Purpose: To assess temperament.

Number of items: 41

Format: For children 5-8 months. Includes 9 categories: activity level, rhythmicity, approach/withdrawal, adaptability, intensity, sensory threshold, mood, distractibility, attention span/persistence.

Reliability: Test-retest reliability coefficients (2 to 3 weeks) ranged from r = .40 to r = .86 (N = 14).

Author: Hubert, N.C. et al.

Article: The study of early temperament: Measurement and conceptual issues.

Journal: *Child Development*, June 1982, *53*(3), 571-600.

Related research: Persson-Blennow, I. and McNeil, T., 1979. A questionnaire for measurement of temperament in six-month-old infants: Development and standardization. *Journal of Child Psychology and Psychiatry and Allied Disciplines*, *20*, 1-13.

3379
Test name: SWEDISH TEMPERAMENT QUESTIONNAIRE

Purpose: To assess temperament.

Number of items: 55 at 12 months, 50 at 24 months.

Format: For infants 12 and 24 months old. Includes 9 categories: activity level, rhythmicity, approach/withdrawal, adaptability, intensity, sensory threshold, mood, distractibility, attention span/persistence.

Reliability: For 12-month-olds, test-retest correlation coefficients ranged from .05 to .84 (3-6 weeks) (N = 11). For 24-month-olds coefficients ranged from .00 to .95 (2-4 weeks) (N = 11).

Author: Hubert, N.C. et al.

Article: The study of early temperament: Measurement and conceptual issues.

Journal: *Child Development*, June 1982, *53*(3), 571-600.

Related research:
Persson-Blennow, I. and McNeil, T., 1980. Questionnaire for measurement of temperament in one and two year old children. *Journal of Child Psychology and Psychiatry, 21,* 37-46.

3380
Test name: TEACHER TEMPERAMENT QUESTIONNAIRE

Purpose: To assess temperament.

Number of items: 64

Format: For children 3 to 7 years. Includes 8 categories: activity level, approach/withdrawal, adaptability, intensity, sensory threshold, mood, distractibility, attention span/persistence.

Reliability: Ranged from r = .69 to r = .87 (N = 10).

Validity: Correlations with Behavioral Styles Questionnaire ranged from r = .18 to r = .46 (N = 78).

Author: Hubert, N.C. et al.

Article: The study of early temperament: Measurement and conceptual issues.

Journal: *Child Development,* June 1982, *53*(3), 571-600.

Related research: Thomas, A. and Chess, S., 1977. *Temperament and development.* New York: Brunner/Mazel.

3381
Test name: TEACHER TEMPERAMENT QUESTIONNAIRE—SHORT FORM

Purpose: To assess teacher' perceptions of children's temperament.

Number of items: 23

Format: Includes 3 factors: task orientation, personal-social flexibility, and reactivity.

Reliability: Alpha coefficients for the three factors were .94, .88, .62, respectively.

Author: Keogh, B.K. et al.

Article: A short form of the Teacher Temperament Questionnaire.

Journal: *Journal of Educational Measurement,* winter 1982, *19*(4), 323-329.

Related research: Pullis, M.E., 1982. *An investigation of the relationship between children, temperament and school adjustment.* Unpublished doctoral dissertation, University of California, Los Angeles.

3382
Test name: THEMATIC APPERCEPTION TEST FOR URBAN HISPANIC CHILDREN

Purpose: To measure thematic apperception.

Number of items: 23 pictures.

Format: Sample pictures presented. Stories told to bilingual interns in either English or Spanish.

Reliability: Inter-rater agreement achieved .80 after training.

Validity: R^2 = .32 to .51 with measures of ego development, trait anxiety, and adaptive behavior.

Author: Malgady, R.G. et al.

Article: Development of a thematic apperception test (TEMAS) for urban Hispanic children.

Journal: *Journal of Consulting and Clinical Psychology*, Dec. 1984, 52(6), 986-996.

Related research: Constantino, G. and Malgady, R., 1983. Verbal fluency of Hispanic, black and white children on TAT and TEMAS. *Hispanic Journal of Behavioral Sciences*, 5, 291-300.

3383
Test name: THERAPEUTIC TALENT INDEX

Purpose: To measure acceptingness, understanding, and openness.

Format: 6-point Likert categories. Sample items presented.

Reliability: Cronbach's alpha = .76.

Validity: Correlated significantly with love (.25), dominance (.28), aggressive-sadistic (-.24), and distrust (-.30), (p<.05).

Author: Jackson, E.

Article: Interpersonal traits and facilitative helping characteristics.

Journal: *Psychological Reports*, Dec. 1985, 57(3-I), 995-999.

Related research: Goodman, G, 1972. *Companionship Therapy*. San Francisco, CA: Jossey-Bass.

3384
Test name: TODDLER BEHAVIOR QUESTIONNAIRE

Purpose: To measure temperament.

Number of items: 60

Format: Includes 8 factors: intensity/activity, regularity, approach/withdrawal, sensory sensitivity, attentiveness, manageability, sensitivity to new foods, adaptability.

Reliability: Test-retest reliability coefficients ranged from r = .64 to r = .87 (N = 26). Alphas ranged from .59 to .77 (N = 357).

Author: Hubert, N.C. et al.

Article: The study of early temperament: Measurement and conceptual issues.

Journal: *Child Development*, June 1982, 53(3), 571-600.

Related research: Hagekull, B. et al., 1980. Behavioral dimensions in one year olds and dimensional stability in infancy. *International Journal of Behavioral Development*, 3, 351-364.

3385
Test name: TODDLER TEMPERAMENT SCALE

Purpose: To measure toddler temperament.

Number of items: 97

Format: Each item was rated on a 6-point scale. All items were combined into nine temperament categories: activity level, rhythmicity, approach/withdrawal, adaptability, intensity of reaction, quality of mood, attention span and persistence, distractibility, threshold of responsiveness.

Reliability: Median test-retest correlation for the nine scales was .81.

Author: Matheny, A.P., Jr. et al.

Article: Toddler temperament: Stability across settings and over ages.

Journal: *Child Development*, Aug. 1984, 55(4), 1200-1211.

Related research: Rullard, W. et al., 1984. Assessing temperament in one to three year old children. *Journal of Pediatric Psychology*.

Field, T. and Greenberg, R., 1982. Temperament ratings by parents and teachers of infants, toddlers and preschool children. *Child Development*, 53(1), 160-163.

Hubert, N.C. et al., 1982. The study of early temperament: Measurement and conceptual issues. *Child Development*, 53(3), 571-600.

3386
Test name: WHAT ABOUT YOU

Purpose: To evaluate personality and biographical traits of creative people.

Number of items: 87

Format: Responses are recorded on a five-point rating scale from "no" to "definitely."

Reliability: Hoyt internal reliability was .95.

Validity: Correlations with other variables ranged from .15 to .73.

Author: Buckmaster, L.R. and Davis, G.A.

Article: ROSE: A measure of self-actualization and its relationship to creativity.

Journal: *Journal of Creative Behavior*, 1985, *19*(1), 30-37.

Related research: Davis, G.A. and Bull, K.S., 1978. Strengthening affective components of creativity in a college course. *Journal of Educational Psychology, 70,* 833-836.

3387
Test name: WIGGINS PERSONALITY INVENTORY

Purpose: To assess self-rated personality.

Number of items: 128

Format: 8-point self-applicability scales.

Reliability: Reliabilities of eight subscales all greater than .80.

Author: Gifford, R.

Article: Projected interpersonal distance and orientation choices: Personality, sex, and social situations.

Journal: *Social Psychology Quarterly*, Sept. 1982, *44*(3), 145-152.

Related research: Wiggins, J.S., 1979. A psychological taxonomy of trait-descriptive terms: The interpersonal domain. *Journal of Personality and Social Psychology, 37,* 395-412.

PREFERENCE

3388
Test name: ACTIVITY PREFERENCE SCALE

Purpose: To identify activity preference.

Number of items: 170

Format: Items consist of randomly ordered pairs of skilled and chance activities.

Reliability: Uncorrected split-half reliabilities ranged from .85 to .89.

Validity: Correlation with the Rotter I-E Scale was r = .19.

Author: Harris, R.M., Jr. and Salomone, P.R.

Article: Toward an abbreviated internal-external locus of control scale.

Journal: *Measurement and Evaluation in Guidance,* Jan. 1981, *13*(4), 229-234.

Related research: Schneider, J.H., 1968. Skill versus chance activity preference and locus of control. *Journal of Consulting and Clinical Psychology, 32,* 333-337.

3389
Test name: BEM SEX-ROLE INVENTORY

Purpose: To measure sex-role orientation.

Number of items: 54

Reliability: Coefficient alphas ranged from .80 to .86.

Validity: Correlations with the: Intellectual Achievement Responsibility Questionnaire ranged from -.41 to .56 (N's ranged from 12 to 404); with Fear of Success Scale ranged from -.37 to .33 (N's ranged from 12 to 404); with sex ranged from .30 to .56 (N's ranged from 26 to 404).

Author: Ireland-Galman, M.M. and Michael, W.B.

Article: The relationship of a measure of the fear of success construct to scales representing the locus of control and sex-role orientation constructs for a community college sample.

Journal: *Educational and Psychological Measurement,* winter 1983, *43*(4), 1217-1225.

Related research: Bem, S.L, 1974. The measurement of psychological androgyny. *Journal of Consulting and Clinical Psychology, 42,* 155-162.

3390
Test name: CHOICE-MONITOR SCALE

Purpose: To measure intrinsic and extrinsic reasons for making choices.

Number of items: 20

Format: Subjects select one of two choices (vocational or activity and check a reason for making it from among 10 alternatives, half extrinsic and half intrinsic).

Reliability: Cronbach's alpha = .65.

Author: Tzuriel, D. and Haywood, H.C.

Article: Locus of control and child-rearing practices in intrinsically motivated and extrinsically motivated children.

Journal: *Psychological Reports*, Dec. 1985, 57(3-I), 887-894.

Related research: Hamlin, R.M. and Nemo, R.S., 1962. Self-actualization in choice scores of improved schizophrenics. *Journal of Clinical Psychology*, 18, 51-54.

3391
Test name: COGNITIVE PREFERENCE READING INSTRUMENT

Purpose: To measure degree of preference for four cognitive modes.

Number of items: 15 paragraphs.

Format: Students indicate the most and least interesting sentences in paragraphs. Sentences written to be easily classified into four cognitive modes.

Reliability: Split-half reliability ranged from .60 to .71.

Validity: Correlations with an alternative cognitive preference measure ranged from .04 to .43.

Author: van den Berg, E. et al.

Article: Index of distinctness: A measure of the intensity of cognitive preferences.

Journal: *Journal of Educational Research*, March/April 1982, 75(4), 197-203.

Related research: van den Berg, E. et al., 1982. The convergent validity of the cognitive preference construct. *Journal of Research in Science Teaching*, 19(5), 337-350.

3392
Test name: COUNSELOR PREFERENCE QUESTIONNAIRE

Purpose: To assess black students' preferences for counselors of their own race.

Number of items: 19

Format: Likert-type.

Reliability: Kuder-Richardson 20 = .85.

Validity: 13 of 17 expert judges had to approve items.

Author: Abott, K. et al.

Article: Counselor race as a factor in counselor preference.

Journal: *Journal of College Student Personnel*, Jan. 1982, 23(1), 36-40.

3393
Test name: EDUCATIONAL ORIENTATION QUESTIONNAIRE

Purpose: To measure and rate characteristics of educational orientation in working with adults.

Number of items: 60

Format: Agreement scale.

Reliability: Test-retest (2 weeks) = .89. Alpha = .94. Item-total correlations ranged from .27 to .40 across subscales.

Author: Hyman, R.B. and Top, D.

Article: Effects of andragogical educational experience on andragogical orientation of nurses.

Journal: *Psychological Reports*, Dec. 1984, 55(3), 829-830.

Related research: Hadley, H.N, 1975. Development of an instrument to determine adult educators' orientation - Andragogical or Pedagogical. Doctoral dissertation, Boston University. *Dissertation Abstracts International*, 35, 75955. University microfilm No. 75-12, 228.

3394
Test name: ENDEMIC IMAGERY QUESTIONNAIRE

Purpose: To measure the appeal of relaxing images and scenes.

Number of items: 10

Format: 5-point Likert response categories. All items presented.

Reliability: Test-retest = .79 (2-week interval).

Author: Saigh, P.A. and Antoun, F.T.

Article: Endemic images and the desensitization process.

Journal: *Journal of School Psychology*, 1984, 22(2), 177-184.

Related research: Saigh, P.A., 1980. The use of endemic images as a means of inducing relaxation and desensitization. *Mediterranean Journal of Social Psychiatry*, 1, 11-16.

3395
Test name: EQUITY SENSITIVITY INSTRUMENT

Purpose: To tap an individual's preference for outcomes versus inputs in a general work situation.

Number of items: 5

Format: Respondents address each item by distributing 10 points between an entitled response and a benevolent response.

Reliability: Coefficient alpha was .83.

Validity: Correlations with other variables ranged from r = -.10 to r = .20.

Author: Huseman, R.C. et al.

Article: Test for individual perception of job equity: Some preliminary findings.

Journal: *Perceptual and Motor Skills*, Dec. 1985, *61*(3-II), 1055-1064.

3396
Test name: FOOD PREFERENCE SURVEY

Purpose: To measure attitudes toward trying new foods.

Number of items: 13

Format: 5-point Likert response categories. Sample items presented.

Reliability: Alpha = .86.

Validity: Correlated .62 (p<.001) with willingness to try unfamiliar food.

Author: Otis, L.P.

Article: Factors influencing the willingness to taste unusual foods.

Journal: *Psychological Reports*, June 1984, *54*(3), 739-745.

3397
Test name: IMAGERY DIFFERENCE QUESTIONNAIRE

Purpose: To determine students' preference for visual or verbal imagery.

Number of items: 54

Format: Items are forced-choice statements.

Reliability: Alpha coefficients were .74 and .72.

Author: Sheckles, M.P. and Eliot, J.

Article: Preference and solution patterns in mathematics performance.

Journal: *Perceptual and Motor Skills*, Dec. 1983, *57*(3-I), 811-816.

Related research: Paivio, A., 1971. *Imagery and verbal processes*. New York: Holt, Rinehart & Winston.

3398
Test name: INSTITUTIONAL/GOAL COMMITMENT

Purpose: To measure importance of college to freshmen.

Number of items: 6

Format: Likert-type items.

Reliability: Alpha = .71.

Author: Pascarella, E.T. and Terenzini, P.T.

Article: Contextual analysis as a method for assessing resident group effects.

Journal: *Journal of College Student Personnel*, March 1982, *23*(2), 108-114.

Related research: Pascarella, E.T. and Terenzini, P.T., 1980. Predicting persistence and voluntary dropout decisions from a theoretical model. *Journal of Higher Education*, *51*, 60-75.

3399
Test name: INTENTION TO SUPPORT UNION SCALE

Purpose: To measure favorable intentions to faculty union membership.

Number of items: 28

Format: 5-point agreement scales (7 items), 7-point bipolar evaluative scales (2 items), 3-point bipolar scales, and 5-point change scale (19 items).

Reliability: Internal consistency ranged from .87 to .88 across two subscales (one reliability not reported).

Author: Zalesny, M.D.

Article: Comparison of economic and noneconomic factors in predicting faculty veto preference in a union representation election.

Journal: *Journal of Applied Psychology*, May 1985, *70*(2), 243-256.

Related research: Terborg, J.R., 1982. University faculty dispositions toward unionization: A test of Triandis' model. Paper presented at the American Psychological Association meeting, Washington, D.C.

3400
Test name: INTERVENTION RATING PROFILE

Purpose: To assess acceptability of interventions.

Number of items: 20

Format: 6-point Likert categories ranging from strongly agree to strongly disagree.

Reliability: Cronbach's alpha = .91 (from previous study, see related research).

Author: Elliott, S.N. et al.

Article: Acceptability of positive and reductive behavioral interventions: Factors that influence teachers' decisions.

Journal: *Journal of School Psychology*, 1984, *22*(4), 353-360.

Related research: Witt, J.C. et al., 1983. Assessing the acceptability of behavioral interventions. *Psychology in the Schools*, *20*, 510-517.

3401
Test name: LEAST PREFERRED CO-WORKER SCALE

Purpose: To measure perception of least preferred co-workers.

Number of items: 8

Format: Bipolar adjective pairs. Sample items presented.

Reliability: Alpha = .85.

Author: Hoffman, E. and Roman, P.M.

Article: Criterion-related validity of the least preferred co-worker measure.

Journal: *Journal of Social Psychology*, Feb. 1984, *122*(first half), 79-84.

Related research: Fiedler, F.E., 1981. Leadership effectiveness. *American Behavior Science*, *24*, 619-632.

Hoffman, E., 1984. An internal dimensional analysis of the least preferred co-worker measure. *Journal of Social Psychology*, *123*, 35-42.

3402
Test name: LOGO SCALE

Purpose: To assess whether students are primarily oriented to learning (LO) or grades (GO).

Number of items: 12

Format: Two-point agree-disagree format. All items presented.

Reliability: Test-retest = .71 (6 weeks). Median item total = .48.

Validity: 34 of 36 students known to be one or the other of the two orientations could be placed in their correct group by LOGO scores.

Author: Eison, J.A.

Article: A new instrument for assessing students' orientations towards grades or learning.

Journal: *Psychological Reports*, June 1983, *48*(3), 919-924.

3403
Test name: MASCULINE GENDER IDENTITY SCALE

Purpose: To measure feminine identity.

Number of items: 20

Format: Multiple-choice. All items presented. Adapted from Feminine Gender Identity Scale.

Reliability: Alpha = .89.

Validity: Discriminates transsexual, homosexual, and heterosexual subjects (69% of subjects classified correctly).

Author: Blanchard, R. and Freund, K.

Article: Measuring masculine gender identity in females.

Journal: *Journal of Consulting and Clinical Psychology*, April 1983, *51*(2), 205-214.

Related research: Freund, K. et al., 1974. Extension of the Gender Identity Scale for Males. *Archives of Sexual Behavior*, *3*, 249-260.

3404
Test name: MIRENDA LEISURE INTEREST FINDER

Purpose: To identify leisure interests.

Number of items: 90

Format: Includes a mixture of activities: games, sports, nature, etc. Employs a 5-point scale from like very much (5) to dislike very much (1).

Reliability: Internal reliability of .87.

Author: McDowell, C.F. and Clark, P.

Article: Assessing the leisure needs of older persons.

Journal: *Measurement and Evaluation in Guidance*, Oct. 1982, *15*(3), 228-239.

Related research: Wilson, G.T. and Mirenda, J.J., 1975. The Milwaukee leisure counseling model. *Counseling and Values*, *20*, 42-46.

3405
Test name: PREFERENCE FOR JOB ENRICHMENT SCALE

Purpose: To measure willingness to have jobs changed and enriched.

Number of items: 6

Format: 6-point Likert format. Sample items presented.

Reliability: Alpha = .85.

Author: Holley, W.H. et al.

Article: Negotiating quality of worklife, productivity and traditional issues: Union members' preferred roles of their union.

Journal: *Personnel Psychology*, summer 1981, *34*(2), 309-328.

Related research: Hackman, J.R. and Lawler, E.E., 1971. Employee reactions to job characteristics. *Journal of Applied Psychology*, *16*, 259-286.

3406
Test name: PREFERRED INSTRUCTOR CHARACTERISTICS SCALE

Purpose: To disclose the level of personal-social or cognitive-intellectual preference students have for teacher behaviors.

Number of items: 36

Format: For each item students select one of two statements expressing a personal-social teacher behavior or a cognitive-intellectual teacher behavior. An example is presented.

Reliability: Test-retest reliability (4 weeks) was .88. Internal consistency reliability coefficient was .90.

Author: Dorhout, A.

Article: Student and teacher perceptions of preferred teacher behaviors among the academically gifted.

Journal: *Gifted Child Quarterly*, summer 1983, *27*(3), 122-125.

Related research: Krumholtz, J.D. and Faquhar, W.W., 1957. The effect of three teaching methods on achievement and motivation outcomes in a how-to-study course. *Psychological Monographs*, *71*(14), 1-26.

3407
Test name: RECREATION EXPERIENCE PREFERENCE SCALES

Purpose: To measure the need-satisfying properties of leisure activities.

Number of items: 82

Format: Includes 41 two-item scales grouped into 18 preference domains. A Likert format utilizing six response options from not important (1) to extremely important (6).

Reliability: Cronbach's alpha internal consistency reliability coefficient for 34 of the two-item scales ranged from .46 to .80.

Author: Tinsley, H.E.A. et al.

Article: Reliability and concurrent validity of the Recreation Experience Preference Scales.

Journal: *Educational and Psychological Measurement*, autumn 1982, *41*(3), 897-907.

Related research: Driver, B.L. and Cooksey, R., 1977. Preferred psychological outcomes of recreational fishing. Proceedings of the Catch-and-Release Fishing as a Management Tool. National Sport Fishing Symposium, Arcata, CA: Humboldt State University.

3408
Test name: ROLE CATEGORY QUESTIONNAIRE

Purpose: To measure cognitive complexity.

Number of items: 2

Format: Respondent writes a 5-minute essay describing a "liked" peer and a "disliked" peer. Descriptive constructs are counted and totalled from each essay.

Reliability: Inter-rater reliability exceeds .90.

Author: Capurso, R.J. and Blocher, D.H.

Article: The effects of sex-role consistent and inconsistent information on the social perceptions of complex, noncomplex, androgynous and sex-typed women.

Journal: *Journal of Vocational Behavior*, Feb. 1985, *26*(1), 79-91.

Related research: O'Keefe, D.J. and Sypher, H.E., 1980. *Cognitive complexity and communication: A critical review of alternative measures*. Unpublished manuscript, Department of Speech Communication, Pennsylvania State University.

3409
Test name: SCALE OF COUNSELING DIMENSION PREFERENCES

Purpose: To assess preferences of bereaved parents for counseling during difficult phases of grieving.

Number of items: 24

Format: Includes items dealing with: action orientation, insight orientation, cognition, conation, structure, and ambiguity.

Reliability: Inter-rater agreement for the 6 dimensions ranged from .83 to .94.

Author: Alexy, W.D.

Article: Dimensions of psychological counseling that facilitate the grieving process of bereaved parents.

Journal: *Journal of Counseling Psychology*, Sept. 1982, *29*(5), 498-507.

Related research: Bowlby, J., 1980. *Loss: Sadness and depression*. New York: Basic Books.

3410

Test name: SCIENCE COGNITIVE PREFERENCE INVENTORY

Purpose: To measure degree of preference for four cognitive modes.

Number of items: 30

Format: Four correct response statements to items are ranked and rated according to preference.

Reliability: Cronbach's alpha ranged from .26 to .90.

Validity: Correlations with an alternative measure of cognitive preference ranged from .04 to .43.

Author: van den Berg, E. et al.

Article: Index of distinctiveness: A measure of the intensity of cognitive preferences.

Journal: *Journal of Educational Research*, March/April 1982, 75(4), 197-203.

Related research: van den Berg, E. et al., 1982. The convergent validity of the cognitive preference construct. *Journal of Research in Science Teaching*, 19(5), 337-350.

3411

Test name: SEX-ROLE IDEOLOGY SCALE

Purpose: To measure prescriptive beliefs about appropriate behavior to men and women.

Number of items: 30

Format: 7-point Likert agreement-disagreement scale.

Reliability: Inter-item Cronbach's alpha (total scale) = .82. Cronbach's alphas across subscales ranged from .28 to .82.

Author: Milo, T. et al.

Article: Conceptual analysis of the Sex-Role Ideology Scale.

Journal: *Psychological Reports*, Aug. 1983, 53(1), 139-146.

Related research: Kalin, R. and Tilby, P., 1978. Development and validation of a Sex-Role Ideology Scale. *Psychological Reports*, 42, 731-738.

3412

Test name: SOCIAL BEHAVIOR INVENTORY—REVISED

Purpose: To measure preference for cooperation and competition by self-report.

Number of items: 25

Format: 5-point Likert type agree-disagree response categories. All items presented.

Reliability: Spearman-Brown reliability ranged from .77 to .78 over two factors.

Validity: Low but significant correlations found with mothers', fathers', and teachers' ratings of behavior and childrens ratings.

Author: Stockdale, D.F. et al.

Article: Cooperative-competitive preferences and behavioral correlates as a function of sex and age of school-age children.

Journal: *Psychological Reports*, Dec. 1983, 53(3-I), 739-750.

Related research: Galejs, I. and Stockdale, D.F., 1980. Cooperative preferences and locus of control of school-age children. *Home Economics Research Journal*, 8, 386-393.

3413
Test name: STUDENT-ATHLETE RECRUITMENT DECISION-MAKING SURVEY

Purpose: To measure importance student athletes attach to coach, campus, athletics, friends, and academics.

Number of items: 59

Format: 5-point Likert scales.

Reliability: Alphas: coach (.95), campus (.93), athletics (.83), friends (.75), academics (.83).

Author: Mathes, S. and Gurney, G.

Article: Factors in student athletes' choices of colleges.

Journal: *Journal of College Student Personnel*, July 1985, 26(4), 327-333.

Related research: Swaim, N.M., 1983. Factors influencing college basketball players to attend selected NCAA Division I colleges, NCAA Division II colleges or NAIA colleges or NCAA Division III colleges. Unpublished master's thesis, Iowa State University.

3414
Test name: TOY PREFERENCE TEST

Purpose: To measure children's sex-role preference.

Format: Consists of a booklet of pictures of toys and the child selects those with which the child would most like to play.

Reliability: Test-retest reliabilities ranged from .011 to .818.

Validity: Correlations with: mother's preference was .204 (daughter) and -.087 (son); father's preference was -.089 (daughter) and -.046 (son).

Author: Newman, R.C. and Carney, R.E.

Article: Cross-validation of sex-role measures for children with correlation of sex-role measures for children and parents.

Journal: *Perceptual and Motor Skills*, June 1981, 52(3), 883-890.

Related research: DeLucia, L.A., 1963. The toy preference test: A measure of sex-role identification. *Child Development*, 34, 107-117.

3415
Test name: UNIONISM SCALE

Purpose: To measure the value of union representation.

Number of items: 6

Format: 6-point agreement scales. All items presented.

Reliability: Internal consistency = .80.

Validity: Correlated .56 and .42 (p<.001) with direct questions about instrumentality of union as a mechanism for change.

Author: Hammer, T.H.

Article: Absenteeism when workers have a voice: The case of employee ownership.

Journal: *Journal of Applied Psychology*, Oct. 1981, 66(5), 561-573.

3416
Test name: VALANCE OF OUTCOMES SCALE

Purpose: To measure importance of instrumental outcomes.

Number of items: 13

Format: 5-point desirability scale.

Reliability: Alphas ranged from .79 to .87 for extrinsic and intrinsic items.

Validity: Does not correlate with pro-strike attitude or locus of control. Does correlate significantly with intention to join a union (r = .27).

Author: Beutell, N.J. and Biggs, D.L.

Article: Behavioral intentions to join a union: Instrumentality X valence, locus of control and strike attitudes.

Journal: *Psychological Reports*, Aug. 1984, 55(1), 215-222.

3417
Test name: WOLOWITZ FOOD PREFERENCE INQUIRY

Purpose: To measure food preferences.

Number of items: 103

Format: Items contrast food preferences (spicy vs. bland, sweet vs. sour, soft vs. hard).

Reliability: KR-20 = .62 for men (N = 73) and .74 for women (N = 122).

Validity: Correlates with orality (.27 for men, -.18 for women), but not for sadism (.10 for men, .13 for women).

Author: Juni, S.

Article: Food preference and orality.

Journal: *Psychological Reports*, June 1983, *52*(3), 842.

Related research: Wolowitz, H.M., 1964. Food preference as an index of orality. *Journal of Abnormal Social Psychology, 69*, 650-654.

PROBLEM-SOLVING AND REASONING

3418
Test name: ANALOGICAL REASONING TEST

Purpose: To measure analogical reasoning of kindergarten and first-grade children.

Number of items: 10

Format: Students supplied the missing word in each analogy. Each response was scored pass (1) or fail (0). Examples are presented.

Reliability: Coefficient alpha was .74.

Validity: Correlation with English proficiency ranged from .01 to .15.

Author: Diaz, R.M.

Article: Bilingual cognitive development: Addressing three gaps in current research.

Journal: *Child Development*, Dec. 1985, *56*(6), 1376-1388.

3419
Test name: ARLIN TEST OF FORMAL REASONING

Purpose: To measure formal reasoning.

Number of items: 42

Format: Consists of 4-response multiple-choice items and includes 9 classical types of thinking operations and schemata.

Reliability: Inter-rater reliabilities ranged from .52 to .97.

Validity: Construct validity coefficients ranged from .55 to .74. Correlations with predictor and criterion variables ranged from -.32 to .45 (N = 218) and -.32 to .47 (N = 259).

Author: Bloland, R.M. and Michael, W.B.

Article: A comparison of the relative validity of a measure of Piagetian cognitive development and a set of conventional prognostic measures in the prediction of the future success of ninth- and tenth-grade students in algebra.

Journal: *Educational and Psychological Measurement*, winter 1984, *44*(4), 925-943.

3420
Test name: BALANCE BEAM TEST

Purpose: To measure proportional reasoning.

Number of items: 16

Format: Multiple-choice.

Reliability: .75.

Author: Linn, M.C. and Swiney, J.F.

Article: Individual differences in formal thought: Role of expectations and aptitudes.

Journal: *Journal of Educational Psychology*, April 1981, 73(2), 274-286.

Related research: Linn, M.C. and Pulos, S., 1980. *Proportional reasoning during adolescence: The balance puzzle.* (Adolescent Reasoning Project, Rep. No. 25.) Berkeley, CA: The University of California, Lawrence Hall of Science.

3421
Test name: BIERI GRID

Purpose: To measure cognitive complexity.

Number of items: 10

Format: Semantic differential.

Reliability: Test-retest = .86.

Author: Wexley, K.N. and Youtz, M.A.

Article: Rater beliefs about others: Their effects on rating errors and rater accuracy.

Journal: *Journal of Occupational Psychology*, Dec. 1985, 58(4), 265-275.

Related research: Tripodi, T. and Bieri, J., 1963. Cognitive complexity as a function of own and provided constructs. *Psychological Reports*, 13, 26.

3422
Test name: COGNITIVE LATERALITY QUESTIONNAIRE

Purpose: To measure hemispheric dominance.

Number of items: 3 left and 3 right hemisphere tests.

Format: Varies by test -- all tests are described.

Reliability: Cronbach's alpha = .80 or more.

Validity: Correctly classifies 95% of brain damaged patients.

Author: Harpaz, I.

Article: Asymmetry of cognitive functioning as a possible predictor for vocational counseling and personnel classification.

Journal: *Journal of Vocational Behavior*, Dec. 1983, 23(3), 305-317.

Related research: Benton, S. and Gordon, H.W., 1979. Assessment of cognitive asymmetries in brain-damaged and normal subjects: Validation of a test battery. *Journal of Neurology, Neurosurgery and Psychiatry*, 42, 715-723.

3423
Test name: COGNITIVE PROCESS QUESTIONNAIRE

Purpose: To measure students' thought processes during periods of teaching-learning.

Number of items: 23

Format: 5-point response categories (usually to almost never, plus don't know). Sample items presented.

Reliability: Alpha - .71 (Alphas vary from .22 to .65 on subscales).

Author: Peterson, P.L. et al.

Article: Students' aptitudes and their reports of cognitive processes during direct instruction.

Journal: *Journal of Educational Psychology*, Aug. 1972, 74(4), 535-547.

3424
Test name: CONCEPTUAL LEVEL ANALOGY TEST

Purpose: To measure abstract reasoning predictive of morbidity and mortality following cardiac surgery.

Number of items: 41

Format: Multiple-choice.

Reliability: Point-biserial correlations between correct item response and total score were all significant (p<.05).

Validity: Significant differences by age, education, and occupation.

Author: Kelleher, W.J. and Townes, B.D.

Article: The conceptual level analogy test: Internal consistency and relationship to demographic variables.

Journal: *Psychological Reports*, June 1984, 54(3), 971-976.

3425
Test name: DECISION-MAKING STYLE SCALE (subscale of the ACDM)

Purpose: To measure how respondents make important decisions. Respondents choose between rational, intuitive, and dependent styles.

Number of items: 30

Format: Dichotomous agree-disagree. Sample items presented.

Reliability: Test-retest ranged from .76 to .85. Internal consistency ranged from .60 to .72.

Author: Phillips, S.D. et al.

Article: A factor analytic investigation of career decision-making styles.

Journal: *Journal of Vocational Behavior*, Feb. 1985, *26*(1), 106-115.

Related research: Harren, V.A., 1978. *Assessment of career decision-making* (ACDM): Counselor/Instructor Guide. Unpublished manuscript, Southern Illinois University.

3426
Test name: DEDUCTIVE/INDUCTIVE REASONING TESTS

Purpose: To measure deductive and inductive reasoning ability.

Number of items: 14 (7 deductive, 7 inductive).

Format: Multiple-choice. Sample items presented.

Reliability: KR-20 (deductive) = .45; KR-20 (inductive) = .42.

Validity: Correlations between each test with 11 other tests (reading, inference, tabular completion, letter series, figure analogies, judgement, logical order, computation, arithmetic reasoning) ranged from .23 to .62.

Author: Colberg, M. et al.

Article: Convergence of the inductive and deductive models in the measuring of reasoning abilities.

Journal: *Journal of Applied Psychology*, Nov. 1985, *70*(4), 681-694.

3427
Test name: FORMAL OPERATIONS ASSESSMENT BATTERY

Purpose: To measure logical reasoning skills.

Time required: 45 minutes.

Reliability: Cronbach's alpha = .83.

Validity: Correlates with Wechsler Intelligence Scale for children (.57 with full scale, .48 with verbal scale, and .24 with performance scale). Correlates .56 with Raven's Progressive Matrices.

Author: Lonky, E.

Article: Logical concept prerequisites to political development in adolescence.

Journal: *Psychological Reports*, Dec. 1983, *53*(3-I), 947-954.

Related research: Arnold, D. et al., 1980. The relationship of two measures of formal operations to psychometric intelligence. Paper presented at the annual meeting of the Eastern Psychological Association, Hartford, Conn.

3428

Test name: FORMAL OPERATIONAL REASONING TEST

Purpose: To assess a subject's comprehension of second-order operations which are used as barometers of formal thought.

Number of items: 25

Time required: 45 minutes.

Format: One sorting problem, 16 proportional logic items, and 8 proportionality items. Sample items presented.

Reliability: Test-retest (sorting problem) ranged from .80 to .81. KR-20 (proportional and proportionality) ranged from .52 to .75.

Validity: Subscales factored with other scales in an interpretable manner.

Author: Roberge, J.J. and Flexer, B.K.

Article: The formal operational reasoning test.

Journal: *Journal of General Psychology*, Jan. 1982, *106*(first half), 61-67.

3429

Test name: INTERPERSONALLY BASED PROBLEM-SOLVING SCALE (IBPS)

Purpose: To assess how consultants facilitate problem-solving.

Number of items: 42

Reliability: Cronbach's alpha = .96.

Validity: Correlates with behavior change (.37); with teacher satisfaction (.71); with problem resolution (.74); with professional growth (.67). All $p < .01$.

Author: Maitland, R.E. et al.

Article: The effects of an interpersonally based problem-solving process on consultation outcomes.

Journal: *Journal of School Psychology*, winter 1985, *23*(4), 337-345.

Related research: Maitland, R.E. et al., 1981. *The interpersonally-based problem-solving scale field test instrument*. Lawrence, KS: University of Kansas.

3430
Test name: INTUITIVE ABILITY TEST

Purpose: To measure ability to reach a successful conclusion based upon insufficient information.

Number of items: 20

Format: Includes verbal-serial, verbal analogy, numerical-serial, and numerical analogy items.

Reliability: Split-half reliabilities ranged from .36 to .91 (N's ranged from 28 to 38). Internal consistency ranged from .27 to .51. Test-retest reliability (3 years) ranged from .50 to .66 (N = 95).

Author: Fallik, B. and Eliot, J.

Article: Intuition, cognitive style and hemispheric processing.

Journal: *Perceptual and Motor Skills*, June 1985, *60*(3), 683-697.

Related research: Westcott, M.R., 1968. *Psychology of intuition*, New York: Holt, Rinehart & Winston.

3431
Test name: INVENTORY OF LEARNING PROCESSES

Purpose: To measure learning processes.

Number of items: 62 (four subscales).

Format: True-false questions. Sample items presented.

Reliability: Ranged from .79 to .88 across subscales.

Author: Alesandrini, K.L. et al.

Article: Visual-verbal and analytic-holistic strategies, abilities, and styles.

Journal: *Journal of Educational Research*, Jan./Feb. 1984, *77*(3), 150-157.

Related research: Schmeck, R.R. et al., 1977. Development of a self-report inventory for assessing individual differences in learning process. *Applied Psychological Measurement*, *1*, 413-431.

3432
Test name: KIRTON ADAPTATION INVENTORY

Purpose: To measure adaptation of innovative styles of problem-solving.

Number of items: 32

Reliability: Internal reliability (alpha) ranged from .85 to .88. Test-retest ranged from .82 to .85.

Validity: Correlates .40 with ratings of innovativeness (p<.001).

Author: Kirton, M.J. and McCarthy, R.M.

Article: Personal and group estimates of the Kirton inventory scores.

Journal: *Psychological Reports*, Dec. 1985, 57(3-II), 1067-1070.

Related research: Kirton, M.J., 1976. Adaptors and innovators: A description and measure. *Journal of Applied Psychology*, 61, 622-629.

3433
Test name: MEANS-ENDS PROBLEM-SOLVING TEST

Purpose: To measure means-ends problem-solving ability.

Number of items: 6

Format: The child is presented the beginning and the outcome of each of six stories. The child is asked to fill in the middle part or to explain how the ending occurred.

Reliability: Inter-rater reliabilities ranged from .86 to .98. Cronbach's alphas ranged from .62 to .88.

Validity: Correlations with other variables ranged from -.02 to .56.

Author: Pellegrini, D.S.

Article: Social cognition and competence in middle childhood.

Journal: *Child Development*, Feb. 1985, 56(1), 253-264.

Related research: Shure, M.B. and Spivack, G., 1972. Means-ends thinking, adjustment and social class among elementary school-aged children. *Journal of Consulting and Clinical Psychology*, 38, 348-353.

3434
Test name: PREACTIVE DECISION EXERCISES

Purpose: To measure teachers' ability to make teaching decisions.

Number of items: 131

Format: Problem situation described and followed by several courses of action that teachers may choose or may not choose. Sample problem and items presented.

Reliability: KR-20 = .72.

Author: McNergney, R.F. et al.

Article: Assessing teachers' planning abilities.

Journal: *Journal of Educational Research*, Nov./Dec. 1983, 77(2), 108-111.

Related research: Frederiksen, N. et al., 1957. The in-basket test. *Psychological Monographs: General and Applied*, 71(9), 1-28.

3435
Test name: PREDICTING DISPLACED VOLUME TEST

Purpose: To assess predictions made about displacement of water.

Number of items: 8

Format: Multiple-choice. Sample items presented.

Reliability: Alpha ranged from .82 (7th grade) to .88 (11th grade).

Validity: Correlates .68 with test using real water and real blocks to displace it.

Author: Linn, M.C. and Pulos, S.

Article: Male-female differences in predicting displaced volume: Strategy, usage, aptitude relationships and experience influences.

Journal: *Journal of Educational Psychology*, Feb. 1983, 75(1), 86-96.

3436
Test name: PROBLEM-SOLVING INVENTORY

Purpose: To measure problem-solving strategies in children.

Number of items: 25

Format: 5-point rating scale for importance of each of 25 items.

Reliability: Alphas ranged from .61 to .75 across subscales.

Author: Fry, P.S. and Addington, J.

Article: Comparison of social problem-solving of children from open and traditional classrooms: A two-year longitudinal study.

Journal: *Journal of Educational Psychology*, April 1984, 76(2), 318-329.

Related research: Heppner, P.P. and Petersen, C.H., 1977. *The development, factor analysis, and validation of a problem-solving instrument.* Unpublished manuscript. Lincoln, NE: University of Nebraska.

3437
Test name: PROBLEM-SOLVING INVENTORY

Purpose: To provide an estimate of self-appraised problem-solving behaviors and attitudes.

Number of items: 32

Format: Includes 3 dimensions: problem-solving confidence, approach-avoidance, and personal control.

Reliability: Reliability ranged from .72 to .90.

Validity: Correlations with decision-making scales ranged from -.55 to .38.

Author: Phillips, S.D. et al.

Article: Decision-making styles and problem-solving appraisal.

Journal: *Journal of Counseling Psychology*, Oct. 1984, *31*(4), 497-502.

Related research: Heppner, P.P. and Petersen, C.H., 1982. The development and implications of a personal problem-solving inventory. *Journal of Counseling Psychology*, 29, 66-75.

3438
Test name: PROBLEM-SOLVING INVENTORY

Purpose: To measure beliefs about problem-solving skills and behavior patterns.

Number of items: 35

Format: 6-point Likert format.

Reliability: Internal consistency ranged from .72 to .90. Test-retest ranged from .83 to .89 across three subscales.

Validity: Significant correlations between subscales and dimensions of coping ranged from .04 to .54 in absolute value.

Author: Ritchey, K.M. et al.

Article: Problem-solving appraisal versus hypothetical problem-solving.

Journal: *Psychological Reports*, Dec. 1984, *55*(3), 815-818.

3439
Test name: PROBLEM-SOLVING INVENTORY

Purpose: To assess attitudes and behaviors associated with effective problem-solving.

Number of items: 35

Format: True-false format.

Validity: Correlates significantly (.47) with rational beliefs. Mothers low in intensity of punishment score high on problem-solving.

Author: Shorkey, C.T. and McRoy, R.G.

Article: Intensity of parental punishments and problem-solving attitudes and behaviors.

Journal: *Psychological Reports*, Feb. 1985, *56*(1), 283-286.

Related research: Heppner, P.P. and Petersen, C.H., 1983. The development and implications of a personal problem-solving inventory. *Journal of Counseling Psychology*, 30, 537-545.

3440
Test name: REVISED INDIVIDUAL DIFFERENCES QUESTIONNAIRE

Purpose: To assess the extent to which an individual typically uses imagery and verbal processes in thinking, studying, and problem-solving.

Number of items: 54

Format: Includes two factors: verbal and imaginal.

Reliability: Coefficient alphas were .72 (verbal) and .74 (imagery).

Author: Fallik, B. and Eliot, J.

Article: Intuition, cognitive style and hemispheric processing.

Journal: *Perceptual and Motor Skills*, June 1985, *60*(3), 683-697.

Related research: Perunko, M., 1982. *Relationships among mental imagery, spatial ability, analytic and synthetic processing and performance on mathematical problems.* Unpublished doctoral dissertation, University of Maryland.
Paivio, A. and Harshman, R.A., 1983. Factor analysis of a questionnaire in imagery and verbal habits and skills. *Canadian Journal of Psychology, 37*, 461-483.

3441
Test name: SHIGAKI-WOLF LOGIC TEST

Purpose: To measure children's class and conditional logic abilities.

Number of items: 33

Format: Includes three or four items to measure each of 10 principles of logic. Subjects are required to generate the appropriate missing element for each syllogism.

Reliability: Test-retest (1 week) reliabilities ranged from .87 to .94 (N = 36).

Author: Shigaki, I.S. and Wolf, W.

Article: Comparison of class and conditional logic abilities of gifted and normal children.

Journal: *Child Study Journal*, 1982, *12*(3), 161-170.

Related research: Shigaki, I.S. and Wolf, W., 1980. Hierarchies of formal syllogistic reasoning of young gifted children. *Child Study Journal, 10*, 87-106.

3442
Test name: TEST OF FORMAL REASONING

Purpose: To assess levels of reasoning.

Number of items: 48

Format: Multiple-choice organized into nine subtests: classification, volume, combinations, isolation of variables, proportions, probability, correlation, mechanical equilibrium, coordination of two frames of reference. A few examples are presented.

Reliability: Coefficients ranged from .52 to .85.

Validity: Kendall's tau ranged from .55 to .74.

Author: Arlin, P.K.

Article: A multitrait-multimethod validity study of a test of formal reasoning.

Journal: *Educational and Psychological Measurement*, winter 1982, *42*(4), 1077-1088.

3443
Test name: TEST OF TEST-WISENESS—REVISED

Purpose: To measure test-wiseness of college students.

Number of items: 41

Format: Includes measures of two test-wiseness elements: deductive reasoning strategies and cue-using strategies.

Reliability: Coefficient alpha was .844.

Validity: Correlations with other variables ranged from -.40 to .70.

Author: Borrello, G.M. and Thompson, B.

Article: Correlates of selected test-wiseness skills.

Journal: *Journal of Experimental Education*, spring 1985, *53*(3), 124-128.

Related research: Ferrell, G.M., 1972. The relationship of scores on a measure of test-wiseness to performance on teacher-made objective achievement examinations and on standardized ability and achievement tests, to grade-point average, and to sex for each of five high school samples. Doctoral dissertation, University of Southern California. *Dissertation Abstracts International*, *33*, 1510-A. University Microfilms No. 72-26,013.

STATUS

3444
Test name: HOME INDEX

Purpose: To measure SES by asking children about parent's home and activities.

Number of items: 22

Format: Factual question format.

Validity: Thirteen items were validated against known father's occupation.

Author: Haller, E.J. and Davis, S.A.

Article: Teacher perceptions, parental social status and grouping for reading instruction.

Journal: *Sociology of Education*, July 1981, *54*(3), 162-174.

Related research: Gough, H., 1949. A short social status inventory. *Journal of Educational Psychology*, *40*, 42-56.
   Robinson, J. et al., 1969. *Measures of occupational attitudes and occupational characteristics.* Ann Arbor, MI: Institute for Social Research.

3445
Test name: INDEX OF EVALUATED INEQUALITY

Purpose: To measure perceptions of the fairness of social inequalities.

Number of items: 5

Format: 4-point agree-disagree format. Sample item presented.

Reliability: Cronbach's alpha = .51.

Author: Smith, K.B. and Green, D.N.

Article: Individual correlates of the belief in a just world.

Journal: *Psychological Reports*, April 1984, *54*(2), 435-438.

Related research: Robinson, R. and Bell, W., 1978. Equality, success, and social justice. *American Sociological Review*, *43*, 65-89.

3446
Test name: INDEX OF PERCEIVED INEQUALITY

Purpose: To measure perceptions of the extensiveness of social inequalities.

Number of items: 20

Format: Agree-disagree response categories. Sample item presented.

Reliability: Cronbach's alpha = .71.

Author: Smith, K.B. and Green, D.N.

Article: Individual correlates of the belief in a just world.

Journal: *Psychological Reports*, April 1984, *54*(2), 435-438.

Related research: Bell, W. and Robinson, R., 1980. Cognitive maps of class and racial inequalities in England and the United States. *American Journal of Sociology*, 43, 320-349.

3447
Test name: OCCUPATIONAL ASPIRATION SCALE

Purpose: To measure the level of occupational prestige.

Number of items: 8

Format: Includes four specific domains and four goal levels. The score for each question ranged from 0 to 9.

Reliability: Test-retest reliability coefficients were .78 (2 weeks) and .88 (5 weeks).

Author: Moracco, J. et al.

Article: A comparison of the occupational aspirations of a select group of military men and women.

Journal: *Vocational Guidance Quarterly*, Dec. 1981, *30*(2), 149-156.

Related research: Haller, A.O. and Miller, I.W., 1963. *The Occupational Aspiration Scale: Theory, structure and correlates.* East Lansing, MI: Michigan State University, Technical Bulletin 288.

3448
Test name: RACIAL SEMANTIC DIFFERENTIAL

Purpose: To assess racial evaluation.

Number of items: 60

Format: Includes five color-person concepts each rated on 12 bipolar scales.

Validity: Correlation with: Tennessee Self-Concept Scale was $r = .02$; with Index of Adjustment and Values (self-ideal) was $r = -.02$; with Index of Adjustment and Values (self-acceptance) was $r = .05$.

Author: Hines, P. and Berg-Cross, L.

Article: Racial differences and global self-esteem.

Journal: *Journal of Social Psychology*, April 1981, *113*(second half), 271-281.

Related research: Williams, J., 1964. Connotations of color names among Negros and Caucasians. *Perceptual and Motor Skills*, 18, 721-731.

3449

Test name: SOCIOMETRIC PEER-RATING SCALE

Purpose: To provide a measure of social status for first- and second-graders.

Number of items: 28

Format: Each child rates every classmate by marking a happy face (likes to play with), neutral face (sometimes likes to play with), or sad face (do not like to play with).

Reliability: Test-retest (7 months) Spearman rho was .69. Split-half corrected Spearman rho was .83.

Validity: Correlations with other variables ranged from -.46 to .88.

Author: Riley, W.T.

Article: Reliability and validity of a cost-efficient sociometric measure.

Journal: *Journal of Psychopathology and Behavioral Assessment*, Sept. 1985, 7(3), 235-241.

Related research: Asher, S.R. et al., 1979. A reliable sociometric measure for preschool children. *Developmental Psychology*, 15, 443-444.

TRAIT MEASUREMENT

3450
Test name: A-B RATING SCALE

Purpose: To measure type A behavior pattern in children.

Number of items: 24

Format: Each item is answered on a 7-point scale arranged as a ladder. All items are presented.

Reliability: Spearman-Brown odd-even correlation coefficient was r = .59 (N = 336).

Author: Wolf, T.M. et al.

Article: Validation of a measure of type A behavior pattern in children: Bogalusa heart study.

Journal: *Child Development*, Feb. 1982, *53*(1), 126-135.

Related research: Bortner, R., 1969. A short rating scale as a potential measure of pattern A behavior. *Journal of Chronic Diseases*, 22, 87-91.

3451
Test name: ADULT SELF-EXPRESSION SCALE

Purpose: To measure assertive behavior.

Number of items: 48

Format: Includes 25 positively worded and 23 negatively worded items. Responses to each item are recorded on a 5-point Likert format (0-4).

Reliability: Test-retest reliability estimate was .89.

Author: Lafromboise, T.D.

Article: The factorial validity of the adult self-expression scale with American Indians.

Journal: *Educational and Psychological Measurement*, summer 1983, *43*(2), 547-555.

Related research: Gay, M.L. et al., 1975. An assertiveness inventory for adults. *Journal of Counseling Psychology*, 22, 340-344.

3452
Test name: AGGRESSION WORD ASSOCIATION TEST

Purpose: To measure aggressive associations.

Number of items: 5 stimulus words denoting aggression embedded in a total of 11 words.

Format: Subjects given 30 seconds to produce 5 associations to each of 11 stimulus words. Primary associations are scored.

Reliability: .72 to .83.

Author: Russell, G.W.

Article: A comparison of hostility measures.

Journal: *The Journal of Social Psychology*, Feb. 1981, *113*(first half), 45-55.

Related research: Gellerman, S., 1956. *The effects of experimentally induced aggression and inhibition on word-association sequences.* Unpublished dissertation, University of Pennsylvania.

3453
Test name: AGGRESSIVE BEHAVIOR SCALE

Purpose: To measure aggressive behavior in children.

Number of items: 10

Format: 0 to 3 severity rating. Sample item presented.

Reliability: Alphas ranged from .78 to .92 across subscales.

Author: Margalit, M.

Article: Perception of parents' behavior, familial satisfaction, and sense of coherence in hyperactive children.

Journal: *Journal of School Psychology*, winter 1985, *23*(4), 355-364.

Related research: Prinz, R.J. et al., 1981. Hyperactive and aggressive behaviors in Childhood: Intertwined dimensions. *Journal of Abnormal Child Psychology, 9*, 191-202.
 Stewart, M.A. et al., 1980. Aggressive conduct disorders of children. *Journal of Nervous and Mental Disease, 168*, 605-610.

3454
Test name: ANGER INVENTORY

Purpose: To provide an index of anger reactions to a wide range of provocations.

Number of items: 80

Format: Each item consists of an anger provoking incident to which the subject responds on a 5-point scale according to the perceived degree of provocation if the incident actually happened.

Reliability: Test-retest reliability coefficient was .17.

Author: Biaggio, M.K. et al.

Article: Reliability and validity of four anger scales.

Journal: *Journal of Personality Assessment*, Dec. 1981, *45*(6), 639-648.

Related research: Biaggio, M.K., 1980. Assessment of anger arousal. *Journal of Personality Assessment*, 44, 289-298.

3455
Test name: ANGER SELF-REPORT

Purpose: To differentiate between the awareness and expression of anger/aggression.

Number of items: 64

Format: Likert-type questionnaire yielding scores for awareness of anger, expression of anger (including subscales for general, physical, and verbal expression), guilt, condemnation of anger, and mistrust.

Reliability: Test-retest reliability coefficients ranged from .28 to .76 for subscales and .54 for total.

Author: Biaggio, M.K. et al.

Article: Reliability and validity of four anger scales.

Journal: *Journal of Personality Assessment*, Dec. 1981, 45(6), 639-648.

Related research: Zelin, M.L. et al., 1972. Anger and self-report: An objective questionnaire for the measurement of aggression. *Journal of Consulting and Clinical Psychology*, 39, 340.

3456
Test name: ARGUMENTATIVENESS SCALE

Purpose: To measure the individual's general trait to be argumentative.

Number of items: 20

Format: A self-report scale on which the subject indicates for each item whether it is almost never true (1), rarely true (2), occasionally true (3), often true (4), or almost always true (5). All items are presented.

Reliability: Cronbach's coefficient alphas were .91 and .86 (N = 692). Test-retest (one week) r's were .87 and .86 (N = 35).

Validity: Correlations with communication predispositions ranged from -.45 to .47. Correlations with behavioral choices ranged from -.39 to .35.

Author: Infante, D.A. and Rancer, A.S.

Article: A conceptualization and measure of argumentativeness.

Journal: *Journal of Personality Assessment*, Feb. 1982, 46(1), 72-80.

3457
Test name: ASSERTION INVENTORY

Purpose: To measure assertion.

Number of items: 40

Format: Responses to each item are first made on a 5-point scale from 1 (none) to 5 (very much), indicating degree of discomfort in various situations. Responses are then made on another 5-point scale from 1 (always) to 5 (never), indicating the probability of engaging in those behaviors.

Reliability: Test-retest (5 weeks) reliability was .87 and .81 (N = 49).

Author: Ramanaiah, N.V. et al.

Article: Personality and self-actualizing profiles of assertive people.

Journal: *Journal of Personality Assessment*, Aug. 1985, *49*(4), 440-443.

Related research: Gambrill, E. and Ritchey, C., 1975. An assertion inventory for use in assessment and research. *Behavior Therapy*, 6, 550-561.

3458
Test name: ASSERTIVE JOB-HUNTING SURVEY

Purpose: To assess self-reported job-hunting assertiveness.

Number of items: 25

Format: Subjects respond on a 1 to 6 point scale as to how likely they would be to respond in the described manner where 1 is "very unlikely" and 6 is "very likely."

Reliability: Cronbach's measure of internal consistency was .82. Test-retest (2 months) correlation was .77.

Validity: Point-biserial correlations with: sex r = .13; with previous job-hunting experience r = .19.

Author: Becker, H.A.

Article: The assertive job-hunting survey.

Journal: *Measurement and Evaluation in Guidance*, April 1980, *13*(1), 43-48.

3459
Test name: ASSERTIVENESS SELF-REPORT INVENTORY

Purpose: To provide a self-report measure of assertiveness.

Number of items: 25

Format: Subjects respond by answering "true" or "false" to each item. All items are presented.

Reliability: Test-retest reliability (5 weeks) r = .81; for females r = .80 and for males r = .96.

Validity: Correlations with the Rathus Assertiveness Schedule were .70 and .63; for females correlations were .69 and .60 and for males correlations were .74 and .77.

Author: Herzberger, S.D. et al.

Article: The development of an assertiveness self-report inventory.

Journal: *Journal of Personality Assessment*, June 1984, *48*(3), 317-323.

3460
Test name: BALANCED F SCALE (SHORT FORM)

Purpose: To measure authoritarianism.

Number of items: 14

Format: Likert format. All items presented for this scale and several others that measure authoritarianism.

Reliability: Alpha = .87.

Author: Ray, J.J.

Article: The workers are not authoritarian: Attitude and personality data from six countries.

Journal: *Sociology and Social Research*, Jan. 1983, *67*(2), 166-189.

Related research: Ray, J.J., 1979. A short balanced F scale. *Journal of Social Psychology, 109*, 309-310.

3461
Test name: BEHAVIORAL ASSERTIVENESS TEST

Purpose: To measure assertiveness.

Number of items: 7

Format: 7 interpersonal situations requiring assertive responses played to subjects on videotape.

Reliability: Inter-rater reliability = .71.

Author: Nesbitt, E.

Article: Use of assertive training in teaching the expression of positively assertive behavior.

Journal: *Psychological Reports*, 1981, *49*(1), 155-161.

Related research: Nesbitt, E.B., 1977. *Comparison of two measures of assertiveness and the modification of non-assertive behaviors.* Unpublished doctoral dissertation, University of Tennessee.

3462
Test name: BELIEFS AND FEARS SCALE

Purpose: To measure pattern of beliefs and fears associated with type A behavior.

Number of items: 48

Format: 7-point Likert response categories.

Reliability: Ranged from .42 to .70 over seven constructs.

Validity: Modest correlations with type A behavior. 9 of 28 correlations significant, but none above r = .30.

Author: Burke, R.J.

Article: Beliefs and fears underlying type A behavior.

Journal: *Psychological Reports*, April 1984, *54*(2), 655-662.

3463
Test name: BUSS-DURKEE HOSTILITY INVENTORY

Purpose: To assess different forms of aggression and hostility

Number of items: 66

Format: Includes 7 subscales: assault, indirect aggression, irritability, negativism, resentment, suspicion, verbal aggression.

Reliability: Test-retest correlations ranged from .64 to .82.

Validity: Correlations with other variables ranged from -.53 to .67.

Author: Selby, M.J.

Article: Assessment of violence potential using measures of anger, hostility and social desirability.

Journal: *Journal of Personality Assessment*, Oct. 1984, *48*(5), 531-544.

Related research: Buss, A.H. and Durkee, A., 1957. An inventory for assessing different kinds of hostility. *Journal of Consulting Psychology, 21*, 343-349.
Biaggio, M.K. et al., 1981. Reliability and validity of four anger scales. *Journal of Personality Assessment, 45*(6), 639-648.

3464
Test name: CHILDREN'S ACTION TENDENCY SCALE

Purpose: To measure aggressiveness, assertiveness, and submissiveness in children.

Number of items: 39

Format: Consists of 13 situations each of which is followed by 3 pairs of responses. The child selects one response in each pair. An example is presented.

Validity: Correlations with observed behaviors ranged from -.60 to .53 for boys (N = 21) and -.54 to .46 for girls (N = 24).

Author: Deluty, R.H.

Article: Behavioral validation of the Children's Action Tendency Scale.

Journal: *Journal of Behavioral Assessment*, June 1984, *6*(2), 115-130.

Related research: Deluty, R.H. 1979. Children's Action Tendency Scale: A self-report measure of aggressiveness, assertiveness and submissiveness in children. *Journal of Consulting and Clinical Psychology*, *47*, 1061-1071.

3465
Test name: CHILDREN'S ASSERTIVE BEHAVIOR SCALE

Purpose: To measure children's assertive behavior.

Number of items: 27

Format: Subjects respond to each item by selecting one of five responses which represent very passive, passive, assertive, aggressive, and very aggressive behavior. All items are presented.

Reliability: Test-retest (4 weeks) reliabilities were .86 and .66. KR-20 internal consistency was .78 and .80.

Validity: Correlation with behavioral observations was .38.

Author: Michelson, L. and Wood, R.

Article: Development and psychometric properties of the Children's Assertive Behavior Scale

Journal: *Journal of Behavioral Assessment*, March 1982, *4*(1), 3-13.

Related research: Michelson, L. and Wood, R., 1980. A group assertive training program for elementary school children. *Child Behavior Therapy*, *2*, 1-9.

3466
Test name: CHILDREN'S AUTHORITARIAN PERSONALITY SCALE

Purpose: To measure authoritarian personality among children in grades 7-11.

Number of items: 20

Format: Yes-?-No format. All items presented.

Reliability: Alpha = .84.

Validity: Correlates .65 with attitude toward authority.

Author: Ray, J.J. and Jones, J.M.

Article: Attitude to authority and authoritarianism among school children.

Journal: *Journal of Social Psychology*, April 1983, *119*(second half), 199-203.

Related research: Jones, J.M. and Ray, J.J., 1984. Validating the school children's attitude toward authority and authoritarianism scales. *Journal of Social Psychology, 122*(first half), 141-142.

3467
Test name: COLLEGE SELF-EXPRESSION SCALE

Purpose: To measure assertiveness.

Format: 5-point rating scale (always to never).

Reliability: Test-retest ranged from .80 to .90.

Validity: Correlated .28 with response latency and .80 with eye contact.

Author: Williams, J.M.

Article: Assertiveness as a mediating variable in conformity to confederates of high and low status.

Journal: *Psychological Reports*, Oct. 1984, *55*(2), 415-418.

Related research: Galassi, J.P. et al., 1975. The college self-expression scale: A measure of assertiveness. *Behavior Therapy, 6*, 217-221.
   Gorecki, P.R. et al., 1981. Convergent and concurrent validation for four measures of assertion. *Journal of Behavioral Assessment, 3*(2), 85-91.

3468
Test name: COLLEGE WOMEN'S ASSERTION SAMPLE

Purpose: To provide a controlled observational measure of assertion.

Number of items: 52

Format: Items are audiotaped and present a brief description of a realistic interpersonal encounter. Subjects respond to each item exactly as they would if actually experiencing it as they hear it.

Reliability: Average coefficient of agreement across all items was .91.

Validity: Correlations with other variables ranged from -.31 to .42.

Author: MacDonald, M.L. and Tyson, P.

Article: The College Women's Assertion Sample (CWAS): A cross-validation.

Journal: *Educational and Psychological Measurement*, summer 1984, *44*(2), 405-412.

Related research: MacDonald, M.L., 1978. Measuring assertion: A model and method. *Behavior Therapy, 9*, 889-899.

3469
Test name: DEL GRECO ASSERTIVE BEHAVIOR INVENTORY

Purpose: To measure assertive, aggressive, nonassertive, and passive aggressive behavior in the college dormitory population.

Number of items: 86

Format: Subjects respond to each item on a 5-point Likert scale from "almost never" to "almost always." All items are presented.

Reliability: Coefficient alphas ranged from .83 to .91.

Validity: Correlations with other scales ranged from -.65 to .58.

Author: Del Greco, L.

Article: The Del Greco Assertive Behavior Inventory.

Journal: *Journal of Behavioral Assessment*, March 1983, *5*(1), 49-63.

Related research: DeGiovanni, I.S., 1978. Development and validation of an assertiveness scale for couples. Doctoral dissertation, State University of New York at Buffalo. *Dissertation Abstracts International*, *39*(9-B), 4573.

3470
Test name: DIRECTIVENESS SCALE

Purpose: To measure domineering, aggressive behavior.

Number of items: 8

Format: Yes-No-Undecided format. All items presented.

Reliability: Alpha = .63.

Author: Ray, J.J.

Article: Achievement motivation as a source of racism, conservativism and authoritarianism.

Journal: *Journal of Social Psychology*, June 1984, *123*(first half), 21-28.

Related research: Ray, J.J., 1976. Do authoritarians hold authoritarian attitudes? *Human Relations*, *29*, 307-325.

3471
Test name: DIRECTIVENESS SCALE

Purpose: To measure directiveness.

Number of items: 14

Reliability: Coefficient alphas ranged from .74 to .79.

Validity: Correlations with dominance was .429; with submissiveness was -.322; with aggressiveness was .241.

Author: Ray, J.J.

Article: Authoritarianism, dominance and assertiveness.

Journal: *Journal of Personality Assessment*, Aug. 1981, *45*(4), 390-397.

Related research: Ray, J.J., 1980. Authoritarianism in California 30 years later - with some cross-cultural comparisons. *Journal of Social Psychology*, *111*, 9-17.

3472
Test name: DOMINANCE SCALE

Purpose: To measure dominance.

Number of items: 30

Format: All items are presented.

Reliability: Coefficient alpha was .89.

Validity: Correlations with rated dominance was r = .54; with rated submissive was r = -.39.

Author: Ray, J.J.

Article: Authoritarianism, dominance and assertiveness.

Journal: *Journal of Personality Assessment*, Aug. 1981, *45*(4), 390-397.

3473
Test name: EMOTIONAL EMPATHY SCALE

Purpose: To measure empathy.

Number of items: 33

Format: Modified for children to 3 response categories (completely disagree, disagree to some extent, completely agree).

Reliability: Children: Alpha = .68. Split-half (adult) = .84.

Validity: Correlates slightly (.11) with social desirability (Crandall, V.C. et al., 1965).

Author: Kalliopuska, M.

Article: Relationship between moral judgement and empathy.

Journal: *Psychological Reports*, Oct. 1983, *53*(2), 575-578.

Related research: Mehrabian, A. and Epstein, N., 1972. A measure of emotional empathy. *Journal of Personality*, *40*, 525-543.

3474
Test name: EMPATHIC RESPONSE INSTRUMENT

Purpose: To measure empathic response of teachers.

Number of items: 15 vignettes (one example given).

Format: Raters judge students' written responses to vignettes on a 5-point scale of empathy.

Reliability: Inter-rater reliability = .90.

Author: Higgins, E. et al.

Article: Effects of human relations training on education students.

Journal: *Journal of Educational Research*, Sept./Oct. 1981, 75(1), 22-25.

Related research: Egan, G., 1974. *The skilled helper*. Monterey, CA: Brooks/Cole.

3475

Test name: EMPATHIC UNDERSTANDING SUBSCALE OF THE BARRETT-LENNARD RELATIONSHIP INVENTORY FORM OS - 64

Purpose: To measure empathy between counselor and client.

Number of items: 16

Format: The client indicates one of three degrees of agreement or disagreement with no neutral ground for each item. A sample item is presented.

Reliability: Test-retest correlation is .89. Spearman-Brown split-half correlations ranged from .82 to .93.

Validity: Correlations with other variables ranged from .033 to .617.

Author: Robinson, J.W. et al.

Article: Autonomic responses correlate with counselor-client empathy.

Journal: *Journal of Counseling Psychology*, March 1982, 29(2), 195-198.

Related research: Barrett-Lennard, G.T., 1972. *Resource bibliography of reported studies using the relationship inventory*. Unpublished manuscript, University of Waterloo, Waterloo, Canada.

3476

Test name: EMPATHY TEST

Purpose: To measure emotional empathy.

Number of items: 33

Format: Includes six subscales. Subjects respond on a scale from -4 (completely disagree) to +4 (completely agree).

Reliability: Split-half reliability was .84 (N = 202). Alpha-coefficient was .79.

Validity: Correlation with Marlowe and Crowne's social desirability scale was .06.

Author: Kalliopuska, M.

Article: Verbal components of emotional empathy.

Journal: *Perceptual and Motor Skills*, April 1983, 56(2), 487-496.

Related research: Mehrabian, A. and Epstein, N., 1972. A measure of emotional empathy. *Journal of Personality, 40,* 525-543.

3477
Test name: FASTE

Purpose: To measure children's empathy.

Format: Subjects are asked how they feel after being shown slides of children experiencing emotions of happiness, sadness, anger, or fear.

Reliability: Test-retest (1 week) reliability was .84.

Validity: Correlations with other variables ranged from -.35 to .83 (entire group); from -.16 to .48 (females); from -.08 to .85 (males).

Author: Marcus, R.F. et al.

Article: Verbal and non-verbal empathy and prediction of social behavior of young children.

Journal: *Perceptual and Motor Skills,* Feb. 1985, *60*(1), 299-309.

Related research: Feshbach, N.D., 1975. Empathy in children: Some theoretical and empirical considerations. *Counseling Psychology, 5,* 25-30.

3478
Test name: FEAR OF NEGATIVE EVALUATION SCALE

Purpose: To measure situation-specific trait anxiety.

Number of items: 30

Format: Contains true-false items.

Validity: Correlations with other variables ranged from .29 to .67.

Author: Smith, T.W. et al.

Article: Irrational beliefs and the arousal of emotional distress.

Journal: *Journal of Counseling Psychology,* April 1984, *31*(2), 190-201.

Related research: Watson, S.R. and Friend, R., 1969. Measurement of social-evaluative anxiety. *Journal of Consulting and Clinical Psychology, 83,* 448-457.

3479
Test name: FRAMINGHAM TYPE A SCALE

Purpose: To assess type A behavior.

Number of items: 10

Format: Respondents indicate extent to which items are self-descriptive. Sample items presented.

Reliability: Alpha = .71.

Author: Matteson, M.T.

Article: Relation of type A behavior to performance and satisfaction among sales personnel.

Journal: *Journal of Vocational Behavior*, Oct. 1984, 25(2), 203-214.

Related research: Haynes, S.G. et al. The relationship of psychosocial factors to coronary heart disease in the Framingham Study. *American Journal of Epidemiology, 107*, 362-383.

3480

Test name: GENERAL POPULATION ASSERTIVENESS CONTINGENCY SCHEDULE

Purpose: To measure assertiveness.

Number of items: 20

Format: Statements are followed by four response categories ranging from "very much like me" to "very much unlike me." All items presented.

Reliability: Cronbach's alpha = .70. Item-total correlations ranged from .-06 to .36.

Validity: Assertiveness correlated -.08 with anxiety and -.13 with mood state (p<.05 or better).

Author: Sundel, M. and Lobb, M.L.

Article: Reinforcement contingencies and role relationships in assertiveness within a general population.

Journal: *Psychological Reports*, Dec. 1982, 51(3-I), 1007-1015.

3481

Test name: HYPOTHETICAL ROLE-PLAYING TEST

Purpose: To provide a behavioral measure of assertion.

Number of items: 12

Format: Includes six refusal items and six general items. A 5-point scale is used. Subjects are instructed to respond as a highly assertive person would.

Reliability: Inter-rater reliability was .88.

Author: Valerio, H.P. and Stone, G.L.

Article: Effects of behavioral, cognitive, and combined treatments for assertion as a function of differential deficits.

Journal: *Journal of Counseling Psychology*, March 1982, 29(2), 158-168.

Related research: Schwartz, R. and Gottman, J., 1976. Toward a task analysis of assertive behavior. *Journal of Consulting and Clinical Psychology, 44*, 910-920.

3482

Test name: IMPULSIVENESS SCALE

Purpose: To measure workplace impulsiveness.

Number of items: 13

Format: Likert.

Reliability: Alpha = .77.

Author: James, L.R. et al.

Article: Perceptions of psychological influence: A cognitive information processing approach for explaining moderated relationships.

Journal: *Personnel Psychology*, autumn 1981, *34*(3), 453-475.

Related research: Barratt, E.S., 1959. Anxiety and impulsiveness related to psychomotor efficiency. *Perceptual and Motor Skills*, *9*, 191-198.

3483

Test name: INDEX OF EMPATHY FOR CHILDREN AND ADOLESCENTS

Purpose: To measure empathy for children and adolescents.

Number of items: 22

Format: Half the items require an affirmative response and half require a negative response to indicate an empathic tendency. All items are presented.

Reliability: Cronbach's alpha coefficients ranged from .54 for first graders, to .68 for fourth graders, to .79 for seventh graders. Test-retest reliability coefficients were r = .74 (1st graders); and r = .83 (7th graders).

Validity: Correlations with other measures ranged from -.57 to .77.

Author: Bryant, B.K.

Article: An index of empathy for children and adolescents.

Journal: *Child Development*, April 1982, *53*(2), 413-425.

Related research: Feshbach, N.D., and Roe, K., 1968. Empathy in six- and seven-year-olds. *Child Development*, *39*, 133-145.

3484

Test name: INNOVATIVENESS SCALE

Purpose: To measure innovativeness.

Number of items: 20

Format: Likert-type format.

Reliability: Split-half = .94. Alpha = .82.

Author: Evans, R.H.

Article: Innovativeness and information processing confidence.

Journal: *Psychological Reports,* April 1985, *56*(2), 557-558.

Related research: Hurt, H.T. et al., 1977. Scales for the measurement of innovativeness. *Human Communication Research, 4,* 58-65.

3485
Test name: INTERPERSONAL JEALOUSY SCALE

Purpose: To measure jealousy.

Number of items: 28

Format: 9-point agree-disagree response categories. Sample items presented.

Reliability: Alpha = .92.

Validity: Significant correlations between jealousy and romantic love were .47 (men) and .41 (women), non-significant correlations between liking and jealousy .05 (men) and .15 (women).

Author: Mathes, E.W. and Severa, N.

Article: Jealousy, romantic love and liking: Theoretical considerations and preliminary scale development.

Journal: *Psychological Reports,* 1981, *49*(1), 23-31.

3486
Test name: MACH IV SCALE

Purpose: To measure Machiavellianism.

Number of items: 20

Reliability: Nunnally (Equation 6-18) = .73.

Validity: Correlated .34 with role ambiguity (Rizzo et al., 1970); -.26 with perceived participation in decision-making (Vroom, 1960); -.35 with job satisfaction (Vroom, 1960); -.28 with job involvement (Lodahl and Kejner, 1965); -.28 with job tension (Kahn et al., 1965); .13 with perceived job performance (Porter and Lander, 1968).

Author: Hallon, C.J.

Article: Machiavellianism and managerial work attitudes and perceptions.

Journal: *Psychological Reports,* April 1983, *52*(2), 432-434.

Related research: Christie, R. and Geis, F, 1970. *Studies in Machiavellianism.* New York: Academic Press.

3487
Test name: MACH V SCALE

Purpose: To measure a respondent's Machiavellian orientation.

Number of items: 20 triads.

Format: Each triad contains: A statement tapping Machiavellianism, a statement unrelated to the Mach item but matched in social desirability, and a statement of different social desirability. Respondents indicate which of the three statements they are in most agreement and in which they are in least agreement.

Reliability: Spearman-Brown adjusted split-half reliability coefficients were .45 and .53. Alphas were .44 and .55

Author: Shea, M.T. and Beatty, J.R.

Article: Measuring Machiavellianism with Mach V: A psychometric investigation.

Journal: *Journal of Personality Assessment*, Oct. 1983, 47(5), 509-513.

Related research: Christie, R., 1970. Scale construction. In R. Christie and F.L. Geis, Eds., *Studies in Machiavellianism*. New York: Academic Press.

3488
Test name: MANIFEST ANXIETY DEFENSIVENESS SCALE

Purpose: To differentiate the highly-trait anxious from those lower in anxiety.

Number of items: 63 (men) and 59 (women).

Format: A self-report questionnaire.

Reliability: Test-retest (2 months) reliability coefficient was .95. Kuder-Richardson 20 coefficient was .91. Split-half (Spearman-Brown correction) reliability was .90.

Validity: Correlations with the Byrne R-S scale was r = .97 (males) and r = .94 (females); with the Taylor Manifest Anxiety Scale was r = .92 (both males and females).

Author: Gard, K.A. et al.

Article: Accuracy in nonverbal communication as affected by trait and state anxiety.

Journal: *Perceptual and Motor Skills*, Dec. 1982, 55(3-I), 747-753.

3489
Test name: MATTHEWS YOUTH TEST FOR HEALTH

Purpose: To assess children's type A behaviors.

Number of items: 17

Format: Items are statements descriptive of type A adults and include competitive achievement striving, impatience, aggressiveness, and easily arousal hostility. The teacher rates the child on a 5-point scale as to how characteristic each statement is of the child.

Reliability: Pearson correlation coefficients over a one-year period ranged from .47 to .59 (N's ranged from 121 to 208). Pearson correlation coefficients over a 3-week period ranged from r = .84 to r = .87 (N's ranged from 121 to 127).

Author: Matthews, K.A. and Avis, N.E.

Article: Stability of overt type A behaviors in children: Results from a one-year longitudinal study.

Journal: Child Development, Dec. 1983, 54(6), 1507-1512.

Related research: Matthews, K.A. and Angulo, J., 1980. Measurement of the type A behavior pattern in children: Assessment of children's competitiveness, impatience-anger and aggression. Child Development, 51, 466-475.

3490
Test name: MEHRABIAN AND EPSTEIN EMOTIONAL EMPATHY SCALE

Purpose: To measure emotional empathy.

Number of items: 33

Format: 8-point agreement scale.

Reliability: Split-half = .84.

Validity: High-scorers have higher rates of helping behavior than low scorers.

Author: Bohlmeyer, E.M. et al.

Article: Differences between education and business students in cooperative and competitive attitudes, emotional empathy and self-esteem.

Journal: Psychological Reports, Feb. 1985, 56(1), 247-253.

Related research: Mehrabian, A. and Epstein, A., 1972. A measure of emotional empathy. Journal of Personality, 40, 523-543.

3491
Test name: NARCISSISTIC PERSONALITY INVENTORY

Purpose: To identify narcissistic personality.

Number of items: 54

Format: A forced-choice test.

Reliability: Coefficient alpha was .86. Correlation between alternate forms (8-week interval) was .72.

Validity: Correlation with the Millon Clinical Multiofial Inventory Narcissistic Scale was .55. Correlation with the Marlowe-Crowne Social Desirability Scale was -.01.

Author: Auerbach, J.S.

Article: Validation of two scales for narcissistic personality disorder.

Journal: *Journal of Personality Assessment*, Dec. 1984, *48*(6), 649-653.

Related research: Raskin, R.N. and Hall, C.S., 1981. The Narcissistic Personality Inventory: Alternate form reliability and further evidence of construct validity. *Journal of Personality Assessment, 45*, 159-162.
    Emmons, R.A., 1984. Factor analysis and construct validity of the Narcissistic Personality Inventory. *Journal of Personality Assessment, 48*(3), 291-300.

3492
Test name: NEGATIVE ASSERTION QUESTIONNAIRE

Purpose: To measure assertiveness by self-report.

Number of items: 17

Format: Yes-No format. Sample items presented.

Reliability: Alpha = .70.

Validity: Correlates -.50 with Fear of Negative Evaluation Scale. Correlates .31 with the Provocative Situation Questionnaire.

Author: Quinsey, V.L. et al.

Article: Assertion and overcontrolled hostility among mentally disordered murderers.

Journal: *Journal of Consulting and Clinical Psychology*, Aug. 1983, *51*(4), 550-556.

3493
Test name: NONPATHOLOGICAL COMPULSIVENESS SCALE

Purpose: To measure compulsiveness.

Number of items: 11

Format: Yes-No.

Reliability: Alpha = .80.

Validity: Three factors extracted: indecision and double-checking, order and regularity, and detail and perfectionism.

Author: Kagan, D. and Squires, R.L.

Article: Measuring nonpathological compulsiveness.

Journal: *Psychological Reports*, Oct. 1985, *57*(2), 559-563.

Related research: Cooper, J., 1970. The Leyton Obsessional Inventory. *Psychological Medicine, 1*, 48-64.

3494
Test name: NOVACO ANGER INVENTORY—REVISED

Purpose: To measure the potential for becoming angry when provoked.

Number of items: 80

Format: Subjects respond to each item on a 5-point scale indicating the degree to which the situation makes them angry. Some items are presented.

Reliability: Pre-posttest correlation was r = .74. Internal consistency was .90.

Validity: Correlations with other variables ranged from .08 to .82.

Author: Selby, M.J.

Article: Assessment of violence potential using measures of anger, hostility, and social desirability.

Journal: *Journal of Personality Assessment*, Oct. 1984, *48*(5), 531-544.

Related research: Novaco, R., 1975. *Anger control: The development and evaluation of an experimental treatment.* Lexington, MA: D.C. Heath.

3495
Test name: OVEREXCITABILITY QUESTIONNAIRE

Purpose: To assess five forms of overexcitability.

Number of items: 21

Format: A free response instrument including five forms of overexcitability: psychomotor, sensual, intellectual, imaginational, and emotional. All items are presented.

Reliability: Inter-rater correlations ranged from .56 to .80.

Author: Piechowski, M.M. and Cunningham, K.

Article: Patterson of overexcitability in a group of artists.

Journal: *Journal of Creative Behavior*, 1985, *19*(2), 153-172.

Related research: Piechowski, M.M., 1979. Developmental potential. In Colangelo, N. and Zaffrann, R.T., Eds., *New voices in counseling the gifted.* Dubuque, IA: Kendall/Hunt.

3496
Test name: NEO INVENTORY

Purpose: To measure personality traits by means of three broad domains.

Number of items: 144

Format: Includes three broad domains of neuroticism, extroversion, and openness. Within each domain are six specific traits and eight-item scales for each specific trait.

Reliability: Internal consistency ranged from .61 to .81 for specific traits. Test-retest reliability (6 months) ranged from .66 to .92. Internal consistency and test-retest for the three domains ranged from .85 to .93.

Validity: Correlation of the three domains with the Self-Directed Search ranged from -.22 to .65 for men (N = 217) and from -.26 to .53 for women (N = 144).

Author: Costa, P.T. et al.

Article: Personality and vocational interests in an adult sample.

Journal: *Journal of Applied Psychology*, Aug. 1984, *69*(3), 390-400.

Related research: McCrae, R.R., and Costa P.T., Jr., 1983. Joint factors in self-reports and ratings: Neuroticism, extroversion, and openness to experience. *Personality and Individual Differences*, *4*, 245-255.

3497
Test name: OBSESSIVE-COMPULSIVE SCALE

Purpose: To measure the degree of obsessive-compulsive traits.

Number of items: 22

Format: Subjects respond to each item as being either true or false. Two items are validity check-items. All items are presented.

Reliability: Test-retest reliability coefficient was .82.

Validity: Correlations with clinicians' evaluations were .79; with roommate evaluations were .45; with other measures ranged from -.57 to .83 (N's ranged from 34 to 114).

Author: Gibb, G.D. et al.

Article: The measurement of the obsessive-compulsive personality.

Journal: *Educational and Psychological Measurement*, winter 1983, *43*(4), 1233-1238.

3498
Test name: PEER RATING INDEX OF AGGRESSION

Purpose: To identify aggressive and nonaggressive children.

Number of items: 9

Format: Children rate all other classmates on a series of aggressive items. An example is presented.

Reliability: Coefficient alpha was .95. Test-retest reliability (over one month) was .91.

Author: Graybill, D. et al.

Article: Effects of playing violent versus nonviolent video games on the aggressive ideation of aggressive and nonaggressive children.

Journal: *Child Study Journal*, 1985, *15*(3), 199-205.

Related research: Walder, L.O. et al., 1961. Development of a peer-rating measure of aggression. *Psychological Reports*, *9*, 497-556.

3499
Test name: PEER RATING OF PERSONALITY TRAITS SCALE

Purpose: To measure and rate college faculty members.

Number of items: 29

Format: 9-point scales followed each of 29 adjectives.

Reliability: Inter-rater reliability ranged from .61 to .94.

Validity: Items factor into two dimensions: achievement orientation and interpersonal orientation.

Author: Erdle, S. et al.

Article: Personality, classroom behaviors and student ratings of college teaching effectiveness: A path analysis.

Journal: *Journal of Educational Psychology*, Aug. 1985, *77*(4), 394-407.

3500
Test name: Q-TAGS TEST OF PERSONALITY

Purpose: To measure hostility.

Number of items: 54

Format: Subject indicates which items are descriptive of self. Items selected primarily from the Minnesota Multiphasic Personality Inventory. The score for an item ranges from 1 to 11.

Reliability: Test-retest = .69.

Author: Roberts, A. and Jenkins, P.A.

Article: Teachers' perceptions of assertive and aggressive behavior at school: A discriminant analysis.

Journal: *Psychological Reports*, 1982, *50*(3-I), 827-832.

Related research: Storey, A.G. and Mason, L.I., 1967. *The Q-Tags Test of Personality*. Montreal: Institute of Psychological Research.

3501
Test name: RATHUS ASSERTIVENESS SCHEDULE— MODIFIED

Purpose: To measure early adolescent assertiveness.

Number of items: 30

Format: Responses to each item are made on a 6-point scale from "very like me" to "very unlike me." All items are presented.

Reliability: Odd-even, split-half, Spearman-Brown adjusted coefficients ranged from .69 to .81 with N's ranging from 25 to 28.

Validity: Correlations with peer rating scores ranged from .25 to .52 with N's ranging from 25 to 28.

Author: Del Greco, L. et al.

Article: The Rathus Assertiveness Schedule modified for early adolescents.

Journal: *Journal of Behavioral Assessment*, Dec. 1981, *3*(4), 321-328.

Related research: Rathus, S.A., 1973. A 30-item schedule for assessing assertive behavior. *Behavior Therapy*, *4*, 398-406.

3502
Test name: REDUCED BEHAVIORAL REHEARSAL ASSERTION TEST

Purpose: To assess the quality of assertive responses under conditions that simulated reality.

Number of items: 12

Format: Items consist of taped situations half of which were specific refusal tasks and half of a general assertive nature. Oral responses were rated on a 5-point scale, ranging from 1 (unqualified nonassertive response) to 5 (unqualified assertive response).

Reliability: Inter-rater reliability was .94.

Author: Valerio, H.P. and Stone, G.L.

Article: Effects of behavioral, cognitive, and combined treatments for assertion as a function of differential deficits.

Journal: *Journal of Counseling Psychology*, March 1982, *29*(2), 158-168.

Related research: Schwartz, R. and Gottman, J., 1976. Toward a task analysis of assertive behavior. *Journal of Consulting and Clinical Psychology*, *44*, 910-920.

3503
Test name: REPRESSION-SENSITIZATION SCALE

Purpose: To measure repression-sensitization.

Number of items: 127

Reliability: Test-retest reliability was .82 (3 months). Internal consistency was .94.

Validity: Correlations with internal-external locus of control were r = .35 (N = 73) and r = .85 (N = 16).

Author: Valliant, P.M. et al.

Article: Variations in locus of control and repression-sensitization in acute schizophrenics, schizophrenic criminals and criminal psychiatric offenders.

Journal: *Perceptual and Motor Skills*, Dec. 1982, *55*(3-I), 919-924.

Related research: Byrne, D. et al., 1963. Relation of the Revised Repression-Sensitization Scale to measures of self-description. *Psychological Reports*, *13*, 323-334.

3504
Test name: REPRESSION-SENSITIZATION SCALE—SHORT VERSION

Purpose: To measure sensitization.

Number of items: 90

Format: Subjects indicate whether each item is true or false of them.

Reliability: Cronbach's alpha was .92.

Validity: Correlations with social anxiety were .63 (college students) and .48 (homosexuals).

Author: Schmitt, J.P. and Kurdek, L.A.

Article: Correlates of social anxiety in college students and homosexuals.

Journal: *Journal of Personality Assessment*, Aug. 1984, *48*(4), 403-409.

Related research: Byrne, D. et al., 1963. Relation of the Revised Repression-Sensitization Scale to measure of self-description. *Psychological Reports*, *13*, 323-334.

3505
Test name: RESPONSE EMPATHY RATING SCALE

Purpose: To measure the empathic quality of counselor behavior.

Format: Includes nine components: intention to enter client's frame of reference, perceptual inference and clarification, accuracy-plausibility, here and now, topic centrality, choice of words, voice quality, exploratory manner, impact. Ratings were made on 5-point behaviorally anchored rating scale.

Reliability: Inter-rater reliability for total empathy was .91. Inter-item reliability (alpha) for total empathy was .82.

Validity: Correlations between empathy components and response modes ranged from -.71 to .61.

Author: Elliott, R. et al.

Article: Measuring response empathy: Development of a multicomponent rating scale.

Journal: *Journal of Counseling Psychology*, July 1982, *29*(4), 379-387.

Related research: Hargrove, D.S., 1974. Verbal interaction analysis of empathic and nonempathic responses of therapists. *Journal of Consulting and Clinical Psychology*, *42*, 305.

3506
Test name: REVISED EMPATHY SCALE

Purpose: To measure perceived empathy.

Number of items: 13

Format: Includes a 6-point response scale.

Reliability: Cronbach's alpha was .79.

Author: Hammer, A.L.

Article: Matching perceptual predicates: Effect on perceived empathy in a counseling analogue.

Journal: *Journal of Counseling Psychology*, April 1983, *30*(2), 172-179.

Related research: Barrett-Lennard, G.T., 1981. The empathy cycle: Refinement of a nuclear concept. *Journal of Counseling Psychology*, *28*, 91-100.

3507
Test name: REVISED F SCALE

Purpose: To measure authoritarianism.

Number of items: 20

Format: Includes 4 factors: leadership/dominance, achievement motivation, interpersonal conflict, and verbal hostility. All items are presented.

Reliability: Ranged from .70 to .79.

Author: Heaven, P.C.L.

Article: Construction and validation of a measure of authoritarian personality.

Journal: *Journal of Personality Assessment*, Oct. 1985, *49*(5), 545-551.

Related research: Heaven, P.C.L., 1984. Predicting authoritarian behavior: Analysis of three measures. *Personality and Individual Differences*, *5*, 251-253.

3508
Test name: SALES TYPE A PERSONALITY INDEX—SHORT FORM

Purpose: To tap type A characteristics.

Number of items: 9

Format: Attempts to measure type A characteristics including: sense of time urgency, challenge of responsibilities, job involvement, speed and impatience, involved striving, and competitiveness.

Reliability: Internal reliability coefficients ranged from .75 to .80. Cronbach's alpha was .76.

Author: Abush, R. and Burkhead, E.J.

Article: Job stress in midlife working women: Relationships among personality type, job characteristics, and job tension.

Journal: *Journal of Counseling Psychology*, Jan. 1984, *31*(1), 36-44.

Related research: Jolly, J.A., 1979. Job change: Its relationship to role stresses and stress symptoms according to personality and environment. *Dissertation Abstracts International*, *32*, 4518B (University Microfilms No. 79-25475).

3509
Test name: SCALE OF TOLERANCE-INTOLERANCE OF AMBIGUITY

Purpose: To measure authoritarianism.

Number of items: 16

Format: 7-point Likert format. Sample items presented.

Validity: Mean correlation with other measures of tolerance of ambiguity is .46.

Author: Tom, D.Y.H. et al.

Article: Influences of student background and teacher authoritarianism on teacher expectations.

Journal: *Journal of Educational Psychology*, April 1984, *76*(2), 259-265.

Related research: Budner, S., 1962. Tolerance of ambiguity as a personality variable. *Journal of Personality*, *30*, 29-50.
  Robinson, J.P. and Shaver, P.R., 1973. *Measures of Social Psychological Attitudes* (rev. ed.). Ann Arbor, MI: University of Michigan.

3510
Test name: SELF-DECEPTION QUESTIONNAIRE

Purpose: To measure denial.

Number of items: 20

Format: Subjects respond as to the extent to which they can answer each item in the affirmative. A 7-point Likert-type scale is employed.

Reliability: Correlations with lateral eye-movements ranged from .15 to .28 (N's ranged from 43 to 16).

Author: Pierro, R.A. and Goldberger, L.

Article: Lateral eye-movement, field dependence and denial.

Journal: *Perceptual and Motor Skills*, Oct. 1982, 55(2), 371-378.

Related research: Gur, R.C. and Sackeim, H.A., 1979. Self-deception: A concept in search of a phenomenon. *Journal of Personality and Social Psychology*, 37, 147-169.

3511
Test name: SELF-REPORT PSYCHOPATHY SCALE

Purpose: To assess personality traits and anti-social behaviors.

Number of items: 22

Format: 1-5 scale.

Reliability: Alpha = .80.

Validity: Correlates .26 with MMPI Psychopathic Deviate Scale (NS); .36 with MMPI Hypomania Scale ($p<.05$); and -.53 with Socialization Scale of CPI.

Author: Hare, R.D.

Article: Comparison of procedures for the assessment of psychopathy.

Journal: *Journal of Consulting and Clinical Psychology*, Feb. 1985, 53(1), 7-16.

Related research: Hare, R.D., 1980. A research scale for the assessment of psychopathy in criminal populations. *Personality and Individual Differences*, 1, 111-117.

3512
Test name: SELF-RIGHTEOUSNESS SCALE

Purpose: To measure self-righteousness.

Number of items: 4

Format: Responses to each item are made on a 5-point rating scale from strongly agree to strongly disagree. All items are presented.

Reliability: Cronbach's alpha was .60. Test-retest correlation coefficient was $r = .53$.

Validity: Correlations with age were $r = -.26$ and $r = -.21$. Correlations with other variables ranged from .05 to .48.

Author: Falbo, T. and Belk, S.S.

Article: A short scale to measure self-righteousness.

Journal: *Journal of Personality Assessment*, April 1985, *49*(2), 172-177.

3513
Test name: SOCIAL RETICENCE SCALE

Purpose: To measure shyness.

Number of items: 22

Format: A self-report instrument.

Reliability: Coefficient alpha was .91. Test-retest reliability was .88 (8 weeks) and .78 (12 weeks).

Author: Jones, W.H. and Russell, D.

Article: The Social Reticence Scale: An objective instrument to measure shyness.

Journal: *Journal of Personality Assessment*, Dec. 1982, *46*(6), 629-631.

Related research: Zimbardo, P.G., 1977. *Shyness*. Reading, MA: Addison-Wesley.

3514
Test name: S-R INVENTORY OF MACHIAVELLIANISM

Purpose: To measure Machiavellianism.

Number of items: 9

Format: 9 situations are followed by six modes of response, each of which was rated on a 5-point scale of how much respondents would be inclined to use it. All items presented.

Reliability: Alpha ranged from .45 to .84 for situations and .72 to .92 for modes of response.

Author: Vleeming, R.G.

Article: Some sources of behavioral variance as measured by an S-R Inventory of Machiavellianism.

Journal: *Psychological Reports*, April 1981, *48*(2), 359-368.

Related research: Endler, N.S. and Hunt, J. M. S-R inventories of hostility and comparisons of the proportions of variance from persons, responses and situations for hostility and anxiousness. In Endler, N.S. and Magnusson, D. (Eds.), 1976, *International Psychology and Personality*. New York: Hemisphere, pp. 288-298.

3515
Test name: THRESHOLD TRAITS ANALOGY

Purpose: To provide a reliable, comprehensive system for defining and establishing the human attributes required to perform a wide variety of jobs.

Number of items: 33

Format: Checklist. All items presented.

Reliability: Spearman-Brown Prophecy Formula = .86. (33 traits, 100 jobs). Inter-form reliability ranged from .42 to .67.

Validity: Validity coefficients all significant (p<.01) for criterion variables, including overall job performance.

Author: Lopez, F.M. et al.

Article: An empirical test of a trait-oriented job analysis technique.

Journal: *Personnel Psychology*, autumn 1981, 34(3), 479-502.

3516
Test name: TOLERANCE FOR AMBIGUITY SCALE

Purpose: To measure ambiguity in members of organizations.

Number of items: 6

Format: 5-point Likert format.

Reliability: Alpha = .69.

Author: Ashford, S.J. and Cummings, L.L.

Article: Proactive feedback seeking: The instrumental use of the information environment.

Journal: *Journal of Occupational Psychology*, March 1986, 58(1), 67-79.

Related research: Norton, R.W., 1975. Measure of ambiguity tolerance. *Journal of Personality Assessment*, 39, 607-619.

3517
Test name: TRAIT FRUSTRATION SCALE

Purpose: To measure trait frustration.

Number of items: 8

Format: 8-point response scale used with each of the 8 items that describes a frustrating situation.

Reliability: Test-retest = .79.

Validity: Frustration scores were related positively but not significantly to aggression.

Author: Bergandi, T.A. et al.

Article: Trait frustration and aggression in adult humans.

Journal: *Psychological Reports*, Dec. 1982, 51(3-I), 815-819.

3518
Test name: TYPE A BEHAVIOR SCALE

Purpose: To measure type A behavior.

Number of items: 14

Format: 7-point bipolar scale.

Reliability: Internal consistency = .49.

Author: Burke, R.J.

Article: Career orientations and type A behavior in police officers.

Journal: *Psychological Reports*, Dec. 1985, *57*(3-II), 1239-1246.

Related research: Bortner, R.W. and Rosenman, R.H., 1967. The measurement of pattern A behavior. *Journal of Chronic Diseases*, *20*, 525-533.

VALUES

3519
Test name: ACCULTURATION SCALE FOR MEXICAN-AMERICAN CHILDREN

Purpose: To assess acculturation of Mexican-American children by responses of teachers and counselors who can report about particular children.

Number of items: 10

Format: Likert format. All items presented.

Reliability: Test-retest (5 week interval) = .97. Alpha = .77. Inter-rater agreement = .93.

Validity: Correlates .76 with the Acculturation Rating Scale for Mexican-Americans. Mean difference between Anglo-Americans and Mexican-Americans was in correct direction and significant (t = 12.62, p<.001).

Author: Franco, J.N.

Article: An acculturation scale for Mexican-American children.

Journal: *Journal of General Psychology*, April 1983, *108*(second half), 175-181.

Related research: Cuellar, I. et al., 1980. An acculturation scale for Mexican-American normal and clinical populations. *Hispanic Journal of Behavioral Science, 2,* 199-217.

3520
Test name: AFFECTIVE WORK COMPETENCIES INVENTORY

Purpose: To measure work attitudes, values, and habits desired by industry and educators.

Number of items: 45

Format: Includes five factors: ambition, self-control, organization, enthusiasm, and conscientiousness.

Reliability: Kuder-Richardson formula 20 reliability estimates ranged from .64 to .89.

Author: Brauchle, P.E. et al.

Article: The factorial validity of the affective work competencies inventory.

Journal: *Educational and Psychological Measurement,* summer 1983, *43*(2), 603-609.

Related research: Kazanas, H.C., 1978. Affective work competencies for vocational education. Columbus, OH: ERIC Clearinghouse for Vocational and Technical Education, The Ohio State University. (ERIC Document Reproduction Service No. ED 166420.)

3521
Test name: ANTI-INDUSTRIAL VALUES SCALE

Purpose: To measure perceived faults of society and to measure perceptions of ideal society.

Number of items: 14

Format: Semantic differential format. All items presented.

Reliability: Cronbach's alpha = .78.

Author: Duff, A. and Cotgrove, S.

Article: Social values and the choice of careers in industry.

Journal: *Journal of Occupational Psychology*, June 1982, 55(2), 97-107.

Related research: Cotgrove, S. and Duff, A., 1980. Environmentalism, middle-class radicalism and politics. *Sociological Review*, 28, 333-351.

3522
Test name: BELIEF IN A JUST WORLD

Purpose: To measure the extent a person believes that people experience the fates that they deserve.

Number of items: 16

Format: Respondents indicate agreement or disagreement with each item on a 6-point scale.

Reliability: Coefficient alpha was .62.

Validity: Correlations with other variables ranged from -.16 to .17.

Author: Smith, C.A.

Article: Organizational citizenship behavior: Its nature and antecedents.

Journal: *Journal of Applied Psychology*, Nov. 1983, 68(4), 653-663.

Related research: Miller, D.T., 1977. Altruism and threat to a belief in a just world. *Journal of Experimental Social Psychology*, 13, 113-124.

3523
Test name: BILLS JUNIOR HIGH SCHOOL INDEX OF ADJUSTMENT AND VALUES

Purpose: To measure self-described values, how subject feels about them, and how subject would like to be.

Number of items: 35

Format: 35 trait words are rated: self, self-acceptance, and ideal self.

Reliability: Test-retest (6 weeks) = .53 to .89 across three types of ratings.

Author: Hines, P. and Berg-Cross, L.

Article: Racial differences in global self-esteem.

Journal: *The Journal of Social Psychology,* April 1981, *113*(second half), 271-281.

Related Research: Bills, R.E. No date. Index Adjustment Values -- Forms: Elementary, Junior High School and High School Manual. University of Alabama, mimeo.

3524
Test name: BIOPHILIA SCALE

Purpose: To measure the meaning of life.

Number of items: 22

Format: Yes-Undecided-No format. All items presented.

Reliability: Alpha = .77.

Author: Ray, J.J.

Article: Attitude to abortion, attitude to life and conservatism in Australia.

Journal: *Sociology and Social Research,* Jan. 1984, *68*(2), 236-246.

Related research: Ray, J.J. and Lovejoy, F.H., 1982. Conservatism, attitude toward abortion and Maccoby's Biophilia. *Journal of Social Psychology, 118,* 143-144.

3525
Test name: CREEDAL ASSENT INDEX

Purpose: To measure general adherence to traditional Christian creeds.

Number of items: 7

Format: Responses to each item are made on a 5-point Likert-type scale ranging from 5 (strongly agree) to 1 (strongly disagree). An example is presented.

Reliability: Cronbach's alphas ranged from .85 to .94.

Author: Hoge, D.R. et al.

Article: Transmission of religious and social values from parents to teenage children.

Journal: *Journal of Marriage and the Family,* Aug. 1982, *44*(3), 569-580.

Related research: King, M.B. and Hunt, R.A., 1975. Measuring the religious variable: National replication. *Journal for the Scientific Study of Religion, 14,* 13-22.

3526
Test name: DEVOTIONALISM INDEX

Purpose: To measure religious devotionalism.

Number of items: 5

Format: Responses to each item are made on a 5-point Likert-type scale ranging from 5 (strongly agree) to 1 (strongly disagree). An example is given.

Reliability: Cronbach's alphas ranged from .84 to .90.

Author: Hoge, D.R. et al.

Article: Transmission of religious and social values from parents to teenage children.

Journal: *Journal of Marriage and the Family*, Aug. 1982, *44*(3), 569-580.

Related research: King, M.B. and Hunt, R.A., 1975. Measuring the religious variable: National replication. *Journal for the Scientific Study of Religion, 14,* 13-22.

3527
Test name: DUALISM SCALE

Purpose: To measure dualism-relativism.

Number of items: 7

Format: 5-point Likert format for rating how often respondents experience a feeling. All items presented.

Reliability: Test-retest = .80.

Author: Ryan, M.P.

Article: Monitoring text comprehension: Individual differences in epistemological standards.

Journal: *Journal of Educational Psychology*, April 1984, *76*(2), 248-258.

Related research: Perry, W.G., Jr., 1968. *Patterns of development in thought and values of students in a liberal arts college: A validation of a scheme*. Cambridge, MA: Harvard University. (ERIC Document Reproduction Service No. ED 024315.)

3528
Test name: ECLECTIC PROTESTANT ETHIC SCALE

Purpose: To measure traditional Protestant beliefs.

Number of items: 18

Format: 5-point Likert format. All items presented.

Reliability: Alpha = .82.

Validity: Correlates with Mirels and Garrett Scale (.36), and Ray Scale (.59).

Author: Ray, J.J.

Article: The Protestant ethic in Australia.

Journal: *Journal of Social Psychology*, Feb. 1982, *116*(first half), 127-138.

3529
Test name: ETHICAL BEHAVIOR RATING SCALE

Purpose: To identify and quantify moral behavior.

Number of items: 15

Format: Includes two factors: Personal moral character and verbal moral assertiveness. Teachers rate students on a 5-point rating scale from (1) never to (5) always. All items are presented.

Reliability: Test-retest reliability coefficient was .54. Coefficient alpha was .96.

Validity: Correlations with the Ethical Reasoning Inventory ranged from -.10 to .37.

Author: Hill, G. and Swanson, H.L.

Article: Construct validity and reliability of the Ethical Behavior Rating Scale.

Journal: *Educational and Psychological Measurement*, summer 1985, *45*(2), 285-292.

Related research: Blasi, A., 1980. Bridging moral cognition and moral action: A critical review of literature. *Psychological Bulletin, 88*, 1-45.

3530
Test name: ETHICAL CONFLICT QUESTIONNAIRE

Purpose: To measure degree of perceived ethical conflict.

Number of items: 20

Format: 7-point scale. All items presented.

Reliability: Test-retest = .84. Interval not reported.

Author: Morrison, J.K. et al.

Article: Ethical conflict among clinical psychologists and other mental health workers.

Journal: *Psychological Reports*, Dec. 1982, *51*(3-I), 703-714.

3531
Test name: ETHICAL REASONING INVENTORY

Purpose: To measure moral reasoning.

Number of items: 26

Format: Multiple-choice format. Stories include six of Kohlberg's moral dilemmas.

Validity: Correlations with the Ethical Behavior Rating Scale ranged from -.10 to .37.

Author: Hill, G. and Swanson, H.L.

Article: Construct validity and reliability of the Ethical Behavior Rating Scale.

Journal: *Educational and Psychological Measurement*, summer 1985, 45(2), 285-292.

Related research: Page, R. and Bode, J., 1980. Comparison of measures of moral reasoning and development of a new objective measure. *Educational and Psychological Measurement*, 40, 317-329.

3532
Test name: FREE WILL-DETERMINISM SCALE

Purpose: To measure beliefs in free will and determinism.

Number of items: 7

Format: Semantic-differential format.

Reliability: Alpha ranged from .62 to .79.

Validity: Student essays that successfully defend a position on the free will-determinism issue correlated with scores on the scale. Correlations ranged from .54 to .59.

Author: Viney, W. et al.

Article: Validity of a scale designed to measure beliefs in free will and determinism.

Journal: *Psychological Reports*, June 1984, 54(3), 867-872.

Related research: Viney, W. et al., 1982. Attitudes toward punishment in relation to belief in free will and determinism. *Human Relations*, 35, 939-949.

3533
Test name: FRIEDMAN'S SCALE

Purpose: To measure degree of agreement with economic-ideological structure of M. and R. Friedman's book, *Free to Choose*.

Number of items: 30

Format: All items presented. Response categories not presented.

Reliability: Item-test correlations ranged from .13 to .65. KR-20 = .80.

Validity: Loads highly (.58) on a factor that measures Western modes of thought and loads only slightly on a factor measuring Eastern modes of thought (.16).

Author: Krus, D.J. and Kennedy, P.H.

Article: Some characteristics of Appalonian and Dionysian dimensions of economic theories.

Journal: *Psychological Reports*, 1982, 50(3-I), 967-974.

3534
Test name: IDEOLOGICAL SCALE

Purpose: To measure traditional religious values.

Number of items: 5

Format: Multiple-choice format.

Reliability: Alpha = .79.

Author: Frost, T.F. and Rogers, B.G.

Article: Attitudes toward technology and religion among collegiate undergraduates.

Journal: *Psychological Reports*, June 1985, *56*(3), 943-946.

Related research: Faulkner, J.E. and DeJong, F., 1966. Religiosity in 5-D: An empirical analysis. *Social Forces*, *45*, 246-254.

3535
Test name: INDEX OF ADJUSTMENT AND VALUES

Purpose: To measure adjustment and values.

Number of items: 35

Format: Includes 35 trait words for which the subject indicates how descriptive it is, how the subject feels about it, and how the subject would like it to be. Provides self-acceptance and self-ideal scores.

Reliability: Test-retest for self-acceptance ranged from .74 to .89 (6 weeks); for self-ideal ranged from .53 to .81 (6 weeks).

Validity: Correlation with Tennessee Self-Concept Scale was .31 (self-acceptance) and -.17 (self-ideal); with racial evaluation scale was -.01 (self-ideal) and .05 (self-acceptance).

Author: Hines, P. and Berg-Cross, L.

Article: Racial differences in global self-esteem.

Journal: *The Journal of Social Psychology*, April 1981, *113*(second half), 271-281.

Related research: Bills, R.E. No date. Index of adjustment and values -- Forms: Elementary, junior high school and high school manual. Mimeographed manuscript, University of Alabama.

3536
Test name: INDIVIDUAL TRADITION-MODERNITY SCALE—REVISED

Purpose: To measure modern attitudes in Chinese adults.

Number of items: 40

Format: 6-point Likert format. Sample items presented.

Validity: Correlates with Kahl's Modernism Scale at .38 for males and .32 for females.

Author: Yang, K-S.

Article: Social orientation and individual modernity among Chinese students in Taiwan.

Journal: *The Journal of Social Psychology*, April 1981, *113*(second half), 159-170.

Related research: Yang, K-S. and Hchu, H-Y., 1974. Determinants, correlates, and consequents of Chinese individual modernity. *Bull. Inst. Ethnol. Academic Sinica.* Taipai, Taiwan, *37*, 1-28. (In Chinese with English summary.)

3537
Test name: JUST WORLD SCALE

Purpose: To measure perception of justice.

Number of items: 20

Format: Paper-and-pencil test. All items are presented.

Reliability: Split-half reliability was .81.

Validity: Correlations with other scales ranged from -.60 to .61.

Author: Ahmed, S.M.S. and Stewart, R.A.C.

Article: Factor analytical and correlational study of Just World Scale.

Journal: *Perceptual and Motor Skills*, Feb. 1985, *60*(1), 135-140.

Related research: Rubin, Z. and Peplau, L.A., 1975. Who believes in just world? *Journal of Social Issues*, *31*, 65-89.

3538
Test name: JUST WORLD SCALE—CHINESE VERSION

Purpose: To measure adherence to the belief in a just world.

Number of items: 20

Format: 6-point Likert format.

Reliability: Alpha = .78.

Validity: Correlated with alienation (r's ranged from .33 to .54, p<.01) and with support for work ethic (.33, p<.01).

Author: Ma, L-C. and Smith, K.B.

Article: Individual and social correlates of the Just World Belief: A study of Taiwanese college students.

Journal: *Psychological Reports,* Aug. 1985 *57*(1), 35-38.

Related research: Rubin, Z. and Peplau, L.A., 1975. Who believes in just world? *Journal of Social Issues*, *31*, 65-89.

3539
Test name: MAGICAL IDEATION SCALE

Purpose: To measure belief in forms of causation that are invalid by conventional standards.

Number of items: 30

Format: True-false format. All items presented.

Reliability: Alpha = .82 (males) and .85 (females).

Validity: Correlation with Eysenck Psychoticism = .32 (males); with perceptual aberration = .68 (males); with physical anhedonia = -.29 (males).

Author: Eckbad, M. and Chapman, L.J.

Article: Magical ideation as an indicator of schizotypy.

Journal: *Journal of Consulting and Clinical Psychology*, April 1983, *51*(2), 215-225.

Related research: Chapman, L.J. et al., 1982. Reliabilities and intercorrelations of eight measures of proneness to psychosis. *Journal of Consulting and Clinical Psychology*, *50*(2), 187-195.

3540
Test name: MAGNITUDE ESTIMATION SCALE FOR HUMAN VALUES

Purpose: To assess human values at a ratio level of measurement. Terminal and instrumental goals are assessed.

Number of items: 18

Format: Subjects rank 18 values, the first of which then receives the value of 100. Respondents enter numbers for subsequent values that are equal to or less than the number given to the prior value in the ranked list.

Reliability: Test-retest (rho) = .73 (terminal) and .72 (instrumental). Rank-value correlations = .78 (terminal) and .78 (instrumental).

Author: Cooper, D.R. and Clare, D.A.

Article: A magnitude estimation scale for human values.

Journal: *Psychological Reports*, 1981, *49*(2), 431-438.

Related research: Rokeach, M., 1967. *Value Summary*, Sunnyvale, CA: Halgren Press.

3541
Test name: MORAL COMMITMENT SCALE

Purpose: To measure organizational commitment.

Number of items: 4

Format: Responses are made on a 5-point scale.

Reliability: Coefficient alpha was .85.

Validity: Correlations with other variables ranged from -.18 to .16.

Author: Werbel, J.D. and Gould, S.

Article: A comparison of the relationship of commitment to turnover in recent hires and tenured employees.

Journal: *Journal of Applied Psychology*, Nov. 1984, *69*(4), 687-690.

Related research: Gould, S. and Penley, L., 1982. *Organizational commitment: A test of the model Working Paper Series*. San Antonio, TX: The University of Texas at San Antonio.

3542
Test name: MORAL CONTENT COMPONENTS TEST

Purpose: To measure the content of moral thought.

Number of items: 50

Format: The subject reads a series of moral dilemmas or stories and then after each the subject ranks statements reflecting possible moral considerations. Includes three factors.

Reliability: Average reliability coefficients were .69 and .75.

Author: Jensen, L. et al.

Article: A factorial study of the Moral Content Components Test.

Journal: *Educational and Psychological Measurement*, autumn 1981, *41*(3), 613-624.

Related research: Boyce, D. and Jensen, L., 1978. *Moral reasoning: Psychological philosophical perspectives*. Lincoln, NE: The University of Nebraska Press.

3543
Test name: MORAL JUDGEMENT SCALE

Purpose: To measure moral judgement.

Number of items: 43

Format: Subjects evaluate each item as to its "rightness" or "wrongness" on a scale from 1 to 5. All items are presented.

Validity: Correlation of each item with locus of control scores ranged from -.26 to .09.

Author: Frost, T.F. and Wilmesmeier, J.M.

Article: Relationship between locus of control and moral judgements among college students.

Journal: *Perceptual and Motor Skills*, Dec. 1983, 57(3-I), 931-939.

Related research: Rettig, S. and Pasamanick, B., 1959. Changes in moral values among college students: A factorial study. *American Sociological Review, 10,* 856-863.

3544
Test name: MYSTICISM SCALE

Purpose: To measure mystical experience.

Number of items: 32

Format: Includes two factors: general mysticism, religious interpretation.

Reliability: Internal consistency reliability correlations included item to total scale .29 to .52 (N = 300); subscale to total scale .39 to .62 (N = 300).

Validity: Correlation with the Religious Experience Episodes Measure was r = .47 (N = 52).

Author: Cowling, W.R. III.

Article: Relationship of mystical experience, differentiation, and creativity.

Journal: *Perceptual and Motor Skills*, Oct. 1985, 61(2), 451-456.

Related research: Hood, R.W., Jr., 1975. The construction and preliminary validation of a measure of reported mystical experience. *Journal of the Scientific Study of Religion, 14,* 29-41.

3545
Test name: NATIVE AMERICAN VALUE-ATTITUDE SCALE

Purpose: To assess attitude-value orientations of elementary age American-Indian children on four dimensions.

Number of items: 64

Format: Auditory dialogues followed by a typical Indian and typical Anglo response. Sample item presented.

Reliability: Alpha = .65 (school goals), .74 (sense of community), .50 (indirectness), .50 (non-interference).

Validity: Anglo responses increased as grade level increases for school goals and non-interference. Increased Indian responses occurred as grade level increases for sense of community and indirectness.

Author: Plas, J.M. and Bellet, W.

Article: Assessment of the value-attitude orientations of American Indian children.

Journal: *Journal of School Research*, 1983, *21*(1), 57-64.

3546
Test name: NATURE OF EPISTEMOLOGICAL BELIEFS SCALE

Purpose: To classify students as dualists or relativists.

Number of items: 7

Format: 5-point Likert scale.

Reliability: Test-retest = .84.

Author: Ryan, M.P.

Article: Conceptions of prose coherence: Individual differences in epistemological standards.

Journal: *Journal of Educational Psychology*, Dec. 1984, *76*(6), 1226-1238.

Related research: Perry, W.G., Jr., 1968. *Patterns of development in thought and values of students in a liberal arts college: A validation of a scheme.* Cambridge, MA: Harvard University. (ERIC Document Reproduction Service No. ED 024315.)

3547
Test name: ORIENTATION TO LEARNING SCALE

Purpose: To measure student orientation to humanistic instructional values.

Number of items: 135

Format: Two equivalent forms, A and B. Responses to each item are made on a 5-point scale from "strongly agree" to "strongly disagree."

Reliability: Odd-even and split-half reliabilities (N = 20) ranged from .93 to .95.

Validity: Correlations with other variables ranged from .119 to .513 (N = 31).

Author: Shapiro, S.B.

Article: The development and validation of an instrument to measure student orientation to humanistic instructional values.

Journal: *Educational and Psychological Measurement*, winter 1985, *45*(4), 869-880.

Related research: Shapiro, S.B., 1983. An empirical value analysis of humanistic approaches to educational psychology. Paper presented at the Western Psychological Association annual meeting, San Francisco.

3548
Test name: PERSONAL SPHERE MODEL

Purpose: To measure people, ideas, and things that are or have been important.

Time required: 10-15 minutes.

Format: Respondents draw symbols of people, ideas, or things important to him or her by connecting them with one, two, or three lines to a symbol for himself or herself. Respondents also cross out connecting lines for interrupted relationships.

Validity: Six factors account for 86% of the common variance. Concurrent validity: Beck Depression Scale correlated significantly with some subscales (sometimes opposite to expected direction). No correlations with fear of success, age, or class in school. Correlation between some subscales and locus of control.

Author: Sollod, R.N.

Article: The personal sphere model: Psychometric properties and concurrent validity in a college population.

Journal: *Psychological Reports*, Dec. 1984, 55(3), 727-736.

Related research: Schmiedeck, R., 1978. *The personal sphere model*. New York: Grune and Stratton.

3549
Test name: POLYPHASIC VALUES INVENTORY

Purpose: To reflect the existence of a broad range of values.

Number of items: 20

Format: Subjects respond to a value-laden situation by selecting a philosophically defensible response ranging between conservative and liberal alternatives. Examples are presented.

Reliability: Average item reliability was r = .63.

Author: Kayne, J.B. and Houston, S.R.

Article: Values of American college students.

Journal: *Journal of Experimental Education*, summer 1981, 49(4), 199-206.

Related research: Roscoe, J.T., 1965. Report of first research with the Polyphasic Values Inventory, *Journal of Research Services*, 5, 3-12.

3550
Test name: PROTESTANT SCALE

Purpose: To measure orientation to work that conforms to the Protestant work ethic.

Number of items: 19

Format: Forced-choice 9-point agreement scale.

Reliability: Alpha = .75.

Author: Ganster, D.C.

Article: Protestant ethic and performance: A re-examination.

Journal: *Psychological Reports*, Feb. 1981, *48*(1), 335-338.

Related research: Mirels, J.L. and Garrett, J.B., 1971. The Protestant ethic as a personality variable. *Journal of Consulting and Clinical Psychology, 36,* 40-44.

3551
Test name: PROTESTANT ETHIC SCALE

Purpose: To measure attitudes toward work.

Number of items: 19

Format: Forced-choice, 9-point response scale ranging from "very strong disagreement" to "very strong agreement."

Reliability: Internal consistency reliability of .75.

Author: Ganster, D.C.

Article: Protestant ethic and performance: A re-examination.

Journal: *Psychological Reports*, Feb. 1981, *48*(1), 335-338.

Related research: Mirels, J.L. and Garrett, J.B., 1971. The Protestant ethic as a personality variable. *Journal of Consulting and Clinical Psychology, 36,* 40-44.

3552
Test name: RAM SCALE—REVISED

Purpose: To measure student philosophical orientation in terms of relative, absolute, or mixed biases or preferences toward issues of knowledge, methods, and values.

Number of items: 36

Format: Includes three scales of knowledge, methods, and values, employing a Likert format.

Reliability: Internal consistency (alpha) estimate for total-scale was .79 and .38, .71, and .76 for subscales of knowledge, methods, and values, respectively.

Author: Wright, C.R. et al.

Article: The RAM Scale: Development and validation of the revised scale in Likert format.

Journal: *Educational and Psychological Measurement*, winter 1983, *43*(4), 1089-1102.

Related research: Brown, G.F. et al., 1977. The relationship of scores

of community college students on a measure of philosophical orientation to the nature of reality to their standing in selected school-related variables.
Educational and Psychological Measurement, 37, 939-947.

3553
Test name: RELIGIOSITY INDEX

Purpose: To measure religiosity among Jews.

Number of items: 7

Format: Guttmann. All items presented.

Reliability: Coefficient of reproducibility = .91.

Validity: Correlates with age and marriage, ideal number of births, mean number of births, and work experience (p<.05).

Author: Hartman, M.

Article: Pronatalist tendencies and religiosity in Israel.

Journal: *Sociology and Social Research*, Jan. 1984, 68(2), 247-258.

3554
Test name: RELIGIOSITY SCALE

Purpose: To measure religiosity.

Number of items: 37

Format: Orthodox-liberal response continuum. Sample item presented.

Reliability: Alpha = .81 and .83 for husbands and wives, respectively.

Author: Filsinger, E.E. and Wilson, M.R.

Article: Religiosity, socioeconomic rewards, and family development: Predictors of marital adjustment.

Journal: *Journal of Marriage and the Family*, Aug. 1984, 46(3), 663-670.

Related research: DeJong, G.F. et al., 1976. Dimensions of religiosity reconsidered: Evidence from a cross-cultural study. *Social Focus*, 54, 866-889.

3555
Test name: RELIGIOUS RELATIVISM INDEX

Purpose: To measure belief that all religions are equally true vs. belief that only followers of Jesus Christ can be saved.

Number of items: 5

Format: Responses to each item are made on a 5-point Likert-type scale ranging from 5 (strongly agree) to 1 (strongly disagree). An example is given.

Reliability: Cronbach's alphas ranged from .73 to .76.

Author: Hoge, D.R. et al.

Article: Transmission of religious and social values from parents to teenage children.

Journal: *Journal of Marriage and the Family*, Aug. 1982, *44*(3), 569-580.

Related research: Hoge, D.R. and Petrillo, G.H., 1978. Determinants of church participation and attitudes among high school youth. *Journal for the Scientific Study of Religion*, *17*, 359-379.

3556
Test name: REST'S TEST OF MORAL COMPREHENSION

Purpose: To measure moral comprehension.

Number of items: 11 item version.

Format: Multiple-choice.

Validity: Reproducibility = .93. Scalability = .84.

Author: Tsujimoto, R.N.

Article: Guttman scaling of moral comprehension stages.

Journal: *Psychological Reports*, 1982, *51*(2), 550.

Related research: Rest, J.R., 1979. *Development of judging moral issues*. Minneapolis: University of Minnesota Press.

3557
Test name: SOCIAL ORDER SCALE

Purpose: To measure acceptance of feminist ideology.

Number of items: 14

Format: 6-point Likert format.

Reliability: Item-total correlations were .40 or higher. Average inter-item correlation = .59. Test-retest = .86 (two weeks).

Author: Koupman-Boydan, P.G. and Abbott, M.

Article: Expectations for household task allocation and actual task allocation: A New Zealand study.

Journal: *Journal of Marriage and the Family*, Feb. 1985, *47*(1), 211-219.

Related research: Worell, J. and Worell, L., 1977. Support and opposition to the women's liberation movement: Some personality and parental correlates. *Journal of Research in Personality*, *11*, 10-20.

3558
Test name: SOCIOMORAL REFLECTION MEASURE

Purpose: To assess non-native values and how they guide reason and reflective sociomoral thought.

Number of items: 15

Format: Paper-and-pencil test in which respondents justify norms by responding to dilemmas.

Reliability: Inter-rater, test-retest, parallel forms, internal consistency generally were in the .70s.

Validity: Correlated .85 with Moral Judgement Interview (Colby, et al.).

Author: Gibbs, J.C.

Article: Facilitation of sociomoral reasoning in delinquents.

Journal: *Journal of Consulting and Clinical Psychology*, Feb. 1984, 52(1), 37-45.

Related research: Gibbs, J.C. et al., 1982. Construction and validation of a simplified, group-administered equivalent to the Moral Judgement Interview. *Child Development*, 53, 875-910.

3559
Test name: SURVEY OF WORK VALUES—MODIFIED

Purpose: To identify intrinsic and extrinsic work values.

Number of items: 54

Format: Includes intrinsic and extrinsic work values. A 7-point Likert format was used. A sample item is presented.

Reliability: Coefficient alpha reliability estimates were .77 (intrinsic work values) and .69 (extrinsic work values).

Author: Phillips, J.S. and Freedman, S.M.

Article: Contingent pay and intrinsic task interest: Moderating effects of work values.

Journal: *Journal of Applied Psychology*, May 1985, 70(2), 306-313.

Related research: Wollack, S. et al., 1971. Development of the Survey of Work Values. *Journal of Applied Psychology*, 55, 331-338.

Hazer, J.T. and Alvarez, K.M., 1981. Police work values during organizational entry and assimilation. *Journal of Applied Psychology*, 66(1), 12-18.

VOCATIONAL EVALUATION

3560

Test name: BEHAVIORAL OBSERVATION SCALES

Purpose: To measure the behavior of managers on the dimensions of support, interaction facilitation, goal emphasis, work facilitation.

Number of items: 75

Format: 5-point Likert response categories. Sample items presented.

Reliability: Alpha ranged from .85 to .92 across subscales.

Author: Wexley, K.N. and Pulakos, E.D.

Article: Sex effects on performance ratings in manager-subordinate dyads: A field study.

Journal: *Journal of Applied Psychology*, Aug. 1982, *67*(4), 433-439.

Related research: Stogdill, R.M. et al., 1962. New leader behavior description scales. *Journal of Psychology, 54,* 259-269.
  Taylor, J.C. and Bowers, D.G. 1972. *Survey of organizations: A machine-scored standardized questionnaire instrument.* Ann Arbor: IRSS, University of Michigan.

3561

Test name: BOREDOM IN DRIVING SCALE

Purpose: To measure boredom among truck drivers while driving on the job.

Number of items: 6

Format: 5-point scales, each point representing the percent of time the driver feels bored. All items presented.

Reliability: Alpha = .86.

Validity: Boredom scores do not differ between "monotonous" and "more stimulating" routes. Scores significantly and positively related to age ($p<.04$), length of residency ($p<.04$), tenure ($p<.03$), health ($p<.05$).

Author: Drory, A.

Article: Individual differences in boredom proneness and test effectiveness at work.

Journal: *Personnel Psychology*, spring 1982, *35*(1), 141-151.

3562

Test name: CLINTON ASSESSMENT OF PROBLEM IDENTIFICATION SKILLS

Purpose: To assess problem identification skills of instructional supervisors.

Number of items: 3

Format: Includes 3 scenarios each of which contains a description of a situation or dilemma with explicit or implied problems to be solved. An example is provided. Two forms are included.

Reliability: Equivalence reliability estimate was .76. Score-rescore coefficients were .71 and .67 for forms A and B, respectively.

Validity: Correlations of forms A and B with the Merrifield-Guilford Seeing Problems test were .42 and .54, respectively.

Author: Clinton, B.J. et al.

Article: The development and validation of an instrument to assess problem identification skills of instructional supervisors.

Journal: *Educational and Psychological Measurement*, summer 1983, *43*(2), 581-586.

3563
Test name: COGNITIVE CONTRIBUTION TEST

Purpose: To measure cognitive contribution of teaching.

Number of items: 8

Format: Likert-type items.

Reliability: .81 to .91.

Author: Neumann, L. and Neumann, Y.

Article: Determinants of students' instructional evaluation: A comparison of four levels of academic areas.

Journal: *Journal of Educational Research*, Jan./Feb. 1985, *73*(3), 152-158.

Related research: Bloom, B.S., 1956. *Taxonomy of Educational Objectives: Handbook I--Cognitive Domain*. New York: David McKay.

3564
Test name: COUNSELING EVALUATION INVENTORY

Purpose: To assess client satisfaction with counseling.

Number of items: 21

Format: Three satisfaction components identified through factor analysis include counseling climate, counselor comfort, and client satisfaction.

Reliability: Test-retest (14 days) reliability (N = 163) ranged from .63 to .78.

Author: Heesacker, M. and Heppner, P.P.

Article: Using real-client perceptions to examine psychometric properties of the Counselor Rating Form.

Journal: *Journal of Counseling Psychology*, April 1983, *30*(2), 180-187.

Related research: Linden, J.D. et al., 1965. Development and evaluation of an inventory for rating counseling. *Personnel and Guidance Journal*, 44, 267-276.

3565
Test name: COUNSELOR BEHAVIOR EVALUATION FORM

Purpose: To assess whether or not trainees observed in counseling interviews performed specific behaviors in the decision-making counseling paradigm.

Number of items: 10

Format: Ratings on each of 10 behaviors are made on a 3-point scale from "clearly displays the behavior" (3) to "completely fails to display the behavior" (1). Scores ranged from 10 to 30.

Reliability: Internal consistency reliability coefficient equivalent to a KR-20 estimate was .85 (N = 216).

Author: Baker, S.B. et al.

Article: Microskills practice versus mental practice training for competence in decision-making counseling.

Journal: *Journal of Counseling Psychology*, Jan. 1984, *31*(1), 104-107.

Related research: Herr, E.L. et al., 1973. Clarifying the counseling mystique. *American Vocational Journal*, 48(4), 66-72.

3566
Test name: COUNSELOR EFFECTIVENESS SCALE

Purpose: To measure client attitudes toward the counselor.

Number of items: 25

Format: Items consist of 7-point semantic differentials. A parallel form was prepared.

Reliability: Coefficient of equivalence was .98.

Author: Ponterotto, J.G. and Furlong, M.J.

Article: Evaluating counselor effectiveness: A critical review of rating scale instruments.

Journal: *Journal of Counseling Psychology*, Oct. 1985, *32*(4), 597-616.

Related research: Ivey, A.E. and Authier, J., 1978. *Microcounseling: Innovations in interviewing, counseling, psychotherapy, and* *psychoeducation.* (2nd ed.) Springfield, IL: Charles C. Thomas.

3567
Test name: COUNSELOR EFFECTIVENESS RATING SCALE

Purpose: To measure client perception of counselor credibility.

Number of items: 10

Format: Items are rated on a 7-point semantic differential scale.

Reliability: Cronbach's alphas ranged from .75 to .90.

Validity: Concurrent validity with the Counselor Rating Form was r = .80.

Author: Ponterotto, J.G. and Furlong, M.J.

Article: Evaluating counselor effectiveness: A critical review of rating scale instruments.

Journal: *Journal of Counseling Psychology*, Oct. 1985, *32*(4), 597-616.

Related research: Furlong, M.J. et al., 1979. Effects of counselor ethnicity and attitudinal similarity on Chicano students' perceptions of counselor credibility and attractiveness. *Hispanic Journal of Behavorial Sciences*, *1*, 41-53.

3568
Test name: COUNSELOR DEVELOPMENT QUESTIONNAIRE

Purpose: To provide a trainee self-report instrument.

Number of items: 157

Format: Includes two subscales: trainee and supervisory needs. Employs a 5-point Likert scale from strongly agree to strongly disagree.

Reliability: Cronbach's alpha ranged from .82 to .88.

Author: Reising, G.N. and Daniels, M.H.

Article: A student of Hogan's model of counselor development and supervision.

Journal: *Journal of Counseling Psychology*, April 1983, *30*(2), 235-244.

Related research: Worthington, E.L., Jr. and Roehlke, H.J., 1979. Effective supervision as perceived by beginning counselors-in-training. *Journal of Counseling Psychology*, *26*, 64-73.

3569
Test name: COUNSELOR EVALUATION INVENTORY

Purpose: To measure counselor effectiveness.

Number of items: 21

Format: Includes 3 factors: counseling climate, counselor comfort, client satisfaction. A 5-point Likert scale is used. Examples are presented.

Reliability: Test-retest (14 days) ranged from .63 to .83.

Author: Ponterotto, J.G. and Furlong, M.J.

Article: Evaluating counselor effectiveness: A critical review of rating scale instruments.

Journal: *Journal of Counseling Psychology*, Oct. 1985, *32*(4), 597-616.

Related research: Linden, J.D. et al., 1965. Development and evaluation of an inventory for rating counseling. *Personnel and Guidance Journal*, 44, 267-276.

Heppner, P.P. and Heesacker, M., 1983. Perceived counselor characteristics, client expectation and client satisfaction with counseling. *Journal of Counseling Psychology*, 30(1), 31-39.

3570
Test name: COUNSELOR EVALUATION AND RATING SCALE

Purpose: To provide a measure of practicum student competence.

Number of items: 27

Format: Responses are recorded on a Likert-type scale of 6 values ranging from 3 (I strongly agree) to -3 (I strongly disagree).

Reliability: Split-half reliability was .95 (N = 45). Test-retest reliability was .94.

Author: Handley, P.

Article: Relationship between supervisors' and trainees' cognitive styles and the supervision process.

Journal: *Journal of Counseling Psychology*, Sept. 1982, *29*(5), 508-515.

Related research: Myrick, R.D. and Kelly, D.F., Jr., 1971. A scale for evaluating practicum students in counseling and supervision. *Counselor Education and Supervision*, *10*, 330-336.

3571
Test name: COUNSELOR INTERVIEW COMPETENCE SCALE

Purpose: To evaluate counselors' interpersonal competence in client interviews.

Number of items: 5

Format: Ratings are made on a 7-point continuum for each of five dimensions: empathy, attractiveness, trustworthiness, interpretation, and expertness.

Reliability: Hoyt coefficients were reported to be .96 and .896. Inter-rater agreement was reported to be .86.

Author: Baker, S.B. et al.

Article: Microskills practice versus mental practice training for competence in decision-making counseling.

Journal: *Journal of Counseling Psychology*, Jan. 1984, *31*(1), 104-107.

Related research: Jenkins, W.W. et al., 1982. *The development of behaviorally anchored rating scales to evaluate counselor interview competence*. Unpublished manuscript, Pennsylvania State University.

3572
Test name: COUNSELOR RATING FORM—SHORT VERSION

Purpose: To assess counselor characteristics of attractiveness, expertness, and trustworthiness.

Number of items: 12

Format: Each item is rated on a 7-point scale from not very (1) to very (7).

Reliability: Coefficient alphas ranged from .63 to .89.

Author: Epperson, D.L. and Pecnik, J.A.

Article: Counselor Rating Form - Short Version: Further validation and comparison to the long form.

Journal: *Journal of Counseling Psychology*, Jan. 1985, *32*(1), 143-146.

Related research: Corrigan, J.D. and Schmidt, L.D., 1983. Development and validation of revisions in the Counselor Rating Form. *Journal of Counseling Psychology*, *30*, 64-75.

Lee, D.Y. et al., 1985. Counselor verbal and nonverbal responses and perceived expertness, trustworthiness and attractiveness. *Journal of Counseling Psychology*, *32*, 181-187.

Vandecreek, L. and Angstadt, L., 1985. Client preferences and anticipation about counselor self-discipline. *Journal of Counseling Psychology*, *32*, 206-214.

Brooks, L. et al., 1982. The effects of nontraditional role modeling intervention on the sex typing of occupational preference and career salience in adolescent females. *Journal of Vocational Behavior*, *26*(3), 264-275.

3573
Test name: COUNSELOR RATING FORM

Purpose: To measure clients' perceptions of counselors'

expertness, attractiveness, and trustworthiness.

Number of items: 36

Format: Includes three scales containing 7-point bipolar items.

Reliability: Split-half reliability ranged from .75 to .92.

Validity: Correlation with congruence measures ranged from -.05 to .41.

Author: Hill, C.E. et al.

Article: Nonverbal communication and counseling outcome.

Journal: *Journal of Counseling Psychology*, May 1981, *28*(3), 203-212.

Related research: Barak, A. and LaCrosse, M.B., 1975. Multidimensional perceptions of counselor behavior. *Journal of Counseling Psychology*, *22*, 471-476.

Banikiotes, P.G. and Merluzzi, T.V., 1981. Impact of counselor gender and counselor sex role orientation on perceived counselor characteristics. *Journal of Counseling Psychology*, *28*, 342-348.

McKitrick, D., 1981. Generalizing from counseling analogue research on subjects' perceptions of counselors. *Journal of Counseling Psychology*, *28*, 357-360.

Heppner, P.P. and Handley, P.C., 1981. A study of the interpersonal influence process in supervision. *Journal of Counseling Psychology*, *28*, 437-444.

Zamostny, K.P. et al., 1981. Replication and extension of social influence processes in counseling: A field study. *Journal of Counseling Psychology*, *28*, 481-489.

Atkinson, D.R. et al., 1981. Sexual preference similarity, attitude similarity, and perceived counselor credibility and attractiveness. *Journal of Counseling Psychology*, *28*, 504-509.

Hubble, M.A. et al., 1981. The effect of counselor touch in an initial counseling session. *Journal of Counseling Psychology*, *28*, 533-535.

Hardin, S.I. and Yanico, B.J., 1981. A comparison of modes of presentation in vicarious participation counseling analogues. *Journal of Counseling Psychology*, *28*, 540-543.

Dowd, E.T. and Bororo, D.R., 1982. Differential effects of counselor self-disclosure, self-involving statements and interpretation. *Journal of Counseling Psychology*, *29*, 8-13.

McCarthy, P.R., 1982. Differential effects of counselor self-referent responses and counselor status. *Journal of Counseling Psychology*, *29*, 125-131.

Porché, L.M. and Banikiotes, P.G., 1982. Racial and attitudinal factors affecting the perceptions of counselors by black adolescents. *Journal of Counseling Psychology*, *29*, 169-174.

Dowd, E.T. and Pety, J., 1982. Effect of counselor predicate matching on perceived social influence and client satisfaction. *Journal of Counseling Psychology*, *29*, 206-209.

Heppner, P.P. and Heesacker, M., 1982. Interpersonal influence process in real-life counseling: Investigating client perceptions, counselor experience level, and counselor power over time. *Journal of Counseling Psychology*, 29, 215-223.

Hackman, H.W. and Claiborn, C.D., 1982. An attributional approach to counselor attractiveness. *Journal of Counseling Psychology*, 29, 224-231.

Ruppel, G. and Kaul, T.J., 1982. Investigation of social influence theory's conception of client resistance. *Journal of Counseling Psychology*, 29, 232-239.

Paurohit, N. et al., 1982. The role of verbal and nonverbal cues in the formation of first impressions of black and white counselors. *Journal of Counseling Psychology*, 29, 371-378.

Heppner, P.P. and Heesacker, M., 1983. Perceived counselor characteristics, client expectations, and client satisfaction with counseling. *Journal of Counseling Psychology*, 30, 31-39.

Corrigan, J.D. and Schmidt, L.D., 1983. Development and validation of revisions in the Counselor Rating Form. *Journal of Counseling Psychology*, 30, 64-75.

Remer, P. et al., 1983. Differential effects of positive versus negative self-involving counselor responses. *Journal of Counseling Psychology*, 30, 121-125.

Heesacker, M. and Heppner, P.P., 1983. Using real-client perceptions to examine psychometric properties of the counselor rating form. *Journal of Counseling Psychology*, 30, 180-187.

Strohmer, D.C. and Biggs, D.A., 1983. Effects of counselor disability status on disabled subjects, perceptions of counselor attractiveness and expertness. *Journal of Counseling Psychology*, 30, 202-208.

Merluzzi, T.V. and Brischetto, C.S., 1983. Breach of confidentiality and perceived trustworthiness of counselors. *Journal of Counseling Psychology*, 30, 245-251.

Lee, D.Y. et al., 1983. Effects of counselor race on perceived counselor effectiveness. *Journal of Counseling Psychology*, 30, 447-450.

Reynolds, C.L. and Fischer, C.H., 1983. Personal versus professional evaluations of self-disclosing and self-involving counselors. *Journal of Counseling Psychology*, 30, 451-454.

Milne, C.R. and Dowd, E.T., 1983. Effect of interpretation style on counselor social influence. *Journal of Counseling Psychology*, 30, 603-606.

Angle, S.S. and Goodyear, R.K., 1984. Perceptions of counselor qualities: Impact on subjects' self-concepts, counselor gender, and counselor introduction. *Journal of Counseling Psychology*, 31, 576-579.

Robbins, E.S. and Haase, R.F., 1985. Power of nonverbal cues in counseling interactions: Availability, vividness, or salience? *Journal of Counseling Psychology*, 32, 502-513.

Ponterotto, J.G. and Furlong, M.J., 1985. Evaluating counselor effectiveness: A critical review of rating scale instruments. *Journal of Counseling Psychology, 32,* 597-616.

Kraft, R.G. et al., 1985. Effects of positive reframing and paradoxical directives in counseling for negative emotions. *Journal of Counseling Psychology, 32,* 617-621.

Suiter, R.L. and Goodyear, R.K., 1985. Male and female counselor and client perceptions of four levels of counselor touch. *Journal of Counseling Psychology, 32,* 645-648.

Corcoran, K.J., 1985. Unraveling subjects' perceptions of paraprofessionals and professionals: A pilot study. *Perceptual and Motor Skills, 60,* 111-114.

3574
Test name: EMPLOYMENT INTERVIEW RATING SCALES

Purpose: To assess potential employees.

Number of items: 7

Format: 7-point rating scales. All items presented.

Reliability: Inter-rater reliability ranged from .39 to .72 across items and age and sex categories. Overall reliability = .70 (p<.001).

Validity: Comparable reliability ratings obtained for males and females and blacks and whites.

Author: Grove, D.A.

Article: A behavioral consistency approach to decision-making in employment selection.

Journal: *Personnel Psychology,* spring 1981, *34*(1), 55-64.

3575
Test name: EVALUATION RATING SCALE

Purpose: To evaluate job applicants (in an experimental setting where raters view taped simulated interviews).

Number of items: 15

Format: Semantic differential. All adjective pairs presented.

Reliability: Alpha = .96.

Validity: Factor analysis showed that the 15 items accounted for 68% of item variance.

Author: Mullins, T.W.

Article: Interviewer decisions as a function of applicant race, applicant quality and interviewer prejudice.

Journal: *Personnel Psychology,* spring 1982, *35*(1), 163-174.

3576
Test name: FACULTY PERFORMANCE CHECKLIST

Purpose: To measure college students' satisfaction with their course and instructor.

Number of items: 64

Format: Students respond to each item with "Yes," "No," or "Does Not Apply." Examples are presented.

Reliability: Coefficient alpha was .88.

Author: Strom, B. and Hocevar, D.

Article: Course structure and student satisfaction: An attribute-treatment interaction analysis.

Journal: *Educational Research Quarterly*, spring 1982, 7(1), 21-30.

Related research: Schuler, G., 1974. *Report of the research team on faculty evaluation*. Unpublished manuscript, Ithaca College.

3577
Test name: GLOBAL DIMENSION APPRAISAL FORM

Purpose: To rate performance of law enforcement personnel.

Number of items: 40

Format: Includes nine dimensions.

Reliability: Inter-rater reliabilities ranged from .53 to .71 (corrected by Spearman-Brown formula).

Validity: Correlations with age ranged from -.28 to .03. Correlations with tenure ranged from -.21 to .15.

Author: Lee, R. et al.

Article: Multitrait-multimethod-multirater analysis of performance ratings for law enforcement personnel.

Journal: *Journal of Applied Psychology*, Oct. 1981, 66(5), 625-632.

3578
Test name: HELPING BELIEFS INVENTORY

Purpose: To measure basic counseling skills.

Number of items: 10 (all nonhelpful response items).

Format: 5-point response categories (almost always helpful to almost never helpful). All items presented.

Reliability: Alpha = .84.

Validity: Correlates .32 with authoritarianism, -.36 with flexibility, -.28 with psychological mindedness (all $p<.01$).

Author: McLennan, P.P.

Article: Helping beliefs inventory: Brief screening measure for training volunteer applicants in counseling.

Journal: *Psychological Reports*, June 1985, *56*(3), 843-846.

3579

Test name: HIGHWAY PATROL PERFORMANCE ASSESSMENT FORM

Purpose: To measure job performance of highway patrol officers.

Number of items: 78

Format: Statements appeared in 3-statement triads, each covering one aspect of the work of patrolmen. 26 triads were grouped into 9 performance areas. Sample items presented. Supervisors check the one statement out of three that best describes job performance of ratee.

Reliability: Triads all exceed the reproducibility of .80. Alpha (computed on triad scores) = .72. Inter-rater reliability = .90.

Validity: Correlations ranged between .62 and .78 with external indicator of job performance. Trooper of the year nominees rated higher than others (p<.001).

Author: Rosinger, G. et al.

Article: Development of behaviorally based performance appraisal system.

Journal: *Personnel Psychology*, spring 1982, *35*(1), 75-88.

3580

Test name: INDEX OF PERFORMANCE EVALUATION

Purpose: To measure performance of managers.

Number of items: 5

Format: 7-point response scales. All items presented.

Reliability: Alpha = .89.

Author: Izraeli, D.N. and Izraeli, D.

Article: Sex effects in evaluating leaders: A replication study.

Journal: *Journal of Applied Psychology*, Aug. 1985, *70*(3), 540-546.

Related research: Bartol, K.M. and Butterfield, D.A., 1976. Sex effects in evaluating leaders. *Journal of Applied Psychology, 61*, 446-454.

3581

Test name: INSTRUCTOR RATING FORM

Purpose: To evaluate instructor performance using a longitudinal approach.

Number of items: 33

Format: 7-point bipolar adjective scales.

Validity: Seven first-order and two second-order factors were identified using the Chain-P technique.

Author: Hundleby, J.D. and Gluppe, M.R.

Article: Dimensions of change in instructor presentations.

Journal: *Journal of Educational Research*, Jan./Feb. 1984, *74*(3), 133-138.

Related research: Luborsky, L. and Mintz, J., The contributions of P-technique to personality, psychotherapy, and psychosomatic research. In Dreger, R.M. (Ed.), 1972, *Multivariate personality research: Contributors to the understanding of personality in honor of Raymond B. Cattell*. Baton Rouge, LA: Claton Publishing Division.

3582
Test name: ISRAELI ARMY QUESTIONNAIRE FOR PERSONALITY AND MOTIVATION MEASUREMENT

Purpose: To measure and predict success in military training.

Number of items: 29

Format: Multiple-choice. "Choose the answer that best describes your behavior."

Reliability: Alpha = .88. (Subscales ranged between .59 and .65.)

Validity: Questionnaire results correlated .34 with some criterion performance, compared to .36 for existing interview scores.

Author: Tubiana, J.H. and Ben-Shakhar, G.

Article: An objective group questionnaire as a substitute for a personal interview in the prediction of success in military training in Israel.

Journal: *Personnel Psychology*, summer 1982, *35*(2), 349-357.

3583
Test name: JOB INVOLVEMENT AND PSYCHOLOGICAL SUCCESS SCALES

Purpose: To measure to what extent a person "eats, sleeps, and lives" his/her job and feelings of competence and success.

Number of items: 10

Format: Likert format.

Reliability: Alpha = .79 (involvement) and .78 (success).

Author: Slocum, J.W., Jr. and Cron, W.L.

Article: Job attitudes and performance during three career stages.

Journal: *Journal of Vocational Behavior*, April 1985, *26*(2), 126-145.

Related research: Hall, T. et al., 1978. Effects of top-down departmental and job change upon perceived employee behavior and attitudes: A national field experiment. *Journal of Applied Psychology*, *63*, 62-72.

3584

Test name: JOB PERFORMANCE SCALES

Purpose: To provide self- and supervisor-ratings of performance.

Number of items: 10

Format: Self-ratings consisted of 3 items, including measures of quantity, quality, and overall performance. Supervisory ratings consisted of 7 items including speed of performance, quality of performance, attitude to the job, initiative, cooperation, punctuality, and ability to learn. Five-point response scales were employed.

Reliability: Alpha coefficients = .93 (self-rating) and .97 (supervisor rating) (N = 166).

Validity: Correlations with other variables ranged from .04 to .37.

Author: Tharenou, P. and Harker, P.

Article: Moderating influence of self-esteem on relationships between job complexity, performance, and satisfaction.

Journal: *Journal of Applied Psychology*, Nov. 1984, *69*(4), 623-632.

3585

Test name: MANAGERIAL PERFORMANCE SCALE

Purpose: To measure eight dimensions of managerial importance (know-how, administration, training, direction, feedback, motivating, innovation, and consideration).

Number of items: 8

Format: 9-point rating scale. Items described.

Reliability: Split-half = .87.

Validity: Convergent validity: superiors-subordinates = .24; self-subordinate = .19; superior-self = .16.

Author: Mount, M.K.

Article: Psychometric properties of subordinate ratings of managerial performance.

Journal: *Personnel Psychology*, winter 1984, *37*(4), 687-702.

Related research: Tornow, W.W. and Pinto, P.R., 1976. The development of a managerial taxonomy: A system for describing, clarifying, and evaluating executive positions. *Journal of Applied Psychology*, *61*, 410-418.

3586
Test name: MANAGERIAL POTENTIAL SCALE

Purpose: To measure managerial competence and managerial interest.

Number of items: 34

Format: Items are from the California Psychological Inventory. Sample items presented.

Reliability: Alpha = .75.

Validity: Correlates .88 (male) and .89 (female) with Goodstein and Schrader Scale.

Author: Gough, H.G.

Article: A managerial potential scale for the California Psychological Inventory.

Journal: *Journal of Applied Psychology*, May 1984, *69*(2), 233-240.

Related research: Goodstein, L.D. and Schrader, W.J., 1963. An empirically-derived managerial key for the California Psychological Inventory. *Journal of Applied Psychology*, *47*, 42-45.

3587
Test name: MULTIPLE ITEM APPRAISAL FORM

Purpose: To rate performance of law enforcement personnel.

Number of items: 40

Format: Includes nine dimensions.

Reliability: Coefficient alphas ranged from .73 to .95. Inter-rater reliabilities ranged from .61 to .80 (corrected by Spearman-Brown formula).

Validity: Correlations with age ranged from -.15 to .09. Correlations with tenure ranged from -.09 to .17.

Author: Lee, R. et al.

Article: Multitrait-multimethod-multirater analysis of performance ratings for law enforcement personnel.

Journal: *Journal of Applied Psychology*, Oct. 1981, *66*(5), 625-632.

3588
Test name: NONVERBAL APPLICANT RATING SCALE

Purpose: To rate applicants on poise, clothing, cleanliness, posture, articulation, voice, answering behavior, and eye contact.

Number of items: 8

Format: 5-point multiple-choice format.

Reliability: Ranged from .62 to .88 across items. (Winer formula for interviewer reliability.)

Validity: Correlations among items ranged from .54 to .90. Mixed sex and race ratings were reported (males rated cleanliness, poise, clothing, posture, articulation, and eye contact lower than females; blacks rated lower than whites on voice intensity and articulation).

Author: Parsons, C.K. and Liden, R.C.

Article: Interviewer perceptions of applicant qualifications: A multivariate field study of demographic characteristics and nonverbal cues.

Journal: *Journal of Applied Psychology*, Dec. 1984, *69*(4), 557-568.

3589
Test name: PERCEPTIONS OF CLASSROOM INSTRUCTOR SCALES

Purpose: To measure student perceptions of classroom teachers.

Number of items: 40

Format: Semantic differential. All items presented.

Reliability: Cronbach's alpha ranged from .72 to .90 across subscales.

Validity: Identical factors (subscales) extracted for males and females.

Author: Bennett, S.K.

Article: Student perceptions and expectations for male and female instructors: Evidence relating to the question of gender bias in teaching evaluation.

Journal: *Journal of Educational Psychology*, April 1982, *74*(2), 170-179.

3590
Test name: PERFORMANCE IMPROVEMENT GUIDE

Purpose: To evaluate student teachers on seven dimensions: Instruction, curriculum, relations to peers and principals, professional qualities, personal qualities.

Number of items: 78 statements.

Format: Respondents rate student teachers on a 6-point scale from (1) strongly disagree to (6) strongly agree.

Reliability: Cronbach's alpha ranged from .56 to .94 across dimensions.

Validity: Valid according to Fiske's multitrait-multimethod test for convergent, but not discriminant, validity.

Author: Wheeler, A.E. and Knoop, H.R.

Article: Self, teacher, and faculty assessments of student teaching performance.

Journal: *Journal of Educational Research*, Jan./Feb. 1982, *75*(3), 178-181.

Related research: Chiu, L.H., 1975. Influence of student teaching on perceived teaching competence. *Perceptual and Motor Skills, 40*, 872-874.

3591
Test name: PRESENTER'S QUALITIES RATING FORM

Purpose: To measure subjects' perception of the presenter's competence.

Number of items: 36

Format: Items are bipolar and rated from 1 to 7. Includes three dimensions: prepared-unprepared, likeable-unlikable, genuine-phony.

Reliability: Coefficient alpha was .87.

Author: Gilver, L.A. et al.

Article: Influence of presenter's gender on students' evaluations of presenters discussing sex fairness in counseling: An analogue study.

Journal: *Journal of Counseling Psychology*, May 1981, *28*(3), 258-264.

Related research: LaCrosse, M.B., 1977. Comparative perceptions of counselor behavior: A replication and extension. *Journal of Counseling Psychology, 24*, 464-471.

3592
Test name: RATING SCALE FOR ENTRY-LEVEL PSYCHIATRIC AIDS

Purpose: To assess potential psychiatric aid employees.

Number of items: 78

Format: 1-5 rating scale format (1 = seldom performs correctly; 5 = performs consistently above average).

Reliability: Alpha ranged between .97 and .99 across rating categories.

Test-retest = .84 (10-14 day interval).

Validity: Correlated .26 with wide range vocabulary test; .24 with personnel tests for industry.

Author: Distefano, M.K. et al.

Article: Application of content validity methods to the development of a job-related performance rating criterion.

Journal: *Personnel Psychology*, autumn 1983, *36*(3), 621-631.

3593
Test name: RATING SCALE FOR JOB-RELATED WORK

Purpose: To measure performance of job-related work.

Number of items: 50

Format: 5-point rating format ranges from 1 (seldom performs correctly) to 5 (performs consistently above acceptable level).

Reliability: Alphas ranged from .91 to .98 across categories of work.

Validity: Correlated (mean validity) .23 with verbal ability test.

Author: Distefano, M.K. and Pryer, M.W.

Article: Verbal selection test and work performance validity with aides from three psychiatric hospitals.

Journal: *Psychological Reports*, June 1985, *56*(3), 811-815.

Related research: Distefano, M.K. et al., 1983. Application of content validity methods to the development of a job-related performance rating criterion. *Personnel Psychology, 36*, 621-631.

3594
Test name: RELATIONSHIP INVENTORY

Purpose: To measure subjects' ratings of the interviewer.

Number of items: 36

Format: Includes 5 subscales: empathic understanding, unconditional regard, level of regard, congruence, and resistance. Responses to each item were made on a 7-point scale from mostly disagree to mostly agree.

Reliability: Cronbach's alphas ranged from .54 to .85.

Author: Lopez, F.G. and Wambach, C.A.

Article: Effects of paradoxical and self-control directives in counseling.

Journal: *Journal of Counseling Psychology*, March 1982, *29*(2), 115-124.

Related research: Strong, S. et al., 1979. Motivational and equipping functions of interpretation in counseling. *Journal of Counseling Psychology*, 26, 98-107.

3595
Test name: RELATIONSHIP QUESTIONNAIRE

Purpose: To measure clients' ratings of counselors' performance.

Number of items: 24

Format: 7-point Likert response categories.

Reliability: Internal consistency ranged from .85 to .90 over two subscales.

Author: Loeb, R.G. and Curtis, J.M.

Article: Effects of counselors' self-references on subjects' first impressions in an experimental psychological interview.

Journal: *Psychological Reports*, Dec. 1984, 55(3), 803-810.

Related research: Sorenson, A.G., 1967. Toward an instructional model for counseling, Occasional report No. 6, Center for the Study of Instructional Programs, UCLA.
  Curtis, J.M., 1981. Effect of therapist's self-disclosure on patients' impressions of empathy, competence, and trust in an analogue of psychotherapeutic interaction. *Psychological Reports*, 48(1), 127-136.

3596
Test name: SALES PERFORMANCE CHART

Purpose: To evaluate salespeople on seven key dimensions: volume, new accounts, selling results, leadership, planning, initiative, resourcefulness.

Number of items: 7

Format: 5-point Likert format.

Reliability: Alpha = .89.

Validity: Actual sales volume correlates .41 with evaluation of sales volume.

Author: Slocum, J.W., Jr. and Cron, W.L.

Article: Job attitudes and performance during three career stages.

Journal: *Journal of Vocational Behavior*, April 1985, 26(2), 126-145.

3597
Test name: SLATER NURSING COMPETENCE RATING SCALE

Purpose: To measure performance of nurses on the job.

Number of items: 84

Format: Supervisors rate observed behaviors. Six behavioral dimensions are scored.

Reliability: Split-half = .98.

Author: Martin, T.N.

Article: Job performance and turnover.

Journal: *Journal of Applied Psychology*, Feb. 1981, *66*(1), 116-119.

Related research: Slater, D., 1967. *The Slater Nursing Competence Rating Scale*. Detroit, MI: Wayne State University College of Nursing.

3598
Test name: SELF-EVALUATED SALES PERFORMANCE MEASURE

Purpose: To provide a self-evaluation of sales job activities.

Number of items: 47

Format: Responses were made on a 5-point scale ranging from "much below average" to "much above average."

Reliability: Cronbach's alpha was .88.

Validity: Correlations with other variables ranged from -.11 to .27.

Author: Motowidlo, S.J.

Article: Relationship between self-rated performance and pay satisfaction among sales representatives.

Journal: *Journal of Applied Psychology*, April 1982, *67*(2), 209-213.

3599
Test name: SESSION EVALUATION QUESTIONNAIRE

Purpose: To measure novice counselors' and their clients' view of counseling session impact.

Number of items: 19

Format: Includes four dimensions: depth, smoothness, positivity, and arousal. All items are bipolar adjectives with responses to each made on a 1-7 scale. All items presented.

Reliability: Coefficient alphas ranged from .78 to .93.

Author: Stiles, W.B. and Snow, J.S.

Article: Counseling session impact as viewed by novice counselors and their clients.

Journal: *Journal of Counseling Psychology*, Jan. 1984, *31*(1), 3-12.

Related research: Stiles, W.B. et al., 1982. Participants' perceptions of self-analytic group sessions. *Small Group Behavior, 13,* 237-254.

3600
Test name: STUDENT EVALUATION OF TEACHING

Purpose: To measure student opinion of teacher behavior and its effect on the student.

Number of items: 8

Format: Rating scales.

Reliability: Internal consistency = .76; Intra-class correlation = .89; Cross-year correlation = .68.

Author: Fox, R. et al.

Article: Student evaluation of teacher as a measure of teacher behavior and teacher impact on students.

Journal: *Journal of Educational Research,* Sept./Oct. 1983, 77(1), 16-21.

Related research: Veldman, D.J. and Peck, R.F., 1979. Student teacher characteristics from the pupil's viewpoint. *Journal of Educational Psychology, 71,* 117-124.

3601
Test name: STUDENT RATINGS OF TEACHERS SCALE

Purpose: To measure student evaluations of teachers.

Number of items: 18

Format: 7-point agreement scale.

Validity: Factors emerged that were similar to Marsh and Ware's five-factor structure of teacher qualities.

Author: Basow, S.A. and Distenfeld, M.S.

Article: Teacher expressiveness: More important for male than female teachers.

Journal: *Journal of Educational Psychology,* Feb. 1985, 77(1), 45-52.

Related research: Marsh, H.W. and Ware, J.E., 1982. Effects of expressiveness, content coverage, and incentive on multi-dimensional student rating scales: New interpretations of the Dr. Fox Effect. *Journal of Educational Psychology, 74,* 126-134.

3602
Test name: STUDENT TEACHER RATING SCALE

Purpose: To measure level of professional development in student teachers.

Number of items: 19

Format: Multiple-choice. Sample items presented.

Reliability: Alphas ranged from .87 to .90 across subgroups.

Author: Hattie, J. et al.

Article: Assessment of student teachers by supervising teachers.

Journal: *Journal of Educational Psychology*, Oct. 1982, *74*(5), 778-785.

3603
Test name: SUPERVISORY STYLES INVENTORY

Purpose: To study supervisors' self-perceptions and trainees' perceptions of their supervisors.

Number of items: 25

Format: Includes three factors: attractive, interpersonally sensitive, and task-oriented. There are two versions: supervisor and trainee.

Reliability: Cronbach's alpha ranged from .70 to .84 for the SSI-S and from .84 to .89 for the SSI-T (N ranged from 105 to 202). Test-retest reliabilities for the SSI-T ranged from .78 to .94 (N = 32).

Author: Friedlander, M.L. and Ward, L.G.

Article: Development and validation of the Supervisory Styles Inventory.

Journal: *Journal of Counseling Psychology*, Oct. 1984, *31*(4), 541-557.

Related research: Stenack, R.J. and Dye, H.A., 1982. Behavioral descriptions of counseling supervision roles. *Counselor Education and Supervision*, *21*, 295-304.

3604
Test name: TEACHER SCORING KEYS

Purpose: To score teacher behaviors measured by existing teacher behavior instruments.

Number of items: 42

Format: Varied with instrument used.

Reliability: Special measures of reliability varied from 0 to .62 with an average of .23. 22 of the 42 were significant at the .05 level.

Validity: Problematic validity revealed by factor analysis.

Author: Medley, D.M. et al.

Article: Assessing teacher performance from observed competency indicators defined by classroom teachers.

Journal: *Journal of Educational Research*, March/April 1981, *74*(4), 197-216.

3605
Test name: TEACHER BEHAVIORS INVENTORY

Purpose: To rate teacher classroom behavior.

Number of items: 60

Format: 5-point frequency scale (1 = almost never to 5 = almost always).

Reliability: SB ranged from .24 to .97 for individual items (median = .76).

Author: Murray, H.G.

Article: Low-inference classroom teaching behaviors and student ratings of college teaching effectiveness.

Journal: *Journal of Educational Psychology*, Feb. 1983, 75(1), 138-149.

Related research: Tom, F.K.T. and Cushman, H.R., 1975. The Cornell diagnostic observation and reporting system for student descriptions of college teaching. *Search*, 5(8), 1-27.

3606
Test name: TEACHER RATING SCALES

Purpose: To measure teacher behavior.

Number of items: 12 behavioral incidents plus 8 judgements.

Format: Judgements made on a 5-point Likert scale. Behavior scales on an 8-point frequency scale.

Validity: Convergent validity ranged from .57 to .70. Discriminant validity ranged from .21 to .47.

Author: Murphy, K.R. et al.

Article: Effects of the purpose of rating on accuracy in observing teacher behavior and evaluating teacher performance.

Journal: *Journal of Educational Psychology*, Feb. 1984, 76(1), 45-54.

Related research: Murphy, K., 1982. Do behavioral observation scales measure observation? *Journal of Applied Behavior*, 67, 562-567.

3607
Test name: TEACHING EFFECTIVENESS INSTRUMENT

Purpose: To measure students' perceptions of teaching practice that contribute to or detract from learning.

Number of items: Varies by respondent.

Format: Students list "things" that contribute to or detract from teaching. Lists then are content analyzed to ascertain the number, variety, and nature of reasons of things cited.

Reliability: Lights coefficients: number (.93); variety (.80); nature of reason (.72).

Author: Cruickshank, D.R. et al.

Article: Evaluation of reflective teacher questionnaire.

Journal: *Journal of Educational Research*, Sept./Oct. 1981, 75(1), 26-32.

Related research: Nott, D.L. and Williams, E.J., 1980. Experimental effects of reflective teaching on preservice teachers' ability to identify a greater number and wider variety of variables present during the act of teaching. Paper. American Educational Research Association, Boston.

3608

Test name: WORK OPINION QUESTIONNAIRE

Purpose: To measure job-related values that predict performance of low income workers at entry-level jobs.

Number of items: 35

Format: 5-point Likert agreement scales. All items presented.

Reliability: Alphas ranged from .66 to .87 across subscales.

Validity: All subscales correlate significantly ($p < .05$) with the Job Performance Index.

Author: Johnson, C.D. et al.

Article: Predicting job performance of low income workers: The Work Opinion Questionnaire.

Journal: *Personnel Psychology*, summer 1984, 37(2), 291-299.

VOCATIONAL INTEREST

3609
Test name: AFFECTIVE COMMITMENT SCALE

Purpose: To assess commitment characterized by positive feelings of identification with, attachment to, and involvement in, the work organization.

Number of items: 8

Format: Responses are made on a 7-point Likert-type scale from strongly disagree to strongly agree. Examples are presented.

Reliability: Coefficient alphas were .88 and .84.

Validity: Correlations with other commitment measures ranged from -.01 to .86.

Author: Meyer, J.P. and Allen, N.J.

Article: Testing the "side-bet theory" of organizational commitment: Some methodological considerations.

Journal: *Journal of Applied Psychology*, Aug. 1984, *69*(3), 372-378.

Related research: Jackson, D.N., 1970. A sequential system for personality scale development. In C.D. Spielberger (Ed.), *Current topics in clinical and community psychology*, (Vol. 2, pp. 61-96). New York: Academic Press.

3610
Test name: ASSESSMENT OF CAREER DECISION-MAKING SCALE

Purpose: To measure progress in career decision-making.

Format: Agree-disagree.

Reliability: Test-retest ranged from .67 to .82 across subscales. Alphas ranged from .67 to .82.

Validity: Subscale intercorrelations presented and resemble previous patterns.

Author: Kahn, M.W. and Weare, C.R.

Article: The role of anxiety in the career decision-making of liberal arts students.

Journal: *Journal of Vocational Behavior*, June 1983, *22*(3), 312-323.

Related research: Harren, V.A. et al., 1978. Influence of sex role attitudes and cognitive styles on career decision making. *Journal of Counseling Psychology, 25*, 390-395.

3611
Test name: CAREER COMMITMENT SCALE

Purpose: To measure commitment to job.

Number of items: 8

Format: 5-point Likert format.

Reliability: Test-retest = .67.

Validity: Correlates significantly with career withdrawal cognitions (-.41) and role ambiguity (-.38).

Author: Blau, G.

Article: The measurement and prediction of career commitment.

Journal: *Journal of Occupational Psychology*, Dec. 1985, *58*(4), 277-288.

Related research: Downing, P. et al., 1978. *Work attitudes and performance questionnaire*. San Francisco School of Nursing, University of California.

3612
Test name: CAREER COMMITMENT SCALE

Purpose: To assess interest in long-term career prospects and advancement.

Number of items: 17

Format: Items are rated on a 5-point scale with scores ranging from 17 to 85.

Reliability: Coefficient alpha was .83.

Author: Koski, L.K. and Subich, L.M.

Article: Career and homemaking choices of college preparatory and vocational education students.

Journal: *Vocational Guidance Quarterly*, Dec. 1985, *34*(2), 116-123.

Related research: Farmer, H., 1983. Career and homemaking plans for high school youth. *Journal of Counseling Psychology*, 30, 40-45.
   Super, D.E. et al., 1978. *The Work Salience Inventory*. New York: Columbia University, Teachers College (mimeographed).

3613
Test name: CAREER DECISION-MAKING QUESTIONNAIRE

Purpose: To assess readiness for career decision-making.

Number of items: 14

Format: Item presented; response categories not presented.

Reliability: Test-retest = .83.

Validity: Factor analysis confirmed the constructs on which the CDM was based. High scorers on CDM likely to be successful users of the SIGI.

Author: Dungy, G.

Article: Computer-assisted guidance: Determining who is ready.

Journal: *Journal of College Student Personnel*, Nov. 1984, 25(6), 539-545.

3614
Test name: CAREER EXPLORATION SURVEY

Purpose: To measure the reactions and beliefs of people to the way they get information about careers.

Number of items: 59

Format: Multiple formats. All items presented.

Reliability: Alphas ranged from .67 to .89 across subscales.

Validity: Factor analysis of items in different populations yielded similar results. Social Desirability did not correlate with CES dimensions. Other validity studies presented.

Author: Stumpf, S.A. et al.

Article: Development of the Career Exploration Survey.

Journal: *Journal of Vocational Behavior*, April 1983, 22(2), 191-226.

3615
Test name: CAREER INDECISION FACTORS SURVEY

Purpose: To measure underlying reasons for career indecision as a means of differential diagnosis and treatment of career problems.

Number of items: 47

Format: Includes six subscales with Likert and semantic differential items, each scaled along 5 points.

Reliability: Coefficient alpha for self-esteem subscale was .83. Coefficient alpha for choice anxiety was .87.

Author: Robbins, S.B. et al.

Article: Attrition behavior before career development workshops.

Journal: *Journal of Counseling Psychology*, April 1985, 32(2), 232-238.

Related research: Robbins, S. et al., 1983. *Career indecision factor survey*. Unpublished manuscript, Virginia Commonwealth University, Richmond.

3616
Test name: CAREER INFORMATION-SEEKING SCALE

Purpose: To measure participants' amount of career information-seeking.

Number of items: 17

Format: Respondents rate their frequency of performance on a 6-point scale for each of the 17 information-seeking behaviors.

Reliability: Internal consistency was .88.

Author: Remer, P. et al.

Article: Multiple outcome evaluation of a life-career development course.

Journal: *Journal of Counseling Psychology*, Oct. 1984, *31*(4), 532-546.

Related research: O'Neill, C.D., 1982. *The differential effectiveness of two dimension-making treatments on college freshmen.* Unpublished doctoral dissertation, University of Kentucky.
  Krumboltz, J.D. and Schroeder, W.W., 1965. Promoting career planning through reinforcement. *Personnel and Guidance Journal*, *44*, 19-26.

3617
Test name: CAREER ORIENTATION INVENTORY

Purpose: To measure degree of expectation and aspiration for a high-level occupation.

Number of items: 17

Format: Semantic differential. All items presented.

Reliability: Hoyt reliabilities ranged from .84 to .85 across sex. Item-total correlations: rho = .86.

Validity: Males tended to have stronger career orientations than females.

Author: Cochran, L.R.

Article: Level of career aspirations and strength of career orientation.

Journal: *Journal of Vocational Behavior*, Aug. 1983, *23*(1), 1-10.

3618
Test name: CAREER ORIENTATION SCALE

Purpose: To measure depth and intensity of interest in a career.

Number of items: 27

Format: Likert format.

Reliability: = .81.

Author: Pedro, J.D.

Article: Induction into the workplace: The impact of internships.

Journal: *Journal of Vocational Behavior*, Aug. 1984, *25*(1), 80-95.

Related research: Greenhaus, J., 1971. An investigation of the role of career salience in vocational behavior. *Journal of Vocational Behavior, 2,* 209-216.

3619
Test name: CAREER PLANNING QUESTIONNAIRE

Purpose: To measure career maturity in 11th grade students.

Number of items: 130

Format: Agree-disagree and multiple-choice. Sample items presented.

Reliability: KR-20s ranged from .71 to .91 across subscales (median = .70).

Validity: Not related to aptitude. Not related to frequency of discussion of plans after high school. Selected subscales correlated with knowledge of duties in occupations and level of certainty about entering occupations.

Author: Westbrook, B.W. et al.

Article: Predictive and construct validity of six experimental measures of career maturity.

Journal: *Journal of Vocational Behavior,* Dec. 1985, *27*(3), 338-355.

Related research: Tittle, C.K., 1982. Career, marriage and family: Values in adult roles and guidance. *Personnel and Guidance Journal, 61,* 154-158.

3620
Test name: CAREER SALIENCE QUESTIONNAIRE

Purpose: To measure the importance of work.

Number of items: 28

Format: All but one item is a five-point response Likert-type. The remaining item is a six-response ranking item.

Reliability: Coefficient alpha was .81. Stability reliability coefficient was .89.

Validity: Correlations with other variables ranged from -.09 to .45.

Author: Thomas, R.G. and Bruning, C.R.

Article: Validities and reliabilities of minor modifications of the Central Life Interests and Career Salience Questionnaires.

Journal: *Measurement and Evaluation in Guidance,* Oct. 1981, *14*(3), 128-135.

Related research: Greenhaus, J., 1971. An investigation of the role of career salience in vocational behavior. *Journal of Vocational Behavior, 1,* 209-216.

3621
Test name: CAREER SALIENCE SCALE

Purpose: To measure extent to which a career is a vital part of peoples' lives.

Number of items: 7

Format: Likert format.

Reliability: Alpha = .83.

Author: Sekaran, U.

Article: Factors influencing the quality of life in dual-career families.

Journal: *Journal of Occupational Psychology*, June 1983, *56*(2), 161-174.

Related research: Sekaran, U., 1982. An investigation of the career salience of men and women in dual career families. *Journal of Vocational Behavior*, *20*, 111-119.

3622
Test name: CENTRAL LIFE INTERESTS QUESTIONNAIRE —MODIFIED

Purpose: To measure the importance of work.

Number of items: 30

Format: Multiple-choice items with three choices. A sample is presented.

Reliability: Stability reliability coefficient was .75.

Validity: Correlations with other variables ranged from -.26 to .45.

Author: Thomas, R.G. and Bruning, C.R.

Article: Validities and reliabilities of minor modifications of the Central Life Interests and Career Salience Questionnaires.

Journal: *Measurement and Evaluation in Guidance*, Oct. 1981, *14*(3), 128-135.

Related research: Dubin, R., 1956. *Central life interests questionnaire.* Unpublished manuscript, Graduate School of Administration, University of California, Irvine.

3623
Test name: CERTAINTY OF OCCUPATIONAL PREFERENCE SCALE

Purpose: To measure how firm occupational aspirations are among secondary school students.

Number of items: 8

Format: 5-point agreement scales. Sample items presented.

Reliability: Internal reliability = .79. Test-retest = .79.

Author: Kidd, J.M.

Article: The relationship of self and occupational concepts to the occupational preferences of adolescents.

Journal: *Journal of Vocational Behavior*, Feb. 1984, 24(1), 48-65.

Related research: Kidd, J.M., 1982. *Self and occupational concepts in occupational preferences and the entry into work: An overlapping longitudinal study.* Unpublished Ph.D. thesis, The Hatfield Polytechnic.

3624
Test name: COMMITMENT SCALE

Purpose: To measure commitment to organization of employment/membership.

Number of items: 15 (continuance); 8 (affective).

Format: 7-point response format. Sample item presented.

Reliability: Alpha = .77 (continuance). Alpha = .87 (affective).

Validity: Continuance did not correlate with Organizational Commitment Questionnaire (r = -.06). Affective did correlate with OCQ (r = .78).

Author: Meyer, J.P. and Allen, N.J.

Article: Testing the "side-bet theory" of organizational commitment: Some methodological considerations.

Journal: *Journal of Applied Psychology*, Aug. 1984, 69(3), 372-378.

Related research: Ritzer, G. and Trice, H.M., 1969. An empirical test of Howard Becker's side-bet theory. *Social Forces, 47,* 475-479.

Mowday, R.T. et al., 1979. The measurement of organizational commitment. *Journal of Vocational Behavior, 14,* 224-257.

Hrebiniak, L.G. and Alluto, J.A., 1972. Personal and role-related factors in the development of organizational commitment. *Administrative Science Quarterly, 17,* 555-573.

3625
Test name: CONTINUANCE COMMITMENT SCALE

Purpose: To assess the extent to which employees feel committed to their organizations by virtue of the costs that they feel are associated with leaving.

Number of items: 8

Format: Responses are made on a 7-point scale from strongly disagree to strongly agree.

Reliability: Coefficient alphas were .73 and .74.

Validity: Correlations with other commitment measures ranged from -.06 to .33.

Author: Meyer, J.P. and Allen, N.J.

Article: Testing the "side-bet theory" of organizational commitment: Some methodological considerations.

Journal: *Journal of Applied Psychology*, Aug. 1984, *69*(3), 372-378.

3626
Test name: EMPLOYMENT COMMITMENT SCALE

Purpose: To provide an index of employment commitment.

Number of items: 6

Format: Responses are made on a 5-point scale from 5 (agree a lot) to 1 (disagree a lot). Separate scales for the employed and unemployed. All items are presented.

Reliability: Alpha coefficients ranged from .64 to .71.

Validity: Correlation with psychological distress ranged from -.22 to .34 (N's ranged from 81 to 636).

Author: Jackson, P.R. et al.

Article: Unemployment and psychological distress in young people: The moderating role of employment commitment.

Journal: *Journal of Applied Psychology*, Aug. 1983, *68*(3), 525-535.

Related research: Warr, P.B. et al., 1979. Scales for the measurement of some work attitudes and aspects of psychological well-being. *Journal of Occupational Psychology*, 52, 129-148.

3627
Test name: EMPLOYMENT IMMOBILITY QUESTIONNAIRE

Purpose: To provide administrators' assessment of how locked-in to their job they feel.

Number of items: 8

Format: The items are combined into a single score.

Reliability: Coefficient alpha was .70.

Validity: Correlations with a variety of variables ranged from r = -.30 to r = .28.

Author: Burke, R.J. and Weir, T.

Article: Occuptional locking-in: Some empirical findings.

Journal: *Journal of Social Psychology*, Dec. 1982, *118*(second half), 177-185.

Related research: Quinn, R.P., 1975. *Locking-in as a moderator of the relationship between job satisfaction and mental health.* Unpublished manuscript, Surrey Research Centre, University of Michigan, Ann Arbor.

3628
Test name: EMPLOYMENT IMPORTANCE SCALE

Purpose: To measure employment importance and work involvement.

Number of items: 3

Format: Multiple-choice. All items presented.

Reliability: Alpha ranged from .34 to .73.

Author: Feather, N.T. and Bond, M.J.

Article: Time structure and purposeful activity among employed and unemployed university graduates.

Journal: *Journal of Occupational Psychology*, Sept. 1983, *56*(3), 241-254.

Related research: Feather, N.T. and Davenport, P.R., 1981. Unemployment and depressive affect: A motivational and attributional analysis. *Journal of Personality and Social Psychology, 41*, 422-436.

3629
Test name: ENGINEERING INTEREST INVENTORY

Purpose: To measure interest in a career in engineering.

Number of items: 111

Format: Formats include a 3-point Yes-Doubtful-No scale, and a 20-point rating scale.

Reliability: Alphas ranged from .68 to .93.

Author: Meir, E.E.

Article: Fostering a career in engineering.

Journal: *Journal of Vocational Behavior*, Feb. 1981, *18*(1), 115-120.

Related research: Dunnette, M.D., 1964. Further research on vocational interest differences among several types of engineers. *Personnel and Guidance Journal, 42*, 484-493.

3630
Test name: FEEDBACK SHEET

Purpose: To measure satisfaction with CHOICES and SDS career exploration experiences.

Number of items: 9

Format: Likert-type response categories.

Reliability: R = .83.

Author: Reardon, R.C. et al.

Article: Self-directed career exploration: A comparison of CHOICES and the Self-Directed Search.

Journal: *Journal of Vocational Behavior*, Feb. 1982, *20*(1), 22-30.

Related research: Talbot, D.B. and Birk, J.M., 1979. Does the vocational exploration and insight kit equal the sum of its parts? A comparison study. *Journal of Counseling Psychology, 26*, 359-362.

3631
Test name: HOME ECONOMICS ATTITUDES SCALE

Purpose: To measure competence and interest in home economics.

Number of items: 66

Format: Multiple-choice.

Reliability: Alpha ranged from .84 to .96 across subscales.

Author: Schumm, W.R. and Kennedy, C.E.

Article: Dimensions of competence and interest in home economics.

Journal: *Psychological Reports*, Dec. 1985, *57*(3-I), 698.

Related research: Nichols, C.W. et al., 1983. What home economics programs do mothers want for sons and daughters? *Journal of Home Economics, 75*, 28-30.

3632
Test name: JOB DECISION STYLE QUESTIONNAIRE

Purpose: To measure manner in which a person chooses a job.

Number of items: 6

Format: Subjects rank six statements as most to least descriptive of themselves.

Reliability: Test-retest (2 weeks) = .87.

Author: Hesketh, B.

Article: Decision-making style and career decision-making behaviors among school leavers.

Journal: *Journal of Vocational Behavior*, April 1982, *20*(2), 223-234.

Related research: Arroba, T., 1977. Styles of decision-making and their use: An empirical study. *British Journal of Guidance and Counseling, 5*(2), 149-158.

3633
Test name: JOB INVOLVEMENT AND SEMANTIC DIFFERENTIAL

Purpose: To measure job involvement.

Number of items: 8

Format: Semantic differential. All items presented.

Reliability: Item-total correlations ranged from .64 to .82 (median = .75). Alpha = .83. Test-retest = .74.

Validity: Correlates .27 (p<.01) with job satisfaction.

Author: Kanungo, R.N.

Article: Measurement of job and work involvement.

Journal: *Journal of Applied Psychology*, June 1982, *67*(3), 341-349.

3634
Test name: JOB INVOLVEMENT SCALE

Purpose: To measure job involvement.

Number of items: 20

Format: 4-point Likert format. Sample items presented.

Reliability: .83 (unspecified).

Author: Drory, A.

Article: Organizational stress and job attitudes: Moderating effects of organizational level and task characteristics.

Journal: *Psychological Reports*, 1981, *49*(1), 139-146.

Related research: Lodahl, T. and Kejner, J., 1965. The definition and measurement of job involvement. *Journal of Applied Psychology*, 65, 24-33.

3635
Test name: JOB INVOLVEMENT MEASURE

Purpose: To measure job involvement.

Format: Responses to each item are made on a 7-point scale from 1 (strongly disagree) to 7 (strongly agree).

Reliability: Coefficient alpha was .86.

Validity: Correlations with other variables ranged from -.06 to .20.

Author: Graddick, M.M. and Farr, J.L.

Article: Professionals in scientific disciplines: Sex-related differences in working life commitments.

Article: *Journal of Applied Psychology*, Nov. 1983, *68*(4), 641-645.

Related research: Lodahl, T. and Kejner, J., 1965. The definition and measurement of job involvement. *Journal of Applied Psychology, 65*, 24-33.

Dubin, R., 1956. Industrial workers' worlds: A study of the central life interests of industrial workers. *Social Problems, 3*, 131-142.

3636
Test name: JOB INVOLVEMENT SCALE

Purpose: To measure job involvement.

Number of items: 4

Format: 5-point Likert format.

Reliability: Alpha = .69.

Author: Ashford, S.J. and Cummings, L.L.

Article: Proactive feedback seeking: The instrumental use of the information environment.

Journal: *Journal of Occupational Behavior*, March 1985, 58(1), 67-79.

Related research: Lawler, E.E. and Hall, D.T., 1970. Relationships of job characteristics to job involvement. *Journal of Applied Psychology, 54*, 305-312.

3637
Test name: JOB INVOLVEMENT SCALE

Purpose: To measure job involvement.

Number of items: 5

Format: Items deal with dislike of the work, reward value of the work, pride and accomplishments from the work, and opportunities to perform well.

Reliability: Coefficient alpha was .82.

Validity: Correlations with other variables ranged from -.16 to .47.

Author: Hammer, T.H. et al.

Article: Absenteeism when workers have a voice: The case of employee ownership.

Journal: *Journal of Applied Psychology*, Oct. 1981, 66(5), 561-573.

Related research: Miller, G.A., 1967. Professionals in bureaucracy: Alienation among industrial scientists and engineers. *American Sociological Review, 32*, 755-768.

3638
Test name: LIFESTYLE INDEX

Purpose: To measure career salience.

Number of items: 9

Format: Multiple-choice.

Reliability: Test-retest ranged from .74 to .81 across items.

Author: Brooks, L. et al.

Article: The effects of a nontraditional role-modeling intervention on sex typing of occupational preferences and career salience in adolescent females.

Journal: *Journal of Vocational Behavior*, June 1985, *26*(3), 264-276.

Related research: Angrist, S.S., 1972. Changes in women's work aspirations during college (or work does not equal career). *International Journal of Sociology of the Family*, *2*, 27-37.

3639
Test name: LIST OF COURSES IN NURSING

Purpose: To measure attractiveness of nursing courses representing nine clinical areas.

Number of items: 90

Format: Yes-Doubtful-No response scale.

Reliability: Split-half = .89. Equivalent test = .82.

Author: Hener, T. and Meir, E.I.

Article: Congruency, consistency and differentiation as predictors of job satisfaction with the nursing profession.

Journal: *Journal of Vocational Behavior*, June 1981, *18*(3), 304-309.

Related research: Peiser, C. and Meir, E.I., 1978. Congruency, consistency, and differentiation of vocational interests as predictors of vocational satisfaction and preference stability. *Journal of Vocational Behavior*, *12*, 270-278.

3640
Test name: MEDICAL CAREER DEVELOPMENT INVENTORY

Purpose: To measure degree of development and readiness to cope with the career of physician.

Number of items: 25

Format: Multiple-choice. All items presented.

Reliability: Alpha = .93 (total). Alphas ranged from .73 to .91 across subscales.

Validity: Did not correlate significantly with sex. Correlated significantly (r = .41) with career planfulness.

Author: Savickas, M.L.

Article: Construction and validation of a physician career development inventory.

Journal: *Journal of Vocational Behavior*, Aug. 1984, *25*(1), 106-123.

3641
Test name: NURSING COURSE ATTRACTIVENESS SCALE

Purpose: To measure the attractiveness of nursing courses.

Number of items: 90

Format: Yes-Doubtful-No format for each items. Sample item presented.

Reliability: Split-half = .89.

Validity: Nurses in specific clinical areas scored higher on that area than mean scores of all nurses for that area (no quantitative measure provided).

Author: Hener, T. and Meir, E.I.

Article: Congruency, consistency and differentiation as predictors of job satisfaction with the nursing profession.

Journal: *Journal of Vocational Behavior*, June 1981, *18*(3), 304-309.

3642
Test name: OCCUPATIONAL RATING SCALE

Purpose: To rate to what degree people believe occupations are "appropriate" for men or women.

Number of items: 14 (occupational titles).

Format: 7-point bipolar rating scale with anchors "appropriate for men" and "appropriate for women."

Reliability: Test-retest = .90 (2 weeks).

Author: Yanico, B.J.

Article: Androgyny and occupational sex-stereotyping of college students.

Journal: *Psychological Reports*, 1982, *50*(3-I), 875-878.

Related research: Shinar, E.H., 1979. Sexual stereotypes of occupations. *Journal of Vocational Behavior*, 317-328.

3643
Test name: ORGANIZATIONAL COMMITMENT QUESTIONNAIRE

Purpose: To assess an affective orientation to the organization.

Number of items: 15

Format: Organizational commitment includes: a strong belief in and acceptance of the organization's goals and values, a willingness to exert considerable effort on behalf of the organization, and a strong desire to maintain membership in the organization.

Responses are made on a 7-point Likert-type scale from strongly disagree to strongly agree.

Reliability: Coefficient alphas were .93 and .89.

Validity: Correlations with other commitment measures ranged from -.06 to .86.

Author: Meyer, J.P. and Allen, N.J.

Article: Testing the "side-bet theory" of organizational commitment: Some methodological considerations.

Journal: *Journal of Applied Psychology*, Aug. 1984, *69*(3), 372-378.
    Mowday, R.T. et al., 1979. The measurement of organizational commitment. *Journal of Vocational Behavior*, *14*, 224-257.
    Graddick, M.M. and Farr, J.L., 1983. Professionals in scientific disciplines: Sex-related differences in working life commitments, *Journal of Applied Psychology*. *68*(4), 641-645.

3644
Test name: ORGANIZATIONAL AND PROFESSIONAL COMMITMENT SCALES

Purpose: To measure commitment to an organization's (or a profession's) goals and values.

Number of items: 15 each for organization and profession.

Format: 7-point Likert scales.

Reliability: Alpha (organization) = .91. Alpha (profession) = .87.

Author: Aranya, N. and Barak, A.

Article: A test of Holland's theory in a population of accountants.

Journal: *Journal of Vocational Behavior*, Aug. 1981, *19*(1), 15-24.

Related research: Porter, L.W. et al., 1974. Organizational commitment, job satisfaction and turnover among psychiatric technicians. *Journal of Applied Psychology*, *59*, 603-609.

3645
Test name: ORGANIZATIONAL COMMITMENT SCALE

Purpose: To measure organizational commitment.

Number of items: 9

Reliability: Cronbach's coefficient alpha was .90.

Validity: Correlation with other variables ranged from -.30 to .52.

Author: Chacko, T.I.

Article: Women and equal employment opportunity: Some unintended effects.

Journal: *Journal of Applied Psychology*, Feb. 1982, *67*(1), 119-123.

Related research: Porter, L.W. et al., 1974. Organizational commitment, job satisfaction, and turnover among psychiatric technicians. *Journal of Applied Psychology, 59*, 603-609.

3646
Test name: ORGANIZATIONAL COMMITMENT SCALE

Purpose: To measure commitment to stay (or leave) employing organization.

Number of items: 4

Format: 5-point Likert format. All items presented.

Reliability: Alpha = .88.

Validity: Correlated -.17 with turnover intentions and -.23 with actual turnover (both p<.001).

Author: Ferris, K.R. and Aranya, N.

Article: A comparison of two organizational commitment scales.

Journal: *Personnel Psychology*, spring 1983, *36*(1), 87-98.

Related research: Hrebiniak, L.G. and Alluto, J.A., 1972. Personal and role-related factors in the development of organizational commitment. *Administrative Science Quarterly, 17*, 555-573.

3647
Test name: ORGANIZATIONAL COMMITMENT SCALE

Purpose: To measure commitment to employing organizations.

Number of items: 15

Format: 7-point Likert format. All items presented.

Reliability: Alpha = .90.

Validity: Correlated -.37 with turnover intentions and -.22 with actual turnover.

Author: Ferris, K.R. and Aranya, N.

Article: A comparison of two organizational commitment scales.

Journal: *Personnel Psychology*, spring 1983, *36*(1), 87-98.

Related research: Porter, L.W. et al., 1974. Organizational commitment, job satisfaction, and turnover among psychiatric technicians. *Journal of Applied Psychology, 59*, 603-609.
   Arnold, H.J. and Feldman, D.C., 1982. A multivariate analysis of the determinants of job turnover. *Journal of Applied Psychology, 67*(3), 350-360.
   Drasgow, F. and Miller, H.E., 1982. Psychometric and substantive

issues in scale construction and validation. *Journal of Applied Psychology*, 67(3), 268-279.

3648
Test name: ORGANIZATIONAL COMMITMENT SCALE

Purpose: To measure "moral" commitment to organizations.

Number of items: 4

Format: 5-point response scales.

Reliability: Alpha = .65.

Author: Werbel, J.D. and Gould, S.

Article: A comparison of the relationship of commitment to turnover in recent hires and tenured employees.

Journal: *Journal of Applied Psychology*, Dec. 1984, 69(4), 687-690.

Related research: Gould, S. and Penley, L., 1982. *Organizational commitment: A test of a model*. Working Paper Series. San Antonio, TX: The University of Texas at San Antonio.

3649
Test name: ORGANIZATIONAL IDENTIFICATION SCALE

Purpose: To measure the extent to which individuals take pride in and have a positive attitude toward their organization.

Number of items: 4

Format: A sample item is presented.

Reliability: Coefficient alpha was .81.

Validity: Correlation with other variables ranged from -.28 to .46.

Author: Gould, S. and Werbel, J.D.

Article: Work involvement: A comparison of dual wage earner and single wage earner families.

Journal: *Journal of Applied Psychology*, May 1983, 68(2), 313-319.

Related research: Patchen, M., 1970. *Participation, achievement, and involvement on the job*. Englewood Cliff, NJ: Prentice-Hall.

3650
Test name: PROPENSITY TO LEAVE INDEX

Purpose: To measure propensity to leave job.

Number of items: 3

Format: 5-point Likert response categories.

Reliability: Median item intercorrelation = .57.

Author: Wright, D. and Thomas, J.

Article: Role strain among psychologists in the midwest.

Journal: *Journal of School Psychology*, 1982, *20*(2), 96-102.

Related research: Lyons, T.F., 1971. Role clarity, need for clarity, satisfaction, tension, and withdrawal. *Organizational Behavior and Human Performance*, *6*, 99-110.

3651
Test name: RAMAK INTEREST INVENTORY

Purpose: To measure attractiveness of occupational titles.

Number of items: 72

Format: Yes-No.

Reliability: Equivalent test = .76.

Author: Gati, I. and Meir, E.I.

Article: Congruence and consistency derived from the circular and hierarchical models as predictors of occupational choice satisfaction.

Journal: *Journal of Vocational Behavior*, June 1982, *20*(3), 354-365.

Related research: Meir, E.I. and Barak, A., 1974. A simple instrument for measuring vocational interests based on Roe's classification of occupations. *Journal of Vocational Behavior*, *4*, 33-42.

3652
Test name: REENLISTMENT DECISIONS QUESTIONNAIRE

Purpose: To measure U.S. Army personnel's perceptions, expectancies, satisfactions, preferences, and intentions in regard to reenlistment.

Number of items: Form 1: 63, Form 2: 59.

Format: Includes four sections of: perception, expectancies, satisfaction, intention and reenlistment.

Reliability: Internal consistency estimates ranged from .70 to .84.

Author: Motowidlo, S.J. and Lawton, G.W.

Article: Affective and cognitive factors in soldiers' reenlistment decisions.

Journal: *Journal of Applied Psychology*, May 1984, *69*(2), 157-166.

Related research: Motowidlo, S.J. et al., 1980. Reenlistment factors for first-term enlisted personnel. Proceedings of the 22nd Annual Conference of the Military Testing Association (pp. 681-690). Toronto: Military Testing Association.

3653
Test name: SELF-ASSESSMENT QUESTIONNAIRE

Purpose: To assist college students in identifying occupations consistent with a major field of study.

Number of items: 107

Format: Includes six scales: appeal, practical, clues, aptitude, skills, and preferences. There are 4 forms.

Reliability: Coefficient alphas for the 4 forms ranged from .81 to .98.

Author: Turner, C.J.

Article: The reliability and factorial validity of the self-assessment questionnaire for liberal arts majors.

Journal: *Educational and Psychological Measurement*, summer 1983, *43*(2), 509-516.

Related research: Malnig, L.R. and Morrow, S.L., 1975. *What can I do with a major in ...?*. Jersey City, NJ: St. Peter's College Press.

3654
Test name: SELF-CONCEPT/ OCCUPATIONAL CONCEPT DISTANCE SCALE

Purpose: To assess similarity between actual and ideal self-concept and perceived occupational concepts.

Number of items: 183 (three 61-item rating scales).

Format: 7-point response scale.

Reliability: Alpha ranged from .70 to .88.

Author: Kidd, J.M.

Article: The relationship of self and occupational concepts to the occupational preferences of adolescents.

Journal: *Journal of Vocational Behavior*, Feb. 1984, *24*(1), 48-65.

Related research: Kidd, J.M., 1982. *Self and occupational concepts in occupational preferences and the entry into work: An overlapping longitudinal study*. Unpublished Ph.D. thesis, The Hatfield Polytechnic.

3655
Test name: SPECIALITY INDECISION SCALE

Purpose: To measure indecision about specialities in professions.

Number of items: 16

Format: 4-point Likert format. All items presented.

Reliability: Alpha = .82.

Validity: One general factor left residual correlations to produce three additional factors.

Author: Savickas, M.L. et al.

Article: Measuring specialty indecision among career-decided students.

Journal: *Journal of Vocational Behavior*, Dec. 1985, 27(3), 356-367.

3656
Test name: VOCATIONAL COMMITMENT QUESTIONNAIRE

Purpose: To measure organizational commitment and correlates of commitment.

Number of items: 56

Format: 5-point Likert agreement scales and multiple-choice. Sample items presented for all scales.

Reliability: Alpha ranged from .64 to .91 across subscales.

Author: Martin, T.N. and O'Laughlin, M.S.

Article: Predictors of organizational commitment: The study of part-time army reservists.

Journal: *Journal of Vocational Behavior*, Dec. 1984, 25(3), 270-283.

Related research: Price, J.L. and Mueller, C.W., 1981. A causal model of turnover for nurses. *Academy of Management Journal*, 24, 543-565.

Ivancevich, J.W. and Matteson, M.T., 1980. *Stress and work: A managerial perspective.* Glenview, IL: Scott, Foresman.

Brayfield, A.H. and Rothe, H.F., 1951. An index of job satisfaction. *Journal of Applied Psychology*, 63, 677-688.

Martin, T.N., 1979. A contextual model of employee turnover intentions. *Academy of Management Journal*, 22, 313-324.

Mowday, R.T. et al., 1979. *Employee-organization linkages: The psychology of commitment, absenteeism, and turnover.* New York: Academic Press.

3657
Test name: VOCATIONAL DECISION-MAKING DIFFICULTY SCALE

Purpose: To assess the number of reasons given by subjects for vocational indecision.

Number of items: 13

Format: Each item is answered either "true" or "false." True responses are summed to provide a total score.

Reliability: KR-20 values ranged from .63 to .86.

Author: Slaney, R.B.

Article: Relation of career indecision to changes in expressed vocational interests.

Journal: *Journal of Counseling Psychology*, July 1984, *31*(3), 349-355.

Related research: Holland, J.L. and Holland, J.E., 1977. Vocational indecision: More evidence and speculation. *Journal of Counseling Psychology*, *24*, 404-414.

3658
Test name: VOCATIONAL DECISION SCALE

Purpose: To measure degree of decidedness, comfort, and reasons for being decided or undecided about a career decision.

Number of items: 38

Format: 5-point Likert format.

Reliability: Test-rest ranged from .36 to .64.

Author: Larson, L.M. and Heppner, P.P.

Article: The relationship of problem-solving appraisal to career decision and indecision.

Journal: *Journal of Vocational Behavior*, Feb. 1985, *26*(1), 55-65.

Related research: Jones, L.K. and Chenery, M.F., 1980. Multiple subtypes among vocationally undecided college students: A model and assessment instrument. *Journal of Counseling Psychology*, *27*, 469-477.

3659
Test name: VOCATIONAL DECISION SCALE - DECIDEDNESS AND COMFORT DIMENSIONS

Purpose: To measure vocational decidedness, comfort, and reasons for undecidedness.

Number of items: 14

Format: Items are rated on a 5-point Likert agree-disagree scale.

Reliability: Test-retest (2 weeks) reliabilities ranged from .61 to .77

Author: Jones, L.K. and Brooks, N.

Article: Outreach: A career exploration kit in the university library.

Journal: *Vocational Guidance Quarterly*, June 1985, *33*(4), 324-330.

Related research: Jones, L.K. and Chenery, M.F., 1980. Multiple subtypes among vocationally undecided college students: A model and assessment instrument. *Journal of Counseling Psychology*, *27*, 469-477.

3660
Test name: VOCATIONAL ROLE PREFERENCE SCALE

Purpose: To measure stereotypical vocational role orientations.

Number of items: 13

Format: Paired occupations, one "female" and one "male," one of which children are to choose as a future job.

Reliability: Test-retest = .81.

Author: Weeks, M.O.

Article: A second look at the impact of nontraditional vocational role models and curriculum on the vocational role preferences of kindergarten children.

Journal: *Journal of Vocational Behavior*, Aug. 1983, *23*(1), 64-71.

Related research: Weeks, M.O. et al., 1977. The impact of exposure to nontraditional vocational role models on the vocational role preferences of five-year-old children. *Journal of Vocational Behavior*, *10*, 139-145.

3661
Test name: WORK INVOLVEMENT SEMANTIC DIFFERENTIAL

Purpose: To measure work involvement.

Number of items: 8

Format: Semantic differential. All items presented.

Reliability: Item-total correlations ranged from .71 to .82 (median .74). Alpha = .83. Test-retest = .78.

Validity: Detailed convergent, discriminate criterion, and concurrent validity data reported.

Author: Kanungo, R.N.

Article: Measurement of job and work involvement.

Journal: *Journal of Applied Psychology*, June 1982, *67*(3), 341-349.

3662
Test name: WORK INVOLVEMENT SCALE

Purpose: To measure psychological involvement in work.

Number of items: 9

Format: 5- and 6-point rating scales.

Reliability: Alpha = .87.

Author: Pistrang, N.

Article: Women's work involvement and experience of new motherhood.

Journal: *Journal of Marriage and the Family*, May 1984, *46*(2), 433-447.

Related research: Lodahl, T. and Kejner, M., 1965. The definition and measurement of job involvement. *Journal of Applied Psychology, 44,* 24-33.

Jiminez, M.H., 1977. *Relationships between job orientation in women and adjustment to the first pregnancy and postpartum period.* Doctoral dissertation, Northwestern University.

Thornton, A. and Camburn, D., 1979. Fertility, sex role attitudes, and labor force participation. *Psychology of Women Quarterly, 4,* 61-80.

3663
Test name: WORK ORIENTATION SCALE

Purpose: To measure discipline and dedication to work as envisaged by Weber's concept of the Protestant ethic.

Number of items: 40 (from California Personality Inventory).

Format: True-False format.

Reliability: Alpha = .75. Test-retest = .70.

Validity: Correlated with CPI scales: well-being (.84); responsibility (.65); self-control (.67); socialization (.65); tolerance (.64); good impression (.66); achievement via conformance (.71); managerial potential (.74). Group norms presented for both males and females, by occupation.

Author: Gough, H.G.

Article: A Work Organization Scale for the California Personality Inventory.

Journal: *Journal of Applied Psychology,* Aug. 1985, 70(3), 505-513.

3664
Test name: WORK PREFERENCE QUESTIONNAIRE

Purpose: To measure job attribute preferences in an ideal job.

Number of items: 26

Format: Multiple-choice. All items presented.

Reliability: Alpha ranged from .43 to .95 across seven factors extracted by factor analysis.

Author: Sterns, L. et al.

Article: The relationship of extroversion and neuroticism with job preferences and job satisfaction for clerical employees.

Journal: *Journal of Occupational Psychology,* June 1983, 56(2), 145-153.

Related research: Barrett, G.V. et al., 1975. Relationship among job structural attributes, retention, aptitude and work values. Technical Report No. 3, The University of Akron, Department of Psychology.

Contract No.
N00014-74-A-0202-0001, NR 151-351. Office of Naval Research (NTIS No. AD-A014466).

3665
Test name: WORK-ROLE SALIENCE SCALE

Purpose: To measure importance of work and career in a person's life.

Number of items: 27

Format: 5-point Likert format. Sample items presented.

Reliability: Alpha ranged from .83 to .90.

Author: Beutell, N.J. and Greenhaus, J.H.

Article: Interrole conflict among married women: The influence of husband and wife characteristics on conflict and coping behavior.

Journal: *Journal of Vocational Behavior*, Aug. 1982, *21*(1), 99-110.

Related research: Greenhaus, J., 1971. An investigation of the role of career salience in vocational behavior. *Journal of Vocational Behavior*, *1*, 209-216.

AUTHOR INDEX

All numbers refer to test numbers for the current volume. Volumes 1 and 2 did not include an author index.

Abbott, M., 3557
Abott, K., 3392
Abraham, I.L., 3112, 3120, 3181
Abush, R., 2638, 3080, 3508
Achenbach, T.M., 2799, 2816
Adams, V.M., 3244
Addington, J., 3206, 3436
Adler, D., 3251
Adler, S., 2630, 2674
Agard, J.A., 2890
Ahl, D., 2724
Ahlgren, A., 2549
Ahmed, S.M.S., 3537
Aiken, L.R., 2740, 2761, 2795
Aiken, M., 3088
Ajzen, I., 2730
Albert, R.S., 2940, 2942
Alcock, J.E., 3211
Alesandrini, K.L., 2712, 3431
Alexander, S., 2440
Alexy, W.D., 3409
Ali Khan, N., 2606
Alker, H., 3272
Allen, N.J., 3609, 3624, 3625, 3643
Allison, S., 2412
Allison, S.N., 2471, 2545
Alluto, J.A., 3624, 3646
Alpert, R., 2433
Alvarez, K.M., 3559
Alyn, J.H., 2393
Ames, C., 3268
Ames, R., 3323
Amidon, E., 2579
Anderson, D.E., 3333
Anderson, G.J., 3094
Anderson, J.G., 2648
Anderson, N.H., 3314
Anderson, T.N., Jr., 3072

Angle, S.S., 3573
Angrist, S.S., 3638
Angstadt, L., 3572
Angulo, J., 3489
Antill, J.K., 3167
Antonak, R.F., 2693
Antonosky, A., 3111
Antoun, F.T., 3394
Aranya, N., 3644, 3646, 3647
Arkin, A.M., 2737
Arkowitz, H., 2603
Arlin, P.K., 3442
Armitage, D., 2375
Arnold, D., 3427
Arnold, H.J., 3647
Arnold, L., 2419
Arnold, S.T., 3271
Arroba, T., 3632
Arvey, R.D., 3326
Asarnow, J.R., 2465
Aschner, M.J., 2823
Ascione, F.R., 2888
Asher, S.R., 2554, 2583, 2923, 3449
Ashford, S.J., 2908, 3288, 3516, 3636
Atkeson, B.M., 2479
Atkinson, B., 2829
Atkinson, D.R., 2698, 3573
Auerbach, J.S., 3491
Austin, B.A., 2765
Authier, J., 3566
Avery, A.W., 3030
Avis, N.E., 3489
Azrin, N., 3022

Bachman, J.G., 2416, 3005
Bachmann, W., 2517, 2642, 3071
Backman, J., 2706, 2714

Bacorn, C.N., 2900
Bailey, D.B., Jr., 2556
Baker, R.W., 2400, 2401, 2611, 3124
Baker, S.B., 3565, 3571
Baldauf, R.B., Jr., 3299
Bander, R.S., 2418, 2430
Bandura, A., 3308
Banikiotes, P.G., 3573
Bank, L., 3141
Banks, M.H., 3081, 3082
Bannerman, J., 2765
Bannon, S.H., 2724
Barak, A., 3353, 3573, 3644, 3651
Baranowski, M.D., 3001
Barbrack, C.R., 2898
Bardo, D.J., 3060
Bardo, J.W., 3060
Barke, C.R., 3158
Barling, J., 2632, 2670, 3002
Barnett, R., 2789
Barratt, E.S., 3482
Barrett, G.V., 3061, 3664
Barrett-Lennard, G.T., 3475, 3506
Barron, F., 3206
Bartal, K.M., 3148
Bartenstein, C., 3230
Bartlett, C.J., 3050
Bartol, K.M., 3580
Basow, S.A., 3601
Bass, P.G., 2984
Bates, J., 3363
Battle, J., 3179
Baur, K.G., 2864
Beamesderfer, A., 2446
Beardsley, D.A., 2702
Beatty, J.R., 3487
Beatty, M.J., 3296
Becerra, R.M., 2790
Beck, A., 2530
Beck, A.T., 2445, 2446, 2476, 2482, 2483, 2485
Beck, J.J., Jr., 2882
Becker, H.A., 3458
Becker, L.A., 2393
Beckwith, L., 2935

Bedeian, A.G., 2542, 2657, 2667, 3288, 3289
Begin, G., 2567
Begley, T.M., 3272
Behuniak, P., Jr., 3234, 3300
Belk, S.S., 3512
Bell, M., 3173
Bell, M.D., 3173
Bell, N.J., 3030
Bell, W., 3445, 3446
Bellet, W., 3545
Belsky, J., 2978, 3025
Bem, S.L., 3389
Ben-Shakhar, G., 3582
Bengston, V., 3028
Benner, E.H., 3213, 3222
Bennett, S.K., 3589
Benton, S., 3422
Berg-Cross, L., 3448, 3523, 3535
Bergandi, T.A., 3517
Berger, E.M., 3296
Berger-Gross, V., 3291
Berman, W.H., 2457, 2974
Bernal, H.H., 3068
Berndt, D.J., 2498, 2534
Bernstein, B., 3109
Bernstein, B.L., 3336
Bernstein, D.M., 2596
Berry, G.L., 2790
Berryman, J.D., 2694
Berscheid, E., 3177
Berzins, J.I., 3294
Betz, N., 3343
Betz, N.E., 2418, 3249, 3256, 3306
Betz, N.M., 3180
Beutell, N.J., 2669, 2703, 2796, 3416, 3664
Beyard-Tyler, K.C., 2700
Bhagat, R.S., 2466, 2488, 2504, 2543
Biaggio, M.K., 3106, 3454, 3455, 3463
Biberman, G., 3368
Bienvenu, M.J., 2897, 2905
Bieri, J., 3421
Bierman, K.L., 2794

Biggs, D.A., 3573
Biggs, D.L., 2669, 3416
Biggs, P., 2760
Bilderback, E.W., 2786
Bills, R.E., 3523, 3535
Birchler, G.R., 2966
Birk, J.M., 3630
Birleson, A.T., 2465
Bizzell, R.P., 3197
Blanchard, R., 3403
Blank, J.R., 2379, 3079
Blasi, A., 3529
Blatt, S.J., 2461
Blau, G., 3344, 3611
Blau, G.J., 3136, 3179
Bledsoe, J.C., 2389, 3151
Blocher, D.H., 3408
Bloland, R.M., 3419
Bloom, B.S., 3563
Blotcky, A.D., 2860
Blumenfield, P.C., 3187
Blyton, P., 2645, 2656
Bobo, J.K., 2803
Bode, J., 3531
Bohlin, G., 3345
Bohlmeyer, E.M., 3490
Bohra, K.A., 2841
Bohrnstedt, G.W., 3177
Bond, M.J., 3628
Bonge, D., 3226
Booth, A., 3023
Booth, R., 2615
Booth, R.Z., 3129
Borg, W.F., 2888
Borg, W.R., 2888
Borko, H., 2739
Bororo, D.R., 3573
Borrello, G.M., 3443
Bortner, R., 3450
Bortner, R.W., 3518
Bovermon, I.K., 3214
Bowen, D.E., 3054, 3066, 3077
Bowen, G.L., 3026
Bowers, D.G., 2889, 3560
Bowlby, J., 2977, 3409

Boyar, J.I., 2447
Boyce, D., 3542
Bradburn, N., 2436
Bradburn, N.M., 2466
Brader, P.K., 2778
Bradley, R., 2553, 3233
Bradley, R.H., 2997, 2998, 3182
Brauchle, P.E., 3520
Bray, D.W., 3145
Brayfield, A.H., 2625, 2634, 3656
Brenner, O.C., 2470
Bretell, D., 2462
Brett, J., 2986
Briggs, L.J., 2387
Brink, T.L., 2475
Brinkerhoff, M.B., 2759
Brischetto, C.S., 3573
Brogan, D., 2746, 2783
Brookover, W.B., 3301
Brooks, G.C., 2784
Brooks, G.C., Jr., 2684
Brooks, L., 3572, 3638
Brooks, N., 3659
Brophy, J., 2911
Brophy, J.E., 2804, 2821
Brown, D., 2415
Brown, D.R., 3199
Brown, D.S., 2574
Brown, G.F., 3552
Brown, R., 3331
Brown, R.A., 2452
Brown, R.D., 2917
Brown, S.A., 3159, 3160
Brown, S.D., 2403, 2977
Browning, D.L., 2959
Brozo, W.G., 2881
Bruch, M.A., 3201
Bruning, C.R., 2716, 3620, 3622
Bryant, B.K., 3483
Bryant, N.D., 2398
Bryne, D., 3504
Buckmaster, L.R., 3285, 3286, 3386
Budner, S., 3509
Buhrmester, D., 3044
Bull, K.S., 3386

Bunting, C.E., 2738
Burke, C., 2391
Burke, P., 3202
Burke, R.J., 2591, 3102, 3462, 3518, 3627
Burkhead, E.J., 2638, 3080, 3508
Burnkrant, R.E., 3376
Burr, R.G., 2641
Burton, R.L., 3229
Busch-Rossnagel, N.C., 3356
Bush, A.J., 2930
Buss, A.H., 3357, 3358, 3463
Butler, M.C., 2641
Butterfield, D.A., 3580
Byrne, B.M., 3301, 3311, 3313
Byrne, D., 3503
Byrnes, D.A., 2424

Cacioppo, J.T., 3367
Cadwell, J., 2739, 2817
Cahn, D.D., 3264
Caillet, K.C., 2585, 2949, 2951, 2955
Caldwell, B.M., 2997, 2998
Caldwell, D.F., 2569, 2636
Callero, P., 3174
Caltabiano, N.J., 3228
Camburn, D., 3662
Campbell, D.J., 2895
Campion, M.A., 3092
Cantwell, D.P., 2502
Caplan, R.D., 2516, 2537
Caplovitz, D., 2436
Capurso, R.J., 3408
Carey, W.B., 2811, 3348, 3364, 3365, 3375
Carlson, G.A., 2465, 2502
Carney, R.E., 3414
Carpenter, P.A., 2392
Carpenter, T.P., 2939
Carson, N.D., 2423
Carter, K.R., 2960
Cate, R.M., 2553, 3041, 3144
Catherall, D., 2559
Caust, C.D., 2455
Cautela, J.R., 2609, 2610

Cecil-Pigo, E.F., 2968, 3018
Cernovsky, Z.Z., 2709
Chabassol, D.J., 2410, 2478, 2500, 2545
Chacko, T.I., 2525, 2526, 3645
Chalmers, B., 3111
Chamberlain, K., 2485
Chambliss, D.L., 2438, 2812
Chan, E., 3338
Chandler, L.A., 2536, 3184
Chapman, L.J., 2507, 3266, 3539
Chapman, L.P., 2507
Chassin, L., 2405, 3202
Chauvin, J.C., 2844
Chemers, M.M., 2843
Chenery, M.F., 3658, 3659
Chess, S., 3356, 3370, 3380
Chickering, A.W., 2788
Chippaone, D., 2899
Chiu, L-H., 3310, 3590
Christensen, A., 2597, 2603, 2978
Christiansen, B.A., 3160
Christie, R., 3486, 3487
Christofferson, J., 2869
Circirelli, V.G., 2990
Cissna, K.N., 3261
Claiborn, C.D., 2868, 2900, 2901, 3165, 3190, 3281, 3573
Clare, D.A., 3540
Clark, E.H., 2665
Clark, P., 3404
Clark, R.M., 3089
Clarkson, P.C., 3086
Cleary, P.A., 2539
Cleland, J., 2552
Clement, P.W., 3056
Clements, D., 2939
Clements, D.H., 2946, 3170
Clinton, B.J., 3562
Clum, G.A., 2530
Cobb, R., 3215
Cobb, S., 2621
Cochran, L.R., 3617
Cohen, B.D., 2923
Cohen, D.B., 2737

Cohen, S., 2501, 2578
Colangelo, N., 3495
Colarelli, S.M., 2537, 3104
Colberg, M., 3426
Coley, L.A., 3240
Collett, L., 2468
Collett, L.J., 2453
Collins, B.E., 3237
Colton, J.A., 3184
Conger, A.J., 2828
Conger, A.S., 3234, 3300
Connell, J.P., 3252
Conners, C.K., 2827
Connolly, J., 2606
Connolly, T., 3085
Conoley, C.W., 3181
Constantino, G., 3382
Constantinople, A., 2955
Cook, R.A., 3262
Cooke, R.A., 2577, 2889, 3116, 3122
Cooksey, R., 3407
Cooley, E., 2581, 3146
Coons, A.E., 2682
Cooper, D.R., 3540
Cooper, J., 3493
Coopersmith, S., 3155, 3197, 3309, 3310
Corcoran, K.J., 3573
Corno, L., 3155
Corrigan, J.D., 3572, 3573
Costa, P.T., 3496
Costa, P.T., Jr., 3496
Cotgrove, S., 3521
Cotter, P., 2544
Couch, A., 3344
Coulson, H.M., 3215
Cowan, G.A., 2580, 2713, 3036
Cowen, E.L., 2801
Cowling, W.R., III, 3544
Crandall, V.C., 3222
Craun, A.M., 2441
Crawford, J.C., 2798
Creech, S., 2736
Crino, M.D., 2904
Cron, W.L., 3583, 3596

Cross, D., 2675
Cross, D.G., 2962, 3014
Crowne, D.P., 2585
Cruickshank, D.R., 3607
Cuellar, I., 2547, 3519
Cummings, L.L., 2908, 3288, 3516, 3636
Cummings, O.W., 2872
Cunningham, J.W., 3096
Cunningham, K., 3495
Cupach, W.R., 2922, 2924, 3261
Curran, J.P., 2602
Curtis, J.M., 2899, 3595
Cushman, H.R., 3605
Cutler, B.L., 2558, 2914

D'Illio, V., 2609
D'Zurilla, T.J., 2409
Dahlquist, L.M., 3242
Daly, E.B., 2531, 3360
Daly, J.A., 2431
Daly, M.J., 3229
Dambrot, F.H., 2726
Damstreegt, D.C., 2869
Daneman, M., 2392
Daniel, R., 2787
Daniels, M.H., 3568
Davenport, P.R., 3628
Davidshafter, C.O., 2708
Davidshofer, C.O., 2374
Davidson, B., 2978, 3361
Davidson, W.B., 2544
Davies, R.A., 2758
Davis, G.A., 3285, 3386
Davis, K.R., Jr., 3373
Davis, L., 3108
Davis, L.E., 2912
Davis, S.A., 3444
De La Garza, J., 2395
Dean, D.G., 2565
Dean, R.S., 2677
DeCharms, R., 3100
Deci, E.L., 2550
Deffenbacher, J.L., 2441
DeGiovanni, I.S., 3469

Dehrenwend, B.S., 2488
DeJong, F., 3534
DeJong, G.F., 3554
DeJulio, S.S., 2682
Del Greco, L., 3469, 3501
DeLucia, L.A., 3414
Deluty, R.H., 3464
DeMan, A.F., 2806, 3168
Demba, M.H., 3331
Derogatis, L.R., 2448, 2539
DeRubeis, R.J., 3090
Desmond, S., 3251
DeSoto, C.B., 2927
DeSoto, J.L., 2927
Dessler, J., 3267
Deszca, E., 3102
Deutsch, G., 2687
Devereux, E.C., 2855
Devlin, P.K., 2580, 2713, 3036
Diaz, R.M., 3418
Dibner, A.S., 2456
Dickstein, L.S., 2460
DiClemente, C.C., 2511
Diekhoff, G.M., 2936
Diener, C., 3268
Diener, E., 2529
DiNola, A.J., 2381
Dishion, T.J., 2818
Distefano, M.K., 3059, 3592, 3593
Distenfeld, M.S., 3601
DiVesta, F.J., 2716
Dixon, D.N., 2900
Dixon, J.C., 2385, 2834
Dodge, K.A., 2613
Doherty, W.J., 3011, 3012, 3045
Dohrenwend, B.P., 3111
Dohrenwend, B.S., 2488, 2543, 3111
Dolan, L., 2994
Dolan, L.J., 2994
Dole, J.A., 2688
Dollinger, S.J., 2490
Domino, G., 2877, 3070
Dorhout, A., 3406
Dornbusch, S.M., 3166
Dosser, D.A., Jr., 3361

Douglas, P., 3246
Dourninck, W.J. van, 2969
Doverspike, D., 3061
Dowd, E.T., 3165, 3573
Dowd, J.J., 2496
Downey, A.M., 2447
Downey, R.G., 2407
Downing, P., 3611
Downs, C., 2904
Doyle, A., 2606
Drasgow, F., 2672, 3647
Dreger, R.M., 3581
Drehmer, D.E., 3366
Dressler, G., 2884
Driscoll, J.M., 2800, 2858
Driver, B.L., 3407
Drory, A., 3561, 3634
Drummond, R.J., 3311
Dubin, R., 2672, 3622, 3635
Dubrin, A.J., 3368
Duff, A., 3521
Duke, M.P., 3255, 3274
Dulaney, E., 2920
Duncan, R.B., 3072
Dungy, G., 3613
Dunham, F.Y., 3183
Dunnam, M., 2810
Dunnette, M.D., 3629
Dupuy, H.J., 2493
Durkee, A., 3463
Durlak, J.A., 2469
Duttweiler, P.C., 3223
Dweck, C., 3268
Dye, H.A., 3603
Dyer, L., 2719

Eagly, A.H., 3212, 3229
Eberhardt, B.J., 3349
Eberly, C., 3269
Eckbad, M., 3539
Edelbrock, C., 2816
Edelbrock, C.S., 2799
Edie, C.A., 2441
Edmonds, V.H., 2980, 3019
Edwards, J.N., 3023

AUTHOR INDEX

Egan, G., 3474
Eggeman, K., 3021
Eidelson, R.J., 3287
Eisenhauer, J.E., 3107, 3290
Eison, J.A., 2757, 3402
Elardo, R., 2969
Eliot, J., 3397, 3430, 3440
Elliott, G.C., 2510
Elliott, R., 3505
Elliott, S.N., 2822, 3400
Ellis, R.A., 3315, 3329
Ellis, R.H., 2815
Ellithorpe, E., 2495
Emmons, R.A., 3491
Endicott, J., 2514
Endler, N.S., 3514
England, G.W., 2686
Englese, J.A., 3302
Epperson, D.L., 3572
Epstein, A., 3490
Epstein, N., 2952, 3287, 3473, 3476
Erdle, S., 3499
Erlenbacher, A., 2375
Erskine, N., 3316
Erwin, T.D., 2958
Estes, T.H., 2741
Etzion, D., 2619
Evanechko, P., 3257, 3337
Evans, D.R., 3106
Evans, R.H., 2907, 3484
Even, B., 2699
Eyberg, S.M., 2979
Ezell, H.F., 3243

Faguhar, W.W., 3406
Faigley, L., 2431
Fairbank, J.A., 2454
Falander, C., 3351
Falbo, T., 3512
Fallik, B., 3430, 3440
Farber, B.A., 2664
Farmer, H., 2996, 3612
Farr, J.L., 3085, 3635, 3643
Farrah, G.A., 3297
Farrell, J., 3028

Fasold, R., 2756
Faulkner, J.E., 3534
Favero, J., 2555, 2564
Fayne, H.R., 2398, 2821
Fazio, A.F., 2474
Feather, N.T., 3628
Feingold, A., 2378, 2680
Feldhusen, J.F., 3250
Feldman, D.C., 3647
Feletti, G.I., 3089
Felton, B.J., 2432
Fenigstein, A., 2605, 3302, 3376
Fenigstein, A.M., 2510
Fennema, E., 3245, 3246
Fergusson, D.M., 2987
Ferrell, G.M., 3443
Ferris, G.R., 2915
Ferris, K.R., 3646, 3647
Feshbach, N.D., 3477, 3483
Feuerstein, M., 2854
Fiebert, M.S., 2760
Fiedler, F.E., 2568, 3074, 3401
Field, T., 2811, 3375, 3385
Fielding, M., 3108
Figley, C.R., 2833
Filsinger, E.E., 2582, 2978, 3554
Fimian, M.J., 2666
Fine, M.A., 3034
Finnerty-Fried, P., 2697, 2755
Fischer, C.H., 3573
Fischer, E.H., 2698, 2743
Fischer, J.L., 2580
Fishbein, M., 2730
Fisher, D.L., 3093
Fisher, S., 3355
Fisher-Beckfield, D., 2409
Flanders, N.A., 2863
Fleishman, E.A., 2682
Flexer, B.K., 3428
Floyd, F.J., 2972
Foa, E.G., 2598, 3144
Foa, U.G., 2598, 3144
Fogarty, R., 2596
Fogerson, L., 3052
Fogl, A., 2877

Foley, T.S., 3120
Fonosch, G.G., 2717
Ford, D.L., Jr., 2628
Ford, M.R., 2848
Forehand, R., 2831
Forfar, C.S., 2453, 2458-, 2460, 2469, 2497
Forness, S.R., 2890
Forsyth, D.R., 3203
Forward, J.P., 3272
Foshay, W.R., 2683
Foster, L.W., 2660
Fox, R., 3276, 3600
Foxworth, M.D., 2665
Foy, D.W., 2825
Franco, J.N., 2547, 3519
Fraser, B.J., 2793, 3078, 3093
Frayer, D.A., 2929
Frederiksen, N., 3434
Freedman, S.M., 2663, 3137, 3140, 3559
Freeman, A.M., 2520
Freiman, D.J., 3061
Frese, M., 2516, 2517, 2627, 2642, 2654, 2658, 3071
Freund, K., 3403
Friedlander, M.L., 3191, 3200, 3603
Friedlander, R.B., 3284
Friend, R., 2604, 3478
Frith, S., 2779
Frost, T.F., 3534, 3543
Fry, P.S., 2475, 2476, 2520, 3206, 3436
Frzystofiak, F., 2651
Fugua, D.R., 2809
Furey, W., 2831
Furlong, M.J., 2901, 3566, 3567, 3569, 3573
Furman, W., 2794, 3044
Fye, S.P., 2535

Gable, R.K., 2745, 3234, 3235, 3300
Gabrys, J.B., 2546
Gaddy, C.D., 3043, 3294
Gadzella, B.M., 2761

Gaffney, L.R., 2595, 2866
Galassi, J.P., 2402, 2403, 3201, 3467
Galejs, I., 3274, 3412
Gambrill, E., 3457
Games, R.G., 2713
Ganster, D.C., 2621, 2752, 3550, 3551
Garbarino, J., 2964, 2982, 2989, 3003
Garber, R.A., 3181
Garcia, E.E., 2933
Garcia-Bahne, B., 2415
Gard, K.A., 3488
Gardner, K.G., 2896
Garfinkel, P.E., 2833
Garner, D.M., 2833
Garrett, J.B., 3550, 3551
Garrison, J.P., 2917
Garrison, K.R., 2917
Garside, R.F., 3342
Gary, L.E., 2790
Gati, I., 3651
Gay, M.L., 3451
Geis, F., 3486
Geis, F.L., 3487
Geisinger, K.F., 2721
Gellerman, S., 3452
Genova, W.J., 3113
Genschaft, J.L., 2903
Gesten, E.L., 2414, 2945
Getter, H., 2576
Gettinger, M., 2821
Getzels, J.W., 2700
Ghiselli, E.E., 3131
Ghowdhary, G.P., 2845
Gibb, G.D., 3497
Gibbs, J.C., 3558
Gibson, H.B., 2737
Gibson, S., 3331
Gidycz, C.A., 2875
Gifford, R., 3028, 3387
Giles, M.B., 2766
Gilver, L.A., 3591
Ginter, E.J., 2427
Giovannoni, J.M., 2790

Glasgow, R.E., 2501, 2578
Glenn, R.N., 3059
Glennon, B., 2509
Gleser, G.C., 3355
Gluppe, M.R., 3581
Godfrey, H.P.D., 2386
Golan, J., 2630, 2674
Goldberger, L., 3510
Golden, S.B., Jr., 3132
Goldfarb, L.A., 2477
Goldfried, M.R., 2409
Goldman, R.D., 2699
Gomez, L.R., 3104
Gomez-Mejia, L.R., 2622
Good, K.C., 2470, 2478, 3129, 3132
Good, L.R., 2470, 2478, 3129, 3132
Good, T., 2911
Goodlad, J.I., 3103
Goodman, G., 3383
Goodman, J.F., 2590
Goodman, Y., 2391
Goodstein, L.D., 3586
Goodyear, R.K., 3573
Gordon, H.W., 3422
Gordon, R.D., 2920
Gorecki, P.R., 3467
Gottfried, A.E., 2404, 3127
Gottman, J., 3481, 3502
Gough, H., 3444
Gough, H.G., 2685, 3135, 3586, 3663
Gould, S., 3541, 3648, 3649
Goyette, C.H., 2828
Graddick, M.M., 3085, 3635, 3643
Graen, G., 2915, 2918
Graen, G.B., 2624, 2916, 2926
Gragne, R.M., 2387
Graham, S., 3282, 3283
Grandjean, B.D., 3068
Granrose, C.S., 2730
Gray, C.A., 2997
Gray, P., 2620
Gray-Toft, P., 2648
Graybill, D., 2528, 3498
Green, B.L., 2514

Green, D.N., 3445, 3446
Green, J.J., 2879
Green, K., 2694
Greenberg, L.S., 2559, 3592
Greenberg, R., 2811, 3375, 3385
Greenberg, R.P., 3355
Greenhaus, J., 3618, 3620
Greenhaus, J.H., 2703, 3665
Greenwood, C.R., 2567, 2824
Greller, M.M., 3083, 3162
Gressard, C., 2727
Gropper, G., 2865
Grossman, J.H., 3366
Grove, D.A., 3574
Guerin, P., Jr., 2596
Guidubaldi, J., 2601
Guise, B.J., 3220
Gullo, D.F., 3170
Gulousen, J., 2912
Gur, R.C., 3510
Gurney, G., 3413
Gurney, R.M., 3164
Guskey, T., 3330
Gutkin, T.B., 3217
Guttman, J., 2859

Haase, R.F., 2434, 3573
Haber, R.N., 2433
Hackett, G., 3249, 3256, 3306
Hackman, H.W., 3573
Hackman, J.R., 2631, 2635, 2653, 3091, 3405
Hadley, H.N., 3393
Hagan, J., 2874
Hage, G., 3088
Hagekull, B., 3384
Hagerty, B.K., 3112
Hahlweg, K., 2913
Hale, W.D., 2448
Hall, B.W., 3332
Hall, C.S., 3491
Hall, D., 3136
Hall, D.T., 3636
Hall, L.E., 2743
Hall, R.H., 2919

Hall, T., 3583
Hall, W.S., 2772
Haller, A.O., 3447
Haller, E.J., 3444
Halliday, M.A., 2370
Hallon, C.J., 3486
Halote, B., 3153
Halpin, G., 2665, 3197, 3222, 3282, 3332
Halsey, A.H., 3109
Hamerlynck, L.A., 3013
Hamilton, M., 2479
Hamilton, V., 2489, 2543
Hamlin, R.M., 3390
Hammer, A.L., 3506
Hammer, T.H., 3118, 3415, 3637
Handal, P.J., 2801
Handley, P., 3570
Handley, P.C., 3573
Hansell, S., 2948
Hansen, G., 2562, 2746, 3006, 3014, 3016, 3041, 3314
Hansen, G.L., 2749, 2750, 3019
Hanson, G.R., 3343
Hanson, R.A., 2952
Hanson, S.L., 2436
Harburg, E., 3358
Hardin, S.I., 3209, 3573
Hare, R.D., 2518, 3511
Hargrove, D.S., 3505
Haring, M.J., 2700
Harker, P., 2631, 3091, 3317, 3584
Harnisch, D.L., 2428
Harpaz, I., 3422
Harrell, T.H., 2442
Harren, V.A., 3425, 3610
Harris, D.B., 3276
Harris, K., 2665
Harris, K.R., 2771, 2917
Harris, R.M., 3225, 3235, 3236, 3237
Harris, R.M., Jr., 3388
Harshman, R.A., 3440
Harter, S., 2593, 3252, 3260
Hartman, B., 3199

Hartman, B.W., 2809
Hartman, M., 3553
Hartup, W.W., 2893
Harvey, D., 2694
Harvey, O.J., 2934
Hasan, R., 2370
Hatfield, J.D., 2633
Hattie, J., 3602
Hawk, J.W., 2763
Hawley, P., 2699
Haynes, S.G., 3479
Haywood, H.C., 3033, 3222, 3390
Hazen, M., 2904
Hazer, J.T., 3559
Hchu, H-Y., 3536
Heavan, P.C.L., 2732, 3507
Heeder, R., 2519
Heesacker, M., 3208, 3210, 3564, 3569, 3573
Heilbrun, A.B., Jr., 2489, 2932, 3135
Heimberg, L., 3156
Heller, R.M., 3050
Helmreich, R., 2614, 3206
Helmreich, R.L., 2704, 3036
Helms, B.J., 3195
Helms, J.E., 2772, 2773
Helwig, J., 2376
Henderson, R.W., 2993, 3076
Hendrix, W.H., 2535
Hener, T., 3639, 3641
Henry, R.M., 2437
Heppner, P.P., 3208, 3210, 3280, 3436, 3437, 3439, 3564, 3569, 3573, 3658
Hereford, C.F., 3032
Herman, M.W., 2696
Herold, D.M., 3083
Herr, E.L., 3565
Herrick, V.E., 2375
Herzberger, S.D., 3459
Hesketh, B., 3632
Heslin, R., 2908
Hicks, L.A., 3231
Higgins, E., 3474

Hill, C.E., 2899, 3063, 3573
Hill, G., 3529, 3531
Himmelfarb, S., 2474
Hines, P., 3448, 3523, 3535
Hirschfield, R.M.A., 2574
Hirschi, T., 2874
Hirschman, E., 3133
Hirschman, E.C., 2512, 2687, 2829, 3271
Hite, L.M., 2426
Ho, R., 2455
Hocevar, D., 2940, 3576
Hock, E., 2513, 2967
Hodapp, V., 2649
Hodges, W.F., 2856
Hoelter, J., 2497
Hoffman, E., 2919, 3401
Hoffman, J.A., 3040
Hoffman, L.W., 3009
Hofman, J.E., 3218
Hogan, H.W., 3189
Hogan, J., 3377
Hogan, R., 3377
Hoge, D.R., 2832, 3525, 3526, 3555
Hoge, R.D., 2606
Hojat, M., 2696
Holahan, C.K., 3322
Holcomb, H., 2823
Holcomb, W.R., 2539
Holden, R.R., 3346
Holland, J.E., 3657
Holland, J.L., 3657
Holley, W.H., 2719, 3405
Hollon, S.D., 2442
Holmes, T.H., 2423, 2481, 2531, 2533
Holt, M.L., 2837
Hong, S-M, 3167, 3230
Hong, S., 2455
Hood, A.B., 2588
Hood, J., 3224
Hood, R.W., Jr., 3544
Hopper, S., 2801
Hoppock, R., 2624
Hops, H., 3024

Horan, J., 2440
Horan, J.J., 2433, 2508
Horn, T.S., 3215, 3260
Hornung, C.A., 2973
Horowitz, J.E., 2921
Horowitz, M.J., 2484
Hosek, J., 2797
Hoskins, R., 2887
House, R.J., 2884, 3267, 3290
Houseknecht, S.K., 2978
Houston, S.R., 3273, 3549
Howard, A., 3145
Howard, K., 3191, 3200
Howard, K.I., 2847
Howe, A.C., 2880
Howell, F.M., 2416, 3005
Hrebiniak, L.G., 3624, 3646
Huba, M.E., 2390
Hubbard, F.O.A., 2742
Hubble, M.A., 3573
Huber, V.L., 3115, 3149
Hubert, N.C., 3342, 3345, 3347, 3348, 3351, 3352, 3357, 3362, 3363, 3364, 3370, 3375, 3378, 3379, 3380, 3384, 3385
Huck, S.W., 2439
Hudson, G.R., 3227
Hudson, W.W., 3000
Huebner, L.A., 2419
Huffman, P., 3047
Humphrey, L.L., 2891, 2945, 3185
Humphries, J., 3103
Hundleby, J.D., 3581
Hunt, J.G., 2884, 3267
Hunt, J.M., 3514
Hunt, R.A., 3525, 3526
Hunter, M.S., 2584
Hurt, H.T., 3484
Husek, T.R., 2440
Huseman, R.C., 3395
Huston, T., 3025
Huston, T.L., 2562, 2704, 2968
Hutchinson, K., 3026
Hyman, R.B., 3393

Ibrahim, A., 2925
Ibrahim, F.A., 3195
Ihilevich, D., 3355
Ihinger-Tallman, M., 2495
Indik, B., 2617
Infante, D.A., 3456
Inglis, J., 2681
Insel, P.M., 3051
Ireland, M.S., 2384, 3354
Ireland-Galman, M.M., 2412, 3389
Irvine, J.J., 2911
Isabella, R.A., 2978
Ishiyama, F.I., 2410, 2478, 2500, 2545
Itkin, W., 2806
Ivancevich, J.M., 2995, 3162, 3656
Ivey, A.E., 3566
Izraeli, D., 3580
Izraeli, D.N., 3580

Jacka, B., 2387
Jacko, E.J., 2439
Jackson, D.N., 3346, 3609
Jackson, E., 3383
Jackson, L.M., 2788
Jackson, P., 3130
Jackson, P.R., 3626
Jackson, S., 2664, 3174
Jackson, S.E., 2626, 2910, 3051
Jacob, T., 3015
Jakubowski, P., 2573
Jamal, M., 2634
James, D.E., 3008
James, L.R., 2661, 3324, 3482
James, N.L., 2549
Janoff-Bulman, R., 3027
Jans, N.A., 2797
Jason, L.A., 2406
Jean, P.J., 2720
Jemison, D.B., 3053
Jenkins, P.A., 3500
Jenkins, W.W., 3571
Jenner, F.A., 2742
Jensen, L., 3542
Jensen, T.B., 2419

Jenson, L., 3042
Jerrell, J.M., 3053
Jiminez, M.H., 3662
Johanson, R.P., 2692
Johnson, B., 2370
Johnson, B.W., 3309
Johnson, C.D., 3608
Johnson, D., 2370
Johnson, D.L., 2999, 3047
Johnson, D.W., 2549, 2707, 2733, 2785, 3058
Johnson, E.S., 3087
Johnson, J., 2463
Johnson, J.H., 2489, 2543
Johnson, P., 2644
Johnson, R.E., 2423
Johnson, R.T., 3058
Johnson, S.M., 2559, 2592, 2629
Jolly, J.A., 3508
Jonah, B.A., 2780
Jones, A.P., 2661, 3095
Jones, J.E., 2896
Jones, J.M., 2723, 3466
Jones, L.K., 3658, 3659
Jones, R.L., 2772
Jones, W.H., 3513
Jordan, T.J., 2421
Jorgenson, D.O., 3121
Joseph, W.B., 3369
Jourard, S.M., 3175, 3263
Jouriles, E.N., 2973
Jungermann, H., 2863
Juni, S., 3417

Kafry, D., 2674
Kagan, D., 3493
Kahn, M.W., 3610
Kahn, R.L., 2638, 2639, 2667, 3054
Kalin, R., 3411
Kalliopuska, M., 3473, 3476
Kalmuss, D.S., 3029, 3046
Kalsounis, B., 2690
Kanner, A.D., 3075
Kanungo, R.N., 3633, 3661
Kaplan, H.I., 2520

Karabel, J., 3109
Karmos, A.H., 2718
Karmos, J.S., 2718
Karnes, F.A., 2844
Kasperson, C.J., 2754
Kassinove, H., 2931
Katerberg, R., 3344
Katz, E.R., 2867
Katz, K., 3054
Kaul, J.J., 3191
Kaul, T.J., 3200, 3573
Kavanaugh, M.J., 2515
Kayne, J.B., 3549
Kazanas, H.C., 3520
Kazdin, A.E., 2482
Keane, T.M., 2454
Keenan, A., 2527
Keinan, G., 2776
Keith, P.M., 2463, 2783, 3295
Kejner, J., 3634, 3635
Kejner, M., 2986, 3662
Kelleher, W.J., 3424
Keller, R.T., 3217, 3315
Kelly, D.F., Jr., 3570
Kelly, E., 3049
Kelly, H.H., 3203
Kelly, I.W., 3172
Kemp, N.J., 2912
Kendall, P.C., 2442, 2891
Keniston, K., 3344
Kennedy, C.E., 3631
Kennedy, P.H., 3533
Keogh, B.K., 2817, 3381
Keple, T.W., 2548
Kerlinger, F.N., 2739
Kernan-Schloss, L., 2384, 3354
Kerr, B.A., 3353
Kida, T.E., 3072
Kidd, J.M., 3623, 3654
Kildea, A.E., 2826, 2928
Kim, Y.C., 2849
King, C.E., 2597
King, D.W., 2782
King, L.A., 2782
King, M.B., 3525, 3526

Kiresuk, T.J., 2898
Kirkwood, W.J., 3278
Kirton, M.J., 3432
Kitson, G.C., 2963
Klaus, D., 2570
Klein, M.F., 3103
Klimoski, R.J., 2686
Knight, R.G., 2386
Knoop, H.R., 3590
Koch, H.L., 2806
Koch, J.L., 2617
Kochenour, E., 2883
Kogan, N.A., 2755
Kolko, D.J., 2570, 2603, 2885
Kolloff, M.B., 3250
Kontos, S., 2390
Korner, A.F., 2811
Kornhauser, A., 2504
Koski, L.K., 2996, 3612
Koss, M.P., 2875
Koupman-Boydan, P.G., 3557
Kourilsky, M., 2396
Kovacs, M., 2450
Kraft, R.G., 2445, 3573
Krahe, B., 3359
Kraut, A.I., 2918, 3291
Krefting, L.A., 2651
Krieschok, T.S., 3280
Krumboltz, J.D., 3406, 3616
Krus, D.J., 3533
Kuh, G.D., 2943
Kukulka, G., 2826, 2928
Kunce, J.T., 2983
Kundert, D.K., 2677
Kunkle, D., 3161
Kurdek, L.A., 2449, 2561, 2605, 2835, 3239, 3240, 3302, 3504,
Kurtines, W., 2957
Kurtzman, C., 2725
Kutner, N., 2783
Kutner, N.G., 2746

LaBaron, S., 2867
LaCrosse, M.B., 3353, 3591, 3753
Lafromboise, T.D., 3451

Lamb, C.W., Jr., 2798
Lamke, L.K., 2978
Lamont, D.J., 3069
Lange, A.J., 2573
LaRossa, R., 2496
Larsen, K.S., 2586, 2695, 2748
Larson, L.L., 2884, 3267
Larson, L.M., 3658
Larzelere, R.E., 2562
Latack, J.C., 2660
Lau, S., 3323
Lauton, G.W., 3652
Lawe, C.F., 2899
Lawler, E., 3136
Lawler, E.E., 2653, 3405, 3636
Lawson, J.S., 2681
Lawton, M.P., 2496, 2506
Leary, M.R., 2551, 2572
Lee, C., 3267
Lee, D.Y., 3572, 3573
Lee, G.R., 2495
Lee, J.Y., 3318
Lee, P.C., 3055
Lee, R., 2668, 3577, 3587
Lefcourt, H.M., 2587, 3157, 3253
Lefcourt, J., 3339
Lefebvre, M.F., 3192
Lefkowitz, J., 2671, 3143
Lefkowitz, M.M., 2502
Leighton, D.C., 2480
Lenihan, M., 3179
Lennox, R.D., 2558
Lent, R.W., 3306
Leonetti, R., 3279
Lerner, R.M., 3275, 3356
Lesser, G.S., 2437
Lessing, E.E., 2838
Lester, D., 2453, 2468
Levenson, H., 3230, 3236
Levine, E.L., 2614, 3328
Levine, J., 2594
Levinger, G., 2968
Levinson, D., 3047
Levy, D.A., 2487
Levy-Shiff, R., 2422

Lewinsohn, P.M., 3101
Lewis, J.M., 2765
Licata, J.W., 3107
Licht, B.G., 3205
Liden, R., 2916
Liden, R.C., 3588
Liebert, R.M., 2523
Lief, H.I., 2781
Likert, R., 2872, 3099
Lin, T., 2899
Lincoln, J.R., 2571
Linden, J.D., 3063, 3564, 3569
Lindgren, H.C., 3142, 3231
Linehan, M.M., 2521
Linkowski, D.S., 2432
Linn, B.S., 2425
Linn, M.C., 3420, 3435
Liska, A.E., 2706, 2714
Litt, M.D., 2499, 2635
Little, L.F., 3010
Litwin, G.H., 3097, 3098
Livch, H., 2468
Llabre, M.M., 2473, 3245
Lloyd, S.A., 2598
Lobb, M.L., 3480
Locke, H.J., 3011, 3015, 3027, 3035
Lodahl, T., 3634, 3635, 3662
Lodahl, T.M., 2986
Loeb, R.G., 3595
Loeber, R., 2818
Loesch, L.C., 2380
Loevinger, J., 2948, 2959
Lohr, J.M., 3226
Lokan, J.J., 3241
Loney, J., 2878
Long, T.J., 2522, 2532
Lonky, E., 3427
Lopez, F.G., 2769, 3594
Lopez, F.M., 3515
Lorge, I., 2697
Lorion, R.P., 2406, 2820, 2945
Louis, M.R., 2636
Lovejoy, F.H., 3524
Lovell-Troy, L.A., 2612
Low, B.P., 3056

AUTHOR INDEX

Lowe, D.R., 2573
Lowe, M.R., 2608-2610
Lowry, N., 2733
Loyd, B.H., 2727
Loyd, D.E., 2727
Luborsky, L., 3581
Ludeke, R.J., 2893
Luenburg, F.C., 3299
Lumby, M.E., 2750
Lumpkin, J.R., 3178
Lunenburg, F.C., 3105
Lyons, T.F., 2542, 2640, 2647, 2657, 3650
Lysy, K.Z., 2852

Ma, L-C., 3538
MacDonald, A.P., Jr., 2713
MacDonald, A.R., 3235
MacDonald, M.L., 3468
Macke, A.S., 2978
Mackey, J., 2549
Mackle, M., 2759
Macklin, M.C., 2722
MacMillan, D.L., 2890
MacPhillamy, D.J., 3101
Madden, M.E., 3027
Madrid, D., 2933
Madsen, C.H., 2822
Maes, W.R., 3333
Magaro, P.A., 2491
Magnusson, D., 3514
Maher, C.A., 2898
Mahoney, T.A., 2651
Maitland, R.E., 3429
Malgady, R.G., 2938, 3382
Malizio, A.G., 2557
Malnig, L.R., 3653
Malouff, J., 2503
Mancini, J.A., 2506
Mandinach, E.B., 3155
Mandler, G., 2430
Mangieri, J., 2937
Mann, B., 2900
Mann, J., 3273
Manuele, C.A., 2618, 2944

Marcus, R.F., 3477
Margalit, M., 3453
Margolin, G., 2966, 3024
Marino, K.E., 3088
Marjoribanks, K., 2985, 3109
Markham, S.E., 2842
Markides, K.S., 3028
Markman, E.M., 3170
Markman, H.J., 2972
Marks, D.F., 2397
Marlowe, D., 2585
Marsh, H.W., 3086, 3303-3305, 3327, 3601
Marshall, R.E., 3089
Martin, H.J., 2586
Martin, J.D., 3240
Martin, T.N., 3597, 3656
Martin, W.H., 2535
Martinetti, R.F., 3193
Maslach, C., 2664
Mason, L.I., 3500
Massey, G.C., 3166
Masson, M.E.J., 2392
Masuda, M., 2531
Matheny, A.P., Jr., 3385
Mathes, E.W., 2575, 2599, 2600, 3006, 3485
Mathes, S., 3413
Matross, R., 2789
Matteson, M.T., 2995, 3479, 3656
Matthews, K.A., 3489
Maw, E.W., 3152
Maw, W.H., 3152
Mayfield, M., 3257, 3337
Mayo, R.J., 3137, 3140
McBroom, L.W., 2416, 3005
McCarthy, J.D., 2832
McCarthy, P.R., 3573
McCarthy, R.M., 3432
McClinton, S.L., 2413
McCormick, E.J., 3095
McCormick, E.K., 3084
McCrae, R.R., 3496
McCubbin, H., 2984
McCubbin, H.I., 2974, 2975

McDavis, R.J., 2909
McDermott, L., 2393
McDevitt, S.C., 2811, 3348, 3375
McDonald, M.P., 3036
McDowell, C.F., 3404
McFall, R.M., 2409, 2595, 2866, 2885
McGaw, B., 2793
McGowan, R.J., 2999, 3047
McGurk, E.A., 2685
McHale, S.M., 2704
McIntire, S.A., 2614, 3328
McIntosh, S.R., 3000
McKitrick, D., 3573
McLennan, P.P., 3578
McLeod, D.B., 3244
McLoughlin, C.S., 2382
McMillan, J.H., 3203
McMurrey, A.D., 3372
McNeil, T., 3378, 3379
McNeill, B.W., 3325
McNergney, R.F., 3434
McRoy, R.G., 3439
Medley, D.M., 3604
Mednick, S.A., 2941
Medway, F.J., 3334
Mehrabian, A., 2952, 3141, 3351, 3473, 3476, 3490
Meier, S.T., 2420, 2646
Meir, E.E., 3629
Meir, E.I., 3639, 3641, 3651
Melzack, R., 2857
Mendelson, B.K., 3176
Meredith, G.M., 2757
Merluzzi, T.V., 3573
Merwin, J.C., 2716
Mevarech, Z.R., 3247
Meyer, J.P., 3609, 3624, 3625, 3643
Michael, W.B., 2377, 2412, 2555, 2564, 2585, 2853, 2949, 2951, 2955, 3153, 3278, 3389, 3419
Michael, W.V., 2394
Michelson, L., 3465
Middlestodt, S.E., 2892
Mihlbauer, T.C., 3079

Mikulecky, L.J., 2763
Miles, G.B., 2909
Miller, A., 2581, 3146
Miller, D.T., 3522
Miller, G.A., 3637
Miller, H.E., 2672, 3647
Miller, I.W., 3447
Miller, J.A., 2392
Miller, L.B., 3197
Miller, M., 2814
Miller, M.D., 2431
Miller, P.A., 2876
Miller, R.L., 3082
Miller, R.S., 2587
Miller, W.B., 3009
Miller, W.R., 2781
Milne, C.R., 3573
Milner, J.S., 2815, 2846, 3350
Milo, T., 3411
Miner, J.B., 3148
Mines, R.A., 2588
Mintz, J., 3581
Mirabile, C.S., Jr., 2848
Mirels, J.L., 3550, 3551
Mirenda, J.J., 3404
Mirowsky, J., 2464
Misanchuk, E.R., 2683
Mitchell, S.E., 3007
Mitchell, S.K., 2997
Mitchell, T.W., 2686
Mitic, W.R., 2435
Mitman, A.L., 2691
Mohr, G., 2516, 2627
Molm, L.D., 3214
Monti, P.M., 2602
Mookherjee, H.N., 3189
Moore, A.K., 3084
Moore, S.M., 3188
Moos, B.S., 3120
Moos, R.H., 2835, 3051, 3120
Moracco, J., 3447
Moracco, J.C., 2620, 3117
Morgan, K.C., 2513, 2967
Morris, J.H., 3243
Morris, L.W., 2523

Morrison, J.A., 2377, 2394
Morrison, J.K., 2519, 3530
Morrow, S.L., 3653
Morse, J.J., 3243, 3317
Moser, J.M., 2939
Moser, R.S., 3259
Moss, G.R., 2452
Moss, H., 2513
Mossholder, KW., 3098
Motowidlo, S.J., 2652, 3207, 3258, 3598, 3652
Mount, M.K., 3585
Mowday, R.T., 3624, 3643, 3656
Muchinsky, P.M., 3349
Mueller, C.W., 3656
Muller, D.G., 3279
Mullins, T.W., 3575
Munoz, D., 2415
Murphy, C.J., 2628
Murphy, G.C., 3265
Murphy, K.C., 2900
Murphy, K.R., 3606
Murphy, V.M., 2481
Murray, H.G., 3605
Myers, A.E., 3125
Myrick, R.D., 3570

Nagy, S., 2676, 3108
Naismith, D.C., 2650
Najman, J., 2458
Nall, R.L., 2872
Nambayan, A., 2767
Napoletano, M.A., 2736
Narayanan, S., 3099
Narikawa, D., 2779
Navran, L., 2921
Neal, W.R., 2694
Nelson, T.L., 2403
Nemo, R.S., 3390
Nesbitt, E., 3461
Nettler, G., 2734
Neumann, L., 3563
Neumann, Y., 3563
Nevid, J.S., 2748
Newfield, J., 3103

Newman, J.E., 2910
Newman, L.F., 3009
Newman, R.C., 3414
Newton, T.J., 2527
Nice, D.S., 2978
Nichols, C.W., 3631
Nichols, J., 3252
Noles, S.W., 3177
Norem-Hebeisen, A., 2785
Norton, R., 2978
Norton, R.W., 3516
Nott, D.L., 3607
Novaco, R., 3494
Nowack, K.M., 3075
Nowicki, S., 3238, 3255, 3274
Nowicki, S., Jr., 3183, 3241
Nowinski, J.K., 2576
Nunn, G.D., 3270
Nye, E.I., 2832

O'Brien, E.J., 3212
O'Connell, J.K., 3219
O'Conner, E.J., 2472, 2623
O'Dell, S.L., 2382
O'Donnell, J.P., 2490
O'Keefe, D.J., 3408
O'Laughlin, M.S., 3656
O'Leary, K.D., 2973
O'Leary, S., 2878
O'Malley, S.S., 2616
O'Neill, C.D., 3616
O'Neill, R., 3305
O'Reilly, C., 2636
O'Reilly, C.A., 2569
Oelke, M.C., 3199
Oetting, E.R., 2819
Okenek, K., 2516, 2517, 2627, 2642, 3071
Oldham, G.R., 2631, 2635, 3091
Olson, D.H., 2592, 2982, 2983
Omizo, M.M., 2897
Oppenheimer, B.T., 2604
Orbach, I., 2538
Oren, D.L., 3166
Ormrod, J.E., 2960

Oros, C.J., 2875
Orthner, D.K., 3026
Osterhouse, R.A., 2429
Ostrum, T.M., 3239
Otis, L.P., 3211, 3396
Ottinger, D.R., 3242
Owens, W.A., 3349
Ozawa, J.P., 2853

Page, R., 3531
Page, R.C., 3104
Page, T.J., Jr., 3376
Paivio, A., 3397, 3440
Palenzuela, D.L., 3196
Palmon, N., 2873
Pandey, J., 2841
Pappo, M., 2411, 2500
Paradise, L.V., 2590
Parham, T.A., 2772, 2773
Parish, T., 3270
Parish, T.S., 3186, 3254, 3269
Parkerson, J.A., 3114
Parrish, T.S., 3038
Parry, G., 3002
Parsons, C.K., 3083, 3588
Parten, M.B., 2861
Pasamanick, B., 3543
Pascarella, E.T., 2399, 2953, 2954, 3049, 3321, 3398
Patchen, M., 3649
Patrick, J., 3084
Pattengill, S.M., 3031
Patterson, J.M., 2975
Paurohit, N., 3573
Payne, B.D., 2428
Pearce, J.L., 3138
Pearlin, L., 2463
Pearlin, L.I., 2457
Pearlman, C., 3150
Pearson, J.E., 2522, 2532
Pearson, P., 3133
Peck, R.F., 3600
Pecnik, J.A., 3572
Pedhazur, E.J., 2739
Pedro, J.D., 3618

Peiser, C., 3639
Pekarik, E.G., 3374
Pellegrini, D.S., 3433
Pendleton, B.F., 3043
Penley, L., 3541, 3648
Peplau, L.A., 3537, 3538
Perry, J.D., 2601
Perry, W.G., Jr., 2958, 3527, 3546
Persson-Blennow, I., 3378, 3379
Perunko, M., 3440
Peters, K., 2546
Peters, L.H., 2472, 2623, 2796
Petersen, C.H., 3280, 3436, 3437, 3439
Peterson, C., 3165
Peterson, D.R., 2807
Peterson, G.W., 3232
Peterson, K., 3248
Peterson, L., 2607
Peterson, M.F., 2577, 2889, 3116, 3262
Peterson, P.L., 3423
Petrie, K., 2485, 2649
Petrillo, G.H., 3555
Pettegrew, L.S., 2839, 3220
Petty, R.E., 3367
Pety, J., 3573
Pfeiffer, E., 2544
Pfeiffer, J.W., 2896
Phares, E.J., 3316
Phelps, J., 2373
Phifer, S.J., 2720
Phillips, J.S., 2663, 3137, 3140, 3559
Phillips, S.D., 3425, 3437
Pichot, P., 2446
Piechowski, M.M., 2852, 3495
Pierro, R.A., 3510
Piers, E.V., 3276
Pierson, D., 3277
Pike, R., 2593
Pines, A., 2619, 2674
Pines, A.M., 2540, 2643
Pinkney, J.W., 2753
Pinsof, W., 2559
Pinto, P.R., 3585

AUTHOR INDEX

Pintrich, D.R., 3187
Piotrowski, C., 3183
Pipes, R.B., 2451
Pistrang, N., 2673, 2870, 2981, 3009, 3662
Plake, B.S., 2417, 2720, 2741
Plas, J.M., 3545
Pliner, J.E., 2415
Plomin, R., 3352, 3358
Pomeroy, S., 2988
Ponterotto, J.G., 2901, 3566, 3567, 3569, 3573
Ponzetti, J.J., 2553
Porche, L.M., 3573
Poresky, R.H., 2563
Porter, L.W., 3143, 3644, 3645, 3647
Posner, J.L., 2540
Power, C.N., 2880
Powers, S., 2395, 3125, 3246, 3253
Powers, W.G., 3026
Prager, K.J., 2837, 3320
Prawat, R.S., 3094, 3238
Prentice, D.S., 2777
Price, J.H., 2864, 2876, 3219, 3251
Price, J.L., 3656
Prien, E.P., 3131
Priesmeyer, M.L., 2983
Primm, J.B., 2957
Prinz, R.J., 3453
Prochaska, J.O., 2511
Prola, M., 2408
Pryer, M.W., 3593
Pulakos, E.D., 3560
Pullis, M., 2817
Pullis, M.E., 3381
Pulos, S., 3420, 3435
Purkey, W.W., 3213

Quay, H.C., 2807
Quinlan, D.M., 2959
Quinn, R.P., 3122, 3627
Quinn, W.H., 2905, 2991, 2992, 3087
Quinsey, V.L., 3492

Raden, D., 2734
Radloff, L.S., 2449, 2464
Rafaeli, A., 2653
Rahe, R.H., 2423, 2481, 2522, 2532, 2533
Rahim, A., 2625, 3065
Ramaniah, N.V., 3457
Ramirez, M., 2753
Rancer, A.S., 3456
Rankin, C.I., 3254
Ransom, G.A., 2394
Raskin, R.N., 3491
Rasmussen, J.E., 2949
Rathe, F.H., 2634
Rathus, S.A., 3501
Ratzlaff, H., 2375
Raulin, M.L., 2486
Ray, J.B., 3284
Ray, J.J., 2458, 2723, 2731, 2732, 2770, 3124, 3126, 3460, 3466, 3470-3472, 3524, 3528
Raymond, M.R., 2744
Rea, R.G., 3226
Reardon, R.C., 3630
Reed, D.M., 2781
Reed, J.G., 2407, 3064
Regts, J.M., 3020
Reifman, B., 2937
Reimer, D.A., 2574, 2977
Reising, G.N., 3568
Reisman, J.M., 2565
Remer, P., 3573, 3616
Remley, T.P., Jr., 3163
Remmers, H.H., 2745
Rentoul, A.J., 3078
Rest, J.R., 3556
Rettig, S., 3543
Revenson, T.A., 2432
Revenstorf, D., 2913
Reynolds, C.L., 3573
Reynolds, C.R., 2524, 2720
Reynolds, W.M., 3153
Riahinejad, A.R., 2588
Rice, D.R., 2690
Rice, R.W., 2843

Rich, Y., 3247
Richards, J.S., 2854
Richardson, G.G., 2374, 2708
Richman, J., 3057
Richmond, B.O., 2524
Ried, D.W., 3224
Rigby, K., 2747, 2805
Riley, W.T., 3449
Ritchey, C., 3457
Ritchey, K.M., 2830, 3438
Ritzer, G., 3624
Rizzo, J.R., 2525-2527, 3288-3289, 3290, 3292
Robbins, E.S., 2434, 3573
Robbins, S.B., 2814, 2883, 3180, 3273, 3615
Roberge, J.J., 3428
Roberts, A., 3500
Roberts, A.D., 2745
Roberts, D.M., 2371, 2372, 2721, 2744, 2786
Robinson, A., 2492
Robinson, E.A., 2979
Robinson, J., 3444
Robinson, J.P., 2563, 2673, 3509
Robinson, J.W., 3475
Robinson, R., 3445, 3446
Robinson, S.L., 2509
Roe, A., 3033
Roe, K., 3483
Roehlke, H.J., 3568
Roff, M., 2601
Rogers, B.G., 3534
Rogers, H.J., 2962
Rohner, R.P., 3031
Rohrkemper, M.M., 2804
Rokeach, M., 3540
Rollins, M.M., 2929
Roman, P.M., 3401
Ronchi, D., 2480
Ronen, R., 3134
Rooparine, J.L., 2861
Roscoe, J.T., 3549
Rose, J.S., 3334
Rosenbaum, M., 2873

Rosenberg, M., 3293, 3295, 3315
Rosenberg, S., 2923
Rosenfield, D., 3154
Rosenkrantz, P., 3319
Rosenkrantz, S.A., 3290
Rosenman, R.H., 3518
Rosenzweig, S., 2528
Rosinger, G., 3579
Rosinski, R.R., 2927
Ross, C., 2464
Ross, G.R., 3227
Ross, S., 2930
Rosse, J.G., 2918
Rossiter, J.R., 2722
Rothbart, M., 3362
Rothbart, M.K., 2840
Rothe, H.F., 2625, 3656
Rotherham, M.J., 2649
Rothstein, M., 3102
Rotter, J.B., 2914, 3225, 3240, 3334
Rotton, J., 3172
Rousseau, D.M., 3122
Rowe, D.C., 3352
Rowland, K.M., 3149
Royal, E.G., 3132
Rubin, Z., 2599, 3537, 3538
Ruggiero, M., 3052
Rullard, W., 3385
Runco, M.A., 2940, 2942
Rundquist, E.A., 3030
Runion, K.B., 3186
Ruppel, G., 3573
Rush, J.C., 3102
Russell, D., 2615, 3181, 3513
Russell, G.M., 3171, 3452
Ryan, M.P., 3527, 3546
Ryan, N.B., 2442
Ryder, R.G., 3012, 3045

Sabatelli, R.M., 2968, 3018
Sachs, J.S., 3119
Sackeim, H.A., 3510
Sackett, P.R., 3073
Sadock, B.J., 2520
Sadowski, C.J., 3100

AUTHOR INDEX

Safran, J.S., 2865
Safran, S.P., 2865
Saigh, P.A., 3394
Saleh, S.D., 2797
Salomone, P.R., 3225, 3235-3237, 3388
Saltzer, E.B., 3340
Sameroff, A.J., 3365
Sampson, D.L., 2798
Sampson, J.P., 2380
Sanchez, A.R., 2698
Sarason, B., 2578
Sarason, I.G., 2402, 2473, 2489, 2508, 2543, 2578
Sarason, S.B., 2430
Saski, J., 2774
Saver, W., 2990
Savickas, M.L., 2483, 2950, 3156, 3157, 3335, 3640
Saxe, J.E., 2371, 2372, 2721
Saylor, C.F., 2450
Scandura, T.A., 2624, 2916
Schaefer, M.T., 2592
Schafer, R.B., 2463, 3298
Schatz, E.M., 3286
Schell, B.H., 2541
Schibeci, R.A., 2793
Schiemann, W., 2918
Schippman, J.S., 3131
Schludermann, E., 2971
Schludermann, S., 2971
Schmeck, R.R., 2420, 3431
Schmelzer, R.V., 2881
Schmidt, J.P., 2605
Schmidt, L.D., 3572, 3573
Schmidt, N., 2561
Schmiedeck, R., 3548
Schmitt, J.P., 2449, 2561, 2835, 3239, 3240, 3302, 3504
Schnake, M.E., 3097
Schneider, B., 3050, 3054, 3066, 3077
Schneider, J.H., 3388
Schoenfeldt, L.F., 3349
Schofield, H.L., 2715

Schon, I., 2758, 2768, 2775
Schooler, C., 2457
Schotte, D.E., 2530
Schrader, W.J., 3586
Schriesheim, C., 2842
Schroeder, M.L., 2518
Schroeder, W.W., 3616
Schuler, G., 3576
Schuler, R.S., 3267
Schumm, W.R., 2980, 3007, 3017, 3631
Schwab, L.O., 2717
Schwab, R.L., 3292
Schwartz, G.E., 2566
Schwartz, J.C., 3003
Schwartz, R., 3481, 3502
Schwartzbach, H., 2492, 3198
Schwarz, J.C., 2971
Schwarzwald, J., 3139
Scott, C., 2908
Scott, J.P., 2531
Scott, K.D., 2842
Scott, K.J., 2883
Scott, N.A., 2446
Scott, W.E., 3115, 3149
Scott, W.E., Jr., 2637
Scruggs, T.E., 2791, 2792
Seagoe, M.V., 2862
Seashore, S., 2569
Sebes, J.M., 2964, 2989
Secord, P.F., 3175, 3263
Sedlacek, W.E., 2684, 2784
Seelbach, W., 2990
Seelbach, W.C., 2991, 2992
Seeman, M., 3339
Segal, S.A., 2833
Seifert, E.H., 2882
Sekaran, V., 3621
Selby, M.J., 3463, 3494
Sells, S., 2601
Semmer, N., 2517, 2642, 3071
Senay, E.C., 2531
Sergiovanni, T., 3277
Sermat, V., 2561
Severa, N., 2575, 3485

Seyfarth, L.H., 2711
Shaha, S.H., 2429
Shamir, B., 3341
Shannon, M., 2690
Shanor, K., 2876
Shapiro, S.B., 3547
Sharkey, C.T., 3284
Sharpley, C.F., 2962, 3014
Shaver, P.R., 3509
Shaw, G.A., 2397, 2941
Shea, M.T., 3487
Sheckles, M.P., 3397
Shephatia, L., 2422
Sherer, M., 3307
Sherman, A.W., 3040
Sherman, J., 3245
Sherman, R.E., 2898
Sherman, T.M., 2766
Shermis, M.D., 2536
Sherwood, J.J., 3298
Shigaki, I.S., 3441
Shinar, E.H., 3642
Shinn, J.M., 3001
Shoham, M., 3139
Shorkey, C., 2871
Shorkey, C.T., 2505, 2774, 3439
Short, J.F., 2832
Shover, P.R., 2563
Shulman, G.M., 3264
Shumate, G.F., 3199
Shure, M.B., 3433
Shuy, R., 2756
Shwebel, A.I., 3034
Sid, A.K.W., 3142
Siegal, L.S., 2969
Siegelman, M., 3033
Siegfried, W.D., Jr., 2906
Sigman, M., 2935
Silber, E., 3313
Silverman, W.H., 3062
Silverstein, A.B., 2847, 3076, 3152
Simard, L.C., 2535
Simmons, R.G., 3312
Sims, E.V., Jr., 2376
Sims, H.P., Jr., 3080

Singer, S., 2961
Sinha, J.B.P., 2845
Siryk, B., 2400, 2401, 2611, 3123
Sjoberg, L., 2494
Slade, P., 2742
Slaney, R.B., 3657
Slater, D., 3597
Slaughter, H.B., 2395
Sleet, D.A., 2862
Slenker, S.E., 3251
Sletto, R.F., 3030
Sloan, V.J., 2779
Slocum, J.W., Jr., 3583, 3596
Smilanski, S., 2422
Smilansky, S., 2861
Smith, C.A., 2637, 2851, 2884, 3522
Smith, D.H., 3138
Smith, H.P., 2798
Smith, K.A., 2707
Smith, K.B., 3445, 3446, 3538
Smith, M.C., 2813
Smith, P., 2754, 2781
Smith, P.C., 2629, 2630
Smith, T.W., 3478
Snow, J.S., 3599
Snow, R.E., 2712
Snyder, D.K., 3020
Snyder, R.A., 3243
Snyder, S.C., 3278
Synder, S.D., 2555, 2564
Solano, C.H., 2810
Sollod, R.N., 3548
Soloman, G., 3161
Solomom, D.J., 3094
Solomon, D., 3273
Somers, M., 2671
Soule, J.C., 3221, 3297
Soutar, G.N., 2675
Spanier, G., 2978
Spanier, G.B., 2436, 2962, 2963, 3014
Spanos, N.P., 2902
Sparacino, J., 2480
Spence, J., 3036
Spence, J.T., 2703, 2704, 3271

Spielberger, C.D., 2402, 2409, 2473, 2508, 3609
Spitzberg, B.H., 2922, 2924, 3261
Spitzer, R.I., 2515
Spitzer, R.L., 2514
Spivack, G., 3433
Springer, S.P., 2687
Squires, R.L., 3493
Srole, L., 2612
Stacy, M., 2844
Stafford, I.P., 2074, 3293
Staines, G.L., 3122
Staley, A.A., 2490
Stapp, J., 2614, 3206
Starker, S., 2384, 3354
Starr, P., 3275, 3312
Start, K.B., 2715
Staton, C.W., 2535
Stauffer, A.J., 2710
Steen, P.L., 2878
Steffensmeier, R.H., 2970, 3048
Stein, M.I., 2725
Stein, S.J., 3013, 3022
Steinberg, L.D., 3052
Steinberg, S.L., 2602
Stenack, R.J., 3603
Stening, B.W., 3169
Stern, A., 2689
Stern, G.G., 3057
Stern, R.M., 3118
Sterns, L., 3664
Stevens, G., 3319
Stevenson, H.W., 2678
Stewart, M.A., 3453
Stewart, R.A., 3296
Stewart, R.A.C., 3537
Stiffman, A.R., 2808
Stigler, J.W., 2383, 2678, 3260
Stiles, W.B., 3599
Stockdale, D.F., 3412
Stogdill, R., 2842
Stogdill, R.M., 2682, 3560
Stokes, J.P., 2965, 2976, 3035, 3039
Stoltenberg, C.D., 3325
Stone, D.L., 2728, 2729

Stone, E.F., 2751
Stone, G.L., 3308, 3481, 3502
Storey, A.G., 3500
Stoudenomice, J., 2836
Stout, J.K., 2540, 2643
Stovall, C., 2784
Strangeland, M., 3106
Straus, M.A., 2973, 3029, 3046
Strickland, B., 3238
Strickland, B.R., 3183, 3241
Stringer, R.A., 3097, 3098
Stripling, R.O., 3163
Strodtbeck, F., 2999
Strohmer, D.C., 2456, 2934, 3573
Strom, B., 2735, 3576
Strong, S., 2769, 3594
Strong, S.R., 2868, 2869, 3190, 3281
Strupp, H.H., 2616, 3119
Stumpf, S.A., 3614
Suarez, E., 2473, 3245
Subich, L.M., 2996, 3209, 3612
Sugawara, A.I., 3318
Suinn, R.M., 2417, 2427
Suiter, R.L., 3573
Sullaway, M., 2978
Summerlin, M.L., 3279
Sundel, M., 3480
Super, D.E., 2996, 3612
Sutton-Simon, K., 2505, 3284
Swaim, N.M., 3413
Swanson, G.E., 2829
Swanson, H.L., 3529, 3531
Swartz, J.P., 2381
Sweeney, G.A., 2433, 2440, 2508
Swensen, C.H., 2959
Swiney, J.F., 3420
Sypher, H.E., 3408
Szapocznik, J., 2807

Tadmor, C.S., 3218
Taft, R., 3360
Talbot, D.B., 3630
Tan, A.L., 2950
Taylor, C., 2791
Taylor, J., 3186, 3270

Taylor, J.B., 2388, 2391, 2756
Taylor, J.C., 2889, 2912, 3560
Taylor, K.M., 2471, 3180
Taylor, M.S., 2379, 3315, 3329
Taylor, O., 2756
Taylor, R.B., 2810
Teborg, J.R., 2629
Teeter, T.A., 3182
Tellegren, A., 2829
Tellenback, S., 2655
Templar, D.I., 2459, 2541, 2764
Tepper, M.E., 3125
Terborg, J.R., 2659, 2894, 3399
Terenzini, P.T., 2399, 2953, 2954, 3049, 3398
Terrell, F., 2560
Terrell, S., 2560
Tesiny, E.P., 2502
Tesler, M., 2857
Teta, D.C., 2519
Tetenbaum, T.J., 2705
Tharenou, P., 2631, 3091, 3317, 3584
Thauberger, P.C., 2443, 2444, 2552
Thayer, P.W., 3092
Thayer, R.E., 2434
Thelen, M.H., 2813
Thomas, A., 2840, 3356, 3370, 3380
Thomas, E.C., 2823
Thomas, J., 2640, 2647, 3650
Thomas, M.L., 2943
Thomas, P.L., 3042
Thomas, R.G., 2716, 3620, 3622
Thompson, B., 3443
Thompson, D.G., 3227
Thompson, D.L., 3235
Thompson, L., 2963, 3004
Thompson, R., 3010
Thompson, S., 2935
Thomson-Rountree, P., 3182
Thornburg, H.D., 3001
Thornton, A., 3662
Thumin, F.J., 2689
Thurlow, M., 2824
Thyer, B.A., 2871

Tiggemann, M., 3255
Tilby, P., 3411
Tinsley, H.E.A., 3209, 3210, 3407,
Tinto, V., 2399
Tippett, J., 3313
Tipton, T.M., 3216
Tisher, R.P., 2880
Tittle, C.K., 3619
Tobacyk, J., 2385, 2834
Tobin, D.L., 2830
Tolchinsky, P.D., 2752
Tolfa, D., 2792
Tolor, A., 2481
Tolsdorf, C., 2589
Tolstedt, B.E., 2965, 2976, 3035, 3039
Tom, D.Y.H., 3509
Tom, F.K.T., 3605
Tomkiewicz, J., 2470
Toobert, D.J., 2818
Top, D., 3393
Topf, M., 2850, 3110
Topkin, W.E., 3123
Topping, C., 2413
Tornow, W.W., 3585
Touhey, J.C., 2759
Townes, B.D., 3424
Tracey, T.S., 2684
Treadwell, T.W., 2579
Triandis, H.C., 3169
Trice, A.D., 3194
Trice, H.M., 3624
Tripodi, T., 3421
Trites, R.L., 2827
Trost, J., 2975
Trusty, F., 3277
Tsai, S-L., 2762
Tseng, M.S., 3235
Tsujimoto, R.N., 3556
Tubiana, J.H., 3582
Tuck, J.P., 2439
Tucker, C.M., 2743, 2921
Tucker, L.A., 3175, 3263
Tuckman, J., 2697
Tully, J., 3202

Tung, W.K., 2546
Turk, D.C., 2457, 2499, 2635, 2974
Turkat, I.D., 2839, 3220
Turner, C.J., 2492, 3198, 3653
Turner, J.L., 2698, 2743
Twentyman, C.T., 2885
Tybout, A., 2908
Tych, A.M., 2947
Tyson, P., 3468
Tzuriel, D., 3033, 3222, 3390

Udry, J.R., 3016
Ungerer, J.A., 2935

Valecha, G.K., 3239
Valencia, R.R., 2993
Valerio, H.P., 3308, 3481, 3502
Valliant, P.M., 3503
Van Bart, D., 2632, 2670, 3002
Van Ijzendoorn, M.H., 3037
Van Til, J., 3138
Vandecreek, L., 3572
VandenBerg, E., 3391, 3410
Vapava, J.R., 2692
Vaughn, E.S., III, 3068
Vaux, A., 2589
Vecchio, R.P., 2568, 2843, 3074
Veit, C.T., 2493
Veldman, D.J., 3600
Velluntino, F.R., 2377
Venkatachalam, R., 3099
Ventura, J.N., 2984
Vera, W., 2760
Verna, G.B., 3186
Vestre, N.D., 2931
Villemez, W.J., 2579
Vincent, J., 2982
Vincent, K.R., 2802, 3372
Viney, L.L., 2947
Viney, W., 3532
Vitale, M., 3154
Vizeltir, V., 3134
Vleeming, R.G., 3302, 3514
Vogel, J., 3374
Vojtisek, J.E., 2491

Volkin, J.I., 3015
Vroom, V.H., 2626

Waddell, F.T., 3141
Waetjen, W., 3299
Wagner, B., 2956
Wagner, F.R., 3243, 3317
Wakabayashi, M., 2926
Walberg, H.J., 3094, 3113
Walder, L.O., 3498
Walker, A.J., 3004
Walker, D.K., 2381
Walker, W.J., 3057
Walkey, F.H., 3230
Wall, S.M., 2590
Wallace, G.R., 3338
Wallace, K.M., 3011, 3015, 3035
Wallston, B.S., 3217, 3339
Wallston, K.A., 3251, 3339
Walsh, J.J., 2700
Walster, E., 2965
Walton, J., 3369
Wambach, C.A., 2769, 3594
Wampold, B.E., 3024
Warburton, D.M., 2489, 2543
Ward, L.G., 3603
Ware, E.E., 3224
Ware, J.E., 3601
Ware, J.E., Jr., 2493
Ware, R., 3371
Warehime, R.G., 2573
Warman, R., 2909
Warr, P., 2632, 2670, 3002, 3130
Warr, P.B., 3626
Wass, H., 2453, 2458-2460, 2469, 2497
Watson, D., 2604
Watson, J.M., 2740, 2795
Watson, S.R., 3478
Watt, N.F., 2870
Weare, C.R., 3610
Weaver, J.R., 2675
Webster-Stratton, C., 2799
Weeks, M.O., 3660
Wegener, C., 2913

Weinberg, J., 2520
Weiner, B., 2859
Weinstein, N., 2850, 3110
Weinstein, R.S., 2892
Weir, T., 3627
Weisberg, P., 2376
Weiss, D.J., 2995
Weiss, D.S., 2685
Weiss, H.M., 2533, 2650
Weiss, R.L., 2966, 3013
Weissberg, R.P., 2414, 2820
Wells, G.R., 3151
Werbel, J.D., 3541, 3648, 3649
Wessberg, H.W., 2610
Wessler, R., 2948
Wessman, A.E., 3335
West, D.J., Jr., 2639
Westbrook, B.W., 3619
Westbrook, M.T., 2981
Westcott, M.R., 3430
Westman, A.S., 2467
Wexley, K.N., 3421, 3560
Weyer, G., 2649
Wheeler, A.E., 3590
Wheeler, K.G., 3256
Wheeler, V.A., 2554
White, D.R., 3176
White, G., 3338
White, G.L., 3128
White, M.C., 2904
White, S.E., 3088
Whiteman, V., 2871
Wiesz, J.B., 2509
Wigfield, A., 2923
Wiggins, J.S., 3387
Wigle, S.E., 3038
Wilcox, L.E., 2891
Wild, B.K., 3353
Wile, D.B., 2896
Wileman, S., 2679
Williams, E.J., 3607
Williams, J., 3448
Williams, J.E., 3318
Williams, J.M., 2540, 2643, 3467
Williams, J.R., 3272

Williams, R.E., 3032, 3233
Williams, V.G., 2881
Williams, W., 2802
Willower, D.J., 2771, 3105, 3107, 3282
Wilmesmeier, J.M., 3543
Wilson, G.T., 3404
Wilson, J., 2787
Wilson, M.N., 2855
Wilson, M.R., 3554
Wilson, R.W., 2864
Wimberly, R.C., 2815
Winefield, A.H., 3255
Winefield, H.R., 3251
Winkworth, J.M., 2881
Wise, P.S., 2600, 2662
Wise, S.L., 2701, 2786, 3067
Witkin, S., 2966
Witt, J.C., 2822, 3400
Wolberg, H.J., 2762
Wolf, F.M., 2483, 3156, 3157, 3335
Wolf, T.M., 3450
Wolf, W., 3441
Wolfe, L.K., 3343
Wolfe, R.N., 2558, 2914
Wollack, S., 3559
Wolman, B.B., 2737
Wolowitz, H.M., 3417
Wood, K., 2906
Wood, R., 3465
Woodrick, C.P., 2753
Woodruff, A.E., 3182
Woodward, H.R., 3100
Worell, J., 3557
Worell, L., 3557
Worley, S.M., 3034
Worthington, E.L., Jr., 3216, 3568
Wright, C.R., 3552
Wright, D., 2640, 2647, 3650
Wright, P., 2907
Wright, P.H., 2548, 2565

Yamamoto, K., 2424
Yamauchi, K.T., 2764
Yang, K-S., 3536

Yanico, B.J., 3079, 3573, 3642
Yogev, A., 3134
Yogev, S., 2986
Young, J., 3090
Youtz, M.A., 3421
Yuker, H.E., 2693, 2702

Zaffrann, R.T., 3495
Zalesny, M.D., 2659, 2894, 3204, 3399
Zalezik, A., 2499
Zamostny, K.P., 3573
Zapf, D., 2654
Zatz, S., 2405
Zeitz, G., 2571
Zelin, M.L., 2886, 3455
Zeltzer, L., 2867
Zemaitis, R., 2455
Zemore, R., 2462
Zeppa, R., 2425
Zigler, E., 2594
Zilberg, N.J., 2484
Zimbardo, P.G., 3513
Zinger, J.T., 2541
Zuckerman, M., 2412, 2471, 2545, 3146, 3147
Zung, W.W.K., 2485
Zuroff, D.C., 3003

SUBJECT INDEX

All numbers refer to test numbers. Numbers 1 through 339 refer to entries in Volume 1, numbers 340 through 1034 refer to entries in Volume 2, numbers 1035 through 1595 refer to entries in Volume 3, numbers 1596 through 2369 refer to entries in Volume 4 and numbers 2370 through 3665 refer to entries in Volume 5.

Abasement, 1720
Aberration, perceptual, 3266
Abidingness, law, 287
Abilit(ies)(y): academic, 766;analytic, 661; cognitive, 2678; conclusions, 2217; cope, stress, 1677; discrimination, 1041, 1249; general reasoning, 2220; human relation, 1714; inductive reasoning, 2209, 2221; information-transformation, 110; intuitive, 3430; letter formation, 1052; mental, 138; occupational, 305; perceptual motor, 2213; performance, 6; problem solving, 1468, 2226; reasoning, 2204; self-concept, 1850; self-estimates, 305, 766, 1428, 1429; supervisor(y), 1019, 2265; verbal, quantitative, 2213; work, 1033
Abortion, attitude toward, 1131
Abrasiveness, self-rated, 749
Abstract(ness): conceptualization, 2216; concreteness, 2200; reasoning, 2201, 2202, 3424
Academic(ally)(s), 388, 621, 675, 2191: ability, 766; ability, confidence, 2147; ability, self-concept, 2128; achievement, 477, 1337; achievement accountability, 467; achievement motivation, 1987; achievement orientation, 228; achievement predictor, 2683, 2684; achievement, university residence, 704; adequacy, peer counseling, 1973; adjustment, 22; advising, perceptions, 1959; advisors, undergraduates, 992; anxiety, 400, 2404; assistant, evaluation, 992; attitude toward, 1126; attribution, 3327; climate, 1335; competence, 2421; curiosity, 1984; environment, attitude, 1126; factors, 527; integration, 2399; locus of control, 3222; motivation, 578, 1985, 3123; orientation, 228; performance, 471; prediction, 231; self-concept, 1395, 2030, 2056, 3153, 3301, 3303; self-concept, elementary school, 2147; self-esteem, 2031, 3154, 3155, 3278; skills, 400; status, college freshmen, 904; success, correlates, 95; success, fear of, 2410; talented elementary students, 1606
Acceptance, 583, 645, 655, 659: blame, 907; disability, 1636; father, 645; loss, 1636; perceived maternal, 759; school, 1070; self, 249, 759, 831, 1105, 1425; social, 1104, 2593
Access, social, 1452
Accidents, pilot, 478
Accountability, academic achievement, 467, 1367
Acculturation, 1696: Mexican-Americans, 2547, 3519

579

Achievement, 1-21, 218, 340-386, 949, 1035-1066, 1596-1624: academic, 477, 1337; academic accountability, 467, 1367; academic, locus of control, 3196; anxiety, 23, 908, 1625, 2433, 2439; artistic and sex role, 877; athletic and sex role, 877; attribution, 3157, 3253; college, 480; competitive, 989; controlled, 989; dynamics, 1631; excellence, 861; first grade, 469, 474; identity, 271, 628, 1286; junior college, 1351; listening, 1043, 1063; locus of control, 3233; mathematics, 1740, 2383; mathematics and sex role, 877; motivation, 1986, 1989, 1990, 1993, 2017, 2019, 2026, 3124-3126, 3141, 3142; see achievement need; motivation, academic, 1987; motivation, junior high, 2028; motivation, men, 1988; need, 23, 204, 210, 712, 721, 727, 744, 986, 1338, 1340, 1345, 1347, 1350, 1353, 2005, 2007, 2009, 2022, 2029; need, children, 715, 718, 737; need, college students, 726; need, disadvantaged students, 722; need, females, 728; need, high school, 729; need, males, 728; need, Mexican-Americans, 738; orientation, 713; phonics, 2398; preschool, 12; pressure for, 496, 647, 673; quantitative, 1043, 1063; reading, 350, 1035, 1036, 1043, 1063; reading, first grade, 602; reading and sex role, 877; responsibility, intellectual, 786; self criticism, 244; standards and sex role, 877; striving, 716; tendency, 2006, 2274; tests, attitude, 2718; verbal, 1063

Acquiescence, 278, 281, 296, 2244: negativism, children, 843

Acting, 568: -out, 2191

Activation, 417: -deactivation, 1839

Active: speech, 397; experimentation, 2216

Activeness, pressure for, 647, 673

Activit(y)(ies), 1339: class, 1380; group, 681; leisure, 198, 268, 3404, 3407; level, 1203, 1870; patterns, 400; preference, 3388; reaction; 1293 stereotypes, girls, 2032; women's attitude toward physical, 791

Actual behaviors, 601

Actualization, self, 214

Acuity, perceptual, 2685

Adaptability, 2285

Adaptive regression, 606

Adequacy, college teachers, 785

Adjective(s): generation technique, 1369; prenominal, 377

Adjustment, 300, 625, 1067, 1398, 3535: academic, 22; adolescent, 3522; behavior, 1238; college life, 22, 2400, 2401, 2409; difficulties, 403; educational, 22-27, 387-402, 1067-1077, 1625-1635; family, 2291, 2992; first grade, 2413; general, 1106; index, 34; kindergarten, 2422; level, 422; marriage, 1299, 2978, 2980, 3011, 3014, 3015, 3019; patient, 418; personal, 37; personal social, 397; premorbid, 421; prisoners, 1678; psychological, 28-43, 403-425, 1078-1089, 1636-1694; rating, 403, 418; retarded, 1033; self, 409; social, 44-70, 426-466, 1090-1116, 1695-1731; trainee, 27; vocational, 1033; widowed, 1693; work, 337

Administrat(ion)(ive)(or), 662: attitudes, 1195; behavior, 1863; educational, 528; guidance, 677; image, 1307; locus of control, 818; morale, school, 1978;

probation, 523; responsibilities, 657; school, 528, 1558; stereotypes, 528; style, 1407, 1408; values, 979

Admission(s): assistance, college, 660; practices and attitudes, 553

Adolescen(ce)(ts)('), 485, 490, 605, 1751: abuse, 2964; alcohol use, 3160; alienation, 2549; assertiveness, 3501; body satisfaction, 756; boys, 848; Chicano, 1696; children behavior, 1844; cognitive functioning, 605; communication, 2897; creative, 133; creatively gifted, 1935; delinquency, 1213; drug use, 562; future time perspective, 772; girls, parents of, 656; girls, social competence, 2595, 2866; goal attainment, 2898; information seeking, 868; late, 498, 646; locus control, 2072; parent relations, 640, 760, 3001, 3030, 3040; peer-relations, 760; perceptions parental, 2156; personality, 854; pre-, 625, 644; rearing, 490; retarded, 1619; self-concept, 1430, 2102; self-expectation, 1432; self-satisfaction, 756; stress, 2435; structure, 760, 1070, 1378, 2175; structure needs, 1991; values, 974, 3523, 3525, 3526; vocational interest, 1591

Adult(s), 485: biographical inventory, 840; career development, 2944; creative, 133, 615; creatively gifted, 1935; development, 2943; interpersonal dependency, 1715; irrational ideas, 1637; locus of control, 3223, 3255, 3274; male self-esteem, 826; perception and recall, 533; self-esteem, 2046, 3312; sex-role concepts, 2132; time perspective, 758; young males, 636

Adverbial clauses, 377

Advisers: characteristics, 994; perceived by students, 993

Advising residence hall groups, 546

Aesthetic: perception, 254; sensitivity, 2034

Affective: assessment, 1802; attitude toward time, 91; attributed, 404; balance, 2426; behavior, 2810; behavior, student, 568; behavior changes, 572; characteristics, 601; cognition, 404; content, 404; developed, 404; dimension, 404; expression, 121, 279; group behavior, 596; interaction, 1217, intimacy, 2965; judgment, 1252; quality of relationships, 640; response, immediate, 429; sensitivity, 98, 428, 429; states, 1638

Affection(ate): nurturant, 652; social, 417

Affectivity, 600: assessment, 1964

Affiliation, 1720: need, 44, 745, 986, 2007; need, Mexican-American, 738; peer, 228; toward others, 1706

Affiliative tendency, 44

African: children, 1740; society, malaise in, 65, 301

Aggress(ion)(iveness), 216, 397, 403, 417, 651, 920, 927, 940, 1510, 1870, 2247, 3452, 3455, 3463, 3470: anxiety, 2437; -assertiveness, 1842; attitude toward, 2706; authoritarian, 2253; behavioral, 1843, 2295, 2800, 2801, 2858; child(ren), 1840, 2277, 2878, 3453, 3464, 3498; -conducive activities, 2190; delay, 1212; interpersonal, 1221; job, 1033; lack of, 2251; peer

related, children, 946; potential, 1476; self, 242
Aging, 407, 415: successful, 33
Agoraphobic: behavior, 2812; cognitions, 2438
Agree(ableness)(ment), 1720: -disagreement, 483; disagreement response set, 281
Aide(s), 577: child-interactions, 577
Ailments, common, 407
Air cadets, 478
Alcohol(ic)(s), 405, 526, 1122, 1674, 3159, 3160: abuse, 2802, 2849; addict, 1639; drug use, 563
Alienat(ed)(ing)(ion), 45, 64, 65, 430, 437, 453, 533, 809, 1090, 1093, 1699, 1701, 1709, 1725: adolescent, 2549; attitudes, 83; conditions, 430; consumer, 1700; cultural, 1093; general, 442, 1091; interpersonal, 1110; manifest, 443, 1103; social, 1098; student(s), 64, 455, 582; university, 465, 1730; work, 2671
Aloneness, 413
Aloofness, 688
Alternate uses, 608
Alternatives, correct, 385
Altitude, high, 571
Altruis(m)(tic), 624, 2317: in children, 926; motivation, 3134
Alumni, follow up, 158
Ambigu(ity)(ous), 2122: intolerance of, 1796; role, 2357, 2525, 3288, 3292; situation, threat perceived, 2077; tolerance (for) (of), 481, 612, 646, 955, 965, 1505, 2245
Ambition, teacher, 1363, 1364
Ambivalence, 2486
American: Catholic priest, 1668; political behavior, 368; values, 1524
American Indian values, 3545
Anagram fluency, 1903
Analog(ies)(y), 887: figure, 2059; verbal, 1065
Analysis, 600: auditory, 1374; early childhood education, 678; schedule, 601; visual, 1041, 1441
Analytic: abilities, 661; empathy, 1370
Anaphora comprehension, 5, 2370
Anatomy test, 658
Anger, 832, 950, 1501, 2246, 2252, 2283, 3106, 3454, 3455, 3494
Anhedonia, 910: physical, 2507
Anomia, 424, 1685, 2563, 2612
Anomie, 1078, 1091, 1638, 1640, 1684: psychological, 413
Anthropology achievement: elementary grades, 1044; concepts, 1269
Anti: -authoritarianism, 481; -democratic attitudes, 77; -intraception, 2253; -sexism, 1123; -social behavior, 578; -war, demonstrators, 552; -worldminded, 1795
Anticipations, personal, 2107
Anxiety, 283, 286, 387, 405, 417, 487, 841, 860, 925, 928, 945, 947, 948, 966, 1496, 1500, 1641, 1642, 1681, 2248, 2270, 2440, 2473, 2523: academic, 400; achievement, 908, 1625, 2433, 2439; aggression, 2437; behavioral, 2456; concept, 1381; death, 410, 1649, 1650, 1651, 2447, 2459, 2541; debilitating, 1625, 1626, 1633, 2240; depression, 773, 1686; elementary children, 933; existential, 1657; facilitating, 1625, 2240; first graders, 948; graduate school, test, 2427; job-induced, 1666; major choice, 1648; manifest, 1478, 2524, 3488; mathematics, 394, 1630, 2417, 2418; neurotic, 749; piano, 2508; preschool, 2509; reactions, 402;

SUBJECT INDEX

self-rating, 911; situational, 26 sixth graders, 947; social, 2604, 2605; state, 1682; -stress, 1643; symptoms 1632, 2441; tension, 1638; test, 25, 26, 32, 209, 387, 392, 393, 395, 396, 398, 399, 401, 402, 713, 1074-1076, 1625, 1627, 1629, 1633-1635, 2428-2430; test, children, 32; trait, 3478; uncertainty, 960; vocational choice, 1648
Anxious(ness): audience, 2551; -fearful, 1872; interaction, 2572; social, 2551
Apathy, 1103
Aphasic, speech, 1887
Apology, -restitution, 381
Appearance: employee, 1007; physical, 593
Apperception: pain, 2095; thematic Hispanic, 3382
Applicant rating, 3588
Application, 600: college, 553
Applied psychology, attitude toward, 1127
Appraisal: see evaluation
Apprehension, 2917
Approach: withdrawal, 2285
Approval: disapproval, teacher, 659; need, 62, 450, 500, 2586; parental, 499; social, 48, 449
Aptitude, 71-75, 467-482, 1117-1121, 1732-1744: community college, 75; employees, 1007; foreign language, 1733; geometry, 74; mental, 72; spatial, 479
Arbitration, 1274
Argumentativeness, 3456
Arithmetic: ability, perception of, 2147; skills, 637, 1038
Arousal: group, 1998; level, 571; seeking need, 2023
Art(s): assessment, 1457; biographical, 2159; music,
attitudes toward, 1841
Arthritis, attitudes, 2767
Articulation, community college, 3163
Aspiration(s): experiences, school related, 472; college students, reality, 740; disadvantaged, 740; educational, college students, 719; occupational, 269, 897, 3623; occupational, high school, 901; student, 2027; vocational, 204, 269
Assault, 2252
Assert(ion)(ive)(iveness), 1702, 2242, 2249, 2256, 2271, 2282, 3457-3459, 3461, 3465, 3467-3469, 3480, 3481, 3492, 3501, 3502: aggressiveness, 1842; behavior, 1873, 2803, 3451; non-, 408; training, 408
Assessment: art, 1457; memory, 2384
Assimilation of meaning, 380
Association(s), 385: dream, 30
Associationalism, 982
Associative: responding, 264; verbal encoding, 1035
Assumptions, looking for, 2215
Assurance, self, 1101, 1427
Athletic: recruitment, 3413; success, 3215
Atmosphere: classroom, 1027; group, 2568, 3074; junior high, 700
Attainment: goals, 714; satisfaction, students, 714
Attitude(s), 23, 76-97, 481, 483-561, 1122-1202, 1745-1838, 2228: abortion, 1131; admission practices, deans, 553; alcohol, 1122; alienation, 45, 64, 65; antidemocratic, 77; Arab-American, 97; authoritarianism, 83; behavior,

1745; black students, 46; business, 84; child rearing, 496, 1148, 3032; children, 497, 1180; children interracial, 1184; children's pictorial, 1770; church, 80; cigarettes, 1122; coffee, 1122; college students, 81, 743, 1530; college student patterns, 222; computer, 2724; conventionality, 2734; counsel(ing)(or), 81, 309, 560, 1173, 2788; creative, 130, 235; cross-cultural, 1153; customer service, 3066; death, 1779; dominating, 504; drug, 1781; drug knowledge, use, 1858; educational, 2738, 2739; employee, 188, 193, 1007, 1156, 2622; father, 645; feminist, liberal, 1767; feminist, nonfeminist, 1834; formation, 83; gender roles, 2746; grade contract, 513; guidance and counseling, 85, 189; impunitive, 481; institutional, 82; intellectual and programmatic, 86; interpersonal, 546; interracial, 517, 1147, 1150, 1183; intimacy, 2579; law-related, 1799; managerial, 523, 1536; marijuana, 1133; masculine, 2759; mathematics, 524; mental, illness, 2736; military service, 81; modern, 3536; money, 2764; mother's, 1803; motivation, upward bound, 217; movie, 2765; multifactor racial, 482, 2766; nationalities, 1135; nonprofessional, 82; office, 3368; parental, 504, 532, 640, 3010; parental, research instrument, 533; peers, 1820; perceived maternal, 759; personal, 535, 593; personnel managers, 1169; policemen's, 1810; political, 536, 537, 1806; premarital intercourse, 2237; privacy, 2751, 2752; procrastination, 2769; professional, 82, 1815; professional-self, 82; protest situational, 1817; pupil, 455, 540; racial, 46, 78, 79, 87, 88, 482, 520, 542, 1812, 1813, 2772, 2773; racial intermarriage, 70; reading, 543, 544, 1787, 1822, 1823; referents, 555; romantic, 2777; scholastic activities, 556; school, 66, 155, 1136, 1149, 1825, 2779; school counselor, 1826; school experience, 1820; school, general, 1820; school orientation, 534; school work, 1820; science, 2793; seat belts, 1828; secondary reading, 1824; self, 1439; self-righteous, 1170; sexual, 2781; sex-role, 1831, 2760, 2783; social, 94, 554, 555, 1527; social responsibility, 94; speaker, 2217; student, 859, 1163, 1188-1190, 1194; student beliefs, 556; students interracial, 535; supervisors, 1023; teachers, 559, 1820; teachers' job-related, 1827; therapist, 96; trusting, 1706; union, 1836, 1837, 3415; United States, 83; university student, 705; upward bound, 45, 217; work involvement, 2797; women, 1134; youth, 1202

Attitude toward: aggression, 2706; art, music, 1841; arthritis, 2767; authority, 1830, 2723, 2747; aviation, 1142; banking, 156; blacks, 1187; black English, 2756; black movement, 542; calculators, 2721; change, 92; church, 80; classroom, 1196; college, 2692; college courses, 151; community, 1312; computer, 115, 152, 2726-2729; controversy, 2707, 2733; cooperation, 1371;

counseling, 189, 2698, 2708; counseling black students, 999; courses, 2735; curriculum, 501; defense, 1197; dental health, 2725; desegregation, 1160; disabled, 2693, 2717; discrimination, 542; dreams, 2709, 2737; drug abusers, 1191; drugs, 1145, 1155, 1210; education, 529, 549, 1167; educational research, 2710; elderly, 2697, 2755; environmental issues, 1152; evangelism, 2711; fees, 2789; female roles, 2742; foreign language, 2744; gifted children, teacher, 558; handicapped, 2702, 2784; homosexuality, 2713, 2748-2750; interracial, 1143, 1168; job, 1346, 2754; job teachers, 557; learning, 540, 2785; mainstreaming, 2694; marriage, family, 1161; mathematics, 153, 2715, 2740, 2761, 2762, 2795; mental illness, 530; Mexican American, 2768; modernity, 1164, 1165; movies, 1166; national groups, 1180, 2798; nonmaternal care, 2967; nuclear disarmament, 2695; nurses, 2696; occupations, 2700; peers, 541; physical activity, 791, 1171; political issues, 1172; pupil control, 2771; psychological help, 1137, 2743; psychological reports and services, 154; reading, 1175, 2741, 2763, 2775; religion, 1178; riots and demonstrations, 482; risk, 2776; school, 540, 541, 1179, 1181, 1771, 2778; school library, 2758; school subjects, 2745; self, 1771; self-control, 2714; sex roles, 552, 2699, 2720, 2782, 2787; social issues, 1146; social studies, 1138; statistics, 2701, 2786; substance use, 2790; suicide, 1192; supernatural phenomena, 1139; teachers, 541, 549, 580, 1771; teaching, 1140, 2691, 2712, 2716; technology, 1162; television commercials, 2722; tests, 1453, 2718, 2791, 2792; time, 91; tutoring, 2794; upward mobility, 1158; whites, 542; witchcraft, 1139; women, 1190, 2703, 2704, 2796; women's liberation, 1200; work, 541, 1199, 2730; working mothers, 2705; youth, 1141

Attraction, 426: interpersonal, 426, 1711
Attractiveness, group, 1712: self-rated, 749, 3275
Attributed effect, 404
Attributes: personal, 561, 692, 1809; physical, 561
Attribution, 3157, 3164-3166, 3203, 3246, 3253, 3254, 3268-3270, 3327
Audience, anxiousness, 2551
Audio-visual, 1
Auditory: analysis, 1374; blending, 1036; memory, 1066; perception, 1613; perception, first graders, 750, 1423; segmentation, 1036, 1037; stimuli, 1233; visual perception, 765; visual rhythm, 750
Authoritarian(ism), 296, 530, 909, 912, 1500, 1807, 2250, 2253, 2258, 2263, 2264, 2293, 3460, 3507, 3509: attitudes, 83; children, 3466; family, 641, 644; principal, 2281; support, 519
Authority: acceptance, 2805; adherence to, 916; attitudes toward, 1830, 2723, 2747; parental, 640; police, 485; rejection by, 499; relations, 400

Autocratic managerial personality, 787
Auto-driving skills, 478
Auto-kinetic, 913
Automaticity, word processing, 2927
Autonomous, achievement, 2298
Autonomy, 214, 218, 949, 1715, 1815, 2367, 3168: child, 2550, 2806; job, 3051; need, 2010
Aviation, attitude toward, 1142
Avoidance, 645: success, 1362
Awareness: failure, 3170; reinforcement, 1416; social, 1417

Babies, social responsiveness, 1235
Back pain, 3192
Bank(ing)(s): attitude toward, 156; climate, 3054; switching, 1307; teller performance, 1537
Beauty, rating, 751
Behavior(al)(s), 562-584, 1203-1246, 1839-1886: academic advisor, 2329; actual, 601; adjustment, 1238; adjustment, school, 1628; affective, 2810; affective group, 596; aggressive, 1843, 2800, 2801, 2858, 2875, 2878, 3453, 3470; alcohol abuse, 2802, 2849; anti-social, 578; anxiety, 2456; assertive, 1873, 2803, 3451, 3481; assessment, neonatal, 1849; authority, 2805; autonomy, 2806; beliefs about, 1847; bizarre, on job, 1033; body sensations, 2812; bulimia, 2813, 2833; change, affective, 572; change, cognitive, 572; change, home economics, 572; checklist, 573; child, 28, 496, 1851, 2831; child abuse, 2815, 2846; child-bearing, 144; children, 1207, 1869, 1870, 2382, 2799, 2816-2818, 2856, 2890, 2891; child's creative, 1926; child's innovative, 1926;

classroom, 390, 565, 566, 574, 578, 581, 681, 718, 1108, 1209, 1211, 1227, 1237, 1854, 1855, 1878, 1885, 2820-2823, 2828, 2865, 2880, 2887, 2888, 3056; combat, 2825; competency, 432; competitive, 2826; consumption, 2829; control problems, 403; coping, 2830; counselee, 427; counselor, 3565; counselor interview, 584; creative, 531; critical interview, 1864; curiosity-related, 1818; daily, 2835, 2836; dating, 253; delinquent, 1213, 2832, 2874; description, 388; deviant, 573; diagnostic, 2838; drug, 569, 2819; early mathematics, 345; employee, 2851; ethical violations, 971; excitability, 2852; exploratory, 1208; facilitative, 432; faculty, 2894; fantasy, 2876, 2886; gender, 1219, 1285; good, student, 578; health, 2864; heterosocial, 2885; home, 1957; hospital, 1861; hyperactive, 2827, 2878; hypothetical, 1745; illness, 2839, 2860, 3220; impaired, 2834; impatient, 1862; indecision, 2809; independent, 651; infant, 2840; information seeking, 2814; ingratiating, 2841; innovative, 432, 621, 1208; instructional, 322; instructional, by tutors, 322; interaction, 585; interaction description system, 596; interpersonal, 1720; interpersonal and administrative, 1863; interpersonal advisor, 2329; intimate, 2837; job, 3052; leadership, 1333, 2843-2845, 2872, 2884, 2889, 2896; loving-rejecting, 149; managers, 3560; maturity, 621, 1206, 1937; modification, 380, 1010;

moodiness, 2801; moral, 981; moral-judgment, 2310; motion sickness, 2848; objectives for writing, 341; organizational, 3065; oppositional, 1225; orientation, 228; noise, 2850; pain, 2854, 2857, 2867; paranoid, 646; parent, 655, 2855, 3033; parent description, 643; pathological 1226, 1310; patient, 1205, 1870; peer influence, 556; preschool, 1872; press, perceived environment, 2050; play, 2861, 2862; problems, 28, 389, 495, 2804, 2807, 2808, 2859, 2866; problem solving, 1232, 2830, 3280; procrastination, 2868, 2869; prosocial in children, 963; protest, 1817; pupil 574, 578; rating, 48, 1845, 2853, 2870; rational, 1679, 1874, 2871; refusal, 1857, 2803; risk taking, 1234; rule-orientation, 2158; self-control, 2873; sexual, 1747; sharing, 62; sleep, 2877; social, 388, 964; stimulus seeking, 2847; student, 601, 737, 2824, 2879, 2881, 2882; student affective, 568; student cognitive, 568; study, 2883; style, 564, 1846, 2811; supervisory, 1241, 2842; system, client verbal, 587; task-oriented, 1854; teacher, 333, 580, 582, 811, 2892, 2893, 3406, 3604-3606; test, 1242; text anxiety, 1074; therapist's, 2197; trainee, 2863; Type A, 1886; verbal, 2248; vocational, 202, 426; withdrawn, 1033

Belief(s): -about-behavior, 1847; children, 535, 2259; client, 3190; human nature, 1522; irrational, 1516, 1665, 2505, 3226, 3228, 3284, 3287; justice, 3522, 3537, 3538; magic, 3539; paranormal, 3211; philosophical, 968; political, 1520, 2318; protestant work ethic, 2319, 3528, 3550, 3551, 3663; religious, 2323; seat belt, 1829; teacher effectiveness, 3330; weather, 3121

Benevolence, 530, 1807

Biodata, 225

Biographical: factors, 1444; information, 212, 703, 1445, 1446; inventory, 213, 1120; inventory, adult, 840; inventory, student, 839; questionnaire, 229, 3349; traits, 3386

Birth, control, 1748: attitudes toward, 1128; paternal reactions, 1958

Black(s), 520, 635: alcoholic men, 1645; children, locus of control, 793; counseling, 2909; cultural mistrust, 2560; English, 1058; English attitude, 2756; ghetto diversity, 1640; history, 157; home environment, 2998; movement, attitude toward, 542; preference toward, 1463; preschool children, 377; school beginners, 566; student attitude, 46; student attitude toward counseling, 999, 3392; students, white colleges, 180; studies, effect of, 88; white student problems, 1980

Blame, acceptance of, 907

Blood donor, salience, 3174

Bloom model, 686

Body: accessibility, tactile, 592; -build, stereotyping, 561; cathexis, 2043, 3175; esteem, 3176; image, 1417; image, peer counseling, 1973; image satisfaction, 2044, 3177; satisfaction, adolescents, 756;

sensations, 2812
Boredom: driving, 3561;
    susceptibility, 2025
Boys: adolescent, personality, 858;
    attitudes, 77; delinquent, 24;
    effeminate, 119, 1219;
    elementary, 389; gender-deviant,
    1218; junior high, 657;
    self-concept, curiosity, 233
Brain damage, 1469
Bulimia symptoms, 2813, 2833
Bureaucracy, 1309
Bureaucratic: personality, 957, 967;
    role, 918
Burnout, 2619, 2628, 2643, 2646:
    college student, 2420; teacher,
    2664
Business: attitudes, 84; education,
    attitude toward, 84; major
    objectives, 661; principles, 661;
    program, graduates, 661; social
    responsibility, 84

Calculators, 2721
Camps, freshmen, 774
Campus, 493: discipline, 682;
    environment, 662, 1311; freedom
    of expression, 586; helpgiver, 993
Capital punishment, 1750
Career: attitudes, 2753; choice,
    influence males on women, 710;
    college alumni, 158;
    commitment, 3611, 3612;
    decisions, 2360; decision-making,
    2206, 3180, 3610, 3613, 3653;
    decisiveness, 2208; development,
    2814; dual, 3043; education, 200;
    exploration, 3630; indecision,
    2207, 2809, 3615, 3655, 3657;
    information-seeking, 3616;
    knowledge, 1040, 2379, 3614;
    medical, 3640; orientation, 1576,
    3617, 3618; patterns, 708; plans,
    175, 202, 3619; preference, 625;
    salience, 3620, 3621, 3638;

women, 1748
Case history, 856
Categorization behavior, 623
Category width, 1271
Cathexis, body, 2043
Causal construct, 2177
Causality, 886: perception, 3181
Censorship, attitude toward, 1125
Certainty, 502
Certification, counselor, 702
Chairman(ship): departmental, 657;
    functions, 657
Challenge: task, 1981
Change(s), 218, 484, 523, 624:
    attitude toward, 92, 1129; dialect,
    105; home economics behavior,
    572; life, 2522; maintenance,
    university residence, 704;
    orientation, 1535; political, 92;
    processes of, 2511; receptivity to,
    301, 976; social, 92; social,
    political and economic, 92;
    teacher, 333; university policy,
    3204; word meaning, 125
Characteristics, college, 171
Cheating, 922
Checklist, symptom, 1663
Child(ren)(s), 377, 380, 402, 403,
    445, 450, 451, 458, 467, 564, 577,
    578, 622, 630, 633, 643, 655:
    abuse, 2815, 2846, 3350;
    academic anxiety, 2404;
    acquiescence-negativism, 843;
    African, 1740; aggression, 946,
    1840, 2277, 2437, 2878, 3453,
    3464, 3498; altruism, 962;
    assertive, 3464, 3465; associative
    response, 264; attitudinal range
    indicator, 497; authoritarian,
    3466; autonomy, 2550, 2806;
    behavior, 28, 496, 1207, 1851,
    1869, 1870, 2811, 2856; beliefs,
    2259; black preschool, 377;
    causal attributions, 3205;
    centered, 1167; centeredness,

SUBJECT INDEX

655; classroom adjustment, 2406; classroom experience, 532; coercive behavior, 2818; cognitive assessment, 2405; cognitive complexity, 2203; cognitive level, 2224, 2678; competence, 2593; comprehension, 355; conceptual style, 603, 1905; conservatism, 1513; counseling, elementary, 25, 28; creative behavior, 1926; creatively gifted, 615; creativity, 2940-2942; curiosity, 723, 733; delay of reinforcement, 239; dependent-independent, 282; depression, 2450, 2465, 2502; development, 138, 625; development, psycho-social, 2945; development, responsibility, 762; disadvantaged, 7, 531, 621; disadvantaged, Mexican-American, 380, 384, 390; disadvantaged, Negro, 376; disadvantaged, preschool, causality, 886; disadvantaged, preschool consequential thinking, 885; disadvantaged, problem-solving, 894; disadvantaged, self-esteem, 830; disobedience, 953; disruptive, 397; disturbed, 38; drug use, 2819; echoic response, 7; egocentricism, 1443, 1485, 1503; ego strength, 3206; eight-year-old, 1771; elementary school, 101, 1043, 1136; elementary school anxiety, 933; emotional disturbance, 1082; entering school, 3; ethnic attitudes, 1184; exploratory behavior, 260; fear, 2490; feelings, family, 41; feelings-judgments, 243; fifth grade, verbal absurdities, 895; first graders, anxiety, 948; first graders, vowel selection, 1045; five to ten years, 382; fourth and fifth grade, school attitudes, 155; fourth-sixth grade, cognitive style, 939; frustration, 2528; future time perspective, 772; handwriting, 2373; gifted, 1124, 3250; guilt, 964; health resources, 2414; home stimulation, 1952; hopelessness, 2482; hospitalization behavior, 1230, 1488; hyperactive, 397, 2827, 2878; impulsive-reflective, 291; innovative behavior, 1926; intellectual ability, 888; intent judgment, 626; interaction aide, 577; intermediate level, science interest, 864; intermediate level, rating subjects, 871; interpersonal attraction, 55; interracial attitude, 1183; introversion-extroversion, 956; investigatory activity, 724; language arts for, 277; learning, 17, 521, 2677; learning disabled, 2853; learning, teachers' perception, 2038; literacy, 3257; locus of control, 754, 797, 799, 2041, 2092, 2101, 2146, 2148, 3182, 3183; loneliness, 2554, 2583, 3241, 3242; management confidence, 2051; manifest anxiety, 1478, 1493, 2524; maturity, 621; mentally retarded, 1759; minority, 502; moral judgment, 977, 2311; moral values, 978; motivation to achieve, 718, 737; normative beliefs, 535; one-year-old, 649; -parent child communication, 640, 646, 654, 3005, 3034; parents, emotionally disturbed, 148; part-whole perception, 19; peer relations, 1104, 2601;

perceptions, 659, 3260;
perception, auditory-visual, 1414;
perception, control, 3252;
perception, environment, 178;
perception, mother behavior, 761; performance attribution, 3268; personality, 842, 927, 1450; phonics, 2398; pictorial attitude, 1770; play behavior, 2861, 2862; play socialization, 61; preference, 1464; prejudice, 1176; preliterate, 1812; preschool, 383, 397, 425, 459, 477, 616-618, 635, 1397; preschool-aged, 2195; preschool anxiety, 2509; preschool cognitive functioning, 59; preschool disadvantaged, 403; preschool disadvantaged, problem solving, 892, 894; preschool frustration, 1229; preschool prejudice, 1174; primary grades, 718; problem behavior traits, 1844, 2799, 2808, 2816, 2831; problem solving, 893, 1468, 3436; prosocial behavior, 963; provocative, 397; psychiatric pathology, 2514; readiness, 1118; rearing, 553, 1304, 2855, 2971, 3042; rearing attitudes, 496, 1148, 3032; rearing problems, 38; reasoning, 3418, 3441; reinforcement, 1853; response styles, 843; retarded, flexibility, 923; reward preference, 261; role taking, 1236; school age, 629; school motivation, 731; security, 3037; self-concept, 230, 807, 3186, 3213, 3221, 3232, 3254, 3279, 3297; self-concept, poverty, 798; self-concept, primary, 763; self-control, 3185; self-enhancement --
self-derogation, 843; self-esteem, 458, 2039, 3197, 3206; self-social construct, 434; self-perception, 3187; sex role, 881, 3188; silent,
397; sixth grade, anxiety, 947; social acceptance, 2593; social behavior, 842, 964; social class, 3189; social competence, 2567, 2606; social desirability, 251, 1708, 2557; social intelligence, 2564; social reinforcement, 725; social responsibility, 58; social situation, 2613; spatial conservation, 1061; stimulus, 1852; stress, 2536, 3184; study conflict, 1466; -teacher, interpersonal perceptions, 2076; teaching rating, 1063; teacher values of disadvantaged, 990; temperament, see, temperament, child and infant; text anxiety, 32, 1076, 1635; twenty-four and thirty-six months, 641; Type A, 3450, 3489; unhappy, 397; verbal absurdities, 895; work values, elementary, secondary, 2317; young, 349, 370, 381

Childhood, 625: early, 623; early education, 658, 678; middle, 412

Choice, 3390: vocational, 1574, 1587, 1594

Chronicity, 421

Church: attitudes, 80, 3062; faith-religion, 1668

Cigarettes, 1122

Clark-Trow subtypes, 714

Class(room): activities, 1380; activities, new, 564; adjustment, 2406; atmosphere, 1027; behavior, 390, 565, 566, 574, 578, 581, 681, 718, 1108, 1209, 1211, 1237, 1854, 1855, 1878, 1885, 2820-2823, 2828, 2865, 2880, 2882, 3056; climate, 583, 3100; environments, 680, 686, 1324, 1539, 3057, 3058, 3078, 3093, 3094; experience, child's, 532; integrated, 2189; interaction, 1261, 1894, 1897; management

SUBJECT INDEX

strategy, 880; methods, junior high school, 700; misconduct, 578; peer performance, 575; planes and procedures, 679; process, 681; quality, 3116; questions, 600; status, 659, 1474; structure, 1969
Classification: job, 3073, 3095; skills, 627, 2946; socioeconomic, 1471
Classifying, 2215
Clerical, 2178: text, 73
Client: assessment, 1080; attitude, counseling, 999; beliefs, 3190; centered counseling, 249; change, 691; expectancy, 3191, 2308, 3210; growth, 646; perception, 227, 309; perception, problem solving, 764; reaction, 589; reaction to interview, 998; satisfaction, 182, 999, 2335, 3059; self-rating, 310; therapist, 2903; verbal behavior system, 587
Climate: bank, 3054; classroom, 3100; counseling, 999; job, 1967; learning, 1323; organization, 1308, 3050, 3097-3099, 3102; school, 3108
Close-mindedness, 413
Closed-mindedness, 2292
Closure, speed, 1612, 1617
Clothing orientation, 875
Coding, 2215
Coffee, 1122
Cognit(ion)(ive), 3, 1255: ability, 2678, 2961; agoraphobic, 2438; affect, 404; assessment, children, 2405; behavioral changes, 572; behavior, infant, 1287; behavior, student, 568; complexity, 47, 1279, 1465, 1913, 2229, 3408, 3421; complexity, children, 2203; complexity, interpersonal, 433; complexity, simplicity, 433; complexity, vocational, 707; components, 1209; control, 913, 924, 1506, 2289; development, 623, 627, 635; differentiation, 2230; difficulty, 1670; egocentricism, 1491; error, 3192; flexibility, 923; functioning, 260, 1121, 2213; functioning, adolescents, 605; functioning, preschool, 59; home environment, 642; impairment, 2681; learning, 175; level, children, 2224; need, 3367; preference, 2179, 3391, 3410; process, 265, 3193, 3423; processing, children, 1905; structure, 218; style, 1479, 1498, 3369; style, field dependence, 815; style, flexibility, 939; style, fourth-sixth graders, 939; tempo, 603, 942; vocational maturity, 1040, 1938
Cohabitation, off campus, 181
Cohesion: gross, 1710; group, 1710, 1711, 2569
Colleagues, evaluation, 1009
Collective: bargaining, 1773; negotiations, 538
College: achievement, 480; activities, 683; adjustment, 2401; admissions assistance, 660; application, 553; aptitude, 1120; assertiveness, 3467-3469; attendance, goals and purposes, 719; business major curriculum objectives, 661; campus dissent, 1098; characteristics, 117, 180; classes, teacher effect, 333; commitment, 206; courses, attitude toward, 151; course evaluation, 1024, 1540, 3064; departments, 3067; environment, 165, 172, 177, 179, 184, 187, 212, 672, 675, 683, 1311; expectations,

662; experience, 675; freshmen, 353, 364, 441, 632, 662; freshmen, academic status, 904; freshmen adjustment, 2420; freshmen, attitudes, 1135; freshmen, characteristics, 67; freshmen, locus of control, 221; freshmen, need achievement, 726; freshmen, socioeconomic status, 904; freshmen, university experience, 904; freshmen, values, 303, 904; freshmen year, 628; head residents, behavior, 1863; importance, 3398; instructor effectiveness, 2338; major prestige, 896; major satisfaction, 872, 876; mathematics anxiety, 2418; men, personal preference, 258; opinions, 231; orientation, 879; performance expectations, 740; routine, 409; satisfaction, 212; student(s), 399, 481, 527, 609, 624, 667, 698; student academic integration, 2399; student adjustment, 22; student alienation, 1091, 1092, 1110; student, anxious, 286, 2604, 2605; student, attitude, 743, 1151, 1152; student, attitude, CAI, 151; student attitude change, 92; student attitude patterns, 222; student behavior, 2881; student, Black, 2909; student burnout, 2420; student career indecision, 2809; students' career planning, 2228, 3653; students failing and superior, 16; students fear of success, 2412, 2471; students' goal and expectations 719, 3049; students' housing needs, 867; students' interpersonal adjustment, 2409; students, Jewish, 503, student's leadership, 2682; students, level of aspiration, 740; students, life changes, 1942; students, life events, 2551; students, locus of control, 3194, 3234; student marijuana, 1131; student motivation, 743; student occupational choice, 719; student optimism, 2408; student peer-rating, 2556; student perceptions, 706; student performance, 1856; student personality, 16; student premarriage counseling, 147; students, reading comprehension, 1615; student relationships, 2588; student response acquiescence, 930; student satisfaction, 663, 1961, 2407; students' self-concept, 2035, 3300, 3305, 3321; student self-esteem, 816, 2139; student, self-interest, male, 199; student, self-regulation, 145; student, situational anxiety, 26; student, social integration, 2399; student stress, 2415, 2423, 2424; student success, 1072, 1073; student, suicide, 1088, 2530; students, text anxiety, 1634, 2302, 2303; students' thoughts, 2403; student time perspective, 782, 783, 790, 805, 834; student transfer, 511; students, unassertive, 286; teacher effectiveness, 1541, 1542, 1551, 1562-1565, 1569, 1570, 1572; teacher perceptions, 785; two year, 171; two year, four year and ideal, 548; and university, 682; women, 1303; women, equalitarianism, 1177; women, inner-outer directedness, 789

Collegial maintenance of standards, 1815
Colonialism, 512
Color meaning, 1774

Combat: behavior, 2825; stress, 2454
Comfort, counselor, 999
Commitment, 214: career, 3611, 3612; college, 206; cultural, 1092; employment, 3626; organizational, 2014-2016, 3541, 3609, 3624, 3625, 3643-3648; vocational, 3656
Communalism, 982
Communication(s), 98-105, 523, 568, 585-601, 1060, 1247-1268, 1887-1902: apprehension, 2917; competence, 2922, 2924; defensive, 1250; dyads, 2905; effectiveness, 99; expectations, 601; facilitative, 1889, 1890; feedback, 2908; index, 76; interpersonal, 1900, 2914, 2920; interviewer, 2906; marital, 2972, 3017; mutual, 98; negotiation, 2918; organization(al), 1898, 1901, 2919; parent-child, 103, 640, 1295, 1297, 2897; patterns, 597; principal teacher, 688; referential, 2923; respect, 2344; satisfaction, 2904; skills, 175, 2913; suggestion, 2902; supervisors, 1023, 2915, 2916, 2926; teacher-student, 2911; verbal-nonverbal, 2921
Community college: aptitude, 75; articulation, 3163; counselor training, 664; faculty attitudes, 1159; freshmen, 472; public, 508; sex role, 3389
Community: employee commitment, 1996; judgment, 1312; participation, 1454; satisfaction, 3060
Companion, imaginary, 1397
Comparing, 2215
Compensation, 663
Competenc(e)(y), 659, 3317: academic, 2421; behavior, 432; children, 2593, 3260; communicative, 2922, 2924; counselor, 3571; educational, 767; female professional, 975, 3243; general social, 636; interpersonal, 446, 1724; language, 380, 384; leader, 1555; managerial, 3586; personal, 1105; premorbid, 2594; presenter, 3591; sense of, 2070; social, 2567; students', 2349; teaching, 1015, 1025
Competit(ion)(ive), 713, 1775, 1802, 2826, 3412: knowledge, 2928
Competitive(ness), 1720: achievement, 989
Complexity, 614: cognitive, 1279, 3408; conceptual, 120, 1421, 1499, 1509; interpersonal, 47; perceptions, 768; sentence, 7; tolerance, 612; work, 268; vocational, 336
Compliance, supervisors, 1005
Composition: ability, 370; evaluation, 1031; written, 370
Comprehension, 5, 15, 349, 355, 1735: age four, 134; anaphora, 5, 2370; counselors, 380, 384; humor, 2378; inferential reading, 1605; languages, 355; listening, 2688; literal reading, 1609; moral, 3556; oral, 365; reading, 14, 20, 1055, 1062, 2688; reading, college students, 1615; sentence, 5; social-moral(s) concepts, 1599, 2308; syntactic, 383; verbal, 1904, 1912, 1915; vocabulary, 365
Compulsiveness, 3493, 3497
Computer, attitude toward, 115, 152, 2724, 2726-2729
Computer science, 2679
Concentration, 645
Concept(s): anthropological, 1269;

attainment, 2924; educational research, 1746; formation, 120, 2213; identification, 884, 2928; justice, 381; masculine-feminine, 114; meaning, 106-125, 602-605, 1269-1279, 1903-1919, 2930; number, 2939; occupational, 1909; people, 502; relationships, 2936; social work, 1277; task, multiple category, 358-363; unpleasant, 35

Conceptual: complexity, 120, 1499, 1509, 2934; development, 135; differentiation, 1273; flexibility, 923; set, 1068; structure, 122, 604; style, 603, 1272, 1906; style, children, 1905; tempo, 604, 1919, 2211

Concrete(ness): abstractness, 2200; experience, 2216; reasoning abilities, 2227

Conditions, job, 1404

Conduct, classroom, 578

Confidence: child management, 2051; information processing, 2907; lack of, 515

Configurations, part-whole, 13

Conflict(s), 796: child study, 1466; ethical, 3530; family, 3003; group, 445; handling, 1865; home-career, 2228; identify, 949; interpersonal, 523, 1950, 2573; locus of, 2085; marital, 2973; model, 616; mode of handling, 1848; non-, 481; personal, 2208; positive choice, 2208; resolution, 1857; role, 1687, 2357, 2526, 2641, 3002, 3289, 3290, 3292, 3341

Conformity, 287, 967, 2290: types, 1731

Congregation, satisfaction, 3062

Congruence, 220, 227, 309, 431, 1538, 2353: cognitive, 34; teacher-student, 175

Conscience development, 638
Consensus, semantic, 1276
Consequences of situations, 266
Consequential thinking, 885
Conservationism, 1776
Conservat(ism)(ive), 555, 1518, 1777, 2257, 2258, 2305, 2731, 2732: children, 1513; dimension, mother's, 2313; -liberalism, 95, 280, 1527; -liberalism, college students, 1835; -radicalism, 1821
Consideration, 688
Constrict(ed)(ion), 408: flexibility, 924; impulsivity, counselors, 961
Constructs: personal, 1305; role, 816
Consultant, reading, 1334
Consultation, 730, 2191
Consumer, alienation, 1700
Consumption/production, 302
Contemporary issues, 485, 498
Content, 596, 689
Continuity, residence, 466
Control(s), 655, 2317: cognitive, 913, 924, 1506; environment, 1997; homicide, 970; imagery, 2052; internal, 238; internal-external, 467, 810; interpersonal, 2075; locus of, See locus of control; maternal, 1954; motor impulse, 386; organization, 1962; parental, 145; perception, 239; personal, 1415; problems, behavior, 403; pupil, 810, 1523, 3105; social, 52, 163; social, in school, 100
Controlling-punitive, 652
Controvers(ial)(y): attitude, 2733; lectures, campus, 586
Conventionalism, 2253, 2734
Cooperation, 338, 397, 1775, 1802, 3412: attitude toward, 1371; student, 24
Coordination, 575: general dynamic, 348; general static, 348

SUBJECT INDEX

Coping: adequacy, 215; behavior, 2830; classroom, 1211; environment, 1095; family, 2984 mechanisms, 3355; strategies, 1085, 2974
Correctional center, 1202
Cosmopolitanism orientation, 2306
Counselee behavior, 427
Counseling, 699: appropriateness, 409, 1336; attitude toward, 2698, 2708, 2788; attitudes of blacks, 999; center, 409, 703, 1313; client attitude, 999; client beliefs, 3190; client expectations, 3191, 3208-3210; client reaction, 311; climate, 999, 2335; disadvantaged youth, 27; effects of, 689; elementary children, 25, 28; elementary school, 70, 671; evaluation, 1000, 3063; expectations, 2058, 3198; follow up, 1010; goals, 1358; individual, 43; influence, 258; information, 2374; interview, student rating, 699; inventory 689; marriage, 146, 240, 1349; micro, 10, 85; need for, 1689; outcome, 34, 500; practicum evaluation, 1003; preference, 3409; pre-marital, 147; rating of, 311; rehabilitation, 692, 1057; relationship(s), 1003, 1268, 2335; relationship, perceptions of, 2037; residence vs. nonresidence, 546; satisfaction, 3564; self-evaluation, 328; sensitivity-repression, 921; skills, 1543, 2343, 3578; student-student, 1000; underachievers, 1069; vocational, 670
Counselor(s), 427, 484, 702, 2909: activity, 584; appraisal position, 665; attitudes, 89, 309, 560, 1173; attractiveness, 2336, 2341, 2342;

behavior, 1543, 3325, 3565; certification, teaching requirement, 702; client, 2899-2901; client perception, 1372; comfort, 999, 2335; competence, 3571; construction-impulsivity, 961; contracts, 665; education, 255; education, graduate, 1004; effectiveness, 307, 312, 316, 325, 1001, 1002, 1057, 1559, 2335, 3566, 3567, 3569; empathy, 309, 3505, 3506; ethical discrimination, 969; evaluation, 999, 1021; evaluation, residence hall, 1006, 1019; experience, 1004; expertness, 2336, 2341, 2342; facilitative conditions, 2344; function, 232; high school, 612, 660; impulsivity-constriction, 961; interpersonal relations, 1003; interest and effort, 1003; interview behavior, 584; nonverbal behavior, 2351; orientation, 2340; paraprofessional residence hall, 2354; perception of counseling, 3200; perception of residence, 1020; performance, 2339, 3599; personal characteristics, 1004; philosophy, 968; preference, 1544, 3392; professional responsibilities, 314, 1003; qualification, 687; rating, 317, 3572, 3573, 3595; rehabilitation effectiveness, 1561; reinforcement, 1545; restrictive-nonrestrictive, 2163; role, 332, 820, 3195, 3199; role concepts, 313; selection, 1004; self-concept, 822, 1426; self-rating, 769; service, 820; stress, 2620; student, 1021; tasks, 837; theory preference, 54;

trainee, 596, 1250, 1317; trainee's effectiveness, 2337; training, 3568, 3570; training, community college, 664; trustworthiness, 2336, 2341, 2342; undergraduate residence, 2355; verbal behaviors, 2351; verbal response, 588; viewed by students, 993
Counting, 345
Couples, married, 648
Courage, social and existential, 1832
Course(s), 527, 667: academic and vocational, 75; attitude, 2735; evaluation, 168, 666-668, 698, 1546, 1547, 3064; expectation, 3158; nursing, 3639, 3641; rating, college, 1024; satisfaction, 175; structure, 667
Courtship, 2597
Co-worker esteem, 1458
Creative(ly): activity, 1921, 2940; attitudes, 130; behavior, 531; behavior, child's, 1926; behavior, disadvantaged, 1922; behavior, underlying elements, 2168; gifted adolescents, 1935; gifted adults, 615, 1935; gifted children, 615; ideas, physics, 1930; inquisitiveness, 578; motivation, 607; person, 1929; personality, 620; potential, engineers, 1933; potential, scientists, 1933; predisposition, 1928; productions, 130, 613; remote associates, 2941; students, 2942; thinking, 1924; thinking, strategies, 615
Creativity, 126-133, 281, 296, 606-620, 688, 861, 1280-1283, 1885, 1920-1935: differences, 132; disadvantaged, 1283; elementary children, 1927, 1932; encouragement, 487; ideational, 619; identification, 133, 1280; leadership, 1925; open

elementary classroom, 1963; student, 36, 303; traits, 3386; women, 840
Credibility, 1888: supervisor, 1556
Criminal psychopathy, 2518
Crises, 628
Critical: evaluation, 369; differences, 981; interview behavior, 1864
Cross-cultural attitude, 1153
Cue interpretations, 1340
Cultural: estrangement, 1700, 1701; mistrust, 2560; values, 516
Culturally disadvantaged: children, 531; intelligence, 72
Culture fair intelligence, 468
Curiosity, 233, 260, 716, 730, 742, 1208, 1778, 3152: academic, 1984; boys, 63; children, 723, 733; -related behavior, 1818; self-appraisal, 2021
Current issues, 498
Curriculum, 502, 527: attitude, 501; choice, motivation, 720; classification by college men, 184; content, 664; development, 1314; evaluation of social welfare, 162; high school, 473; objectives, 694; people, 502; perceptions, 694; priorities, black history, 157; ratings of, 706; use, 501
Customer service, 3066
Cynicism, 1103, 2253: freedom from, 481; police, 943; political, 537
Czechoslovakia: social stratification, 268

Daily activity, 567, 3075
Data, collecting, 2215
Dating, 503, 593, 2603: behavior, 253; marriage, 503; motivation, 3128
Daydreams: assessment, 3354;

SUBJECT INDEX

attitude, 2737; inventory, 858
Deactivation, 417: -activation, 1839
Dean(s) attitudes, and admissions practice, 553
Death: acceptance, 2458; anxiety, 410, 1649-1651, 2447, 2459, 2541; attitude, 1779; concern, 411, 1652, 2460; confrontation, 2444; fear, 1081, 2453, 2467-2469, 2497; threat, 1691
Debating, 1765
Debilitating anxiety, 1625, 1626, 1633
Decision(s): confidence, 2223; difficulty, 2180; executive, 2346; flexibility, 2223
Decision-making, 2270: career, 3180, 3610, 3613; dilemma, 1939; economic, 2396; faculty, 3262; group, 2912; policy, 2910; strategies, 2223; styles, 2205, 3425; teacher, 835, 3434; values, 2314; vocational, 1579, 3632
Decisiveness, 2265: peer counseling, 1973
Decoding, visual-social cues, 1619
Deduct(ion)(ive), 887, 3426: logic, 2202
Defense: mechanism, 850, 1653, 3355; policy, attitude toward, 1197
Defensive(ness), 255, 299, 421, 845, 1725: communication, 1250
Deference, 1720
Deficiency: goal, 1994; need, 1355
Definitions: confidence in, 125; work, 354
Delay, 403
Delinquency, 378, 656, 1213, 1221, 1244, 1245, 2832, 2874
Delinquent: boys, 24; girls, 463; girls, parents of, 656; juvenile, 519; personality, 853, 855, 857
Delivery, 596

Democratic values, unmet, 2055
Demographic data, 2173
Demonstrators, anti-war, 552
Denial, 3510
Dental Health, attitudes, 2725
Dependability: people, 2288; supervisors, 1023
Dependen(ce)(cy)(t), 281, 830, 927, 1500, 1720, 2205, 2206: emotional, 931; -independence, 400; interpersonal, 2574; job, 1034; marital, 3029, 3046; persistence, 216; political, 512; social, 434; work, 1034
Depress(ion)(ive), 417, 420, 841, 1088, 1089, 1638, 1644, 1645, 1654, 1664, 1670, 1681, 2442, 2445, 2446, 2449, 2461, 2463, 2464, 2479, 2498, 2534, 2546: anxiety, 773, 1663; anxiety-irritation, 1686, 2621; children, 2450, 2465, 2502, 2503; geriatric, 2475, 2520; patients, 420; proneness, 2462; self-assessment, 1692; sense of, 1962; symptomatology, 1644
Deprivation: foreign student, 1094; social, 466
Description: job, 1321; managers, 1447
Descriptive rating scales, 215
Desegregat(ed)(ion): attitudes, 1160; schools, 452
Desirability, social, 49, 62, 251, 281, 296, 2557, 2585
Desire to work: paid employment, 3130; woman, 1995
Despair, sense of, 1684
Destructiveness, 2253
Detachment, 989, 1720
Determiners, specific, 385
Determinism, 2571, 3532
Development(al), 134-140, 621-639, 1284-1292, 1936-1944: adult,

2943, 2944; child, 137, 625;
classification, 2946; cognitive,
623, 627, 635, 2961; conceptual,
135; conscience, 638; curriculum,
1314; ego, 136, 629, 1944, 2948,
2959; ego identity, 628, 2949,
2950; ego stages, 245, 2951;
emotional, 637, 2952; Eriksonian
stages, 632; infant, 625, 631,
1050; intellectual, 637, 1515,
2953, 2954, 2958; kindergarten
children, 1289; mental, 2956;
moral, 139, 638, 2957; motor,
634, 637; newborn, 1284;
numbers, 2939; perceptual
motor, 477; physical, 637;
Piagetian, 2960; psychosocial,
632, 1941, 2945, 2947, 2955;
pupil, 637; responsibility in
children, 762; sex role, 137;
social, 637; staff, 3112, 3113;
status, 481; strategy, 880; verbal
ability, 1300; vocational, 1291
Deviance, 1803
Deviant: behavior, 573; role, 3202
Devotionalism, 982
Dexterity, mental, 1738, 2689
Diagnosis, 421
Dialect: black, non-standard, 1046;
change, 105; training, 105
Differences, creativity, 132
Differentiation: conceptual, 1273;
psychological, 1417
Diffusion, identity, 628
Directedness: college women, 789;
inner-outer, 789
Directions and commands,
comprehension, 380, 384
Directiveness, 583, 3470, 3471:
primary teachers, 936
Direct object: punishment, 654;
reward, 654
Disab(ility)(led), 515, 1780:
acceptance, 1636; attitude
toward, 2693, 2717; persons,
1751, 1780; self attitude, 752;
student facilities, 1315
Disadvantaged, 432, 1452, 1510:
American Indian youth, 375;
children, 7, 531, 612; children,
adjustment, 27; children, creative
behavior, 1922; children, delay of
reinforcement, 239; children,
problem solving, 892, 894;
children, self-esteem, 830;
children, social responsibility, 58;
children, teacher values, 990;
creativity, 1283; job-conditions,
1318; job placement, 1445; job
satisfaction, 1577;
Mexican-American children, 380,
384, 390; Negro, 342, 350, 376;
preschool children, 7, 403;
preschool children, causality,
886; preschool children,
consequential thinking, 885;
school beginners, 434; skills,
arithmetic/reading, 1038;
students, 679; students,
aspiration level, 740; tolerance,
1508; work attitudes, 1199, 1531;
work requirements, 1246; youth,
group counseling, 53
Disapproval, 659
Discipline, 625, 1748: campus, 682;
formal, 880; inconsistent, 655;
methods for residents, 546;
program, 682; self, 589-591, 593,
598, 599
Discomfort, 1725
Discontentment, political, 1976
Discrimination, 76, 1041: ability,
1249; attitude toward, 542;
complexity, 1908; letter, 1051;
oral, 1421; right-left, 814, 1943;
self, 1431; sex, 3085; visual, 356,
357, 1412, 1442; word, 356, 357,
602
Discussion, 1295, 1297
Disengagement, 688

SUBJECT INDEX

Disobedience; children, 953
Disorganization, proneness, 2513
Disorientation, 1079
Dissent(ion), 484, 625
Dissertations, reading, 20
Distance, 2224: comfortable, 436; interpersonal, 436, 451, 2596; proxemic, 68; psychological, 50, 56; social 63
Distraction, overlapping, 385
Distress, 2466, 2539: psychological, 35, 2493
Distributive justice, 234
Distrust, 1103: political feelings, 1975; Upward Bound Student, 45
Disturbed children, parents of, 148
Diver training, 1288
Divergent: production(s), 110, 111, 129, 1920; thinking, 608
Dogmatic thinking, 953
Dogmatism, 95, 227, 294, 926, 1483, 2258, 2260, 2261, 2287, 2294; client, 309; counseling client, 309
Dominance, 1720, 3472: father, 647, 673; mother, 647, 673; parental, 229, 1301; -submissiveness, 2291
Draft, 1748
Draw a: car, 846; dog, 1117
Dream(s) 2709: analyzing, 1655; associations, 30; incident, 1655
Drinking, 1748
Driving, boredom, 3561
Dropout(s), 401, 645, 651, 653: potential, 391; prediction, school, 476; self-esteem, 827
Drug(s), 343: abuse, 344, 505, 1042, 1220; attitude, 1145, 1155, 1191, 1781; behavior, 569; hyperactivity, 1203; illegal use of, 1785; issues, 506; knowledge, 343, 344, 1042, 1600; knowledge, use, attitudes, 1858; reasons for use, 569; sources of, 569; use, 485, 507, 569, 1130, 1204, 1210, 1214, 1215, 1228, 1698, 2223, 2819; use, adolescent, 562; use, alcohol, 563
Dualism, 3527, 3546
Dyad(ic): affective behavior, 2810; communication, 2905, 2911; counselor-client, 227; feelings in, 237; marital, 2962, 2978; members perceptions, 102; parent-child, 2979; trust, 2562
Dying, fear of, 406, 1650, 1651, 2444, 2447, 2453, 2467-2469, 2497
Dynamics, 1885
Dysphoric feeling, 416

East-West, 1782
Eating habits, restraint, 1876
Echoic response, preschool children, 7
Economic: change, 92; decision-making, 2396; ideology, 3533
Education(al), 268: adjustment, 22; administrator, 528; aspirations, college student, 719; attitude toward, 529, 549, 1167, 2738, 2739; competence, 767; drug, 1130; early childhood, 71, 678; flexibility, 131; forces, teacher, 2057; goals, 511, 3068; graduates, 685; graduate counselor, 1004; guidance effort, 687; handicapped, 583; innovation, receptivity toward, 1784; opinions, 529; orientation, 3393; preference, 200; psychology, 684; quality, 663; research, 1752, 2710; set, 1068, 1350; vocational, 305-339
Effectiveness: advisor, 2329; college course, 2338; college instructor, 2338; college teacher(s), 1541, 1542, 2334; college students' perception of instructors, 2358;

communication, 99, 148;
counselor, 307, 312, 316, 325,
  1001, 1002, 1559, 2335, 3566,
  3567, 3569; counselor trainee's,
  2337; elementary guidance, 316;
  instructor, 329; judgment by
  child, 243; organizational
  practices, 1972; peer counseling,
  1973; perceptual, 214; personal,
  214; practice teaching, 690;
  psychological, 1449; speakers,
  1765; teacher, 335, 1026, 1030,
  3607; teaching, 2333, 2347
Efficacy, 976, 3204, 3331
Effort, 575
Ego: -centrism, 579, 1109, 1480,
  1484, 1485; closeness-distance,
  913; cognitive, 1491;
  development, 135, 136, 629, 1944,
  2948, 2959; functioning, 1417;
  identity, 949, 2241, 2949, 2950;
  identity development, 628, 2951;
  identity status, 628; involvement,
  3359; organization, 749;
  permissiveness, 3360; role-taking,
  1503; strength, 2164, 3206;
  sufficiency, 1929
Egotism, 417
Elaboration, 861
Elderly: attitudes toward, 2697,
  2755; care, 2990; mental
  competence, 2385; morale, 2506;
  stress, 2531
Elementary: anaphora
  comprehension, 2370; children,
  attitudes, 1136; children, client
  centered approach, 249; children,
  creativity, 1927, 1932; children,
  interracial attitudes, 1168;
  children, teacher-pupil relations,
  256; first grade adjustment, 2413;
  grades, 3-6, 696; grades,
  anthropology, 1044; guidance, 31;
  reading, 1455, 1460; school, 388,
  389, 540, 595, 622, 688, 701, 1723,
  1756, 1770; school, academic
  self-concept, 2147; school boys,
  389; school child anxiety, 933;
  school children, 21, 101, 456,
  491, 626, 1043; school climate,
  1323; school counseling, 70, 315,
  316, 671; school, English second
  language, 1598; school
  environment, 1316; school, inner
  city, 990; school openness, 1963;
  school perceptual abilities, 2098;
  school principals, 1680; school
  reading attitude, 1822; students
  academically talented, 1606;
  student teachers, 495, 701;
  teachers, 341, 488; teacher
  evaluation, 1036; visual
  discrimination, 2394
Embed(ded)(ness), 1417: figures,
  770, 1386
Emotion(al)(s), 404, 593: arousal,
  1231; control, peer counseling,
  1973; dependence, 931, 1638;
  development, 637; distance, 1103;
  factors, 138; maturity, 621, 2952;
  reliance, 1715; self assessment,
  2165; social climate, 583; -social
  state, 578; state, immediate, 416;
  support, university residence,
  704; types, 3361; withdrawal, 405
Emotionality, 403, 944, 1641
Emotive imaging, 2063
Empath(ic)(y), 220, 227, 235, 328,
  429, 757, 771, 1100, 1385, 1387,
  1438, 2243, 2268, 3476, 3490:
  children, 3473, 3477, 3483;
  counselors, 309, 3475, 3505, 3506;
  police, 781; teachers, 3474;
  understanding, 431, 1370, 1538,
  2344, 2353
Emphasis, 688
Empiricism, 301, 976
Employability, 310, 320: attitude(s),
  188, 193, 1007, 1156, 2622;
  behavior, 2851; commitment,

1996; evaluation, 1007, 1016, 3574, 3575; motivation, 205; perceptions, 3326; rating, 327, 692; satisfaction, 164; self-evaluation, 1008; work relations, 1116; work values, 1532
Employee: appearance, 1007; aptitude, 1007
Employment: commitment, 3626; desire for, 3130; immobility, 3627; success, 241
Encoding, associative verbal, 1035
Encopresis, 846
Encounter groups, psychological state, 841
Encouragement, parental, 713
Engaged couples, 597
Engineer(ing)(s): career interests, 3629; correlates with success, 212; creative potential, 1933; motivation, 1366; performance, 1557; self perception, 829; students, 42, 95
English: black non-standard, 1046; invitation/comprehension, 1046; pressures for, 647, 673; proficiency, 1732; sound-symbol relations, 366
Enhancement, self, 1994
Enthusiasm, 679: toward learning, 540; toward school, 540
Enuresis, 846
Environment(al): assessment, 672; campus, 662; classroom, 1324, 1539, 3057, 3058, 3078, 3093, 3094; college, 165, 172, 184, 187, 212; community, 1060; control, 1997; coping, 1095; effects upon, 3069; forces, 673; geographic, 3070; issues, attitudes, 1152; learning, 473, 673, 686, 3076, 3109, 3114; living, 3087; medical school stress, 2419; orientation, 302; perception, 179; preserving the natural, 1776; press of, 704; psychosocial, 1960; satisfaction, 1965; school, 1316; stress, 3071; treatment, 1310; uncertainty, 3072; university, 1440
Envy, interpersonal, 439
Equalitarianism, 537, 1123, 1177
Equality, 301: ethnic, 976
Erikson(ian): ego epigenesis, 628; stages of development, 245, 632; theory, 628, 629, 949
Eroticism, 1157
Esprit, 688
Esteem: co-worker, 1458; father, 788; self, see Self-Esteem; self, adult male, 826; self, children, 458; self, college student, 816; self, high school students, 827; self, pre-adolescent, 825; self, student, 792
Estrangement: cultural, 1700, 1701; political, 1977; self, 430, 457
Ethic(al)(s), 1815, 3529: behavior, violations, 971; conflict, 3530; discrimination, counselors, 969; norms, business, 84; Protestant, 3528, 3550, 3551, 3663; reasoning, 3531
Ethlanguage, pressure for, 647, 675
Ethnic, 301: differences in development of responsibility, 762; equality, 976
Ethnocentrism, 1144
Etiology, interpersonal, 530
Evaluat(e)(ing)(ion)(ive), 481, 600, 689, 694, 2215: academic, assistants, 992; colleagues, 1009; composition, 1031; course, 168, 666-668, 698, 1545; courses, college, 1024, 1540, 1547; counseling, 311, 1000, 3063; counselor, 999, 3599; critical, 369; educational-vocational counseling, 311; elementary

guidance, 316; elementary teacher, 1036; employee, 1016, 3574, 3575; faculty, 1548, 3576; guidance, 687; inservice, 1319; interview for teaching, 1015; job, 1016, 1027, 3061; lesson, 1027; middle school, 1326; nurses, 3597; practice teaching, 690; psychotherapy, 1080; residence counselor, 1006; staff, 3112, 3113; stress, 1627; student counselors, 1021; student teachers, 3590, 3602; supervisor(s), 1007, 1017, 1023, 2332; teachers, 698, 997, 1009, 1014, 1022, 1027-1029, 1032, 1550, 1551, 3581, 3589, 3600, 3601; teaching method, 698, 3563

Evangelism, 2711
Events, 3101: life, 3111
Examination(s), 666: attitude toward, 248; reaction toward, 16
Excel, desire to, 713
Exchange, leader-member, 1896
Exertion, physical and mental, 709
Exhaustion, 2540
Exhibition, 1720
Existential(ism), 2296: anxiety, 1657; confrontation, 2443; social courage, 1832
Expectation(s): athletic success, 3215; college, 662, 740, 3049; communication of, 601; course, 3158; counsel(ing)(or), 1382, 2058, 3191, 3198, 3208-3210; parental, 1302; pay, 3258; reinforcement, 44, 69; survey, 719; task success, 3207; therapist, 3336; work, 3122
Experience(s), 694: college, 675; counselor, 1004; recent, 1290; religious, 1514; time, 1400, 1420
Explanation, 666
Exploratory behavior, 260
Expressing feelings, 1753

Expression(s), 1725: affective, 121, 279; feelings, 500; openness to, 481, 500; stimulus, 38
Expressive: dimensions, 594; style, 594
External: cognition, 2187; -internal locus of control, 2049; sensation 2187
Extracurricular activities, 675
Extraneous clues, 385
Extrasensory perception: attitude toward, 1139
Extroversion, 841: introversion, 390, 749; children, 956; students', 2349
Eye: contact, 1257; -hand coordination, 2143

Face saving, 1352
Facilitat(ing)(ive): anxiety, 1625; behavior, 432; communication, 1889, 1890
Facilities: disabled student, 1315; materials, junior high, 700
Factors, emotional, 138
Factually set, 1068
Faculty, 586, 595, 662: attitudes, 1159; behavior, 2894; college classification by, 184; decision-making, 3262; evaluation, 698, 999, 1009, 1014, 1022, 1027-1029, 1032, 1548, 3576; needs, 1356; orientations, 1788; policy making, 174; roles, 509; -student perceptions, academic advising, 1959; -student relations, roles, 675, 695; teaching, 2331; union membership, 3399
Failure: avoidance, 1833; awareness, 3170; fear of; 19, 204, 392, 1342; motivation to avoid, 209; risk, 713; success, 526, 1373; threat, 713
Fairness of system, 487

SUBJECT INDEX

Family, 141-149, 593, 640-656, 1161, 1293-1306, 1945-1958, 3047: adjustment, 2991, 2992; authoritarianism, 641, 644; background, 625; communication, 2905; conflict, 3003; coping, 2984; dual career, 3043; elderly, 2990; harmony, 466; independence, 976, 2999; interaction, 597, 2986; learning environment, 2985; maltreatment, 2989; orientation, 2302; parental, 593; relations, 141, 142, 645, 1296, 2982, 2983; relationships, 1951; relations, peer counseling, 1973; richness, 466; role, 302; social support, 2988; ties, 302; well-being, 2987

Fantasy, 40, 1243, 2886: projections, 579; sexual, 2876

Fat, fear of, 2477

Fatalism, 985

Father(s): acceptance, 645; attitudes, 645; dominance, 647, 673; esteem, 788; identification with, 434, 830; relationship with, 653

Fatigue, 841, 1670

Fear, 253: children, 2490; dying, 406, 1081, 1650, 1651, 2453, 2467-2469, 2497; failure, 19, 204, 392, 1342; fat, 2477; psychotherapy, 2451; rating of, 414; success, 1658-1660, 1667, 2410-2412, 2470, 2471, 2478, 2500, 2545; survey, 1966

Feedback, 2908: amount of, 487; analysis, 1259; interpersonal, 1899; job, 3083; teacher, 333, 1885

Feelings, 593: dysphoric, 416; expressing, 1753; expression of, 500, 773; inadequacy, 773; inferiority, 515; openness, 293; perception, 102; personal, 804; positive-negative, 555; sensitivity to, 500; toward school, 1825; toward whites, 2157

Fees, attitudes, 2787

Felt figure replacement, 440

Female(s): career choice, 710; need achievement, 728; professional competence, 975, 3243; professors, 1754; social roles, 1755

Femin(ine)(inity)(ism)(ist), 1789, 1790: -antifeminist, 1791; attitudes, 1834; ideology, 3557; liberal attitudes, 1767; -masculinity, 795, 927; orientation, 1768; rating scale, 284

Field dependence, 770, 776, 815, 3231: practice, 1317

Figure: analogies, 2059; copying, 1734; drawing, 888; human, 32

Film test, 765

Financial comfort, 215

Firearm registration, attitude toward, 1125

Fireman: job perception, 1012; leadership, 1549

First grade(rs), 371, 374: achievement, 469, 474; anxiety, 948; auditory perception, 750; home environment, 1946; racial attitude, 1813; readiness, 1118; readiness for, 1735; reading achievement, 602

Five-year-olds, 1744

Flexibility, 15, 481, 893: conceptual, 923; cognitive, 923, 939; constricted, 924; educational, 131; interpersonal, 217; perceptual, 923; rigidity, 1486; speed, 15; spontaneous, 923

Fluency: anagram, 1903; ideational, 1911

Focus(ing), 596, 1859
Follow-up, student counseling, 1010
Food preference, 3396, 3417
Foreclosure, 628
Foreign: language aptitude, 1733; language attitude, 2744; policy, 510
Foreigners, attitude toward, 2798
Foreman, perception of job, 1012; production, 1013; responsibilities, 1011
Formal reasoning abilities, 2227
Formalistic, 2186
Form discrimination, 2143
Fourth, fifth and sixth grade, 1647
Fraternit(ies)(y): activities, 486; social, 300, 486
Free: speech commitment, 973; time, 570
Freedom, expression, campus, 586; from cynicism, 481; students, 586
Freshmen: camp experience, 774; year, college, 628
Friend(lines)(s)(ship), 447, 1097, 2565: identification with, 434, 830; negro-white, 452
Frustration(s), 796, 1216, 2472: delay, 1212; job, 2623; reactions to, 1675, 2528; response, 1229
Functional literacy: high school, 1611; reading skills, 1602
Functioning, facilitative, 1716
Future: goal success expectancy, 220; orientation, 207, 301, 976; time perspective, 50, 56

Games, 1218
Gender, 1219: behavior, 1285; identity, 630, 3403; role attitude, 2746; role, middle childhood, 243
General ability, perceptions, 2147
General anxiety, 1638
General information, 1738
Generations, relations, 76
Genuineness, 328, 1438: facilitative, 2344
Geograph(ic)(y), 347, 3070: Japan, 351
Geometry, 4, 474: aptitude, 74
Geriatric: depression, 2475, 2520; hopelessness, 2476; outpatients, 2566
Gestalt completion, 1617
Gifted: adults, creative, 615; children, 1124, 1387; children, creative, 615, 1283, 2940, 2942; children, self-concept, 3250; children, teacher attitude, 558; teacher, 1049
Girls: adolescent, 2866; delinquent, 463; delinquent, parents of, 656; social competence, 2595
Goal(s): attainment of, 714; college, 719; deficiency, 1994; educational, 511, 3068; job, 709; marital, 3021; Neotic, 821; orientation, 400; personal, 829; pre-counseling, 1358; success, future expectancy, 2020; therapy, 1365; vocational, 511
God, 1748
Grad(es)(ing), 487: attitude toward, 166, 2757; contract attitude, 513; contract system, 513; high school, 700; practices, 1748; predictor, 75; systems, 487
Graduate(s): business programs, 661; education, 685; programs, 676; school, case of entry, 487; students, 528; student education, 131; students' environmental perception, 2062; student intellectual attitude, 86
Grammatical: clues, 385; structure, 380
Grandparents, foster, 33
Grapheme-phoneme, 366
Graphic expression, 715
Gratification, postponement, 207
Grievance, 2656

Grooming, hygiene, 1603
Group(s): activity, 681; arousal, 1998; atmosphere, 2568, 3074; attractiveness, 1712; behavior, affective, 596; behavior, self perception, 778; cohesion, 1710, 1711, 2569; conformity, 445; counseling disadvantaged, 53; decision-making, 2912; direction by supervisor, 1005; interaction, 1722; judgment, 1392; minority, 480; need strength, 1999; participation, 53; practicum, 1259; process, 523, 880; religious, 183; work, 598
Guidance: administrator, 677; assessment, 687; classes, elementary, 31; counseling attitudes, 85, 189; director's roles, 318; function, 325; needs, elementary, 31; practices, 185; process, 687; school evaluation, 687; state director, 318, 697
Guilt, 289, 841, 1638, 1670, 2247, 2252, 2279, 2284: dispositional, 2276; -innocence, 381

Habits, 593: work, 1033, 1047
Handicapped, 1756, 2702: attitude toward, 2784; children, 1384, 1386, 1388, 1390, 1411, 1433, 1435-1437; children, mainstreaming, 1783, 2694; educationally, 583; preschoolers, 1597
Handwriting: children, 2373; cursive, 2375; kindergarten, 1051; legibility, 2376
Happiness, 1661: marital, 3022
Harmony: familial, 466; within group, 1711
Hazard perception, 2065
Head start, 637
Health: behavior, 2864; engenderingness, 1487; habits, 1220; locus of control, 2066, 3217-3219, 3251, 3339; mental, 42; opinion, 2067; organizational, 1330; physical, 215, 2860; resources, 2414; self-perception, 779; status, 2835
Hebrew, visual discrimination, 2377
Helpgivers, campus, 993
Helping dispositions, 2267, 3578
Helplessness: institutional, 1670; learned, 1670
Heterosocial: assessment, 2570; behavior, 2885
Hierach(ical)(y), 695: influence, 1892; occupational, 269
High school, 436, 471: achievement motivation, 729; alienation, 1090; counselors, 612, 660; curriculum, 473; functional literacy, 1611; occupational aspiration, 897, 901; personality, 851; seniors, 517; sex education, 668; social studies, 601; stress, 2481; students, 401, 472, 645, 650, 653; students, self-esteem, 827; vocational plans, 1590
Higher education, opportunities, 167
Higher learning, 347
Higher order need strength, 2000
Hindrance, 688
History: black, 157; case, 856; school, 625; social, 466
Hobbies, 593
Home, 497, 516: behavior, 1957; economics, behavioral change, 572; economic interest, 3631; environment, 1294, 1298, 1947; environment, cognitive, 642; environment, first graders, 1946; index, 344; interview, 647; learning environment, 647, 2993, 2994, 2997, 2998; observation,

1948; self-esteem, 2064; stimulation, 642; stimulations, child's, 1952, 2969; teachers, 572
Homemaker, 2995, 2996
Homicide, control, 970
Homonyms, 11
Homophobic, 514
Homosexuals, 514: attitude toward, 2713, 2748-2750
Hopelessness, 413, 1662, 1684, 2483: children, 2482; geriatric, 2476
Horizontality, 2224: principle, 1624
Hospital(ization): behavior, 1861; children, 1230; projective test, 1488
Hostil(e)(ity), 146, 919, 1500, 1681, 1720, 3500: -aggressive, 1872, 3452, 3463; indirect, 2252; press, 1342; wit, 2278
Housing: issues, 319; needs, 867
Human: figure drawing, 32; nature, philosophy, 980, 1522; relations, ability to facilitate, 1714; resources, 3078; values, 1529
Humor, 2278: children's preference, 1456; perceptiveness, 2378, 2680
Hydrostatic principle, knowledge, 1623
Hygiene, grooming, 1603
Hyperactiv(e)(ity), 1203: child, 397, 2827, 2878; -distractable, 1872
Hypersensitivity, 236
Hypnosis, 2902
Hypothesizing, 2215

Ideal: self, 252, 759; teacher, 679
Idealism, 2296
Ideas, 575, 3548: data, 2317
Ideational: creativity, 619; expressive style, 594; fluency, 1907, 1911
Identification, 640: concept, 884; creativity, 133; father, 434, 830; figures, 228; letter, 12; minority, 434; mother, father, teacher and friend, 434, 830; numerical, 12; parents, 143; peer group, 100; religious, 988; resolution, young adults, 2166; role, 331; sex role, 1461; status, 2237, 2238; subcultural, 95
Identity: achievement, 271, 628, 1286; conflicts 949; diffusion, 628; ego, 949; ego development and status, 628; gender, 630, 3403; Jewish-American, 1403; perceived, 3261; personal, 796; sex role, 3294
Ideology: economic, 3533; feminist, 3557; mental health, 1807; pupil control, 1819, 3105
Ignoring, 504
Illness: acceptance, 2432; behavior, 2839; mental, 1807; perceived, 3220
Image(s), 1281: administrator, 1307; factor, 683; science, scientists, 1794
Imagery, 265, 753, 784, 794: control, 2052; endemic, 3394; preference, 3397; production, vividness, 2153; self-reported, 777; self-reported vividness, 2118; vividness, 1375, 2040
Imaginative thinking, 1282
Imagining, emotive, 2063
Immaturity, 855-857
Immediate recall, 2217
Impairment, memory, 2386
Impersonal(ity)(ization), 695, 967
Implied meaning, 1278
Importance, 1318
Imposition on others, 746
Impulse: aggression, 1638; control, motor, 386; inhibition, 386
Impulsiv(e)(eness)(ity), 481, 845, 986, 3482: constriction, counselors, 961; reflection, 285,

290, 291, 1490, 1494; responding, 2262; -reflection, 2170
Impunitive attitudes, 481
Inadequacy, 515: feelings, 773, 1402
Incapability, political, 2111
Income, 268
Incomplete sentence(s), 400, 806
Indecision, career, 2809, 3655, 3657
Indecision, vocational, 3657-3659
Independen(ce)(t), 228, 282, 301, 397, 481, 1771, 2317: behavior, 651; -dependence, 400; family, 976, 2999; judgment, 612, 614; need, 1343; political, 512; pressure, 647, 673; rebellious, 481; teacher, 578; university environment, 704
Index, tension, 1667
Indian youth, disadvantaged, 375
Individualism, 989, 2571
Individualiz(ation)(e)(ed), 681: reading instruction, 545; reinforcers, 2018; studies, 6; study in institution, 169
Induction, 887
Inductive: logic, 2202; reasoning ability, 2209, 3426
Industrial: problems, 150; psychology, attitude toward, 1127; rehabilitation, 515; work groups attitudes, 1127
Infan(cy)(t), 623: characteristics, 1940; development, 625, 1050, 1287; language, 2935; psychological development, 631; temperament, see: Temperament, child and infant
Inference(s), 2217: social, 114
Inferential reading comprehension, 1605
Inferiority, feelings, 515
Inflectional performance, 17
Influence, hierarchical, 2236: in counseling, 258; leader, 1554; psychological, 3324; work, 2626, 2653
Information, 575: acquisition, 1; amount, 2223; biographical, 703; community life, 1060; institutional, 150-193, 657-706, 1307-1336, 1959-1983; job training, 709, 3079; processing, 605, 2907; processing style, 443; seeking, adolescents, 868; seeking, careers, 3616; seeking strategies, 2223, 2814; sex, 2393; symbolic, 107; transformation abilities, 106-108
Ingratiating behavior, 2841
Inhibition(s), 1720, 1870: impulse, 386; motor, 59; reciprocal, 389
Initiative, 949, 2265, 2842, 3131: supervisors, 1023
Inmates, prison, 91
Inner-outer directedness, 789
Innocence-guilt, 381
Innovati(on)(veness), 3484: behaviors, 432, 621; educational, 1784; university residence, 704
Inpatient behavior, mood, 1862
Inquisitiveness, creative, 578
Insecurity, 515
Inservice evaluation, 1319
Insight, 1385
Institution(al)(s): attitudes, 82; authority, attitudes, 2747; helplessness, 1670; information, 150-193, 657-706, 1307-1336, 1959-1983; political, 1806; procedures, 682
Instruction(al): attitude toward, 2712; behavior, 322; programmed, 153; television, problems, 488; threat of, 488; values, 3547
Instructor, 527, 667: behavior, 2863; effectiveness, 329; evaluation, 698, 997, 1009, 1014, 1022,

1027-1029, 1032, 3581; quality, 667; university, 680
Integrat(ed)(ion), 517: attitude, 79; classrooms, 2189
Integrative complexity, 1910, 2214, 2934
Integrity: of man, 915; of social agents, 2288
Intellectual(ity), 624, 986: ability, children, 888; achievement responsibility, 786; development, 637, 2953, 2954, 2958; efficiency, 2251; environment, 2993, 2994; growth, university residence, 704; locus of control, 3222; pragmatism, 95, 1515; pragmatic attitudes, 86; pressure for, 647, 673; self-confidence, 2073
Intelligence, 1117, 2265, 2689: children, 2677; culturally disadvantaged, 72; culture fair, 468; developmental, 1055; evaluated, 247; social, 1096, 1099, 1100, 2555, 2564; verbal, 887
Intensity, 2285
Intent(ionality): accidental, 381; judgment of, 622
Interaction, 68, 237: aide-child, 577; analysis, 427, 1049; anxiousness, 2572; behavioral, 585; behavior description, 596; classroom, 1105, 1894, 1897; counselor-client, 1253; family, 597; group, 1722; interpersonal, 448; interracial, 1143, 1745; marital, 240, 3024, 2035; mother, 1300; mother-child, 1953; parent-adolescent, 640; parent-child, 646, 1301, 1955; pupil, 1027; supervisor, 1248; teachers, 333, 1029; verbal, 596, 1261
Interconcept distance, 1908
Interest(s), 194-203, 593, 707-711: effort, counselors, 1003; information seeking, 868; job, 709; judgment of, 626; occupations, 196, 199, 201, 3629, 3631; parental, 650; patterns, 472; political, 537; religious, 1580; residence counselor, 1019; school, 391; science, intermediate, children, 864; social, 249; value, 1535; work, 757
Intermarriage, racial, 90
Internal: cognition, 2187; scanning, 1914; sensation, 2187; work motivation, 2001
Internal-external control, 50, 56, 238, 267, 576, 810, 1368, 1393, 1396, 1399, 1401, 1405, 1046, 1413, 1434, 2049, 2181: university freshmen, 221
Internationalism, 1795
Interorganizational relations, 1893
Interpersonal, 621, 625: adequacy, peer counseling, 1973; adjustment, college student, 2409; administrative behavior, 1863; aggression, 1221; alienation, 1110; attitudes, 546; attraction, 426, 1711; behavior, 1720; cognitive-complexity, 433; communication, 1900, 2920; competenc(e)(y), 446, 1724; complexity, 47; conflict, 523, 1950, 2573; contact, 328; control, 2075; dependency, adults, 1715, 2574; distanc(e)(ing), 436, 451, 2596; effectiveness, 2576; envy, 439; etiology, 530; feedback, 1899; flexibility, 217; index, 447; interaction, 448; jealousy, 2575; judgment, 1717; orientation, 54, 67, 216; perception, 428, 433; perceptions, teacher-child, 2076; problem, 892; pursuing, 2596; reflexes, 448; regard, 681; relations, 51, 431, 464, 575, 1102,

1256, 1668, 2548, 2577, 2588;
relations, counselors, 1003;
relations, self-perceptions, 780;
relations university residence,
704; relationships, 1716;
relationships, locus of control,
2087; seniority, 428, 444;
sensitivity, 1663, 1681, 1718,
2269, 2288; situations, 1721;
skills, 431; style, 1489; support,
2578; trust, 954, 1504, 2914; value
constructs, 2304
Interpretat(ing)(ion)(ive), 600, 689,
1448: data, 1607
Interracial: attitudes, 517, 1150,
1198; attitude, students, 535;
interaction, 1745
Interrogative patterns,
recognition, 380, 384
Intervention: acceptability, 3400;
federal, 79
Interview(ing), 587, 589:
assessment, 3162; behavior,
counselor, 584; client reaction,
998; counseling, 699; home, 647;
maternal, 927; rating, counseling,
699; reaction, 589, 998; residents,
546; schedule, 471; teaching,
evaluation, 1015; techniques,
medical students, 2330
Interviewer(s): knowledge of laws,
1018; rating, 803, 3594;
screening, 1013; self-disclosure,
104, 2906; trustworthiness, 938
Intimacy, 688, 1257, 2580, 2592,
2837, 2965, 3004: attitude, 2579;
physical, 3039; social, 2587
Intolerance: general, 1792; trait
inconsistency, 2078
Intrinsic: -extrinsic job outcomes,
1786; motivation, 481, 1994, 3127,
3136, 3138, 3140; task motivation,
3137
Introspection, 481

Introversion: -extraversion, 292,
390, 749; children, 956;
occupational, 292; social, 1670
Intrusiveness, 655
Intuitive, 2205, 2206: ability, 3430
Invasion, privacy, 1320, 2079
Investigatory activities,
children, 724
Involvement: family, 2986; job,
1322, 2002, 2003, 2671, 3583,
3620, 3633-3637; maternal, 578;
positive, 655; university
residence, 704; work, 3661, 3662
Irrational beliefs, 1516, 1637, 1665,
2505, 3226, 3227, 3284, 3287
Irritability, 1638, 1670, 2552
Irritation, 2627, 3075:
anxiety-depression, 1686, 2621
Isolated child, 397
Isolation, 1093: perceived, 453;
social, 437, 1110, 1727
Issues, housing, 319
Item distractors, 173
Italian stereotype, 3228

Japanese: Americans, 520;
geography, 351
Jealousy, interpersonal, 2575, 3006,
3485
Jewish: American identity, 1403;
college students, 503; religiosity,
3553
Job(s), 457: aggression, 1033;
attributes required, 1040;
attitude, 1346, 2754; autonomy,
3051; bizarre behavior, 1033;
burnout, see: Burnout; career
key, 2379; characteristics,
3080-3082, 3088; classification,
3073, 3095; clerical, 73; climate,
1967, 3052; complexity, 3091;
complexity, perception, 2083;
conditions, 1404; conditions,
clerical, 2178; dependence, 1034;

description, 1321; design, 3092; discrimination, 3085; duties, 1040; education required, 1040; equity, 3395; evaluation, 1016, 3061; feedback, 3083; foremen perception, 1012; foremen responsibilities, 1011; frustration, 2623; goals, 709; grievance, 2656; hunting, 3458; induced anxiety, 1666; information and training, 709, 3079; interest, 197, 709; interview performance, 1736, 2350; involvement, 1322, 1737, 2002, 2003, 2364, 2671, 3583, 3633-3637; knowledge, supervisors, 1005, 2380; need fulfillment, 3143; outcomes, 1534; outcomes, intrinsic-extrinsic, 1786, 3136, 3138; performance, 2647, 3584; performance, evaluation of, 1016, 1537, 1553, 1566; performance, perception, 3267; physical and mental exertion, 709; physical surroundings of, 709; police, 3577, 3579; pressure, 1687; prestige, 273; problems, 1968; proficiency, 320; quitting, 3650; rating, 3096; rating of residence counselors, 1019; relations with associates, 709; relations with employers, 709; recruiters, 518; robustness, 3107; satisfaction, 709, 1575, 1577, 1578, 1581, 1586, 1588, 1589, 1592, 1594, 1668, 2320, 2363, 2365, 2367, 2368, 2624, 2625, 2629-2637, 2657, 2659, 2668, 2670, 2673, 2675; security, 709, 1687, 2367; selection, 1040, 3632; status, 2645; stress, 2621, 2641, 2642, 2649, 2650, 2654, 2658; structure, 3084; tedium, 2643, 2674; tension, 2638-2640, 2667; time demand, 2644; values, 321; viewpoints, 546

Journals in sociology, prestige, 906

Judgment, 9, 890: affect, 1252; analysis, 2183; children's, 626; clinical, 215; concepts, 2936; group, 1392; independence of, 612; interest, 622, 626; interpersonal, 1717; moral, 139, 622, 626, 633, 638, 852, 1519, 1599, 2210, 3543; supervisors, 1023; teacher, 1059; visual, 1115

Junior college: motivation, 1351; student ability, 766; transfers, 1311

Junior high school, 1799: abstract reasoning, 884; achievement motivation, 2028; atmosphere, 700; boys, 651; classroom methods, 700; grading, 700; knowledge of work, 711; materials and facilities, 700; need achievement, 729; skills, 700; students, 700; teachers, 700; teachers, student-centeredness, 1867

Justice: conceptions, 381, 3522, 3537, 3538; distributive, 234; social, 381

Juvenile delinquency, 519

Kindergarten, 352, 356, 357, 540: adjustment, 2422; children, development, 1289; handwriting performance, 1051; performance, 2381; racial preference, 1459; reading, 352; sex role, 874, 881, 883

Kindness, 113, 1270

Kinesthetic sensitivity, 1421

Knowledge: behavioral principles, 2382; careers, 3614; drugs, 343, 344, 1042, 1600; laws, interviewers, 1018; of accident avoidance, 1622; morphographic, 2387; music, 2389; organization

SUBJECT INDEX

of subject matter, 679; personal traits, 862; political, 368; reproductive, 1056; rules of the road, 1622; supervisors, 1023; words, 342; work, 711
Kuder Preference Test, 10

Labor, division of, 695
Laboratory, 1182
Lack of social support, 1638
Language, 21: ability, 384; arts, 12, 637; arts, pre-first graders, 277; competence, basic, 380, 384; comprehension, 355; infant, 2935; informal, 378; negative, 2933; oral, 1275; performance, 1035; proficiency, 376; skills, 1597; street, 378
Late adolescent(s), 498: males, 646
Latency, 585
Laterality assessment, 1881, 2681, 2687, 2690, 3422
Law(s): abidingness, 287; and order, 1797; enforcement personnel, 3577, 3579, 3587; knowledge of, 1018
Leader(ship): behavior, 1241, 1333, 1866, 2084, 2843, 2845, 2872, 2884, 2896; creativity, 1925; firemen, 1549; influence, 1544; initiative, self-concept, 2056; -member exchange, 1986, 2915, 2916, 2926; motivational style, 2184; opinion, 2104; qualities, 338; satisfaction, 2345; students, 2349, 2684, 2844; style, 941; style, supervisors, 1023; teacher, 1057; technical competence, 1555
Learn(er)(ing), 494: attitude toward, 540, 2785; behavior, 2829; behavior, perception of, 838; behavior in classrooms, 838; children's, 521, 2677; climate, 1323; cognitive, 175; disabled, 2853; enthusiasm for, 540; environment, 473, 647, 673, 686, 1298, 1324, 1371, 2985, 3076, 3089, 3109, 3114; grades vs. true, 487; higher, 347; inflectional principals, 17; materials, 1325; memory, 8; preference, 3402; process, 488, 3431; readiness, 2193; self-concept, 1389, 3213, 3299; student perceptions, 175; style, 2216; tasks, 1868
Learning disabled, children, phonics, 2398
Lectures: controversial, 586; quality, 3085
Legibility, 1052, 2376
Leisure activities, 198, 268, 870, 2185, 3404, 3407
Lesson, evaluation, 1027
Length, 2224
Letter: discrimination, 1051; formation, 1052; identification, 12; sound translation, 1062
Level of arousal, 2291
Level of aspiration, self-concept, 2056
Level of regard, 227, 309, 431, 2353
Liberal-conservative, 95, 280, 1527
Liberal dimension, mother's, 2313
Liberalism, 555, 2258
Liberalism-conservatism, college students, 1835
Libertarian democracy, 1799
Library, attitude, 2758
Lie scale, 499
Life: change(s), 1290, 2522, 2532, 3009; changes, college students, 1942; events, 2581, 3111; experience, 1719, 3373; experiences, women's liberation, 861; history, 1288; imagined, 3193; inventory, 2836; irritants, 3075; meaningfulness in, 821, 3524; perspective, 2047;

satisfaction, 33, 415, 2504, 2529; statuses, perception, 2047; stress, 2533, 2543; style, 268, 1800
Lifestyle orientation, 2186
Liking, 460, 2582
Line Meanings, 608
Linguistic competence, 1121
Listening, 1735, 2913: achievement, 1043; comprehension, 2688
Literacy: basic occupational, 1038; child understanding, 3257, 3337; functional, 1611
Literal reading comprehension, 1609
Locative prepositional, 377
Locus of conflict, 2085
Locus of control, 50, 221, 239, 310, 320, 1368, 1383, 1393, 1396, 1399, 1401, 1406, 1413, 1434, 1628, 2068, 2071, 2074, 2088-2091, 2093, 2094, 2102, 2150, 3166, 3171, 3178, 3222-3225, 3230, 3233-3240, 3244: administrators, 818; adolescents, 2072; adult(s), 2033, 2100, 3194, 3196, 3255, 3272, 3274; black children, 793; children, 754, 797, 799, 2041, 2092, 2101, 2146, 2148, 3182-3187, 3205, 3241, 3242, 3252; health, 2066, 3217-3219, 3251, 3339, 3340; intellectual, social physical, 2086; internal-external, 576, 2049, 2081, 3164; interpersonal relationships, 2087; mental health, 2096; peer counseling, 1973; preschool, primary, 2113; rehabilitation clients, 29; teacher, 3332-3334
Logic(al), 474, 884: ability, children, 3441; additions, 19; connectives, 123; operations, 2946
Loneliness, 1703-1705, 1729, 2552-2554, 2561, 2615: children, 2583
Long-term memory, 1601

Love: addiction, 2584; punishment, symbolic, 654; reward, symbolic, 654; romantic, 2599, 2600; sickness, 3012
Loving, styles, 1871
Lower class, 349: children, test anxiety, 1076
Loyalty: supervisor, 1005; teacher, 1883
Lunar effects, 3172

Machiavelliansim, 1492, 1517, 1721, 3486, 3487, 3514
Magic, 3539
Majors, college, 222, 662
Maladjustment, 2492
Malaise, African society, 65
Male(s): influence on female career choice, 710; need achievement, 728; self-esteem, 826; sex-role attitude, 2760; young adult, 636
Management, 388: strategy, classroom, 880; style, 1333
Manager(ial)(s): attitudes, 523, 1536; autocratic personality, 787; behavior, 3560; changes in practice, 1129; description, 1447; needs, 1348; positions, 3104; rating, 1560, 3580, 3585, 3586; sex-role stereotypes, 1482; traits, 2265
Manifest: alienation, 443, 1102; anxiety, 29, 1478, 1493, 1647, 2524, 3488; needs, 211, 2005; rejection, 496
Marginality, 249
Marijuana, 353, 1214, 1223: attitude toward, 1133
Marital: activities, 3013; alternatives, 3016; communication, 2972, 3017; conflict, 2973; dependency, 3029, 3046; instability, 3023; interaction, 3024, 3025; quality, 3026; relationships, 1766, 3018,

3021; satisfaction, 2976, 3007, 3020, 3022, 3027, 3028, 3035
Marri(age)(ed), 503, 593, 1056, 1161: adjustment, 648, 1299, 2962, 2978, 2980, 3011, 3014, 3015, 3019; complaints, 2966; counseling, 146; couples, 648; dating, 503; difficulties, psychiatric patients, 773; interaction, 240; jealousy, 3006; reward, 3041; satisfaction, 648, 1305; students, 1349; termination, 2963, 2968, 2977
Masculine: attitudes, 2759; transcendence, 1757
Masculinity-femininity, 795, 927, 2265; concepts, 114
Masochistic-self effacing personality, 787
Mass media, 302
Mastery, 301
Materials and facilities: junior high school, 700; learning, 1325
Maternal: acceptance, perceived, 759; attitude, perceived, 759; controls, 1954; encouragement measure, 651; interview, 927; involvement, 578; perceived nuturance, 646; responsiveness, 2273; vocalization, 649; warmth, 652
Mathematics, 4, 19, 21, 508, 525, 1758, 2371: achievement in, 1740, 2383; anxiety, 394, 1630, 2417, 2418; attitude, 153, 524, 2715, 2740, 2761, 2762, 2795; attribution, 3246; early behaviors, 345; lecture, quality, 3086; locus of control, 3244; remedial, 508; self-concept, 1409, 3247, 3248; self-efficacy, 3249; stereotype, 3245
Maturity, 2265: adult vocational, 1936; behavior, 621, 1206, 1937;

children, 621; emotional, 621; personal, 636; reading, 1053; social, 636; students', 2349; vocational, 308, 2618
Meaning: assimilation of, 380; concept, 106-125, 1269-1279; implied, 1278; unusual, 1914
Meaningful(ness): in life, 821; words, 360
Meaninglessness, 413, 424, 1700
Mechanics, word association, 119
Mechanization, attitude toward, 1162
Media therapy, 98, 307
Medical career, 3640
Medical school: learning environment, 3089; stress, 2425
Memorizing, 2215
Memory, 8, 11, 13, 18, 116, 117, 358-363, 382, 600, 1738, 2385: assessment, 2384; auditory, 1066; early, 134, 848; immediate and remote, 2213; impairment, 2386; long-term, 1601; performance, 382; remote, 1601; short-term, 18; span, 1388, 1436, 1437; symbolic implications, 116; vision-spatial, 2152; visual, 2397
Mental: ability, 138; aptitude, 72; competence, 2385; development, 134, 2956; dexterity, 1738, 2689; effort, 3161; health, 42; health ideology, 530, 1807; health, locus of control, 2096; health, locus of origin, 1801; health, psychodynamic, 880; illness, 530, 1772, 1807; illness, attitude toward, 530, 2736; impairment, 2834
Mentally retarded children, 1759
Merit, 502
Methods, 694: disciplining, residents, 546
Mexican-Americans, 472, 549:

acculturation, 2547, 3519; achievement need, 738; attitudes towards, 2768; disadvantaged children, 380, 384, 390; power need, 738; rejection need, 738; workers' status, 902

Middle school: evaluation, 1326; teachers, student-centeredness, 1867

Migrant children placement, 21

Militancy, 1495

Military: experience, 518; morale, 1971; reenlistment, 3652; service attitudes, 81; training success, 3582

Ministers, protestant, 519

Minority: children, 502; groups, 480; group rights, 79; identification, 434; youth, 1587

Mistrust, 2247: cultural, 2560

Mobility: physical, 1707; upward, 1158, 3145

Modernism, 301, 302

Modernity, 1327, 2309: attitudes, 1164, 1165, 3536

Money, 593, 2317, 2764

Monosyllabic: nonsense, 374; words, 374

Mood, 416, 1083, 2275, 2285, 2494: impatient behavior, 1862, 2801; objective, 417, 1496; psychological, 1669; sad, 1670; state, 2457

Moonlighting, 226

Moral: behavior, 981, 3529; code, 981; commitment, 3541; comprehension, 3556; development, 139, 638, 2957; evaluation, 1745; judgment, 622, 626, 633, 638, 852, 1519, 1599, 2210, 2301, 3543; -judgment, behavior, 2310; judgment, children, 2311; reasoning, 2212, 2218, 2219, 2222, 3531, 3558; structure, children, 977; social values, 472; thought, 3542; values, children, 978

Morale, 415, 443, 444: elderly, 2495, 2496, 2506; military, 1871; school administrator, 1680, 1978

Moralism, 624

Moratorium, 628

Morphographic, transfer and knowledge, 2387

Mosaic: construction, 611; test, 138

Mother(s), 578: attitude, 1803; child care, 2967; children's perception, 761; -child interaction, 649, 1300, 1953; daughter, 3004; dominance, 647, 673; identification with, 434, 830; relations with, 419; role of, 652, 2970, 2981; working, 655

Motion picture, 1384, 1386

Motion sickness, 2848

Motivation, 204-210, 712-747, 1337-1366, 1984-2029, 3135: academic, 578, 3123; achievement, 712, 721, 1338, 1340, 1347, 1350, 1353, 1986, 1987, 1989, 1990, 1993, 2017, 2019, 2026, 3124-3126, 3141, 3142; achievement, children, 718, 737; achievement, men, 1988; altruistic, 3134; college, 208; college student, 743; creative, 607; curricula choice, 720; dating, 3128; effectance, 3150; employee, 205; esteem, 1360; face saving, 1353; factors, academic, 1985; fear of failure, 1342; internal work, 2001; intrinsic, 730, 1994, 3127, 3136-3138, 3140; junior-senior high school achievement, 729, 2028; to manage, 3148; novelty, 717; peer, 732; parental, 1945; power, 3129, 3132; safety, 1360; school, 731, 737, 2004, 3151; structure, 687; success avoidance, 1362; teacher, 1029; training, 338, 3139;

Upward Bound, 45; upward mobility, 3145; vindication, 746; vocational choice, 720; work, 487, 1341, 1344, 1366
Motor: activity, 397; development, 634, 637; impulse control, 386; inhibition, 59; perceptual, 469; proficiency, 348, 634; speed, 1610
Motoric expressive style, 594
Mountain sickness, 571
Movement, 502
Movies, 1436: attitude toward, 1166, 2765
Multifactor social attitude, 482
Multiracial attitudes, 2766
Murray's needs, 211
Music and art: attitude toward, 1841; knowledge, 2389
Mutual communication, 98
Mysticism, 3544

Nationalities, 1135: attitude toward, 2798
Naturalism, 529
Naughtiness, 622, 626
Navy, satisfaction, 2661
Need achievement, 204, 210, 721, 744, 986, 1340, 1345, 2265: children's, 715; college students, 726; disadvantaged students, 722; females, 728; males, 728
Need(s): affiliation, 745, 986; affiliation, Mexican-American, 738; approval, 450, 500; arousal seeking, 2023; assessment, 1329; cognition, 3367; deficiency, 1355; desire, 2008; disposition, 601; financial reward, 2265; for achievement, 2005, 2009, 2022, 2029; for affiliation, 2007; for autonomy, 2010; housing, 867; independence, 1343; interpersonal, 51; manifest, 211, 2005; power, 2265; psychological, 1339; satisfaction, 1348, 1354, 1356, 1357, 2012, 1213, 3277; satisfaction, job related, 2011, 3143; -satisfying, leisure activities, 2185; security, 2265; self-actualizing, 2265; self-peer, 1359; strength, 2182; strength, growth, 1999; strength, higher order, 2000; to achieve, 2007; vocational, 323
Negativism, 2252: -acquiescence, children, 843
Negotiation(s): collective, 538; groups, 324; latitude, 2918; role force, 324
Negro: disadvantaged, 342, 350; white student friendship, 452
Neighborhood youth corps, 563
Neonatal behavioral assessment, 1849
Nervousness, 1683
Network: peer, 2591; personal, 2589
Neurologic status, 1284
Neurotic(ism), 39, 43, 405, 853, 855-857: anxiety, 749; manifestations, 36; symptoms, 2480
Newborn, 1284
Ninth grade, 347, 351
Noetic goals, 821
Noise sensitivity, 2099, 2850, 3110
Nonassertive, 408
Nonconformity, 481: orientation, 228
Nonfeminist attitudes, 1834
Nongraded school, 574
Nonsense: monosyllabic units, 374; trigrams, 363
Nonverbal, applicant rating, 3588; rigidity, 1477; verbal, 2921; visual discrimination, 2377
Normlessness, 437, 454, 1093, 1640, 1700, 1701, 1709
Notes, student, 379

Noun(s): plural forms, 367; possessive, 377
Novelty: -experiencing, 21; motivation for, 717, 3133
Nuclear disarmament, 2795
Number(s), 345, 474, 2224: concepts, 2939; joining, 478
Numerical, 1738: identification, 12
Nurs(es)(ing): attitude toward, 2996; courses, 3639, 3641; rating, 3596; role conflict, 3289; school of, 694; stress, 2639, 2648; union, 2669
Nurses aides, 3377
Nurturance, 1720: perceived maternal, 646
Nurturant-affectionate, 652

Obedience, four year olds, 60
Object: orientation, 2317; permanence, 140; scale, 635; sorting, 1273
Objectives: curriculum, 694; residence counseling, 546
Objectivity-subjectivity, 1769
Obscene words, 1274
Observation, 574, 730
Observing and inferring, 2215
Obsessive compulsive, 1663, 1681, 3493, 3497
Occupation(al)(s), 1060, 2237: ability, 305; aspiration, 269, 897, 3623; aspiration, high school student, 897, 901; attitude toward, 2700; choice, 1587; choices, college students, 719; concept, 1909, 3654; interest, 197, 199, 301; inventory, 711; knowledge, 2379; literacy, basic, 1038; preference, 874; prestige, 273-275, 897, 900, 2239, 3447, 3651; prestige, psychology, 903; rating, 3096; satisfaction, 709; self-efficacy, 3256; status, 276, 1470; stereotypes, 270, 3642;

strain, 1686; stress, 2620, 2665, 2666; titles, 707; values, 2315
OCS stress reaction, 1672, 1673
Off-campus cohabitation, 181
Office opinion, open, 1805
Old people, 1760
Onomatopoeia, 1281
Open-mindedness, 935, 2259, 2292
Openness, 214: elementary school, 1963; to experience, 2162
Operant conditioning, delinquent boys, 24
Operational thought, 889
Opinion(s): about education, 529; health, 2067; leadership, 2104; open office, 1805; personal, 612; pupil, 541, 1820; student, 95
Opportunities, 694: higher education, 167
Opposites, word, 2
Oppositional behaviors, 1225
Optimism, 2487, 3156: college student, 2408
Oral: comprehension, 365; form discrimination, 1421; P/S language, 1275; traits, 934; vocabulary, 380, 384
Organization(al), 575: behavior, 3065; characteristics, 1333, 1970; choice, 2105; climate, 176, 1308, 3050, 3097-3099, 3102; climate description, 688; commitment, 2014-2016, 3541, 3609, 3624, 3625, 3643-3648; communication, 1898, 1901, 2904, 2919; community, 1453; control, 1962; employee commitment, 1996; health, 1330; need satisfaction, 1354, 1357; order, university residence, 704; practices effectiveness, 1972; preference, 259; pride, 3649; research, 1331; structure, 1332; subject matter, 679; supervision, 1023
Organized demeanor, 1885

SUBJECT INDEX

Organizers, advance, 8
Orientation, 2213: achievement, 248, 713; career, 1576, 3617, 3618; college, 879; environmental, 302; future, 207, 301; goal, 400; interpersonal, 54, 67, 216; lifestyle, 2186; other, 989; peer group, 534; person, 1994; professional, 539; research, 1816; school, 547; work, 2676
Originality, 617, 861, 1281
Outcomes, instrumental, 3416
Outpatients, geriatric, 2566
Overexcitability, 3495
Overprotection, 496
Overt aggression, 1638

Pain: apperception, 2095; behavior, 2854, 2867; pediatric, 2857
Paintings, assessment, 1457
Panic, 2438
Parachute jumpers, 406
Paragraph completion, 120, 891, 1498, 1499
Paranoid: behavior, 646; ideation, 1681
Paranormal belief, 3211
Paraplegics, 418
Parent(al)(ing)(s), 451, 498, 1304, 3036: adolescent interaction, 640, 3001, 3030; approval, 499; as teacher, 1808; attitude, 144, 504, 532, 533, 640, 1148, 1193, 3010; authority, 640; behavior, 643, 655, 1295, 3033; behavior, loving-rejecting, 149; -child communication, 103, 640; -child interaction, 646, 1955, 2979, 3005; child rearing, 2855, 2971; child relations, 148, 654, 3034; control, 145; delinquent girls, 656; disturbed children, 38; dominance, 229, 1301; encouragement, 713; expectation, 1302; family, 593; frustration, 1216; identification, 143; interest, 650; motivation, 1945; normal adolescent girls, 656; perceptions, 1956; punishment intensity, 1949; questionnaire, 463; rating, 643, 1303; relations, adolescent, 760; satisfaction, 3008; support, 640, 3038; transition to, 3048; warmth, 3031
Participation, 1687: group, 53; psychological, 1419
Passive speech, 397
Past, remembered, 812
Paternal reactions to birth, 1958
Pathological behavior, 1226, 1310
Patient(s): adjustment, 418; behavior, 1870; depressive, 420; psychogeriatric, 2213; schizophrenic, 306; symptoms, 1663; terminally ill, 1656; therapist, 995; therapy, 191
Pattern(s): activity, 400; communication, 597; copying, 801; meanings, 608
Pay, 2367, 2651, 2652, 3258
Peer(s), 497, 516, 523: acceptance, 1105; affiliation, 228; aggressiveness in children, 946; attitude toward, 541; classroom performance, 575; counseling effectiveness, 1973; evaluation, 1168, 3374; group, 163; group orientation, 534; influence on behavior, 556; network, 2591; perceptions, 256; rating, 802, 2556, 3449; relations, 70, 397, 472, 675, 2601; relations in adolescents, 760; roles, 2590, 3259; self-esteem, 2064; tutoring, 1240
Penmanship and neatness: children, 2373; perception of, 2147
People: concepts, 502; liking, 2582;

test, 535
Perceived: decision-making, 3262; depth of interaction, 1722; environment, behavioral press, 2050; external barriers, 2208; identity, 3261; isolation, 453; lunar effects, 3172; maternal nuturance, 646; power, 3214 problems, black/white somatotype, 3263; students, 1980; stress, 2501; supervision influence, 2359; work influence, 2653

Perception(s), 1, 227-256, 748-838, 1367-1443, 2030-2157, 2280: academic climate, 1335, 3322; adequacy by college teachers, 785; aesthetic, 254; alcohol consumption, 3159, 3160; attractiveness, 3275; auditory, first graders, 750; auditory, Spanish language-oriented children, 1613; auditory and visual stimuli, 765; authentic ability, 2147; body, 3175-3177; boss, 3326; campus by student, 187; causes, 3181, 3327; children, 659, 1414; classroom, 1227; client, 227, 2336; college environment, 177; college students, 706; college students of instructor effectiveness, 2358; competence, 3243; complexity of, 768; control, 239, 3168, 3252; counseling session, 3200; counselor-client, 1372; counselor role, 332, 3199; counselor by students, 993; curriculum, 694; environment by children, 178; environment by employee, 164; environmental, 179; features, 1391; first graders, 1423; general ability, 2147; graduate students' perception, 2062; hazard, 2065; illness, 3220; instructor's, 2349; interpersonal, 428, 433; job by firemen, 1012; job by foreman, 1012; learning behavior, 838; life stresses, 2047; marriage, 240; maternal acceptance, 759; maternal attitude, 759; mathematics, 3245, 3249; mental effort, 3161; mother by child, 761; of appraisal interview and supervisor, workers, 2036, 3162; of counseling relationship, 2037; of job complexity, 2083; of leadership behavior, 2084; of parental reactions of birth, adolescents, 2156; of penmanship and neatness, 2147; of reading and spelling ability, 2147; of role conflict, role ambiguity, 2121, 3341; parent, 1956, 2045; part/whole, 124; part/whole, in children, 19; peer, 256, 2045; performance, 3267; personal control, 1415; preprofessional teacher training, 1982; principal, 1407; problem solving, 764, 3280; psychological influence, 3324; psychologists, 3265; reality, 3173; recall, adults, 533; residence counselors, 1020; reversals, 813; role, 2123; school, 700, 2045, 3055; self, 748, 2045, 3260, 3270, 3273; self-control, 3185; self-perception, children, 3187; sex role, 2110, 3167, 3188; stereotypes, 3169, 3318, 3319; stressors, 3184; student, 175; student/faculty, about academic advising, 1959; teachers by students, 1027; teachers of administrators, 1408; teachers of students, 24; team teaching, 334; understanding, 3264; unmet democratic values, 2055; visual, 801, 808, 1735; work, 1404

Perceptual: aberration, 3266;

SUBJECT INDEX

ability, 1121; ability, elementary school, 2098; acuity, 2685; effectiveness, 214; flexibility, 923; handicapped, 1384, 1386, 1387, 1390, 1411, 1435, 1436; motor, 469, 1597; motor ability, 2213; motor development, 417; -motor skill, from discrimination, fine eye-hand coordination, visual motor match, 2143; rigidity, 1377; speed, 1604, 1608, 1618
Performance: ability, 6; child attribution, 3268; clinical, medical students, 2356; college expectation, 740; college student, 1856; employees, 1007; engineer, 1577; index, 636; inflectional, 17; job, 1553, 1566, 2647, 3584; job interview, 2350; kindergarten, 2381; language, 1035; managerial, 3585; memory, 382; principal, 1558; similies, 1054; social, 2608-2610; student, 568; teachers, 997, 1027; work, 3593
Permanence, object and person, 140
Persistence/dependence, 216
Person orientation, 1994
Person permanence, 140
Personal: adjustment, 37; anticipations, 2107; attributes, 561, 692, 1809, 2171, 3269-3271; attitudes, 535, 593; characteristics, 657; characteristics, counselor, 1004; constructs, 1305; control, 3272; goals, 829; growth, university residence, 704; identity, 796; manager, 1169; maturity, 636; needs, 1356; opinion, 612; problems, 419; skills, 3320; social adjustment, 397; space, 1107, 1418; traits, knowledge of, 862; understanding, 175; values, 1521; worth, 2367, 2614
Personalistic, 2186
Personality, 211-226, 839-863, 1444-1452, 2158-2174, 3372, 3387: active-passive, 848; adolescent, 854; adolescent, boy, 848; aggressive-sadistic, 787; agreeing tendency, 3344; assessment, 2171; bureaucratic, 957, 967; children, 842, 927, 1450; college freshmen, 223; competitive-narcissistic, 787; cooperative-overconventional, 787; creative, 620; delinquents, 853-857; disadvantaged, 1452; disorder, 405; docile-dependent, 787; enuresis, 846; happy-sad, 848; high school, 851; Holland types, 3343; integration, 847, 849; Jungian, 3371; locus of control, see: Locus of Control; managerial-autocratic, 787; narcissistic, 3491; rebellious-distrustful, 787; responsible-hypernormal, 787; persuasiveness, 3353; psychopathology, components, 3346; Rorschach, 224; self-effacing-masochistic, 787; semantic differential, 1451; style, 2169; teacher, 1027; traits, 615; vocational preference, 194
Personnel: ratings of, 706; student, 859
Perspective, 2224: life, 2047
Pessimism, 1103, 1662, 1670, 2483, 2487
Pharisaic virtue, 1170
Pharmacological rating, 1228
Phenomenology, 2296
Philosoph(ical)(y): belief, 968; counselor, 968; human nature, 980, 1522; orientation, 3552
Phobic anxiety, 1681

Phoneme-grapheme, 366
Phonemic, 380: discrimination, 380, 384
Phonetic generalization, 371, 374
Phonics, 1048: achievement, 2398
Physical: ability, middle childhood, 244; ability, students', 2349; activity, 265; activity, attitude, 1171; activity, women's attitude, 791; appearance, 593, 3275; attributes, 561; condition, 578, 593; contact, 649; development, 637; environment, community, 1060; intimacy, 3039; surroundings, job, 709; symptoms, 773
Physics, creative ideas, 1930
Physiognomic reactivity, 1506
Physiological reactions, 395
Piaget(ian), 635: development, 2960
Piano anxiety, 2508
Picture: -frustration, 1675; interpretation, 1085, 1448; school, 738; stories, 113
Pilot accidents, 478
Peace group members, 510
Plan(fulness)(ning), 501, 986
Plans: career, 175, 202, 3619; procedures in class, 679
Play, 40, 1208, 1218, 2861, 2862
Pleasantness, 417
Pleasure, 2507
Plural formation patterns, 367
Police, 1666, 3577: attitudes, 1810; authority, 485; cynicism, 943; empathy, 781; motivation, 205; rating, 3577, 3579, 3587; recruits, 443, 444; tasks, 257; women, 1666; work, 257
Policies and procedures, 663
Political: activity, 576; attitude, 536, 537, 1172, 1806; behavior, American, 368; belief, 593, 1520; change, 92; cynisicm, 537;

dependence, 512; discontent, 1976; distrust, feelings of, 1975; efficacy, sense of, 537; estrangement, 1977; future time perspective, 832; incapability, 2111; independence, 512; institutions, 1806; interest, 537; knowledge, 368; orientation, democratic, 1799; orientation, superintendents, 972; preference, 873; protest, 1197; sciences skills, 369; tolerance, 537; trust, 537
Politics, 2237
Poor, 522
Popularity, 556: self-perceived, 458
Population control, 1811
Positive regard, 220: unconditional, 227, 309
Positive reinforcement, 2188, 2189
Possessive nouns, 377
Possessiveness, 504, 655, 2584
Post-treatment awareness, 1416
Potential: series learning, 1743; success, 338
Poverty, 522: children, self-concept, 798
Power(ful), 52, 268, 485, 659, 2253: motivation, 732; need, Mexican-American, 738; others, 1405, 1406; perceived, 3214; seeker, 3368; social, 460, 1112, 3129, 3132; socialized activities, 732; supervisor, 1231
Powerlessness, 413, 437, 809, 1093, 1700, 1701, 1709, 2112
Practical significance, 696
Practice(s): guidance, 185; teaching, effectiveness, 690; teacher, student evaluation of, 690
Practicum: counselor evaluation, 1003; group, 1259
Pragmatism, 2296: intellectualism, 95, 1515
Preadolescent, 625, 644: self-esteem, 825

SUBJECT INDEX

Preceptual scanning, 421
Pre-college testing program, 480
Pre-counseling training, 2374
Prediction(s): academic, 231, 232; school success, 71
Predictive index, 475
Predisposition, creative, 1928
Preference(s), 257-263, 864-883, 1453-1464, 2175-2199, 3390: activity, 3388; cognitive, 2179, 3391, 3410; competition, 3412; counselor, 1544, 3392, 3409; educational, 200; food, 3396, 3417; friend, 434; humor, 1456; imagery, 3397; job enrichment, 3405; learning, 3402; mother, father, teacher and others, 55; occupational, 874; organizational, 259; political, 873; professor, 866; racial, 865, 1459; reading, 1460; recreation, 3407; roommate, 262; sex-role, 2181, 3314, 3389, 3411; skin, 1463; social, 789; student, 263; task, 205, 2178; teacher, 866, 880; toys, 883; teacher behavior, 3406; vocational, 194, 195, 213, 305; work, 692, 708, 3395, 3664; worker, 3401
Prejudice, 281, 296, 482, 1174, 1185, 1187: anti-black, 2297; projective, 1176
Preliterate: children, 1812; children, racial attitude, 1814
Premarital counseling, 147
Premorbid: adjustment, 421; competence, 2594
Prenominal adjectives, 377
Preparation, 666
Prepositional phrases, locative, 377
Prereading, 352
Preschool, 578: achievement, 12; anxiety, 2509; behavior, 1872; children, 383, 397, 425, 459, 477, 616, 617, 635, 1397; children, black, 377; children, disadvantaged, 403; children, frustration, 1229; children, handicapped, 1597; children, prejudice, 1174; children, reflexivity, 1490; children, self-perception, 835; primary locus of control, 2113; problem solving, disadvantaged children, 892, 894; program, 642; to primary, 390; racial attitude, 1814; screener, 1714; social-emotional behavior, 1237
Presentation, self, 2558
Presenter competence, 3591
Press(ure), 487, 1666: achievement, 496, 647, 673; activeness, 647, 673; English, 647, 673; ethlanguage, 647, 673; independence, 647, 673; intellectuality, 647, 673; job, 1687
Prestige, 269, 2317: among sociology journals, 906; college major, 896; occupational, 269, 273-275, 897, 900, 3447, 3651; perception of vocational, 204
Priesthood, 1668
Priests, American Catholic, 1668
Primary: children, reinforcement preferences, 739; grade, 367; grade children, 718; grades, primary and elementary, 1743; grades, reading attitude, 1775; grades, reading comprehension, 14; preschool locus of control, 2113; roles, 73; self-concept, 2114, 2115; teacher directiveness, 936
Principal(s), 484, 495: elementary school, 1680; evaluation, 1558; perception, 1407; role, 538; teacher, 595; teacher communication, 688
Principalization, 850

Principle(s): business, 661; identification, 884
Print, awareness, 2390
Privacy: attitude, 2751, 2752; invasion, 1320, 2079
Probability, 2224
Probation administrators, 523
Probing, 689
Problem(s): assessment, 1674; behavior, 28, 389, 495, 2807; behavior control, 403; behavior traits, children and adolescents, 1844; centeredness, 583; child-rearing, 38; client, 1080; conduct, 2251; educational, 131; educational-vocational, 38; elementary school, 1108; emotional, child, 1082; industrial, 150, 151; instructional television, 488; job, 1968; sexual marital, 38; social interpersonal, 38; solving, 264-267, 456, 884-895, 1465-1469, 2200-2234, 3316, 3429, 3435, 3437-3440; solving ability, 2226; solving, adequacy, 764; solving, behavior, 3280; solving, children, 893, 1468, 3433, 3436; solving, client perceptions, 764; solving, disadvantaged children, 892, 894; solving, interpersonal, 2576; solving, preschool, 892; solving, skills, 2225; solving, strategies, 1467, 3432; solving, teacher, 1232, 2804; solving, therapist perception, 764; student, 1336, 2859; supervisor, 996; wives, 1306
Procedure(s), 600, 694, 695: sampling, 161
Processing: activity, 577; cognitive, 3193; reactive, 421
Procrastination, 3281: attitudes, 2769; behavior, 2868, 2869
Production, 676, 688: consumption, 302; foreman, 1013
Productivity, creative, 130

Profession, employee commitment, 1996
Professional(ism), 326, 327, 1816: activities, 657; attitudes, 82, 1815; commitment, 1815; identification, 1815; orientation, 539; responsibilities, counselors', 1003; role orientation, 539; self-attitudes, 82
Professors: female, 1754; preference for, 866
Proficiency, job, 320
Program: innovation, 160; planning, 694
Programmed instruction, 153
Prohibitions, 649
Project: complexity, 3103 Head Start, 637
Projection(s), 41, 850: fantasy, 579; role, 2512
Projectivity, 2253
Promotion, desire for, 2359
Pronunciation, 371
Propensity, social, 2611
Property, 593
Proportion, 1614
Protest: behavior, 1817; situational attitude, 1817
Protestant ministers, 519
Provocative child, 397
Proverbs, 1818
Pro-worldminded, 1795
Proxemic distance, 68
Psychiatric aide employees, 3592
Psychiatric: behavior, 1205; complaints, 773; evaluation, children, 2514; marital difficulties, 773; outpatients, 1681; patients, 489, 1654; progress, 2452; symptoms, 2515, 2539; treatment, 773, 3120; vocational problems, 773
Psychiatric rating, 405, 1079
Psychodynamic mental health, 880
Psychological: adjustment, 28-43,

421; androgyny, 2176; anomie, 413; dependence, 2199; distance, 50, 56; distress, 35, 2493; health, attitude, 1137; help, attitude, 2743; influence, 3324; moods, 1669; needs, 1339; reports and service, attitude toward, 154; separation, 3040; state, 841; stress, 2517; testing, 1127; well-being, 2493

Psychologist: attitudes, 154; perceived, 3265; stress, 2662

Psychology: attitude toward, 1127; occupations in, 142, 903

Psychopath(ic)(y), 855-857: criminal, 2518

Psychopathology, dimensions of, 412, 2448, 3346

Psychosexual maturity, 1668

Psychosocial: development, 632, 1941, 2945, 2947, 2955; environment, 1960

Psychosomatic complaints, 2480, 2516

Psychotherapists and patients, 306

Psychotherapy, 1137: check list, 2519; evaluation, 1080; fear of, 2451; process, 2352, 2616

Psychotic symptoms, 773, 853

Psychoticism, 1681

Public exposure to sexual stimuli, 1761

Public policy issues, 1797

Public school(s), 687: teaching, 539

Pun, 613

Punishment: capital, 1750; direct object, 654; parental intensity, 1949; symbolic love, 654

Punitive-controlling, 652

Punitiveness, attitudes, 2770

Pupil: affect, 1217; attitude, 455, 540; behavior, 574, 578; control, 810; control ideology, 1819, 2117, 2771, 3105, 3282, 3283; development, 637; evaluation, 3374; ideal, 1929; information acquisition, 1; interaction, 1027; interest by teacher, 1027; observation by teacher, 1027; opinion, 541, 1820; ratings, 2870; ratings by teachers, 297, 298; responses, 1267; self-esteem, 3276; teacher, 600

Q sort, 822, 831, 1678

Qualit(ies)(y), 681: class, 3116; college departments, 3067; education, 663; leadership, 338; mathematics, lecture, 3086

Quantitative, achievement, 1043, 1063; aptitude, 1732

Questions, classroom, 1266

Races, tolerance of, 1792

Racial: academic predictor, 2684; attitudes, 46, 78, 79, 87, 88, 482, 520, 542, 1147, 1176, 1804, 1812, 1813; attitude, first grade, 1813; attitude, preliterate children, 1814; attitude, preschool, 1814; evaluation, 3448; factors, 386; identity attitudes, 2772, 2773; intermarriage attitudes, 90; preference, 865, 1459; relations, 76, 99; stereotype, 520, 1154

Radicalism, 280, 529: -conservatism, 1821

Rapport: with students, 33; teacher, 1891

Rating: applicant, 3588; college course, 1024; counseling interviews, 699, 3594; counselor, 35, 72, 3573, 3595; curriculum, 706; managers, 3580; peer, 2556; police, 3577, 3579, 3587; sales person, 3596, 3598; scales, descriptive, 215; students, 24; teacher, 1028, 2395; work

trainee, 338
Rational, 2205, 2206: behavior, 1679, 1874, 2774, 2871
Rationality, 1679, 2931
Reaction, counseling, 311
Reactive, inhibition, 399
Readers, retarded, 340
Readiness, for first grades: reading, 352, 356, 357, 1118; school, 469; vocational planning, 470; words, 337
Reading, 2, 12, 15, 21, 340, 516, 543, 1048: achievement, 350, 1035-1037, 1043, 1063, 1598; achievement, first-grade, 602; adult and college, 20; and spelling ability, perception of, 2147; attitude, 543, 544, 1175, 1787, 1822, 1823, 2741, 2763, 2775; attitude, elementary school, 1822; black and white students, 2; comprehension, 14, 20, 1055, 1062, 1609, 2388, 2688; comprehension, college students, 1615; consultant, 1334; difficulty, source of, 340; failures, 475; formal, 352; functional skills, 1602; informal, 350; input, 372; instruction, fourth grade, 544; instruction, individualizing, 545; kindergarten, 352; levels, 375; maturity, 1053; miscue, 2391; oral, 2388, 2391; performance, 1744; pre-, 352; preference, 1455, 1460; rate, 1039; readiness, 352, 356, 357, 1121; retention, 1616; skills, 366, 1038; span, 2392; storage, 373; teacher survey, 545; teaching in content classrooms, 1763; teaching of, 559
Real estate, success, 2686
Realism: color, 830; size, 434, 830, 2296
Reality, perceptions, 3173
Rearing adolescents, 490

Reasoning, 889, 1738: ability, 2204; ability, formal, 2231, 3419, 3428, 3442; abilities, concrete, 2227; abstract, 2201, 2202, 3424; abstract, junior high, 884; analogical, 3418; deductive-inductive, 3426; logical, 3427, 3441; moral, 2212, 2218, 2219, 2222, 3531, 3558; proportional, 3420; scientific, 2232
Rebellious independence, 481
Recall, 4, 8, 346, 359, 360, 361, 382: perception, adults, 533
Receptivity to change, 301
Reciprocal inhibitions, 399
Recognition, 2, 363, 366, 374, 663: interrogative patterns, 380, 384; word, 342
Reconstruction, 13
Recruit(ers)(ment): job, 518; student athletes, 3413
Referential communication, 2923
Referral, 2191: process, 2119
Reflection, 689: impulsivity, 285, 290, 291, 1490, 1494, 2170, 2272
Reflective observation, 2216
Reflectivity, 2262
Reflexes, interpersonal, 448
Refusal behavior, 1857, 2803
Regard: level, 1538; unconditional positive, 431
Regression, adaptive, 606
Rehabilitation, 337: clients, 29; counseling, 692, 1057; counselor effectiveness, 1561; gain, 693; industrial, 515; services, 182; vocational, 691
Reinforcement: by others, 44; children, 1853; contingencies, 1434; counselors, 1545; delay of, 58, 239; expectation, 69; positive, 2188, 2189; preferences, primary children, 739; social, 725, 2925;

social, for retardates, 725
Reinforcers: effectiveness, 734; effect on children, 282; individual, 2018; survey for therapy, 735; teacher, 736
Rejection, 69, 583: by authority, 499; manifest, 496; need, Mexican-American, 738; sensitivity to, 44, 1726; verbal, 585
Relatedness behavior, 432
Relations: family, 141, 142, 645; intergenerational, 99; interpersonal, 50, 51, 431, 464, 575, 1102, 2577; job, with associates, 709; job, with employees, 709; mothers, 419; other people, 593; parent-child, 148; parent-daughter, 1303; racial, 99; school community, 1827; social, 1106; students, 679; teacher-pupil, 256
Relationship(s), 431, 884: affective, quality of, 640; counseling, 1003, 1268, 2899-2901; family, 1951; father, 653; interpersonal, 1256, 1716, 2548, 2588; intimate, 2580, 2592; inventory, 309, 1262, 1538; marital, 1766, 3018; peer, 397, 472, 675, 2601; residence counselor, 1019; self-other, 1728; sibling, 3044; spouse, 3045; student-teacher, 2416; supervisors, 1023; therapeutic, 330, 2559; therapist, 995
Relative clauses, 377
Relativism, 3527: religious, 3555
Religion, 485, 593, 2237: attitude, 1178; commitment, 982; conventional orientation to, 2312; dogma, 983; experiences, and activities, 675, 1514, 1580; groups, 183; identification, 988
Religiosity, 2322, 3553, 3554

Religious: beliefs, 2323, 3525, 3526; experience, mystical dimensions, 2324; relativism, 3555; values, 3534
Remedial mathematics, 508
Remembered past, 812
Reminiscence, 812
Remote: associates, 610; associational ability, 610; remote, 1601
Repression, 293, 612, 840: sensitivity, 951, 1502, 3503, 3504; sensitivity in counseling, 921
Reproductive, knowledge, 1056
Research: and thinking skills, 1606; article rating, 693; concept-educational, 1746; education, 1752; organizational, 1331; orientation, 1816; teacher orientation, 550
Resentment, 1638, 2252
Residence: assistants, 1487; continuity, 466; counseling positions, candidates, 546; counselor, 1006; counselor evaluation, 1006; counselor, job rating, 1019; counselor, objectives for, 546; counselor relationships, 1019; counselor, student perception, 1020; environment, university, 704; innovative university, 704; interest, 1019; residence vs. nonresidence counseling, 546; roommate preference, 262; viewpoints, 546
Residents: interviews with, 546; methods of discipline, 546
Resignation, 2278
Resolution, conflict, 1857
Resources, 575: human, 3077
Respect, 3366
Responding, associative, 264
Response: acquiescence, college

student, 930; echoic, 7; styles, children, 843; system, verbal, 588
Responsibilit(ies)(y), 16: counselor, 314; development, ethnic differences, 762; development in children, 58, 762; for others, 1687; intellectual achievement, 786; school counselors, 314; social, 58, 462, 915, 1113
Responsiveness, 666: maternal, 2273
Restraint, eating habits, 1876
Restrictiveness, social, 530, 1807
Retail bargaining, 1762
Retail store manager, 1560
Retardates: social inference, 1114; social reinforcement, 725
Retarded, 405, 479: adolescents, 1619; children, flexibilities, 923; readers, 340; reading, 1616; work adjustment, of, 1033
Retirement, reasons for early, 669
Reversals, perceptions of, 813, 850
Reward(s): by supervisor, 1005; contingency, 2120; direct object, 654; level, 2598, 3144; marriage, 3041; preference, 261; symbolic love, 654
Rhythm, auditory visual, 750
Rhythmicity, 2285
Right-left discrimination, 1943
Rigidity, 917, 1377, 1477, 1486, 1500, 2286
Riots and demonstrations, attitudes toward, 482
Risk orientations, 1786
Risk taking, 861, 1077, 1234, 2160, 2161, 2172, 2255, 2776
Rod and frame, 776, 815
Role(s), 3053: ambiguity, 1687, 2357, 2525, 3288, 3289, 3292; ambiguity, perceptions, 2121; choice, 869; concepts, counseling, 313, 3199; conflict, 1687, 2122, 2357, 2526, 2641, 3002, 3289, 3292; conflict, counselors, 314; conflict, perceptions, 2121, 2123; consistency, 1461; constructs, 219, 816; counselor's, 332; deviant, 3202; expectations, 3291; family, 302; female, attitude, 2742; force, negotiators, 324; graduate student, 2426; guidance director's, 318; identification, 331; mother, 652, 2970; orientation, 263; orientation, professional 539; peer, 2590; perception, teachers, 2038; primary, 713; projection, 2512; repertory, 1465; sick, 1239; strain, 1667; stress, 2525-2527; student, 2590; taking, 579, 1096, 1236, 1503, 3259; vocational, 3660; work, 2672
Romantic: attitudes, 2777; love, 295, 2599, 2600
Roommate preference, 262
Rule(s), 695: conformity, 967; -orientation behavior, 2158

Sad mood, 1670
Safety: practice, supervisor's, 1073; traffic, 1622
Sales person, rating, 3596, 3598
Salience, 1422: career, 3260, 3621, 3638; work, 2672; work role, 3665
Sampling procedures, 161
Satisfaction: attainment of students, 714; body image, 2044; body in adolescents, 756; client, 182, 999, 3059; college major, 872; college student, 663, 1961, 2407; communication, 2904; community, 3060; congregation, 3062; counseling, 3564; course, 175; employee, 164, 2362; environment, 1965; job, 709, 1575, 1577, 1578, 1581-1586, 1588, 1589, 1592, 1595, 1668,

2320, 2624, 2625, 2629-2637, 2657, 2659, 2668, 2670, 2675; leadership, 2345; life, 33, 415, 2504, 2529; marital, 648, 2967, 3007, 3020, 3027, 2038, 3035; Navy, 2661; need, 1356; occupational, 709; parental, 3008; pay, 2652; student, 159; task, 2663; training, 310, 320; university student, 705; work, 178, 2673; work schedule, 2660
Scales, recommended, 666
Scanning, 612: internal, 1914, 2932
Schedul(e)(ing), 694: modular, 1328
Schizophreni(a)(c)(s), 526, 1084, 1085, 1224, 1504, 2491: patients, improvement, 306; socialization, 1111
Scholastic: activities and attitude, 556; potential in women, 1739; women's potential, 1119
School(s), 491, 494, 497, 516, 532: acceptance, 1070; administrators, 528; administrator morale, 1680, 1978; attitude toward, 66, 155, 540, 541, 1136, 1149, 1181, 1825, 2778, 2779; attitude, peer counseling, 1973; beginners, black & white, 655; behavior, 1238; behavior adjustment, 1628; bureaucratic structure, 695; children, 629; climate, 3108; -community relations, 1827; competence, 460; counselor attitude, 1826; desegregated, 452; disadvantaged, 434; drop-out prediction, 476; elementary, 1723; elementary-inner city, 990; enthusiasm toward, 540; feelings toward, 1825; guidance evaluation, 687; history, 625; interest, 391; last year, 494; motivation, 737, 2004, 3151; nongraded, 574; nursing, 694; organization, 695; orientation, 547; orientation attitude, 534; perception of, 700, 3055; picture stories, 738; principal, 3107; psychologist stress, 2662; rating, 548; readiness, 469; related experiences and aspirations, 472; satisfaction, general, 2147; self-esteem, 2064; sentiment, 1179; situations, 700; situations, student survey of, 700; subjects, attitudes, 2745; subjects, ratings intermediate grade, 871; success, prediction of, 71; work, 593
Science: aptitude, 1732; attitudes, 2793; interest, intermediate children, 864
Scientists, creative potential, 1933
Screening interviewee candidates, 1013
Seat belt: attitudes, 1828, 2780; beliefs, 1829
Second-language, elementary school English, 1598
Secondary: reading attitude, 1824; school, 1787; social studies, 600; student, 368, 369, 537, 549; students' attitudes, 93; students' political attitude, 537; teacher evaluation, 1030
Security, 502, 2317: child, 3037; job, 709, 1687
Seeking professional psychological help, 1764
Selection: counselor, 104; job, 3632; supervisors, 1017
Self-, 241, 250, 494, 499, 551: acceptance, 252, 759, 831, 1425, 1880, 2125; acceptance, social, 499; actualization, 214, 2367, 3285, 3286; adjustment, 409; aggression, 242; appraisal, 472; appraisal, curiosity, 2021; assessment depression, 1692;

assessment of emotions, 2165; assurance, 1101, 1427, 2265; attitude, 1439; attitude of disabled, 752; centrality, 249; concept, 219, 230, 243, 252, 255, 300, 472, 755, 759, 787, 796, 798, 823, 824, 1279, 1376, 1389, 1394, 1395, 1402, 2108, 2109, 2123, 2127, 2129, 2130, 2171, 2239; concept, academic, 2030, 3153, 3301, 3303; concept, academic interest and satisfaction, 2056; concept, actual ideal, 748; concept, adolescent, 2103; concept, anxiety, 1381; concept, blood donor, 3174; concepts, children, 807, 3186, 3213, 3221, 3232, 3250, 3254, 3279, 3297; concept, college students, 2035, 3300, 3305; concept, counselor, 822; concept, crystallization, vocational, 2155; concept, global, 1398; concept, leadership and initiative, 2056; concept, learner, 3299; concept, level of aspiration, 2056; concept, male college students, 199; concept, math, 1409, 3247, 3248; concept, middle childhood, 243; concept of ability, 1850; concept of academic ability, 2128; concept, primary, 2114, 2115; concept, primary children, 763; concept spouse, 3298; concept, stability, 2145; concept, student, 1424, 3304, 3321; concepts, general adequacy, peer, teacher-school, academic, physical, 2069, 3338; confidence, 338; confidence, intellectual, 2073; confidence, social, 1715; consciousness, 1880, 2510, 3202, 3376; control, 2714, 2873, 3185; criticism, 244; deception, 3510; derogation, 2131; description, 749, 1369;

directed classroom, 1969; directed learning readiness, 1742, 2193; disclosure, 104, 589, 590, 591, 593, 598, 599, 1254, 1258, 1263-1265, 1895, 1899, 1902; discrimination, 1431; efficacy, 3180, 3216, 3256, 3306-3308; enhancement, 1994; enhancement derogation, children, 843; esteem, 213, 246, 249, 272, 286, 296, 434, 499, 515, 636, 788, 800, 817, 2053, 2054, 2061, 2082, 2124, 2126, 2133, 2135-2138, 2140, 2141, 2149, 3212, 3229, 3293-3296, 3309, 3311, 3314, 3315; esteem, academic, 2031, 3154, 3155, 3278; esteem, adults, 2046; esteem, adult males, 826; esteem, children, 458, 2039, 3197, 3206; esteem, college students, 816, 2139; esteem, disadvantaged children, 830; esteem, dropouts, 827; esteem, high school students, 827, 3313; esteem, low, 1670; esteem, preadolescent, 825; esteem, pupil, 3276; esteem, school, home, peer, 2064; esteem, student, 792, 2134, 3310; esteem, task, 3328, 3329; estimate ability, 766; estrangement, 430, 457, 1701; evaluated intelligence, 247; evaluation, 828; evaluation, employee, 1008; expectations, 212, 1432; focus, 1484; global, 1793; ideal, 252, 759; involvement, 796; justification, 746; needs, 3316; non-professional attitudes, 82; other relationships, 1728; peer, 1359; perceived popularity, 458; perception, 748, 755, 819, 829, 3273; perception, children, 3187, 3260; perception, counselor,

1426; perception, engineering students, 829; perception, gifted, 1124; perception, group behavior, 778; perception, health, 779; perception, interpersonal relations, 780; perception, preschool, 835; perception, pupil, 1105; poverty, children, 798; presentation, 2558; rated ability, 305; rated abrasiveness, 749; rated anxiety, 911; rated attractiveness, 749; rated occupational interest, 196; rating, 550, 1410; rating clients, 310; rating, college students, 248; rating, counselors, 769; realization, 2317; regard, 556; regulation, college student, 145; rejection, 449; report, 551; respect, loss of, 515; rightousness, 3512; satisfaction of adolescents, 756; social, 1728; social constructs, 830; social constructs, children, 434; subordination, 967; value, 400; worth, 1880
Semantic: classes, 358; differential, 307, 1180, 1181, 1192; flexibility, 210; implications, 266, 359; transformations, 11, 127; units, 3360
Sensation seeking, 2023-2025, 2172, 3146, 3147
Sense of competence, 2070
Sensitivity, 283, 443, 444: aesthetic, 2034; affective, 98, 428, 429, 1252; interpersonal, 428, 444; noise, 2099, 2850, 3110; personal feelings, 500; repression, 951; repression in counseling, 921; to rejection, 1726; training, 186, 220
Sensitization-repression, 1875
Sensory expressive style, 594
Sentence: completion, 796, 863; complexity, 7; construction, 377; elements, elaborative, 377; imitation, 376, 377
Separation problems, 397, 2975, 2977, 3040
Series learning potential, 1743
Set: educational, 1068, 1350; size, 345
Sex, 593: discrimination, 3085; education course, high school, 668; -exaggerated concern, 2253; information, 2393; role(s), 284, 288, 552, 795, 878, 2194, 2195, 3167; role achievement standards, 877; -role adoption, 2192; -role, artistic achievement, 887; role, athletic achievement, 877; -role attitude, 1831, 2720, 2760; -role, attitude toward, 552, 2699, 2782, 2783, 2787; role, children, 881, 3188; -role, concepts, adult, 2132; role development, 137; -role, female, 2303; role identity, 3294; role, kindergarten children, 883; role, mathematics achievement, 877; role, mechanical achievement, 877; role orientation, 874, 3389; -role perceptions, 2110; -role preference, 2181, 3414; role, reading achievement, 877; role, social skills, 877; -role socialization, 2360; -role stereotypes, 1482, 2196, 3318, 3319
Sexual: attitudes, 2781; behavior, 485, 1747, 2875; fantasy, 2876; goings-on, 2253; ideology, 3411; marital problems, 38; stimuli, public exposure to, 1761; symbolism, 114; thoughts, 1260
Shop, attitude toward, 1182
Shyness, 3573
Sight-sound, 1

Sight word, 2937
Silent child, 397
Similarities, 608, 619
Simil(e)(ies): appreciation, 2938; performance, 1054
Simultaneous movement, 348
Situational response, 1462
Sixth-grade pupils, 659
Skill(s), 661: academic, 400; arithmetic, 637; auditory blending, 1036; auditory segmentation, 1037; auto-driving, 478; classification, 627; communication, 175, 2913; counseling, 1543, 3578; functional reading, 1602; interpersonal, 431; junior high school, 700; leading process, 1860; personal, 3320; problem-solving, 2225; reading, 336; reasoning, 3427, 3428; research and thinking, 1606; social, 1697, 2602, 2608-2610; supervisors, 3652; utilization of, 1687; work, 338; writing, 364
Slang, 1058
Sleep: behavior, 2877; disturbance, 1870
Small group, 596
Smoking, 1748
Sociability, 1099, 1720, 1870: student, 24
Social, 624, 2173: acceptance, 1104; acceptance, children, 2593; access, 1452; achievement, 2298; adjustment, 44-70; affection, 417; affiliation, 2367; alienation, 1098; and existential courage, 1832; anxiety, 2604, 2605; anxiousness, 2551; approval, 48, 449, 2586; attributes, 561; attitude(s), 554, 555, 1513, 1527; behavior, 388; behavior, children, 842, 963, 964; behavior, positive/negative, 390; change, 92; class, children, 3189; closeness, 1723; competence, 425, 459, 1719; competence, adolescent girls, 2595; competence, children, 2567, 2606; competence, general, 636; constructs, children, 434; contact, intimate, 1707; control, 52, 174; dependency, 434; deprivation, 466; desirability, 49, 62, 251, 281, 296, 435, 438, 441, 449, 450, 2557, 2585; development, 637; diffusion, 460; distance, 63, 535, 1144, 1184, 1185, 1723; egocentricism, 1109; emotional, 1108; fraternities, 486; functioning, 2607; future time perspective, 832; history, 466; inequality, 3445, 3446; inference, 1114, 1619; institutions, 1060; integration, 2399; intelligence, 1096, 1099, 1100, 2555, 2564; interest, 249; interpersonal problem, 38; intimacy, 2587; introversion, 1670; isolation, 437, 1110, 1709, 1727; issues, 1146; justice, 381; life, 663; maturity, 636; morals concepts, comprehension, 1599, 2300; moral values, 472; nonconformity, 1725; orientation, 1101; orientation, university residence, 704; performance, 2608-2610; personal adjustment, 397; power, 460, 1112, 3129, 3132; preference, 789; problems, 419; propensity, 2611; reinforcement responsiveness, 725; relations, 456, 464; relations, middle childhood, 244; responsibility, 58, 462, 915, 1113; responsibility, attitudes, 94; responsiveness, 1235; restrictiveness, 530, 1807; roles, 461; roles, females', 1755; schemas, 440; self-acceptance, 499; self-confidence, 1715;

situations, children, 2613; skills, 1697, 2602; skills, sex role, 877; stratification, 268; studies, attitude, 1138; studies, elementary school, 1060, 1282; studies, high school, 601; studies programs, secondary school, 600; studies, student teachers, 600; support, 215, 2578, 2988; vocabulary, 252; welfare concern, 462; welfare curriculum, 162; withdrawal, 50, 56; work concepts, 1277; work majors, 674
Socialization, 61, 236, 855-857: children's play, 60; schizophrenic, 1111
Society, 497
Sociocentric, 2186
Socio-economic status, 270, 277, 482, 898, 899, 1471-1473; college freshmen, 904; low, 1065; preschool children, 59
Socio-emotional: climate index, 583; problematic, 578
Sociology departments, 676, 685
Sociometric: analysis of students, 1695; measure, 214; nominations, 1713
Solitude, 2317
Somatic: concern, 405, 1079; discomfort, 571
Somatization, 1663, 1681, 1870
Somatotype, perceived, 3263
Sound-symbol relationship, 366
Space, 747: personal, 1107, 1418; relations, 1738
Spanish, 380: visual discrimination, 2394
Spatial: ability, 1061; aptitude, 479; egocentricism, 1485; orientation, 1433; orientation and visualization, 2042, 2048, 2106, 2116, 2144; relations, 2060; visualization, 2097

Speakers, 1765, 2913
Speech, 388: active, 397; aphasic, 1887; forms, private, 1491; imitation, 349; passive, 397
Speed, 1361: of closure, 1612, 1617; motor, 1610; perceptual, 1604, 1608, 1618
Spelling, 108: and reading ability, perception of, 2147; sound, 1062
Spouse: abuse, 3000; relationship, 3045; self-concept, 3298
Stability of self-concept, 2145
Staff, 523, 3112, 3113
State anxiety, 1682, 2440
State guidance office function, 697
Statistics: attitude toward, 2701, 2786; basic, 2372
Status, 268-277, 896-906, 1470-1475, 2235-2239: academic, college freshmen, 904; classroom, 659; concern, 1475; developmental, 481; distance, Mexican-American migrants, 902; ego identity, 628; family, 2987; identity achievement, 271; jobs, 273, 275, 276, 2645; occupational, 276, 1470; socioeconomic, 270, 482, 898, 899, 1471-1474, 3444; socioeconomic, college freshmen, 905
Stereotype(s), 2253, 3169: banking, 156; body build, 561; girls, activity, 2032; Italian, 3228; mathematics, 3245; occupational, 270, 3642; political, 1186; racial, 520, 1154, 1198; sex role, 1482, 2196, 3318, 3319; vocational role, 3660
Stimulation, 666: auditory, 1233; home, 642; seeking, 741
Stimulus: child, 185; expressions, 38; seeking, 2847; varying input need, 1992
Strain: occupational, 1686, 2627,

2638; role, 1667
Stratification, social, 268
Street language, 378
Stress: 423, 841, 1672, 1673, 1677, 1687, 2434, 2466, 2488, 2489, 2501, 2532, 2535, 2537, 2543: administrative, 2617; adolescent, 2435; children, 2536; combat related, 2454; coping behavior, 2830; counselor, 2620; elderly, 2531; environmental, 3071; evaluative, 1627, 1694; high school, 2481; job related, 2621, 2638, 2639, 2641, 2642, 2649, 2650, 2654, 2658; life events, 2531, 2533; medical school, 2419, 2425; nursing, 2639, 2648; psychological, 2517; role, 2525-2527; school psychologist, 2662; subjective, 1086, 2484; teacher, 2655, 2665, 2666, 3117; undergraduates, 833, 2415, 2423
Striving, achievements, 716
Structure(d): bureaucratic, 1309; cognitive, 218; conceptual, 604; job, 3084; need for, 2208; need for in adolescents, 760, 1070, 1378, 1991; organizational, 1332; situation, 656
Student(s), 581, 662, 680: ability, junior college, 766; academic aspiration, 2027; academic attitude, 1126; activism, 1483, 2879; activities, university, 705, 1293; adolescent, 1430; affective behavior, 568; alienated, 455, 582; aspiration, disadvantaged, 740; athlete, 3413; attainment satisfaction, 714; attitudes and beliefs, 556, 859, 1160, 1163, 1188-1190, 1193, 1194; autonomy, 333; behavior, 578, 603, 737, 2824; -centered characteristics, 581; -centered classroom, 1969; -centeredness, junior high,

middle school teachers, 1867; cognitive behavior, 568; cognitive processing, 3423; counselor, 1021; counselor contacts, 665; disadvantaged, 679; drug attitudes, 1145; effects on white fifth-grade, 88; engineering, 829; evaluation of teachers, 690, 698, 1009, 1014, 1022, 1027, 1029, 1032, 1562-1565, 1567-1572; evaluation of instructors, 2348; efforts, 2349; faculty perceptions about academic advising, 1959; faculty relations, 675, 694; feelings toward whites, 2157; foreign, 1094; freedom, 586; graduate, 528, 2426; high risk, 1189; high school occupational aspiration, 897, 901; influence, university residence, 704; interracial attitudes, 535; junior high school, 700; learning environment, 3114; male high school occupational aspiration, 901; notes, 379; opinion, 95; outcomes, 687; perception, 175, 3322; perception of advisers, 993; perceptions of teacher, 1027; performance aspects, 568; performance attribution, 3323; personal, 859; philosophical orientation, 3552; preference, 263; problem behavior, 2589; relations with, 679; roles, 2590; satisfaction, 159, 1071; satisfaction, university, 705; self-concept, 1429, 3304; self-esteem, 2134, 3310, 3313; social work majors, 674; sociometric analysis, 1695; stress, 2415, 2423, 2424; suicide, 1087, 1088; superior, 680; survey of school situations, 700; teacher, 701; teacher, concerns of, 701; teacher, elementary school, 495,

701; teacher evaluation, 3590, 3602; teacher relationships, 2416, 2911; teachers, social studies, 600; test anxiety, 387; -student counseling, 1000; tutors, 322; university, 442, 586; white & black, 2
Study: habits, 23, 1105, 2883; individualized, 6; practices, 169; strategy, 1072, 1073
Style: behavioral, 564; categorization, 1464; cognitive, 1479; ideational expressive, 594; instructional, 288; interpersonal, 1489; leader's motivational, 2184; supervisors, 3603
Sub-cultural identification, 95
Submission, 2253
Submissiveness, 1720, 3464
Substance, 2224: use, attitudes, 2790
Substitution, symbol, 340
Success: athletic, 3215; avoidance, 1362, 2228; computer science, 2679; employment, 241; failure, 526, 1373; fear of, 1658-1660, 1676, 1833, 2410, 2411, 2470-2471, 2478, 2500, 2545; military training, 3582; negative consequences, 2455; potential, 338; scholastic, 74
Suffering, 417
Suggestibility, 279, 914, 2902
Suicid(al)(e), 1088, 2521, 2538: attitude toward, 1192; contemplation, 1087; ideators, 2530; intent, 1688; potential, 1671, 2485
Summarizing, 2215
Super-ego complaints, 773
Superintendent(s): behavior, 1307; political orientation, 972
Superior students, 680
Supernatural phenomena, 1139

Superstition, 2253
Supervisor(s): ability, 1019, 2265; attitude, 1023; beginning, 996; behavior, 1241, 3325; communication, 1023; compliance, 1005; counselor, 1317; credibility, 1556; dependability, 1023; evaluation of, 1017, 1023; group direction, 1005; initiative, 1023; interaction, 1248; job knowledge, 1005, 1023; judgment, 1023; knowledge, 1023; leadership style, 1023; loyalty of, 1005; organization, 1023; power, 1231; problems of, 996; relationships, 1023; rewards by, 1005; safety practice, 1023, 1073; satisfaction with, 1552; selection of, 1017; skills, 3562; style of, 183, 3603; subordinate, 2915, 2916; teaching, 1023; training needs, 1005
Support, 689: parental, 640, 3038; social, 2578
Suspicion, 2252
Symbol: recognition, 1118; substitution, 112, 340; transformations, 126
Symbolic: classes, 361; implications, 129, 362; love-punishment, 654; love-reward, 654; units, 363
Symbolism, sexual, 114
Symptom(s): anxiety, 2441; checklist, 425, 1084, 1663; neurotic, 2480; patients', 1663; physical, 773; psychiatric, 2515, 2539; psychopathology, 2448; psychotic, 773
Synonyms, 3
Syntactic: comprehension, 383; contrasts, 383; principle, 383; structures, 349, 355
Syntax, 5
Synthesis, 600

Taboo words, 1274
Tactics, 1882
Tactile body accessibility, 592
Talent, therapeutic, 3383
Target game, 618
Task(s): arousal, 3149; concern by teacher, 333; challenge, 1981; complexity, 3115; effectiveness, 214; motivation, 3137; orientation, 1101; orientation, positive/negative, 390; -oriented behavior, 1854; preference, 205, 2178; satisfaction, 2317, 2663; success, 3207
TAT, 204, 268, 726, 929
Teacher(s), 483, 484, 494, 566, 581, 621: affect, 1217; ambition, 1363, 1364; approval-disapproval, 659; attitude, 557, 559, 1167, 1195, 1196; attitude toward, 541, 549, 580; attitude toward gifted children, 558; behavior, 580, 582, 811, 2887, 2888, 2892, 3406, 3604-3606; burnout, 2664; -centered characteristics, 581; -centered, classroom, 969; characteristics, 684, 1022; -child, interpersonal perceptions, 2076; college, effectiveness, 2334; constellation of forces, 2057; decision making, 836, 3434; desirable, 679; directiveness, 936; effectiveness, 1026, 1030, 3331, 3607; elementary, 341, 348, 2691; evaluation, 698, 997, 1009, 1014, 1022, 1027-1029, 1032; evaluation by colleagues, 1541, 1542, 1550, 1551; evaluation by students, 1022, 1562-1565, 1567-1572, 3589, 3600, 3601; evaluation, secondary, 1030; feedback, 1885; ideal, 679; identification with, 434, 830; independence, 578; interactions, 1029, 1251; interest in pupils, 1027; interpersonal relations, 2577; job-related attitudes, 1827; junior high school, 700; knowledge, drug, 1130; leadership style, 1507, 2889; leisure activities, 870; locus of control, 3332-3334; loyalty, 1883; militancy, 1495; moonlighting, 226; motivation by, 1029; observation of pupils, 1027; of mentally retarded, 154; orientation toward research, 550; perception of administration, 1408; perception of children's learning, 2038; perceptions of counselor role, 332; perception of students, 24; performance, 997, 1027; personality, 1027; preference, 866, 880; presentation, 1029; primary directiveness, 936; principal, 595; promotion, 1364; pupil, 600; pupil control, 1523; pupil relations, 256, 1266, 1267; rapport, 1891; rating of sex role development, 136; rating of student, 24, 297, 298, 1043, 1063, 2890, 2891; ratings, 1028, 2395; ratings of composition, 1059; reinforcing behaviors, 736; role perception, 2038; secondary school, 2347; stimulation by, 1029; stress, 2655, 2665, 2666, 3117; student perceptions of, 1027; student relationships, 2416, 2911; style, 333, 1571; survey reading, 545; temperament, 1884; tests, 1029; training, perceptions, 1982; value of disadvantaged, 990; verbal pattern, 1255
Teaching, 492: assessment, 1029; attitude toward, 1140, 2716; by supervisors, 1023; competence, 1015, 1026; effectiveness, 335, 2333, 2347, 3330; faculty, 2331;

method, 679; method, evaluation of, 698; observation, 1015; of reading, 559; practice, 690; process, 488, 3536; public school, 539; rating, 1025; reading in content classrooms, 1763; style(s), 694, 882; urban school success, 1593
Team teaching, 334, 1140
Technology, attitude toward, 1162
Tedium, 2540, 2643, 2674
Television: commercial attitudes, 2722; instructional, 488; watching behavior, 1207
Temperament, 1846, 2291, 3356: child and infant, 2254, 2285, 2811, 2817, 2840, 3342, 3345, 3347, 3348, 3351, 3352, 3357, 3358, 3362-3365, 3370, 3375, 3378-3381, 3384, 3385
Tempo, conceptual, 604
Temporal experiences, 2080
Tendenc(ies)(y): affiliative, 44; to achieve, 2006
Tendermindedness, 529
Tenseness, 1641
Tension, 1079, 1666, 1690, 2542, 2638, 2639: index, 1667; job, 2640, 2667
Test(s): anxiety, 25, 26, 32, 209, 392, 393, 395, 396, 398, 399, 401, 402, 713, 1074-1076, 1625, 1627, 1629, 1633, 1635, 2428-2430: anxiety, college students, 1634; anxious students, 387; attitude toward, 1453, 2791, 2792; behavior, 1242; clerical, 73; graduate students, 2427; parameters, 161; taking skills, 1620; wiseness, 385, 1064, 1620, 1621, 3443
Testing: practices, 190; program, pre-college, 480
Text(books), 666: appraisal, 1983; evaluation, 1325; quality, 667
Theft, 1244
Theory, preferences, 54
Therapeutic: outcome, 3119; relationships, 330, 2559; talent, 3383
Therapist: assessment of, 995; attitudes, 96; behavior, 2197; client, 2903; expectancy, 3336; perception, problem solving, 764; relationship with, 995; self-disclosure, 1254
Therapy: goals, 1365; rating, 3090; reinforcers for, 735; relationship, 1262; session, 191
Thinking, 568, 730: complex integrative, 891; consequential, 815; creative, 1924; divergent, 608; dogmatic, 953; doing, 216; imaginative, 1282; overinclusive, 1224; sexual, 1260; skills, 2215
Thoughtfulness, 987
Thoughts: covert, 3201; positive and negative, 2402, 2403
Threat, 299: of instruction, 488; perceived in ambiguous situations, 2077; reaction to, 346
Thrust, 688
Ties, family, 302
Time: adolescents, 772; affective attitude toward, 91; experience, 1400, 1420; future perspective, 772; job demand, 2644; perspective, adults, 758; perspective, children, 772; perspective, college students, 782, 783, 790, 805, 834; perspective, future, 775, 806, 832, 3335; perspective, political future, 832
Time learning vs. learning for grades, 487
Tolerance: ambiguity, 481, 612, 646, 955, 965, 1505; bureaucratic,

1508; complexity, 612; delay, 1212; political, 537
Toughness, 2253
Toy preference, 883, 3414
Tradition(al)(ism), 624, 967: family, 3047; nontraditional values, 493, 3536
Traffic safety, 1622
Trainee: adjustment, 27; counselor, 596
Training, 661: behavior, 2863; counselor, 3568, 3570; dialect, 105; information, job, 709; judgment, 9; military, 3582; motivational, 3139; needs, supervisors, 1005; satisfaction, 310, 320; satisfaction, rehabilitation clients, 29; sensitivity, 186, 220
Trait(s): anxiety, 3478; frustration, 3517; inconsistency, intolerance, 2078; measurement, 278-299, 907-967, 1476-1510, 2240-2295, 3496, 3499, 3511, 3515; oral, 934; personality, 615; rating, 2251; worker, 339
Transcendence, 41
Transfer(s): student, college, 511; university, 192
Transformations, 106, 107, 111, 112, 117, 126-128, 267: word, 11
Translation, 600
Transportation, community, 1060
Traumas, early, 625
Treatment: environment, 1310, 3120; need of psychiatric patients, 773
Trust, 949, 958, 1497, 3366: dyadic, 2562; interpersonal, 954, 1504, 1718, 2269, 2914; political, 537; supervisor, 2359
Trustworthiness, 258, 2151: interviewer, 938; of human motives, 2288
Turning: against object, 850; against self, 850
Tutor(ing)(s): attitudes, 2794; observation of, 322; peer, 1240; student, 322, 2893
Type A Behavior, 1886, 3450, 3462, 3479, 3489, 3508, 3518

U-Tube, 1623
Unconditional positive regard, 227, 309, 1538
Unconditionality of regard, 2353
Underachievers, 400, 1069
Underdeveloped countries, 512
Undergraduate(s), 675, 683: as academic advisors, 993; stress, 833
Understanding, 689: empathetic, 1370; instructions, 1361; perceived, 3264; personal, 175
Unemployment, 515
Union: attitude, 1836, 1837, 2669, 2719, 3118, 3415; faculty membership, 3399
United States attitudes, 83
University, 509, 660, 704, 903: alienation, 465, 1730; counseling center, 409, 703; entrants, 708; environment, 1440; environment, independence, 704; experience, college freshmen, 904; faculty needs, 1356; instructors, 680; residence, academic achievement, 704; residence, change and maintenance, 704; residence, emotional support, 704; residence, innovation, 704; residence, intellectual growth, 704; residence, interpersonal relationships, 704; residence involvement, 704; residence, order and organization, 704; residence, personal growth, 704; residence, social orientation, 704; setting, 680; student activity, 705; student attitude, 705; student

influence, 704; student rigidity, 1486; transfers, 192, 218
Unusual meanings, 1914
Upward Bound Students, 45: locus of control, 238; self-esteem, 248; self-estimated intelligence, 247
Upward mobility, 3145

Valence, 2895
Valuelessness, 413
Values, 300-304, 968-991, 1398, 1511-1535, 2296-2328, 3535, 3540, 3549: acculturation, 2547, 3519; adolescents, 974, 3523; American, 1524; anti-industrial, 3521; children's, 66; Christian, 3525, 3526; clarification, 1511, 1533; college freshmen, 904; college students, 2308; constructs, interpersonal, 2304; cultural, 516; decision-making, 2314; educational administrators, 979; guidance practices, 185; human, 1529; instructional, 3547; instrumental, 2326; interest, 1535; job, 321; moral and social, 472; occupational, 2315; orientation, work, 2307; other-centered, 1526, 2327; perceptions of unmet democratic, 2055; prescriptive, 991; prescriptive in adolescent, 974; proscriptive, 991; self, 400; self-centered, 2327; social 1528; system, adolescent's, 2325; teachers, 990; terminal, 2326; traditional/nontraditional, 493; vocational, 1512; western, 976; women's role, 1530; work, 2320, 2321, 2328, 3520, 3559, 3608; work, intrinsic and extrinsic, 2316
Vandalism, 1245
Variety, tendency toward, 959, 1054
Verbal, 1738: absurdities, children, 895; achievement, 1043, 1063; analogy, 1065; automaticity, 2927; behavior, 2248; behavior system, client, 587; behavior, teacher, 583; checklist, 561, 1198; comprehension, 1904, 1912, 1915; development, 1300; hostility, 2252; incorporation, 585; information, 373; intelligence, 887; interaction, 596, 1261; nonverbal, 2921; originality, 1281; pattern, 1255; rejection, 585; response, counselor, 588; response system, 588; self-disclosure, 590; skills, 397
Verbalizer-visualizer, 1916
Vietnam, attitude toward, 81
Vigor, 502
Vindication motivation, 746
Visual: analysis, 1041, 1441; -auditory memory, 1066; -auditory perception, 765, 1414; -auditory rhythm, 750; discrimination, 356, 357, 1412, 1442, 2377, 2394; imagery, 265; imagery, vividness of, 2154; integration, 1596; judgment, 1115; matching, 285; memory, 2397; -motor coordination, 1118; -motor match, 2143; perception, 801, 808, 1735; perspectives, 1443; -social cues, decoding, 1619
Visualization: spatial, 2097; spatial orientation, 2042, 2048, 2106, 2116, 2144
Visualizer-verbalizer, 1916
Visuo-spatial memory, 2152
Vividness: imagery, 2040; of imagery production, 2153; of visual imagery, 2154
Vocabulary, 3, 4, 354, 377: comprehension, 365; oral, 380, 384; sight word, 2937; social, 252
Vocalization: age four, 134;

maternal, 649
Vocational, 10: adjustment, 1033; behavior, 202, 426; choice, 193, 204, 269, 1574, 1594; choice anxiety, 1648; choice motivation, 409, 707, 720; cognitive complexity, 707; commitment, 3656; complexity, 336; conflict, 2641; counseling, 670; decidedness, 2234; decision-making, 1579; development, 1291; evaluation, 305-339, 992-1034, 1536-1573, 2329-2359; goals, 511; home economics, teachers, 572; indecision, 2233, 3657-3659; identification, 212; interest, 1574-1595, 2360-2369; maturity, 308, 636, 639, 1040, 1291; maturity, adult, 1936, 2618, 2944; needs, 323; orientation, women, 2198; planning readiness for, 470; plans, 1590; preference, 194, 195, 2369; problems, psychiatric patients, 773; rehabilitation, 691; rehabilitation clients, 310; role orientation, 3660; self-concept crystallization, 2155; training, 3139; values, 1512
Volume, 2224
Vowel selection, forced, 1045

War, 1748
Warmth, 328, 937, 1438: maternal, 652; parental, 3031; self-rated, 749; teacher, 1027
Water level, 1624
Weather beliefs, 3121
Weight, locus of control, 3340
Well-being, 2474, 2493, 2499, 2544, 2987
Welfare, 1748
White(s), 520: school beginners, 566
Widowers, 1693

Widows: adjustment-depression of, 1693; coping, 2974
Wi(fe)(ves): dependency, 3029; problem, 1306; separation, coping, 2975
Willingness, 568
Witchcraft, 1139
Withdrawal, 2191: behavior, 1033; emotional, 405; social, 50, 56
Women('s), 1766, 1767, 1800: attitude toward, 1190, 2703, 2704, 2796; attitude, toward physical activity, 791; attitude, women's liberation, 1200; careers for, 1748; college, 1304; creativity, 840; desire to work, 1995; heterosocial assessment, 2570; inner-outer directedness, 789; liberation group, 1505; liberation members life experiences, 862; managers, attitudes toward, 1838; married, 1128, 1134; rights, 1766; role choice, 869; scholastic personality, 1119; scholastic potential, 1739; social situations, 1731; status of, 179; values, 1530; vocational orientation, 2198
Word(s): association, 871; association, mechanics, 119; definitions, 354; discrimination, 356, 357, 602; fluency, 1917, 1918; knowledge of, 342; meaning, 1276; meaning changes, 225; meaningful, 360; monosyllabic, 374; obscene, 1274; opposites, 2; recognition, 2, 342; representation, 602; segmentation, 602; sounds, 1374
Work: ability, 1033; adjustment of retarded, 1033; alienation, 2671; attitude toward, 541, 1199; complexity, 268; components, 1341; conditions, 1040, 1404; dependence, 1034; ethic, belief in, 2319, 3550, 3551;

expectations, 3122; fields of, 1040; group, 598; habits, 297, 388, 1033, 1047; importance, 3622; influence, 2626, 2653; interest, 747; involvement, 2361, 2797, 3628, 3661, 3662; knowledge by seventh graders, 711; load, quantitative, 1687; load, variation in, 1687; motivation, 487, 1341, 1344, 1366; motivation, internal, 2001; nonwork conflict, 3341; orientation, 2676; performance, 1573, 3593; preference, 692, 708, 3664; quality, 338; quantity, 338; readiness, 337; relations, 193, 1116; requirements, 1246; -role salience, 2235, 2672, 3665; satisfaction, 178; schedule satisfaction, 2660; situation profile, 1974; skill, 338; tedium, 2674; tension, 2667; trainee rating, 338; values, 1531, 1532, 2320, 2321, 2328, 3520, 3559, 3608; value, intrinsic and extrinsic, 2316; value orientation, 2307

Worker('s): perception of appraisal interview, 2036; perception of supervisors, 2036; preference, 3401; traits, 339
Working: attitude, 2730; class affinity, 2265; conditions, 663, 667, 3097; mother, 655, 2705
World minded, 1201
Worry-emotionality, 1694, 2523
Writing, apprehension, 2431
Writing skills: basic, 364; behavioral objective, 341; cursive, 2375
Written composition, 370, 1059

Yielding, social, 1115
Youth, 531: attitude, 1201; attitude toward, 1141; vocational maturity, 1938

Zygosity, 1292

Withdrawn from CCSU